PHYSICS OF THE AIR

PHYSICS OF THE AIR

BY

W. J. HUMPHREYS, C.E., Ph.D.

*Meteorological Physicist (Retired, Collaborator), United
States Weather Bureau; Author of "Weather Proverbs
and Paradoxes," "Rain Making and Other Weather
Vagaries," "Fogs and Clouds," "Snow Crystals"
(with Wilson A. Bentley), "Weather
Rambles," etc.*

THIRD EDITION
FIFTH IMPRESSION

McGRAW-HILL BOOK COMPANY, Inc.

NEW YORK AND LONDON

1940

THE MAPLE PRESS COMPANY, YORK, PA.

PREFACE TO THE THIRD EDITION

This third edition of "Physics of the Air" contains no radical departure from either the plan or the scope of the second. Its justification is in the elimination of a few errors and the inclusion of much additional information, especially that of recent date. To every critic I hereby extend my sincere thanks, and I especially thank my friends and colleagues, Dr. E. W. Woolard and Mr. R. T. Zoch, for their many helpful comments, and Mr. C. M. Lennahan for his efficient aid in reading proof.

W. J. HUMPHREYS.

WASHINGTON, D. C.,
October, 1940.

PREFACE TO THE SECOND EDITION

The first edition of this book is out of print. It also is out of date, hence a new edition is in order. An additional Part, Meteorological Acoustics, has been included, and many paragraphs and topics have been added. Nothing in the older work has been discarded, though various portions have been rewritten and rearranged. For the convenience of the special student, references are given to important original sources—not all, but enough at least to start him in the right direction.

It would have been more consistent and elegant, perhaps, if the metric system of units had been used exclusively, but that was impracticable, as it would have required numerous awkward conversions of original data; and also unnecessary, since every scientist who, musically speaking, has begun to play tunes and quit just running scales, is quite familiar with both systems.

In the course of this revision, many helpful suggestions were accepted from my friend and colleague, Mr. E. W. Woolard, whom I earnestly thank for his unfailing kindness and ever ready cooperation.

W. J. HUMPHREYS.

WASHINGTON, D. C.,
December, 1928.

PREFACE TO THE FIRST EDITION

The physical phenomena of the earth's atmosphere are exceedingly numerous and of great importance. Nevertheless, the explanations, even of those well understood, still remain scattered through many books and numerous journals. Perhaps this is because some of the phenomena have never been explained, and others but imperfectly so, but, however that may be, it is obvious that an orderly assemblage of all those facts and theories that together might be called the *Physics of the Air* would be exceedingly helpful to the student of atmospherics. An attempt to serve this useful purpose, begun in a course of lectures at the San Diego Aviation School (Rockwell Field) in 1914, led to the production of the following chapters—revised and reprinted from the *Journal of The Franklin Institute*, 1917, 1918, 1919, 1920.

The author begs to express his indebtedness to Prof. C. F. Marvin, Chief of the United States Weather Bureau, for numerous helpful criticisms; to Dr. C. F. Brooks, Editor of the *Monthly Weather Review*, for many excellent suggestions; to Prof. C. F. Talman, Librarian of the United States Weather Bureau, for valuable aid in locating original sources; and to Major R. B. Owens, D. S. O., Secretary of The Franklin Institute, for his encouraging interest in the work and invaluable attention to the details of its publication.

CONTENTS

PART I

MECHANICS AND THERMODYNAMICS OF THE ATMOSPHERE

CHAPTER

PART IV

ATMOSPHERIC OPTICS

PART V

FACTORS OF CLIMATIC CONTROL

PHYSICS OF THE AIR

PART I

MECHANICS AND THERMODYNAMICS OF THE ATMOSPHERE

CHAPTER I

OBSERVATIONS

Before discussing any of the physical laws of the atmosphere, it will be instructive briefly to consider the kind of observational data upon which they are based; that is, to enumerate the meteorological phenomena which commonly are measured, and to indicate in each case the type of instrument generally used. No effort will be made to describe apparatus in detail, nor to discuss the minutiæ of every correction. These important matters are fully taken care of by observers' instructions issued by the United States Weather Bureau and other meteorological services.[1] Besides, they pertain to the technique of the collection of data rather than to the science deduced therefrom, which latter, and not the former, is the object of the present discussion.

MEASURED PHENOMENA

Temperature.—Probably the most obvious, satisfactory definition of temperature describes it as *that thermal state of an object which enables it to communicate heat to other objects*. Whenever the heat interchange that always takes place between two objects in thermal communication results in a net loss to the one and gain to the other, the temperature of the former is said to have been higher than that of the latter. If, however, there is no net loss or gain by either, the objects are said to have the same temperature.

Detection of net loss or gain of heat may be accomplished in any one of many ways, some of which are change of volume, change of state, change of electromotive force, and change of electrical resistance. All these, according to circumstances, afford convenient means of comparing the temperatures of different objects, and of establishing a scale for

---

[1] See also COVERT, R. N., "Meteorological Instruments and Apparatus Employed by the United States Weather Bureau," *J. Optical Soc. Am. and Rev. Sci. Insts.*, **10**; 299–425, 1925, and KLEINSCHMIDT, E., "Handbuch der Meteorologischen Instrumente," 1935.

Fig. 1.—Thermometer shelter and rain gage for cooperative observers.

ready reference. Thus, the ordinary mercury thermometer, the alcohol thermometer, adapted to low temperatures, and others of this nature, are based on the fact that the coefficient of volume expansion of the contained fluid is greater than that of the vessel. Such thermometers, though capable of a high degree of accuracy, are not adapted to cheap and convenient registration, except of extremes; that is, the maximum or minimum temperature reached since the last adjustment. Nevertheless, differential expansion does afford several means of obtaining continuous mechanical registration of temperature. The most compact and satisfactory apparatus of this kind in general use consists essentially of a curved closed tube of oval cross-section—a Bourdon tube—completely filled with a suitable liquid. Inequality of expansion between tube and

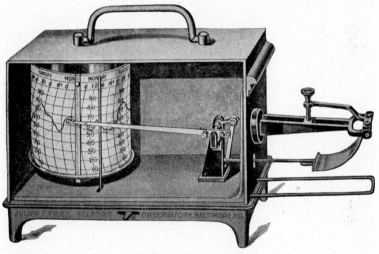

Fig. 2.—Thermograph.

liquid in this case demands change of volume, and that in turn changes the curvature of the tube.[1] Hence, by making one end of the tube fast and connecting the other with a tracing point, a complete record of temperature changes may be obtained on a moving surface. The unequal expansion of the two sides of a bimetallic strip is also utilized in obtaining temperature registration.

Variation with temperature of electrical resistance, and of the electromotive force at a thermal junction, both provide means of measuring temperature changes to a high degree of accuracy.

In the case of the atmosphere, however, temperature commonly is measured at fixed times, and whenever desired, by the readings (corrected when necessary) of a good mercurial, or, in very cold regions,

---

[1] For the theory of this extensively used gage, see LORENZ, H., *Z. Ver. deut. Ing.*, **54**; 1865, 1910.

alcohol, thermometer exposed to full circulation of the air, but protected from both solar and sky radiation.   An excellent shelter for this purpose, with maximum and minimum thermometers in place, is shown in Fig. 1. Normally, of course, the door is closed.   A continuous but less accurate record of atmospheric temperature may be, and very commonly is, secured by the use of either a bimetallic or a Bourdon tube thermograph (Fig. 2).   The connection between the thermal element and the tracing point may be either mechanical, as shown, or electrical.   In the latter case, the two may be separated any desired distance, the first placed outdoors, say, and the second conveniently located in an office.   Other methods of measuring and even of continuously recording the temperature of the air have been devised, though at present they are but sparingly used, and then, as a rule, only for special purposes.

Pressure.—The pressure of the atmosphere, upon the distribution of which winds and storm movement so vitally depend, ordinarily, is not determined.   Measurements, however, equally good for intercomparison, are made to which it is directly proportional, and from which pressures readily might be computed in dynes per square centimeter, or any other specified units.   On land, the measurement usually taken for this purpose is the height of the barometric column; that is, the difference in level between the two free surfaces of a continuous mass of mercury, one of which is open to the atmosphere, the other *in vacuo*, slightly corrected for temperature effects, capillarity, scale errors, and degree of vacuum. From this corrected height and the local force of gravity, the actual air pressure is easily computed.   Further, by reducing the barometric heights simultaneously observed at different places to what they presumably would be if the stations all had a certain common level—for which operation appropriate equations are used—data are obtained which, when plotted on a map of the region concerned, show the approximate pressure distribution, from which, in turn, the strength and course of the winds during the next 12 to 24 hours may be closely predicted.

As a rule, the mercurial barometer is read by eye and only as occasion may require, but it also has been so constructed as to give excellent continuous records.

The aneroid, or, as its name implies, non-liquid, barometer, though involving many sources of error, is conveniently portable and capable of fairly satisfactory use in many places—on kites, aeroplanes (as altimeters) etc.—where the mercurial barometer would be wholly impracticable. It consists essentially of a disk-like vacuum cell, or series of such cells, a few centimeters in diameter, whose corrugated, flexible top and bottom are held apart by a short, stiff spring.   Any change in the atmospheric or external pressure obviously must lead to a corresponding flexure of the spring, which motion may be communicated to either an index hand or a recording pen. In the ordinary barograph (Fig. 3) the pen commonly is actuated by a number of aneroid cells placed in series.

Most aneroids, whether single- or multiple-celled, require careful attention and frequent comparison with a standard mercurial instrument. They also are inherently subject to lag errors due to the imperfect elasticity of the cells that vary according to the pressure conditions and the characteristics of the particular instrument, and which, for accurate readings, must always be allowed for.

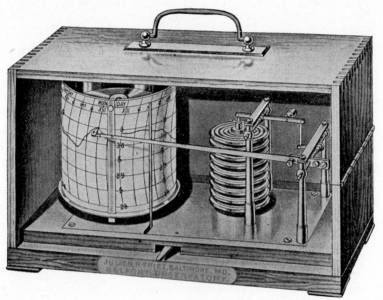

Fig. 3.—Barograph.

Wind Velocity.—The velocity of the wind may be determined by triangulation on most, but not all, types of clouds, balloons, and other floating objects; by noting the speed of rotation, easily automatically recorded, of a windmill anemometer, air meter, or other similar device, and applying the necessary corrections; by the pressure on a flat surface squarely facing the wind; by the difference in level between the two free surfaces of a liquid in a U-tube or equivalent vessel when one surface is protected and the other exposed to the full force of the wind; and by a great many other but generally less accurate methods.

The Robinson cup anemometer, especially the three- or four-cup form[1] (Fig. 4), appears to be the most convenient and reliable wind-velocity instrument wherever it can be properly exposed. The theory of its action, however, is but imperfectly understood.[2] Rapid velocity changes, manifesting themselves in irregular puffs, and of great importance to the

[1] PATTERSON, J., *Trans. Roy. Soc. Canada*, January, 1926; DINES, J. S., *Meteorol. Mag.*, **71**; 133, 1936; MARVIN, C. F., *M. W. R.*, **62**; 115, 1934.

[2] CHREE, *Phil. Mag.*, **40**; 63, 1895.

aviator, the architect, and the engineer, generally are observed and recorded by some quick-acting pressure apparatus, such as the Dines pressure tube anemometer, or the Pitot tube, or Venturi tube.

The Pitot tube, of which the Dines anemometer is a modification, consists of a tube with a "dynamic" opening facing the wind, or current of other fluid, and one or more "static" openings facing at right angles to the direction of the flow.   When the respective openings communicate with closed chambers the head h of the fluid in question that would balance the difference between the dynamic and the static pressures in

F_{IG}. 4.—Three-cup anemometer.

a perfect instrument (the best gives very nearly theoretical values) is found by applying Bernoulli's principle, $p + \frac{1}{2}\rho V^2 =$ constant, at each of the openings, assuming ρ constant; or from the fact that it must be such as alone would give a back velocity out of the tube equal to the forward velocity into it.   Hence,

$$h = \frac{V^2}{2g},$$

in which V is the velocity of the current, and g gravity acceleration; all in c.g.s. units.

In practice, the pressure difference is given by a column of liquid, a compressed spring, or other device, differentially connected with the two chambers, dynamic and static.   In each case

$$V = \sqrt{2gcp},$$

when p is the corrected reading of the indicator in whatever terms, and c the value of h per unit of p. If, for instance, p is dynes per square centimeter, c is the thickness in centimeters of a horizontal layer of the air, say, that would produce a gravity pressure of 1 dyne per square centimeter; and similarly for other types of graduation.

The Venturi tube, which measures velocity of flow in exactly the reverse manner to that of the Pitot tube, that is, by decrease of pressure, consists of two oppositely directed hollow cones joined together coaxially by a short throat of uniform cross-section. The angular opening of the receiving cone, which may have a short cylindrical mouth, is relatively large, while the discharge cone is comparatively long and tapering.

Let this tube be mounted parallel to the wind whose velocity V_0 it is proposed to measure, and let r be the ratio of the cross-section of the mouth to that of the throat, in which the velocity, therefore, is rV, nearly (change in density being slight), if V is mouth velocity and r is small. If the flow through the tube is smooth (in good tubes it is very nearly so), the pressure against the wall of the mouth cylinder and that against the throat are each less than the outside static pressure. Furthermore, if h_1, h_2, and h_3 are the heads of the current atmosphere that would give the static (without velocity), mouth, and throat pressures, respectively, then, if density is constant, and it is, nearly, when the constriction is slight,

$$h_2 + \frac{V^2}{2g} = h_3 + \frac{r^2 V^2}{2g} = h_1,$$

and

$$V = \sqrt{2g(h_1 - h_2)} = \frac{1}{r} \sqrt{2g(h_1 - h_3)} = \sqrt{\frac{2g(h_2 - h_3)}{r^2 - 1}}.$$

To determine V by this method, it clearly is only necessary to connect the mouth and throat cylinders through small openings to the opposite sides of a manometer, or either opening to one side of a manometer the other side of which is connected to a static chamber. If, as in the Pitot tube, p is the manometer reading and c the value of h per unit of p,

$$V = \sqrt{2gcp_1} = \frac{1}{r} \sqrt{2gcp_2} = \sqrt{\frac{2gcp_3}{r^2 - 1}}$$

for the several connections, as indicated.

When the throat constriction is small, it may be assumed that the wind velocity V_0 is substantially the same as the mouth velocity V.

Similarly, a small flat disk, set parallel to the wind, and provided with a tube running from a minute opening near its middle to a suitable manometer, also gives the wind velocity.

Let h_1 and h_2 be the static and tube pressures, respectively. Then, as before

$$\frac{V^2}{2g} + h_2 = h_1,$$

and

$$V = \sqrt{2g(h_1 - h_2)} = V_0, \text{ closely.}$$

When the Venturi tube is decidedly constricted, $r = 10$, say, the density of the passing air, or other gas, has one value in the open, another in the mouth, and a third in the throat. Hence, the equations that give the relation of velocity to pressure are different from those above for constant density.

Let V_0, ρ_0, p_0; V_1, ρ_1, p_1; and V_2, ρ_2, p_2 be the velocity, density, and pressure outside, in the mouth, and in the throat, respectively. Let, at first, $V_0 = 0$.

Since the air passes through the tube adiabatically, the sum of the potential and kinetic energies of the unit mass remains constant, hence (see Chapter II)

$$\frac{p_0}{\rho_0(\gamma - 1)} = \frac{p_1}{\rho_1(\gamma - 1)} + \frac{V_1{}^2}{2} = \frac{p_2}{\rho_2(\gamma - 1)} + \frac{V_2{}^2}{2}.$$

Since, if T is absolute temperature,

$$\frac{\rho_1}{\rho_2} = \frac{p_1}{p_2}\frac{T_2}{T_1} = \frac{p_1}{p_2}\left(\frac{p_2}{p_1}\right)^{\frac{\gamma-1}{\gamma}} = \left(\frac{p_1}{p_2}\right)^{\frac{1}{\gamma}}$$

(see Chap. II), and, if A is area of cross-section

$$A_1\rho_1 V_1 = A_2\rho_2 V_2,$$

therefore

$$V_1 = \left\{\frac{2p_0}{\rho_0(\gamma - 1)}\right\}^{\frac{1}{2}}\left\{1 - \left(\frac{p_1}{p_0}\right)^{\frac{\gamma-1}{\gamma}}\right\}^{\frac{1}{2}} =$$

$$\frac{\left\{\dfrac{2p_1}{\rho_1(\gamma - 1)}\right\}^{\frac{1}{2}}\left\{1 - \left(\dfrac{p_2}{p_1}\right)^{\frac{\gamma-1}{\gamma}}\right\}^{\frac{1}{2}}}{\left\{\left(\dfrac{A_1}{A_2}\right)^2\left(\dfrac{p_1}{p_2}\right)^{\frac{2}{\gamma}} - 1\right\}^{\frac{1}{2}}}.$$

$$V_2 = \left\{\frac{2p_0}{\rho_0(\gamma - 1)}\right\}^{\frac{1}{2}}\left\{1 - \left(\frac{p_2}{p_0}\right)^{\frac{\gamma-1}{\gamma}}\right\}^{\frac{1}{2}} =$$

$$\frac{\left\{\dfrac{2p_1}{\rho_1(\gamma - 1)}\right\}^{\frac{1}{2}}\left\{1 - \left(\dfrac{p_2}{p_1}\right)^{\frac{\gamma-1}{\gamma}}\right\}^{\frac{1}{2}}}{\left\{1 - \left(\dfrac{A_2}{A_1}\right)^2\left(\dfrac{p_2}{p_1}\right)^{\frac{2}{\gamma}}\right\}^{\frac{1}{2}}}.$$

Since

$$p = \rho g h,$$

V_1 and V_2 can also be expressed in terms of gravity acceleration and the heads of the current atmosphere necessary to produce the several pressures.

To use a Venturi tube of this type to measure wind velocity, it is necessary to know, by experiment or otherwise, the relation between the velocity of the open air and that of the stream in the mouth when facing the wind. That is, to know k for all values of V_0 in the expression

$$V_0 = kV_1$$

Obviously, a Pitot and a Venturi tube can easily be combined by connecting the dynamic opening of the first and the throat of the second to opposite sides of a manometer, and the reading of the latter thereby made approximately double that given by either tube alone.

Wind velocities at considerable heights in the free air commonly are obtained by triangulation on suitable clouds, or small free balloons.

Wind Direction.—The direction of the wind, as the term is used in meteorological literature, always means the direction *from* which the wind is blowing at the place in question. It may be determined approximately by the course of smoke, drifting clouds, or other floating objects, by the set of a wind vane (Fig. 5), drift of a pennant, flexure of trees, or other simple methods. Various devices for automatically recording this direction, either in its entirety or for selected points only, are possible, the simplest, perhaps, being electrical and under control of contacts made by a rod connected to and rotated by the wind vane. In common practice, only a small number of directions, usually eight, are registered, each covering an angle of 45 degrees. That is, a wind from any point between W. 22.5° S. and W. 22.5° N. is registered as a west wind; and similarly for the other octants. This division may seem very coarse, but it is sufficient for most meteorological uses.

Humidity Definitions.—The mixture of water vapor with the permanent gases of the atmosphere has occasioned a number of "humidity problems" over which the student is in danger of becoming more or less confused. And this danger is increased by the use in this connection of the same word by recognized authorities to connote quite different ideas. For the sake of clearness, therefore, this subject will be briefly discussed under several sub-heads.

1. *Absolute Humidity.*—Two entirely different definitions are in use for the common expression "absolute humidity:"

a. The mass of water vapor per unit volume.

b. The gas pressure exerted by the water vapor per unit area.

According to the first definition, the absolute humidity may be expressed in terms of any units of mass and volume, as, for instance, grams per cubic meter.

According to the second definition, it may be expressed in terms of any units of force and area—dynes, say, per square centimeter; or any

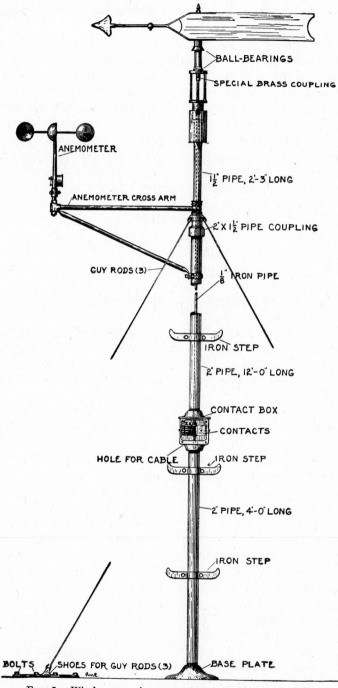

BALL-BEARINGS

SPECIAL BRASS COUPLING

ANEMOMETER

$1\frac{1}{2}$ PIPE, 2'-3' LONG

ANEMOMETER CROSS ARM

$2'' \times 1\frac{1}{2}''$ PIPE COUPLING

GUY RODS (3)

$\frac{1}{8}''$ IRON PIPE

IRON STEP

2' PIPE, 12'-0" LONG

CONTACT BOX

CONTACTS

HOLE FOR CABLE

IRON STEP

2' PIPE, 4'-0" LONG

IRON STEP

BOLTS   SHOES FOR GUY RODS (3)   BASE PLATE

FIG. 5.—Wind vane and anemometer support, pattern, 1913.

measurable pressure effect, such as height of the mercury column the vapor pressure would sustain.

Accepting the simple definition (a) as being correct, as every one does, it remains to show the equivalence to it of definition (b). This relation follows at once from the well-known fact that the pressure exerted by any constituent in a uniform mixture of gases is to the total pressure as the number of its molecules per given volume is to the total number of the mixture in the same volume. Vapor pressure, therefore, varies directly as vapor density, or mass per unit volume. Hence the two definitions (a) and (b) of absolute humidity are equivalent to each other, for any given temperature except in so far as the water vapor departs from an ideal gas, a departure that may be quite appreciable near the point of saturation.

2. *Relative Humidity.*—Different definitions are also in use for the expression "relative humidity:"

a. The ratio of the actual quantity of water vapor present in a small volume to the saturation quantity, that is, to the amount that would just saturate an equal volume at the same temperature.

b. The ratio of the actual to the saturation pressure of water vapor at the same temperature.

In these definitions the expressions "saturation quantity" and "saturation pressure" refer to the maximum quantity of water vapor per unit volume and maximum pressure of water vapor per unit area, respectively, that can exist in the presence of a flat surface of pure water, at the given temperature.

3. *Specific Humidity.*—The term "specific humidity," means the weight of water vapor per unit weight of moist air. It is a conservative property so long as neither evaporation nor condensation occurs in the air concerned, independent of temperature, pressure, and volume—a fingerprint, as it were, of any given air mass.

4. *Mixing Ratio.*—The ratio of the mass of water vapor in a small volume to the mass of the rest of the air in the same volume; or, say, the number of grams of water vapor per kilogram of dry air.

5. *Dew Point.*—The expression "dew point," as used in humidity tables and elsewhere, means simply that temperature at which, without change of pressure, saturation is just reached. It might also be defined as that temperature at which the saturation pressure is the same as the existing vapor pressure.

6. *Saturation Deficit.*—"Saturation deficit," a term much used by plant physiologists, is susceptible of several definitions, especially: (1) amount of water vapor, in addition to that already present, per unit volume, grams per cubic meter, say, necessary to produce saturation at the existing temperature and pressure; (2) difference between actual and saturation pressure; (3) ratio of the vapor pressure deficit to the

saturation pressure at the existing temperature. The third is relative, the others absolute.

It should be noted that absolute humidity, relative humidity, and saturation deficit refer to the state of a *volume* in respect to water vapor, and that the amount of vapor required to produce saturation is independent, nearly, of the kind or density of any other gas present, provided they do not react on each other.

Humidity, Instrumentation.—The absolute humidity, in the sense of mass of water vapor per unit volume, can be determined by noting the increase in weight of phosphorus pentoxide or other suitable drying agent on absorbing a known volume of the vapor. This direct determination of the humidity, however, is impracticable for routine observations.

On the other hand, as partial pressure ratios are independent of temperature, the determination of the absolute humidity in the sense of vapor pressure merely requires measuring the loss of pressure due to absorption of the vapor in a closed space, for which there are several devices;[1] or, as more commonly practiced, finding the dew point and referring it to a table of predetermined saturation pressures. Similarly, the difference between the current and dew-point temperatures is sufficient to determine, from suitable tables, the relative humidity.

The dew point may be found by any one of several slightly different methods, all of which have for their basis the determination of that temperature at which moisture just begins to collect on a cooling surface. A thin-walled silver tube, burnished on the outside, is an excellent vessel for the cooling mixture. The temperature of the liquid, if well stirred, and that of such a tube will be very nearly the same; and, besides, the dulling of the surface promptly reveals the slightest condensation.

It should be noted, however, that if carefully taken the observed temperatures of the silver hygrometer will be slightly below the actual "dew point." This is because the initial deposit is in the form of minute droplets, whose vapor pressure is greater than that of a flat surface at the same temperature, in accordance with the equation,[2]

$$\Delta p = \frac{2T\rho_v}{R(\rho_w - \rho_v)},$$

which may be derived as follows:

Let R be the radius of a capillary tube standing in a vessel of water (Fig. 6); h the height of the water in the tube when saturation is attained and all air removed; T the surface tension; ρ_w the density of the water; ρ_v the average density through h of the saturated vapor; and g the gravity acceleration. Then, obviously,

$$2\pi RT = \pi R^2(\rho_w - \rho_v)gh;$$

[1] Shaw, A. N., *Trans. Roy. Soc. Canada,* **10**; 85, 1916.

[2] Thomson, Sir William, *Proc. Roy. Soc. Edin.,* **7**; 63, 1870; *Phil. Mag.,* **42**; 448, 1871.

and

$$\Delta p = \rho_v g h,$$

being the difference between the vapor pressures at the inner and outer surfaces.

Hence

$$h = \frac{\Delta p}{\rho_v g} = \frac{2T}{R(\rho_w - \rho_v)g},$$

and

$$\Delta p = \frac{2T\rho_v}{R(\rho_w - \rho_v)}.$$

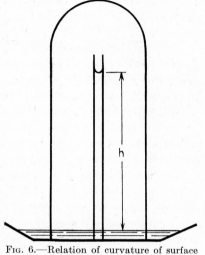

At ordinary temperatures and for droplets whose radii are 10^{-4} cm. (a possible size) the temperature depression, or error, amounts roughly to $0.02°$ C. According to the equation, the error obviously might have any value, though actually it seems always to be small; that is, this, too, like many other physical equations, has its limitations.

Fig. 6.—Relation of curvature of surface to saturation vapor pressure.

In taking humidity measurements the observer must be careful that his presence does not affect the amount of moisture in the air under examination—he must stand to the lee of his apparatus.

Although the dew-point apparatus and other absolute hygrometers are extremely simple in theory, they generally are too complicated in structure and too difficult to manipulate to be suitable for routine observations.[1] On the other hand, the psychrometer, presently to be explained, which depends on the maximum cooling of water by evaporation when amply ventilated, is less obvious in theory,[2] but both simple in construction and easy to use.

A convenient form of the psychrometric equation is:

$$e = e' - AB(t - t'),$$

[1] For a general discussion of hygrometry see *Phys. Soc. Lon.*, **34**, February, 1922; Glazebrook, "Dictionary of Applied Physics," Vol. 3; and Bongards, Hermann, "Feuchtigkeits Messung," 1926. See also Whipple, F. J. W., *Proc. Phys. Soc.*, **45**; Pt. 2, 307, 1933, and Brooks, D. B., and Allen, H. H., *J. Wash. Acad. Sci.*, **28**; 121, 1933.

[2] Ivory, *Phil. Mag.*, **60**; 81, 1822; August, *Ann. Phys.*, **5**; 69, 1825; Apjohn, *Trans. Roy. Irish Acad.*, 1834; Regnault, *C. R.*, **20**; 1127–1220, 1845; **35**; 930, 1852; Maxwell, Encyc. Brit., 9th Ed., "Diffusion," 1878; Stefan, *Zeit. Oest. Gesell. für Meteorologie*, **16**; 177, 1881; Ferrel, Annual Report, Chief Signal Officer, Appendix 71, "Hygrometry," 1885; Carrier, *Trans. Am. Soc. Mech. Eng.* **33**; 1005, 1912; Grossmann. *Ann. Hydr.* **44**; 577, 1916.

in which

    t = the air temperature.
    t' = the temperature of a vigorously ventilated wet-bulb thermometer.
    e = the vapor pressure.
    e' = the saturation pressure at temperature t'.
    B = barometric pressure.
    A = a number that, in the case of ample ventilation, varies only with t', when e is constant, and with it but slowly.

Obviously, the relatively cool wet bulb gains heat by conduction from the adjacent atmosphere and loses heat through evaporation. There is also absorption and emission of radiation, but when the ventilation is ample—3 meters per second or more—the net gain or loss of heat by this process is negligible in comparison with that by conduction or evaporation, respectively. Radiation effects may be still further reduced by surrounding the thermometer and its stem with a suitable wet-lined, reflecting shield, preferably of the Dewar-bulb type. For most purposes, however, the use of a shield is unnecessary. It may be assumed, then, that the equilibrium or steady temperature of an amply ventilated wet-bulb thermometer is that at which the heat it gains by conduction from the passing air is equal to the heat it loses by evaporation.

The details of the processes of evaporation and heat conduction involved are not all fully known. But it is known that when radiation effects are excluded, the equilibrium temperature is measurably independent of the rate of ventilation, which, under these conditions, is only a convenient means of quickly attaining a steady state. In the extreme case of simple molecular diffusion in an otherwise stagnant atmosphere, it seems safe to assume that the space immediately adjacent to the wet surface is fully saturated at the temperature of the wet bulb, and that heat is supplied by molecular bombardment of the air. Furthermore, if the temperature is not affected by ventilation (all radiation effects excluded) it seems that identically the same conditions just stated, or their equivalents, must hold whatever the ventilation.

In so far as these assumptions are true, it follows that during a steady state the gain of heat Q per unit time, say, is given by the equation

$$Q = ms(t - t'),$$

in which m is the mass of previously free air, temperature t, that during the time in question comes into actual contact with the wet-bulb, temperature t', and s its average specific heat, at constant pressure, between these temperatures.

Also, since gas pressure at any temperature is proportional to the number of molecules of whatever kind or kinds per unit volume,

$$Q = \frac{e' - e}{B} rmL_t',$$

in which e' is the saturation vapor pressure at the temperature t', e the vapor pressure in the free air, B the current barometric pressure, r the ratio of the molecular weight of water to the equivalent molecular weight of the free air, and L_t', the latent heat of evaporization at the temperature t'.

Hence, equating the two values of Q:

$$e = e' - AB(t - t'),$$

in which

$$A = \frac{s}{rL_t'}.$$

The value of A, therefore, varies slightly, but, to known amounts with e (s is greater for water vapor than for dry air), and t'. At $t' = 0°$ C. it also depends upon the phase, liquid or solid, of the evaporating water. But as vapor pressure at $0°$ C. is the same over ice as over water, it seems that the abrupt change of A at this temperature must be accommodated by an equivalent opposite change in the value of $t - t'$.

The general agreement between this theory and the best psychrometric observations, such as those of Hazen, Marvin and others of the Weather Bureau (Signal Corps),[1] while not perfect, is sufficiently close to make it doubtful which is in greater error, and thus to increase confidence in each. See also M. W. R., 61,300, 1933.

When e, e', and B are expressed in millimeters of mercury under standard conditions and t and t' in centigrade values, observation gives $e = e' - 0.000660B(t - t')(1 + 0.00115t')$, approximately.

In practice, t and t' commonly are obtained with a properly constructed and adequately ventilated (usually whirled) psychrometer carrying both a wet- and a dry-bulb thermometer. The sling psychrometer (Fig. 7), whirled by hand, is a simple device for this purpose. The observer has only to note the air temperature, the wet-bulb depression (that is, difference between the wet- and dry-bulb temperatures), and barometric pressure. With these values he reads off from tables the vapor pressure and the dew point.

Assmann's aspiration psychrometer (Fig. 8), however, appears to be the most accurate instrument for this purpose. This consists of two parallel double-walled tubes, silvered to minimize radiation effects, containing a wet- and a dry-bulb thermometer, respectively, united into a common duct and surmounted by a small ventilating fan.

If the wet bulb is stationary in the instrument shelter and kept wet by distilled water; or slowly dripping, to avoid accumulation of salts, if tap water is used; then,[2] in terms of millibars and centigrade degrees, to a fair approximation, $e' - e = \frac{4}{5}(t - t')$.

[1] *Annual Report Chief Signal Officer*, Appendix 24, 1886.
[2] WHIPPLE, F. J. W., *Meteorol. Mag.*, **65**; 57, 1930.

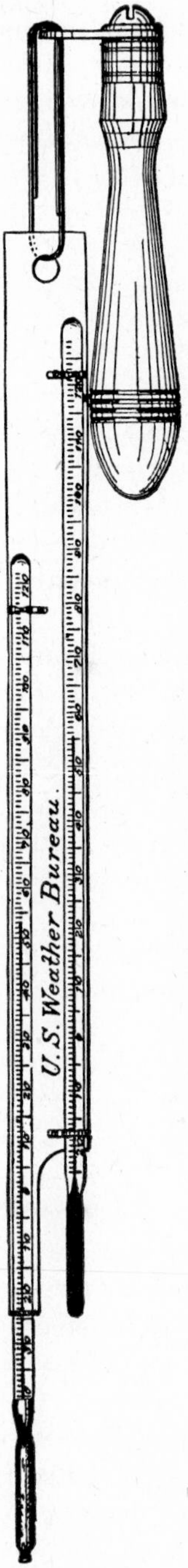

Several kinds of instrument for automatically recording humidity have been devised, but of these only the hair hygrometer is in general use. Its response, however, is much slower than that of electrical hygrometers now being developed.[1] The hair hygrometer resembles some forms of thermograph except that the actuating member instead of being a thermal element is a strand of clean hairs, freed of oil, that increase in length with the relative humidity. With reasonable care the data thus obtained on a calibrated scale are both consistent and fairly reliable.

The most elaborate psychrometric tables are the Aspirations-Psychrometric-Tafeln, 2. auf., K. Preuss. Meteorolog. Institut. Brief tables, up to 100° C., are given by Awberry and Griffiths.[2]

For very low temperatures the thermometers in the Assmann psychrometer can be replaced by batteries of thermo elements, connected through a galvanometer from the readings of which $t - t'$ can be found.[3] The value of t is obtained with a separate thermometer.

Cloudiness.—The degree of cloudiness generally is expressed in tenths (estimated) of the sky actually overcast, regardless of the thickness, or thinness of the cloud. For mean cloudiness over the earth see the memoir there on by C. E. P. Brooks.[4]

Kinds of Clouds.—As an indication of the approaching weather and general state of the atmosphere, the kind (or kinds) of clouds present is more important than the mere total percentage of cloudiness. For convenient reference clouds have been divided into four primary and ten secondary (combination, alto, and fracto) forms. These are:

Primary Forms.—Cirrus—or curl cloud; stratus—or layer cloud; cumulus—or wool-pack cloud; and nimbus—or rain cloud.

Combination Forms.—Cirrostratus, cirrocumulus, stratocumulus, cumulonimbus, and nimbostratus.

Alto Forms.—Altostratus and altocumulus.

Fracto Forms.—Fractostratus, fractocumulus, and fractonimbus.

Fig. 7.—Sling psychrometer.

[1] Dunmore, F. W., *J. Research, Nat. Bur. Standards,* **23**; 701, 1939.

[2] *Proc. Phys. Soc.,* 44; Pt. 2, 132, 1932.

[3] Malmgren, Finn, *Geophys. Pub.* **4**; No. 6, 1926, Oslo.

[4] *Roy. Meteorolog. Soc. Mem.,* **1**; No. 10, 1927.

The foregoing names are used in the International Cloud Classification, now generally accepted.

It will be noted that several names possible in accordance with this scheme of nomenclature are omitted, even though a few of them have occasionally been used in certain other schemes of classification. Thus there is no cirronimbus, for the reason that rain clouds never have the cirrus form; no altocirrus, because cirri usually are high; no altonimbus,

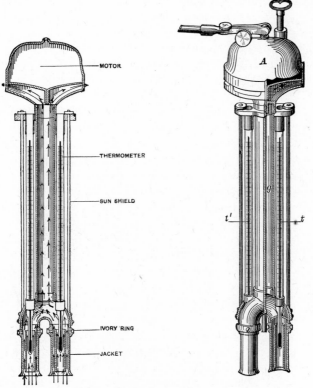

FIG. 8.—Aspiration psychrometer.

because rain clouds, except the cumulonimbus, are never high; and no fractocirrus, because cirri are always broken and detached.

Most of these clouds may be grouped according to their respective altitudes:

Upper Clouds.—Cirrus, cirrostratus.

Intermediate Clouds.—Cirrocumulus, altostratus, altocumulus.

Lower Clouds.—Stratocumulus, nimbus, fractonimbus, stratus, fractostratus.

Convection Clouds.—The cumulus, fractocumulus, and cumulonimbus (base), all caused by convection, chiefly thermal, vary in altitude from low to intermediate.

Precipitation.—The amount of precipitation is measured as the actual or, in case of snow, equivalent, depth of horizontal water layer. The details in respect to the manner of catching and measuring precipitation have been greatly varied. The measuring, of course, is simple enough, but it is far from easy to secure a correct catch, owing chiefly to the influence of the vessel itself on the wind currents over and about its mouth and the consequent effect on the amount of precipitation actually caught. The details of a simple rain gage are shown in Fig. 9, and its installation

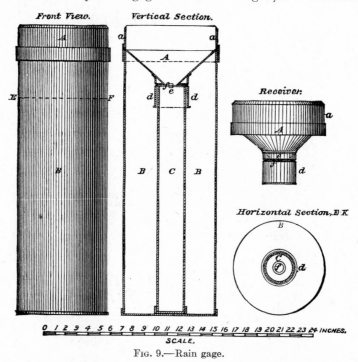

Fig. 9.—Rain gage.

in Fig. 1. Many gages are provided with a small tipping bucket just beneath the spout of the receiving funnel, by which the time of occurrence and rate of each rainfall are electrically recorded at any desired place.

Evaporation.—Evaporation is measured in terms of the depth of a flat layer of water, of area equal to that of the evaporating surface. This, too, like precipitation, has been measured by many kinds of apparatus, some of which have been designed with the view of simulating the surface of leaves, or meeting other special conditions. Many attempts have also been made to find from theoretical considerations a correct equation between rate of evaporation and the various factors upon which it depends, such as shape of surface, extent of surface, temperature of the superficial layer, temperature of the air, humidity, barometric pressure, wind velocity, and anything ese that might be considered of importance.

A few special cases, such as evaporation from flush circular and elliptical water surfaces at constant temperature and in absolutely stagnant atmosphere, appear to have been completely analyzed.[1] But this work, however ingenious, has contributed very little to the solution of the general problem, because in Nature water surfaces are of irregular outline, and all the factors that control evaporation are in such a maze of flux and reflux as to render equation testing and evaluation of constants

Fig. 10.—Sunshine recorder.

of doubtful accuracy and value. Evaporation, therefore, like most biological and many other phenomena, must be observed and measured; it cannot be computed very accurately as a function of given conditions (for discussion see Chap. XV).

Sunshine.—Sunshine generally is expressed in terms both of hours of its actual and percentage of its possible duration. It is recorded automatically, usually through electrical contact made or broken by the movement of a mercury piston in the stem of a vacuum-enclosed black-bulb differential air thermometer (Fig. 10); by charring on prepared cards in the focus of a glass sphere; or by photographic traces on sensitized paper.

[1] STEFAN, *Sitzb. K. Akad.*, **73**; 943, 954, 1881.

Fig. 11.—Forty-foot steel wind instrument tower; typical installation for high office building.

Radiation.—In relation to the atmosphere, radiation from three sources is of importance: from the sun, from the sky, and from the earth. Each may be measured integrally (that is, in terms of the amount of that energy delivered per minute, say, per unit normal area at the place of observation), or spectrally (that is, as distributed according to wave length). The first kind of measurement, the integral, usually is made by some type of pyrheliometer, and the second (so far applied only to solar and sky radiation) by a bolometer.

Electrical Condition.—Measurements of the electrical condition of the atmosphere generally are confined to the vertical potential gradient, determined by any one of several methods, ionization, and the consequent conductivity.

Optical Phenomena.—Various optical phenomena of the atmosphere are observed and recorded. These include, especially, mirages, sky colors, sky polarization, rainbows, coronas, and halos. For several of them—mirages, sky colors, and rainbows—mere eye observations are sufficient. Sky polarization, however, cannot be measured or even detected without the aid of suitable apparatus, while the data pertaining to halos and even coronas are far more valuable when they include accurate angular measurements.

Visibility.—The usual method of measuring visibility, a thing of great importance to the aviator, is the crude one of noting the maximum distance at which such objects as trees, houses, hills, and mountains, or their larger details, can be recognizably seen by the unaided normal eye. Poor visibility is owing to loss of light from object to observer by absorption, scattering, and reflection, and, in far greater measure, to the veiling glare due to diffusion by fog and dust in the line of sight. The theory of visibility is well known,[1] but at present this element is not very generally and reliably measured. When the air is filled with smoke or other particles that coagulate, visibility through it increases with time. If n is the number of such particles per unit volume, then

$$\frac{1}{n_2} - \frac{1}{n_1} = k(t_2 - t_1).$$

That is, the volume per gram increases linearly with time, or

$$-\frac{dn}{dt} = kn^2.$$

k is about the same for all smoke materials, but increases with the fineness of the granules. It therefore is a measure of the probability of collision due to the Brownian movement. Such particles may be driven together also by supersonic air waves, and even by a very high-

[1] JONES, L. A., *J. Franklin Inst.*, **188**; 363, 1919; *Phil. Mag.*, **39**; 96, 1920; MIDDLE-TON, W. E. K., "Visibility in Meteorology," Univ. of Toronto Press, 1935.

pitched sound, and the visibility in the small region so affected may be thereby improved. However, hissing the air clean over an aerodrome is not yet a practical procedure.

Typical Installation.—A typical roof installation of the more common meteorological instruments is shown in Fig. 11. The wind vane is at the top of the tower, the whirling Robinson cup anemometer just below and to the left of the vane, and the sunshine recorder slightly lower, on the cage or platform railing. The thermometer shelter, with the door open, is in the lower portion of the tower. Finally, two rain gages—one simple, the other tipping-bucket—are shown in the lower left corner of the picture.

SOURCES OF METEOROLOGICAL INFORMATION

As a further introduction to a discussion of the physics of the air, it will be helpful to consider a sort of vertical cross-section of the atmos-

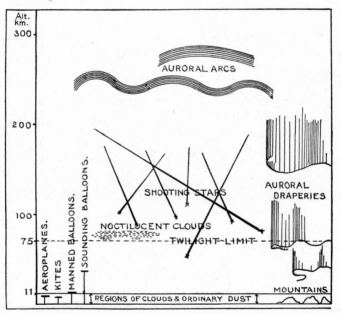

Fig. 12.—Sources of meteorological information.

phere as a whole with reference to the *sources* of meteorological information concerning each particular level. Other cross-sections that show its temperature, pressure, density, and composition at various heights will be given later. Figure 12, an adaptation of Wegener's profile of the atmosphere,[1] indicates the principal present sources of this information and the distribution of meteorological phenomena at various levels.

[1] *Phys. Zeitsch.*, **12**; 170, 1911.

Mountains and other irregularities of the earth's surface make it practicable to examine the atmosphere minutely and to record continuously all its changes at every height from sea level up to nearly six kilometers. In fact, many continuous records have already been obtained at the summit station on El Misti, Peru, whose altitude is 5852 meters. Occasional and partial records have been obtained by this means as far up as about 9 kilometers, or to near the top of Mount Everest. But

Fig. 13.—Launching meteorological kite.

all such records, whether obtained at high levels or low, of course are more or less affected by the surface conditions. Hence, some means of obtaining observations and records other than apparatus carried about on the surface of the earth is essential to a knowledge of the conditions and movements of the free atmosphere. One obvious source of information as regards motion only, and which has been extensively used, is the observation of drifting clouds, which occur at all levels from the bottom of the atmosphere up to 11 kilometers, or thereabouts, in middle latitudes, and occasionally, in the tropics, even above 15 kilometers.

There are several methods of determining the height, direction of motion, and velocity of clouds, but all depend upon simple processes of triangulation. Thus, simultaneous theodolite observations made on the same spot in a cloud from two stations whose elevations and distance apart are known obviously furnish all the data necessary for an easy and fairly accurate determination of the height of the particular spot in question, while a single subsequent observation by either instrument on this spot, provided the time interval between the first and second observations is known, clearly gives all the additional data necessary to the determination of its velocity and direction of travel—assuming uniform motion and constancy of level. Excellent results, also, are gotten with the range

Fig. 14.—Sounding balloons.

finder, and from cloud negatives simultaneously obtained with photo-theodolites provided with fiducial lines. In this way, if several successive exposures are made, the height and movement of each distinguishable point in the cloud can be determined, and therefore not only the height and drift of the cloud as a whole, but also its dimensions and something of its internal motions. However, the general motion of the wind at the point observed and time of observation, though interesting and often valuable, is by far the chief information about the atmosphere that clouds give, and, indeed, some, such as those formed by air billows over mountain crests and elsewhere, do not give even this. Besides, they are not always present, so that on clear days even this modicum of information about the upper air would be impossible to obtain if we had no other means of investigation. But there are others, the most fruitful

Fig. 15.—Sounding balloon.

of which is the carrying of self-registering thermometers, barometers, hygrometers, and the like into the free air by means of:

a. Kites (Fig. 13) to over 9 kilometers, the record being 9.74 kilometers—little used at present.

b. Aeroplanes; present limit about 17 kilometers.

c. Manned balloons; maximum elevation, roughly, 22 kilometers.

d. Sounding balloons (Figs. 14 and 15), with a record of about 36 kilometers.

e. Radiosondes, sounding balloons with equipments that radio the temperature, pressure, and humidity of the air at frequent intervals, hence at many levels, though not over the same spot, for the balloon drifts with the wind.

Upper air movements are also shown by the flights of pilot balloons (small balloons without apparatus); record 39 kilometers.

The registering apparatus sent aloft by these various methods furnish reliable information concerning the composition (including humidity), temperature, pressure, direction of motion, and, in some cases, velocity of the air, from the surface of the earth up to the greatest height reached. And it is this automatically recorded information, gathered, with but little exception, since the beginning of the twentieth century, that has so greatly extended our accurate knowledge of meteorology, and done so much to make of it an interesting and profitable branch of both theoretical and applied physics.

Beyond the reach of the pilot balloon, or, for the present, at elevations greater than 39 kilometers, our information of the atmosphere is limited to such deductions as properly may be drawn from the height of the twilight arch—roughly, 75 kilometers; heights of the nacreous and noctilucent clouds, 28 and 82 kilometers, respectively; the reflection of sound, at around 40 kilometers; radio phenomena, to about 250 kilometers; the paths of shooting stars, rarely, if ever, seen as high as 200 kilometers; and the phenomena of the auroras, those curious and but partially explained electrical discharges that seldom occur at a lower level than 90 kilometers, but up to nearly 1000.

The above, obviously, are all, or nearly all, the means by which our knowledge of the atmosphere has been obtained. Up to 35 kilometers it is comparatively well known, but beyond that level only deductions, growing less certain with increase of elevation, can possibly take us at present, or at any time until higher soundings have been made.

CHAPTER II

SOME THEORETICAL RELATIONS BETWEEN TEMPERATURE, PRESSURE AND VOLUME IN THE ATMOSPHERE

In order to acquire a clear understanding of the causes of the actual distribution of temperature in the atmosphere, it will be convenient, first, to consider some of the thermodynamic equations of gases, especially those that give relations between temperature, pressure, and volume.

Dry Air.—If to a unit mass of air or other gas at constant pressure p a quantity of heat dQ be supplied, the energy so added will divide itself into two parts. One portion will change the temperature of the gas and the other will change its volume. Hence, if the work, incident to the expansion, is expressed in its heat equivalent, or if each portion of the energy is expressed in heat units and not in units of work, then, equating like unto like,

$$dQ = C_v dT + A p dV \tag{1}$$

in which C_v is the specific heat of the gas in question at constant volume, dT and dV the resulting changes in temperature and volume, respectively, and A the reciprocal of the mechanical equivalent of a unit of heat.

But to secure the relations desired, the relation of p to T, for instance, when both are variable, it is necessary to have an additional equation involving dT, dp, and dV. From Boyle's and Charles' laws, we have such an equation, namely,

$$pV = \frac{p_0 V_0}{T_0} T,$$

which expresses the fact that for a given quantity of gas the product of pressure and volume varies directly as the absolute temperature T. So long, then, as the quantity of gas involved and its temperature are constant, so also is the product pV. But when this quantity is one gram and the temperature $0°$ C., it is convenient to speak of the quantity, $p_0 V_0 / T_0$, as the characteristic constant R of the gas in question. In general, then, for 1 gram,

$$pV = RT, \text{ equation of state}$$

in which the value of R, apart from units, depends solely upon the kind of gas.

27

Hence, differentiating,

$$pdV + Vdp = RdT. \tag{2}$$

To find the relation between dp and dT, it is only necessary now, by aid of equation (2), to eliminate dV from equation (1); thus

$$dQ = C_v dT + A(RdT - Vdp). \tag{3}$$

When p is constant, $dQ = C_p dT$, where C_p is the specific heat at constant pressure; hence, equating this value of dQ to that given by equation (3) with $dp = 0$, we have the important relation

$$C_p - C_v = AR.$$

This excess of the specific heat at constant pressure over the specific heat at constant volume is simply the amount of heat necessary to perform the external work incident to expansion as a result of increasing the temperature 1° C.; substituting in equation (3), we get

$$dQ = C_p dT - A \cdot V dp.$$

In the case of an *adiabatic* process (that is, a process in the course of which no heat is either given to or taken from the gas involved by conduction or radiation, such as closely obtains in the case of rapidly rising or falling air), $dQ = 0$, and

$$\frac{dT}{dp} = \frac{AV}{C_p} = \frac{ART}{pC_p}. \tag{4}$$

From this it appears that the limiting ratio of the change of temperature to the change of pressure, in an adiabatic process, is directly proportional to the absolute temperature and inversely proportional to the pressure.

In the case of dry atmospheric air at ordinary temperatures $C_p = 0.240$, and $C_v = 0.171$, regarded here as "standard" values. Hence, for such air,

$$dT = dp \frac{ART}{0.240p}.$$

But

$$R = \frac{p_0 V_0}{T_0} = \frac{p_0}{\rho_0 T_0},$$

from which, assuming p_0 to be the pressure in dynes per square centimeter when the barometer, under gravity $g = 981$ cm. per second per second, and at 0° C. stands at 760 mm., and ρ_0 the corresponding density of dry air at 0° C., it follows that, numerically,

$$R = \frac{1033.2 \times 981}{0.001293 \times 273} = 2.871 \times 10^6.$$

And as

$$A = \frac{1}{4.185 \times 10^7},$$

therefore,

$$dT = \frac{dp}{p}\frac{T}{3.4984},$$

and

$$\frac{dT}{T} = 0.2858\frac{dp}{p}.$$

In the special case where the pressure is one atmosphere (barometer reading 760 mm.) and the temperature 0° C. (273° Abs.), such as often happens on the surface of the earth, an adiabatic change of pressure represented by 1 mm. of the barometer produces a temperature change given by the equation,

$$dT = \frac{1}{760}\frac{273}{3.4984} = 0°.10268 \text{ C.}$$

From equation (4) we get

$$\frac{dT}{T} = \frac{dp}{p}\frac{AR}{C_p}.$$

Hence

$$\log_e\frac{T_1}{T_2} = \frac{AR}{C_p}\log_e\frac{p_1}{p_2}$$

or, Poisson's equation,

$$\frac{T_1}{T_2} = \left(\frac{p_1}{p_2}\right)^{\frac{AR}{C_p}} = \left(\frac{p_1}{p_2}\right)^{\frac{C_p-C_v}{C_p}} = \left(\frac{p_1}{p_2}\right)^{0.288}$$

or,

$$\frac{p_1}{p_2} = \left(\frac{T_1}{T_2}\right)^{3.47}.$$

Also, by substituting for T_1 and T_2 their values from $pV = RT$,

$$\frac{p_1}{p_2} = \left(\frac{\rho_1}{\rho_2}\right)^{C_p/C_v}; \rho = \text{density.}$$

If we wish to find the rate of adiabatic cooling with change of height dh, a matter of great meterological importance, it is necessary to find the value of dp in terms of dh and substitute it in equation (4). It must be remembered, too, that pressure p decreases as the height h increases.

But $-dp = 981\rho dh$, where ρ is the density of the gas in question, or

$$-dp = \frac{981dh}{V} = \frac{981pdh}{RT}.$$

Hence, by substitution in equation (4), as explained,

$$-\frac{dT}{dh} = \frac{981A}{C_p} = \frac{1}{10239}. \tag{5}$$

That is, the adiabatic rate of decrease of temperature of absolutely dry air with increase of height is 1° C. per 102.39 meters.

Humid Air.—The natural atmosphere is not absolutely dry. Hence, as the specific heat of water vapor at constant pressure, roughly 0.47, is greater than that of dry air, 0.240, it follows that the adiabatic rate of decrease of temperature with increase of height is less in the actual atmosphere than that computed above for dry air. The C_p becomes C_p', as given by the equation

$$C_p' = \frac{(C_p\rho + C_p''\rho_w)}{(\rho + \rho_w)},$$

in which ρ, ρ_w are the densities of the dry air and the water vapor, respectively, and C_p'' the specific heat at constant pressure of water vapor at ordinary temperatures. If, for instance, 3 percent of the atmospheric pressure is owing to water vapor, we may put $\rho = 97$, $\rho_w = 1.866$, and find that $C_p' = 0.2416$; substituting this value in equation (5) gives 1° C. per 103.07 meters as the adiabatic gradient so long as the temperature is distinctly above the dew point.

Clearly, when the temperature of the atmosphere decreases with increase of height at the adiabatic rate, any portion of it transferred without gain or loss of heat from one level to another has, at every stage, the same temperature and density as the adjacent air, and therefore, if abandoned at rest, will neither rise nor fall. If, however, the temperature decreases at a less rate, an isolated mass of air, on being adiabatically lifted or depressed, becomes colder and denser or warmer and rarer, respectively, than the adjacent air, and consequently, if abandoned, will return to its initial level. Finally, if the temperature decreases at a greater rate, an isolated mass of air, on being elevated or depressed, will become warmer and lighter or colder and denser than the adjacent air, and, if permitted, will continue to rise or fall, respectively, until arrested by a change in the temperature gradient, or, if descending, perhaps even by the surface of the earth.

In short, the atmosphere is in neutral, stable, or unstable equilibrium in respect to strictly adiabatic processes according as the temperature decrease with increase of height is the same as, less than, or greater than the adiabatic rate, whatever that may be, or, according as its potential temperature (the temperature any portion would have if brought adiabatically to some given pressure) is constant, increases or decreases with height.

Others, also, of the above equations for dry air have to be appreciably modified to adapt them to the atmosphere as it actually is. Thus, since the constants of the various gases of the atmosphere differ from each other, it is only as an approximation that for the natural air we can write

$$p = \rho RT.$$

To be exact we should write, for instance

$$p = R_N(\rho_N + a\rho_w + b\rho_o + \cdots)T,$$

in which R_N is the gas constant for nitrogen, ρ_N, ρ_w, ρ_o, etc., the current densities of the nitrogen, water vapor, oxygen, etc., respectively, and a, b, etc., the ratios of the density (under like conditions) of nitrogen to those of the several other gases in question. However, as the relative amounts of the chief constituents of the atmosphere, except water vapor, are very nearly constant it is sufficient for all practical purposes to put

$$p = R(\rho + a\rho_w)T, \tag{6}$$

in which R is the gas constant of normal dry air, ρ the current density of the dry air, ρ_w the density of the water vapor present and a the ratio of the density of dry air to that of water vapor, that is, 1.608, nearly.

If the density of the air mixture is ρ' then

$$\rho' = \rho + \rho_w,$$

and from equation (6)

$$p = \rho' R\left(1 + 0.608\frac{\rho_w}{\rho'}\right)T \equiv \rho' R'T \equiv \rho' RT',$$

in which T' is the *virtual temperature*, or temperature at which dry air at the same pressure would have the same density as that of the current air, a fictitious value convenient for calculations, hence much used in aerological work.

Again, Poisson's equation in the form

$$\frac{p_1}{p_2} = \left(\frac{T_1}{T_2}\right)^{\frac{C_p}{AR}}$$

has to be modified through both the C_p and the R. If for each unit mass of dry air there are w units of water vapor this exponent becomes

$$\frac{C_p}{AR}\left[\frac{1 + \dfrac{C_p''w}{C_p}}{1 + aw}\right] = 3.50\left(\frac{1 + 1.96w)}{1 + 1.608w}\right),$$

in which C_p'' is the specific heat of water vapor at constant pressure, and a the ratio of the weighted mean molecular weight of dry air to that of water vapor. But w seldom is large enough to increase the value of the exponent by more than 1 per cent, and therefore commonly may be neglected.

Water vapor also frequently causes another and most important change in the temperature gradient. As soon as condensation sets in, the latent heat of vaporization, and, if ice is formed, of fusion, is liberated, and thus the rate of temperature decrease with altitude is reduced. The amount of this reduction, often at least half the original value, depends, of course, slightly upon what becomes of the condensed vapor. If it is carried along with the rising air the process remains adiabatic, except as modified by conduction and radiation, but if, as in great measure must happen, it is left behind as precipitation, then the process becomes that special case of the nonadiabatic which von Bezold, followed by others, has called pseudoadiabatic. This whole subject has been more or less discussed by several writers, but most fully, first, by Hertz[1] and, later, by Neuhoff.[2]

Undoubtedly much of the condensation drops out, or begins to drop out, as soon as formed, so that the actual temperature gradient, while lying somewhere between the really adiabatic and the "pseudoadiabatic" curves, probably follows the latter more closely than the former. Presumably, therefore, in practice it would be better, or at least quite as well, to determine the latter gradient (the adiabatic will be considered later, under "Condensation," in Chap. XV) and then to add such corrections to it as the circumstances of individual cases suggest. The main curve can be determined as follows:

As before,

$$dQ = C_v dT + A p dV.$$

But

$$pV = RT,$$

(R being appropriate to the existing mixture of air and water vapor). Hence

$$\begin{aligned} dQ &= C_v dT + A(RdT - Vdp) \\ &= (C_v + AR)dT - AVdp \\ &= C_p dT - AVdp \end{aligned} \tag{7}$$

But

$$-dp = g\rho dh,$$

where g is gravitational acceleration.

Therefore,

$$dQ = C_p dT + gAdh.$$

[1] *Deutsch. Met. Zeit.*, i; 421, 1884.
[2] *Abh. K. P. Met. Inst.*, i; No. 6, Berlin, 1900.

Now the heat dQ is added as the result of a quantity of water vapor dw being extracted. Hence

$$dQ = -sdw,$$

in which s is the heat of vaporization, and therefore,

$$-sdw = C_p dT + gAdh.$$

From this equation it is obvious that to obtain the ratio of dT to dh in terms of measurable quantities it is necessary and sufficient to express dw in similar terms.

But

$$w = \rho 0.622 \frac{e}{b},$$

in which w is the total mass of water vapor per cm.³, ρ the density of dry air at the current temperature and pressure, 0.622 the ratio of the molecular weight of water vapor to the weighted mean of the molecular weights of the constituents of dry air, e the partial pressure of the water vapor in terms of centimeters of mercury, and b the height, also in centimeters, of the barometer.

Hence

$$\frac{dw}{w} = \frac{de}{e} - \frac{db}{b}.$$

But, if D is the density of mercury,

$$-Ddb = \rho dh = \frac{pdh}{RT} = \frac{Dbgdh}{RT}.$$

Hence

$$-\frac{db}{b} = g\frac{dh}{RT}.$$

and

$$dw = w\frac{de}{e} + wg\frac{dh}{RT}.$$

Hence, by substitution,

$$C_p dT + sw\frac{de}{e} + swg\frac{dh}{RT} + gAdh = 0$$

or

$$\left(C_p + sw\frac{de}{edT} \right) dT + \left(\frac{sw}{RT} + A \right) gdh = 0$$

and

$$\frac{dT}{dh} = -\frac{g\left(A + \frac{sw}{RT} \right)}{C_p + sw\frac{de}{edT}}. \tag{8}$$

All the terms on the right-hand side of this equation are known for any definite temperature and assumed value of dT. From this equation, therefore, tables can be written and curves constructed that give the "pseudoadiabatic" gradient under all conditions of temperature and pressure.

Entropy and Potential Temperature.—In studying the energy of the atmosphere, it often is convenient to use the temperature-entropy diagram, in which one of the coordinates is the absolute temperature on the thermodynamical scale, and the other, called entropy, a quantity such that the product of a limiting change in it by the absolute temperature (an area on the diagram) shall be equal to the corresponding change of thermal energy per unit mass of the substance in question. In symbols, writing φ for entropy,

$$d\varphi = \frac{dQ}{T}.$$

But from equation (7),

$$dQ = C_p dT - AVdp = C_p dT - \frac{ARTdp}{p}.$$

Hence $d\varphi$, because it is a function of dQ, the change in energy, is a function of both T and p, the things affected by that change in energy. Evidently, then, we can arbitrarily mark our scale of entropy zero at any chosen values of T and p, and count only its changes between this and other temperature-pressure states. Let these chosen values be T_0 and p_0. In meteorological problems 100° is a convenient value for T_0, since lower temperatures of the atmosphere do not occur; and the bar, or 10^6 dynes per square centimeter, approximately one atmosphere, for p_0.

If θ is the potential temperature corresponding to p_0, that is, the temperature to which dry air in the state (T, p) would come if adiabatically brought to the pressure p_0, then from Poisson's equation

$$T = \theta\left(\frac{p}{p_0}\right)^{\frac{AR}{C_p}}.$$

Hence, substituting for dQ

$$d\varphi = C_p\frac{dT}{T} - AR\frac{dp}{p} = C_p d\log\left\{\theta\left(\frac{p}{p_0}\right)^{\frac{AR}{C_p}}\right\} - AR\frac{dp}{p} = C_p\frac{d\theta}{\theta}.$$

and

$$\varphi = C_p\log\theta + \text{constant or } \varphi_1 - \varphi_2 = C_p\log\frac{\theta_1}{\theta_2}.$$

Therefore, when the pressure on a given mass of dry air is increased or decreased adiabatically from one value to another, the quantity of heat produced or consumed, respectively, is numerically proportional to the absolute temperature at which the change is made. Also, from this equation, wherever the potential temperature is constant, as throughout a completely stirred mass of dry air, the entropy also is constant. Hence an isentropic surface (surface over which the entropy is constant) is an equipotential-temperature surface.

Though the surface is the same no matter by which of these names, "isentropic" or "equipotential-temperature," we call it, one's concept may not be equally clear in the two cases. The meaning of the term "potential temperature" is readily understood and easily remembered, whereas to most people "entropy" is an eel-like term—the more firmly one tries to grasp its meaning the more quickly it slips away. But "equipotential-temperature surface" is too cumbersome to say and too long to write. Then abbreviate; take the initials of the three words and call it "e.p.t." surface, or, shorter still, "ept" surface, and know what it is!

The Entropy of Humid Air.—Let an aspiration psychrometer meet the following conditions, as it may to any required approximation:

1 That there be no net radiation gain or loss by the thermometer element.

2. That there be no addition of heat to, or subtraction from, the system, air, water vapor, and water, within and passing through the psychrometer.

3. That the exit air be saturated. This assumption is not necessary, but convenient.

4. That the pressure be constant.

Let T be the absolute temperature of perfectly dry intake air (if not fully dry, some of the following equations will need slight but obvious changes); T' the absolute temperature of the wet bulb; C_p and C_p' the specific heats of dry air and of water vapor, respectively, at constant pressure; and x the mass ratio of water vapor to dry air in saturated air at the temperature T'.

Then, counting from the freezing point, the heat in $1 + x$ grams of saturated air at the temperature T' is $(C_p - C_p'x)$ $(T' - 273)$, which, since the process is adiabatic, is equal to the heat in the initial stage, $C_p(T - 273) + x(T' - 273)$. That is, as Normand[1] has shown:

1. The heat content of any air equals the heat content of the same air saturated at its wet-bulb temperature minus the heat content of the liquid water required so to saturate it.

2. The wet-bulb temperature of air adiabatically cooled, whether much or little, by evaporation into it from spray or other source, is constant. Therefore the wet-bulb potential temperature (wet-bulb temperature reduced to some standard pressure) is an exceedingly con-

[1] *Memoirs Indian Meteorological Department*, **23**; Pt. 1, 1921.

servative property of the atmosphere—a voucher that is well-nigh a fingerprint in air-mass analysis.

3. If the wet-bulb temperatures of several portions of air are equal, that of their mixtures will be the same, however different their actual temperatures.

Furthermore, since the quantity of heat added to an object divided by the current absolute temperature of that object is the change in its entropy, the entropy per gram of dry air at the absolute temperature T, counting from 0° C. is

$$C_p \int_{273}^{T} \frac{dT}{T} = C_p \log\frac{T}{723}.$$

Similarly, the entropy of $1 + x$ grams of saturated air at the absolute temperature T', also from 0° C. is, since the specific heat of water is one,

$$C_p \log \frac{T'}{273} + x \log \frac{T'}{273} + \frac{Lx}{T'},$$

in which L is the heat of vaporization of a gram of water at the absolute temperature T'.

But

$$C_p \log \frac{T}{273} = C_p \log \frac{T'}{273} + \frac{Lx}{T'}, \text{ nearly,}$$

since $Lx = C_p(T - T')$, and

$$\log \frac{T}{T'} = \frac{T}{T'} - 1 - \frac{1}{2}\left(\frac{T}{T'} - 1\right)^2 + \frac{1}{3}\left(\frac{T}{T'} - 1\right)^3 \cdots = \frac{T}{T'} - 1, \text{ nearly,}$$

which is true for all ordinary values of T/T'.

Hence, as first shown by Normand,[1]

The entropy of any air approximately equals the entropy of the same air saturated at its wet-bulb temperature *minus* the entropy of the liquid water required so to saturate it.

Equivalent Temperature.—Since the give and take of heat in the processes of condensation and evaporation, respectively, are large, it follows that the actual temperature of a given mass of humid air is determined, in part, by the amount of water that has just undergone one of these changes in it. And, since these processes are of frequent occurrence, the temperature of such a mass of air is no assurance of its identity. However, on warming the air at a particular level, say that of condensation, by the heat of condensation of all the water vapor in it, a temperature is obtained that generally is nearly enough constant, at the initial pressure, to identify the air in question for at least a day or two.

[1] *Loc. cit.*

If T_E is the equivalent absolute temperature, then, clearly, where there are w grams of water vapor to 1 gram of dry air,

$$T_E = T_c + \frac{L_c w}{C_p},$$

in which T_c is the condensation temperature, L_c the latent heat of vaporization of water at this temperature, T_c, and C_p the specific heat of dry air at constant pressure.

T_c and the corresponding pressure p_c can be computed, as explained in Chap. XV, under "Condensation Due to Dynamic Cooling." In practice, however, they are picked out on a large Neuhoff diagram or other suitable graph. A slightly different and, perhaps, more nearly constant value of T_E is obtained by dropping out all condensed water as soon as formed, and for L_c substituting L_m, the weighted mean value of the heat of condensation as the vapor gradually is exhausted incident to cooling by convection. Of course, tables and graphs that give the values of L_m can be prepared in advance.

Equivalent Potential Temperature.—The equivalent potential temperature θ_E is found by reducing the equivalent temperature to its value at a standard pressure, p_0. Hence

$$\theta_E = T_E \left(\frac{p_0}{p_c}\right)^{\frac{AR}{C_p}}.$$

Temperature Changes of a Rising (or Falling) Isolated Mass of Air.— The above discussion of the temperature decrease with increase of height of dry air applies only to an atmosphere whose potential temperature is the same throughout, such as it would be on thorough adiabatic mixing. As a matter of fact, the actual potential temperature of the atmosphere rarely, if ever, is uniform, and hence it is of some interest to trace the temperature changes with change of height of an isolated mass of air, or other gas, as it rises or falls adiabatically through an atmosphere whose potential temperature is non-uniform.

This subject has been discussed by several authors, but most concisely, perhaps, by Exner in his "Dynamische Meteorologie," and, in substance, as follows:

Let the absolute temperature at a given point within the adiabatically cooling (or warming) isolated mass of air be T, and that of the surrounding air at the same level, and where the pressure, therefore, is also the same, T'. Then, as already explained, at any point within this mass

$$\frac{dT}{dp} = \frac{ART}{pC_p}$$

whatever the cause of the pressure change dp.

Now, let dp be due wholly to change of level of the isolated mass in the surrounding air; then

$$-dp = \frac{gpdh}{RT'}.$$

Hence the temperature gradient of (not within) the rising mass at the place in question is given by the equation

$$\frac{dT}{dh} = -\frac{gAT}{C_pT'} = -a\frac{T}{T'},$$

in which a is the adiabatic temperature gradient. That is, the rising air will cool at a greater or less rate than the "adiabatic" according as its temperature is higher or lower than that of the adjacent atmosphere, and by roughly 0.4 of one per cent of the adiabatic rate for each 1° C. difference.

Let the height under consideration be h, and let the temperature of the free air decrease uniformly with ascent. Then, if T_h' is the temperature of the free air at the level h, and T_0' its temperature at the surface,

$$T_h' = T_0' - lh,$$

in which l is the uniform lapse-rate, or ratio of temperature change to change of height, of the free air. Hence

$$(dT)_h = -a\frac{T_h dh}{T_0' - lh},$$

or

$$\frac{(dT)_h}{T_h} = -a\frac{dh}{T_0' - lh},$$

and

$$\log T_h = \frac{a}{l} \log (T_0' - lh) + \text{a constant}.$$

If T_0 is the initial or surface temperature of the rising mass, then

$$\frac{T_h}{T_0} = \left(\frac{T_0' - lh}{T_0'}\right)^{\frac{a}{l}}$$

Hence, in general, the cooling with height is given by the equation

$$\left(\frac{dT}{dh}\right)_h = -a\left(\frac{T_0' - lh}{T_0'}\right)^{\frac{a-l}{l}}\frac{T_0}{T_0'}.$$

When the temperature of the free air has the "adiabatic" distribution, or $l = a$,

$$\frac{dT}{dh} = -a\frac{T_0}{T_0'}.$$

That is, the rising air then also cools at a constant rate, but one more or less different from the "adiabatic," except in the special case when it has the same initial temperature as the adjacent air.

When $l = 0$, or the temperature of the free air remains constant with height, as it does in the isothermal region, the value of dT/dh clearly can not be determined from the above equation. However, from

$$T_h = T_h' = T_0\left(1 - \frac{lh}{T_0'}\right)^{\frac{a}{l}},$$

it appears that when $l = 0$,

$$T_h = T_0 e^{\frac{-ah}{T_0'}},$$

and

$$\left(\frac{dT}{dh}\right)_h = -a\frac{T_0}{T_0'}e^{\frac{-ah}{T_0'}}.$$

Hence in an isothermal region the rate of cooling of a rising mass of air decreases with height.

Finally, from the equation

$$T_h = T_0\left(\frac{T_0' - lh}{T_0'}\right)^{\frac{a}{l}},$$

it appears that where $T_h = T_h'$

$$T_h = T_0' - lh,$$

or that the rising air comes to the temperature of the surrounding atmosphere, and thus into a position of rest, at the height

$$h = \frac{1}{l}\left[T_0' - \left(\frac{T_0'^a}{T_0^l}\right)^{\frac{1}{a-l}}\right].$$

If, for instance, $l = a/2$, $T_0' = 290°$ Abs., and $T_0 = 300°$ Abs., then $h = 1.99$ kilometers, approximately; whereas, if the rising air cooled according to the adiabatic rate (1° C. per 102 meters), as usually assumed, the value of h would be 2.05 kilometers.

If the roughly approximate value of the adiabatic rate, 1° C. per 100 meters, is used, the above values of h become 1.93 kilometers and 2 kilometers, respectively.

Change of Lapse Rate Due to Adiabatic Vertical Convection.— Again following Exner, let a thin horizontal layer of air of thickness δz be lowered adiabatically, without lateral expansion or contraction, to a new level and let its thickness there be $\delta z'$. Let the corresponding temperatures, pressures, densities, and lapse rates at the lower surface in its two positions be T, T'; p, p'; ρ, ρ'; and l, l', respectively. Then, from Poisson's equation, putting $AR/C_p = k$; $dp/dz = b$; and $dp'/dz' = b'$;

$$\frac{T'}{T} = \left(\frac{p'}{p}\right)^k \text{ and } \frac{T' + l'\delta z'}{T + l\delta z} = \left(\frac{p' + b'\delta z'}{p + b\delta z}\right)^k.$$

Expanding and retaining only the significant terms, we get

$$T' + l'\delta z' = T\left(1 + \frac{l}{T}\delta z\right)\left(\frac{p'}{p}\right)^k\left(1 + \frac{k}{p'}b'\delta z'\right)\left(1 - \frac{k}{p}b\delta z\right), \text{ virtually.}$$

Again retaining only the significant terms, substituting for T' its value from the first equation, and noting that $b = -\rho g$, $b' = -\rho'g$, and that $\delta z/\delta z' = \rho'/\rho$, we finally get

$$l' = \frac{p'}{p}\left(l + \frac{Ag}{C_p}\right) - \frac{Ag}{C_p}. \tag{9}$$

But p' and p are unequal, since they pertain to different levels, hence l' and l also are unequal; that is, vertical convection changes the lapse rate, except in the special case when l has the adiabatic value, $-Ag/C_p$. If, for example, a layer of air having initially half the dry adiabatic lapse rate—colder above than below by about 1° C. per 200 meters difference in level—should descend until the pressure at some point in it became doubled, then at that point, *not elsewhere*, its lapse rate would be zero.

All the above is, as explained, on the assumption that there is no lateral expansion or contraction. Suppose, however, that the horizontal cross-section of the convecting air changes from s at one level to s' at the other. Then, since $\delta z/\delta z' = \rho's'/\rho s$, clearly, in this case,

$$l' = \frac{s'p'}{sp}\left(1 + \frac{Ag}{C_p}\right) - \frac{Ag}{C_p}. \tag{10}$$

Equations (9) and (10), it should be noted, do not represent an ado about nothing, or at most just some rare and unimportant event, but are evaluations of the ceaseless changes in the lapse rate that, however unsuspected, occur with every variation of the barometer and every change of level no matter how produced.

Lapse Rate in Non-adiabatic Convection.—If dQ in equation (1) is not zero, then we may put $dQ = BdT$, as Emden[1] does, and obtain the expression

$$0 = (C_v - B)dT + ApdV,$$

which, by substitution, gives

$$\frac{dT}{dh} = -\frac{g}{R}\frac{C_p - C_v}{C_p - B}.$$

[1] *Met. Zeit.*, **33**; 353, 1916.

From this, one may pass on to various other equations. Linke,[1] for instance, putting $dT/dh \equiv l$, and $H_l = -T_0/l$, gives the easily derived, and perhaps sometimes useful, equations:

$$T = T_0(1 - h/H_l)$$

$$\frac{dp}{p} = -\frac{gdh}{RT} \equiv -\frac{g}{l}\frac{dT}{dh}\frac{dh}{RT}$$

$$p = p_0\left(\frac{T}{T_0}\right)^{\frac{-g}{Rl}} = p_0\left(1 - \frac{h}{H_l}\right)^{\frac{-g}{Rl}}$$

$$h = H_l\left[1 - \left(\frac{p}{p_0}\right)^{-\frac{Rl}{g}}\right]$$

$$\rho = \rho_0\left(1 - \frac{h}{H_l}\right)^{\frac{-g}{Rl}-1}.$$

Work of Expanding Air.—If the mass m of air expands adiabatically, clearly

$$mC_v dT_v + mC_p dT_p = 0$$

in which dT_v and dT_p are the change in temperature due to change of pressure at constant volume, and change in temperature due to change in volume at constant pressure, respectively, and C_v and C_p the specific heat at constant volume and constant pressure, respectively. The first term is the heat consumed due to change of pressure at constant volume, and the second the heat consumed due to change of volume at constant pressure. The sum of the two is zero because the whole process is adiabatic.

But, as explained above

$$pV = RT.$$

Hence, for V constant

$$\frac{dT}{dp} = \frac{V}{R},$$

and for p constant

$$\frac{dT}{dV} = \frac{p}{R}.$$

Substituting

$$mC_v\frac{Vdp}{R} + mC_p\frac{pdV}{R} = 0.$$

Putting $C_p/C_v = \gamma$, we get

$$\log (pV^\gamma) = \text{constant},$$

Hence,

$$pV^\gamma = \text{constant}.$$

[1] *Met. Zeit.*, **36**; 143, 1919.

The work w therefore, each initial unit volume at pressure p_1 can do on expanding to volume V is given by the equation

$$w = p_1 \int_1^V \frac{dV}{V^\gamma} = \frac{p_1}{\gamma - 1}\left(1 - \frac{1}{V^{\gamma-1}}\right)$$

and the total potential energy E per unit volume at pressure p_1, or work it can do on expanding to an infinite volume, by the equation

$$E = \frac{p_1}{\gamma - 1}.$$

If the expansion is isothermal, $pV = $ constant, as explained above, and, per unit volume,

$$w = p_1 \log V$$
$$E = \infty.$$

Work Done on a Mass of Ascending Air.—As shown by D. Brunt,[1] if p, ρ, T are the pressure, density, and absolute temperature, respectively, of non-ascending air at a particular level, and p, ρ', T' the like values at the same level of a second quantity of air buoyed up through the first, then, per unit mass of this lighter air,

$$dw = g\frac{\rho - \rho'}{\rho'}dh = (T' - T)\frac{\rho g dh}{\rho T} = -R(T' - T)d \log p,$$

The negative sign is required since p decreases with increase of height.

If, then, a graph, having T for the abscissa and $\log p$ for the ordinate, is constructed on the same diagram for both the ascending and the surrounding air, the area between these curves and the constant pressure lines, appropriate to the heights h_1 and h_2, will be proportional to the work done by the denser air on the lighter in pushing it up from the lower to the higher of the given levels. The number of ergs per gram of the ascending air, per square centimeter of the enclosed area, is determined by the scales of the coordinates.

[1] *Quart. J. Roy. Meteorol. Soc.*, **57**; 431, 1931.

CHAPTER III

OBSERVED VERTICAL TEMPERATURE GRADIENTS

The temperature of the surface air is well known at many places and at various heights, from sea level up to about 6 kilometers. But the temperature records obtained by the aid of kites and balloons, both manned and free, show that the mountain air temperatures generally differ materially from the temperature of the free air at the same height and latitude.

According to Hann and Süring,[1] the average temperature of the surface decreases approximately at the rate of 1° C. per each 180 meters, 200 meters, and 250 meters increase of height on mountains, hills, and plateaus, respectively. In the free atmosphere, however, the result is quite different. Here the decrease of temperature with increase of altitude, except at very great heights is, roughly, the same at most parts of the world, for the reason explained below.

The records obtained by kites, manned balloons, and sounding balloons all agree, of course, so far as they apply to the same levels, but as the free or sounding balloon, with its automatically registering apparatus, has gone far higher than either manned balloons or kites, and as ascensions by it have been quite numerous, only the records thus obtained are considered in what follows. Again, and for the sake of still further uniformity, the first part of the discussion is confined to those records which were obtained at Munich, Strassburg, Trappes, and Uccle, four European stations of about the same latitude and more or less similar climates. The records of vertical temperature distribution have been divided also according to season, winter (December, January, February, and March) and summer (June, July, August, and September), and prevailing type of weather, or, to be more exact, the height of the barometer, high, low, and neutral. Spring and fall observations have been omitted owing to the transitional nature of these seasons, or the overlapping and confusion at these times of summer and winter conditions.

Average Vertical Distribution of Temperature during Summer and during Winter.—When these data were assembled, the middle of 1918, all the available records of the stations mentioned were used, 185 winter records and 231 summer records. A larger number of flights would, of course, furnish a somewhat more reliable average, but, as the several stations gave substantially the same results, it would seem that no great

[1] "Lehrbuch der Meteorologie," 4th Ed., p. 125.

change would be made in the season averages, however large the number of combined observations, nor, indeed, have the many subsequent flights, to 1939, indicated any such change.

Figure 16 gives the average winter and summer vertical temperature gradients of the stations in question, or the graphs obtained by plotting the average temperatures (derived from the average of the observed temperature gradients) of the given season against the corresponding heights at which they were obtained.

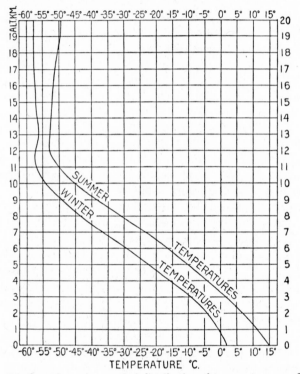

Fig. 16.—Winter and summer vertical distribution of temperature over Europe.

A number of interesting points are brought out by these two curves, each of which calls for an explanation. Among other things, the two gradients are, roughly, parallel to each other throughout their whole range. This is because the temperature of the atmosphere from top to bottom is determined by the same factors in the winter that determine it in the summer; that is, by radiation, conduction, and convection, all mainly from the surface of the earth and the lower atmosphere, and since each of these factors commonly is less in winter than in summer, it follows that usually their combined result, the temperature of the higher atmosphere, must also be less then at every level; hence, presumably, the substantial parallelism of the two gradients in this case.

Again, it appears, as shown by the figure, that up to about $2\frac{1}{2}$ kilometers the temperature decreases less rapidly with increase of elevation during winter than it does during summer. The reason for this, while not quite obvious, will become apparent from the following considerations:

The surface of the earth, which is a much better radiator than the atmosphere, often cools, especially during clear nights, to a decidedly lower temperature than the air 100 meters or so above it. Hence, late at night, when the sky is clear and the wind is light, the temperature near the surface usually increases with increase of height, and even when there is sufficient wind to prevent this "temperature inversion," as it is called, the lower atmosphere still is colder than it otherwise would be. Obviously, too, the amount of this surface cooling, and therefore the magnitude of the temperature inversion, depends jointly upon the rates of radiation to and from the sky and the time involved. Now the rate of the output of surface and lower air radiation is less in winter than in summer, both because of their lower temperatures at that time and because the atmosphere then contains less water vapor, its chief radiating constituent. Nevertheless, even though the radiation loss from the surface of the earth and adjacent air is greater in summer than in winter, the concurrent radiation gain from the upper air may, perhaps, usually render the difference, or net loss, somewhat less.

At any rate, partly for this reason, it may be, but mainly because of the relatively greater length of the nights and greater dryness and consequent diathermacy of the atmosphere, the total surface cooling, and therefore the morning temperature inversions, is much more pronounced in winter than in summer. Hence, the average decrease of temperature with increase of height through the first 1 or 2 kilometers is decidedly less during the colder than during the warmer season, a condition still more pronounced, and extending to greater levels, in high latitudes.

Another peculiarity shown by the curves is the fact that between the heights of approximately 4 and 8 kilometers the temperature decreases rather more rapidly during winter than summer. Throughout this region the temperature of the atmosphere depends in part upon convection from lower levels and in part upon its gain and loss of heat through radiation. But even this midair, or radiational, change in temperature can result only in immediate convection. Consequently, so long as saturation is not reached, the convectional temperature gradient must be very approximately that of a totally dry atmosphere. If, however, condensation takes place, the latent heat of vaporization becomes sensible heat, and the decrease of temperature with increase of altitude is correspondingly less. When a condensation temperature gradient is once established in this mid-region of the atmosphere it tends to persist, even after condensation has ceased and the clouds have evaporated, because, what-

ever condition—the presence or absence of sunshine, for instance—produces a temperature change in one part of it is likely to produce similar
temperature changes in other parts, and therefore approximately the
same variation for each level, a variation which would leave the general
temperature gradient substantially as before.   Furthermore, the true
condensation gradient frequently is renewed for cloudless skies seldom
last long.   We should, then, expect to find the average vertical temperature gradient following, roughly, the gradient for saturated air for the
given temperature, and such, indeed, are the gradients actually found,
except during winter in high latitudes.

Hence, as the atmosphere between the levels of 4 and 8 kilometers
is quite out of the reach of surface inversions, and as it is also warmer
and more humid during summer than during winter, we should expect
the summer temperature of this region to decrease less rapidly with
increase of altitude than does the winter temperature, precisely as balloon
records show to be the case.

As just stated, the winter temperature gradient in high latitudes
usually differs from that of the rest of the world; commonly being less to
much less.   In most places heat is carried upward by convection, and
condensation gradients thus established that tend to persist and frequently are renewed.   Where, however, the surface is continuously cold
the atmosphere does not ascend, but, on the contrary, slowly descends,
owing to the ceaseless outflow of the lower air, incident to the thermally
established high pressure.   In this case the free air loses heat by radiation and gains heat by absorption and by compression; but through the
lower several kilometers radiation by the atmosphere exceeds its absorption, as is presently explained.   Indeed, if it did not, then the added
dynamical or compressional heating soon would arrest descent.   Now,
as the outflow is shallow the descent necessarily is slow, and as radiation
exceeds absorption the lapse rate thus established must be less than
the adiabatic.   Clearly, too, the extent of this departure will, in general,
be the greater the slower the descent.

To sum up: Where heat is carried up by convection the lapse rate is
approximately the adiabatic for saturated air; and where it is not carried
up, this rate is less to much less than the adiabatic for dry air.

Another point brought out by Fig. 16 is the fact that up to 8 kilometers, or thereabouts, the ratio of the decrease of temperature to
increase of height itself increases with height.   The explanation of this
phenomenon is precisely the same as that of the difference between the
winter and summer gradients from 4 to 8 kilometers.   That is to say, it
depends upon the amount of water vapor necessary to produce saturation at the various levels, since the less this vapor is in proportion to the
total gases present the more nearly does the actual temperature gradient
follow the adiabatic curve for dry air.

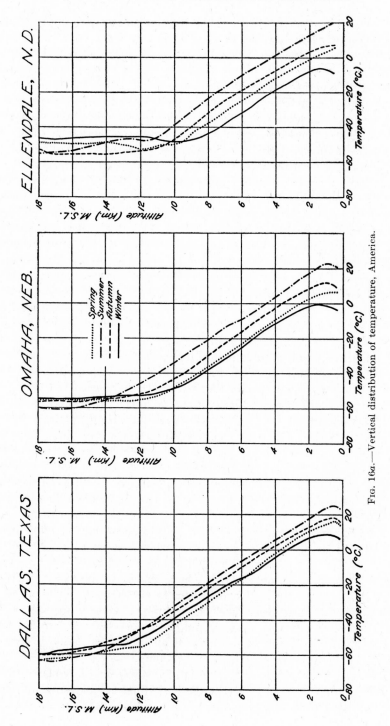

Fig. 16a.—Vertical distribution of temperature, America.

One striking feature of each of the temperature gradients is its gradual change, between the levels of 9 and 12 kilometers, from a rapid decrease of temperature with increase of height to an approximately isothermal condition. Normally, however, the temperature gradient changes from a rapid to practically a zero decrease of temperature with increase of height, much more abruptly than one would infer from the given curves. But this more or less abrupt change varies considerably in altitude from day to day. Therefore, when a large number of actual gradients are averaged an *apparent* gradual transition is indicated.

Two other features calling for some attention often are in the lower portion of a recorded summer gradient; namely, the fact that through the first $\frac{1}{2}$ kilometer the temperature decreases but slowly, and the further fact that through the second $\frac{1}{2}$ kilometer it decreases more rapidly than anywhere else, short of very considerable altitudes. Now many of the observations from which summer gradients are constructed are obtained during the early forenoon. Hence the average slow decrease of temperature with increase of elevation is the result only of ordinary morning inversions. On the other hand, the rapid decrease of temperature through the second $\frac{1}{2}$ kilometer is expressive of the adiabatic gradient of unsaturated air that commonly exists during summer afternoons up to a level of at least 1 kilometer. In this case it has persisted in its upper portion throughout the night, and has been modified, as explained, by temperature inversions only in its lower half.

Figure 16*a*, from *Monthly Weather Review Supplement* 38, by C. M. Lennahan, gives the mean temperatures from the surface to well up into the stratosphere at three points in America. Here, contrary to the conditions shown in Fig. 16, the stratosphere is warmer in winter than in summer. This may be owing to such seasonal changes in the humidity and cloudiness of the lower air, as would cause the tropopause (base of the stratosphere) to be highest and coldest in summer, just as, and presumably for the same reason, it is higher and colder in tropical than in extra-tropical regions.

Atmospheric Stratification.—Almost every individual sounding of the atmosphere shows more or less stratification—layer upon layer of air differing more or less from each other in lapse rate, humidity, and direction and velocity of movement. The warmer an upper layer the less likely it is to be penetrated by convection from below—a cooling process— or itself to fall to a lower level—a warming process. The first would put relatively dense air in light, and the second light air in dense, an unstable situation in either case. In many cases convection is arrested by one of these layers as by a physical ceiling.

Not only is the atmosphere generally stable in the respect of one layer to another, but also within the individual layers, especially when they are free from cloud, and the less the lapse rate the greater this stability. An obvious measure of this stability would be the force of restitution per unit mass of air per unit vertical displacement; but this force is directly proportional to the difference between the densities of the displaced and the then surrounding air. In symbols,

$$S = \frac{a - b}{T},$$

where a is the adiabatic, and b the current, lapse rate, and T the absolute temperature of the surrounding air at the final position.

Why the Atmosphere Is Stratified.—The chief factors that cause stratification of the atmosphere are: (1) the running of colder air under warmer air; (2) the flow of warmer (actually or potentially) and, usually, more humid air over colder and drier air; (3) turbulence, by which the adiabatic gradient is approached through the disturbed air by mixing, making it colder at the top and warmer at the bottom—most pronounced in the lowest, or surface, layer, because turbulence, due to friction, is greatest there; and (4) convection and overflow, especially vigorous in the thunderstorm.

Why the Temperature of the Atmosphere Decreases with Increase of Height.—It is not, perhaps, obvious why the temperature of the atmosphere should rapidly decrease with increase of height, except near the surface at the time and place of a temperature inversion, as it does through at least the first several kilometers, as shown by Fig. 16. Essentially, however, this phenomenon depends on the following facts:

1. The atmosphere, as is known from observation, transmits, directly and by scattering, to the surface of the earth 42 per cent, roughly, of the effective radiation received from the sun, that is, nearly half of the portion absorbed and not lost by reflection. Consequently, it is this surface, where the energy absorption is concentrated, and not the atmosphere, through which it is diffused, that is chiefly heated by insolation. The heated surface in turn warms the air above it, partly by contact and partly by the long wave-length radiation it emits, and of which the atmosphere is far more absorptive than it is of the comparatively short wave-length solar radiation.

2. Furthermore, and this is an equally vital part of the explanation, the lower atmosphere (below about 10 kilometers), under all ordinary conditions, emits more radiant energy than it absorbs. It is these two phenomena, (*a*) the net loss of heat by radiation (cooling above), and (*b*) the surface heating (warming below), that together establish and maintain the vertical convections of the atmosphere under which, since the descending portions grow warmer through compression and the ascending colder through expansion, the whole of the convective region is made to decrease in temperature with increase of height.

But since the coefficient of absorption of the air, as of other objects, changes but little, if at all, with temperature, while its emissive power decreases rapidly as it grows colder, and since the intensity of the incident terrestrial (including atmospheric) radiation remains roughly constant up to an altitude of many kilometers beyond the first 4 or 5 kilometers, it follows that the upper limit of the convective region is not, as formerly supposed, the outermost limit of the atmosphere, but at that height at which the temperature is so low that the loss of heat by radiation is no longer in excess of, but is now equal to, its gain by absorption. Beyond this level as high up as this equality holds, temperature does not decrease, or does so but slightly, with increase of height; nor would it so decrease, at least at nothing like the present rate, beyond any level, however low, at which absorption and radiation became equal.

In short, then, through the first 10 kilometers or so the higher the air the colder it is, because (1) owing to its transparency to solar radiation it is heated mainly at the surface of the earth, and (2) at ordinary temperatures it emits more radiation than it absorbs. These together usually so affect the density of the atmosphere as to induce vertical convections, and thereby to establish and maintain, throughout the region in which they are active, a rapid decrease of temperature with increase of height. This is the gross state of the atmosphere, on which, however, there often are superimposed relatively small disturbances in the form of temperature inversions.

Temperature Inversions.—It often happens that at one or more levels the temperature of the air increases, more or less, with increase of height, instead of decreasing. Such a temperature inversion normally occurs at the surface of the earth (not over the ocean) on still, clear nights, because this surface, being a good radiator, cools faster on such occasions than does the free atmosphere, and, in turn, by contact, correspondingly chills the adjacent air. Even a very gentle wind greatly decreases the intensity of this morning inversion by distributing, through turbulence, such loss of heat as does occur to a greater mass of air.

Another common cause of temperature inversions is turbulence induced by friction. The masses of air forced to higher levels cool by expansion, and those brought to lower levels are warmed by compression, until an adiabatic gradient is established from top to bottom of the agitated layer. In this way the upper portion of this layer becomes colder than it otherwise would have been, and therefore colder than the air next above it. Hence a temperature inversion is thereby established at the interface between the turbulent air beneath and the undisturbed air above.

The running of cold air under warm air and the flow of warm air over cold air, both common phenomena, are two other ways, and the only others of importance, by which temperature inversions may be, and frequently are, effected.

CHAPTER IV

THE ISOTHERMAL REGION, OR STRATOSPHERE

Of all the conditions indicated by the temperature gradients of Figs. 16 and 16a, by far the most surprising, and most difficult fully to explain, is the approximately isothermal state of the upper atmosphere so far as explored. Indeed, the discovery of the fact that the temperature of this portion of the upper atmosphere changes but little with altitude, and the supplementary discovery of its physical explanation, constitute one of the most important advances in modern meteorology.

The exploration of the atmosphere by small balloons carrying meteorological instruments was suggested in 1809,[1] but the idea was first carried out by Hermite[2] on Mar. 21, 1893, when the height of 16 kilometers was attained. In April, 1898, Teisserenc de Bort,[3] with improved apparatus, began at Trappes, France, a long series of frequent atmospheric soundings. Among other things, he soon found temperature records that indicated something unsuspected: either errors in the thermometers themselves or surprising temperature conditions in the upper atmosphere. However, numerous temperature records subsequently obtained by himself and many others in various countries and with different kinds of apparatus have shown that, in general, the temperature of the instrumentally explored portion of the upper atmosphere actually does change but little with change of height. Indeed, as a rule, the change is so small that the whole region characterized by this approximate constancy of temperature has been called the "isothermal region." At present it is called the "stratosphere," though the older and less used term certainly is more suggestive of its distinguishing characteristic.

Physical Explanation of the Existence of the Stratosphere.—The height at which this region begins, and its temperature, both depend upon season, upon storm conditions, and upon latitude; but, while all these are important details, they are secondary to the fact that there is an isothermal region at all.

As soon as observations left no doubt of the actual existence of an isothermal region, many explanations of it were proposed, but for a number of years all such suggestions proved unavailing. Finally, however, independently and nearly simultaneously, the generally accepted expla-

[1] *Ann. Harvard Obs.*, **68**; pt. 1, p. 1.
[2] *L'Aérophile*, **1**; 45, 1893.
[3] *C. R.*, **129**; 417, 1899.

51

nation occurred to Gold[1] of England and Humphreys[2] of America.   The same subject has also been discussed at length by Emden,[3] Milne,[4] and Pekeris.[5]   The key to the explanation is this: The temperature of every portion of the atmosphere is determined, in part at least, by counteracting radiation—radiation absorbed and radiation emitted—and wherever these two are equal there is substantial constancy of temperature.

Gold's method of procedure was to take the best-known data concerning atmospheric absorption and radiation and to obtain, by the aid of suitable mathematics, a general solution of the problem.   The chief difficulty in the application of this direct and elegant method, apart from the troublesome equations involved, is that due to our imperfect knowledge of the necessary radiation and absorption constants.   Numerical values in these particulars are not accurately known and certainly not easy to determine.

On the other hand, the solution offered by Humphreys, while not so direct, reduces the necessary mathematics to a minimum.   In brief, it is as follows: Since the average yearly temperature of the atmosphere at any given place does not greatly change, it follows that the absorption of solar radiation by the earth as a whole is substantially equal to the total outgoing earth radiation, and (see Chap. VI) in amount approximately equal to that which a black or perfectly radiating surface, equal in area to the surface of the earth, would emit if at the absolute temperature 246°.   Further, since at ordinary atmospheric temperatures water vapor, in considerable quantity, absorbs and, presumably, also radiates in the main as does a black body at the same temperature, while dry air is exceedingly diathermanous, it follows that the planetary radiation of the earth is largely water vapor radiation.

Now the records of sounding balloons show that at some height, in general about 11 kilometers above sea level in middle latitudes, the average temperature ceases to decrease with increase of height.   Individual flights show many peculiarities that call for special explanation, but the purpose here is to consider only the general explanation of the main effect, and therefore average conditions are considered.

If, then, as is approximately true, the temperature does not decrease with increase of altitude above 11 kilometers, at least not below the height to which instruments have been taken, it follows that this must be the limit of anything like a marked vertical convection.   And from this in turn it follows, since conduction is negligible, that the upper atmosphere must be warmed almost wholly by absorption of radiation, in part

[1] *Proc. Roy. Soc.*, **82**; 43, 1909.
[2] *Astrophys. J.*, **29**; 14, 1909.
[3] *Sitzb. K. Bayr. Akad. Wis.*, p. 55, 1913.
[4] *Phil. Mag.*, **44**; 872, 1922.
[5] *Beitr. Geophys.*, **23**; 377, 1930.

solar and in part terrestrial; but exactly how much of the final temperature of the upper atmosphere is due to the one source of heat and how
much to the other it is impossible to say.   However, there are certain
facts that seem clearly to indicate the relative importance in this respect
of the two sources.   Thus the summer and winter gradients, as given in
Fig. 16, show a difference of temperature in the stratosphere of only about
the amount that might be expected on the assumption that the temperature of the upper air is wholly dependent upon the radiation from below.

Figure 16a, however, shows that at the places it represents the
stratosphere normally is warmer in winter than in summer, or just the
reverse of the conditions shown by Fig. 16.   This difference presumably is
owing to the much greater height of the tropopause (base of the stratosphere) at the American stations in summer than in winter and that, in
turn, to the greater heights to which given quantities of water vapor are
carried in the summer than in winter.   The higher water vapor is
carried the colder it, along with the other constituents of the air, becomes,
and the less the radiation it, and they, send into the stratosphere.   Where
this condition is quite pronounced, the stratosphere must be correspondingly cold, as it is, owing, presumably, to this cause in tropical regions.
At any rate, the fact that at the places represented by Fig. 16a the
stratosphere is warmer in winter than in summer does not disprove the
idea that the temperature of this upper air is mainly determined by
radiation from below.

It should be noted, too, that the seasonal gradients given in Fig. 16
were obtained at latitudes near to 50°, where the number of hours of
summer and winter sunshine, respectively, differ greatly, and therefore
where the seasonal temperatures of the stratosphere, if essentially determined by absorption of solar radiation, should differ somewhat correspondingly.   But, since no such great difference in these temperatures
exists, it would appear that the temperature of the stratosphere must be
due chiefly to absorption of long wave-length radiation given off by the
earth beneath and by the water vapor and other constituents of the
atmosphere at lower levels, and to only a very minor degree to the absorption of solar radiation.   If, now, we knew the volume and spectral
distribution of the outgoing radiation and the coefficient of absorption,
wave length by wave length, of the air in the stratosphere and its radiation exponent (how its rate of radiation varies with temperature), we
clearly could compute the equilibrium temperature of this portion of
the upper air to a tolerably close approximation.   But we do not have
the necessary information in sufficient detail to give much confidence
in this line of attack.   A much easier approach to this problem, therefore,
will be offered here, though it does not provide a perfect solution.

As stated above, the radiation up through the stratosphere, being
mainly from the earth and water vapor beneath, is, roughly, black-body

radiation, appropriate, however, to varying temperatures through the spectrum—lower for that from the clouds, for instance, and higher for that from the earth beneath—and its normal intensity about that which would obtain if the atmosphere were replaced by a world-enclosing black shell at 246° Abs. Hence, to obtain a first approximation to the temperature of the stratosphere, we may consider only the radiation into it from below and regard that as coming from a world-enclosing black surface at the absolute temperature 246°. Obviously this surface could be regarded as of infinite length and breadth in comparison to any height attained by sounding balloons, and therefore as giving radiation of equal intensity at all available altitudes.

Consider two such black surfaces, parallel and directly facing each other, at a distance apart small in comparison to their width, having the absolute temperature T_2, and let an object of any kind whatever be placed at the center of the practically enclosed space. Obviously, according to the laws of radiation, the final temperature of the object in question will also be T_2, very nearly. If, now, one of the parallel planes should be removed, the uncovered object would be in substantially the same situation, so far as exposure to intensity of radiation is concerned, as is the air in the stratosphere in its exposure to the radiation from below, and its spectral distribution also would be roughly of the same general order. Of course, each particle of the upper air receives some radiation from the adjacent atmosphere, but this is small in comparison to that from below and may, therefore, provisionally be neglected. Hence the problem, as an approximation, is to compute the temperature to which an object, assumed to be infinitesimally small, to fit the case of a gas, will come when exposed to the radiation of a single black plane of infinite extent.

Now, whether between the parallel planes or facing but one, the object in question is in temperature equilibrium when, and only when, it loses as much energy by radiation as it gains by absorption. Furthermore, so long as its chemical nature remains the same, its coefficient of absorption is but little affected by even considerable changes in temperature. Therefore, whatever the nature of the object, since it is exposed to twice as much radiation when between the two planes as it is when facing but one, it must, in the former case, both absorb and emit twice as much energy as in the latter. Or, using symbols,

$$E_2 = 2E_1$$

in which E_2 and E_1 are the quantities of heat radiated by the object per second, say, when between the two planes and when facing but one, respectively.

Again,

$$E_2 = K_2 T_2{}^{n_2}$$

and

$$E_1 = K_1 T_1{}^{n_1}$$

in which T_2 and T_1 are the respective absolute temperatures of the object under the given conditions, and K and n its radiation constants.

For every substance there are definite values of K and n which, so long as the chemical nature of the object remains the same, do not rapidly vary with change of temperature. Hence, assuming $K_2 = K_1$ and $n_2 = n_1$, we have, from the equation

$$E_2 = 2E_1$$
$$T_2 = \sqrt[n]{2}\,T_1.$$

From this it appears that there must be some minimum temperature T_1 below which the radiation of the earth and lower atmosphere will not permit the upper atmosphere to fall, though what it is for a given value of T_2 depends upon the value of n.

Presumably the radiation of the upper atmosphere is purely a thermal radiation, and, therefore, in full agreement, as is the thermal radiation of water vapor, carbon dioxide, and certain other gases, with the Kirchhoff[1] law. In other words, the ratio of emission to the coefficient of absorption for any given wave length, presumably, is wholly a question of temperature, and is numerically equal to the radiation of a black body at the same temperature and wave length. In symbols,

$$\left(\frac{He}{h}\right)_{\lambda,t} = (E)_{\lambda,t}$$

in which H is the incident energy, h the energy absorbed, and e the energy emitted by the body or gas in question at the wave length λ and temperature t, and E the black-body emission at the same wave length and temperature, all per equal area and time.

To fix the ideas, let the body of gas under consideration be a shell 1 centimeter thick, surrounding the earth at a fixed distance—20 kilometers, say, above sea level—and let the black body be a very thin shell at the same temperature inside and outside, that may, if we wish, take the place of the gas shell. Now, since nearly all the incident radiation under consideration, the radiation of the earth and its atmosphere onto a shell at 20 kilometers elevation, or anywhere else in the isothermal region, comes from below, we may assume it, or its normal equivalent, to be substantially the same for all levels of the upper atmosphere, and assume the emitted radiation to be all the energy sent out by the shell on *either* or on *both* sides; only, whatever the assumption for one shell, the same must be made for the other.

Returning to a consideration of the temperature of the upper atmosphere under the influence of radiation from the lower levels: Since the

---

[1] Pringsheim, "Congrès International de Physique," **2**; 127, Paris, 1900.

composition of the upper atmosphere is not appreciably changed by a change of even 50° C., it follows that such a change of temperature will not materially alter its coefficient of absorption. Hence a change in the intensity of the incident radiation H will make substantially the same proportionate change in the rate of absorption h, whatever the alteration in temperature. In short,

$$\frac{H}{h} = K, \text{ a constant, presumably.}$$

Hence

$$\frac{e_{\lambda,\, t_1}}{e_{\lambda,\, t_2}} = \frac{E_{\lambda,\, t_1}}{E_{\lambda,\, t_2}},$$

or

$$\frac{e_{\lambda,\, t_1}}{E_{\lambda,\, t_1}} = \frac{e_{\lambda,\, t_2}}{E_{\lambda,\, t_2}}.$$

Unfortunately, nothing is known of the spectral distribution of the energy radiation of the cold upper atmosphere, though possibly it is of the irregular, but more or less continuous broad band, type. If this is its distribution, and if for each wave length the increase of black body radiation, for a small increase of temperature, is proportional to the total radiation at that wave length, which it is to a rough first approximation, then to about the same average approximation,

$$\frac{e_{t_1}}{e_{t_2}} = \frac{E_{t_1}}{E_{t_2}},$$

in which the symbols stand for the total radiation of all wave lengths.

But from the Stefan law in regard to the total radiation of black bodies, we know that

$$\frac{E_{t_1}}{E_{t_2}} = \frac{T_1^4}{T_2^4}$$

in which T_1 and T_2 are the respective absolute temperatures.

Hence, as explained above, if the spectral distribution of the radiation of the upper atmosphere is continuous, or nearly so (no matter how irregular), and not confined chiefly to lines with zero radiation between them, it follows that in the equation,

$$T_2 = \sqrt[n]{2}\, T_1$$

the numerical value of n must be 4, roughly. But, as already explained, the value of T_2 is substantially 246° absolute; hence, on the assumption that $n = 4$, it follows that $T_1 = 207°$ absolute. And this is the average value, approximately, that observation gives up to the greatest heights yet attained.   The probable temperature at great heights, 40 kilometers and more, is in doubt.[1]

Whatever the facts in regard to the radiation constants of the atmosphere, the laws of radiation and absorption appear to demand that the temperature of the upper atmosphere shall change but little with change of height so far as its composition is constant.   Besides, while the exact value of this temperature—the temperature of the stratosphere—is, of course, best determined by actual observation, it also may be computed approximately from the known intensity of outgoing radiation, together with the thermal properties of the gases of the atmosphere.

Doubtless solar radiation affects the temperature of the stratosphere to some extent, but, presumably, not very much, since the radiation from the lower levels seems competent not only to produce an isothermal condition in the upper levels, but also to maintain them at substantially the observed temperature.   Further, the lower atmosphere obviously is slightly warmed and its radiation correspondingly increased by return radiation from the upper, but this presumably does not affect the general validity of the above reasoning, which is based on the action of the *total* outgoing radiation.

Given the isothermal condition of the upper atmosphere, it follows that the heated surface air can, under favorable circumstances, rise until, but only until, by expansion it has cooled down to that temperature (the temperature of the stratosphere) below which the radiation from below will not allow it to fall.

The existence of an upper isothermal region and the vertical temperature gradient (Fig. 16) suggests rational explanations of a number of otherwise obscure meteorological phenomena—why the clouds of a given region have a fairly well-defined maximum height; why this height differs between summer and winter; why it is a level of maximum cloud formation, and the like—but all these are special phenomena that will be discussed independently later on.

INEQUALITY OF SEASONAL TEMPERATURE CHANGE OF LOWER AND UPPER ATMOSPHERE

As just explained, if T_2 is the absolute temperature of the black surface that gives off radiation equivalent to that sent out by the convective portion of the atmosphere and T_1 the absolute temperature of the isothermal region, then

$$T_1 = \frac{T_2}{\sqrt[4]{2}} = 0.84 T_2, \text{ roughly.}$$

[1] LINDEMANN and DOBSON, *Proc. Roy. Soc.*, **102**; 411, 1923; **103**; 339, 1923.
SPARROW, *Astrophys, J.*, **63**; 90, 1926.
GOWAN, E. H., *Proc. Roy. Soc.*, **120**; 655, 1928; **128**; 531, 1930.
GUTENBERG, B., *Beitr. Geophys. Köppen Band*, **87**; 1931.
VEGARD, L., and TÖNSBERG, E., XI; No. 2, 1935.

E. Hopf[1] finds, with Milne and Eddington,

$$T_1 = 0.82T_2.$$

Hence the greater T_2, or the warmer the lower atmosphere, if its composition remains the same, the greater the difference between T_1 and T_2, or the greater the contrast between the temperature of the lower atmosphere and that of the stratosphere. This is in keeping with the observed fact (Fig. 16), that the seasonal difference in the temperature of the stratosphere, while in the same sense as that of the lower atmosphere, is not so great as is the latter. Because of seasonal differences in the composition of the lower atmosphere, especially in the average amount and distribution of water vapor, there can be no constant relation between the above temperature differences—only the qualitative relation as given, and even this may be reversed, as shown by Fig. 16a.

HEIGHT OF THE STRATOSPHERE

If H_1 is the height and T_1 the temperature of the under surface of the isothermal region above the level H_0, whatever that may be, whose temperature is T_0, then

$$H_1 = H_0 + \int_{T_0}^{T_1} \frac{dH}{dT} dT.$$

As above explained, the greater the temperature of the lower atmosphere, the greater the difference between this temperature and that of the stratosphere, or, in symbols, the greater T_0 the greater $T_0 - T_1$, and therefore the greater H_1, provided the lapse rate is no larger—and it varies but little. Hence the isothermal region should be at a greater height during summer than during winter. Another way of showing this same thing is as follows:

Let the difference between the summer and winter temperatures of the lower atmosphere be ΔT_2 throughout, and the corresponding difference between the temperatures of the upper atmosphere ΔT_1, then, according to the above theory, $\Delta T_1 = 0.84\Delta T_2$, roughly. This, as already explained, is a radiation result. The inequality or $0.16\Delta T_2$ is produced by convection. Now if h is the change in elevation corresponding to 1° C., we have

$$\Delta H = 0.16\Delta T_2 h.$$

But, ΔT_2, winter to summer, is roughly 12° C., and h about 110 meters. Hence the change in the seasonal height of the stratosphere, if there is constancy in atmospheric composition, and other conditions, except temperature, is, roughly,

$$\Delta H = 0.16 \times 12 \times 110 = 211.2 \text{ meters.}$$

[1] *Monthly Notices Roy. Astronom. Soc.*, **90**; 287, 1930.

It must be distinctly noted, however, that many disturbing elements, such as quantity and distribution of water vapor, frequency and extent of cirrus clouds, and the like, so modify these simple relations that they apply only to average conditions, nor everywhere even to these.

STORM EFFECTS ON TEMPERATURE GRADIENTS

The average of a season's (winter or summer) vertical temperature gradients gives a fairly regular curve, and, of course, the same would be true of the average of these averages, or what might be called the annual gradient for any given locality. However, each particular flight yields its own temperature-altitude curve, which differs more or less from others of the same place and season, especially in the values of the gradients in the first 2 or 3 kilometers, in the absolute temperatures at other levels, and in the location of the upper inversion.

With the view of determining the causes of some of these flight-to-flight irregularities, both the summer and the winter records from which the corresponding seasonal gradients were determined (all in Europe) were grouped, according to the heights of the barometer at the times and places of observation, into "highs," "neutrals," and "lows." Thus the "highs" belong to barometric readings of 5 mm. or more above, and the "lows" to readings of 5 mm. or more below, the seasonal normal, and the "neutrals" to the various intermediate values, all reduced to sea level.

Figure 17 shows the winter averages, respectively, of 54 highs, 72 neutrals, and 59 lows. Commonly, as the figure shows, a high barometer in the winter is accompanied by low surface temperatures, a slow decrease of temperature up to the height of about 3 kilometers, relatively warm air, in general, between the levels of 2 and 9 kilometers, a high upper inversion, a cold stratosphere, and a marked minimum temperature in its lower portion. A winter low, on the contrary, and in comparison with a high of the same season, is accompanied by warm surface temperatures, a more rapid decrease of temperature with increase of elevation through the first 3 kilometers, relatively cold air from, roughly, 2 to 9 kilometers height, a low upper inversion, and a warm stratosphere.

The normal barometer, as one would expect, is accompanied by intermediate values in all particulars.

The corresponding summer gradients (averages, respectively, of 32 highs, 161 neutrals, and 38 lows), given in Fig. 18, show, except near the surface, where the lows remain cold and the highs warm, the same characteristics as do those of winter.

Both the summer and the winter curves follow exactly the averages of the observations, as per the accompanying table.

An obvious contributing cause of these differences in temperature is the warming of the air by compression and its cooling by expansion incident to barometric changes; an amount which, starting with dry air at 0° C., is given, as explained on page 28, by the equation

$$\frac{dT}{dp} = \frac{78}{p},$$

in which p is the pressure, expressed in millimeters of mercury, and dT the change of temperature in degrees Centigrade.

According to Figs. 17 and 18, the temperature at the altitude of 4 kilometers is considerably warmer both winter and summer in the regions

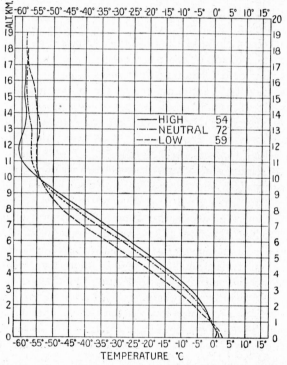

HIGH 54
NEUTRAL 72
LOW 59

TEMPERATURE °C

FIG. 17.—Temperature gradients at different pressures, winter.

of high barometric pressure than it is in the regions of low pressure. But to secure a temperature difference of 7° C., say, as a result of pressure change only, would require a rise or fall of the barometer at this level of about 40 mm., or something like 70 mm. at sea level; and, since this is several-fold the average pressure change, it is obvious that the observed temperature differences, often more than 7° C., cannot in the main be accounted for in this way, though, of course, the pressure effect must be present to some extent.

Another contributing cause of temperature differences, generally associated with the height of the barometer, is the clear and cloudy con-

TABLE I.—AVERAGE TEMPERATURES, CENTIGRADE (FROM AVERAGE TEMPERATURE GRADIENTS) FROM 416 SOUNDING BALLOON FLIGHTS AT TRAPPES, UCCLE, STRASSBURG, AND MUNICH, 1900–1912. TEMPERATURE T; NUMBER OF CASES N

Altitude in kilometers above sea level	Winter								Summer							
	High		Neutral		Low		Mean		High		Neutral		Low		Mean	
	T	N	T	N	T	N	T	N	T	N	T	N	T	N	T	N
0.0	0.67	43	1.61	55	2.85	49	1.72	147	15.54	29	14.82	121	13.58	28	14.76	178
0.5	0.87	43	1.01	55	1.77	49	1.23	147	13.98	29	13.90	121	11.93	28	13.60	178
1.0	-0.63	54	-0.49	72	-0.80	59	-0.63	185	12.39	32	12.12	161	9.98	38	11.81	231
1.5	-1.56	54	-1.77	72	-3.50	59	-2.26	185	9.57	32	9.34	161	7.23	38	9.03	231
2.0	-2.75	54	-3.76	72	-5.92	59	-4.16	185	7.09	32	6.54	161	4.55	38	6.29	231
2.5	-4.60	54	-6.10	72	-8.66	59	-6.48	185	4.37	32	3.84	161	2.12	38	3.63	231
3.0	-6.92	54	-8.65	72	-11.75	59	-9.14	185	2.00	32	1.19	161	-0.49	38	1.02	231
4.0	-12.69	54	-14.69	72	-18.44	59	-15.30	185	-3.16	32	-4.16	161	-5.74	38	-4.28	231
5.0	-19.22	54	-21.49	72	-25.91	59	-22.24	185	-8.74	32	-9.83	161	-11.33	38	-9.93	231
6.0	-26.18	54	-28.40	72	-33.37	59	-29.33	185	-15.11	32	-16.15	161	-17.86	38	-16.29	231
7.0	-33.27	54	-35.80	71	-40.83	59	-36.63	184	-22.18	32	-23.12	161	-24.80	38	-23.26	231
8.0	-40.83	53	-43.10	70	-47.13	59	-43.63	182	-29.82	32	-30.59	161	-32.34	38	-30.77	231
9.0	-48.05	50	-49.70	67	-51.33	57	-49.63	174	-37.62	31	-38.08	159	-39.77	37	-38.27	227
10.0	-54.85	48	-54.30	64	-54.23	53	-54.33	165	-45.32	31	-44.88	155	-44.57	36	-44.87	222
11.0	-59.65	44	-56.50	56	-55.03	47	-56.83	147	-52.62	31	-50.08	149	-48.37	34	-50.07	214
12.0	-60.75	38	-56.80	45	-54.93	37	-57.23	120	-57.02	30	-52.68	133	-49.97	30	-52.87	193
13.0	-59.05	34	-56.70	34	-54.23	30	-56.33	98	-57.62	27	-52.78	117	-48.27	27	-52.77	171
14.0	-58.35	26	-57.70	22	-54.73	24	-56.53	72	-56.82	22	-52.48	104	-47.87	21	-52.37	147
15.0	-58.85	17	-58.20	16	-55.43	16	-57.13	49	-55.32	18	-52.38	81	-47.37	17	-51.97	116
16.0	-58.55	11	-58.30	12	-56.43	10	-57.33	33	-55.32	13	-51.68	61	-48.17	8	-51.57	82
17.0	-58.65	5	-58.00	9	-57.63	7	-57.63	21	-54.82	9	-51.18	36	-47.37	4	-51.07	49
18.0	......	..	-58.30	6	-57.83	5	-57.63	13	-53.82	8	-50.38	22	-46.97	3	-50.17	33
19.0	......	..	-58.20	5	......	..	-57.63	8	......	..	-49.88	17	......	..	-49.57	21
20.0	......	..	......	..	......	..	-57.63	5	......	..	-48.98	15	......	..	-48.97	18

dition of the sky, or the humid and the dry state of the atmosphere. A barometric high, as we know, commonly is accompanied by clear skies and a dry atmosphere, while in the region of a low the sky ordinarily is overcast, the atmosphere relatively moist, and precipitation abundant— conditions that have much to do with air temperatures. Thus, generally, at the end of any consecutive 24 hours of clear weather the surface of the earth will be warmer in the summer time and colder in the winter because

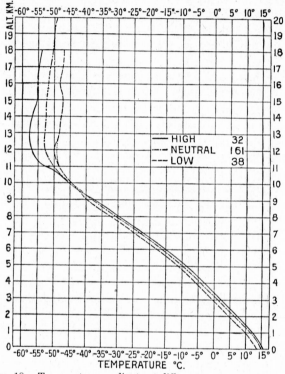

Fig. 18.—Temperature gradients at different pressures, summer.

of the unequal lengths during those seasons of the day and night. On the whole, the earth gains heat, especially in clear weather, during summer and loses it in the winter. A cloud covering, however, greatly reduces, through return radiation, the rate of this gain or loss, and therefore during winter the surface temperature is lowest when the barometer is high and the sky clear, while it is warmest when the barometer is low and the sky so overcast as to decrease the net radiation loss.

In the summer time, as explained, the conditions of gain and loss of heat are the reverse of those during winter. Consequently the highest summer surface temperatures accompany the high barometer, or clear weather, especially of afternoons, while the lowest accompany cloudy skies.

When the barometer is distinctly above normal the temperature fall with increase of altitude near the stratosphere generally follows approximately the adiabatic curve for dry air. When, however, the barometer is low the temperature gradient usually is far less constant at all elevations. In many cases the temperature gradient over varying heights is essentially the adiabatic curve for saturated air at the prevailing temperature and pressure; that is, a fall of temperature per given change in altitude is less, other things being equal, the greater the amount of uncondensed moisture present.

Since the temperature of the stratosphere depends essentially upon the amount of radiation received from the lower atmosphere, it follows that, on the average, the temperatures of the two regions must vary in the same sense, or warm and cool together, and this, indeed, is just what happens in Europe as the winter and summer gradients of Fig. 16 indicate. It is surprising, therefore, when we find the temperatures of these regions varying in the opposite sense, the one getting warm while the other is getting cold. But it must be remembered that the lower atmosphere is warmed convectionally, in large part, while the upper air is warmed almost wholly by radiation. Hence whatever increases radiation from the lower air, increase of humidity or temperature, or both, must tend to increase the temperature of the isothermal region, and whatever decreases this radiation, decrease of humidity or temperature, or both, must decrease its temperature below that which it otherwise would have. Now the average seasonal change of the lower atmosphere is primarily one of temperature, while the average storm difference of a given season appears to be largely one of humidity. The high temperature of summer obviously affords a more abundant radiation than the relatively low temperature of winter and should give a warmer stratosphere. Similarly, the different intensities of radiation from humid and relatively dry air would lead one to expect the stratosphere to be warmer over a cyclonic than over an anticyclonic area.

Another important factor, presumably the controlling one, in the temperature contrasts between cyclonic and anticyclonic regions is the vertical movement of the atmosphere, upward in the former, downward in the latter. Probably at least a large portion of the anticyclonic excess of air that gives the increase of pressure and makes good the loss by outflow is fed in at considerable altitudes, though below the stratosphere. If the air movement is as here supposed, there necessarily must be dynamical heating throughout the lower atmosphere, partly because of the initially increased pressure, but mainly through descent. At the same time, the stratosphere would be more or less lifted and cooled by the resulting expansion.

Conversely, if, as there is much reason to believe, the chief removal of atmosphere over cyclonic areas is also from considerable altitudes, but below the stratosphere, the lower atmosphere must be dynamically cooled, partly by virtue of the immediately decreased pressure, but chiefly through ascent. The stratosphere would be lowered and its temperature thereby increased. It seems likely, too, that under these conditions there would be a somewhat continuous slow movement of air from the stratosphere down into the region of the troposphere (convection region), with, of course, counterflows elsewhere and subsequent readjustments of the level of the stratosphere as temperature and other conditions changed.

Radiation intensity, change of barometric pressure, and vertical circulation, therefore, appear all to contribute to the lowering of the temperature of the troposphere and raising that of the stratosphere in cyclonic regions. Conversely, they appear equally to contribute to the raising of the temperature of the troposphere and lowering that of the stratosphere in anticyclonic regions. It must not be supposed, however, that these are all the factors that affect the cyclone and anticyclone, for many of them are largely produced and maintained by purely dynamical causes.

The above temperature conditions are averages, respectively, for the whole of cyclonic and anticyclonic areas. Subdivisions of these areas show temperature contrasts between their several quadrants, owing, in part at least, to differences in horizontal wind direction and the distribution of condensation and evaporation. This interesting detail, however, scarcely belongs to a discussion of the stratosphere, but rather to an account of the two types of weather concerned, under which heads it will receive further consideration.

RELATION OF THE STRATOSPHERE TO LATITUDE

It is well known that both the height and temperature of the stratosphere are functions of latitude. In the northern hemisphere, during summer, the under surface of the stratosphere gradually rises from about 10 kilometers above sea level at latitude 60° to approximately 15 kilometers at the equator, while the temperature correspondingly changes, roughly, from −45° C. to −70° C. Similar altitude and temperature changes of the stratosphere with latitude obtain, so far as observed, during all seasons and in both hemispheres, though the exact cause, or causes, of these variations is not known.

Changes in the amount of radiation from below and changes in the diathermacy of the upper air at once occur as possible explanations of the above latitude effects. The warm surface temperatures of equatorial regions necessarily cause, through vertical convection, abundant cloudiness at high altitudes. These clouds, in turn, intercept much of the radiation from below, either reflecting or absorbing it. The portion reflected obviously does not directly warm the cloud, but somewhat raises the temperature of the troposphere, while a portion of that which is absorbed merely produces evaporation rather than a change of temperature. Hence, presumably, the high clouds of equatorial regions, and also the considerable humidity there at great altitudes, owing to the persistent vertical convection, raise the level and thereby decrease the temperature of the effective radiating surface, thus diminishing the intensity of the radiation that reaches the stratosphere, and permitting its temperature to be correspondingly low.[1]

Some of the heat thus absorbed in the lower atmosphere conceivably may manifest itself in an acceleration of interzonal circulation in equatorial regions and an increase of outgoing radiation at higher latitudes.

There is, of course, abundant cloudiness over the higher latitudes as well as in equatorial regions, but there the atmosphere is more generally descending instead of ascending, the clouds low, the humid layer shallow, and consequently the effective radiating surface and the stratosphere comparatively warm.

Conceivably, too, the composition of the stratosphere may differ with latitude. Because of auroral concentration and because of any poleward drift there may be of the upper atmosphere, perhaps there is more ozone, intensely absorptive of earth radiation, over high than over low latitudes. Doubtless, also, there are local differences in the water vapor content of the stratosphere, but at most the absolute humidity of this region must be exceedingly small, as is obvious from its excessively low temperature, and from the fact that marked temperature changes of the upper atmosphere, amounting at times to 20° C., or more, rarely, if indeed ever, produce clouds above the high cirrus; that is, above the upper levels of the troposphere.

As previously stated, the essential cause of the relation of the temperature of the stratosphere to latitude is not known, but it seems probable that this relation may depend, in part at least, upon the distribution of clouds, water vapor, and ozone, and therefore that each deserves further observation and study in this connection.

The recorded increase of temperature with increase of height in the stratosphere is owing, in part at least, to insolation and insufficient ventilation of the thermal element.[2]

Although thermometers have never been carried higher than about 35 kilometers, nevertheless a number of determinations have been made, from different theoretical considerations, of the temperature of the very high atmosphere, but they vary over so wide a scale—from near the absolute zero to well above that of molten iron—that it seems more likely

[1] HUMPHREYS, W. J., *Mount Weather Bull.*, **4**; 129, 1911.

MÜGGE, R., *Zeit. Geophys.*, **2**; 63, 1926.

[2] BALLARD, J. C., *M. W. R.*, **62**; 45, 1934.

DINES, L. H. G., *M. O. Prof. Notes*, No. 67, 1935.

that all are wrong than that all are right! The following is a partial list of recent papers on this subject: MARTYN, D. F., and PULLEY, O. O., *Proc. Roy. Soc.*, **154**; 482, 1936; PEKERIS, C. L., *Proc. Roy. Soc.*, **158**; 650, 1937; VEGARD, L. and TÖNSBERG, E., *Geophys. Pub.*, **12**; No. 3, 1938; HULBERT, E. O., *J. Opt. Soc. Amer.*, **28**; 227, 1938. See also Chap. V of this book.

CHAPTER V

COMPOSITION, PRESSURE, AND DENSITY OF THE ATMOSPHERE

Composition of Surface Air.—In the previous discussions the actual composition of the atmosphere was of little or no importance. In some that follow however, barometric hypsometry, for instance, or the determination of altitude from pressure, it is a factor that cannot always be neglected. It will be convenient, therefore, before considering such subjects, to note of what substances the atmosphere consists and in what proportions they occur.

If we disregard such obviously foreign things as dust, fog, and cloud, then whatever remains appears to be ideally homogeneous, under ordinary conditions, and in many discussions, such as most of those of the previous pages, it conveniently may be so treated. The Greek philosophers, indeed, regarded the atmosphere as one of the four elements that singly and combined constituted the whole of the material universe. To them it was an element in the strictest sense—a thing that cannot be divided into dissimilar parts.

In reality it is not even a single substance like water, much less a single element, but a mixture of a number of gases and vapors that radically differ from each other in every particular; nor are even the relative percentages of the several distinct constituents really constant. The story of the chemical conquest of the atmosphere, from the calcination and combustion experiments of the seventeenth and eighteenth centuries that established its complexity down to the refined analyses of the present day that note and account for even the faintest traces, is full of instruction and inspiration. However, it is practicable to give here only some of the final results.

The chief independent gases that are blended into a dry atmosphere at the surface of the earth, and their respective volume percentages, are as follows:[1]

Element	Nitrogen	Oxygen	Argon	Carbon Dioxide	Neon	Helium	Krypton
Volume, per cent...	78.09	20.95	0.93	0.03	0.0018	0.00053	0.0001

The actual volume percentage of each constituent of dry air appears to vary slightly, and of course every determination of it is subject to experimental errors. Hence values that differ a little from the above are given by some authors. Thus, in the fifth edition of Hann and Süring's

[1] PANETH, F. A., *Quart. J. Roy. Meteorol. Soc.*, **63**; 433, 1937.

"Lehrbuch der Meteorologie" the figures for nitrogen, oxygen, and hydrogen are 78.08, 20.95, and $<10^{-3}$, respectively; while Moureu and Lepape[1] give for argon, neon, and helium, 0.9323, 0.0018, and 0.0005.

In addition to these elements, hydrogen and xenon, in relatively minute amounts, are permanent constituents of the atmosphere. There also are many substances, such as radio-active emanations, the oxides of nitrogen, ozone (mainly in the upper air, a mere trace in the lower), and, above all, water vapor, that are found in varying amounts. Of these, only water vapor commonly forms an appreciable percentage of the total atmosphere, a percentage that depends chiefly upon temperature in the sense that, for any given pressure, the higher the temperature the greater the possible, and usually the actual, percentage of water vapor. This relation holds up to the boiling point of water at the given pressure, when, assuming saturation, there is nothing but water vapor present, as in the spout, for instance, of a vigorously boiling kettle.

Because of this relation of water vapor to temperature its volume percentage decreases in the lower atmosphere from the equator towards the poles, while that of each of the other constituents of the atmosphere correspondingly increases. The annual average values, quoting from Hann and Süring,[2] are:

	Nitrogen	Oxygen	Argon	Water Vapor	Carbon Dioxide
Equator.....................	75.99	20.44	0.92	2.63	0.02
50° N......................	77.32	20.80	0.94	0.92	0.02
70° N......................	77.87	20.94	0.94	0.22	0.03

Except for the change in the amount of water vapor, the composition of the surface atmosphere, still (1940) under minute investigation, is substantially the same at all parts of the earth, though a trifle richer in one or more of the denser elements in rising than in falling air.[3] Its composition varies distinctly, however, with increase of height beyond 20 kilometers.[4] But a detailed discussion of this problem requires the use of barometric hypsometry.

BAROMETRIC HYPSOMETRY

Let ρ be the density of the atmosphere at the height h, and p its pressure in dynes per square centimeter. Then at the level h the decrease in pressure $-dp$ due to the increase in height dh is given, neglecting the velocity effect on weight, by the equation,

$$-dp = \rho g dh, \tag{1}$$

in which g is the acceleration of gravity at the point in question.

[1] C. R. **183**; 171, 1926.
[2] "Lehrbuch der Meteorologie," 4th Ed., p. 5.
[3] Moles, Batuccas, and Payà, C. R., **172**; 1600, 1921.
[4] Paneth, F. A. Nature, **139**; 180, 220, 1937.

To within practically negligible limits the density of the atmosphere is directly proportional to the pressure—*Boyle's law;* inversely proportional to the absolute temperature—*Charles' law;* and directly proportional to the sum obtained by adding together the molecular weights of the several gases present, each multiplied by the ratio of its partial pressure (the pressure which it alone produces) to the total pressure—*Avogadro's law.*

If, now, ρ_0 is the density of dry air at the temperature 0° C., and under the pressure p, then

$$\rho = \rho_0 \frac{\left(1 - 0.378\frac{w}{p}\right)}{1 + at} \tag{2}$$

in which w is the partial pressure of the water vapor present, t the existing temperature in degrees Centigrade, and a the coefficient of gas expansion, or $\frac{1}{273}$, at 0° C. or, more nearly, 0.00367, since air is not a perfect gas— see Van der Waals' equation.

Substituting the value of ρ, as given by equation (2), in equation (1), we have

$$-dp = \rho_0 g \frac{\left(1 - 0.378\frac{w}{p}\right)}{1 + at} dh. \tag{3}$$

Further, let H be the height of the "homogeneous" atmosphere, or height it would have if everywhere at the same temperature and pressure, and therefore of constant density. Obviously, according to Boyle's law, the value of H is independent of the actual value of the pressure. If, for instance, the amount of gas is doubled, p becomes doubled and the density doubled, and consequently H remains unchanged. Similarly for any other multiple or submultiple of the pressure.

At any given place the pressure p clearly is equal to the continuous product of the gas density, local acceleration of gravity, and homogeneous height; therefore

$$p = \rho_0 g H. \tag{4}$$

Hence, substituting in equation (3)

$$-dp = \frac{p}{H} \frac{\left(1 - 0.378\frac{w}{p}\right)}{1 + at} dh. \tag{5}$$

But, as is seen from equation (4), H is inversely proportional to g. Hence before we can assign a numerical value to H it is necessary to specify the value of g to which it applies. Now the height of the "homogeneous" atmosphere corresponding to temperature t and gravity g is found by multiplying any barometric height b, representing, under gravity g, a pressure p, by the ratio of the density of mercury at the temperature for which b was determined to the density of dry air at the given temperature t, and assumed pressure p.   For $0°$ C. and normal gravity G (that is, the value of gravity acceleration at sea level at latitude $45°$ N.),

$$H_G = 7991 \text{ meters.}$$

Therefore H, or, specifically,

$$H_g = 7991 \frac{G}{g} \text{ meters.}$$

Hence, substituting in equation (5), and measuring in meters,

$$-7991 \frac{dp}{p} = \frac{\left(1 - 0.378 \frac{w}{p}\right)}{1 + at} \frac{g}{G} dh. \tag{6}$$

Integrating this from h_0, p_0 to h, p, we have

$$7991 \log_e \left(\frac{p_0}{p}\right) = \int_{h=o}^{h=h} \frac{\left(1 - 0.378 \frac{w}{p}\right)}{1 + at} \frac{g}{G} dh. \tag{7}$$

However, the exact integration is not practicable, since t and the ratio w/p both are more or less irregular and variable functions of h. The value of g is also a function, but, for any given place, a fixed one, of h. Nevertheless, when the coincident values of p, t, and w are closely known, as they may be, it is possible to determine with equal accuracy the corresponding values of h; that is, to obtain an approximate solution of the above equation.   This, of course, is most accurately done by dividing the total height into intervals over each of which t and the ratio w/p both change very nearly uniformly.

If at the elevation h_0 we have the ratio w_0/p_0 and at h the ratio w/p, then, when $h - h_0$ is not too great, we may, with but little error, assume the ratio constant and its value for the interval in question to be

$$\frac{\left(\dfrac{w_0}{p_0} + \dfrac{w}{p}\right)}{2} = W. \tag{8}$$

Also, if the temperature varies approximately uniformly between the given levels, we can assume, again with but little error, the mean, t_m, of the two limiting temperatures to be that of the whole layer between h and h_0.   Finally, as the value of g changes but little through all attainable levels in the atmosphere, its mean value, g_m, between the two levels, may be used as a very close approximation.

Hence, with all these approximations,

$$h = 7991 \log_e \left(\frac{p_0}{p}\right) \frac{1 + at_m}{1 - 0.378W} \frac{G}{g_m}. \tag{9}$$

It will be noticed that since $1 + at = T/273$, in which T is the absolute temperature, $T_M/273$ should, theoretically, be used in place of

$1 + at_m$, where T_M is the harmonic mean $\left(\dfrac{n}{T_M} = \dfrac{1}{T_1} + \dfrac{1}{T_2} + \cdots + \dfrac{1}{T_n} \right)$ of the absolute temperatures (average) of the equally spaced short intervals between the given levels. Probably, however, this refinement is seldom justified by the data, except for elevations greater than 4 or 5 kilometers.

If, instead of natural logarithms with base e, ordinary logarithms with base 10 are used, equation (9) becomes

$$h = 18{,}400 \log_{10}\left(\frac{p_0}{p}\right)\frac{1 + at_m}{1 - 0.378W}\frac{G}{g_m}. \tag{10}$$

Now g_m differs in general from G both because of difference in latitude and because of difference in elevation. Thus the shape of the earth causes the value of gravity so to vary at sea level that at latitude l

$$g_l = G(1 - 0.00264 \cos 2l + 0.000007 \cos^2 2l),$$

while with elevation it varies inversely, nearly, as the square of the distance from the center of the earth.

Let R be the radius of the earth at the place of observation, and d the elevation at which the value of g is desired. Then $\dfrac{g_0}{g_h} = \dfrac{(R + d)^2}{R^2}$, nearly (increase of g due to mass of air left below is negligible), and, to the same approximation.

$$g_h = g_0\left[1 - 2\frac{d}{R} + 3\left(\frac{d}{R}\right)^2 - 4\left(\frac{d}{R}\right)^3 + \cdots \right]. \tag{11}$$

But even if d is as great as 10 kilometers, the fraction d/R is still so small, roughly $\frac{1}{637}$, that an error of less than 1 in 135,000 will be made by writing

$$g_h = g_0\left(1 - 2\frac{d}{R} \right).$$

Hence, finally,

$$g_{l,d} = G(1 - 0.00264 \cos 2l + 0.000007 \cos^2 2l)\left(1 - 2\frac{d}{R} \right), \text{ nearly,}$$

and

$$h = 18{,}400 \log_{10}\left(\frac{p_0}{p}\right)\frac{1 + at_m}{1 - 0.378W}\frac{1}{(1 - 0.00264 \cos 2l + 0.000007 \cos^2 2l)}$$
$$\frac{1}{\left(1 - 2\dfrac{d}{R} \right)} \text{ nearly.} \quad (12)$$

But as the quantity of water vapor in the atmosphere seldom amounts to more than 2.5 per cent of the total gases present, it follows that

$$\frac{1}{1 - 0.378W} = 1 + 0.378W,$$

to within 1 part in 10,000. Similarly,

$$\frac{1}{1 - 0.00264 \cos 2l + 0.000007 \cos^2 2l} = 1 + 0.00264 \cos 2l - 0.000007$$

$\cos^2 2l$, usually to within 1 part in 1,000,000 and

$$\left(\frac{1}{1 - 2\frac{d}{R}} \right) = 1 + 2\frac{d}{R},$$

when $d = 10$ kilometers, to within 1 part in 100,000.

Hence, for convenience, if $d = \dfrac{h_0 + h}{2}$, we may write as a close approximation,

$$h = 18,400 \log_{10} \left(\frac{p_0}{p} \right)(1 + at_m)(1 + 0.378W)(1 + 0.00264 \cos 2l -$$

$$0.000007 \cos^2 2l)\left(1 + \frac{h_0 + h}{R} \right). \quad (13)$$

If standard gravity g_s, that is, 980.665 cm./sec.^{2}, is used instead of normal gravity G, the term $1 + 0.00264 \cos 2l - 0.000007 \cos^2 2l$ in equation (13) must be replaced by the term $1 + \dfrac{g_s - g_l}{g_s}$, and the coefficient 18,400 changed in the ratio G/g_s.

Since the two pressures p_0 and p occur in this equation as a ratio, it is correct and customary to substitute for them the corresponding barometric readings—properly corrected, of course, for t and g. But as the value of g, in turn, depends upon h, the evaluation of the latter would appear to require a series of approximations. Rigidly this is true, but, as the value of g varies so little through attainable altitudes, a very rough approximation to the value of h is sufficient for the altitude correction of g.

Obviously, in general, the recorded values of t, W, and the barometric reading b are all in error, and therefore it will be well to see what effects such errors have on the computed value of h.

Assuming an error to be in b only, amounting to db, we have from equation (13), substituting b_0/b for p_0/p and using natural logarithms,

$$dh = -7991\frac{db}{b}(1 + at_m)\,(1 + 0.378W)\,(1 + 0.0026 \cos 2l)\left(1 + \frac{h_0 + h}{R} \right)$$

or, very approximately,

$$dh = -7991\frac{db}{b}(1 + at_m).$$

Hence the greater the altitude, or the smaller the value of b, the more important become the errors in pressure. Under the reasonable conditions that $t_m = 0°$ C., $db = 1$ mm., and $b = 500$ mm., corresponding to an altitude of, roughly, 3350 meters, the error $dh = 16$ meters, nearly. Hence, to avoid serious errors in barometrically ascertained altitudes, the value of b must be determined with great care.

Assume, now, an error in the mean temperature amounting to dt; then $dh = 18,400 \log_{10} (b_0/b)\, adt$, approximately.

Hence

$$\frac{dh}{h} = \frac{adt}{1 + at_m} = \frac{dt}{t_m + 273} = \frac{dt}{T},$$

in which T is the absolute temperature.

Again, let $b = 500$ mm., $t_m = 0°$ C., and $dt = 1°$ C. Then

$$dh = 12.25 \text{ meters, approximately.}$$

Clearly, then, to avoid considerable errors in hypsometric altitude determinations the temperature must also be known very closely.

Finally, assume an error in the value of W, that is to say, in $\left(\dfrac{w_0}{p_0} + \dfrac{w}{p}\right)/2.$

As there should be no error of consequence in w_0, assuming it to be the vapor tension at the surface of the earth, it follows that the chief error is likely to be in w, the vapor tension at the elevation where the total pressure is p.

Let w and p both be expressed in terms of barometric height, then

$$dh = 18,400 \log_{10}\left(\frac{b_0}{b}\right)(1 + at_m)0.378\frac{dw}{2b}.$$

If, as above, we let $b = 500$ mm., then w will usually be less than 4 mm. Hence, assuming $b_0 = 760$ mm., $t_m = 0°$ C., and a 25 per cent or 1 mm. error in w,

$$dh = 1.25 \text{ meters, approximately.}$$

Hence an error in the value of the humidity produces only a small effect on the altitude determination in comparison with that due to an error of the same order in either the temperature or the total pressure.

Errors in the force of gravity, whether from latitude or from elevation, have already been shown to be very small.

For all ordinary purposes, therefore, altitudes in meters may be determined by the greatly simplified equation,

$$h = 18,400 \log_{10}\left(\frac{b_0}{b}\right)(1 + at_m). \tag{14}$$

Obviously, these hypsometric formulae apply only to so much of the atmosphere as is of substantially constant composition, since the same "homogeneous" altitude, 7991 meters, is assumed throughout. Clearly, too, this condition of constant composition must apply, very approximately, up to the greatest altitude to which vigorous vertical convection extends, or in middle latitudes, as we shall see later, to an elevation of about 11 kilometers above sea level.

Beyond this level, up at least to the greatest altitude yet reached by sounding balloons and presumably much higher still, the temperature changes comparatively little with change of elevation. Hence in this region there can be relatively little vertical movement of the atmosphere, and therefore a chance, apparently, for the several gases, oxygen, nitrogen, and others, to distribute themselves, each as though it alone were present.

For any region in which this separation obtains it would be sufficient for most purposes to use the simple equation,

$$-dp = p\frac{dh}{H},\tag{15}$$

in which p is the partial pressure of the gas under consideration at the place in question, dh the change in elevation, and H the virtual height of the given gas, or its height, assuming its density throughout to be the same as at the initial level, necessary to produce the pressure p. This equation neglects any changes in the force of gravity, but, as already explained, such changes are small, and therefore the equation as it stands gives a close first approximation. It is not convenient, however, for numerical calculations, but for this purpose can be put into the following form:

$$\log_{10} p = \log_{10} p_0 - \frac{0.434295}{H}(h - h_0).\tag{16}$$

Equation (14) is applicable as far up as the composition of the atmosphere is essentially constant, or to an elevation of about 20 kilometers,[1] while above that level, where, owing to the practical absence of vertical convections, each gas tends to be distributed more or less as though it alone were present, equation (16) perhaps may be used, with, of course, the proper value of H for each gas considered.

This value is given by the following equation:

$$H = 7991\frac{D_a}{D}\frac{T}{273},$$

in which T is the absolute temperature, D_a the density of dry air, and D that of the gas in question, both at the same pressure (no matter what) and at 0° C.

[1] Paneth, F. A., Nature, **139**; 220, 1937.

Instead of determining height from pressure observations, one often wishes to compute the pressure at a given height from the pressure p_0 at some other height and the intervening virtual temperature distribution, which, as explained in Chap. II, provides for the water vapor.

Let gravity be considered as constant, and let T_m be the mean virtual temperature between the two heights h_0, h. From equation (9)

$$h - h_0 = H \log \left(\frac{p_0}{p}\right)\frac{T_m}{273};$$

but, from equation (4),

$$H = \frac{273R}{g};$$

hence

$$p = p_0 e^{\frac{-g(h-h_0)}{RT_m}}.$$

If T_m is constant, evidently

$$\frac{\Delta p_0}{p_0} = \frac{\Delta p}{p}.$$

That is, when the mean temperature is constant, changes of pressure at different levels are of like sign and proportional to the respective original pressures.

If T_m is variable,

$$\frac{\Delta p_0}{p_0} = \frac{\Delta p}{p} - \frac{g(h - h_0)\Delta T_m}{RT_m{}^2}.$$

Standard Atmosphere.—In aeronautics and ballistics, considerable use is made of a "standard atmosphere," characterized by the uniform decrease of temperature with increase of height according to the equation

$$t = 15 - 0.0065h,$$

in which t is the temperature in degrees Centigrade at the height h meters above sea level, and by the further fact that at sea level the barometer reading is 760 mm. While not strictly accurate, it gives very nearly the average values up to the level at which $t = -55°$ C., its assumed limit, and generally is sufficient for practical purposes.

COMPOSITION AND PRESSURE OF THE ATMOSPHERE AT DIFFERENT LEVELS

Since vigorous convection does not extend into the stratosphere, it formerly was generally supposed that therefore the density of each gas in this region must decrease with increase of height, precisely as it would if no other gas were present. On this assumption and on the further assumption that the temperature of the stratosphere has the same value, whatever the height, it is easy to compute the composition, pressure, and density of the air at all levels, given the readings of the thermometer and barometer at some particular height, as, for example, 11° C. and 760 mm., at sea level. Calculations based on such assumptions have been made, using equation (14) for the troposphere and (16) for the stratosphere. However, analyses of samples of the atmosphere from various levels have shown that its composition is constant, except for decrease of water vapor, up to about 20 kilometers above the surface. Indeed, for computing the pressure and density of the air at various heights, it would be best, perhaps, to assume its composition to be the same throughout. This conclusion rests on the following facts: (a) Winds and variations in temperature have been observed and measured in the stratosphere up to 30 kilometers or more above sea level; (b) the reflection of sound from great heights, indicating a region there of at least warm air; (c) the return of wireless waves from different and changing levels, indicating diurnal variations of temperature in the high atmosphere; and (d) the spectral proof that both oxygen and nitrogen extend out to the ultimate limits of the aurora, certainly 1000 kilometers. These conditions must keep most, if not all, portions of the upper air in a perpetual state of greater or less agitation and, therefore, its composition much the same throughout.

It is true that the amount of ozone in the atmosphere varies with height and has its maximum density at around the 25-kilometer level, but, although this gas is of vital importance in some respects, in mass it is only a mere trace and does not alter the foregoing conclusion that, at least roughly, the composition of the air is the same, top to bottom, except in respect to water vapor. It is true also that the atmosphere is ionized far more at some levels than at others, but even a thousand million ions per cubic centimeter would not measurably alter the percentage composition of the air. Finally, as previously stated, careful analyses by F. A. Paneth[1] indicate that beyond the 20-kilometer level the percentage of helium increases, whereas that of oxygen decreases. But the change is so small that, before accepting it as proved, one would like to see the results of the analyses of many more samples of air from much greater heights.

Some have supposed that any hydrogen that might reach the outer atmosphere would quickly be lost owing to the high velocity of its molecules, but Jeans[2] has shown that this is not true. Another cause of doubt about the composition and density of the outer atmosphere is the spectrum of the aurora. This, at every level, even up to 1000 kilometers, shows only nitrogen bands and a few "forbidden" oxygen lines, including the "auroral line."[3] The absence of the spectra of hydrogen and helium

[1] *Nature*, **139**; 220, 1937.

[2] "Dynamical Theory of Gases," Chap. XV.

[3] McLennan and Shrum, *Proc. Roy. Soc.*, **108**; 501, 1925.

does not disprove the presence in minute amounts of these elements; in fact, it seems all but certain that helium, at least, must be present. Furthermore, the heights at which meteors appear and disappear, and their relative brightness between these levels, have raised questions about the density distribution, hence the temperature, of the upper air that have been quite differently answered.[1] Then, too, the position and exact nature of the Kennelly-Heaviside and Appleton layers, or E and F layers, as they more commonly are called, so vital to radio communication,

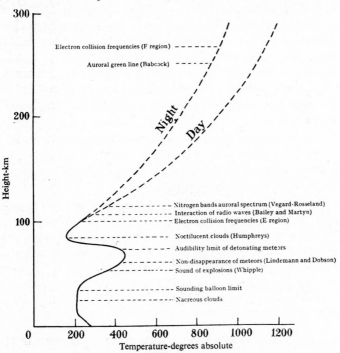

FIG. 19.—Temperature of the atmosphere to great heights. (*Martyn and Pulley.*)

and the cause or causes of the observed variations in the amount of ozone[2] are unsolved problems. In short, our knowledge of the atmosphere becomes rapidly more and more speculative with increase of height beyond 35 kilometers; hence all tables and diagrams representing it are correspondingly uncertain.

Figure 19, copied from a paper by D. F. Martyn and O. O. Pulley,[3] gives the best information, actual and inferential, that we now have on the average distribution of temperature with height. We know by direct measurement what it is up to about 35 kilometers above the

[1] LINDEMANN and DOBSON, *Proc. Roy. Soc.*, **102**; 411, 1923; **103**; 339, 1923; SPARROW, *Astrophys. J.*, **63**; 90, 1926.

[2] DOBSON, HARRISON, and LAWRENCE, *Proc. Roy. Soc.*, **114**; 521, 1927.

[3] *Proc. Roy. Soc.*, **154**; 455, 1936.

surface; and from the "reflection" of sound by the sky it is inferred that shortly above the 35-kilometer level the temperature rapidly increases with height to some value greater, perhaps much greater, than that at the surface. Such a warm layer of air presumably would lead to convection above it and consequent cooling, but to what height and minimum temperature we do not know. We do know, however, that on rare occasions a cirrus-like cloud is seen at about 82 kilometers above sea level. It is doubtful what the material of this cloud is, but it might be crystals of ice[1] if the temperature there were of the order of 160° Abs. But, whatever the temperature in this region, it probably is much greater at levels two or three times as high, though at very great heights such gases as are present may not have a temperature at all, or at least not in the same sense that the surface air has. It may be erroneous, therefore, to interpret in terms of temperature the phenomena that so interpreted have led to the conclusion that the very high atmosphere is hotter than molten iron.

DENSITY OF THE ATMOSPHERE

The pressure and density of the air at all levels, up to the height of 40 kilometers, are given in the accompanying table and shown by Figs. 20 and 21, respectively.

In computing the pressure and density values in the accompanying table the complete hypsometric equation was used. That is, the effect of water vapor and of both the latitude and altitude changes of gravity were all allowed for. No allowance, however, was made for the probable change with altitude in composition of the upper atmosphere because (*a*), the exact amount of this change is not certain, and (*b*), at most, it could not alter the values at the level of even 40 kilometers by more than about 1 per cent.

MASS OF THE ATMOSPHERE AND OF ITS CONSTITUENTS

The exact calculation of the mass of the atmosphere and of its constituents is beset with serious difficulties.[2] However, since but little gas of any kind extends beyond the 100-kilometer level, as we know from auroral and meteoric phenomena, it seems that both rotational and decrease of gravity effects must be small, and that, since the world average height of the barometer at the surface of the earth, whose area is 51×10^{17} cm.[2], is 74 centimeters,[3] the mass A of the atmosphere is close to the minimum value[4] given by the equation

$$A = 74 \times 13.5951 \times 51 \times 10^{17} \text{ grams.}$$

[1] HUMPHREYS, W. J., *M. W. R.*, 61, 228, 1933.

[2] JEANS, "The Dynamical Theory of Gases," Chap. XV. MASCART, *Bull. Astron.* (2), Pt. 1, **3**; 331.

[3] HANN and SÜRING, "Lehrbuch der Meteorologie," 5th Ed., p. 258.

[4] WOODWARD, *Bull. Am. Math. Soc.*, **6**; 143, 1900.

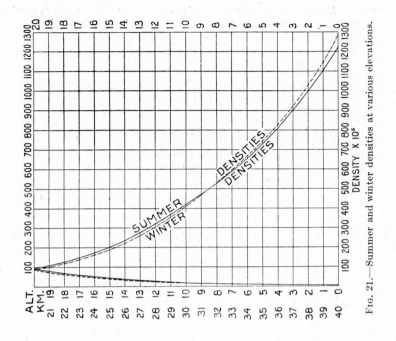

Fig. 21.—Summer and winter densities at various elevations.

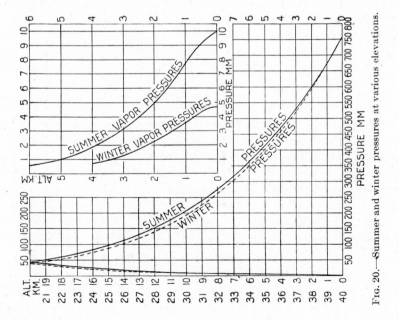

Fig. 20.—Summer and winter pressures at various elevations.

PHYSICS OF THE AIR

TABLE III.—AVERAGE GRAMS PER CUBIC METER ($\rho \times 10^6$, ρ = DENSITY) AND MILLI-
METERS PRESSURE (TOTAL, AND WATER VAPOR) FROM 231 SUMMER AND 185 WINTER
SOUNDING BALLOON FLIGHTS AT TRAPPES, UCCLE, STRASSBURG, AND MUNICH,
1900–1912

Altitude kilometers above sea level	Summer			Winter		
	Total pressure	Vapor pressure	Grams per cubic meter	Total pressure	Vapor pressure	Grams per cubic meter
0.0	762.55*	10.46	1224.42	763.35*	4.69	1287.58
0.5	718.75	9.17	1159.17	717.42	4.35	1212.31
1.0	677.24	7.81	1099.61	674.11	3.56	1147.23
1.5	637.81	6.21	1046.50	633.12	2.93	1084.23
2.0	600.31	4.97	995.19	594.37	2.27	1025.03
2.5	564.67	3.97	945.56	557.71	1.71	970.08
3.0	530.82	3.12	897.73	522.99	1.30	919.87
4.0	468.23	1.87	808.07	458.91	0.72	826.62
5.0	411.93	1.06	726.57	401.32	....	743.33
6.0	361.32	0.57	653.35	349.62	....	666.41
7.0	315.84	.....	587.39	303.34	....	596.05
8.0	274.98	.....	527.26	261.94	....	530.41
9.0	238.39	.....	471.70	225.37	....	468.61
10.0	205.77	.....	418.94	193.19	....	410.34
11.0	176.95	.....	368.66	165.19	....	355.20
12.0	151.80	.....	319.03	141.11	....	303.43
13.0	130.14	.....	273.51	120.55	....	259.22
14.0	111.58	.....	234.50	102.99	....	221.46
15.0	95.67	.....	201.06	87.99	....	189.20
16.0	82.03	.....	172.40	75.18	....	161.66
17.0	70.34	.....	147.83	64.24	....	138.13
18.0	60.32	.....	126.77	54.89	....	118.03
19.0	51.73	.....	108.72	46.91	....	100.87
20.0	44.37	.....	93.25	40.09	....	86.20
21.0	38.05	.....	79.97	34.26	....	73.67
22.0	32.64	.....	68.60	29.28	....	62.96
23.0	27.99	.....	58.82	25.02	....	53.80
24.0	24.01	.....	50.46	21.39	....	45.99
25.0	20.60	.....	43.29	18.28	....	39.31
26.0	17.67	.....	37.14	15.63	....	33.61
27.0	15.16	.....	31.86	13.36	....	28.73
28.0	13.01	.....	27.34	11.42	....	24.56
29.0	11.16	.....	23.45	9.77	....	21.01
30.0	9.58	.....	20.13	8.35	....	17.95
31.0	8.22	.....	17.28	7.14	....	15.35
32.0	7.05	.....	14.82	6.10	....	13.12
33.0	6.05	.....	12.72	5.22	....	11.24
34.0	5.19	.....	10.91	4.46	....	9.59
35.0	4.46	.....	9.37	3.82	....	8.21
36.0	3.83	.....	8.05	3.27	....	7.03
37.0	3.28	.....	6.89	2.79	....	6.00
38.0	2.82	.....	5.93	2.39	....	5.14
39.0	2.42	.....	5.09	2.04	....	4.39
40.0	2.08	.....	4.37	1.75	....	3.76

* Normal for the season.

Similarly, taking the average amount of water vapor in the atmosphere to be the equivalent of a layer of water over the entire earth 2.54
centimeters deep, a value of the order deducible by Hann's equation[1] from

[1] "Lehrbuch der Meteorologie," 4th Ed., p. 245.

Arrhenius'[1] values of average humidity, the mass W of the water vapor is given, closely, by the equation

$$W = 2.54 \times 51 \times 10^{17} \text{ grams.}$$

Finally, the approximate mass M of any of the constituent gases of the atmosphere is given by the equation, the first term of which applies to the troposphere and the second to the stratosphere.

$$M = (A - W)Vm'/m.$$

V is the volume percentage of the gas in question in dry air; m' the molecular weight of the gas; and m the virtual molecular weight of dry air. The results are given in the following table:

MASS OF THE ATMOSPHERE AND ITS CONSTITUENTS

Substance	Volume percentage dry air	Molecular weight	Total mass, kilograms
Total atmosphere...............	....	....	$51,300,000 \times 10^{11}$
Dry air.......................	100.00	28.97*	$51,170,000 \times 10^{11}$
Nitrogen......................	78.09	28.02	$38,648,000 \times 10^{11}$
Oxygen.......................	20.95	32.00	$11,841,000 \times 10^{11}$
Argon........................	0.93	39.88	$655,100 \times 10^{11}$
Water vapor..................	....	18.02	$130,000 \times 10^{11}$
Carbon dioxide...............	0.03	44.00	$23,320 \times 10^{11}$
Neon.........................	0.0018	20.0	636×10^{11}
Krypton......................	0.0001	82.9	146×10^{11}
Helium.......................	0.00053	4.00	37×10^{11}
Ozone........................	....	48.00	30×10^{11}
Xenon........................	0.000008	130.2	18×10^{11}
Hydrogen.....................	0.00005	2.02	2×10^{11}

* Virtual.

The volume percentages here accepted are those given by F. A. Paneth.[2] This value, however, is omitted in the case of both water vapor and ozone, because each is variable in respect to place, time, and height. The amount of water vapor is computed on the assumption, supported by observation, that, normally, it is just sufficient to cover the entire earth with a layer 2.54 cm. (1 inch) deep.

The only one of these several gases about which there still are reasonable doubts as to the approximate values of its volume percentage and total mass is hydrogen. Unusual difficulties beset the measurement of this constituent of the atmosphere. At best it is present only as a

[1] *Phil. Mag.*, **41**; 264, 1896.
[2] *Quart. J. Roy. Meteorol. Soc.*, **63**; 433, 1937.

mere trace, and even this is likely to become contaminated in the course of separation and measurement.

Change of Density with Height.—Since

$$\rho = \frac{p}{RT},$$

therefore

$$\frac{d\rho}{\rho} = \frac{dp}{p} - \frac{dT}{T} = -\frac{273dh}{TH} - \frac{dT}{T}.$$

Level of Constant Density.—Density is constant where pressure contraction equals temperature expansion. Let v, p, ρ, T, and ΔT be the volume, pressure, density, absolute temperature, and change of temperature, respectively, of a quantity of air at the height h above sea level, H the homogeneous height of the atmosphere above h, and $k\Delta T/T$ the average ratio of the change of the absolute temperature along the column of air below h. The ρ is constant where

$$\frac{\text{pressure contraction}}{v} \equiv -\frac{\delta v}{v} = \frac{\delta p}{p} = \frac{k\Delta T \rho gh}{T\rho gH} =$$

$$\frac{\text{temperature expansion}}{v} \equiv \frac{\Delta v}{v} = \frac{\Delta T}{T},$$

that is, when $kh = H$. But since, on the average, the temperature lapse, except in the lowest 1 or 2 kilometers, follows the saturation adiabat, k is less, but not greatly less, than unity, and h correspondingly greater than H. For such levels (where $kh = H$) in middle latitudes k is approximately 0.85, as may be determined from observations, or computed from saturation adiabats, and H roughly 7 kilometers. At higher latitudes (lower temperatures) k and H are both slightly less, and at lower latitudes both are a little greater. Hence, at 8 kilometers above sea level, the density of the atmosphere is approximately the same in all parts of the world and all seasons of the year. Furthermore, density grows greater below 8 kilometers and less above, both with the waning of summer and the increase of latitude, and, conversely, less below 8 kilometers and greater above, both with the coming of summer and the decrease of latitude.

CHAPTER VI

INSOLATION

Factors of Insolation.—The temperature variations of the atmosphere, both as to time and to place, and also the actual average temperature for any given locality, all obviously are of the utmost importance within themselves, and of equal importance indirectly through such meteorological elements as humidity, precipitation, wind direction, wind velocity, and nearly everything else that contributes to the sum total of both weather and climate. Hence it is imperative that in any general discussion of meteorology some consideration be given to the question of the source, or sources, of the heat energy necessary to these conditions, where it is delivered, and how distributed.

A little heat is given to the surface of the earth and the atmosphere surrounding it by conduction from the heated interior, a little as a result of certain chemical changes, some from tidal action, and another small amount by the absorption of stellar and lunar radiation. But the sum total of all these several amounts is so small in comparison to that which results from the absorption of solar radiation that for even a close approximation to the total amount of thermal energy given to the atmosphere it is sufficient to consider the sun as its only source.

The rate at which energy is delivered per unit horizontal area at any place on or above the surface of the earth directly from the sun—the intensity of the vertical component of the sunshine at that place, or the local *insolation*—depends upon:

a. The solar output of radiation.

b. Distance from the sun.

c. Inclination of the rays to the plane of the horizon, or solar elevation.

d. Transmission and absorption by the atmosphere, above the given place.

These factors, then, determine the earth's heat income, and will be considered *seriatim*. How the heat is conserved, distributed, and expended also are important problems, which will be taken up later.

SOLAR OUTPUT OF RADIATION

There is no *a priori* reason for assuming that the total output of radiation from the sun must remain strictly constant from age to age, from year to year, or even from day to day. Neither is there any known *a priori* reason for supposing that the solar radiation must greatly vary, either periodically or irregularly.   Hence it is distinctly a subject for continuous and careful observation, a sort that, fortunately, is already well under way.   Beginning with the summer of 1905, Abbot and Fowle, of the Astrophysical Observatory of the Smithsonian Institution, and others working with them, have made at various favorable locations in the United States, South America, Asia, and Africa numerous determinations of the solar constant, or intensity of the solar radiation (normal to that radiation) received, increased by the transmission loss through the atmosphere and reduced to its value at "mean solar distance"—a technical expression implying a distance equal to half the major axis of the earth's orbit.

The mean value of the solar constant during the period 1905–1926 was within 1 per cent of 1.94 calories per square centimeter per minute; while apparently satisfactory individual values varied from 1.85 to 2.02 calories.[1]   This mean value was later corrected by Abbot and Aldrich,[2] owing to improvements in the absolute pyrheliometer, to 1.893 + the totally absorbed energy of unknown amount in the ultraviolet region. The magnitude of these variations, however, has, in general, decreased with improvement of equipment, of method of operation, and of atmospheric conditions, until the daily changes have come within the range of experimental errors.   But this gives all the greater confidence in the variation trends, when simultaneously found in different parts of the world, or coincident with other solar phenomena, or both.   There appear to be irregularly recurring trends of one or two periods in a month,[3] and more certainly one that substantially follows the sun-spot curve, and indicates a 2 per cent, or more, greater solar constant at the times of spot maxima than at spot minima.

Now, any change whatever in the intensity of the radiation absorbed by the earth during several months necessarily leads to about the same change in the average intensity of the radiation lost by the earth.   But as the earth radiates roughly as a "black" body, hence, in proportion to the fourth power of the absolute temperature, and as the effective absolute temperature of the earth as a full radiator is roughly 246° Abs., it follows that a long-continued 2 per cent change in the solar constant would, if everything else remained the same, change this effective temperature by about 1.25° C.   Clearly, though, not everything else is the same, for according to extensive statistical evidence the average temperature of the earth as a whole, but most pronounced in equatorial regions, is a little higher at the times of spot minima when the solar constant is least, than at the times of spot maxima when it is greatest.   It may be that at the times of spot maxima, and more frequent and extensive auroras, the

[1] Abbot, C. G., "Beiträge zur Geophysik," **16**; 361, 1927.

[2] *Smithsonian Misc. Col.*, **87**; No. 15, 1932; **92**; No. 13, 1934.

[3] Abbot, C. G., *loc. cit.*, p. 365.

turbidity of the upper atmosphere is increased and the average surface insolation correspondingly decreased; or, possibly, the amount of cirrus haze is increased. Perhaps, the ozone in the upper air varies in amount with the sun-spot period and thereby alters the temperature of the surface, being a blanketing agent, owing to its powerful absorption of earth radiation. However, all these are but little more than speculative guesses; many data are yet needed to establish the facts, and to determine their causes.

The changes of the output of solar radiation appear to be very small in the green and infragreen, but to increase rapidly from that point with decrease of wave length to possibly 100 per cent in the far ultraviolet.[1] Evidently this is not primarily a temperature effect, but the actual cause is unknown.

Changes in the temperature and temperature distribution of the atmosphere obviously must entail variations in the strength of the winds and other weather elements. Hence, in so far as increase or decrease of the solar constant leads to alterations in the temperature of the air, whether in the same sense or the opposite, it must affect the run of the weather. But logical as this argument may be, official meteorological services have not yet been able to make much use of the current value of the solar constant in predicting the coming weather. This, however, is no reason for now lessening the study of the sun, since the information thus obtained promises to be of predictive value, not only of some sort for the weather, long-range probably (really a climatic swing), but also for other things. It promises, for instance, the foreknowledge of marked changes in the intensity of the antirachitic region of the ultraviolet, so important to animal health, growth, and propagation. And, anyhow, weather prediction is not the only end of knowledge.

DISTANCE FROM THE SUN

If the apparent disk of the sun radiated equally all over, it would be strictly accurate to say that the intensity of its energy received at any particular point is directly proportional to the solid angle subtended by it at that point. But it does not radiate equally from all parts, either in amount or kind. The quantity of radiation per unit area of the apparent solar disk decreases from center to circumference, while at the same time the spectral region of maximum intensity gradually shifts to longer and longer wave lengths. Hence, the intensity of the total solar radiation at a given point cannot be rigidly proportional to the solid angle in question. This departure, however, from exact proportionality must in most cases be wholly negligible. Besides, the solid angle subtended by the sun at the surface of the earth is so small that but little error would be made in

[1] ABBOT, C. G., *loc. cit.*

problems of total radiation by regarding it as strictly zero and therefore applying without correction the law of inverse squares.

At aphelion the distance of the earth from the sun is, roughly, 1.034 that at perihelion. Hence the intensity of the sunshine at perihelion, other things being equal, must be approximately 1.069 that at aphelion. And, since the earth may be regarded as a full radiator at about 246° Abs., it follows that its effective temperature must be greater when a maximum than when a minimum by about 1.7 per cent of the average value, or, roughly, by 4° C.

All these calculations assume complete equilibrium between radiation and absorption, and, while there necessarily is some lag, an approach to equilibrium, as a little calculation will show, probably comes much sooner than one might suppose to be the case. Hence northern winters are not only shorter but also warmer than they would be if they occurred at times of aphelion instead of, as they do, at times of perihelion; while the winters of the southern hemisphere, during which the earth is farthest removed from the sun, have now a maximum both of duration and severity.

Notwithstanding—really, because of—the marked difference between the perihelion and aphelion intensities of the solar radiation at the limit of the atmosphere, it is easy to show that the total amount of solar energy that comes to the earth as a whole is constant per constant angular travel along its orbit; and that each hemisphere, regardless of the perihelion phase, or exact date on which perihelion occurs, receives during the course of a whole year exactly the same amount of solar radiation as does the other. This is shown as follows:

Let S be the solar distance, $d\theta$ the angle at the sun swept over by the earth in the time dt. Then, from the law of equal areas,

$$S^2 d\theta = C dt,$$

in which C is a constant.

Also, if dQ is the amount of solar energy incident upon the earth, radius R, in the time dt,

$$dQ = \frac{I_1 \pi R^2}{S^2} dt,$$

in which I_1 is the intensity of the radiation at unit solar distance. Hence

$$dQ = \frac{I_1}{K} d\theta,$$

or the energy received by the earth from the sun, assuming the solar output to be constant, is directly proportional to the angular distance between the initial and final radii vectors. Since the direction of the earth's axis is practically fixed in space, it follows that, to the same degree of approximation, each hemisphere must be inclined toward or from the sun over exactly one-half the angular orbit, and hence that the total yearly amount of heat received by one hemisphere is the same as that received by the other, and also that the earth as a whole gets precisely the same amount of radiant energy in the period it takes to round the aphelion half of its orbit that it does while in the perihelion half—what it loses by distance it exactly makes up by time.

It must not be supposed that this equality of heat supply means equality of world temperatures. Indeed, it means quite the reverse, for the equal quantities are delivered in unequal times; the aphelion time being longest, therefore the world temperature is then the lowest, except in so far as there may be a temperature lag, or, perhaps, counter land and water effects, during this period, and shortest with highest tempera-

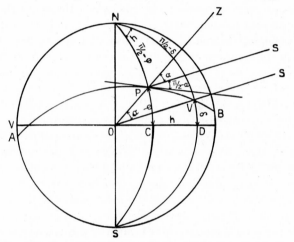

Fig. 22.—Relation of insolation to latitude, declination, and hour angle.

ture, as previously explained, through the perihelion time. As a matter of fact, there are even overbalancing counter-effects that make the average world temperature lower during the northern winter, the season in which perihelion occurs, than it is in July, the aphelion month. This is owing, chiefly, to the far greater extent of land in the northern hemisphere than in the southern, since it gets much colder than the ocean surface in winter and much warmer in summer.

SOLAR ALTITUDE

Leaving out, for the present, all questions of atmospheric absorption, it is obvious that the insolation is directly proportional to the sine of the angle of solar altitude, or to the cosine of the sun's zenith distance. But neither of these angles is directly known, and therefore they can be expressed only in terms of those that are known. Each, however, is a function of latitude, of the time of day, expressible as an hour angle, and solar declination, as will be explained by the aid of Fig. 22.

Let P be the point of observation, with its zenith at Z, and let the sun be off in the direction OS or PS. Clearly, then, the plane of OZ and OS intersects the surface of the earth in a great circle, and the angle ZOS, measured by the arc PV of this circle, is equal to the sun's zenith distance. But in the spherical triangle NPV it is obvious that the arc NV, V being directly under the sun, is the codeclination, NP the colatitude, and the angle h at N, measured by the arc CD on the equator, the hour angle, or angle through which the earth must turn to bring the meridian of P directly under the sun. Hence

$$I_n = I \cos \alpha = I(\sin \varphi \sin \delta + \cos \varphi \cos \delta \cos h),$$

in which I_n is the insolation at the surface, I the intensity of the solar radiation at the given place, φ the latitude of the point P, δ the solar declination, and h the hour angle, as explained.

To find the amount of solar energy delivered at a given point we have the equation

$$dQ = I_n dt = \frac{I(\sin \varphi \sin \delta + \cos \varphi \cos \delta \cos h)dh}{\omega}$$

in which dh is the change in the angle h in the time dt, and ω the angular velocity of the earth with reference to the sun, or $\pi/12$ radians per hour. To obtain the total energy delivered per unit area in the course of a day we may consider I and δ constant for that time, and therefore write

$$Q = \frac{2I(\sin \varphi \sin \delta H + \cos \varphi \cos \delta \sin H)}{\omega}$$

in which H is the hour angle between noon and sunrise or sunset.

H obviously is a function of φ and δ. Thus at sunrise, say, $\alpha = \pi/2$,

$$\cos \alpha = 0 = \sin \varphi \sin \delta + \cos \varphi \cos \delta \cos H,$$

and

$$\cos H = - \tan \varphi \tan \delta.$$

Hence

$$Q = \frac{2I \sin \varphi \sin \delta(H - \tan H)}{\omega}.$$

Now φ, the latitude of the place in question, is known, and δ, the solar declination for any given day, is obtainable from an ephemeris. Hence, assuming a constant output of solar energy and allowing for variations in solar distance, the relative per diem amounts of insolation delivered to the earth (outer atmosphere) at different latitudes and different times may readily be computed. A few of these values, in terms of the total insolation received at the equator on the day of the vernal equinox, are given in the following table (recomputed), and the complete data for all seasons and all latitudes in Fig. 23, both of which are copied from Davis' "Elementary Meteorology," Ginn & Company:

Latitude	0°	+20°	+40°	+60°	+90°	−90°
March 20...............	1.000	0.940	0.766	0.500	0.000	0.000
June 21.................	0.882	1.044	1.107	1.093	1.201	0.000
September 22...........	0.987	0.927	0.756	0.494	0.000	0.000
December 21............	0.941	0.676	0.357	0.056	0.000	1.283
Annual total...........	348	329	275	198	144	144

Elaborate tables and graphs of such values have been published by Angot.[1]

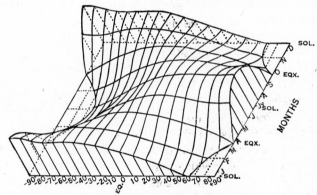

Fig. 23.—Relation of insolation to season and latitude.

TRANSMISSION AND ABSORPTION

The rate of solar output of energy, distance from the sun, length of day, and solar altitude are all, as above explained, of vital importance in determining the amount of radiant energy delivered to unit horizontal area during any interval of time—any consecutive 24 hours, say. But they give only the quantity of insolation delivered, and not the amount of energy actually absorbed by air and earth and thereby rendered effective in maintaining their temperatures. This smaller quantity, the absorbed energy, depends not only upon the total insolation and therefore upon each of the above factors, but also upon at least two others; namely, reflection and scattering. Thus it is obvious that all the solar radiation which is reflected back to space, whether by clouds or by the surface of the earth, is immediately and completely lost, so far as heating the atmosphere is concerned, and that the same is also true of that smaller

[1] *Ann. Bur. Cent. Météorol.*, Pt. I, 1883.

portion lost through the process of scattering, whether by dust particles or by air molecules.

The total loss of solar energy by these two processes, reflection and scattering, amounts, according to Abbot, Fowle and Aldrich,[1] to about 43 per cent for the whole earth. This estimate is based largely on the reflecting power, 78 per cent, of a dense cloud, and the observed cloudiness. It is all but certain, however, that the recorded cloudiness is larger than the actual amount in terms of 78 per cent reflectors, owing to the fact that even the faintest trace of condensation is regarded as "cloud," and the sky therefore frequently reported to be completely covered when, as a matter of fact, the sun is shining at nearly full value. Furthermore, the sunshine is depleted by roughly one-tenth its original value before reaching the clouds. From these several facts it seems that the unused or lost solar energy is about 38 per cent of the whole. This value may be considerably in error, but it appears to be as good as can be obtained from the available data and therefore is here provisionally adopted.

When solar radiation is minutely analyzed spectrally it exhibits thousands of irregularities in the wave-length distribution of energy that were present even before the outer atmosphere was reached. The minima, indicating strong absorptions in the solar atmosphere, constitute the well-known Fraunhofer lines.

In addition to the vast number of intensity deficiencies, absorption or Fraunhofer lines, as they are called, inherent in solar radiation, there are many similar deficiencies resulting from its passing through the oxygen, carbon dioxide, water vapor, ozone, and possibly other substances of the atmosphere. Carbon dioxide, water vapor, and ozone also strongly absorb the long wave-length earth radiation. Oxygen and water vapor absorb in many exceedingly restricted regions, so restricted, indeed, that in mere appearance they are indistinguishable from the narrow Fraunhofer lines. And in addition to these numerous narrow lines there are a number of broad absorption bands, certainly of water vapor, ozone, and carbon dioxide. Oxygen, too, seems to have a broad band in the region of exceedingly short wave lengths. Presumably all these bands are simply aggregates of large numbers of individual lines.

Whatever the actual process of absorption, it is certain that to within observational errors the amount of energy absorbed increases arithmetically with the intensity of the incident radiation and, for monochromatic radiation, geometrically with the quantity of the absorbing material passed through, provided it is all under the same physical condition. Thus, if $I_{0\lambda}$ is the initial intensity of a parallel beam of monochromatic radiation, and $aI_{0\lambda}$ its intensity after passing normally through a homogeneous layer of absorbing material of unit thickness, then its

[1] *Ann. Astrophys. Obs. Smithsonian Institution*, **4**; 381, 1922.

intensity after traversing a distance of m units in the same material is given by the equation

$$I_\lambda = I_{0\lambda}a^m.$$

In the case, also, of scattering of monochromatic radiation, the extinction progresses according to the same laws that apply to absorption. That is to say, it is always a constant fraction of the remaining radiation that gets through a unit quantity of the scattering material.

The coefficients both of direct absorption and of extinction by scattering (see Chap. VII, Part IV) are radically different for radiations of different wave lengths. But if $I_{0\lambda}$ is the initial intensity of the radiation of a given wave length and $aI_{0\lambda}$ its intensity after it has passed normally through a layer of absorbing material of unit thickness, then after normal transmission through layers m and n units thick, respectively,

$$I_{m\lambda} = I_{0\lambda}a^m, \text{ and } I_{n\lambda} = I_{0\lambda}a^n.$$

Hence,

$$a = \left(\frac{I_{m\lambda}}{I_{n\lambda}}\right)^{\frac{1}{m-n}}, \text{ and } I_{0\lambda} = I_{m\lambda}\left(\frac{I_{m\lambda}}{I_{n\lambda}}\right)^{\frac{m}{n-m}}.$$

Now, in the case of the atmosphere, while in a vertical direction there is homogeneity neither in dust content nor in density, there frequently is approximate horizontal homogeneity over considerable distances in respect to both conditions; and by observing the sun at different angles of elevation a considerable and, at such times, allowable range in the ratio of m to n can be obtained for the atmosphere as a whole.

For simplicity it is desirable to take $n = 2m$, from which

$$I_{0\lambda} = \frac{I^2_{m\lambda}}{I_{2m\lambda}} \text{ (equation of Bouguer).}$$

When both $I_{m\lambda}$ and $I_{n\lambda}$ are measured, as they may be anywhere, $I_{0\lambda}$, or the intensity of the radiation outside the atmosphere, is thereby also determined nearly as closely. This equation, however, is accurate only when the transparency of the air is the same at the times of both observations. If the sky is clearer at the time the sun is viewed through the greater air path, $I_{2m\lambda}$ evidently will be too large and $I_{0\lambda}$ correspondingly too small; similarly, if at that time the sky is less clear, $I_{0\lambda}$ will be too large. Neither, as Langley showed long ago, is it permissible to drop the λ and apply the equation so modified to the whole, or even any considerable portion, of the solar radiation.

Let the intensities of the several monochromatic radiations be A_0, B_0, C_0, etc., and their respective coefficients of transmission a, b, c, etc. Then their combined residual intensities after passing through the thicknesses m and $2m$ of the absorbing medium will be, respectively,

$$A_0a^m + B_0b^m + C_0c^m +, \text{ etc. } = R_m$$

and

$$A_0 a^{2m} + B_0 b^{2m} + C_0 c^{2m} +, \text{etc.} = R_{2m}.$$

Hence the initial intensity, as computed by the Bouguer equation, is

$$R_0 = \frac{R_m{}^2}{R_{2m}}.$$

But the difference between the actual and the computed initial intensity is

$$A_0 + B_0 + C_0 + , \text{etc.} - R_0 =$$
$$A_0 + B_0 + C_0 + \text{etc.} - \frac{(A_0 a^m + B_0 b^m + C_0 c^m + \text{etc.})^2}{A_0 a^{2m} + B_0 b^{2m} + C_0 c^{2m} + \text{etc.}} =$$
$$\frac{A_0 B_0 (a^m - b^m)^2 + A_0 C_0 (a^m - c^m)^2 + \cdots + B_0 C_0 (b^m - c^m)^2 + \text{etc.}}{A_0 a^{2m} + B_0 b^{2m} + C_0 c^{2m} + \text{etc.}}.$$

An occasional term in the numerator of this final fraction may reduce to zero, since possibly $a = k$, $c = l$, etc., but in general no two of the coefficients, a, b, c, etc., are equal to each other. Hence every term in the numerator, except the few zero ones, if such exist, and consequently the fraction as a whole, is both real and positive. The Bouguer equation, therefore, when applied to complex radiation, always gives too small a value for the initial intensity.

Clearly, then, to determine to the highest degree of accuracy the intensity of the radiation reaching the outer atmosphere (that is, the amount per unit normal surface per unit time) it is necessary first to analyze it into the spectroscopic components and then either to determine the initial intensity of each or else to adopt some equivalent process. The direct method of measuring the energy in each small spectral range would be very tedious, and, besides, would involve a difficult instrumental standardization; hence the following method has been found more convenient:

1. Analyze the solar radiation and obtain, with the bolometer, the relative distribution of energy through the spectrum for different solar altitudes but, as nearly as possible, constant sky conditions.

In each case the value of m, the air mass, as it is called, is practically proportional to the secant of the solar zenith distance except near the horizon. Hence when the solar altitudes at which the bolograms were taken are known, the ratios of the corresponding m's, being the ratios of the respective zenith distance secants, are also known.

2. Measure with a pyrheliometer the rate at which solar energy, exclusive of sky radiation, is delivered per unit normal area during the same time that one of the bolograms is being obtained.

3. Extrapolate, according to the Bouguer equation, each portion of the bolograms to zero atmosphere and thus obtain the initial bologram, or energy distribution through the solar spectrum outside the atmosphere.

4. Measure the areas between the base line, corresponding to zero radiation, and the two bolograms, the extrapolated and the one corresponding to the pyrheliometric reading.

5. From these areas A_0 and A, respectively, and the observed solar intensity I, compute I_0, the intensity of solar radiation outside the atmosphere, by the equation

$$I_0 = I \frac{A_0}{A}.$$

The ratio of A_0 to A evidently varies with the transparency of the atmosphere, and so too does the radiation from the sky round about the sun. Hence, after their mutual relation has been determined, to obtain I_0 it is only necessary to make a single measurement of I and of this radiation; a process that both increases the number of possible observations and avoids the errors incident to the continuous change of sky conditions.[1]

When expressed in terms of gram-calories per square centimeter of normal surface per minute, and reduced to mean solar distance, the average value of I_0 is about 1.94.

As stated above, careful estimates show that about 38 per cent of this radiant energy is wholly lost, leaving some 62 per cent directly absorbed, 2 parts by the earth, 1 part by the atmosphere. And since the air usually is around nine-tenths opaque to terrestrial radiation, it follows that approximately 58 per cent of the incident solar energy ultimately heats the atmosphere.

The more conspicuous notches in the bolometric curve coincide with water-vapor absorption bands, from which it is inferred that most of the direct absorption of solar energy in the atmosphere is due to water vapor. All these bands, however, are of longer wave length than the region of maximum intensity in the solar spectrum, as are also the absorption bands of carbon dioxide and the stronger bands of ozone. Nitrogen and argon have no known absorption bands, while oxygen, the only other important constituent of the atmosphere, has only one, and that in the extreme ultraviolet or Schumann region, except some fine lines in the red. Further, the general absorption of all three is so feeble that, to a first approximation, it may be regarded as wholly negligible. Hence, atmospheric absorption of radiation, whether solar or terrestrial, obviously is due almost wholly to water vapor, carbon dioxide, and ozone; and, since the approximate amount of carbon dioxide in the atmosphere is always known and the quantities of water vapor and ozone at least often determinable, it frequently is possible, by the aid of laboratory data,

[1] ABBOT, FOWLE, and ALDRICH, *Ann. Astrophys. Obs. Smithsonian Institution*, **4**; 79, 1922.

to know roughly the actual absorption in any portion of the spectrum due to all of these substances, either singly or jointly.

In the presence of organic material at ordinary temperatures, ozone soon reverts to ordinary oxygen—a sufficient reason, perhaps, why only traces of it are found in the lower atmosphere. In the stratosphere, on the other hand, where there can be but little of anything oxidizable and where the temperature is about $-55°$ C. in mid-latitudes, and even lower in the tropics, it obviously is far more stable. Hence, since extreme ultraviolet radiation, such as there is every reason to believe is emitted by the sun, on passing through cold dry oxygen converts much of it into ozone, it long appeared exceedingly probable that this substance must exist to appreciable amounts in the outer air where, indeed, it later was found spectroscopically by Ångström,[1] Fabry and Buisson,[2] Fowler and Strutt,[3] and Abbot.[4] Strutt[5] also proved, spectroscopically, that it is not nearly so concentrated in the lower atmosphere as in the upper.

A very searching investigation of the vertical distribution of ozone, based on many spectroscopic examinations of the zenith sky light near (before and after) sunrise and sunset, has been made by Götz, Meetham, and Dobson.[6] They found that roughly one-fourth of the ozone is in the troposphere; that its density is greatest at around 25 kilometers above sea level; that its percentage of the total air present is greatest at close to 35 kilometers; that its center of gravity is at approximately 22 kilometers; and that its greatest changes in amount occur between the levels of 10 and 20 kilometers. However, the total amount of ozone in a vertical column of a given cross-section and its distribution along this column vary widely with the state of the weather, season, and latitude—so widely, in fact, that a generalized graph of them, as now known, would be more misleading than informative.

A distribution of ozone very similar to the above was found by Coblentz and Stair[7] at Flagstaff, Arizona, in June, 1938.

The form of the solar energy spectrum curve outside the atmosphere as determined by Abbot and Fowle and its comparison with "black-body" curves at 6200° and 7000° Abs. are given by Fig. 24 (a copy of Fig. 29, Vol. 3, *Annals of the Astrophysical Observatory of the Smithsonian Institution*). The curve of terrestrial radiation intensities, on the other hand, is not known, but it obviously must be within that of a full radiator at the earth's temperature, and in most parts well within, because of the universal presence and great depth, with decrease of temperature with

[1] *Arkiv för Matematik, Astronomi och Fysik.*, **1**; 395, 1914.

[2] *J. Phys.* (5), **3**; 196, 1913.

[3] *Proc. Roy. Soc.*, **93**; 77, 1917.

[4] *Proc. National Acad.*, **4**; 104, 1918.

[5] *Nature*, **100**; 144, 1917; *Proc. Roy. Soc.*, **94**; 260, 1918.

[6] *Proc. Roy. Soc.*, **145**; 416, 1934.

[7] *J. Research, Nat. Bur. Standards*, **22**; 604, 1939.

increase of altitude, of the highly absorptive substances, water vapor especially, carbon dioxide, and ozone. That is, it must be everywhere within, and mostly far within, the black-body curve for 287.2° Abs., as

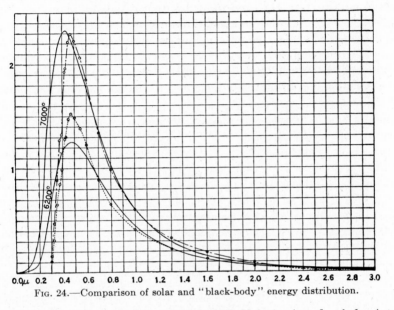

Fig. 24.—Comparison of solar and "black-body" energy distribution.

shown in Fig. 25, copied from Plate XX, Vol. 2, *Annals of the Astrophysical Observatory of the Smithsonian Institution* (Abbot and Fowle).

The absorptions of earth radiation by water vapor, carbon dioxide, and ozone are shown in Fig. 26. The outer or enveloping curve, a copy of Fig. 25, gives the intensity distribution of radiation from a black

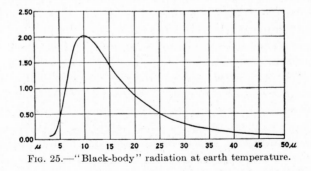

Fig. 25.—"Black-body" radiation at earth temperature.

body at the temperature 287.2° Abs. The area of this curve below the irregular full line, at least up to 20μ, and, presumably, through much, if not all, the region of longer wave lengths, shows the absorption of vertical earth radiation by a column of 3 grams of water vapor per square centimeter cross-section, as estimated from laboratory measurements made by Fowle.[1] The amount of water vapor assumed, 3 grams per square centimeter cross-section of the column, is a little more than the average amount in the atmosphere as a whole. The areas below the two broken curves show the absorption by carbon dioxide above sea level, as computed from the experimental data of Schaefer,[2] and Rubens and Aschkinass.[3] Finally, the area below the dotted line gives some idea of the absorption of earth radiation by ozone, estimated from the observations of G. Hettner, R. Pohlman, and H. J. Schumacher.[4] The amount of absorption by ozone is uncertain for several reasons, but chiefly

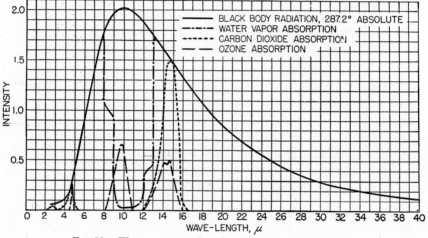

FIG. 26.—Water vapor, carbon dioxide, and ozone absorption.

because the quantity of it in the atmosphere, the equivalent, on the average, of a layer 3 mm. thick,[5] at normal temperature and pressure, appears to vary widely,[6] being greatest, it seems, when the barometer is low, during winter and spring, and in high latitudes; and least when the barometer is high, during summer and autumn, and in low latitudes.[7]

It appears, then, as shown by Fig. 26, that the absorption of radiation directly from the earth by water vapor is quite imperfect (others have found water vapor to be even less absorptive between 8μ and 13μ than here indicated) even when the surface is at sea level; that carbon dioxide

[1] *Smithsonian Misc. Col.*, **68**; No. 8, 1917. See also HETTNER, *Ann. Phys.*, **55**; 476, 1918.

[2] *Ann. Phys.*, **16**; 93, 1905.

[3] *Ann. Phys.*, **64**; 584, 1898.

[4] *Z. Phys.*, **91**; 372, 1934.

[5] FABRY and BUISSON, *Astrophys. J.*, **54**; 297, 1921; *J. Phys.*, **2**; 197, 1921.

[6] DOBSON, HARRISON and LAWRENCE, *Proc. Roy. Soc.*, **114**; 521, 1927; BUISSON, *C. R.*, **186**; 1229, 1928.

[7] For detailed information about atmospheric ozone, see Conference on Atmospheric Ozone, *Quart. J. Roy. Meteorol. Soc. Supplement* to Vol. 62, 1936.

does not appreciably affect the amount of this absorption in the region of its bands, that being already complete, or nearly so, owing to the presence of water vapor; and that, since ozone absorption is very strong where that of water vapor is weakest and imperfect and earth radiation at its maximum, the presence of this gas in the atmosphere has a distinct heat-conserving or warming effect.

It is also obvious that, although each of these substances is an effective absorber in the region of appreciable to strong solar radiation, their joint effect on earth radiation is far greater, so much so, indeed, that they produce a very marked greenhouse effect. Whatever the absorption of water as a vapor may be, as a cloud it is nearly a perfect absorber of all terrestrial radiation.

DISPOSAL OF SOLAR RADIATION

Since the average temperature of the earth remains sensibly constant, it is evident that all the radiant energy reaching the outer atmosphere is somehow disposed of. This disposal is 38 per cent by reflection and scattering, processes of nullification so far as thermal effects are concerned, and 62 per cent by absorption and re-radiation. Therefore, if the solar constant is 1.94 calories per square centimeter per minute, the effective black-body temperature of the earth as a radiator to space—its planetary temperature—is given by the equation

$$T^4 = \frac{\dfrac{0.62 \times 1.94}{4}}{8.22 \times 10^{-11}}.$$

Hence

$$T = 246° \text{ Abs.}$$

If all the radiation from the sun were absorbed, the earth's planetary temperature, obtained by writing 1.00 in place of 0.62 in the above equation, would be 277° Abs., or about 10° C. below the actual average temperature of the surface air. This difference evidently is owing to the coefficient of transmission of the atmosphere being greater for the incoming solar radiation than for the outgoing earth radiation.

Let S be the total solar energy per second incident on the earth, t the fraction of S that reaches the surface of the earth directly and by scattering (sun and sky radiation), a the fraction that is absorbed in the atmosphere, E the total radiant energy leaving the surface of the earth, t_1 the fraction of E that gets through the atmosphere directly, a_1 the fraction that is absorbed; then, since half the absorbed energy (at least to a first approximation) is radiated out to space and half in to the earth, if there is no reflection of earth radiation.

$$E\left(t_1 + \frac{a_1}{2}\right) = S\left(t + \frac{a}{2}\right).$$

If t_1 is 0.12, and it is approximately, $a_1 = 0.88$, and

$$0.56E = S\left(t + \frac{a}{2}\right). \qquad (1)$$

Now, $t + a = 0.62$, but we do not know at all closely the average value of either t or a. Perhaps it would not be greatly wrong to assume $t = 0.42$ and $a = 0.20$. This gives $E = 0.93S$, and $T_0 = 272°$ Abs., where T_0 is the average black-body surface temperature of the earth.

This estimate, about 15° C. below the actual average temperature of the surface air, is uncertain for several reasons. The value of $t + a$ is not accurately known, while that of each separately is even more doubtful. Possibly a little more earth radiation than the amount assumed passes out through the atmosphere directly, thereby slightly lowering the required surface temperature. On the other hand, it seems certain that clouds must, to some extent, reflect terrestrial radiation, but that is not important. If the amount of outgoing radiation reflected were, on the average, 5 per cent of the whole (it probably is much less), the values of a_1 and t_1 would be about 0.84 and 0.11, respectively, instead of 0.88 and 0.12, and the corresponding value of T_0 275° Abs., a gain of only 3° C. Furthermore, the processes of evaporation, condensation, and convection, especially mechanical or turbulence convection incident to winds, all change the temperature of the surface from that which would obtain if they did not occur. Finally, and most important of all, the earth is not, as assumed, a black body, and does not radiate as one. To radiate at the same rate per equal area its temperature must be appreciably higher than that of a black body. Hence the difference of 15° C. found above between the actual average temperature of the surface of the earth and its computed value, on the assumption that this surface is a full or perfect radiator, is in the right direction and probably not far wrong in amount.

As explained by W. H. Dines,[1] the earth and the air afford three major heat-balance problems, namely, heat gain and heat loss of the earth as a whole; heat flow to and from the surface; and heat gain and loss by the atmosphere.

The following catalogue of what becomes of the solar radiation received by the earth is based on the best values available. The larger terms are well supported by observation, and therefore such errors as may still exist in the smaller ones are unimportant.

Some of these values are quite surprising, especially the value of 105 for the total radiation of the surface of the earth in contrast with 42 for all the solar radiation it gets, both direct and scattered, and 100 for what it would get if there were no intervening atmosphere at all. This apparent contradiction results from the fact that the surface of the earth receives far more radiation from the clouds and radiating gases of the

[1] *Quart. J. Roy. Meteorol. Soc.*, **43**; 151, 1917.

atmosphere, water vapor and carbon dioxide especially, than it does from the sun. In short, the earth is in a tolerably effective "greenhouse," and the resulting temperatures are correspondingly different from what one intuitively might expect them to be.

EFFECTS OF CLOUDS ON INCOMING AND OUTGOING RADIATION

As stated above, a dense cloud reflects about 78 per cent of incident solar radiation, but, according to the experiments of Rubens and Laden-burg,[1] it absorbs and emits long wave-length, or earth, radiation very much as does a black body. Hence, since (see Fig. 26) the atmosphere is transparent to 0.1 to 0.2 of the outgoing radiation and imperfectly, however highly, absorptive of the rest, it follows that the undersurface of a stratus cloud, or cloud sheet, at any level, being cooler than the vapor and surface beneath, receives and absorbs, both day and night, more radiant energy than it emits and that its upper surface, being warmer than the air above, receives and absorbs less by night but more by day (owing to the added sunshine) than it gives out. Also, since, with increase of height, temperature in the cloud realm decreases and water vapor thins out, the higher the cloud the greater these several inequalities between absorption and emission.

Whenever, on the whole, the gain of heat by the cloud in this way is greater than the loss, its temperature and also that of the containing air should increase, and both then be pushed up to a higher level (unless in the meantime the superjacent air has been equally heated) and thereby cooled to a lower temperature than they had before they were warmed and the cloud thus thickened and deepened, except insofar as it might evaporate into drier air above. Similarly, when the cooling is in excess of the heating, the cloud is carried to a lower level, correspondingly warmed by the consequent compression of the air it is in and more or less evaporated.

All these cases of convection within the cloud (it cannot rise or fall throughout simultaneously) tend to break it up into cells, manifested by cloud in the ascending portions and by clear sky, or, at least, thinner cloud, in the descending parts. Also, the cooling on top leads to a slight temperature inversion analogous to that which occurs at the surface of the earth on calm, clear nights.

Furthermore, dense low clouds, radiating approximately as black bodies and having nearly the same temperature as the earth beneath, prevent appreciable surface cooling by night. On rare occasions, when the cloud is the warmer of the two, the temperature of the surface increases throughout the night. On the other hand, high cirrus clouds, since they are far colder than the earth, and also because but little of their radiation can penetrate through the water vapor beneath, allow

[1] *Verhandl. D. Physik. Ges.*, **11**; 16, 1909.

the surface to cool nearly as much at night as it would if the sky in every direction were perfectly clear.

The above considerations offer an obvious rational means of computing the loss of heat from the surface of the earth on still nights and the consequent minimum temperature. But it is an impracticable method; hence only empirical equations thus far have been used for this purpose.

Another important factor in the disposal and distribution of the radiant energy received by the surface of the earth is the nature of that surface. Its efficiency, both as a radiator and as an absorber, varies from place to place—a surface of dry sand, for instance, differs in these respects from a grass sod, and both differ from a forest covering—hence surface heating and cooling are more or less irregularly distributed over all land areas. Over water these local differences do not occur. Here, however, until a covering of ice is formed, or at least until the surface water has cooled to a temperature near the freezing point, the temperature changes but little from day to night and but slowly from season to season. At night the drop in temperature normally is very small, because, as soon as the surface water is even minutely cooled, it sinks, except when it already is close to freezing, and thereby forces warmer water to the top, a convectional process that distributes the loss of heat throughout a large amount of material, and hence entails but a small drop in temperature, whereas on land the supply of heat by conduction from the soil is from only a very shallow layer, and the temperature change is therefore correspondingly great. During the daytime, when the surface receives more heat than it gives off, dry soil just gets hotter, whereas from damp soil, from growing vegetation, and, especially, from water, much of the absorbed energy converts the liquid into a gas without change of temperature. This vapor then goes with the winds to other places, both near and far, where it is condensed and where, incident to condensation, it gives back the energy of evaporation in the form of heat. In this way, and also by the circulation of the atmosphere and of all the seas, large and small, the heat supplied to the air and the earth, however locally and irregularly, is so spread to all parts of the world as to approach equality of distribution—an equality always approached but never attained.

PLANETARY TEMPERATURE AND ABSORBING SHELL

Let the earth be surrounded by an absorbing but non-reflecting shell in the stratosphere; ozone, for instance. Let S be the average normal intensity of the solar radiation outside this shell and let aS be the portion of S arrested by it through absorption and scattering jointly. Then since, to a first approximation, $aS/2$ is sent out to space by scattering and reradiation, the actual intensity of the incoming radiation just within the shell is $S(1 - \frac{a}{2})$. Similarly, if E is the average intensity of the earth radiation reaching the shell and bE the portion arrested, its intensity just outside is $E(1 - \frac{b}{2})$. Hence for the steady state,

$$E\left(1 - \frac{\overline{b}}{2}\right) = S\left(1 - \frac{\overline{a}}{2}\right),$$

or

$$E = S\frac{2 - a}{2 - b}.$$

That is, E is greater than, equal to, or less than, S, according as b is greater than, equal to, or less than a. For instance, let $b = 0.2$ and $a = 0.02$, values that perhaps are of the right magnitude for the ozone. Then $E = 1.1S$. That is, the intensity of the earth radiation is 10 per cent greater than it would be if there were no absorbing layer at all, and the planetary temperature raised from 277° Abs. to 284° Abs.

All changes, therefore, in the amount of ozone, or other similarly absorbing material, in the outer atmosphere must more or less affect the average temperature of the earth. Hence variations in the ultra-violet radiation from the sun, because of the changes thus induced in the amount of ozone, must, so far as the action just explained alone is concerned, change the average temperature of the lower air—increase or decrease it according as the quantity of ozone in the upper air is made larger or smaller. We might, therefore, suspect that the paradox of the earth being coolest when the solar radiation is greatest, and warmest when that is least, might be owing to the amount of ozone in the strato-sphere varying inversely with the number of sunspots and value of the solar constant. But observations indicate that, in general, the amount of ultraviolet radiation and, presumably, therefore, also of ozone increases with spot activity. Hence we suspect that there may be some other action of ozone that tends to reduce the temperature of the lower air, and this we find in its strong tendency to induce condensation and therefore to render humid air at least hazy; for clearly a greater general prevalence of cirrus and cirrus haze during spot maxima than during spot minima also would account for this paradox, because such clouds, owing to the size of their particles, shut out the short wave-length solar radiation more effectively than they shut in the long wave-length earth radiation. And perhaps these clouds really are generally most prevalent during spot maxima, and therefore at least a contributing factor in the cause of the observed temperature changes.[1]

[1] ROKUZYÔ, T., and C. S. CHOW, *Proc. Phys.-Math. Soc. Japan*, **4**; 47, 1922.

CHAPTER VII

ATMOSPHERIC CIRCULATION: GENERAL PRINCIPLES

INTRODUCTION

Since the atmosphere is a fluid whose viscosity is not only small but also well known, one might suppose, with respect to any given portion, that it would be quite as easy, through the equations of thermodynamics and hydrodynamics, to foretell its every movement and future position as by the equations of celestial mechanics to predict an eclipse or an occultation. But this is far from being the case, and for many reasons. Thus the irregularities of surface heating and surface friction, and the action of mountains, themselves irregular and broken, in deflecting winds, both horizontally and vertically, complicate the problem beyond exact solution. Besides, there are even discontinuities in the amount of atmosphere involved. Water vapor is added in large amounts by evaporation to the volume of circulating gases, mainly in the regions of "highs," while equal average quantities are withdrawn (not simultaneously) by precipitation, chiefly in the regions of "lows." Hence an exact mathematical solution of the problem of world-wide circulation does not seem possible. Nevertheless, many details of this circulation are clearly understood from physical considerations and admit of at least approximate analyses. Some of these details pertain equally to all the more general winds, and therefore a discussion of them will be given independently as a common introduction to the more extended accounts of certain types of atmospheric circulation that follow under the captions Monsoons, Hurricanes, Trade Winds, Cyclones, etc.

Atmospheric circulation, whether manifesting itself in a monsoon, for instance, or in only a gentle lake breeze, is a gravitational phenomenon induced and maintained by temperature and humidity differences. This can be well illustrated by the flow of water between two adjacent tanks when connected by an upper and a lower pipe and kept at different temperatures.

Let the two tanks A and B (Fig. 27) be filled to the same level slightly above the upper pipe u, and let them have the same temperature. Under these conditions there will be no flow of water from either tank to the other. Now let the pipes be closed and let the water in tank A be equally warmed throughout. It will expand, providing its original temperature was not below 4° C., and if the cross section is of constant area the amount of water above each level in A, at and below the initial surface, will be

102

increased in proportion to its distance from the bottom. Hence the pressure due to gravity is everywhere throughout the original volume correspondingly increased—the maximum increase being at the level of the initial surface. If the lower pipe *l* be now opened, there still will be no flow of water from either tank to the other. But if the upper pipe be opened, water will flow from *A* to *B*, and in so doing will decrease the pressure on all parts of *A* and increase it on all parts of *B*. If *l* also is open, water will flow from *B* to *A*. If both pipes are left open and the water in *A* kept constantly warmer than the water in *B*, there will be continuous circulation of the water from *A* to *B* through the upper pipe and from *B* to *A* through the lower. Obviously, the same results could be obtained by applying a cooling process to *B* instead of a warming one to *A*. That is, since the circulation in question is a gravitational phenomenon induced by a temperature difference between the water in the two tanks, it clearly is immaterial how this temperature difference is established, whether by heating the one tank or by cooling the other; similarly in the case of the atmosphere. If two adjacent columns of air of the same composition, or the masses of such air over two

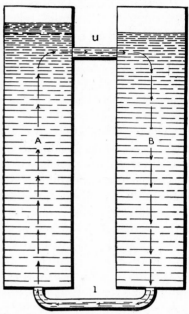

Fig. 27.—Circulation between warm and cold tanks.

adjoining regions, whether large or small, are kept at different temperatures, there will exist, through the action of gravity, a continuous overflow from the warmer to the colder, and an underflow from the colder to the warmer. Neither does it make any difference in this case how the inequality of temperature is established and maintained, whether by heating the one section or by cooling the other. If the two columns are kept at the same temperature, but if the absolute humidity of one is made greater than that of the other, there will be an overflow of air from the more humid column to the drier and an underflow from the drier to the more humid—increase of absolute humidity decreasing density as does increase of temperature.

VERTICAL CONVECTION OF THE ATMOSPHERE

General Considerations.—Vertical convection of the atmosphere may be divided into two classes: (*a*) mechanically forced convection, as the rise of air on the windward side of a mountain or other obstruction and its fall on the leeward side; (*b*) thermal convection.   The latter, involving both warming and cooling, is by far the more important; in fact, it either constitutes or is associated with all natural air movements.   It commonly is said to consist of the rising of warm air and the sinking or flowing in of cold air to take its place; but, while this describes the phenomenon of thermal convection, it seems to imply the false concept that warm air has some inherent ascensional power, whereas, in reality, thermal convection is only a gravitational phenomenon, consisting in the sinking of relatively heavy air and the consequent forcing up of air which, volume for volume and under the same pressure, is relatively light.

The terms "heavy" and "light" are used here advisedly instead of "dense" and "rare," because it is the relative *weights* of two adjacent masses of air of equal volume under the same pressure and not their *densities* that determine which shall fall and which shall be raised.

Three factors enter into the question of weight per unit volume when pressure is constant: (*a*) temperature, (*b*) composition, and (*c*) horizontal velocity, including speed and direction.   The first of these weight factors varies widely and is very effective.   A change in temperature by any given amount $\mp t$, say, changes the original weight per unit volume W_1 to the new weight $W_1 \pm w$ in the ratio,

$$\frac{W_1}{W_1 \pm w} = \frac{T \mp t}{T} \text{ (Charles' or Gay-Lussac's law)},$$

in which T is the original absolute temperature.   Thus if the original temperature is that of melting ice, and it is increased or decreased by 1° C., the weight per unit volume will be decreased or increased, respectively, 1 part in 273.

The effect of the second of the above weight factors, the composition of the atmosphere, is obvious from the following consideration: Since the number of gas molecules per unit volume under a fixed temperature and pressure is independent of the nature of the gas—Avogadro's law—it follows that under these conditions an increase or decrease of water vapor, say, in the atmosphere, implies a corresponding decrease or increase of the other molecules present, mainly nitrogen and oxygen.   Now the equivalent molecular weight of dry air is approximately 28.96 and the molecular weight of water 18; hence a change in the water vapor, the only constituent of the atmosphere that appreciably varies, amounting to 1 per cent of the total number of gas molecules present, alters the weight per unit volume by $\frac{1096}{2896} \frac{1}{100} W$, in which W is the weight of the unit volume of dry air under the same conditions of temperature, pressure, and gravity.   On very warm days water vapor may amount to 5 per cent or more of the total gas molecules present, and the air, therefore, be, roughly, 2 per cent lighter than it would be if perfectly dry.   Of course, changes from saturation to utter dryness, or the reverse, do not occur in nature, but a variation of as much as 50 per cent in the absolute humidity at a given place does occur through evaporation, condensation, and air movement.   Hence on very hot days a change of 1 per cent in the weight per unit volume of the lower air as a result of altered composition alone is quite possible, and indeed often occurs.   This produces a difference in buoyancy of the same order as that caused by a 3° C. change in temperature and therefore may be decidedly important.

The third factor that affects weight and convection, namely, horizontal velocity, while comparatively small, occasionally may be of some importance.   Its numerical value can easily be computed.   Let NS (Fig. 28) be the axis of the earth's rotation, and let P at latitude ϕ

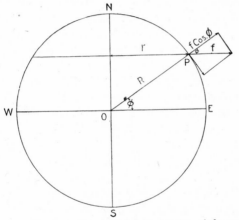

Fig. 28.—Decrease of weight due to rotation of the earth.

be the point under consideration.   The centrifugal force f exerted by the mass m at the point P is given by the equation

$$f = mr\omega^2,$$

in which ω is the angular velocity of the earth's rotation, and r the distance of P from the axis.   Numerically,

$$\omega = \frac{2\pi}{86,164}.$$

Since the mean radius of the earth is about 6368 kilometers, and since weight equals mass times gravitational acceleration, or $981m$, approximately, in the c.g.s. system, it follows that at latitude 40°

$$f = \frac{w}{378}, \text{ roughly,}$$

in which w is the weight of the object considered, while the decrease, δw, in the weight, or the component of f at right angles to the surface, is given by the equation

$$\delta w = -f \cos 40^\circ = -\frac{w}{494}, \text{ about.}$$

At latitude 40° a velocity of 22.4 meters per second (50 miles per hour) from east to west is equivalent to decreasing ω^2 by 1 part in 8, approximately, and an equal velocity from west to east to increasing it a like amount. That is, at latitude 40° a given mass of air in a west wind of 22.4 meters per second (50 miles per hour) weighs less than an equal amount in an east wind of the same velocity by about 1 part in 1976: similarly for other latitudes in proportion to their cosines. Hence, other things being equal, an east wind tends slightly to underrun an adjacent west wind.

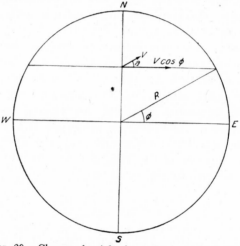

Fig. 29.—Change of weight due to horizontal velocity.

The above special solution of this problem may suffice for most purposes, but the following outline and conclusions of a more general solution probably will be of interest.

Referring to Fig. 29, let $V \cos \phi$ be the horizontal velocity of the surface of the earth at latitude ϕ, v the horizontal velocity of the air with reference to the surface, α the angle between the east direction and the path, and assume the earth to be spherical and concentrically homogeneous. Further, let mg_0 be the gravitational pull on the mass m, or the weight the mass m would have when at rest if the earth were non-rotating, and let mg be the actual force normal to the surface, very nearly its true weight. Then,

$$mg = mg_0 - m\frac{(V \cos \phi + v \cos \alpha)^2}{R} - \frac{m(v \sin \alpha)^2}{R}$$

$$= mg_0 - \frac{m(V \cos \phi)^2}{R} - \frac{mv(2V \cos \phi \cos \alpha + v)}{R}$$

But, $mg_0 - \dfrac{m(V \cos \phi)^2}{R} =$ the normal force of the mass m when at rest on the surface of the rotating earth. Hence, when the mass m is given a horizontal velocity v, its still-weight W is changed by an amount ΔW given by the equation

$$\Delta W = -mv\frac{(2V \cos \phi \cos \alpha + v)}{R}.$$

The exact equations that apply to the actual surface of the earth are more complicated than those given here, but the numerical values are very nearly the same.

Since the latitude is limited by 0° and 90°, it follows that the sign of the change (that is, whether the change consists of a decrease or increase from the still-weight) depends upon the value of α, or the direction of motion. Obviously, whenever $\cos \alpha$ is positive, or the velocity has an *easterly* component, the change of weight is *negative*—maximum when ϕ and α are both zero, or when the motion is east on the equator. Similarly, since $2V \cos \phi$ is nearly always large in comparison with v, the change of weight ordinarily is *positive* whenever the velocity has an appreciable westward component. This increase of weight clearly is a maximum when $\phi = 0°$ and $\alpha = 180°$, or when the motion is west on the equator.

Further, the direction of the wind in order that there be no change of weight is conditioned by the equation

$$- \cos \alpha = \frac{v}{2V \cos \phi}.$$

But, as above stated, $2V \cos \phi$ nearly always is large in comparison with v, and therefore the direction conditioned by zero change in weight commonly has only a small westerly component. For example, let $v = 44.7$ meters per second (100 miles per hour) and let $\phi = 60°$. Then, under these somewhat excessive conditions, for zero effect, $\cos \alpha = -\frac{1}{10}$, about, or the direction along which there is no change of weight is less than 6° west of the meridian.

From the above it appears that of the three factors that alter the weight of a given volume of air and thereby determine whether it shall rise to higher levels, sink to lower, or remain where it is, temperature is by far the most important, and horizontal velocity the least important. As a rule, the former alone need be considered.

Local Convection.—There are two distinct ways of thermally inducing convection: (*a*) by *heating below*; (*b*) by *cooling above*. Each is of great importance, both in general atmospheric movements and also in those restricted or local winds to which special names have been given. Where heating alone occurs the rising air does not return, but remains in equilibrium at its new level, where its final temperature is the same as that of the adjacent atmosphere. Similarly, when cooling alone occurs the sinking air does not again immediately rise. In other words, neither heating nor cooling, acting alone, can produce closed circulation in which the same mass passes through a complete cycle of positions, though, of course, a compensating movement must occur somewhere. A strong local uprush, for instance, except in the case of the thunderstorm, to be explained below, is nearly always compensated by a wide settling, so gentle that it cannot be measured. Similarly, restricted downrushes of air, again except in connection with the thunderstorm, are compensated by wide and gentle upward movements.

Whatever the type of atmospheric disturbance under consideration, the most important general facts to remember are: that all vertical movements of the air are accompanied by dynamical heating or cooling; that rising air in the absence of condensation cools, roughly, at the adiabatic rate of about 1° C. for each 103 meters increase of elevation; that descending air warms at substantially the same rate; and, especially, that since the current lapse rate generally is much less than the adiabatic, dynamical cooling usually limits upward convection to a small range, while, quite as commonly, downward convection is arrested, not at and by the surface of the earth, but in mid-air by dynamical heating.

This stability of the atmosphere just emphasized, and briefly discussed in Chap. III, prevents the weather from being fitful and erratic. For instance, it postpones the heat thunderstorm to the latter portion of a hot spell, or until progressive convection has established an adiabatic lapse rate up to the condensation level; makes rain widespread and gentle instead of local and intense, and the air at flying levels smooth and comfortable instead of rough and bumpy; and produces many other effects of like nature. The fact, therefore, that the atmosphere usually is more or less stable vertically is a matter of very great meteorological significance.

Interzonal Drift.—Although the movement of the air is mainly from east to west within the Tropics and from west to east in middle latitudes, it nearly always has a north-south component, even where steadiest and most persistent. Also, at most places, especially in the temperate zones, the winds frequently are largely to wholly north or south, usually for a few hours to a day or two, and, in places, nearly continuously for an entire season. All this circulation is, of course, owing to horizontal pressure gradients incident, directly or indirectly, to differences of temperature. It is not in general a uniform and smooth circulation, but, however tortuous its path and turbulent its manner, a major net result is the perpetual maintenance of counter interzonal or latitudinal drifts; courses that through the rotation of the earth entail important effects that must be carefully considered.

Change of Velocity with Change of Latitude.—The velocity of the
earth's surface at and near the equator, as a little calculation shows, is
about 1675 kilometers (1040 miles) per hour from west to east, while,
with reference to this surface, the velocity of the atmosphere from east to
west in the same region is only a small fraction of this value. In reality,
therefore, the atmosphere of equatorial regions is also moving from west
to east with a great velocity, though not so great as that of the surface
of the earth itself.

Let, then, r_1 be the distance of the mass m_1 from the axis of rotation
of the earth, and ω_1 its angular rotation about this axis; r_2 and ω_2 the
corresponding values for m_2; and so on for the entire earth, including
the atmosphere. Then, in the absence of extraneous forces, the sum
total of the angular momenta is constant, or, in symbols,

$$m_1 r_1{}^2 \omega_1 + m_2 r_2{}^2 \omega_2 + \cdots \equiv \Sigma m r^2 \omega = \text{constant.}$$

Let, now, the position of m_1, a given mass of air, say, be so changed that
r_1 becomes r_1'. Then, either ω_1 must so change as to keep

$$m_1 r_1{}^2 \omega_1 = m_1 r_1'{}^2 \omega_1' \qquad \text{(law of equal areas),}$$

or else the rest of $\Sigma m r^2 \omega$, after deducting $m_1 r_1'{}^2 \omega_1'$, must be so changed
as to retain constant the sum $\Sigma m r^2 \omega$.

If $m_1 r_1{}^2 \omega_1$ gains from or loses to the rest of $\Sigma m r^2 \omega$, it clearly must do
so through a mutual push or pull between the masses concerned. Hence,
if a given mass of air were forced poleward or equatorward, and there
were no interfering constraint, the absolute value of its east-west component would not remain constant, as often is supposed, but actually
increase or decrease in proportion with the secant of the latitude. But
the winds do not blow according to this simple law. It operates, of
course, but so also do the modifying constraints, and both must be considered, for the final result is their joint product.

Law of Conservation of Areas.—The law of the conservation of
areas as applied to the atmosphere is of sufficient importance to justify
its brief demonstration. It should be definitely noted that the law of the
conservation of areas applies only to objects held on their course by an
extraneous push or pull directed all the time to the same center or axis,
as illustrated by the movements of the planets about the sun, and not at
all to projectiles or to airplanes or other self-propelled objects. The
rotation of the earth beneath any one of these, though changing its
direction, does not alter its speed.

Let O (Fig. 30) be the center about which a mass m is moving with
the linear velocity v_1 along the circular arc AB whose radius is r_1. Let
m be constrained to follow its path by a central force; that is, a force
directed towards O. For instance, let it move over a frictionless horizontal plane, and be kept in its orbit by the tension on a weightless string

connecting it with the center O.   At B let the tension on the string be so increased that the mass m will be drawn in the distance BH in the same time that, undisturbed, it would have reached E.   During this time the path will be something like BC.   If the tension again becomes constant with the value appropriate to the point C, the new orbital velocity will be v_2 along the arc CD of radius r_2.

By taking the time interval smaller and smaller, the velocity along BH, however irregular, approaches uniformity as its limit, while BE and BC both approach straight lines.   With the two component velocities along BE and BH, respectively, uniform it is obvious that the resultant

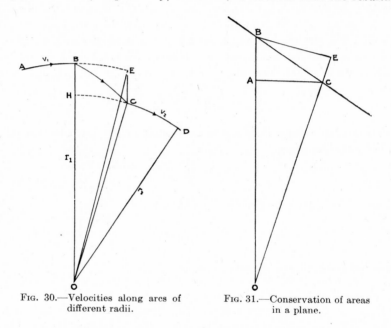

FIG. 30.—Velocities along arcs of   FIG. 31.—Conservation of areas
          different radii.   in a plane.

velocity along BC must also be uniform.   The problem of vectorial areas reduces, therefore, to finding the general relation of a radius vector to the component of the corresponding orbital velocity normal thereto. This relation may be shown as follows:

Let BC (Fig. 31) be a rectilinear section of the orbit, usually of infinitesimal length, along which the velocity is uniform, and let OB and OC be two radii.   From B draw BE perpendicular to OC extended, and from C draw CA perpendicular to OB.   Hence

$$\frac{AC}{BE} = \frac{v_1}{v_2}$$

in which v_1 and v_2 are the components of the uniform velocity along BC at right angles to OB and OC, respectively.   But from the similarity of the triangles *OAC* and *OEB* it follows that

$$\frac{AC}{BE} = \frac{OC}{OB},$$

and, therefore, that

$$\frac{v_1}{v_2} = \frac{OC}{OB}.$$

That is, $rv = k$, a constant, in which r is the radius vector and v the component of the orbital velocity at right angles thereto.

But, by elementary geometry,

$$rv = 2a,$$

in which a is the rate at which area is covered by the movement of r. Hence whatever the portion of the orbit, the radius vector sweeps over equal areas in equal intervals of time, or whatever the points selected,

$$\frac{v_1}{v_2} = \frac{r_2}{r_1}.$$

The kinetic energy E_1 of the mass m while on the arc AB (Fig. 30) is given by the equation

$$E_1 = \frac{1}{2}mv_1{}^2.$$

Similarly, its kinetic energy along *CD* is given by

$$E_2 = \frac{1}{2}mv_2{}^2.$$

These are unequal, the difference being

$$\frac{m}{2}(v_2{}^2 - v_1{}^2),$$

and it will be interesting to find the source of inequality.

At all parts of the orbit the tension f on the string is given by the equation

$$f = \frac{mv^2}{r}$$

and the work, dw, done on shortening the radius by the small amount dr is expressed by the equation

$$dw = -\frac{mv^2}{r}dr.$$

But since

$$rv = k, v = \frac{k}{r},$$

and

$$dw = -\frac{mk^2}{r^3}dr.$$

Hence on shortening the string from r_1 to r_2 the work becomes

$$W = mk^2 \int_{r_2}^{r_1} \frac{dr}{r^3} = \frac{m}{2}\left(\frac{k^2}{r_2{}^2} - \frac{k^2}{r_1{}^2}\right).$$

But

$$k^2 = v^2 r^2 = v_1{}^2 r_1{}^2 = v_2{}^2 r_2{}^2 = \text{etc.}$$

Hence

$$W = \frac{m}{2}(v_2{}^2 - v_1{}^2).$$

But this is identical with the value already found for the difference between the kinetic energies of m at the distances r_1 and r_2 from O.

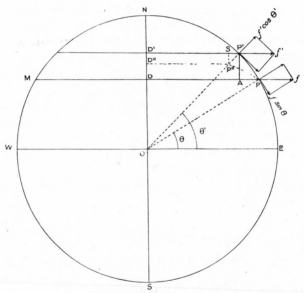

Fig. 32.—Conservation of areas on a sphere.

That is, this difference is equal to and due to the work done on m by the tension on the string while decreasing the radius from r_1 to r_2.

Consider now the velocity of a quantity of air or other mass moving as a unit frictionlessly over the surface of the earth. Let the mass m, regarded as a point (in the case of an extended body it is Σmvr that remains constant), be at P (Fig. 32) rotating around the axis NS on the small circle MP and held to the surface by gravity directed towards the center O. If v is the linear velocity of m, it follows that the radially directed force f is expressed by the equation

$$f = \frac{mv^2}{r} = \frac{mv^2}{DP}.$$

On forcing this mass to a higher latitude, to P', say, work is done against the horizontal component of f. But from the similarity of triangles it is obvious that at every point along the arc PP', $f \sin \theta$, the force to overcome, is to f, the centrifugal force, as the rate of approach to the axis is to the rate of progress along the meridian. Thus the work done in going from P to P' is the same as that which would be done in shortening the radius DP to DA. But, as above explained, this work on m, or transfer of energy to it, must appear as so much additional kinetic energy, friction being excluded. Hence the orbital velocity v' at P' is to the orbital velocity v at P as DP is to $D'P'$. That is, the conservation of areas holds likewise in this case, where the radius vector is the normal from the moving mass to the axis of rotation.

This same law holds also on the slightly flattened earth. To make this clear, let PP'' be a portion of a greatly flattened meridian, and let the mass m be taken from P to P' as before, and thence to P''. From P' to P'' the work is against the force $f' \cos \theta'$, and obviously equal to the work against f' over the distance $P'S$. Hence the orbital velocity of m at P'' is to its orbital velocity at P as DP is to $D''P''$.

Suppose a quantity of quiet air, air moving strictly with the surface of the earth, at, say, latitude 30°, is forced to higher latitudes, as it actually is by pressure gradients due to temperature differences, what, according to the law of the conservation of areas, would be its final surface velocity at, say, latitude 60°?

At latitude 30° its orbital velocity, being the same as that of the surface, is, approximately,

$$v = \frac{2\pi 3957 \cos 30°}{24} = 897.2 \text{ miles per hour} = 401.1 \text{ meters per second.}$$

At latitude 60° its orbital velocity, from the principle stated, would be

$$v' = v \frac{\cos 30°}{\cos 60°} = 1554 \text{ miles per hour} = 694.7 \text{ meters per second.}$$

while at latitude 60° the orbital velocity of the surface is

$$s = \frac{2\pi 3957 \cos 60°}{24} = 518 \text{ miles per hour} = 231.6 \text{ meters per second.}$$

Hence the velocity of the transferred air in question with reference to the surface would be

$$v' - s = 1036 \text{ miles per hour} = 463.1 \text{ meters per second.}$$

As a matter of fact, no such enormous velocities of the wind as the principle of the conservation of areas would lead one to expect in the higher latitudes are ever found, either at the surface or at other levels. This, however, does not argue against the applicability of the principle itself, but only shows that in the case of atmospheric circulation there are very effective damping or retarding influences in operation.

The resistance due to the viscosity of the atmosphere is one of these retarding influences, but its effect probably is very small. A larger effect doubtless comes from surface turbulence induced by trees, hills, and other irregularities. A still greater velocity control is that incident to vertical convection, by which all the lower portion of the atmosphere is made to have more nearly the same velocity. In this way, largely, even the more distinct poleward and equatorward currents eventually are intermingled and brought to a common state. Finally, the east-west pressure gradients of cyclones and anticyclones greatly reduce the velocity effect due to change of latitude. The eastward urge of the poleward winds is ever present, of course, but so too is the westward urge of the equatorward winds—equal in mass to the poleward, but shallower, on the whole, and more affected by surface drag.

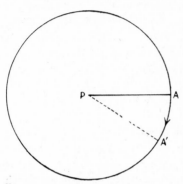

Fig. 33.—Deflection, at pole, due to earth's rotation.

The situation is very complex, but while our most extensive or planetary winds are prevailingly from the west in middle latitudes, and from the east in equatorial regions, owing to the conservation of angular momentum, nevertheless the actual direction and speed of the wind at any particular time and place are determined by the latitude, surface interference and current pressure gradient, however established, as explained in the next few sections.

Deflection Due to the Earth's Rotation.—The effect of the rotation of the earth on the direction of the wind is extremely important to the science of meteorology. It therefore is necessary to understand clearly that there is such an effect, and how it is produced. To this end, let P (Fig. 33) be one pole of the earth—the south pole, say—assume the surface to be flat, which it very approximately is close about any point, and let a particle of air cross it in the direction PA with the uniform velocity v; let the earth rotate in the direction AA' with the angular velocity ω, and let the distance which the air particle under consideration has gone from P in the brief time dt be such that

$$PA = dr = v\,dt.$$

Let the meridian along which the particle started as it left P have the position PA' at the end of the time dt, or when the particle, keeping a constant direction in space, has arrived at A. Obviously, the velocity with which the earth moves under the particle increases directly with the distance from P. But as this latter is directly proportional to the time dt since the particle left P, v being a constant, it is clear that the distance ds travelled normally to the instantaneous meridian may be expressed in terms of a constant acceleration a in the direction opposite to that of rotation. That is,

$$ds = \frac{1}{2}a(dt)^2.$$

Also

$$ds = dr\omega dt = vdt\omega dt = v\omega(dt)^2.$$

Hence,

$$\frac{1}{2}a(dt)^2 = v\omega(dt)^2,$$

or

$$a = 2\omega v.$$

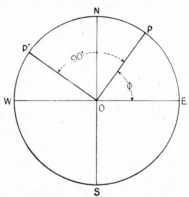

Fig. 34.—Deflection, not at pole, due to earth's rotation.

Since a force is measured in terms of mass times acceleration, it follows that the west-east deflective force f that would keep a mass m, of atmosphere, or anything else, next the pole in the same meridian, or the east-west force that, if the earth were still, would produce the given motion with reference to its surface, is given by the equation

$$f = ma = 2m\omega v,$$

where v and ω have the values above assigned.

Let the moving particle under consideration be not at one of the poles, but at some other point, such as P (Fig. 34) at latitude ϕ. Resolve the angular velocity ω, about ON, into its components about the right-angled axes OP and OP'. These components, as is well known, are $\omega \sin \phi$ about OP and $\omega \cos \phi$ about OP'.

Now all points on and exceedingly close to the equator of a rotating sphere have sensibly the same velocity around the axis, hence the direction and velocity of horizontally moving particles at P are affected by the component of rotation about OP only, and not at all by the component about OP'.

That is, at N, as already explained,

$$a = 2\omega v, \text{ and } f = 2m\omega v,$$

while at latitude ϕ, where the angular rotation is $\omega \sin \phi$,

$$a = 2\omega v \sin \phi, \text{ and } f = 2m\omega v \sin \phi,$$

to the right (going forward with the particle) in the northern hemisphere, to the left in the southern.

From this simple equation it follows that the deflective force due to the rotation of the earth acting on a quantity of moving air (that is, the force that, assuming the earth to be still, measures the existing tendency of wind to change its direction with reference to any great circle along which it is moving) is:

a. Directly proportional to its mass.

b. Directly proportional to its horizontal velocity.

c. Directly proportional to the angular velocity of the earth's rotation.

d. Directly proportional to the sine of the latitude of its location.

e. Exactly the same whatever its horizontal direction.

f. Always at right angles to its instantaneous direction and therefore wholly without influence on the speed with reference to the surface.

g. Opposite to the direction of the earth's rotation. Hence to the right, or clockwise, in the northern hemisphere; to the left, or counter-clockwise, in the southern.

Since the deflection acceleration is all the time at right angles to the path, it follows that an object moving freely over the surface of the earth would describe an endless series of curves. At each point on this path the acceleration at right angles to it, measured with reference to the surface of the earth, is given, as explained, by the equation

$$a = 2\omega v \sin \phi,$$

in which the terms have the values assigned above. It is also given by the well-known equation for acceleration along a radius of curvature. That is,

$$a = \frac{v^2}{r},$$

in which, since the force is tangent to the earth, $r = R \tan \alpha$ where R is the radius of the earth, and α the angle subtended at the center of the earth by the radius of the path at the point under consideration. Hence, when the only deflective influence is that due to the earth's rotation,

$$r = \frac{v}{2\omega \sin \phi}, \text{ and } \tan \alpha = \frac{v}{2R\omega \sin \phi};$$

and rate of deflection $v/r = 2\omega \sin \phi$.

That is, the greater the linear velocity of the moving object over the surface of the earth, and the nearer it is to the equator, the greater the radius of curvature. On the equator the radius of curvature is infinite, or the path a straight line. However, unless moving along the equator the object soon crosses to the other hemisphere and its direction of curvature changes, as is well shown by the summer wind tracks over the Indian Ocean.

Rate of Change of Wind Direction.—The theoretical rate of change of wind direction at any *point* on the surface of the earth obviously is the angular velocity ω' of the earth about an axis passing through its center and the point in question. This change of direction, therefore, clockwise in the northern hemisphere, counter-clockwise in the southern, occurs at a rate *wholly independent* of wind velocity, and is given by the equation

$$\omega' = \omega \sin \phi,$$

in which ϕ is the latitude of the place under consideration and ω the angular velocity about the axis through the north and south poles. Note that this rate of change of direction of a wind stream at a fixed point on the surface of the earth is just half that of a particle of air in this stream—rate of deflection, v/r.

But, as the earth turns completely around during a sidereal day, $\omega = 2\pi/86,164$ per second $= 15° \, 2' \, 28''$ per hour, or $15°$ per hour, roughly. Hence

$$\omega' = 15° \sin \phi \text{ per hour, roughly.}$$

The approximate values of ω' corresponding to different latitudes may conveniently be tabulated as follows:

EARTH ROTATION IN DEGREES PER HOUR AT DIFFERENT LATITUDES

φ	0°	5°	10°	15°	20°	25°	30°	35°	40°	45°
ω'	0.00°	1.31°	2.61°	3.89°	5.14°	6.36°	7.52°	8.63°	9.68°	10.64°
φ	50°	55°	60°	65°	70°	75°	80°	85°	90°	
ω'	11.52°	12.32°	13.02°	13.63°	14.13°	14.53°	14.81°	14.98°	15.04°	

It must be clearly understood that the above values of rate of change of direction are based on the assumption that there is no friction and no disturbing horizontal pressure gradient, neither of which is true with reference to actual winds. Nevertheless, the values obtained are important, since they indicate the natural torque of the atmosphere, or its tendency to rotate when set in motion by pressure gradients.

It is interesting and quite practicable, as Whipple[1] has shown, to compute the path of a frictionless mass over the rotating earth when its direction and velocity are given for any definite point, but this will be omitted, since in the case of the actual atmosphere, because of viscosity, turbulence, surface obstacles, horizontal pressure gradients, etc., the departures from theoretical values are so great that it seems hardly necessary or even safe to go beyond the above simple and general relations.

[1] *Phil. Mag.*, **33**; 457, 1917.

Centrifugal Deflecting Force of Winds.—Usually the course of a wind is curved, from which we infer that there is a force *on* the moving air that bends it to its path, and an equal reaction *by* this air that measures its tendency to deflect from its actual course to one less curved. The value of this centripetal force f in the plane of the orbit, not the plane of the horizon, or, of its equal, the inertial or centrifugal pressure by the air, is given, on the assumption that the earth is not rotating, by the equation

$$f = \frac{mv^2}{r},$$

in which m is the mass concerned, v its linear velocity, and r the radius of curvature of the path at the place and time under consideration, or radius of the "small circle" in which the air is then moving.

Relative Values of Centrifugal and Rotational Components.—The ratio between the two deflective forces, rotational and centrifugal (centrifugal action of the earth's rotation and centrifugal action due to curvature of path), varies greatly with the velocity of the wind, radius of curvature of its path, and latitude of its location. Within 20°, at least, of the equator cyclonic storm winds commonly move on curves whose radii are comparatively small, 150 kilometers (93.2 miles) or less, in which case the centrifugal deflective force generally is greater than the rotational. In middle and higher latitudes, however, the average radii of cyclonic wind paths usually are much larger, say 600 kilometers (373 miles), and the rotational deflective force greater than the centrifugal.

A few numerical examples will be interesting. No effort has been made to get average values, but only such as presumably often occur.

RATIOS OF DEFLECTIVE FORCES UNDER GIVEN CONDITIONS

Latitude	Radius of curvature, miles	Gradient velocity, miles per hour	Rotational force / Centrifugal force
10°	20	80	$\frac{1}{44}$
20°	30	70	$\frac{1}{13}$
30°	100	50	$1\frac{0}{19}$
40°	400	40	$1\frac{2}{3}$
50°	400	35	$1\frac{4}{3}$
60°	400	35	$2\frac{6}{5}$

In tropical cyclones, therefore, the pressure gradient is balanced mainly by the centrifugal force, while in those of middle latitudes it is balanced chiefly by the rotational deflective force.

Ordinarily, except in the neighborhood of a well-marked low, the radius of curvature is much larger than any of the values above assumed, and consequently the ratio of rotation to centrifugal force correspondingly greater.

Total Horizontal Deflecting Force.—If the path of the air is at all curved, as it usually is, its total *horizontal* deflecting force, F, due to its velocity is given by the equation

$$F = 2m\omega v \sin \phi \pm \frac{mv^2}{r},$$

in which $r = r' \sec \alpha$, r' and α being the linear and angular (as seen from the center of the earth) radii respectively of the "small circle" in which the air is moving, or $r = R \tan \alpha$, R being the radius of the earth, and the other symbols having the meanings given above. The positive sign is used, or the deflective forces are additive, in the northern hemisphere when the course of the wind is counter-clockwise; in the southern hemisphere when the course is clockwise. The negative sign is used in each case when the sense of rotation is reversed. In cyclones, therefore, the total deflecting force is equal to the sum of the centrifugal and rotational deflective forces; in anticyclones to their difference.

When the winds become approximately steady the deflective force obviously is balanced against the gravitational pressure gradient. In symbols,

$$\frac{1}{\rho}\frac{dp}{dn} = 2\omega v \sin \phi \pm \frac{v^2}{r},$$

in which ρ is the density of the air, dp the slight difference between the pressures at the ends of the short horizontal distance dn at right angles to the path at the place considered. The meanings of the other symbols are given above. If the gradient is zero (that is, if the air moves without lateral restraint), $r = \dfrac{v}{2\omega \sin \phi}$ as previously shown, or $R \tan \alpha = \dfrac{v}{2\omega \sin \varphi}$; also, from the equation just given, $2\omega v \sin \phi \pm \dfrac{v^2}{r} = 0$. Hence, under the assumed conditions, $r = R \tan \alpha = \infty$; that is, $\alpha = 90°$, or the path is a great circle. However, these latter equations have but little more than a theoretical interest, since, without the driving force of a pressure gradient, wind velocity can neither be acquired nor (because of friction) maintained.

GRADIENT WIND

Gradient Velocity.—That velocity of the air at which the deflective force due to the rotation of the earth and the centrifugal force jointly balance the horizontal pressure gradient is called the gradient velocity. It does not occur near the surface of the earth, owing to surface friction, including turbulence, but "from kite observations, it appears that at 1500 feet above the surface the agreement [between the observed and 'gradient' velocities] is generally very close,"[1] especially in the absence of thunderstorms and other local disturbances. This does not mean that the wind has the same velocity at all levels beyond $\frac{1}{2}$ kilometer, but only that above this height the velocity of an approximately steady wind is very nearly the gradient velocity appropriate to the atmospheric density, horizontal pressure gradient, and latitude at the place in question.

If the sense of rotation is that which exists in a cyclone, the two deflective forces are additive, as stated above, and the gradient velocity is given by the general equation

$$v = \pm\sqrt{\frac{r}{\rho}\frac{dp}{dn} + (r\omega \sin \phi)^2} - r\omega \sin \phi, \tag{A}$$

in which the sign of the radical remains to be determined.

But obviously $v = 0$ when $dp/dn = 0$, as there can be no wind without a pressure gradient, from which it follows that the sign of the radical is positive, and that actually

$$v = \sqrt{\frac{r}{\rho}\frac{dp}{dn} + (r\omega \sin \phi)^2} - r\omega \sin \phi. \tag{B}$$

Theoretically this wind at any place is *along* the corresponding isobar, parallel, roughly, through the first kilometer of elevation, to the sea-level isobar, and always in such direction that one moving with it will have the *lower* pressure to his *left*. It must be distinctly noted, however, that the above equations presuppose absence of friction and the attainment of a steady state. They therefore give the approximate wind velocity and direction only for levels above the reach of appreciable surface turbulence, and even there in the cases only of smooth and regular isobars. Near the surface where the velocity is checked by friction the wind direction is correspondingly deflected toward the region of lower pressure.

In the c.g.s. system of units:

$v =$ centimeters per second.

$dp/dn =$ difference in dynes pressure per square centimeter, per centimeter horizontal distance at right angles to isobars. $r = r' \sec \alpha$; $r' =$ radius of curvature, in centimeters, of wind path at time and place of observation, *not distance to the center of the low;* $\alpha =$ angular radius (measured from the center of the earth) of the "small circle" along which the wind is moving. Ordinarily r differs from r' by less than 1 part per 100, and therefore, in practice, they may be assumed to have equal values.

$\rho =$ grams of air per cubic centimeter.

$\omega =$ angle through which the earth turns per second, $2\pi/86,164$.

$\sin \phi =$ natural sine of the angle of latitude.

[1] SHAW, "Forecasting the Weather," 2d Ed., p. 84.

If the path of the wind is straight (that is, if there is no centrifugal force), the equation for gradient velocity is

$$v = \frac{\dfrac{dp}{dn}}{2\omega\rho \sin \phi}.$$

In anticyclonic regions gradient winds, as explained, obey the equation

$$\frac{1}{\rho}\frac{dp}{dn} = 2\omega v \sin \phi - \frac{v^2}{r}$$

or

$$v = r\omega \sin \phi \pm \sqrt{(r\omega \sin \phi)^2 - \frac{r}{\rho}\frac{dp}{dn}}. \tag{C}$$

As above,

$$v = 0 \text{ when } \frac{dp}{dn} = 0.$$

Hence, in this case, the sign of the radical is negative and

$$v = r\omega \sin \phi - \sqrt{(r\omega \sin \phi)^2 - \frac{r}{\rho}\frac{dp}{dn}}. \tag{D}$$

Obviously, then, as pointed out by Gold,[1] steady anticyclonic winds cannot become intense, since the maximum possible velocity is given by the equation

$$v_{max} = r\omega \sin \phi.$$

For example, if $r = 500$ kilometers, and $\phi = 40°$,

$$v_{max} = 23.4 \text{ meters per second} = 52.3 \text{ miles per hour.}$$

The gradient that produces this velocity is given by the equation

$$\frac{dp}{dn} = \rho r(\omega \sin \phi)^2.$$

On substituting this gradient in the equation above for straight winds, it appears that it would give the velocity,

$$v = \frac{\rho r(\omega \sin \phi)^2}{2\rho\omega \sin \phi} = \frac{1}{2}r\omega \sin \phi.$$

That is, the limiting velocity of anticyclonic winds,

$$v_{max} = r\omega \sin \phi,$$

is just twice that which the corresponding pressure gradient would give to straight winds.

Note that v_{max} is exactly the same as the velocity of the surface of the earth at the point in question about the center of curvature of the isobar, but in the opposite direction.

[1] *M. O.*, No. 190, "Barometric Gradient and Wind Force," London, 1908.

Since "for the time being, we may regard the gradient winds as the best estimate we can give of the actual winds at, say, 1500 feet above the surface,"[1] it seemed advisable to construct tables (see Appendix I), one for cyclonic, the other for anticyclonic conditions, that give the theoretical wind velocities in meters per second, kilometers per hour, and miles per hour for various latitudes, radii of curvature, and pressure gradients, as indicated, each to be used in conjunction, of course, with the current weather map, corrected, if need be, by estimation or by special reports, for the hours that have elapsed since the observations were made from which it was constructed.

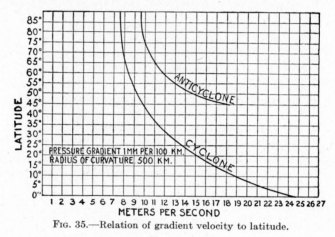

Fig. 35.—Relation of gradient velocity to latitude.

As the equations demand and the tables indicate, the winds of an anticyclone, gradient for gradient, latitude for latitude, and curvature for curvature, are stronger, often much stronger, than those of a cyclone. This may seem to be flatly contradicted by the fact that anticyclones are characterized by relatively light winds, but the contradiction is only apparent, for, as the equations show, steep gradients cannot obtain in anticyclonic regions, nor, therefore, heavy winds except near their borders, or when r is large. Hence, in general, strong anticyclonic winds cover only a narrow strip of territory, and their duration, therefore, is comparatively brief.

Figs. 35, 36, and 37 represent, respectively, the effect of latitude, pressure gradient, and radius of curvature on the "gradient" velocity, other things in each case being constant.

Surface gradients and surface isobars, when well defined and in the absence of local disturbances, may be used for approximate values up to heights of, roughly, 2 kilometers, except wherever the horizontal temperature gradient is steep and opposite in direction to the horizontal pressure gradient. In such cases the temperature tends to weaken and

[1] SHAW, "Forecasting the Weather," 2nd Ed., p. 89.

finally reverse the pressure gradient with increase of height. Hence, since the temperature gradient is nearly always more or less poleward,

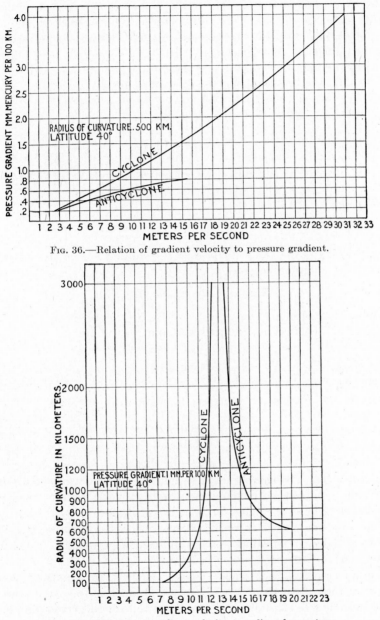

Fig. 36.—Relation of gradient velocity to pressure gradient.

Fig. 37.—Relation of gradient velocity to radius of curvature.

in extra-tropical regions the east wind generally is the shallowest and the least likely to have, at a height of 2 kilometers, say, the direction and velocity computed from the surface system of isobars; and the west wind the deepest, with direction and velocity closest in agreement with the values thus computed. In short, with increase of height the isobars, usually closed on the surface, tend to open out and roughly to follow the parallels of latitude with the decrease of pressure directed poleward, at least to well above the troposphere.

Gradient Velocity Nomogram.—The general gradient velocity equation, $F = 2m\omega v \sin \phi \pm mv^2/r$, reduces, on dividing by m, to

$$2\omega v \sin \phi - \frac{1}{\rho}\frac{dp}{dn} = \pm\frac{v^2}{r},$$

the upper sign being used for anticyclones and the lower for cyclones.

A straight line nomogram that solves this equation has been constructed by Herbert Bell, after the method developed by Prof. d'Ocagne in his "Traité de Nomographie." The solution is as follows:

Writing

$$u = -\frac{20}{\rho}\frac{dp}{dn} \text{ and } w = 10^5\omega \sin \phi,$$

u and w being scales along the lines $x = -10$ and $x = 10$, respectively, the velocity equation becomes

$$2500u + vw = \pm 50{,}000\frac{v^2}{r},$$

which is linear in u and w.

If, then, a network is constructed of the two families

$$x = 10\frac{v - 2500}{v + 2500} \tag{1}$$

and

$$y = \pm\frac{50{,}000\dfrac{v^2}{r}}{v + 2500}$$
$$= \pm\frac{6.25 \times 10^6}{r}\frac{(10 + x)^2}{10 - x}, \tag{2}$$

the point c, say, determined by equations (1) and (2) from values of v and r, will be collinear with the point A on the u scale, fixed by the given value of dp/dn, and the point B on the w scale indicated by the latitude.

The resulting diagram, with gradients in terms of millimeters difference of barometer reading per 100 kilometers, velocity in meters per second, and $\rho = 0.0011$, is given in Fig. 38.

To find the gradient wind velocity, connect the known pressure gradient (marked on lower left border of the diagram) and the latitude of the place in question (given on the upper right border) with a straight edge or stretched string and note where it cuts the curve representing the radius of curvature of the local isobar. For *cyclones* the vertical through this point gives the required velocity in meters per second. For *anti-*

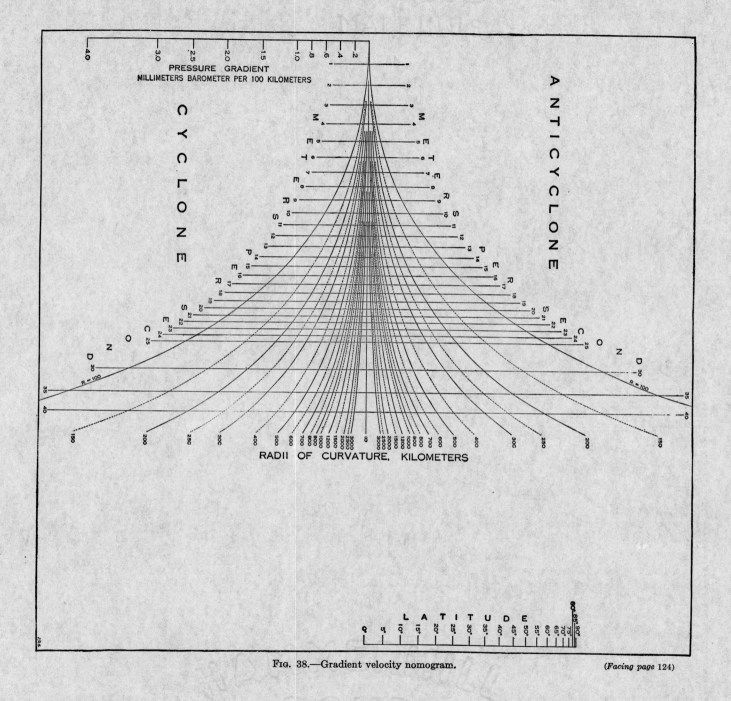

Fig. 38.—Gradient velocity nomogram.

(Facing page 124)

cyclones two velocities are thus indicated, but the *smaller* is the one to take, since it alone is physically possible (see equations (C) and (D), page 121).

This nomogram should be used in conjunction with the surface distribution of pressure only in the absence of local disturbances, thunderstorms, squalls, etc., or strong horizontal temperature gradients; where the pressure gradient is well defined—isobars smooth, and for elevations between, roughly, 500 and 2000 meters.

Automatic Adjustment of Winds in Direction and Velocity.—In discussing the more extensive winds it is convenient to consider the earth as stationary and the air as moving over it without friction under the influence of three distinct horizontal forces: (1) the deflective force, due to the earth's rotation; (2) the horizontal component of the centrifugal force, due to the curvature of the path; and (3) the horizontal or gradient pressure, due to gravity. The first two are at right angles to the course of the wind and therefore help to control its direction, but do not alter its speed. The latter, however—that is, the gradient pressure—affects both the direction and

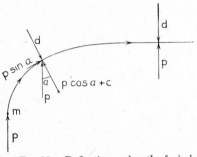

Fig. 39.—Deflection and path of winds in frictionless flow under a force of constant magnitude and constant geographic direction.

the speed. Furthermore, as the velocity depends upon the horizontal pressure alone, and as the other forces depend in turn upon the velocity, and are zero when it is zero, it follows that of the three forces only the gradient pressure is independently variable.

Consider, then, the result of applying a horizontal pressure p of constant magnitude and constant geographic direction to a small mass m of air, free, as above assumed, from friction: Let m (Fig. 39) be the mass in question initially at rest with reference to the surface of the earth, and let it be acted on by the force p, exactly poleward, say. Immediately the mass moves, under the applied pressure p, the deflective force d becomes operative, thus curving the path (to the right in the northern hemisphere, to the left in the southern) and introducing the centrifugal force c. So long, however, as the angle between the path and the force p is less than 90° there still will be a component of the latter in the line of motion; accordingly the speed of m will continue to increase, and therefore also the deflective force d. If this angle should exceed 90°, the force p would have a component opposite to the direction of motion, which consequently would be slowed up and d thereby correspondingly decreased. In the end, therefore, a poleward force along the meridians on an object free to move gives it an exactly west to east velocity of such magnitude that, except in very high latitudes, the resulting deflective force is nearly equal to the horizontal pressure—the horizontal component of the centrifugal force being then comparatively small, except near the poles. Whatever the direction of the gradient force, whether poleward, as above assumed, or any other, the final motion is normal thereto.

A change in the magnitude but not in the direction of p, above, would only shift the latitude of the path and change the velocity so as to be nearly proportional to p. However, p is not the same in either direction

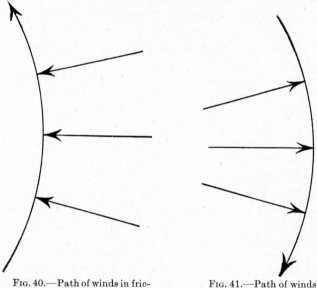

FIG. 40.—Path of winds in frictionless flow under a converging force.

FIG. 41.—Path of winds in frictionless flow under a diverging force.

or magnitude all along the course a stream of air actually takes. Hence such a stream does not indefinitely remain compact but sooner or later swirls about a low, or cyclone, that it overtakes; or, more frequently, it deflects in the anticyclonic sense and loses its identity through diffusion with winds of other sources.

If the horizontal pressure is not everywhere in the same direction, but converges, as in Fig. 40, or diverges, as in Fig. 41, the path, in adjusting itself normally to the directions of this pressure, obviously curves, as in cyclonic and anticyclonic regions, respectively.

In all cases, then, where friction is negligible, the wind automatically follows approximately the isobar of its position, with substantially the gradient velocity.

CHAPTER VIII

ATMOSPHERIC CIRCULATION:
GENERAL PRINCIPLES (*Continued*)

VARIATION OF WIND WITH HEIGHT

Irregularities, Gusts or Puffs.—Though the wind at an altitude of 200 meters or more is comparatively steady, except in very rough or mountainous regions, near the surface of the earth any appreciable wind that may exist is always in a turmoil, owing to surface friction that checks the lower layer while the layers above tumble forward and down, and to numerous obstructing objects that block its course and introduce cross-currents. Hence its direction constantly changes through many degrees, while the velocity irregularly but persistently fluctuates from one extreme to another. At one instant the actual velocity may be anything up to 50 per cent or more greater than the average velocity, while a second or two later it may be fully 50 per cent less than the average. The greater the average velocity the greater, roughly, in the same proportion, the absolute change, as illustrated by Fig. 42. So great, indeed, are these irregularities that places near the surface of the earth not more than 15 meters (50 feet) apart, though having the same average wind direction and velocity, commonly have different, often very different, simultaneous directions and velocities, and therefore, for the instant, radically different winds. When thermal convection is active and there is appreciable wind, there are major eddies, or blocks of air, $\frac{1}{2}$ to 1 mile in length, in the direction of the wind, and about $\frac{1}{8}$ mile broad and, in these larger masses, many irregular and much smaller eddies. In a surface inversion, these eddies are relatively small and tend to be damped out.

Furthermore, this turbulence in the lower air, whether induced by a relatively warm surface or caused by obstacles in the path of the wind, prepares the way for—makes easier—more turbulence. The lapse rate in a stratum of air thus thoroughly mixed up is, by virtue of this mixing, rendered adiabatic. Hence, when a limited mass—a gob—of this air is given a vertical impulse, it goes right on to the top or bottom surface of the agitated layer, except to the extent that it may be checked by mere friction.

If the depth of the adiabatic layer is great, 500 meters or more, the major eddies, due apparently to thermal convection and producing marked gusts and distinct lulls, may average, roughly, 1500 meters in length, in the direction of the wind, and 400 meters in width. These great thermally induced gusts, however, are accompanied by much smaller interference eddies, 15 to 30 meters in diameter, due to houses, trees, and other surface irregularities. When the agitated layer is shallow, as it is when the lapse rate is distinctly less than the adiabatic, interference eddies alone occur.[1]

These facts are of great importance with reference to the wracking effect winds have on houses, bridges, and other structures. They also deeply concern the aviator when starting and landing. But, however valuable for many reasons an exact knowledge of surface air movements would be, it is obvious that they defy all formulae, and that mathematical equations can no more predict the course and speed of a given portion of turbulent surface air than they can mark the path and fix the velocity of water in the swirls and eddies of a mountain torrent. Nevertheless, the average effect of a group of wind eddies, like the average effect of a large number of gas molecules, does profitably yield to mathematical discussion, and it is possible now, from the classical papers of Ekman,[2] Åkerblom,[3] Taylor,[4] Hesselberg and Sverdrup,[5] Richardson,[6] Jeffreys,[7] Giblett[8], and others, to formulate very concisely the major effects of turbulence on the direction and velocity of the winds so affected, that is, all those of the lower atmosphere. To this end it will be convenient (though there are other ways of arriving at the same result) to take over the equations of Ekman's oceanographic paper[9] and, by turning the z-axis up into the air, solve for winds, instead of, as his problems demanded, down into the water for the ocean drift.

Ekman Spiral.—Ekman assumed a straightaway wind blowing over an initially quiet body of water of great extent and considerable depth, and found what would be the resulting movements of the water on the attainment of a steady state. In what follows the atmosphere will be considered at rest, with reference to the solid earth, with a broad straightaway current of water (or drift of land surface, prairie sod, say) flowing under it, and the resulting steady-state movements of the air determined. Clearly, the two problems, the effect of wind on water drift, and of a water current on air drift, are identical, except as to the numerical values

---

[1] For an excellent discussion of eddies, see *Geophys. Mem.*, 54, 1932.

[2] On the Influence of the Earth's Rotation on Ocean Currents," *Arkiv Mat. Astr. Fysik*, 1905.

[3] "Sur les courants les plus bas de l'atmosphère," *Nova Acta Reg. Soc. Upsaliensis*, 1908.

[4] "Eddy Motion in the Atmosphere," *Phil. Trans.*, **215**; 1–26, 1915; On the Theory of Diffusion by Continuous Movements, *Proc. London Math. Soc.*, **20**; 196, 1922.

[5] *Geophys. Inst. Leipzig*, Ser. 2, Heft 10, 1915; *Beit. z. Phys. Atmos.*, **7**; 156–166, 1917.

[6] *Proc. Roy. Soc.*, **96**; 9–18, 1919; **97**; 354–373, 1920.

[7] *Proc. Roy. Soc.*, **96**; 233–249, 1919.

[8] *Geophys. Mem.*, **54**; 1932.

[9] *Loc. cit.*

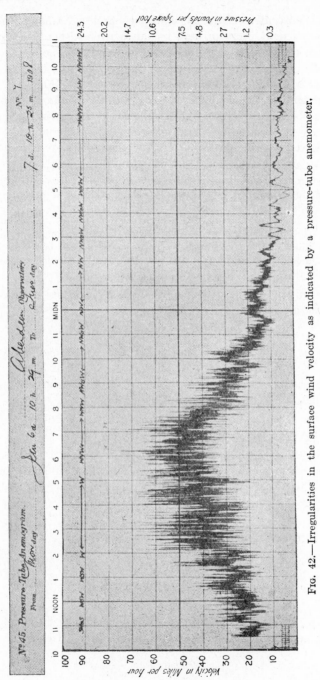

FIG. 42.—Irregularities in the surface wind velocity as indicated by a pressure-tube anemometer.

of certain constants. Hence the equations used by Ekman in the solution of the ocean drift problem may be taken over without change for the solution of the similar wind problem. Clearly, too, the final results will be directly applicable to all steady winds, whether over land or over water, for a wind is only motion as between earth and air.

Mathematical Theory.—Let the origin of the rectangular coördinates x, y, and z be on the surface (land or water) of the earth, z being vertical and positive upwards, and the positive direction of y 90° counter-clockwise from the positive direction of x, as seen from above. Let

u, v = the velocity components of the air drift in the directions of x, y;

X, Y = the x, y components of extraneous forces per unit cube of the air;

ρ = the density of the air, regarded constant, which it is, roughly, through at least the first half kilometer;

μ = the coefficient of drag, or eddy viscosity, of the air, considered constant through the eddy layer—an allowable first approximation—and, by definition, the drag per unit area between two parallel layers of the medium a unit distance apart moving past each other with unit velocity.

t = the time.

Then, in the northern hemisphere (or, with proper change of signs, the southern),

$$X = 2\rho v\omega \sin \varphi; \qquad\qquad Y = -2\rho u\omega \sin \varphi,$$

in which ω is the angular velocity of the earth's rotation, and φ the latitude.

Furthermore, since the drag-producing velocity is the relative velocity of superjacent layers, it evidently is equal to

$$\frac{\partial^2 u}{\partial z^2}\delta z^2$$

in the direction of x, per δz increase of height. Hence the drag, in this direction, per unit cube (opposite faces a unit distance apart and having unit area) is

$$\mu\frac{\partial^2 u}{\partial z^2}.$$

But the force per unit cube in the direction of x also is

$$\rho\frac{\partial u}{\partial t},$$

or its mass times its acceleration in that direction.

Similarly for the forces in the direction of y.

Finally, since, by assumption, u and v vary only with time and height, there are no other forces in the direction of x or y. Hence

$$\frac{\partial u}{\partial t} = 2v\omega \sin \varphi + \frac{u}{\rho}\frac{\partial^2 u}{\partial z^2},$$

$$\frac{\partial v}{\partial t} = -2u\omega \sin \varphi + \frac{\mu}{\rho}\frac{\partial^2 v}{\partial z^2}.$$

For steady motion, and on writing

$$\frac{\rho\omega \sin \varphi}{\mu} = a^2,$$

these equations reduce to

$$\frac{\partial^2 u}{\partial z^2} + 2a^2v = 0,$$

$$\frac{\partial^2 v}{\partial z^2} - 2a^2u = 0,$$

the general solution of which is

$$u = C_1e^{az} \cos (az + k_1) + C_2e^{-az} \cos (az + k_2),$$
$$v = C_1e^{az} \sin (az + k_1) - C_2e^{-az} \sin (az + k_2),$$

in which C_1, C_2, k_1, k_2, are arbitrary constants.

Clearly, the drag is zero, hence u and v are zero, when z is infinite. Indeed the drag is approximately zero at half a kilometer, or thereabouts, above the surface, since at that level the speed and direction of the wind are practically what they would be under the existing horizontal pressure gradient if the atmosphere were a perfect fluid.

If, then, u and v are each to be zero when z is infinite, obviously C_1 is zero. Hence

$$u = C_2e^{-az} \cos (az + k_2)$$
$$v = -C_2e^{-az} \sin (az + k_2),$$

and

$$\frac{du}{dz} = -aC_2e^{-az}\{\sin (az + k_2) + \cos (az + k_2)\}$$

$$= -a\sqrt{2}C_2e^{-az} \sin (az + k_2 + 45°)$$

$$\frac{dv}{dz} = aC_2e^{-az}\{\sin (az + k_2) - \cos (az + k_2)\}$$

$$= -a\sqrt{2}C_2e^{-az} \cos (az + k_2 + 45°).$$

If the tangential drag of the surface on the air is T, and in the positive direction of y, then

$$\mu\left(\frac{du}{dz}\right)_{z=0} = 0, \quad -\mu\left(\frac{dv}{dz}\right)_{z=0} = T.$$

Hence

$$k_2 = -45°$$
$$C_2 = \sqrt{u_0^2 + v_0^2} = V_0$$
$$u = V_0e^{-az} \cos (45° - az)$$
$$v = V_0e^{-az} \sin (45° - az)$$
$$V_0 = \frac{T}{\mu a\sqrt{2}} = \frac{T}{\sqrt{2\mu\rho\omega \sin \varphi}}. \tag{1}$$

Since the tangential drag T of the water (or land) on the air is, by assumption, in the positive direction of y, and, of necessity, in the direction of the surface movement with reference to the air, it follows from the equations (1) that, in the northern hemisphere, the drift of the air just above the surface ($z = 0$, components u and v of V_0 equal to each other and positive) is 45° to the right of the direction of the surface current relative to the air. In the southern hemisphere the air drift is 45° to the left of the surface current.

Since the value of a is independent of height, z may be counted from any level, provided T is the drag between the superjacent layers of air at that level, and V_0 the corresponding drift velocity. Hence the projection of the drift envelop onto the ground or water surface is an equiangular, 45° or 135°, spiral about the initial contact point of air and surface.

The relations between the air and surface movements are shown in Fig. 43 (as over water $i = 20°$ or less—over land the angle i is 30° or more), in which wa is the contact position of certain adjacent air and surface particles at a given instant, w' the position of the same surface particle at a given subsequent instant, and a' the position, at the same subsequent instant, of the initial air particle. That is, with reference to the earth beneath, ww' is the direction and speed of the surface, and aa' the consequent direction and speed of the air. Hence $a'w'$, inclined 135° to aa', is the direction and speed of the surface with reference to the air, and, of course, $w'a'$ that of the air with reference to the surface. That is, $w'a'$ is the theoretical direction and speed of the surface wind. Actually, however, this law of the winds does not hold close to the ground, where the drag is much greater than it is at a moderate height. Here z, as used in the foregoing equations, must be counted from a short distance above the surface.

It should be noted in this connection that since the angle $w'a'w$ between the directions of the surface wind and the "drift wind" has to be 135°, therefore the speed of the surface wind decreases as its inclination to the isobar increases, becoming zero as this angle reaches its limit, 45°.

From equations (1) it is further obvious that the angle between the directions of the driving surface and the resulting air drift increases uniformly with height, two right angles for each π/a gain therein; and also that the velocity of the drift continuously decreases as the height grows greater, falling to the $e^{-\pi}$th, or, approximately, the one twenty-third part of its initial value for any π/a ascent.

The speeds and directions of the drift currents at the heights 0, $\pi/10a$, $2\pi/10a$, and so on, of which wa'' is an example, are shown in Fig. 43, projected onto the surface, or xy plane. The direction and velocity of this actual wind at the height corresponding to the drift wa'' are given by $w'a''$, and similarly for other heights.

If we assume the turbulence drag to be substantially zero at that level at which the wind, as we go up, attains the direction of the isobars, that is, where the angle of inclination i (Fig. 43) becomes zero, and call this height H, then, clearly

$$H = \frac{3\pi}{4a} = \frac{3}{4}\pi\sqrt{\frac{\mu}{\rho\omega\sin\varphi}}. \tag{2}$$

To find the total momentum given to the air per unit of time by the drag T, let F_x be the total flow in the positive direction of x across a strip of infinite height and unit width at right angles to x, and F_y the similar total flow in the direction of y. Then

$$F_x = \int_0^\infty u\,dz = V_0 \int_0^\infty e^{-az}\cos(45° - az)dz = \frac{V_0}{a\sqrt{2}} = \frac{T}{2\rho\omega\sin\varphi},$$

$$F_y = \int_0^\infty v\,dz = V_0 \int_0^\infty e^{-az}\sin(45° - az)dz = 0.$$

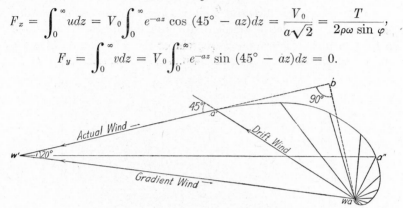

Fig. 43.—The equiangular wind spiral.

Hence the integrated momentum of the drift wind is 90° to the right of the direction of the surface flow with reference to the air, and its value per second per strip of unit width at right angles to this direction and infinite height (practically, to the level of gradient direction),

$$\rho F_x = \frac{T}{2\omega\sin\varphi}.$$

Since the above discussion applies to any velocity, between air and earth in any direction, let, as we may, $w'a'$ (Fig. 43) be the direction and velocity of the surface wind, and let i be the inclination angle, or angle between the direction of the "surface wind" (wind at bottom of region of constant eddy viscosity, say 10 meters above the surface) and the direction of the isobar, or direction of the gradient wind. Then, on the assumption that the viscosity is constant up to the gradient-direction level, and from there on zero, the gradient velocity is given by $w'a$, determined by drawing $a'a$ so as to make the angle $w'a'a$ 135°.

From Fig. 43, it also is evident that the surface wind W_s is given, in terms of the gradient wind W_g, by the equation

$$W_s = W_g(\cos i - \sin i),$$

and the drift wind W_d by the equation

$$W_d = W_g \sin i \cdot \sqrt{2}.$$

The figure also shows that, theoretically, the wind attains gradient velocity both below and above the level of gradient direction, and that at this level the velocity is distinctly in excess of the gradient value. All these surprising deductions have actually been observed.

Since H, the height of the gradient-direction wind, is given by observation, we have, from equation (2), in known terms

$$\mu = \frac{16H^2\rho\omega \sin \varphi}{9\pi^2}.$$

Clearly, then, the direction and velocity of the wind at different heights up to the level of gradient direction furnishes, as indicated by Fig. 43, a means of determining whether or not μ is essentially constant.

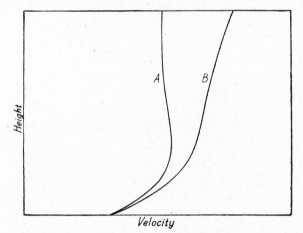

Fig. 44.—Theoretical relation of wind velocity to height; A, constant gradient per unit mass; B, gradient per unit mass increasing linearly with height.

This has been done, and the assumption that normally μ is substantially constant with height fully sustained,[1] however much it may vary with the roughness of the surface and velocity of the wind.

If the driving forces X, Y, per unit mass, hence the gradient wind, are the same at all levels, as above assumed, then the speed of the actual wind varies with height substantially as indicated by curve A, summer type (Fig. 44). If, however, these forces increase linearly with height, this speed will vary as indicated by curve B, winter type.

OBSERVATIONS

The foregoing, like mathematical analyses in general, tells us unequivocally not what may happen but what must happen, provided, of course, the premises are both accurate and complete. But certain of the above primary assumptions are only approximately true; hence in this case,

[1] Taylor, *Phil. Trans.*, **215**; 1, 1915; Whipple, *Quart. J. Roy. Met. Soc.*, **46**; 39, 1920.

too, as is the rule, it is necessary to compare the theoretical deductions with the observed facts—the "must be" with the "is."

The averages of the wind velocities at various heights in the lower atmosphere, from observations made daily, or nearly so, over a period of several months, give a curve of the same general type as the theoretical ones shown in Fig. 44. This is well illustrated by Fig. 45, a typical example from many based on observations covering several years at Drexel, Nebraska, and kindly furnished by W. R. Gregg, U. S. Weather Bureau. Clearly, then, so far as change of velocity is concerned, the

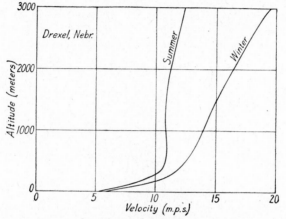

Fig. 45.—Average, over several years, wind velocity at all heights, from surface to 3 kilometers, at Drexel, Nebraska.

assumptions on which the theoretical analysis is based seem to be substantially correct. And the same is true of the wind direction, since, as long known, the angle between this direction and that of the current isobar decreases with increase of elevation, to approximately zero at ½ kilometer, or thereabouts, above the surface.

Physical Theory.—Now that we have seen from the mathematical theory of the way of the wind what, under certain conditions, must happen, and from the observations that what "must happen" really, in effect, does happen, there remains only the necessity of explaining why it happens—of giving the common sense or physics of it, thereby supplementing the logical proof and observational testimony by a peaceful understanding. To this end the exactly similar problem, as already explained, of finding the steady state of initially quiet deep water, as induced by a wind of constant direction and velocity, will be considered, being easier to visualize, presumably, than the action of a water current on initially still air.

Let, then, *aa'* (Fig. 46) represent the steady direction and velocity of the surface air. The water, being free to flow, and on a rotating sphere, will deflect from the wind direction—to the right in the northern hemisphere. Let ww' be the final or steady direction and velocity of the surface water. Numerically, at latitude ϕ,

$$ww' = 7.9 \times 10^{-3} \frac{aa'}{\sqrt{\sin \varphi}}$$

nearly.[1] Clearly, then, $w'a'$ is the direction and velocity of the wind with reference to the moving surface of the water—but little different from aa', its geographic direction and velocity. Hence the drag of the air on the water, T per unit surface area, is in the direction $w'a'$. But the water,

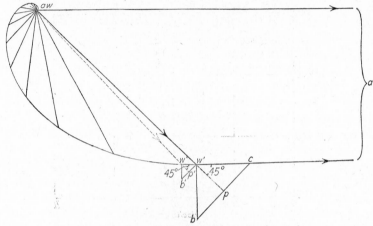

Fig. 46.—Ocean drift induced by a steady wind.

being free to move, automatically adjusts its motion so as to balance this force by the corresponding force incident to earth rotation. That is, in each vertical column of water of unit cross-section there is a momentum M at right angles to $w'a'$ of such magnitude that

$$T = 2M\omega \sin \varphi.$$

Now the connecting medium between the wind above and the moving water beneath the surface layer is that surface layer, however thin. Hence the reaction on this surface by the momentum M at right angles to $w'a'$ is the same, this being the resultant of all the subsurface momenta, as would obtain if the neutralizing components parallel to $w'a'$ did not exist. Hence the drag of the under water on the surface is in the direction $w'b$ normal to $w'a'$. Furthermore, the component of this water drag normal to the direction of surface flow is equal and opposite to that of the wind drag, there being no other horizontal forces operating on it. If, therefore, wp is the direction of surface flow and if pc, normal thereto, represents the component of T in that direction, then pb, equal and opposite to pc, similarly represents the component of the water drag on the surface at right angles to the direction of flow.

[1] Durst, Quart. J. Roy. Met. Soc., 50; 115, 1924.

From the similarity of triangles and the fact that $bw'a'$ is a right angle, it follows that $pw'a'$ is half a right angle. Hence, under the conditions assumed as to steady winds and initially still deep water, the final direction of surface drift makes an angle of 45° to the direction of the wind with reference to the water surface—to the right in the northern hemisphere, to the left in the southern.

Consider next the water as made up of separate layers, each moving as a solid and connected to its neighbors by interfacial viscosity, and let ww'' be the direction and velocity of the second layer. Clearly, then $w''w'$ is the direction and velocity of the first or surface layer with respect to the second. Also, exactly as before, we find that the drift of this second layer is 45° to the right (northern hemisphere) of the direction of the first layer with respect to the second.

In this manner any depth may be reached, however thin the separate layers. Hence the projection of the envelop of the radii vectors of the water drifts onto the surface is a 45° (or 135°) equiangular spiral about any common starting point of wind and water.

Since the above directional relations are independent of velocity, it follows that the amount of spiraling is directly proportional to depth, provided the viscosity, here owing to turbulence convection, is constant. Hence, from the direction and velocity of the surface drift and of the drift at any known depth the movement of the water at any other depth may be determined graphically. Also from these observed drifts the viscosity readily can be determined.

Exactly similar conclusions, arrived at in precisely the same way, apply to the atmosphere, as already explained.

The Half-kilometer Maximum and One-kilometer Minimum Velocities.—Although the above theory requires a maximum wind velocity at some level and smaller velocities at greater heights, it accounts for a difference of but a few per cent, and therefore only partially, at most, for the fact that on many individual days a well-defined maximum velocity occurs at the height of about $\frac{1}{2}$ kilometer, and an equally distinct minimum—often even less than that at the surface—near the 1-kilometer level. This great difference between the minimum above and the maximum below may result from any one of several causes, or combinations of some of them. Thus, on the poleward border of a cyclone, or equatorward border of an anticyclone, the wind changes from easterly near the surface to westerly at some height, often about 1 kilometer. In such cases the velocity obviously falls to a minimum at the level of direction reversal. Again, with increase of height, there usually is considerable, and at times very great, change in the direction of the isobars, gradual as a rule, but often rather abrupt. When the air through the level of this change of isobar direction is continuously well mixed, as it frequently is, its mean velocity is reduced. If, for instance, equal masses having equal and opposite speeds are mixed, their velocity becomes zero; if originally at right angles to each other, their velocity, on the principle of the conservation of linear momentum, is reduced about 30 per cent; and similarly for any other distribution of gradients and convectional interchange. This, too, accounts for a minimum velocity when, but only when, the mixing is confined to the layers in question—a state that must occur under certain fairly common conditions, as will be explained directly. Above the 1-kilometer minimum, and therefore beyond the usual reach of both mechanical and thermal turbulence, the speed of the wind normally goes on increasing with increase of height through the next several kilometers, but not indefinitely. This will be considered later.

During clear afternoons, especially in summer, the lower kilometer, roughly, of the atmosphere appears to be well mixed through both mechanical and thermal convection, and therefore to have the distribution of wind velocity and direction indicated by the Ekman spiral (Fig. 43), except as modified, as indicated above, by special storm conditions or directions of isobars.

The decided minimum velocity near the 1-kilometer level, when not associated with great change of direction, is essentially a phenomenon of the early morning and, presumably, of much of the night, and not, as just explained, of the afternoon. Apparently, then, there must be at these times two layers of turbulent mixing, one near the surface and another about 1 kilometer above, with a stratum between through which convection does not extend. The surface layer is turbulent owing, evidently, to surface friction. The upper layer must be turbulent when partially clouded, as it frequently is, due to the greater loss of heat by the clouds than by the clear air between them—a form of thermal convection. This will give a minimum velocity at the upper level in the common case of very differently directed isobars through the stratum in question. Finally, the intermediate layer will be free from interchange with the surface air owing to the absence, at night, of thermal convection and its insufficient ascent during the early forenoon; and also free from interchange with the upper layer, since the dynamical heating of the falling masses does not permit sufficient descent.

Accordingly the aviator might anticipate roughish flying, during warm afternoons, all the way from the surface up to a height of rather more than 1 kilometer, and smooth beyond that; and of early mornings a rough layer, perhaps 200 to 300 meters thick, on the surface, then a smooth layer, and above that again another rough layer—the first cloud level—and lastly the usual smooth air of the greater altitudes. And these are just the conditions that the aviator often does encounter.

The generally present maximum velocity of the wind at the height of about half a kilometer and minimum at near 1 kilometer above the surface obviously are phenomena of considerable importance to the aviator. Hence, though already known to many, they merit much further study, and more use than has yet been made of them.

Wind Velocities from the Ekman Spiral.—Since the maximum wind velocity occurs, on the average, at the height of about 500 meters, therefore, as shown by inspection, the several radii in Fig. 43, from the spiral center, corresponding to the heights 0, $\pi/10a$, *et cetera*, may be regarded as applying, roughly, to the levels: near the surface, 75 meters, 150 meters, 225 meters, and so on, respectively, above the surface. Hence, to get the probable direction and speed of the wind at any level up to 500 meters, draw a straight line, such as $w'a'$, Fig. 43, which shall represent the surface wind; at the end a' draw another straight line, 135° from $w'a'$, and to the right (for the northern hemisphere) as viewed from w'; and make i = the observed or assumed angle between the surface wind and local isobar. Next, lay off about the spiral center wa a series of radii at steps of 18°, or any other convenient interval, from the initial radius aa', and connect a' with a by means of a spiral so drawn that it shall cut all radii from a at 45°. To this end it is convenient to compute the relative lengths of the several radii and lay them off accordingly before drawing the spiral. From this construction one has: surface wind, $w'a'$; gradient wind, $w'a$; probable wind at the heights of 75 meters, 150 meters, and so on, w' to terminus of proper radius. In Fig. 43, $w'a''$ represents the direction and velocity of the wind 300 meters above the surface, of course in terms of the surface velocity. That is, if the surface velocity is v, the approximate average velocity 300 meters above the surface is

$$V = v\frac{w'a''}{w'a'}.$$

The velocities at other heights are similarly obtained.

Or, if one prefers, he may use for the wind velocities a previously computed table, such as the following:

APPROXIMATE AVERAGE WIND VELOCITIES AT DIFFERENT HEIGHTS

Height	Over water $i = 20°$	Over land $i = 30°$
Surface:	v	v
75 meters	$1.305v$	$1.729v$
150 meters	$1.512v$	$2.232v$
225 meters	$1.642v$	$2.561v$
300 meters	$1.717v$	$2.758v$
375 meters	$1.751v$	$2.862v$
450 meters	$1.759v$	$2.902v$
525 meters	$1.752v$	$2.902v$
Gradient level	$1.673v$	$2.732v$

Similar tables may be computed for other values of i.

It must be remembered that the above wind velocities are only approximate average values, and therefore to be used in individual cases only when it is impracticable to obtain the actual values by direct observations.

From careful theoretical considerations, in which the individual eddies, or parcels, are supposed continuously to exchange momentum with the surrounding air, O. G. Sutton,[1] following Ertel,[2] derives the simple expression,

$$\frac{v}{v_1} = \left(\frac{h}{h_1}\right)^{\frac{n}{2-n}},$$

for moderate heights, a few feet to 200, say, in which v and v_1 are the mean wind velocities at the heights h and h_1, respectively, and n is a number, 0 to 1, though commonly about 0.25, that varies with the vigor of the vertical interchange that, in turn, depends on the intensity of the insolation, mainly, and the condition and nature of the surface.

Empirical Wind Velocity Equations.—Above the thin surface layer the wind increases so nearly regularly with height that its approximate velocity at any level, up to 300 to 400 meters elevation, may be computed by an empirical equation. Several such equations have been proposed, but the best, perhaps, that covers the whole range, is Chapman's[3]

$$v = a \log h + b,$$

in which v is the velocity at the height h above the ground, a and b constants—not universal, but only for a given time and place, and also numerically dependent, of course, on the units employed. Individual winds often are erratic and not computable.

To use this equation one must have the simultaneous velocities of the wind at two appreciably different heights, from which to find the current values of the variable constants a and b.

A similar equation

$$v = a \log (h + c) + b$$

had previously been found by Hellmann.[4]

However, for heights from 16 to 300 or 400 meters above the surface, especially over open country, the wind velocity can be quickly and even more closely computed by Hellmann's[5] other equation

$$\frac{v}{v_0} = \left(\frac{h}{h_0}\right)^{\frac{1}{5}},$$

in which h is the height in meters above the surface for which the velocity

[1] *Proc. Roy. Soc.*, **146**; 701, 1934.
[2] *Met. Zeit.*, **50**; 386, 1933.
[3] *Professional Note* No. 6, *M. O.*, 232*ff*, 1919.
[4] *Sitzb. K. Preuss. Akad. Wiss.*, p. 191, 1917.
[5] *Loc. cit.*, p. 194.

v in meters per second is to be computed, and h_0 the known height (not less than 16 meters) at which the velocity v_0 is measured. Brodtke[1] finds that $v = 1.2 + 1.79h^{0.246}$ meters per second; h in meters.

Horizontal Pressure Gradient and Elevation.—Because of the actual distribution of insolation over the earth the temperature of the lower atmosphere, as shown by observation, is warmest, on the average, in equatorial regions and coldest beyond the polar circles, with intermediate values over middle latitudes. Hence, since the temperature of the air above the earth depends mainly upon convection and radiation from below, it follows that the latitude distribution of temperature in the upper air must be substantially the same as that at the surface; that is, warmest within the tropics and coldest in the polar regions, with intermediate values between. And this, indeed, according to kite and balloon records, does apply at each level up to 10 to 12 kilometers, or to fully three-fourths of the air mass. At much higher levels, 15 to 20 kilometers, the rare atmosphere is coldest over equatorial regions and warmest over high latitudes, as previously explained in the discussion of the stratosphere. This inverse condition, however, does not everywhere apply to the winter and summer atmospheres of the same place. On the contrary, in many regions the atmosphere is warmer, on the average, at all explored levels during summer than during winter, and warmer, so far as known, over regions whose temperatures are relatively high than over others of the same latitude that are comparatively cold.

As a crude first approximation to conditions as they actually exist, assume (1) that the temperature distribution is the same along all meridians, (2) that the temperature change from one latitude to another is the same for all levels, and (3) that sea-level pressure is the same at all latitudes. Assumption (1) approximates the conditions over much the greater portion of the southern hemisphere, but, on account of the irregular distribution of land and sea, has to be modified for any detailed study of the winds of the northern hemisphere. Assumption (2) conforms roughly to average conditions between the thermal equator and latitude 50° to 60°, except near the surface and at altitudes above 10 to 12 kilometers. This is well shown by Fig. 47 referring to the northern hemisphere during its summer, and copied from Süring's paper[2] on the present state of knowledge concerning the general circulation of the atmosphere. Assumption (3), as applied to normal pressure, is also approximately true except for restricted areas, whose secondary and local effects will not here be discussed.

Consider an atmosphere of the same composition throughout, and having initially the same temperature at any given elevation, resting on a horizontal plane. Let the temperature be uniformly increased from

[1] *Met. Zeit.*, **35**; 313, 1918.
[2] *Z. Gesell. Erdkunde*, p. 600, 1913.

north to south, say, and by the same amount from top to bottom, thus simulating the temperature distribution that actually obtains in the earth's atmosphere over middle latitudes, as above explained. From the hypsometric and gas equations,

$$p = p_0 e^{-\frac{gh}{RT_m}}, \text{ and } pV = RT,$$

it appears that at the height h, the horizontal pressure gradient, obviously directed from the warmer toward the colder region, is given by the equation

$$\frac{dp}{dn} = \frac{T \delta T}{T_m{}^2} hg\rho_h, \qquad (3)$$

in which δT is the change in temperature per centimeter distance along

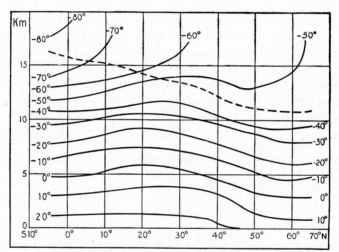

Fig. 47.—Relation of temperature to altitude and latitude. (*After Süring.*)

the meridian, T the absolute temperature, and ρ_h the density, each at the height h, and T_m the mean absolute temperature of the column.

By assumption δT is constant, while $T/T_m{}^2$ is nearly constant up to at least 12 kilometers—slowly decreasing to the base of the stratosphere and then slowly increasing—and, as shown by Fig. 21, the product $h\rho_h$ also roughly constant between 5 and 12 kilometers—increasing up to 8 or 9 kilometers and then decreasing. Therefore, under the given assumptions, not greatly different from average conditions, the horizontal pressure gradient in the case of straightaway, or planetary, winds is approximately constant throughout the upper half of the troposphere, and even slightly into the stratosphere.

This conclusion is fully supported by observations, as shown by Fig. 48, referring to the northern hemisphere during its summer, and also copied from Süring's paper.[1]

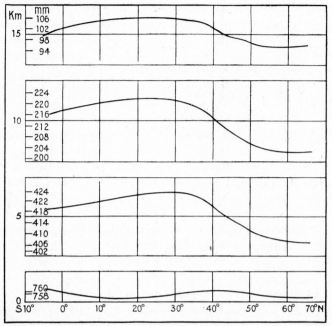

Fıg. 48.—Relation of pressure to altitude and latitude. (*After Süring.*)

Constancy of Mass Flow: Egnell's Law.—If the upper winds are so nearly straight, as they frequently are, that the cyclostrophic effect is negligible, one may write

$$\frac{T\delta T}{T_m{}^2}hg\rho_h = 2\rho_h\omega v \sin \varphi$$

as the relation between the horizontal pressure gradient and the wind velocity at the height h and latitude φ. But, as just explained, the first half of this equation is roughly constant between the levels of 5 and 12 kilometers; hence so also is the product $\rho_h v$, or mass flow per second, say, per unit area cross-section between these levels, at any given latitude. That is, above any fixed place the velocity of straight or nearly straight winds in the upper half of the troposphere increases with height at roughly the same rate that the density of the air decreases. This relation between the density and velocity of the atmosphere at different levels is known as Egnell's law,[2] determined empirically by himself, as previously by H. H. Clayton,[3] from cloud observations.

[1] *Loc. cit.*

[2] *C. R.*, **136**; 360, 1903.

[3] *Am. Meteorol. J.*, **10**; 177, 1893.

Relation of Wind Velocity to Altitude above 5 Kilometers.—As just explained, $h\rho_h$ is roughly constant between the levels of 5 and 12 kilometers, and, in the case of straight winds, so also is $\rho_h v$ above any given place. Hence, between these levels and over a fixed locality, the velocity at any point in a planetary wind is roughly proportional to the height of that point above the surface. In nearly all cases, except in regions of great altitude, it will be sufficient here to use heights as measured from sea level, and not from the actual surface.

Above the troposphere over the regions between the thermal equator and latitude 50° to 60° the horizontal temperature gradient decreases, and presently even reverses with increase of height, as shown by Fig. 47, and therefore the corresponding pressure gradient also decreases, as shown by Fig. 48. Hence, the mass flow, ρv, likewise decreases with elevation above this critical level. Further, the decrease of the horizontal pressure gradient, and consequently of ρv, with altitude in the stratosphere appears usually to be more rapid than that of the density alone, from which it follows that the wind velocity generally must have its maximum value at or below the base of the stratosphere.

Level of Maximum Horizontal Pressure Gradient.—The level of maximum horizontal pressure gradient (level of maximum value of ρv, not of v) obviously may be found by equating to zero the derivative with respect to h of the right-hand portion of (3), and solving for h. To simplify the equations, let the lapse rate l be uniform, let zero subscripts indicate surface conditions, and substitute for ρ_h its value in terms of height and surface temperature and density. The expression thus obtained, to be differentiated with respect to h, equated to zero, and solved for h, is

$$\frac{(T_0 - lh)\delta T}{\left(T_0 - \dfrac{lh}{2}\right)^2} h g \rho_0 \frac{T_0}{T_0 - lh} e^{\frac{-gh}{R\left(T_0 - \frac{lh}{2}\right)}}.$$

This gives

$$h = \frac{2T_0}{Rl^2}(\sqrt{R^2l^2 + g^2} - g).$$

Corresponding, then, to the uniform lapse rates 6° and 7° C. per kilometer, and surface temperature 280° Abs., the levels of maximum gradient are 8.134 and 8.113 kilometers, respectively; and similarly for other values of l and T_0.

Season of Greatest Winds.—From the above discussion it is obvious that the general wind will be swiftest whenever the temperature contrast between the air of higher and lower latitudes is greatest. But the temperature of the atmosphere in low latitudes does not change through the year nearly so much as does that of higher latitudes. Hence, the maximum horizontal temperature gradient, and therefore normally the greatest pressure gradient and strongest winds, must occur during winter.

Latitude of Greatest Winds.—The place of strongest winds clearly is that at which the horizontal pressure gradient divided by the sine of the latitude is greatest. In the northern hemisphere, according to Fig. 48, this occurs in the summer at about latitude 45°. It is obvious, however, since the pressure gradient depends in general upon the latitude rate of temperature change, that the belt of maximum winds must shift more or less from season to season—poleward with the coming of summer, equatorward with the onset of winter.

Hours of Greatest and Least Winds.—On land, but not appreciably at sea, the velocity of the surface wind has a well-defined daily period. Over level regions this velocity is least, on the average, about sun-up and greatest from 1 to 2 p.m. The change is larger on clear days than on cloudy, and also most pronounced in summer, when it reaches an average altitude of about 100 meters, and least in winter, when it rises to only about 40 meters.

The physical explanation of this diurnal variation was given long ago by Epsy. During the night, when there is no thermal convection, surface friction, in the case of light to moderate winds, holds the lower air comparatively quiet, while the upper glides over the lower with but little restraint. During the day, however, and especially during clear, summer days, thermal convection and the accompanying turbulence so mix the surface layers of the air with those next above as to bring both to a more or less common velocity, which is greater than the undisturbed or night surface velocity, and less than that of the undisturbed upper layers before their mixture with the lower. Since, however, these changes of velocity depend only on the intermingling, no matter how effected, of upper (faster) and surface (slower) currents, it is evident that when the wind is strong enough to produce abundant mechanical turbulence the added thermal convection cannot, and it does not, produce much contrast between the day and night velocity—the intermingling being already well nigh perfect.

Daily changes of wind velocity also occur on mountain tops, where the maximum is at night and the minimum by day, or just the reverse of the velocity changes that occur near the surface over plains. Three factors, possibly more, combine to produce this result: (*a*) Contraction of the lower air by night, thus bringing air of slightly higher levels, possibly 15 meters (50 feet) or so, and therefore of somewhat greater velocity down to the mountain top. (*b*) The presence by day and absence by night of surface disturbances, due to convection, in the air flowing over the mountain. (*c*) Overflow from the region of maximum expansion to the region of maximum compression. Since the greatest expansion of the lower air usually occurs at 3 to 4 p.m. and its greatest compression at 5 to 6 a.m., it follows that the overflow will be from west to east, or with the prevailing winds, through the night, and from east to west, or against them, during most of the day; that is, from sun-up to 3 or 4 p.m.

Diurnal Shift of the Wind.—The average direction of the wind changes slightly during the day, both over plains and on mountain tops, the tendency being for it always to follow the sun, or, rather, the most heated section of the earth. That is, the wind tends to be east during the forenoon, south (in the northern hemisphere) during the early afternoon, and west during the late afternoon and early evening. This does not mean that at each instant the wind really blows directly from the then warmest region, but that the actual changes through the day in the average hourly wind directions can be accounted for by a velocity component away from that region. The whole sequence results from the thermal expansion of the atmosphere (progressive from east to west), which causes an increase of pressure and consequently an outward flow at all levels above the surface. The area covered is so vast that the time involved, only a few hours, is insufficient for the completion of the convection circuit, so that even the surface winds are *away* from the most heated regions, as stated, and not toward them, as in sea and land breezes, for instance. The compensating or return current occurs at night, when the component, outside the tropics at least, is from the higher latitudes. In reality the entire phenomenon is only a diurnal surge, a flux and reflux, of the atmosphere due to diurnal heating and cooling.

Normal State of the Atmosphere.—From the above explanations of the causes of general winds, especially those that pertain to cloud levels, it appears that the normal state of the atmosphere is one of considerable velocity with reference to the surface of the earth. In middle latitudes, at least, this velocity is from west to east more or less along parallels of latitude and so great as nearly to balance the latitudinal pressure gradient due to the zonal distribution of insolation. Calms, therefore, in this region must be regarded as disturbances of the atmosphere, and indeed often are comparatively shallow, with normal winds above.

Equatorial East to West Winds.—East to west winds are quite as general and constant in equatorial regions as are west to east winds in middle latitudes. Along its borders, roughly 30° N. and 30° S., this equatorial belt of east to west winds is very shallow. Toward the equator its thickness increases, as a rule, until it reaches at least the limit of vertical convection. There are, however, great irregularities in these winds, just as in those of higher latitudes on either side of it. But the general conditions are as stated and require explanation.

The only obvious cause of east to west and west to east general or planetary winds is interzonal circulation, to which, indeed, they usually are regarded as being entirely due. Heating in equatorial and cooling in polar regions necessarily produce a more or less vigorous interchange of air, but, as already explained, one that is profoundly modified by earth rotation.

Assume, as initial conditions, uniformity of surface temperature and absence of local convection, and let the earth and the atmosphere be everywhere rotating at the same rate, so that there shall be no winds of any kind. Let the temperature of the surface and the atmosphere now be decreased in proportion to the distance from the equator. There will be a poleward overflow and an equatorward underflow, but the air that starts toward either polar region will quickly assume an eastward component, while the under- or countercurrent will have a westward component. In the absence of friction or other disturbing factor, the upper air moving under a pressure gradient from lower toward higher latitudes would approach along an asymptotic spiral a certain limiting parallel, where the deflecting force due to its final velocity would equal the pressure gradient across that circle. At the same time the east to west undercurrent would give a deflective force counter to the equatorward gradient. Hence, perhaps, equilibrium would soon be reached with west to east upper winds balancing the poleward pressures and east to west lower winds balancing the equatorward pressures, and thus further interzonal circulation prevented.

But surface friction, viscosity, local convection, and other disturbing factors so restrict the approach to equilibrium velocities that interzonal circulation is continuous, though of varying intensity, both local and general. Hence the eastward-moving upper air must gradually reach the surface and reach it as an eastward wind. In its subsequent course to lower latitudes it will become a westward wind, as already explained. In general, then, the areas of planetary atmospheric descent are the regions of west to east winds, while the similar areas of ascent are regions of east to west winds. Doubtless, too, these phenomena are accentuated at the surface—that is, the eastward and the westward surface winds are stronger than they otherwise would be—by the intermingling of the air of different levels through innumerable local convections.

What latitude establishes the boundary between the east and west winds? This important question has no answer, unless height is considered. At the surface the boundary is several degrees nearer the equator during winter than in summer, but its average latitude is, roughly, 30° to 32°. Near its border the east to west winds are very shallow, but in general they increase in depth as the equator is approached until they extend to the limit of vertical convection.

If the temperature distribution were the same along all meridians, and gradually varied from highest at the equator to lowest at the poles, it would seem that the area of ascending air would be substantially the same as the area of descending air (really a trifle larger, because of the higher temperature and consequent greater volume of the ascending air), and therefore that the surface borders between east and west winds would be approximately 30° on either side of the equator. But temperature is not distributed in this ideal way. There are restricted areas which are exceptionally warm, at least during a portion of the year, and others that are exceptionally cold; hence one would expect the area of ascent to be only roughly equal to the area of descent, and therefore the boundaries in question to be, as they are, only approximately at latitudes 30° N. and 30° S.

The velocity of the west to east winds of middle and higher latitudes and the velocities of east to west winds of equatorial regions obviously depend ultimately upon the rate of interzonal circulation. If this circulation were zero, surface friction, facilitated by local vertical convections, soon would greatly diminish and finally eliminate any cross-meridian velocity that originally might obtain. On the other hand, an extremely vigorous interzonal circulation would lead to violent east to west winds, partly because velocity is not altered by mere deflection and partly because there would then be less time for the latitude (conservation of area) effects on the velocity to be minimized by convectional turbulence—the total number of such disturbances becoming larger and their cumulative effects therefore greater with increase of time. Hence the moderate east winds of equatorial regions and west winds of higher latitudes that actually exist are due to the fact that the interzonal circulation itself is moderate, and this in turn to the further fact that the interzonal pressure gradient, which these winds balance, is not very great.

It appears, then, (a) that the temperature gradient, directed in general from the equatorial toward the polar regions, establishes an upper pressure gradient in the same direction and a lower in the opposite direction; (b) that in the absence of friction or other disturbance these pressures would produce east to west and west to east gradient winds with but little or no interzonal circulation; (c) that as the winds actually are more or less checked by surface friction, turbulence, convection, etc., they fail to attain full gradient velocities, and therefore cross the isobars at a small angle, except near the surface, where this angle is much larger, and thus maintain a correspondingly vigorous interzonal circulation even in the absence of cyclones and anticyclones; (d) that the actual west to east winds of the middle and higher latitudes and the east to west winds of equatorial regions are due chiefly to their approach to gradient directions, and, finally, (e) that the strength of any steady wind is proportional, approximately, to the gradient pressure, and its direction substantially normal thereto.

Probable Interzonal Circulation of the Stratosphere.—The primary circulation just explained involves all the atmosphere from the surface of the earth up to at least the highest cloud levels, but there is reason to believe that it does not extend to the greatest altitudes. Indeed, it appears probable that far above the uppermost clouds there may be another primary or fundamental circulation in reverse direction to that of the lower. This inference is based on the fact that the stratosphere is so much warmer in high than in low latitudes that seemingly there must be an overflow of air from the former to the latter and a corresponding return; that is, a primary circulation in the stratosphere in which the upper branch is from the polar (in this case warmer) toward the equatorial (in this case colder) regions and the under from the equatorial toward the polar regions, with, of course, longitudinal components in each due to the earth's rotation. In a sense the upper circulation, if it exists as inferred, is the mirror image of the lower, though more regular. Such circulation obviously implies a level of equal pressure, which indeed appears to exist at the height of about 20 kilometers. This inference as to the existence of a counter circulation at great altitudes is further supported by observations of noctilucent clouds[1] and of the drift of meteor trails.[2]

CLASSIFICATION OF WINDS

All the above is entirely general and of universal application. Gravity and temperature differences enter directly or indirectly into all atmospheric circulations, both the fundamental and continuous circulation that exists between the warm equatorial and cold polar regions, and those secondary circulations that occur only locally and occasionally. Nevertheless, clearness in any detailed discussion of all winds requires, first, an exact statement of what a wind is, and then a grouping of the various kinds according to some basis of classification suitable to the purpose in view. Accordingly, we shall agree that, as here used, the term "wind" means "air in motion relative to the surface of the earth." This does not restrict the term, as some definitions do, to air movements perceptible to the senses, nor to those near, and parallel to, the surface of the earth, nor to the naturally caused, but is all inclusive in every particular.

If, now, one were discussing the dynamics of the atmosphere he would, of course, do so in terms of equations between the three forces on a given quantity of air, gravity, hydrostatic pressure and friction, and the resulting tangential and normal accelerations thereof; and might well, as Jeffreys[3] has done, classify the winds according to the dominant acceleration term, or chief reaction to the driving force. This gives three distinct classes: (1) vortex, or cyclostrophic, winds, such as tropical cyclones, tornadoes and waterspouts, in which the velocity is high, the path a relatively small approximate circle, and the acceleration mainly radial; (2) long-path or geostrophic winds, as anticyclones, extratropical

[1] STÖRMER, *Univ. Obs. Oslo,* 1933.

[2] OLIVIER, *Proc. Amer. Phil. Soc.,* **72**; 215, 1933.

[3] *Quart. J. Roy. Met. Soc.,* **48**; 29, 1922.

cyclones, monsoons, etc., which change direction but slowly, owing to acceleration, relative to fixed coordinates in space, essentially equal and opposite to the acceleration of the surface of the earth under an isolated object moving frictionlessly over it at that place, as explained later; (3) short-path surface winds—sea breeze, mountain winds, glacier winds, and many others—in which the driving force does but little more than overcome frictional resistance, and move the air approximately in the direction of the pressure gradient.

But it is helpful also to assort the winds according to the way by which the driving force is established and maintained. This scheme does not, nor does any other, unmistakably allocate every wind to a definite class, but it does give the following convenient groups which will be considered separately:

a. Winds due chiefly to local heating—whirlwinds, cumulus convection, valley breezes, sea breezes.

b. Winds due to local cooling—land breezes, mountain breezes, glacier winds, bora, mistral, Norwegian fallwinds, continental fallwinds.

c. Winds due to simultaneous adjacent local heating and local cooling —thunderstorm winds.

d. Winds due to widespread heating and cooling—monsoons, trades, antitrades, tropical cyclonic winds, extratropical cyclonic winds, anticyclonic winds.

e. Forced winds, or winds caused by other winds—eddies, foehns (Chinooks), tornadoes.

CHAPTER IX

ATMOSPHERIC CIRCULATION (*Continued*)

WINDS OF LOCAL ORIGIN

WINDS DUE TO LOCAL HEATING

Whirlwinds.—During clear, calm summer afternoons, particularly during a dry spell when vegetation is parched and the ground strongly heated, dust whirls often develop, and occasionally travel considerable distances before losing their identity. The flatter the region, the more barren, the hotter the surface, and the quieter the air, the more violent these whirls become. Hence, level deserts are especially frequented by such winds, amounting at times to violent storms, though never more than a few meters in diameter. The development of these storms in which convection is strong is not simple, but an understanding of them will help materially to an understanding of convection due to heating in less obvious cases.

It is well known that those regions in which violent dust or sand whirls occur are also the places where inferior mirages are most frequent. The reason for this coincidence is the fact that the density gradient of the atmosphere essential to the production of a mirage simulating a lake, namely, an increase of density with elevation, is most favorable to strong vertical convection. Under these conditions the air is in that same unstable equilibrium that applies to a column of liquid whose under layer is lighter than the upper—whose under layer is oil, say, and upper layer water.

At first sight it might seem that no such condition of considerable extent can occur in nature; that as soon as the under layer became specifically lighter than the one next above, they would change places. Whenever a cork, for instance, is let go under water it bobs up. Similarly, a balloon rises, without exception, whenever the combined weight of gas, envelop, etc., is less than that of the atmosphere displaced. Why then should not surface air, whenever it becomes specifically lighter than the air above it, also rise immediately? This undoubtedly is just what a limited volume of light air would do if actually surrounded on all sides by heavier air. But surface air is not completely surrounded by other air; its condition is somewhat analogous to that of a cork whose flat surface is pressed against the bottom of a vessel of water. The cork in this case does not rise, simply because it is pressed down by water above

151

and not pushed up by water beneath. Similarly, warm air covering an extensive flat surface is pressed down by the superincumbent atmosphere and not pushed up by denser air below—there is no denser air below to push it up.

Obviously, though, even surface air under the given conditions is in an unstable condition. Hence it is important to determine that vertical temperature gradient which reduces superjacent layers of air to the same density.

Auto-convection Gradient.—Suppose the atmosphere is perfectly quiet, what temperature gradient must any layer of it have in order that it may just initiate its own convection?

Clearly this gradient must be such that density shall just increase with elevation. That is, the ratio $d\rho/dh$ must be just positive. Since

$$\rho = \frac{p}{RT} \text{ and } dp = -\rho g dh,$$

therefore, as T decreases with increase of h,

$$\frac{d\rho}{dh} = -\frac{p}{RT^2}\left(\frac{dT}{dh} + \frac{g}{R}\right).$$

Hence,

$$\frac{d\rho}{dh} = 0,$$

when

$$-\frac{dT}{dh} = \frac{g}{R} = \frac{981}{2.871 \times 10^6},$$

that is, when the lapse rate is 1° C. per 29.27 meters.

That is, in order that an under layer shall have the same density as the next above it the temperature must decrease at the rate of 1° C. per 29.27 meters increase of altitude, or 3.51 times faster than the adiabatic rate of 1° C. per 102.81 meters. In order that the lower layer shall be distinctly lighter than the upper, the temperature decrease with increase of altitude must be four or five times the adiabatic rate. Indeed, a much greater lapse rate than the autoconvective often occurs close to the surface,[1] as shown by the road mirage.

Obviously, an extensive layer of warm, light air cannot all rise at the same time. It must rise locally and in streams, if at all. Similarly, the upper air must settle locally, if at all. And this is just the way the convective interchange usually does take place near a heated surface, as is evident from the marked shimmering—apparent trembling or rapid waving of objects—seen closely over a stretch of desert, open field, house

[1] Malukar, S. L., and Ramdas, L. A., *Indian Jour. Phys.*, **6**; 495, 1932.

roof, etc., on clear, calm, summer days, a phenomenon due to irregular refraction incident to irregular density. The rapidity of this trembling, and the fact that it applies to the smallest details seen, evidence the great number and small size of the unequally heated rising and falling masses of air. It also is well known that marked shimmering does not extend far, usually only a few meters, above the surface. Evidently, therefore, the rising columns do not long retain their identity, but through turbulence and diffusion soon mix with the surrounding air and thereby eliminate the marked irregularities of temperature and density. In this way heat is carried up from the surface when the lapse rate is superadiabatic, and down when it is subadiabatic, with, in each case, as in every other type of atmospheric stirring, a closer approach to the isentropic or adiabatic gradient.

It might seem that the rising portions would ascend with great velocity and that the reservoir of warm air would be quickly exhausted. But the ascent is surprisingly slow. The acceleration a is given by the equation

$$a = g\frac{T' - T}{T},$$

in which T' is the absolute temperature of the rising air and T that of the surrounding cooler air. If, for instance, $T' = 302°$ Abs., and $T = 300°$ Abs., $a = 6.54$ centimeters per second per second; and even this small value rapidly decreases, through mixing of the warmer and cooler air. Hence it is evident that the velocity of ascent of the small, fitful leaks of warm air over a broad uniform plane cannot be at all great. It must be remembered, however, that this driblet sort of circulation is very different from that which can, and does, occur over a small island, for instance, where the rising mass is too united and large to be rapidly mingled with the surrounding air. Not only is this leakage of hot air over a plain generally slower than one might expect, but even such rate of loss as there may be is continuously balanced, or nearly so, by freshly warmed air so long as the surface is heated by insolation.

It occasionally happens, however, that because of some disturbance an unusually large volume of warm air breaks through and rises in a columnar form. Such a column necessarily produces a chimney-like draft, since the air composing it is warmer and therefore lighter than the adjacent air on the outside. Hence, however established, such a column of warm air will maintain its integrity, or, rather, perpetuate itself, so long as the air that is forced into it from the base is warm and light. Pictet,[1] for instance, reports observing a dust whirl near Cairo, Egypt, that began on a small sand mound, remained stationary for nearly 2

[1] HILDEBRANDSSON and TEISSERENC DE BORT, "Les Bases de la Météorologie dynamique," **2**; 286–288.

hours, then, in response to a gentle breeze, wandered away, but maintained its sharply defined outlines and great altitudes until lost in the distance, more than 3 hours later, or about 5½ hours after its inception.

In this connection it apparently cannot be too strongly emphasized that the ascending air is not "drawn" up any more than air is "drawn" up a chimney. In each case the weight of the column of warm air is less than the weight of an adjacent equal column of cooler air, and the static unbalance is compensated kinetically; that is, air is forced up the column in question, as up a chimney, because of, and in proportion to, the difference between its density and that of the cooler descending air outside. Even a *vena contracta*, or constricted section, is formed in the column a short distance—1 to 5 meters often—above the surface, as, and for the same reason that, such a constriction occurs in a jet of any fluid shortly after its issuance from an ordinary orifice.

The incoming air is almost certain to be directed to one side of the center of the rising column, and, as the angular momentum thus established tends to remain constant, a correspondingly vigorous whirl is developed as the place of ascent is approached that gathers up such loose materials as dust, straws, leaves, etc. Furthermore, this rotation remains the same, whether clockwise or the reverse, though the details of how it does so are, perhaps, not fully understood.

The diameters of these whirls (seldom more than a few meters near the ground) are too small for the direction of their gyration to be greatly influenced by the rotation of the earth. Hence nearly as many turn in one sense as in the other. They have even been reported to reverse, but it is probable that the apparent changes were only optical illusions similar to that which causes the cup anemometer to seem to reverse its rotation.

The height to which the whirling column rises (that is, the distance between the base of the column and its mushroom capital), the violence of the whirl, and, in some measure, even its duration, all depend upon the amount of surface heating and the extent to which the lower temperature gradient has been made greater than the adiabatic. When this heating is slight, only those small and gentle dust whirls with which all are familiar can be generated and sustained. When, however, the heating is pronounced, as it often is over level, desert regions, the whirl may assume almost tornadic violence. But, however violent, this sort of storm is never a tornado; it originates near the surface and is sustained by the supply of warm air from below, while the true tornado is generated and developed by conditions that occur at the cloud level.

When dust whirls pass on to regions where the surface air is not so strongly heated—over bodies of water, for instance, or green vegetation— they no longer are fed with air relatively so light and, as a rule, quickly come to rest. Naturally, too, their frequency varies with topography, ground covering, latitude, season, and time of day. Thus they are most frequent of afternoons and least of early mornings, most likely to occur during summer and fall and least during winter and spring; most generally found in tropical and semitropical countries and least in regions of high latitude; more numerous over barren surfaces than over water and succulent vegetation; and, finally, more favored by level regions than by irregular and broken ground.

Whirlies.—On the slopes of Adélie Land, the home of the blizzard, sharply delimited violent "whirlies," as Sir Douglas Mawson calls them, a few yards to 100 yards or more in diameter, are very frequent near the time of equinox. They approach the tornado in violence, and, since they occur in otherwise calm air and spin almost like a solid—just a few feet between hurricane wind and dead calm—they must originate between passing currents overhead and from there burrow down, as vortices do, until plugged up by the surface beneath.

Cumulus Convection.—An interesting and important case of rapid vertical convection resulting from the local application of heat and consequent establishment of strong horizontal temperature contrasts is that displayed by the turbulence of the cumulus cloud. That strong vertical and irregular movements of the air often occur in large cumulus clouds is known from the rapid boiling and rolling motions of their upper portions, from the descriptions of aeronauts who have been caught up in the heart of a thunderstorm, and from the formation of hail within them. This latter phenomenon implies very definitely, for the smallest stones, an uprush of at least 8 to 10 meters per second (20 miles per hour). This, in turn, on the theory of the chimney-like action of a warm central column of air, would demand the equivalent of a column 1500 meters high and 1° C. warmer throughout than the surrounding atmosphere at the same level. Large stones imply a much greater velocity.

The chief cause of the horizontal temperature contrasts necessary to this rapid uprush obviously is the difference between the current temperature gradient of the surrounding atmosphere and the adiabatic gradient of the saturated air within the cloud itself, full details of which will be given in the chapter on the thunderstorm.

The common level, therefore, of a considerable number of detached but neighboring cumuli is one of rather vigorous convection—up within the clouds and down between them—however free from turmoil the atmosphere may be at other altitudes.

Valley Breeze.—During warm, clear days, when there is but little or no general wind, a gentle breeze, known as the valley breeze, often blows up the sides of mountains. The strength of this breeze varies greatly, owing to the size of the mountain, the material of its covering, and the conditions of its surroundings. The cause of some of these variations can be understood by reference to Fig. 49.

Case 1.—Mountain Slope Connecting Wide Plateaus of Different Level. Let *AD* be the upper plateau, *BC* the lower, and *AB* the slope connecting them. Further, let the insolation be vertical, or the sun directly overhead. If, now, the slope *AB* is barren, or nearly so, it will become strongly heated and the adjacent air correspondingly expanded. As this lighter air is buoyed up by the adjacent denser atmosphere there results a draft in toward the side of the mountain. But this draft is all along the mountain slope from top to bottom, and thus in a measure the warm air is held in against the mountain side. Hence, the updraft along the side of the mountain is analogous to that in a chimney.

In addition to this obvious chimney effect of the mountain, there is, in the case under consideration, another source of upward winds that causes them to blow up along even shaded and cool ravines; unless snow-filled and very cold, in which circumstance local density is the

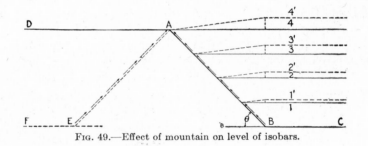

Fig. 49.—Effect of mountain on level of isobars.

controlling factor and air drainage, or a downward flow of the air, usually prevails, as will be more fully explained later. The early morning isobaric levels, 1, 2, 3, etc., are raised by heating during the day to higher levels, 1′, 2′, 3′, etc. From any point directly above the foot of the mountain the amount of this expansion obviously drops off, as indicated in the figure, as the side of the mountain is approached. Hence a pressure gradient is established toward the mountain side and plateau beyond. If both plateaus are broad, a perceptible breeze of several hours' duration up the mountain slope and onto the higher plateau may be induced in this manner. Such winds grow stronger as the top of the mountain is approached. At night, after sufficient cooling has taken place, the winds reverse.

To form some idea of the possible magnitude of these effects, let the difference in level between *AD* and *BC* be 1.6 kilometers (1 mile), and let the air between these levels be warmed on the average 5.5° C. (10° F.); then the increase of barometric pressure at *A* will be about 2.5 mm. (0.1 inch), with proportionate increases along the side of the mountain—quantities quite sufficient to produce a decided breeze.

Similar overflow winds occur also on the slopes of the isolated mountain, *BAE*, whenever the air on the opposite sides is unequally heated.

Thus the landward side of a coast mountain, for instance, on a still, warm day should have a breeze blowing up it and out to sea.

Case 2.—Isolated Mountain in the Midst of a Uniformly Heated Plain.— Here, too, the sides of the mountain are heated and corresponding upward currents induced. There also is expansion of the air over the adjacent plains and a tendency to establish pressure gradients towards the mountain, as in the case just discussed. But, however great this expansion, the gradients thus produced never cause, in the present case, more than a negligible wind. To make this statement obvious: Let the ridge *A* of the mountain be 1.6 kilometers (1 mile) above the plains *EF* and *BC*; let the width of the base *EB* be 3.2 kilometers (2 miles), and let the air be heated the same over one plain as over the other. Let the temperature increase of the air during the day be 5.5° C. (10° F.), or, suppose, 1 part in 50 of the absolute temperature. Under these conditions the compensating flow of air from the two sides must amount jointly to 1 part in 50 of the volume of the mountain; that is, the horizontal flow of the air from either side of the given mountain must average, from top to bottom, 1 part in 50 of 0.8 kilometer (0.5 mile). If, further, this is extended over a period of 10 hours, as it might be, the average velocity would amount to only about 1.5 meters (5 feet) per hour—certainly an imperceptible breeze.

Clearly, then, the breezes that ascend mountain sides on still, clear days have two causes: (*a*) a chimney or draft effect due to surface heating —always present—and (*b*) a pressure gradient effect due to expansion of the air over an adjacent plain or valley—present only when this expansion is unequal on the opposite sides of the mountain, or when the base levels are decidedly unequal on the opposite sides.

Sea Breeze.—Whenever a strongly heated region adjoins one whose surface is less heated, a local circulation from the one to the other obtains, unless prevented by winds of a larger system. Thus along the seashore, beside a lake and even at the edge of a favorably situated forest, a breeze (sea breeze, lake breeze, and forest breeze, respectively) of greater or less strength sets in during dry summer forenoons, after the land surface has become sufficiently warmed to establish decided convection.

Since the sea breeze obviously ceases at that level where the barometric pressure is the same above the land that it is above the water, and since the change of pressure with change of altitude is a function of temperature, it follows that its depth, never great, may easily be computed by replacing certain general terms of a suitable equation by observed temperature and pressure data. To develop such an equation:

Let ρ be the density of the air, then

$$-dp = \rho g dh,$$

in which $-dp$ is the small decrease in pressure corresponding to the small increase dh in height, and g the gravitational acceleration.

From the general equation

$$pV = RT = \frac{p}{\rho},$$

in which p is the pressure, V the specific volume, R the gas constant, and T the absolute temperature, it follows that

$$\rho = \frac{p}{RT}.$$

Therefore,

$$-\frac{dp}{p} = \frac{gdh}{RT}.$$

Hence, integrating from p_0, corresponding to $h = 0$, to p, corresponding to $h = h$, if T is independent of h, which, as a first approximation, its average value may be assumed to be,

$$\log_e \frac{p}{p_0} = -\frac{gh}{RT}.$$

The value of the first half of this equation obviously remains the same when the corresponding, but more convenient, barometric readings b and B are substituted for p and p_0, respectively.   Hence, also,

$$\log_e \frac{b}{B} = -\frac{gh}{RT}.$$

But the top of the sea breeze clearly is where there is no horizontal difference of pressure, or where $db = 0$, when h is constant.   Hence, on differentiating this equation, keeping h constant, it is seen that

$$db = dB\left(\frac{b}{B}\right) + \frac{bgh}{RT^2}dT,$$

and that the depth of the breeze h is given by the equation

$$h = -\frac{dB}{dT}\frac{RT^2}{gB}.$$

Consider a typical case: Let the sea-level reading of the barometer on land, less that at sea, or $dB = 0.5$ mm.; let the temperature over the land exceed that over the sea by $dT = 5°$ C.; let $T = 300°$ Abs.; let B, the sea-level barometer reading at sea, be 760 mm. R for dry air $= 2.871 \times 10^6$.   Then the depth or thickness, h, of the sea breeze is given by the equation

$$h = \frac{0.5}{5}\frac{2.871 \times 10^{10} \times 9}{981 \times 760} = 34{,}657 \text{ cm.} = 347 \text{ meters, approximately.}$$

The sea breeze, usually, as just explained, not more than 500 meters deep, starts on the water, seldom attains a greater velocity than 4.5

meters per second (10 miles per hour: the greater the temperature contrast the stronger the breeze), and extends inland, growing feebler and warmer, to a distance of only 16 to 40 kilometers (10 to 25 miles).

In a very important sense the circulation involved in this and all other local air convections is incomplete, since in such cases the path along which a given particle of the atmosphere flows is open and not closed. That is, the air that goes up over the heated land, in the case of the sea breeze, for instance, does not itself return by way of the water; it simply spreads out at the top of its ascent where its new temperature (above assumption of constancy of temperature not strictly correct), acquired by adiabatic expansion, is the same as that of the adjacent atmosphere, while the return branch, or down-flowing portion of the circulation, is broad and gentle. Hence the surface air always flows from the cooler toward the warmer mass. By day the sea or lake breeze is on shore, because the soil gets warmer than the evaporating water, and the similar forest breeze, always feeble, away from the woods.

Winds Due to Cooling

Land Breeze.—By night, when the direction of the horizontal temperature gradient is the reverse of that during the day (that is, when the water surface is relatively warm and the soil cool, because of its rapid radiation), the direction of the surface wind is also reversed or offshore. This is the well-known land breeze.

Besides being reversed in direction and occurring at night instead of by day, the land breeze further differs from the sea breeze, usually, in being very much the weaker of the two, even though aided by the gravity flow of the cooler surface stratum of air. This is because (a) the temperature contrast between land and water is less by night than by day, and (b) the surface friction over land, which retards the land breeze, is greater than the water friction that affects the sea breeze. Hence, while the latter, as above stated, reaches 16 to 40 kilometers (10 to 25 miles) inland, the former seldom extends more than 8 to 10 kilometers (5 to 6 miles) to sea.

The depth of the land breeze, usually less than that of the sea breeze, obviously may be computed in precisely the same manner as the latter.

Mountain Breeze, or Gravity Wind.—During clear nights when there is but little or no general wind, there usually is a flow of the surface air, commonly most pronounced in ravines, down the sides and along the basin of every valley. At most places this movement is gentle to very slow, but in those exceptional cases where the valley is long and rather steep, especially if covered with snow and free from forest, and still better if fed by a gently sloping plateau, the down-flowing air current may attain the velocity of a gale and become a veritable aerial torrent. This drainage flow is known indifferently as the mountain breeze, or mountain wind; also canyon wind, katabatic wind, and gravity wind.

For simplicity let there be no general wind; let the cross-valley profile be the arc of a circle, and let the covering of the walls be everywhere the same. But even thus simplified the problem of air drainage still requires the consideration of temperature changes of the free air, of the surface air, and of the surface itself.

Free Air.—Largely, perhaps almost wholly, because of the dust and vapor always present, the lower atmosphere emits and absorbs radiation

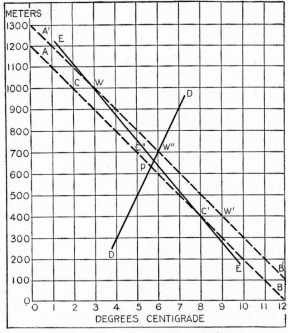

FIG. 50.—Assumed temperature gradients.

abundantly through much the greater portion of the spectrum. But during clear nights the loss, in the lower air at least, is usually, if not always, greater than the gain. However, even on such nights when radiation losses are greatest, the lower air, neglecting surface influences, cools too slowly and, on any given level, too nearly uniformly to produce more than very scattered and very feeble convection currents.

Suppose, though, that a limited mass of free air is cooled to a temperature below that of the adjacent atmosphere at the same level, as must happen at night within a small isolated cloud. What will be the result?

This problem, interesting within itself and essential to the present discussion, can easily be solved graphically. To this end let AB and $A'B'$ (Fig. 50) be two adiabatic gradients of the free air, indicating a temperature decrease of 1° C. for each 100 meters increase in elevation (the customary approximate value), and let *EE* be any actual temperature gradient different from the adiabatic—in this case, for simplicity, assumed to be 1° C. per 120 meters change of elevation. If, under the given conditions, a limited mass of air at an elevation of 1000 meters, say, be cooled 1° C., or its position in Fig. 50 be shifted from *W* to *C*, it will immediately become denser than the neighboring air of the same level, and therefore sink. As it sinks, if there is no interchange of heat by conduction, it will warm up adiabatically and finally come to equilibrium where the adiabatic gradient *AB* intersects the actual gradient *EE*, or at *C'*, where the falling air will have reached, through compression, the same temperature as the then adjacent atmosphere. That is, under the above gradient, a limited mass of air at any sufficient elevation cooled 1° C. will drop 600 meters, and in so doing increase its temperature by 6° C., or become 5° C. warmer than it originally was before the initial cooling. Similarly, if the original limited mass of air, with elevation and temperature indicated by *C'*, say, be warmed 1° C., it will be forced to assume a new equilibrium level and temperature indicated by *W*. When the vertical temperature gradient is "reversed"—temperature increasing with elevation as indicated by *DD* of the figure—the final gain in temperature is less than the initial loss. If, for example, the initial cooling is from *W''* to *C''*, *P* will be the point of equilibrium and the final temperature will be less than the initial. In short, when air whose temperature decreases with elevation is warmed, it proceeds at once to get colder than it was at first, as is evidenced by every cumulus cloud; and when cooled it quickly gets warmer than it originally was, as evidenced by the disappearance of small isolated clouds after sundown. If this gradient is reversed, that is, if the temperature increases with elevation, there still will be dynamical heating and cooling as before, but to an extent less than the initial cooling and heating, respectively. An initial temperature change different from the one just assumed, 1° C., would, of course, produce, under the same temperature gradient, correspondingly different alterations in level and final warming or cooling, provided always that the process is wholly adiabatic and that it takes place well above the surface of the earth. As a matter of fact, there necessarily is some interchange of heat between the moving limited mass of air and the surrounding stationary atmosphere. In so far, however, as the falling mass of air *gains* heat by conduction or radiation, its equilibrium is reached at a correspondingly *higher* level and *colder* temperature. Similarly, so far as the rising mass of air loses heat by conduction or radiation, its equilibrium is reached at a correspondingly *lower* level and *warmer* temperature.

It must be clearly understood that all the above reasoning applies only to free air. When the surface air of a level region or valley basin of negligible slope loses heat it gets *colder* and not warmer, simply because it cannot acquire dynamical heating by falling to a lower level—it is already at the bottom. It must also be noted that the paradoxical results under discussion, "cooling by warming," as Shaw[1] has called it, and its counterpart, warming by cooling, apply to isolated masses of air. When the whole of each layer of air of the same level undergoes the same temperature change, and when this change is but slightly different from that of the next higher or lower level, as obviously is the case over flat regions on still, clear nights, there can be but little local convection, and, therefore, but little dynamical heating. There still will be night cooling, however, of the free air through at least the lower kilometer or more, but it will be distributed approximately uniformly and nowhere localized in that manner which, as just explained, is essential to marked convection.

Valley Surface.—Since all portions of the valley surface are equally exposed, or nearly so, to the sky, and since the covering is uniform, it follows that on clear nights each portion must lose heat by radiation at a rate that varies closely only with its temperature. At the same time the surface also acquires heat partly by absorption and partly by conduction. But during still, clear nights the net loss of heat by the valley surface, whatever its nature, is more rapid than is the net loss of heat by the slowly radiating free air. Indeed, it may even be assumed, as a rough approximation, that the atmosphere neither emits nor absorbs radiation; that only the surface covering is effective in these respects, and hence that all temperature changes of the valley air are results of heat conduction to or from the valley surface and of dynamical heating or cooling.

Surface Air.—Any change in the temperature of the surface is communicated in greater or less measure by conduction, radiation, diffusion, and convection to all the neighboring atmosphere. But as chilled air tends to fall vertically, appreciable cooling, in this case, extends through only a relatively thin surface layer, as often is obvious to one on crossing a ravine.

Consider then a thin layer of air close to the surface of one of the valley walls, and follow its movements and temperature changes on a still, clear night. As the surface cools, which it does everywhere, the temperature of the adjacent air is also reduced and its density thereby correspondingly increased. Hence as soon as this cooling has proceeded to a lower temperature than that of the free atmosphere at the same elevation, the surface air on the valley walls begins to flow to lower levels, overrunning, of course, any pockets of colder air that may be in its path. The turbulence resulting from this flow continuously, and at all places along its course, causes more or less of the initially chilled air to be separated from the surface, there abandoned, temporarily or permanently, and underrun by other air. Clearly, too, the amount of turbulence and

[1] "Forecasting the Weather," 2nd Ed., p. 213.

consequent depth of the affected layer, or amount of interchange between free air and surface air, vary owing to velocity of flow, slope of surface, nature of covering, etc.

If the mass of a unit volume of this cooled air is w grams more than that of an equal volume of free air at the same level its contribution f to the total force producing, or tending to produce, drainage, or flow down the sides of the valley, is given by the equation

$$f = gw \sin \theta,$$

in which g is the local acceleration of gravity and θ the angle of slope at the particular place along the valley wall where the small quantity of air under consideration happens to be. Sin θ varies, of course, from a minimum at the bottom of the valley, where it is 0 if the valley happens to be level, to a maximum where the sides are steepest. The value of the other variable w depends on the difference between the temperature of the cooled air in question and that of the free atmosphere at the same level. A steady state, always more or less closely approached, obviously would give

$$gw \sin \theta = KV^n$$

in which K is the coefficient of whatever opposition (friction, etc.) is encountered per unit volume due to the drainage velocity V down the slope, and n a numerical exponent.

Since w is proportional to δT, or difference in temperature between the surface air and free air at the same level, it follows that if δT, and therefore w, remains constant, that is, if the rate of temperature loss by the descending air through conduction to the surface is equal to the rate of its temperature gain over the free air of identical levels, owing to compression during descent, then

$$\frac{1}{mS_p}\frac{de}{dt} = \left(A - \frac{dT}{dh}\right)V \sin \theta$$

where de/dt is the rate of loss of heat by the mass m of air to the surface at any given place, S_p the specific heat of air at constant pressure, A the adiabatic gradient, dT/dh the actual vertical temperature gradient in the free air at the given level, and V the velocity in meters per second of the flow down the slope at the same level.

Clearly, then, V must increase with increase of de/dt. Also V must vary with dT/dh, but always be positive (downhill) so long as dT/dh is less than A, which it nearly always is except near the surface under strong insolation. If the temperature gradient of the free air should be super-adiabatic (dT/dh greater than A), V would become negative, or the surface air would need to flow uphill to maintain δT constant. Actually, however, the air would flow down and not up the cooling surface. That is, if the free air were in this unstable condition, δT, as applied to any given mass of surface air, instead of tending to remain constant, would rapidly increase.

The more rapid the loss of heat by the surface the more rapid also the loss of heat by the adjacent air, and the swifter its flow, if the slope is sufficient; but, on the other hand, the swifter the flow the more rapid the dynamical gain of heat, and also the greater the retarding effect of surface friction. Hence an automatic adjustment between free-air gradient, velocity of flow, and rate of loss of heat to the radiating surface is always in operation. Furthermore, as this automatic adjustment prevents the air next the surface from becoming greatly colder than the free air at the same level, and as the latter cools only slowly, it follows that the temperature along the valley walls cannot decrease at all rapidly except below the inversion level (the nearer the bottom the more pronounced), as presently explained.

Initially, when the temperature of the free air everywhere over the valley decreases with elevation, the speed of the surface air down at least the steepest portions of the cooling walls is quite certain to be sufficient to make its dynamical gain of heat exceed its conduction loss and therefore to cause its temperature to increase with descent. As the bottom of the valley is approached, however, the rate of vertical descent and the consequent dynamical heating become less and less, and finally cease altogether, except in so far as there is drainage along the valley. At and near the bottom, then, where the dynamical heating is absent, or small, the temperature of the surface and the adjacent air necessarily decreases more or less rapidly. In a short while, therefore, the valley basin begins to fill with a river of cold air. The first incoming air doubtless overflows the original bottom layer, but in so doing gets separated from the cooling surface, and in position itself to be underrun by such other air as has cooled to a lower temperature, and this in turn by still colder air, and so on. In this way a temperature inversion is established in the valley. Below the inversion level (level of maximum temperature) the surface flow, though still active, is so decreased in rate of descent that the contact cooling exceeds the dynamical heating. The surface air could not otherwise here underrun the free air since the temperature of the latter decreases, as explained, with decrease of altitude below the inversion level. Above the inversion level the temperature of the down-flowing air, since it cannot anywhere greatly differ from that of the free air at the same elevation, necessarily increases, in general, with descent.

A valley wall produces local cooling up in the atmosphere, guides the resulting drainage of cold air and more or less controls its velocity, while the temperature gradient of the free air (modified over the valley bottom by the inflow from the sides) limits and largely determines the ratio of velocity of flow to rate of loss of heat (not cooling) by the surface air.

In the case, therefore, of well-defined valleys it appears that there must be on either side a belt at substantially the same elevation as the then inversion level along which during still, clear nights the dynamical heating and the contact cooling of the descending surface air are exactly equal. Above this level, descending air grows continuously warmer; below it, continuously cooler. Later in the night the inversion level attains a practically stationary elevation, and then intersects the valley walls in what are known as the "thermal belts."

In this connection it may be interesting to note that there are many practices in recognition of the above facts of air drainage. Thus, for instance, the mountain camper tents above, and not below, his night fire, so as to avoid the smoke; the Swiss peasant builds his cottage on a knoll to keep above the valley flood of cold air; and the orchardist seeks the "thermal belt" to escape killing frosts.

Mountain Convections.—Vertical convections on the sides of mountains, due to temperature contrasts of different origin from those already mentioned, are also well known, and, though rarely, if ever, producing more than a gentle breeze, are worth mentioning. Thus, a considerable shower during the afternoon of a warm summer day, for instance, may leave the atmosphere, level for level, distinctly cooler than the side of a neighboring mountain. Consequently the air will then flow up the adjacent slopes and occasionally carry with it masses of detached fog, or "steam," that gradually merge into a long billow-like crest cloud. Similarly, as the cooler air on the clearing side of a cyclone invades a mountainous region, the relatively warm slopes often, when the general winds are light, induce rising currents. And as these currents also frequently are laden with patches of "steam" cloud the familiar mountain saying: "When the fog rises the rain is over," is well justified.

On the other hand, the air on the stormy side of a cyclone is nearly always warmer during winter, and also frequently warmer during the other seasons, than are the mountains; and therefore on these occasions, as it passes over them, downward currents are induced along their slopes, a circumstance that equally justifies this other common saying of the mountain dweller: "While the fog descends it will continue to rain."

Glacier Winds.—It is well known that a draft of cold air often is found blowing out from a cave-like opening in the lower end of a glacier, hence called glacier wind. Similar winds, blowing out during summer and in during winter, occasionally are found at the mouths of caves, called blowing caverns, on the sides of hills or mountains. In the volcanic mountains of Japan such places are numerous and extensively used for cold storage.[1] In each case the explanation of the phenomenon is the same and obvious. The cavity extends quite through the glacier, or earth, as the case may be, from its lower to its higher openings. Let this

[1] Suzuki, S. and T. Sone, *Tohoku Univ. Sci. Reports,* **3**; 101–111.

difference in elevation be 250 meters; let the average temperature of the air inside the cavity be 0° C., and of that outside at the same level 15° C. The density of the inner air will be to that of the outer approximately as 19 to 18, and the pressure head, producing an inverse chimney effect, about 14 meters. Neglecting friction—usually, however, an extremely important factor—this would give the exit air a computed velocity of about 16.6 meters per second (37.1 miles per hour), a very appreciable gale. The velocity or strength of this wind, other things being equal, varies as the square root of the difference in level between the lower and upper openings.

In the case of a glacier, drainage obviously obtains in substantially the same manner, whether the air passes in a concentrated stream through a cavity or along a crevice within the ice, or merely flows in a broad sheet over the top surface. Clearly, too, the same sort of aerial cascades (exaggerated mountain winds) must occur, especially during summer nights, over any banks of snow that may exist in the upper and steeper reaches of canyons and mountain valleys. Such winds necessarily are shallow and therefore, when swift, a treacherous source of danger to the landing aviator.

The Bora.—From the above explanation and examples of aerial drainage it is obvious that similar winds must often blow down steep slopes that separate high, snow-covered plateaus or mountain ranges from adjacent bodies of relatively warm water. Thus when an anticyclone covers such a region, during winter, the surface air becomes very cold and correspondingly dense until, unless otherwise dissipated, it overflows restraining ridges, or drains away through passes and gaps. Clearly, too, this flow must be most frequent, and strongest, during the early morning, since that is the coldest time of the day, and least frequent during mid-afternoons. In many instances during anticyclonic weather the air, as it leaves the snow fields, is so cold that, in spite of dynamical heating, it even reaches the sea at freezing temperatures and very dry. When, however, the drainage is amplified, if not even started, by the pressure gradients (to which the final velocity bears no special relation) due to a properly situated "low," it usually is associated with a counter-cyclonic current above and, therefore, accompanied by rain, sleet, or snow.

Probably the best known of all these violent fallwinds is the *bora* of the northeast Adriatic, especially at Trieste, Fiume, and Zengg. The boras of these places, however, are not from the north, as the name implies, but rather from the northeast and east-northeast.

Another excellent example of this kind of wind occurs at Novorossisk, a Russian port on the northeast coast of the Black Sea, where it blows down from a nearby pass in the mountains, occasionally with destructive violence. Probably, also, the brief but sudden and violent williwaws of steep, high-latitude coasts have a similar origin.

Mistral.—Another instance of convection due essentially to cooling is the well-known mistral, or dry, cold, northerly wind of the Rhône Valley. Here the more or less persistent winter flow, over the warm waters of the Gulf of Lyons to the south, and the frequent highs, over the snow-covered plateaus of southeastern France to the north, often coöperate in such manner as to produce extensive air drainage down the lower Rhône Valley. In general, the cause of the mistral, and its action, is the same as that of the bora. It is less violent, however—its path less steep, and, therefore, itself not so distinctly an aerial cataract. Similar winds occur, of course, under like circumstances in other parts of the world, but the mistral is the best known of its class.

Santa Ana.—The Santa Ana is a fierce wind down the Santa Ana canyon of Southern California and out 25 to 50 miles to sea. It originates in much the same way as do the bora and the mistral, but is less fitful than the former and more violent than the latter.

Norwegian Fallwinds.—An extensive fallwind, which, because of its importance and the fact that it is more or less unique, deserves especial mention, frequently occurs during winter along the coast of Norway. Sandström,[1] in one of his interesting atmospheric studies, describes it as follows:

In winter, as one steams along the northwest coast of Norway, there is frequent opportunity to observe a peculiar meteorological phenomenon. Fine weather prevails over a narrow strip along the coast, while a heavy bank of cloud is visible out to seaward. Of course, coastwise traffic is greatly favored by this fine-weather strip and takes full advantage of it. Throughout this zone of fine weather prevails a cuttingly cold wind so strong that one can scarce stand against it when on deck. The maximum velocity of this wind is attained near shore, where the water is whipped up into whirls and miniature waterspouts. Evidently the wind here plunges down upon the water from above, and with great force.

Upon leaving the steamer and travelling inland up the mountain slopes on skis, strong head winds oppose progress. This easterly wind is still very strong on the great divide of the Scandinavian Peninsula. But observations of the cloud caps on the highest peaks of the range show that a westerly wind is blowing at those great altitudes. It is clear that a lively interchange of air between the North Atlantic Ocean and the continent is taking place above the Scandinavian highlands. This exchange takes place along either side of a glide surface whose altitude above the ground at the divide may be estimated at about 1000 meters. In fact, at the kite station Vassijaur it proved almost impossible to raise the kites above that level, evidently because they there encountered a glide surface through which they cannot pass, since the wind has opposite directions on the two sides of this surface, and therefore calm must prevail at the glide surface itself. The altitude of this glide surface decreases to the Atlantic Ocean. The air below this surface flows toward the west, and above the surface it flows toward the east.

[1] *Mount Weather Bull.*, **5**; p. 129, 1912.

Continental Fallwinds.—From the above discussion of winds that result from surface cooling it is obvious that they are of very general occurrence, especially during cold weather and down the valleys and slopes of high, snow-covered regions.   Hence one would expect drainage winds to obtain to a greater or less extent, during winter, over the middle- and high-latitude regions of every continent.   Where the elevation and slope are slight, however, as they are, with but minor exceptions, over all North America east of the Rocky Mountains, over Russia, and over Siberia, except the eastern portion, this drainage necessarily must be comparatively sluggish.

On the other hand, there are two regions of continental extent— Greenland, with an area of about 827,000 square miles, and Antarctica, with an area of, roughly, 4,600,000 square miles—that are ideally located for, and perfectly adapted to, the production of strong and almost continuous fallwinds.

Greenland, as is well known, is continuously covered with an enormous ice cap that rises to a gently rounded plateau of, roughly, from 2000 to 3000 meters (7000 to 10,000 feet) elevation.   This plateau, whose crest runs approximately north and south, has been crossed several times —six in all—at as many different places, and, in each case, nearly constant down-slope or drainage winds, of greater or less strength, were experienced.

Throughout its great area, therefore, Greenland is a region of almost perpetual aerial cascades and cataracts.   The continuous refrigerative influence of its enormous ice cap, covering an area eighteen times that of the state of Pennsylvania and rising at places to an elevation of over 3 kilometers (2 miles), not only controls the direction and velocity of nearly all local winds, but obviously must affect, to some extent, the general circulation of the middle and higher latitudes of the whole northern hemisphere—an important circumstance that will be taken up later.

Antarctica, according to the reports of all its explorers, is quite as completely covered with ice as is Greenland, and it also rises, more or less dome-like, to fully as great altitudes.   Hence it would seem that its general effect on the movement of the air must be very similar to that of its great counterpart in the northern hemisphere—an inference now fully borne out by the many accounts and records of those who have skirted its coasts, crossed its plateaus, or wintered on its borders.   Sir Douglas Mawson, for instance, who spent many months during 1912–1913 at Adélie Land, latitude 67° S., on the edge of the continent, almost directly south of Tasmania, reports an average wind velocity for an entire year, from the interior toward the sea, of more than 22.4 meters per second (50 miles per hour).   "Day after day," he says, "the wind fluctuated between a gale and a hurricane."   Velocities of 100 miles, and over, per hour occurred, and gusts of even much greater velocity occasionally were recorded. These measurements were made at the main station on the declivitous border that connects the inner ice plateau with the ocean. Back some distance inland, where the slope is gentle, the winds were less severe. At sea, also, these continental drainage winds decreased in intensity with increase of distance from shore, and ceased altogether at a distance of about 300 kilometers (187 miles), where the westerlies became effective. Obviously, therefore, this particular station was located in one of the windiest places in the world—in an aerial cataract where the cold drainage air of the ice plateau rushes down a steep coastal slope to the sea.

Similar winds of varying intensity, and irregular duration, are reported all along the Antarctic border, from every inland station, and from end to end of every exploring trail. Clearly, then, the winds of Antarctica, though due essentially to cooling, nevertheless, because of the extensive area they cover, belong also to those great circulations that are strongly influenced by earth rotation, and therefore constitute an important part of the general circulation of the atmosphere, under which head they will again be considered.

Wind Due to Simultaneous Adjacent Local Heating and Local Cooling

Thunderstorm Winds.—Shortly, say twenty minutes or so, before the rain of a thunderstorm reaches a given locality the wind at that place, generally light, begins to die down to an approximate calm and to change its direction. At first it usually is from the south or southwest in the extratropical portion of the northern hemisphere; from the north or northwest in the corresponding portion of the southern, and in both more or less directly across the path of the storm itself. After the change, it blows for a few minutes rather gently, directly toward the nearest portion of the storm front, and finally, as the rain is almost at hand, abruptly, and in rather violent gusts, away from the storm and in the same direction, roughly, that it is traveling, a direction that usually differs appreciably from that of the original surface wind. Generally this violent gusty wind lasts only through the earlier portion of the disturbance, and then is gradually, but rather quickly, succeeded by a comparatively gentle wind, which, though following the storm at first, frequently, after an hour or so, blows in the same general direction as the original surface wind.

The chief cause of these and all other winds peculiar to the thunderstorm, except those within the cumulus cloud itself, is the juxtaposition of warm air, immediately in front of the rain, and a column, or sheet, of cold air, through which the rain is falling. How this temperature distribution is established, and what the results are, will be explained later in the chapter on the thunderstorm.

CHAPTER X

ATMOSPHERIC CIRCULATION (*Continued*)

WINDS DUE TO WIDESPREAD HEATING AND COOLING

Monsoons.—Summer monsoons and winter monsoons, for convenience discussed together, bear the same relation to summer and winter that sea breezes and land breezes bear to day and night. It is the temperature contrast between land and water that establishes the circulation that manifests itself on the surface as a sea or land breeze, in the one case, and as a seasonal or monsoon wind in the other. The direction of the surface wind in either case is always from the cooler toward the warmer of the adjacent regions; from the ocean toward the land, by day, as a sea breeze and, during the warmer season, as a summer monsoon; from the land toward the ocean, by night, as a land breeze and, during the colder season, as a winter monsoon. Hence, monsoons may be regarded as sea and land breezes of seasonal duration, and might very well be classed with the latter, under some common appropriate caption. Because of the immense areas involved, however, it cannot be said of them, as of sea and land breezes, that they are caused by mere local temperature differences. Besides, the duration of a land or sea breeze is so brief that it covers only a narrow strip along the coast, as already explained; while the monsoon winds extend far from the coast, both inland and to sea, and the directions of the former, since their paths are always short, are but little affected by the rotation of the earth, while the courses of the second are greatly modified by this important factor.

The prevailing directions of monsoon winds, except where distinctly modified by the general circulation, are given by the following table and by Figs. 51 and 52:

DIRECTION OF MONSOON WINDS

Hemisphere	Season	Land south	Land west	Land north	Land east
Northern	Summer	N. E.	S. E.	S. W.	N. W.
Northern	Winter	S. W.	N. W.	N. E.	S. E.
Southern	Summer	N. W.	N. E.	S. E.	S. W.
Southern	Winter	S. E.	S. W.	N. W.	N. E.

Since monsoons depend upon seasonal temperature contrasts between land and water, it is obvious that winds of this class must be most pro-

Fig. 51.—Prevailing directions of monsoon winds, northern hemisphere.

nounced where such contrasts are greatest—that is, in temperate regions —and least developed where the temperature contrasts are smallest—

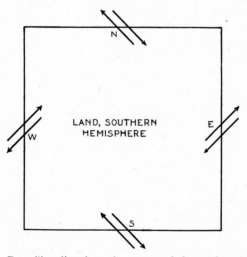

Fig. 52.—Prevailing directions of monsoon winds, southern hemisphere.

that is, in equatorial and polar regions. It is even possible for secondary monsoons to develop, or for a monsoon to occur within a monsoon. This merely requires a favorably situated inland sea, such as the Caspian.

In such cases monsoons, or seasonal winds, prevail between the inland sea and the surrounding land, and, in turn, between the continent as a whole and the adjacent oceans; just as, and for the same reason that, on a still greater scale, there is a constant circulation between the perpetually warm equatorial regions and those about the poles that are continually cold.

Another comparison between these several winds, the semi-daily (land and sea breeze), semi-annual (monsoon), and perpetual (interzonal), that is interesting and instructive concerns their depth. As already stated, the land and sea breezes seldom reach greater depths than 100 to 500 meters; the winter monsoon of India has a depth, roughly, of 2000 meters, and the summer monsoon 5000 meters; while the general or interzonal circulation involves the whole of the troposphere with a depth of 10 to 12 kilometers, and probably also, though perhaps to a less vigorous degree, even the stratosphere.

If the term *monsoon* be extended, as it properly may, to include all winds whose prevailing directions and velocities undergo distinct alterations as a result of seasonal changes in temperature, it clearly follows that this class of winds is well nigh universal. Nevertheless, it is generally thought of in connection with only those places where it is most strongly developed, and especially where the seasonal winds are more or less oppositely directed. Among these places are: India (Indian monsoons, owing largely to conditions over central Asia, are the most pronounced of all, but by no means the simplest,[1] and have been most fully studied), China, the Caspian Sea, Australia, and portions of Africa.

In the United States the chief monsoon effects are in the eastern portion, where the prevailing winds are northwest in winter and southwest in summer, and in Texas, where the prevailing winds are also northwest in winter, but southeast in summer.

Trade Winds.—As previously stated, in equatorial ocean regions, or, roughly, over the oceans between latitudes 30° N. and 30° S., the winds usually have an east to west component. In the northern hemisphere they blow rather constantly from the northeast, becoming east-northeast and finally nearly east winds as the equator is approached. Similarly, in the southern hemisphere, starting from the southeast, they gradually back through east-southeast to nearly east. In each case they blow "trade;" that is, in a fixed or nearly fixed direction. It is because of this steadiness of direction and not because of any relation they may have to the paths of commerce that they are called trade winds. Along each border of this belt, or along both the northern and southern horse latitudes, calms are frequent, while such winds as do occur generally are light and variable in direction. Besides, the barometric pressure is high, humidity low, and sky clear. Hence it generally is inferred that

[1] SIMPSON, *Quart. J. Roy. Met. Soc.*, **47**; 151, 1921.

throughout the horse latitudes the air is descending. This evidence, however, as applied to places other than the centers of maximum pressure is not quite conclusive—it only shows that the air is not ascending.

Another narrow belt of calms or light variable winds, known as the region of the doldrums, approximately follows the equator (more exactly the thermal equator), where the two systems of trade winds, the northern and the southern, come together. Here, however, the barometric pressure is low, humidity high, and skies often filled with cumulus and other clouds that give conclusive proof of strong ascending currents.

Trade winds in the sense here used—that is, nearly constant winds blowing in a westerly direction—do not occur on land except along coasts and over islands. Besides being well-nigh peculiar to the oceans, they are even different from ocean to ocean, and also, since they tend to follow the thermal equator, somewhat different in latitude and intensity from season to season.

According to Shaw[1] the average velocities of the Atlantic trade winds are as follows:

TRADE-WIND VELOCITIES, ATLANTIC OCEAN

	Jan.	Feb.	Mar.	April	May	June	July	Aug.	Sept.	Oct.	Nov.	Dec.	Year	
N. E. trade....	10	11	11	12	11	10	9	7	8	6	8	10	9.4	Miles per hour
S. E. trade....	14	13	13	12	11	12	12	15	17	15	16	15	13.8	Miles per hour

From this it appears that the trades are strongest during the winter when their counterpart, the system of westerly winds of higher latitudes, is strongest; and weakest during the summer when their counterpart is weakest. It also appears that the southeast trades, or those pertaining to the southern hemisphere, are about one-third stronger than the northeast trades, due probably to the greater extent of the southern oceans and consequent less surface friction—the same reason, doubtless, that the westerly winds of the southern hemisphere are stronger, on the average, than the westerlies of the northern hemisphere.

The trade winds of the Pacific Ocean are weaker than those of the Atlantic and not so constant in direction. On the Indian Ocean the trades are confined to the southern hemisphere. North of the equator the winds of this ocean, being controlled by the adjacent continent, are distinctly of the monsoon type.

The seasonal shifting in latitude of the trade regions and belt of doldrums is shown by the following table, copied from Hann's "Lehrbuch," 4th Ed., p. 469:

[1] M. O., **203**; 9, 1910.

SEASONAL LATITUDE LIMITS OF TRADE WINDS AND DOLDRUMS

	March		September	
	Atlantic	Pacific	Atlantic	Pacific
N. E. trade.......	26°–3° N.	25°–5° N.	25°–11° N.	30°–10° N.
Doldrums........	3° N.–Equator	5°–3° N.	11°– 3° N.	10°– 7° N.
S. E. trade.......	Equator–26° S.	3° N.–28° S.	3° N.–25° S.	7° N.–20° S.

Antitrade Winds.—As the heated and expanded air of equatorial regions overflows to higher latitudes it, necessarily, is deflected by the rotation of the earth. That portion which goes north changes from an east wind near the equator to a southeast, south, southwest, and, finally, at about latitude 35° N., a more nearly west wind. Similarly, that portion which goes south becomes northeast, north, northwest, and, finally, at about latitude 30° S. a more nearly west wind. These and the following statements apply to average conditions, but, frequently, not to the actual state, since the antitrades are subject to rapid and marked changes. It should be noted also that the antitrades, being counter currents over the trades, necessarily are restricted to the same regions, namely, the semitropical oceans.

At great altitudes, 10 to 15 kilometers, the east to west velocity near the equator is, roughly, 36 meters per second (80 miles per hour). Hence its west to east velocity around the axis of the earth is about 428 meters per second (957 miles per hour). As this air, assuming it to start from the equator and neglecting viscosity effects, moves to higher latitudes its west to east velocity must so increase, according to the law of the conservation of areas, that at about 16° N. or S. its angular velocity will be the same as that of the earth, and, itself, therefore, be moving only poleward in the plane of the meridian. The exact latitude, however, at which the antitrades move directly poleward depends upon the position of the thermal equator and therefore varies with the seasons. Thus during August and September, when the center of the doldrums is, roughly, 8° N., the inflection of the northern antitrades occurs somewhere between latitudes 20° N. and 25° N. At other seasons, because the doldrums are then nearer the equator, the place of inflection is also less removed. Beyond the turning point, wherever that may be, these upper or antitrade winds become westerly, and, except as modified by local disturbances, tend, as previously explained, to reach, under the influence of the poleward pressure, a limiting or gradient velocity, and to follow parallels of latitude. However, there are innumerable disturbances, mainly due to the distribution of land and water, that cause constant and abundant interzonal circulation, which feeds and indefinitely maintains the antitrade wind portion of the general or planetary atmospheric circulation.

The height of the antitrades (depth of the trades) is greatest, at any given place, during summer and least during winter. It also decreases with latitude, becoming zero, on the average, at about 30° N. and S. Thus during winter their height over Cuba, 22° N., is about 3.5 kilometers; over Hawaii, 19° 30′ N., about 3 kilometers; over Jamaica, 17° N., 6.5 kilometers; and over Trinidad, 12° N., 8 kilometers. But, whatever their height, it is always the same as the depth of the trades, of which they are but the overhead continuation. Indeed, the trade winds, as they approach the equator, ascend and gradually flow off poleward, thus producing in each hemisphere a great antitrade branch of the general circulation, which, in turn, becomes the westerlies of higher latitudes. These, in their turn, are confused by storms and other local disturbances, but after few or many vicissitudes, as circumstances may determine, ultimately return to a similar starting point, only to begin another of their endless cyclic journeys through trades, antitrades, westerlies, and the innumerable secondary winds such a course implies.

Tropical Cyclones.—A tropical cyclone—the cyclone of the Indian Seas, the hurricane of the West Indies, Revillagigedo Islands, and South Pacific, and the typhoon of the West Pacific and China Sea—consists of a vast whirl of rapidly moving air currents surrounding a calm and relatively small center or vortex.

Distinction between Tropical and Extratropical Cyclones.—Although tropical and extratropical cyclones have many similarities, such as low-pressure centers, abundant precipitation, same instantaneous wind directions, and the like, and although it may be impossible to say just when a tropical cyclone on its way to higher latitudes becomes extratropical in character, nevertheless they usually differ from each other in several important respects. Among these differences are: (*a*) The isobars of the tropical cyclone generally are more symmetrical and more nearly circular than those of the extratropical. (*b*) The temperature distribution around the vortex of the tropical cyclone is practically the same in every direction, while about the extratropical it is very different. (*c*) In tropical cyclones rains are torrential, especially near the center, and, in stationary, or nearly stationary, storms, more or less equally distributed on all sides of the center; in the extratropical, rains usually are much lighter and very unequal in different quadrants. (*d*) Tropical cyclones usually have calm, rainless centers 8 to 50 kilometers (5 to 31 miles) or more in diameter, while the extratropical rarely show this characteristic whirl phenomenon. (*e*) Tropical cyclones are most frequent during the summer and autumn of the hemisphere in which they occur, while the extratropical are strongest and most numerous during winter. (*f*) Tropical cyclones often move to higher latitudes, where, from roughly 30° on, they are no longer tropical but in characteristics, as well as position, distinctly extratropical; the extratropical, on the other hand, never invade the region of the tropical nor assume its distinctive characteristics. (*g*) The pressure drop of the tropical cyclone generally begins with the winds; in the extratropical it usually begins much sooner. (*h*) The tropical cyclone has no anticyclone companion; the extratropical usually has—to the west. (*i*) The tropical cyclone normally has no line of discontinuity, no cold front or windshift line; the extratropical cyclone usually has.

Place of Occurrence.—Tropical cyclones occur over the warmer portions of all oceans except, possibly, the south Atlantic. They are most numerous, however, in the west Atlantic (including the Gulf of Mexico), Bay or Sea of Bengal, and west Pacific (including the China Sea), where their annual frequencies are, for those of greater than minor intensity, roughly, about 4, 8, and 24, respectively. They seldom originate closer than 5° or 6° to the equator but most frequently between latitudes 10° and 20°, and always, or nearly always, as shallow disturbances in a region of unsettled weather and increasing convectional showers in a belt of doldrums, hence, at higher latitudes during summer than during winter when, indeed, they seldom occur at all.

Size and Shape of Storm.—The diameter of the tropical cyclone varies greatly. Near their origin some storms may be no more than 80 kilometers (50 miles) across, while others, when well developed, may have diameters of 300 to 1500 kilometers (187 to 932 miles). The clouded area incident to typhoons, always much more extensive than the surface storm, may be even 3000 kilometers (1864 miles) across.

The shape of the storm as given by any single isobar, except the very outer ones, commonly is nearly circular. The several isobars, however, are not concentric, but all crowded in the direction of that anticyclonic region which the storm, as a whole, then is skirting, hence, usually on the poleward to eastward side, in the direction of the neighboring "high-pressure belt."

Direction of Wind.—The direction of the surface wind is spirally in at an angle of 30°, roughly, to the isobars, counter-clockwise in the northern hemisphere, clockwise in the southern. At an elevation of only 700 to 800 meters the inflow is said to cease, and above this level the circulation is outward. These horizontal motions, aided by the drag of the centrifugated droplets, necessitate a correspondingly strong upward component around the vortex or inner portion of the storm, and a slower downward component over a much greater surrounding area.

Velocity of Wind.—The velocity of the wind in a tropical cyclone also varies greatly from one storm to another, and even more from one to another portion of the same storm. Near the center, or within the eye, of the storm, which may have any diameter from 8 to 50 kilometers

(5 to 31 miles) or more, the wind is very light and the sky clear or only partially covered with high clouds. Away from this center, especially on the right-hand side (going with the storm), the winds often reach destructive velocities of 40 to 50 and even 60 meters per second (90 to 112 or even 134 miles per hour), but decrease in violence rather rapidly with increase of distance from the center, dropping to only moderate winds of 50 to 60 kilometers (31 to 37 miles) per hour at a distance of, say, 300 kilometers (187 miles).

Direction of Travel.—Tropical cyclones of the northern hemisphere first move west, then usually northwest. Many turn north at latitude 20° to 25°, roughly, and finally move away to the northeast. In the southern hemisphere the corresponding directions of travel of the tropical cyclone are: west, southwest, south, and, finally, southeast.

Velocity of Travel.—The velocity of the tropical cyclone as a whole, or of its center, varies from almost zero near its place of origin, and also at and near its place of inflection when this happens to be abrupt, to perhaps 800 kilometers (497 miles) per day. Over the Bay of Bengal, Arabian Sea, and China Sea the velocity averages about 320 kilometers (199 miles) per day. Over the south Indian Ocean the velocity ranges from 80 to 320 kilometers (50 to 199 miles) per day. Over the west Atlantic the average velocity before and during recurvature is about 420 kilometers (260 miles) per day, but after recurvature—that is, when moving northeast over middle latitudes—about 640 kilometers (398 miles) per day.

Origin and Maintenance.—Since tropical cyclones originate in a belt or region of doldrums where convectional rains are frequent and heavy, and since they rarely occur closer than 5° or 6° to the equator, it follows that both vertical convection and earth rotation are essential to their genesis.

The atmosphere of a doldrum belt becomes very warm and humid, and therefore frequently is in a state of vertical convection. The upward branches of this convection are nearly always limited to very restricted areas, where they break through, as it were, and often give rise to local thunderstorms. Occasionally, however, heating and expansion must take place more or less uniformly over a comparatively extended region. So long as the upward current is gentle and restricted to a small area, the compensating inflow from the sides is also gentle and can produce only a cumulus cloud and perhaps a thunderstorm. In the event that such a storm is formed, the inflowing countercurrent to the ascending warm air is replaced by an equivalent column, or sheet, of descending cold air (air cooled by the partial evaporation of the falling rain) immediately to the rear. That is, the loss of warm surface air is compensated by a similarly concentrated and vigorous downflow of cold upper air. Hence, rotary circulation, since it depends upon horizontal inflow from all, or at least several, sides, is not possible in the case of ordinary thunderstorms, whatever their location.

On the other hand, an approximately equal expansion of the air over a relatively large area, whether caused by an increase of temperature, or vapor density, or by both, must lead to an overflow above and a corresponding surface inflow around the outer borders.

Obviously the rate of volume overflow at any time is proportional to the area in question, while the corresponding inflow is proportional to the boundary multiplied by the average normal component of the wind. If the area is circular with radius R, it follows that the rate of outflow above is proportional to πR^2, and the rate of inflow below to $2\pi R V_n$, in which V_n is the average radially inward component of the wind at the distance R from the center. But as the two currents compensate each other except as modified by precipitation, explained below, it follows that V_n, other things being equal, is proportional to R. Hence, when the area involved is rather large, 100 miles, say, in diameter, the relatively shallow and spirally moving compensating or return current may become very perceptible. This at once feeds the entire rising column with excessively humid air that renders it an even better absorber than before, of both insolation and terrestrial radiation, and increases its rate of expansion, thus initiating, perhaps, a widespread condensation. If so, the latent heat thus set free, while it does not actually raise the temperature of the air, reduces the rate of adiabatic cooling from approximately 1° C. to about 0.4° per 100 meters increase of elevation, and thereby establishes, within the rising column, temperatures distinctly higher than those of the surrounding air at the same level. In this way the circulation is accelerated, and, thereby, the rate of condensation and freeing of latent heat increased until—through growth of size, restricted supply of water vapor, and other causes—a limiting, somewhat steady, state is attained.

When the conditions here described occur at some distance from the equator, the rotation of the earth deflects the inflowing air and establishes a rotation around the region of lowest pressure—an effect all the more likely to occur (perhaps rarely else does occur) when the existing convection takes place along the doldrum boundary between the rather oppositely directed (not opposing) trade winds, the one from higher latitudes, the other from across the equator.[1] But whatever the radius of curvature, the angular momentum remains constant—the law of the conservation of areas obtains—except as modified by friction and viscosity, and therefore, since surface drag is effective at but small elevations, the atmos-

---

[1] The highly favorable influence of oppositely directed neighboring winds on the genesis of the tropical cyclone was first stressed by A. Thom, in his book, "An Inquiry into the Nature and Cause of Storms," London, 1845, but, of course, without the strong argument therefor that can now be made, based on the influences of earth rotation and the conservation of areas.

phere at only 100 to 200 meters above the water may, as it moves inward, soon reach that velocity at which its deflective force is equal to the horizontal pressure gradient. When such velocity is reached, as it obviously may be at any appreciable altitude, inflow at that place necessarily ceases. Near the water, however, this limiting velocity is prevented by surface friction and turbulence. Hence, as soon as the whirl is well established, it must be fed almost exclusively by the lowest and, therefore, most humid air. In this way a maximum amount of precipitation, and, through it, a maximum amount of thermal energy, is secured—a condition important to the maintenance of the tropical cyclone, as is evident from the fact that it tends to go to pieces over dry land, especially before it has recurved and become essentially extratropical.

Of course, similar atmospheric expansions may, and doubtless do, occur in the doldrums when they are on, or very close to, the equator, but in this case a whirl is impossible, and, therefore, a low so initiated will soon fill by gentle, somewhat radial, winds from all sides and at considerable altitudes, or, at most, mere local thunderstorms will develop.

From the above it is evident that the seat, so to speak, of the tropical cyclone is where the sustaining energy is supplied, that is, where condensation is taking place. Hence the movement of the air at this level, and not at the surface, determines the course of the storm.

It has been suggested that tropical cyclones may be eddies mechanically generated by the mutual drag between two passing streams of air, much as whirls are formed along the side of a ship. But there are several objections to this hypothesis, one, at least, of which is fatal, *viz.*, the fact that the maximum possible linear velocity of particles in such a whirl, because equal to only the relative velocity of the parent streams, could never closely approach that of hurricane winds.

Energy.—The energy of the hurricane varies exceedingly from storm to storm, but always is enormously great. Horiguti,[1] in his detailed study of the typhoon, finds that, in the Okinawa typhoon, latent heat was freed by condensation at a rate equivalent to about 12×10^{11} horsepower. This storm, approximately 700 kilometers in radius, remained nearly stationary for 10 days or more, and during that time the rate of its mechanical dissipation of energy was of the order of 27×10^9 horsepower.

[1] *Mem. Imp. Marine Obs. Kobe,* **3**; 162, 1928; **5**; 1, 1932.

CHAPTER XI

ATMOSPHERIC CIRCULATION (*Continued*)

WINDS DUE TO WIDESPREAD HEATING AND COOLING (*Continued*)

EXTRATROPICAL CYCLONES

General Remarks.—The strong winds and heavy precipitations of middle latitudes are associated with the occurrence of low barometric pressure, while gentle winds and clear skies as commonly are associated with the occurrence of high barometric pressure. Hence the cyclone, or that system of winds that accompanies and surrounds any considerable region of minimum pressure, and the anticyclone, or that system of winds that belongs to and encircles a region of maximum pressure, deserve and have received a vast amount of observation and study. Nevertheless, in many respects—in their origin, in their temperature distributions, and in the laws of their movements—cyclones and anticyclones still remain in great measure the meteorological mysteries they have always been. However, since the midlatitude interzonal circulation occurs largely through cyclones and anticyclones, it evidently must do so owing to certain causes, and these appear to be mainly the rotation of the earth and the frictional connection, including turbulence, between it and the atmosphere.[1]

Although the cyclones and anticyclones of extratropical regions are as closely associated and as fully the complements of each other as are hills and hollows, it nevertheless will be convenient to consider them independently. It will also be convenient first to summarize the facts of observations, and then to string these facts together on the thread of a provisional theory.

Size.—The area covered by an extratropical cyclone, the largest of all distinctive storms, nearly always amounts to millions of square kilometers. In North America the average diameter of these storms is estimated to be, roughly, 2500 kilometers (1553 miles), which probably is not greatly different from their average diameter on other continents. Over the North Atlantic their diameters are still larger, while the greatest of all in size is the semipermanent or winter Aleutian "low," which appears usually to be much larger than the traveling cyclones of the Atlantic or even the great semipermanent Icelandic "low."

Direction of Movement of the Cyclonic Center.—The direction the center of a cyclone travels, wherever it may be located, is substantially

[1] EXNER, *Sitzb. Wien*, **IIa**; Bd. 137, p. 189, 1928; JEFFREYS, *Quart. J. Roy. Met. Soc.* **52**; 85, 1926; **53**; 401, 1927.

the same as that of the higher clouds or of the atmosphere at 4 to 10 kilometers above sea level. In general, therefore, the cyclones of middle latitudes travel from west to east, with (in the northern hemisphere) a southerly dip over continents and a northerly deflection over oceans. Cyclones, for instance, that develop between latitudes 30° and 45°, in the western United States, usually turn northeast before reaching the Mississippi River. Farther west they may move east, or even somewhat southeast. Another and more useful generalization is that at any particular time the center of the cyclone travels parallel to the surface isobars in the warm sector of the disturbance.

Locus of Maximum Cyclonic Frequency, or Chief Paths of Cyclonic Storms.—Probably no part of the earth's surface more than 3° or 4° from the equator is wholly free from cyclonic storms, but the frequency of their occurrence varies greatly with respect to both time and place. Beginning with the West Pacific: During summer and fall many cyclonic storms come from the general region of the Philippines, or off the coast of China, and move northeast across, or on either side of, Japan. Winter and spring cyclones enter on this same general course at latitudes 30° to 40°; some, presumably, being of oceanic origin, while others, obviously, either develop within, or cross over, China. In any case, the general track of these storms is along the Japanese and Kurile Islands, and thence east over the Bering Sea. The main path is then southeast across the Gulf of Alaska, with the storms, including off-shoots from the Aleutian "low," crossing onto the continent anywhere between latitudes 40° and 60°, but apparently most frequently in the general neighborhood of Vancouver Island. These Pacific storms usually cross the continent nearly from west to east, dipping slightly south over the Great Lakes, and finally leave it by way of Newfoundland. A smaller number of storms from the North Pacific dip far south, somewhat like the Mediterranean branch mentioned below, to about latitudes 35° to 40°, but usually recurve west of the Mississippi and join the main course as they reach the Atlantic. Those that originate in or cross over the central and southern portions of the United States, as also those that come from the Gulf of Mexico, move northeast and gradually merge their paths with that of the Pacific storms anywhere from the Great Lakes to the Newfoundland Banks. Other cyclones coming up from the Florida and West Indies regions follow the coast, not far off shore, and also merge their paths with that of the others in the neighborhood of Newfoundland. Halfway or more across the Atlantic the path of maximum storm frequency breaks up into at least three distinct routes. The main route turns far north, usually by way of the Norwegian Sea, then southeast, entering Russia in the neighborhood of the White Sea, and passing on toward Central Asia. A second route turns southeast and crosses Europe generally along the northern side of the Mediterranean, and then turns north either across

Hungary toward northwest Russia or by way of the Black Sea toward Central Asia. A third, and least frequented, route, commonly running just south of Ireland, appears to cross both the North and the Baltic Sea, and then, like the others, to move on toward Siberia and central Asia. The cyclonic storms of central and northern Asia do not appear to be very numerous. Nevertheless, their track of maximum frequency seems to turn south, as does the similar track over North America, as far as Lake Baikal, thence probably to the Sea of Okhotsk and across, or to the south of, Kamchatka, to the main storm path north of the Aleutians, as already explained.

In the southern hemisphere the path of maximum storm frequency appears closely to follow the 60° parallel of latitude. Presumably it dips poleward at both the Ross and the Weddell Sea, as each of these is a region of semipermanent low pressure.

It must be remembered, in this connection, however, that in both the southern hemisphere and the northern, cyclonic storms occur almost everywhere, and, therefore, that the routes above described are only paths of maximum cyclonic frequency and not of exclusive travel. Furthermore, it is seldom that an individual storm endures long enough to follow any of these paths even half way around the earth.

Velocity of Travel.—The velocity with which the center of a cyclonic storm moves along its path varies greatly. It depends upon the season, being fastest in winter and slowest in summer; upon location, being faster in America than in Europe, for instance; and finally, upon the individual storm.

The following table gives average velocities of cyclonic centers for different parts of the northern hemisphere. Those pertaining to the United States were computed from a table of average 24-hour movements as determined by Bowie and Weightman[1] from 16,239 observations, covering the years 1892–1912, inclusive. The others are from Hann and Süring's "Lehrbuch der Meteorologie."[2]

AVERAGE VELOCITY OF CYCLONES IN METERS PER SECOND

(For the United States the velocity is also given in miles per hour)

	United States	Japan	Russia	North Atlantic	West Europe	Bering Sea
Winter..........	(34.9) 15.6	12.4	10.8	8.2	8.0	8.5
Spring..........	(27.5) 12.3	11.1	9.2	8.3	7.2	8.5
Summer.........	(24.4) 10.9	7.8	8.0	7.4	6.6	10.3
Fall.............	(27.5) 12.3	10.6	9.6	8.3	8.2	9.3
Year............	(28.6) 12.8	10.5	9.4	8.05	7.5	9.1

[1] *Monthly Weather Review, Supplement* 1, p. 8, 1914.
[2] 4th Ed. p. 529.

Frequency.—The frequency of the occurrence of cyclonic storms varies not only from place to place, as already explained, but also at any given place, or even over an extensive area—probably an entire hemisphere—according to season. Tropical cyclones, it will be recalled, are far more frequent during summer and early fall than during winter. Mid-latitude cyclones, on the other hand, have exactly the opposite relation of frequency to season, being, in general, most numerous in winter and least numerous in summer. Exceptions to this rule apply to the paths of tropical cyclones next after the recurvature, provided we regard such storms as having then become extratropical. Perhaps exceptions also apply to certain regions on the poleward sides of the main cyclonic routes, since these are farthest north in summer and farthest south in winter. This, however, is not certain. A statistical investigation might show that even the greatest increase due to latitude shift is more than compensated by the general seasonal decrease in frequency.

When all storms are counted that appear in the United States or Southern Canada, whether short or long lived, weak or intense, it appears[1] that the frequency of summer (June, July, and August) "lows" is to that of winter (December, January, and February) "lows" approximately as 5 to 8. On the other hand, if only long-lived cyclones are considered, it appears[2] that in the United States the frequencies of summer to winter storms are about as only 2 to 9, and those of Europe as 3 to 10.

In either case, then—that is, whether only the longer lived and more intense "lows" are counted, or whether all, of whatever magnitude and duration, are included—it seems that cyclonic storms are most frequent during winter and least frequent during summer. Further, the extratropical storms of winter are not only more numerous than those of summer, but also, in general, longer lived, more intense, and faster moving.

Direction of Winds.—From the directions of winds in and about a region of low barometric pressure, as given on synoptic charts, (Fig. 112) for instance, it is often, perhaps usually, inferred that cyclonic winds circulate spirally inward and upward and then outward and upward, counter-clockwise in the northern hemisphere, clockwise in the southern, around a storm axis. This indeed is, in general, the course of the winds in tropical cyclones, especially in those that are violent and of small diameter, as the eye of the storm and directions of cloud movements clearly indicate, but it does not apply to extratropical cyclones, except, perhaps, to the occasional ones of great violence and small diameter. Extratropical cyclones rarely have clear centers, as they would if the

[1] Bowie and Weightman, *Monthly Weather Review, Supplement* 1, p. 7, 1914.
[2] U. S. Weather Bureau *Bull.* A, p. 6, 1893.

circulation about them was closed or along spiral paths of repeated turns. Neither, in general, is a closed circulation indicated by the movements of the clouds. Again, it often happens that the velocity of the forward moving wind of a cyclone is less than that of the storm itself, so that instead of flowing around the storm center it necessarily is left behind.

Synoptic weather charts, therefore, show instantaneous wind directions, but not wind paths, which however can be found for surface winds.[1] This is because the storm condition itself is moving forward—moving, indeed, with a velocity nearly always comparable to, and, at times, even faster than, that of the lower winds themselves.

The main body of the storm winds, those below an elevation of 4 or 5 kilometers, except everywhere near the surface, and also generally about the poleward side above 2 to 3 kilometers elevation, blow, in the cyclonic sense, roughly parallel to the surface isobars. This does not mean that the path of any given particle of air is around and around the center of low pressure, because, as above explained, both this center itself and its system of isobars usually are in rapid transit. Near the surface the velocity is so slowed down that the deflection forces no longer balance the horizontal pressure, and therefore the winds of this level are directed inward at a considerable angle across the isobars. Through the poleward half of the storm area the horizontal temperature gradient is nearly always opposite in general direction to the horizontal pressure gradient at the surface. With increase of elevation in this section therefore, the pressure gradient usually weakens from the start and later reverses at the height of only a few kilometers—often less than 1 kilometer; while the winds first increase (where the surface drag rapidly decreases) to a maximum, then decrease, and later more or less reverse in direction.

Deflection Angle.—The angle between the surface wind direction at any place within a cyclonic storm and the normal to the corresponding

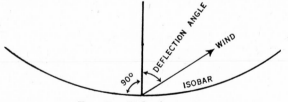

Fig. 53.—Deflection angle.

isobar, the "deflection" angle (Fig. 53), is greatest, or the surface winds most nearly parallel to the isobars, (*a*) when the winds are swiftest and thus develop the strongest deflective forces—therefore greatest to the south and east of the storm center and least to the north and west, (*b*) when the velocity of the storm as a whole is least, (*c*) in the summer time, because during this season the storm movement is less than during

[1] SHAW, "Forecasting Weather," 2nd Ed., Chap. IX.

other seasons, (d) over water where it is roughly 80°, because the surface drag is less here than over land where the "deflection" angle averages only 40° to 50°. It varies greatly, however, from quadrant to quadrant of a moving storm, both over land and over sea.

It is important to note also that usually the deflection angle does not greatly change with distance from the center. This follows from the fact that the horizontal pressure, the wind velocity, and the consequent surface friction and percentage loss of gradient velocity all are roughly constant in any given direction from the center, so long as only points distinctly within the storm area are considered.

With increase of elevation and consequent decrease of surface drag the deflection angle over land gets larger by 25° or 30°, or more, in the first kilometer. Beyond this elevation it still gains, but relatively very slowly. At an elevation of several kilometers the velocity of the air is decidedly greater than that of the storm, and therefore air that may have risen to this level is carried forward. Hence the main outflow of the extratropical cyclone is toward the east.

Wind Velocity.—As just stated, the pressure gradient and wind velocity are roughly constant along any given radius from the storm

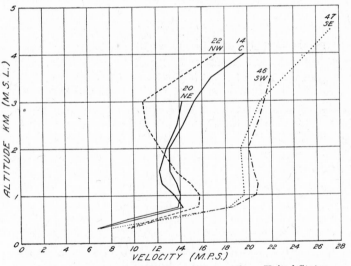

Fig. 54.—Cyclonic wind velocity, winter, northern United States.

centre. This is because at middle and higher latitudes the deflective force is essentially geostrophic (due to the rotation of the earth) and to only a small extent cyclostrophic (due to circular motion). The winds, however, often are different in different portions of the storm area, and commonly strongest in its southern and eastern quadrants, where the isobars are most crowded and the direction of the winds, roughly, that of the storm movement.

The actual average velocity of the wind in the different quadrants of a cyclone and at different elevations is given in the following table by

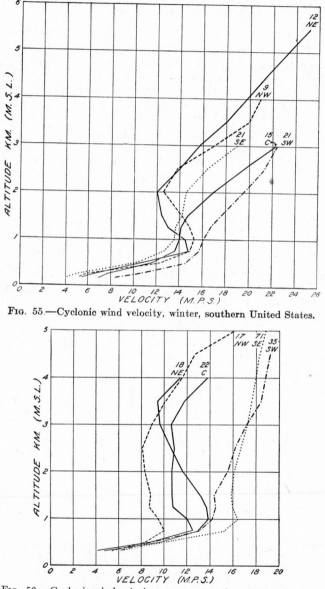

FIG. 55.—Cyclonic wind velocity, winter, southern United States.

FIG. 56.—Cyclonic wind velocity, summer, northern United States.

Peppler,[1] based on a large number of measurements made during 1903–1908, at Lindenburg; latitude 52° 10′ N.; longitude, 14° 15′ E. Approxi-

[1] *Beiträge Physik freien Atmosphäre*, **4**; 95, 1911.

CYCLONIC WIND VELOCITY IN METERS PER SECOND AND (MILES PER HOUR)

Altitude		Surface 122 m.	500 m.	1000 m.	1500 m.	2000 m.	2500 m.	3000 m.	3500 m.	4000 m.
South quadrant	Winter	6.16 (13.8)	14.75 (33.0)	15.09 (33.8)	15.32 (34.2)	15.79 (35.3)	16.85 (37.7)	18.28 (40.9)	19.25 (43.1)	20.30 (45.4)
	Summer	5.42 (12.1)	9.64 (21.6)	10.69 (23.9)	11.31 (25.3)	12.22 (27.3)	12.91 (28.9)	14.08 (31.5)	15.69 (35.1)	17.21 (38.5)
	Year	5.84 (13.1)	12.24 (27.4)	12.93 (29.0)	13.38 (30.0)	14.07 (31.4)	14.94 (33.4)	16.24 (36.3)	17.53 (39.2)	18.81 (42.1)
West quadrant	Winter	6.70 (15.0)	13.47 (30.1)	13.39 (30.0)	13.93 (31.2)	14.75 (33.0)	16.18 (36.2)	17.31 (38.7)	17.31 (38.7)	
	Summer	5.66 (12.7)	9.45 (21.2)	9.89 (22.1)	9.91 (22.1)	10.17 (22.7)	10.65 (23.8)	11.40 (25.5)	12.07 (27.0)	12.62 (28.2)
	Year	6.06 (13.5)	11.34 (25.4)	11.52 (25.7)	11.80 (26.4)	12.34 (27.6)	13.29 (29.8)	14.23 (31.9)	14.56 (32.6)	
North quadrant	Winter	4.72 (10.5)	8.85 (19.8)	8.95 (20.0)	9.00 (20.1)	9.09 (20.4)	9.07 (20.3)	9.32 (20.8)	8.52 (19.0)	8.02 (17.9)
	Summer	4.84 (10.8)	7.85 (17.6)	8.37 (18.7)	8.45 (18.9)	8.81 (19.7)	9.11 (20.4)	10.26 (22.9)	10.63 (23.8)	10.63 (23.8)
	Year	4.79 (10.7)	8.36 (18.7)	8.66 (19.4)	8.72 (19.5)	8.94 (20.0)	9.08 (20.3)	9.78 (21.9)	9.57 (21.4)	9.32 (20.8)
East quadrant	Winter	4.50 (10.1)	10.45 (23.4)	10.02 (22.4)	10.43 (23.4)	10.58 (23.7)	11.64 (26.0)	12.11 (27.1)	13.37 (29.9)	14.59 (32.7)
	Summer	4.11 (9.2)	8.22 (18.4)	8.64 (19.4)	8.77 (19.6)	8.98 (20.1)	9.50 (21.3)	9.50 (21.3)	9.81 (21.9)	11.86 (26.5)
	Year	4.34 (9.7)	9.37 (20.9)	9.37 (20.9)	9.64 (21.6)	9.82 (21.9)	10.61 (23.7)	10.84 (24.3)	11.62 (26.0)	13.25 (29.7)

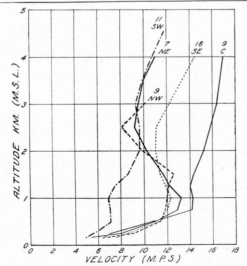

FIG. 57,—Cyclonic wind velocity, summer, southern United States.

mately the same average cyclonic wind velocities occur also in the United States, at least east of the Rocky Mountains, as shown by Figs. 54–57, kindly furnished by the Aerological Division of the U. S. Weather Bureau, in which the velocity is given in meters per second, and the height in kilometers above mean sea level. The letters indicate the section of the storm area and the figures the number of cases averaged. This subject has been discussed in greater detail by L. T. Samuels.[1]

Convection.—The vertical movements of the air, whether up or down, in an extratropical cyclone, or between such a cyclone and a neighboring anticyclone, are not known with much detail and accuracy. However, since the cyclone moves eastward with the air currents directed inward across the isobars, it is obvious that ordinarily the chief air convergence, due in part to increase of latitude, and hence the principal vertical convection, must be on the front or east side. Temperature also usually helps to locate the chief upflow in this quadrant, since its winds necessarily are from lower latitudes, and, therefore, relatively warm.

This localization of the uprising air explains why, other things being equal, most of the precipitation due to cyclonic storms occurs to the east and southeast (northeast in the southern hemisphere) of their centers.

Other things, however, are not always equal. Thus an extensive plain rising, gradually, to great elevations, may slope in such direction that the mechanical or forced convection over it on any side of a cyclonic center may approach, or even exceed, the thermal convection to the east. The Great Plains east of the Rocky Mountains illustrate this point. Here precipitation in the case of "stagnant" or slow-moving lows usually is most pronounced to the north of the center where the winds are persistently up the slope not alone of the surface, but of the cold air as well. Here, too, contrary to rule, the rear of the winter cyclone, being from the Pacific, and also heated, in places, by descent, is warmer than the front. The wind shift does not always imply clear and colder. Also on the Pacific coast of North America, for instance, where the ocean is to the immediate west, the heaviest rains are to the south and west of the cyclonic center.

Velocity of Travel and Amount of Precipitation.—It is well known that the velocity of travel of an extratropical cyclone and the amount of precipitation accompanying it are to each other, roughly, in inverse ratio. This is simply because the slower the storm travels, the longer the winds blow into it at any given place and, therefore, other things being equal, the greater the duration and the amount of the precipitation at that place. In extreme cases very fast moving cyclones may give but little or even no precipitation.

Classification.—Cyclones occur in extratropical regions with so great frequency that several such storms are nearly always present in each hemisphere. Naturally, they have been much studied and, therefore,

[1] *M. W. R.*, **54**; 195, 1926.

variously classified, especially according: to duration, as semipermanent and migratory; to season of occurrence, as summer and winter; to zone of origin, as tropical and extratropical; and to the place from which first reported, as, for instance (referring to only those within or near the United States), Alberta, North Pacific, South Pacific, Northern Rocky Mountain, Colorado, Texas, East Gulf, South Atlantic, and Central.

All these classifications are useful, but not adapted to the present purpose, which is to group the cyclones, as far as practicable, according to their more important causes. Perhaps this end will be fairly well served by dividing them into *thermal, insolational,* and *mechanical.*

Thermal. *Due to Relatively Warm Water.* — The name semipermanent cyclone—for which the alternate name, thermal cyclone, is here proposed, for reasons that will appear below—or semipermanent "low," has been given to that system of winds of any region over which the barometric pressure habitually, or seasonally, averages lower than for the surrounding regions. The term generally is used as though it applied to but one and the same cyclone, however it might wander or even for a time wholly disappear. Thus, one always says *the* Icelandic "low," not *an* Icelandic "low." Similarly, *the* Aleutian "low," not *an* Aleutian "low." But, as stated, this applies only to average conditions. In reality there is no one permanent Icelandic "low," for instance, that retains its identity wherever it may be, but only a series of lows which cross, originate over, or, on invading, become intensified over, practically the same restricted region.

There are several semipermanent cyclones in various parts of the world. The most nearly continuously active of these, at least in the northern hemisphere, and at all seasons apparently productive of many migrating cyclones, in the form, perhaps, of offshoots, or secondaries, lies southeast of Greenland and southwest of Iceland. Another such region, active during winters only and known as the Aleutian "low," lies along and to the south and southeast of the Aleutians, extending into and including the Gulf of Alaska. The Norwegian Sea and, possibly, the Sea of Okhotsk are other such high-latitude regions. The Gulf of Lyons is a low-pressure haunt during winter, as is also the Black Sea, and the Caspian Sea, as its monsoon winds definitely show. The Gulf of Mexico, over which occasional winter cyclones appear to generate, may likewise be added to the above list.

In the southern hemisphere the regions of most persistent lows are the Ross Sea and its counterpart, the Weddell Sea, on the other side of the Antarctic continent.

All the above regions have surfaces warmer than those that at least partially surround them. The circulation induced by such temperature distribution is converted into a system of cyclonic winds by the deflective force due to the earth's rotation. The warm waters off the coast of Greenland and Iceland, for instance, necessarily maintain the atmosphere above at higher temperatures, level for level, than that of the neighboring ice caps. Hence a practically continuous overflow of air from the one place, with compensating drainage and inflow from the other, is enforced by the existing and perpetually maintained distribution of unequal surface temperatures. These temperature contrasts are most pronounced, and the resulting Icelandic "low" most intense, during winter; but it prevails through summer also, for the simple reason that the necessary temperature gradients, though weakened during this season, are not obliterated, the water remaining always warm in comparison with the ice-caps of both Greenland and Iceland, which persist from season to season and from year to year.

The Aleutian "low," on the other hand, is merely seasonal: it prevails only while the adjacent Alaskan and Siberian regions are snow covered and relatively cold. When this snow is gone the temperature gradients are even reversed, and the off-shore drainage of winter is replaced by the on-shore winds of summer. Similar considerations and explanations obviously apply to all the other regions frequented by semipermanent cyclones.

Of Foehn Origin.—It has long been recognized that a secondary cyclone sometimes originates on the north side of the Alps when the foehn, or warm mountain wind, is strong. And, if here, the same presumably is true also of many other places. Indeed, cyclones appear occasionally to start at the times of well-defined foehn (Chinook) winds along the eastern slopes of the Rocky Mountains, both in the United States and in Canada, and perhaps even in Alaska. In these cases the crossing winds may cool slowly, owing to the liberated heat of condensation, on the west side of the range, and then rapidly warm, being dry, with descent on the eastern side, thereby establishing a steep temperature gradient between the locus of descent and much, at least, of the surrounding region. Hence, with the cessation of the flow of the foehn, convection over the heated area may become pronounced, and occasionally a secondary cyclone begun.

Insolational. *Of Land Origin.*—Since gulfs and seas flanked by relatively cold land areas induce, as explained, more or less permanent cyclones, it follows that peninsulas flanked by relatively cold water should also be generators of cyclonic wind systems. Similarly, any area of sufficient size that becomes heated, through insolation, to temperatures above those of the adjacent regions, should likewise induce, or tend, to induce a circulation of the cyclonic type. The Spanish Peninsula shows, during summer, the phenomenon in question. It also occurs over the Alaskan peninsula, onto which summer winds blow from the Gulf of Alaska, from Bering Sea and from the Arctic Ocean, obviously producing, through rotational deflection, a distinct cyclonic circulation. Similarly, the Great Plains often show daylight, or insolational lows, from which occasional cyclonic storms appear to originate, or by which a feeble passing cyclone is strengthened. Also many start over northwestern Australia.

Of course, entire continents show low average pressure during summer and high during winter, while in each case the opposite condition applies to the oceans. Such conditions, however, are not productive of storms, because the areas involved are hypercyclonic in size—so large, in fact, that they only modify the general or planetary circulation, without producing local disturbances within it. Neither do temperature contrasts, between areas that are very small in comparison with that of the average cyclone, produce extensive precipitation, but mere local disturbances quickly smoothed out by the general circulation, or, at most, only thunder showers. In short, for the development of cyclones by temperature contrasts, the warm area must be neither too large nor too small, neither continental in extent nor, in size, a mere island or bay.

Mechanical.—The mechanical "low" is divisible into two classes: (1) permanent—in reality not a cyclone at all in the ordinary sense of a low center with enclosing isobars—and (2) migratory—the characteristic cyclone of middle latitudes. In the first class, certainly, and presumably in the second also, the low pressure is rather the *result* than the *cause* of the associated winds. Indeed, in the case of any steady wind, except those near the surface, or close to the equator, its sustaining force (force in its direction) is small, in comparison with the deflective force at right angles to its path, due to the rotation of the earth.

Permanent.—There are two well-developed, permanent lows of this type (mechanical) and also an imperfectly developed third. These are: (*a*) the equatorial low, which roughly follows the equator through its entire course, due partly to the relatively high temperature and the usual high absolute humidity of this belt and partly to the right and left deflective forces of the westward winds of the northern and southern hemispheres, respectively; (*b*) the Antarctic trough, encircling Antarctica generally between 60° and 70° S. and having an annual average pressure of about 740 mm., mechanically sustained jointly by the northward pressure of the swift west winds over the oceans and the southward pressure of the east to west component of the vigorous southeast air drainage or fallwinds of Antarctica; (*c*) the Arctic trough, irregular in outline and intensity and apparently only fragmentary.

Migratory.—The great majority of extratropical cyclonic storms are migratory, and apparently originate either by breaking off from or in some manner being induced by the semipermanent and insolation lows, or by somehow forming at almost any other place, especially along the more frequented storm paths. The genesis, development, and detailed structure of these storms have been the subjects of many studies and speculations. Nevertheless, they are still imperfectly understood, and, furthermore, such understanding of them as we have is a composite of so many, and, in some cases, so nearly identical contributions, that it is not practicable completely to analyze them and correctly accredit each bit and portion.

Former, or Convectional, Theory of the Cyclone.—It formerly (very roughly from 1850 until 1915) was generally believed that the extra-tropical cyclone is initiated by thermal convection, and maintained largely by the liberated heat of condensation. These causes are shown to be inadequate by the facts that: (1) cyclones are more numerous during winter than summer; (2) occasionally a well-developed extratropical cyclone is accompanied by little precipitation, or even none at all; and (3) sounding balloon records have shown that the temperature of the troposphere in the cyclones of some regions, at least (certainly England and continental Europe), usually is lower than that of the anticyclone.

Present Theory of the Origin and Maintenance of the Extratropical Cyclone.—Since, in general, the surface of the earth is perpetually warmest in the region between the tropics and coldest at high latitudes, the atmosphere must somehow continuously circulate back and forth between these areas of maximum temperature contrast, however many and howsoever important secondary circulations it may experience in so doing. Furthermore, as explained in Chap. VII, if this air were entirely free from all constraint, except the support of the surface, it would move along approximate circles of radius

$$r = \frac{v}{2\omega \sin \varphi},$$

in which v is its linear velocity, ω, the angular rotation of the earth, and φ, the latitude of the place in question. However, from the movements of clouds and balloons and from surface observations as well, we know that normally the course of the wind is widely different from that which it would take if wholly free from horizontal restraint. Clearly, then, moving air is subject not only to the vertical force that sustains its weight but also to a horizontal force that in part determines its path. Obviously, too, this force is a mechanical shove, the shove of the atmosphere toward which the moving air presses as it tends to deflect incident to the rotation of the earth. In order, then, that a current of air in the northern hemisphere should flow toward the Arctic along a meridian, it must be constrained by an eastward increase of pressure, and that increase must continue across (along a parallel of latitude) the whole width of the northward-moving sheet. Therefore, this sheet cannot extend clear around the earth, since to do so would imply that the pressure is greater at the end of the circuit than at its beginning—one and the same place— an obvious impossibility. And the same argument holds for winds in general in both hemispheres. Therefore, along any great circle there normally are differences of pressure, which is high in some places and low in others. In short, the interzonal circulation of the atmosphere must develop, or be effected through the agency of, cyclones and anticyclones.

This same conclusion, namely, that the interzonal circulation of the atmosphere must develop, and be by way of, cyclones and anticyclones, can also be derived mathematically.[1] Finally, the fact that it does circulate in that way is direct and positive proof that it must circulate in that way.

As previously explained, the tendency to conservation of areas, or angular momentum, deflects poleward-moving winds toward the east and equatorward winds toward the west. That is, to a great extent, in mid-latitude regions the warmer wind blows eastward and north-eastward, and the colder air from higher latitudes blows westward and southwestward—the one alongside the other. This condition, as now long known, and much longer suspected, is the immediate cause of the great majority of mid-latitude cyclones.

Let v_1, ρ_1, be the velocity (westward), and density, respectively, of the cold poleward air; and v_2, ρ_2, the velocity (eastward), and density, of the warm equatorward air. Then the dynamic push poleward per cubic centimeter of the cold air, at the interface between the westward and eastward currents, is $2\rho_1 v_1 \omega \sin \varphi$, and the gradient poleward push against it of the warm air $2\rho_2 v_2 \omega \sin \varphi$ (that being the gradient, or poleward push per cubic centimeter, in the warm air at the place in question), where φ is the latitude, and ω the angular velocity of rotation of the earth; and the gravity push equatorward per cubic centimeter of the same air, $g(\rho_1 - \rho_2)$ tan β, where β is the slope of the interface. In the case of equilibrium, obviously

$$\tan \beta = 2\omega \sin \varphi \frac{(v_1\rho_1 + v_2\rho_2)}{g(\rho_1 - \rho_2)}$$
$$= 2\omega \sin \varphi \frac{(v_1 T_2 + v_2 T_1)}{g(T_2 - T_1)},$$

in which T_1 and T_2 are the absolute temperatures of the cold and the warm air, respectively.

For instance, if, at latitude 70°, v_1 and v_2 are each 10 meters per second and if the temperatures of the currents are 270° Abs. and 280° Abs., respectively, all of which are reasonable values, then $\beta = 26' 26''$, a rise of the interface at the rate of a little more than ¾ mile in 100 miles along the meridian—in this case. Obviously, though, the same equations hold whatever the directions of the passing winds, so long as an object between them would be rolled counter-clockwise, looked at from

[1] JEFFREYS, HAROLD, *Quart. J. Roy. Meteorol. Soc.*, **48**; 29, 1922.

above.   Also the angle of the slope increases with the sine of the latitude, relative velocity of the passing currents, and decrease of their temperature difference.

Let, then, such a dynamical equilibrium be established, and, to be specific, let the interface intersect a "level" earth along a parallel of high latitude, and, finally, let the balance or equilibrium be upset, as probably it usually is before it gets fully established. This unbalance could be effected by changing the speed or direction of either current, or by altering the barometric pressure on either side of the boundary; causes which in turn could be established in several ways. To be further specific let the westward velocity of the cold air be greatly reduced by an obstruction, say, at a particular place. Immediately it will assume an equatorward component at that place, which component will again, owing to the rotation of the earth, increase (unless prevented) the westward velocity. The intruding cold air, by interfering with the flow of the warm, will lead to a reduction of pressure on its lee, or (in this case) eastern side. This will maintain the unbalance, and always to the lee of the intruding cold air. Furthermore, the outflow of cold air from its reservoir evidently must be compensated by an equivalent inflow of warm air, and, of course, like other flows, chiefly where the weakening of the obstruction is greatest; in this case, on the east side of the low pressure, owing to the resulting modifications in the course of the isobars. These, presumably, will tend to be elliptical with the major axis, roughly, along the eastern edge of the intruding cold air, and with the lowest pressure close to the cold reservoir, or within the bend, or elbow, of the cold border. Clearly, too, the poleward flow of the warm air will cause it to increase its eastward speed, thus accentuating the decrease of pressure and all the attending phenomena, towards some ultimate steady state. Finally, since the deflected warm current will be on the east side (in the assumed case) of the cold intrusion, and much deeper, the latter being shaped rather as a thin wedge; and, since its eastward velocity is greater, in nature at least, than the westward of the polar air; therefore, the place of interchange, and its accompanying low pressure, will travel eastward along the border of the cold reservoir, or interface, between the two systems of winds, and continue to do so until the interchange itself creates, for a time, its own undoing, or by change of position encounters unfavorable conditions. As the break continues to move forward, the winds to the rear will persistently renew the barrier, thereby permitting not a general collapse but only a traveling breach, of greater or less width, as determined by the supplies of air available for interchange, topography, nature of the surface, and distribution of temperature.

It was assumed above that the disturbance to the dynamical equilibrium began with the cold air; it might quite as well have been with the warm, since in either case the countercurrents would be simultaneous.

As already stated, the above course of general reasoning lacks mathematical exactness—for the actual atmosphere such does not exist, and certainly would be very difficult to supply—nevertheless, it is in general accord with the phenomena of the extratropical traveling cyclone, by which, naturally, it was suggested, and which it, in turn, helps to explain. That is, although the actual atmosphere is not a perfect gas, nevertheless it is so highly fluid that if we knew the behavior of the one, presumably we could roughly infer that of the other, under like circumstances. We therefore assume that the actual cold polar air and warm equatorial air can flow in opposite directions, separated by an almost discontinuous interface, sloping gently downward from the colder side almost to the surface, well within the warmer current. And this condition does occur, briefly, at any given place, and irregularly, but over and over again without end.

Now, as is well known, the polar regions always are relatively cold and the equatorial comparatively warm; hence, the atmosphere continuously tends to circulate interzonally, and to come to a state of dynamic equilibrium. But, as it is slightly viscous, and the surface of the earth rough and irregular, complete dynamical equilibrium does not and cannot obtain. On the contrary, surface friction and turbulence so check the speed of the lower winds that they flow, not parallel to the isobars, but diagonally across them, from a region of higher pressure towards one of lower pressure. From this one might hastily suppose that there could be an equatorward surface flow of cold air all around any parallel of middle to higher latitude, and a poleward overflow from at least the tropical regions. But that would entail, through the conservation of areas, or angular momentum, upper winds in the polar regions so great that they would, through wave action, completely mix the higher and lower air, thereby breaking an important link in the chain of events. Besides, we know, from direct observations with pilot balloons, that there is no circumpolar whirl of very great velocity. And we also know, of course, that while cold north winds are frequent in middle latitudes, and beyond, they are not continuous at any given place, but alternate irregularly with winds from other directions. Therefore, and for other reasons, as explained above, we believe that a large part of the interzonal circulation of the middle and higher latitudes *must* occur in the form of cyclones—the way it *does* occur—and that these cyclones commonly must start (and they seem usually so to start) as breaks in pseudodynamic barriers between relatively cold and warm currents of air. Most of these breaks, apparently, occur along the border of the polar (north or south) reservoir, including the winter land reservoirs of high latitudes, but many others appear elsewhere. For instance, a trough of low pressure, roughly along the Mississippi Valley, with northerly winds on the west and southerly on the east, is almost certain to develop cyclones as long as it lasts; sometimes in such quick succession that a third or even a fourth may have begun before the first is off the map. Similarly, and under like circumstances, secondary lows often occur over the western Atlantic, a winter phenomenon, off the coast of the United States, and also in various other parts of the world, such as the western Pacific, in winter—in short, wherever there are oppositely flowing currents, having contrasting temperatures, and so directed as to give low pressure between them.

As already stated, this break in the dynamic partition that initiates the cyclone can be effected in various ways. However, it appears to be facilitated by regions of relatively high temperature, such as the Ross and the Weddell Seas, when open, and the Atlantic southwest from Iceland; and, in winter, the Pacific off the Aleutians, the northwest corner of the Gulf of Mexico, portions of the Mediterranean, and, to a greater or less extent, many others. A particularly effective cause of a large break, and the development of an extensive and vigorous storm, is the intrusion of a minor disturbance, or small cyclone, from some other place, no matter how far removed. For instance, a tropical cyclone may cross an ocean, perhaps, in 10 days, recurve, lose most of its intensity, and then develop again into a large and vigorous storm—now an extratropical cyclone, initiated by the intrusion, at the right time and place, of a disturbance sufficient to start the exchange between the cold and the warm currents. Somewhat similarly, a low may cross the Rocky Mountains to the Mississippi Valley as a feeble disturbance, as such lows frequently are, owing presumably to difficult access to abundant cold air on the one side and warm on the other; then turn northeastward and, now, with access to both reservoirs free and easy, at least so far as topography is concerned, rapidly develop into a large and vigorous storm.

After the break and the consequent cyclone are well established, the warm and the cold winds no longer flow past each other in parallel, opposite, directions, but largely over and under each other in a traveling quasiswirl. In front, that is, on the side toward which the storm is approaching, the direction of flow of the cold air remains much as it was— from the east, suppose. The warmer air, under the new disposition of pressure, is deflected, in this case, northward and slowly upward over the cold air, and, thereby, commonly cooled to the state of cloud formation and precipitation. The lower portion of the elevated air appears to turn backward, at least with reference to the position of the storm center, and, often, to carry precipitation to the poleward and rear quadrant. The higher winds move on, less and less deflected from their original course with increase of height, and carry with them portions of the higher storm clouds. The line of intersection of the interface between the cold and warm currents in the front part of the storm with the surface generally is called the "warm front," an appropriate name given to it by V. Bjerknes.

To the rear of the storm, and equatorward from its center, the intruding cold air runs forward and underflows the warmer wind. The line of surface intersection in this region Bjerknes calls the "cold front." It is the familiar wind-shift line, or line along which the direction of the wind greatly and rapidly changes—from southwest, for instance, to northwest, usually accompanied by an appreciable to considerable change in temperature and humidity. In fact, there are, in this case, an almost abrupt change of winds, from one air mass to another of very different origin, an abrupt increase of pressure, and an inward break in the directions of the isobars. This line has also long been known as the squall line, because all along it sudden gusts, squalls and, in summer, thunderstorms, are very common, owing to the vigorous ascent here of the warm air, caused by being lifted by the lower part of the oncoming colder air or to being partially to wholly entrapped by the faster moving higher layers. This portion of the cyclone also nearly always is accompanied by precipitation, not gentle and long continued, as in the front of the storm, but rather in the form of heavy showers of short duration, the so-called clearing-up shower, followed by lower temperature and a clear sky.

During the most vigorous stage of the cyclone, only one-third, or less, of its area is covered by the warm winds. The rest is covered by winds of polar origin. Normally, too, the following cold wind eventually gains on the storm as a whole. The cold front swings around until the warm segment soon is completely separated from its tropical supply. Hemmed in, now, on all sides, the entrapped warm air is lifted up from mother earth, still swirling a little, no doubt, dynamically and otherwise cooled until it is just like the air all about and its identity thus quickly and wholly lost in that natural Nirvana—the snow-covered latitudes—of every well-behaved cyclone.

Such, then, in a general way, is our present concept of the genesis, course, and final disappearance of a typical extratropical cyclone. In variety, it is endless, but all are alike in consisting of oppositely directed warm and cold currents; in having the warmer air in front and the colder to the rear; in having a low-pressure center; and in ultimately reaching high latitudes, unless forcefully prevented; where, owing to occlusion, or separation from the warm winds and capture by the cold, it quickly becomes but a common portion of the frigid air cap, and, as such, soon returns to lower latitudes in the counter, or cold side, of one or more new cyclones, there to warm up for another, but different, journey toward the realm of ice and snow—back and forth, in an endless sequence of weather and weather changes.

Possible Cyclones in the Stratosphere.—As previously stated, there seems to be good reason to believe that there is a well-defined interzonal circulation in the stratosphere, between the warm polar and cold tropical portions of this region. If so, are there not, then, cyclones in the stratosphere, and anticyclones, too, perhaps? Since the friction between the stratosphere and troposphere evidently is slight, and turbulence very small—marked turbulence would give an adiabatic, not an isothermal gradient—it follows that an interzonal circulation, if of over- and underrunning, or non-interfering currents, would lead to winds of very great velocity in the stratosphere of high latitudes. But observations, on sounding balloons, and on the drift of high volcanic dust, all have shown only moderate winds in the stratosphere, and of varying directions. If, then, there is a marked circulation in the stratosphere between high and low latitudes, and it seems practically certain that there must be, it evidently is under the control, in part, of north-south isobars, or east-west gradients, since in this way, and, so far as we can see, in this way only, an abundant latitude circulation can occur without excessive longitude velocities. Evidently, too, an east-west gradient cannot continue in the same sense all around the earth; even once around would give the impossible condition of two different pressures at the same place—the starting point. Hence, if there are north-south isobars in the stratosphere, they must be in the form of closed curves, and that means a more or less alternate distribution of high pressures and low pressures.

We know, from sounding balloon observations, that the base of the stratosphere, at any given place, rises and falls, often a kilometer or more; that, in general, it is highest over anticyclones and lowest over cyclones; that the higher it is, the colder it is; and that to a greater or less extent this change of temperature extends to great heights. Now this is exactly what must occur in the stratosphere, if locally lifted or lowered bodily;[1] hence, we infer that such lifting and lowering does occur over anticyclones and cyclones, respectively.

Let a stratospheric column be dropped bodily a distance dh, and let the surrounding air come in until equilibrium is again established. At each level there, obviously, will result a change in pressure directly proportional to the pressure at that level. That is, throughout the column

$$\frac{dp}{p} = K, \text{ a constant.}$$

But, as is well known,

$$\frac{dT}{T} = C\frac{dp}{p},$$

in which T is the absolute temperature, and C a constant, 0.2858 for dry air. Hence, since T is constant, roughly, in the stratosphere, dT also is constant, and the upper air remains vertically isothermal, whatever the pressure increase or decrease. An increase of pressure in the stratosphere, such as presumably takes place over cyclones, *increases* its

[1] SHAW, "Perturbations of the Stratosphere," *M. O.* **202**; 47, 1909.

temperature, while a decrease of pressure, such as probably occurs over anticyclones, correspondingly *decreases* its temperature. In each case the pressure effect presumably is slightly enhanced by the coincident change in the intensity of radiation from below.

Suppose the temperature of the stratosphere over a cyclone should differ from that at the same place over the following anticyclone by 10° C., what, according to the above conception, will be the approximate change of boundary level? Let h be this change, and let the temperature of the stratosphere be 220° Abs. Then since

$$\frac{dp}{p} = \frac{dh}{H},$$

in which H is the height of the homogeneous atmosphere, about 6450 meters at the assumed temperature, it follows that

$$\frac{10}{220} = 0.2858\frac{h}{H}, \text{ roughly,}$$

and

$$h = 1 \text{ kilometer approximately.}$$

That is, the temperature of the stratosphere will increase or decrease at the rate of approximately 10° C. per kilometer enforced fall or rise, respectively, under the influence of cyclonic and anticyclonic disturbances.

In this connection, it should be noted that, on the average, and at least over the British Isles and continental Europe, the changes of pressure at the height of even 9 kilometers is substantially the same as at the surface. Evidently, therefore, in such cases, cyclones and anticyclones in the troposphere extend, also, well up into the stratosphere. This observed approximate equality of pressure changes, at widely different levels, implies, also, certain temperature relations. From the equation

$$p = p_0 e^{\frac{-gh}{RT_m}} \qquad \text{(see Chap. V)}$$

in which p_0 and p are the pressures at the surface and height h, respectively, and T_m the mean absolute (virtual) temperature of the air between these levels, it appears that, if T_m is constant,

$$\frac{\Delta p}{\Delta p_0} = \frac{p}{p_0}.$$

That is, at the height of 9 kilometers, where the pressure is less than one-third that at the surface, the change in pressure should also be less than one-third the surface change, and not, at Dines found, substantially the same. If T_m also changes, then

$$\frac{\Delta p}{p} = \frac{\Delta p_0}{p_0} + \frac{gh\Delta T_m}{RT_m^2}.$$

Hence the change of pressure at the base of the stratosphere can equal (as often it does) that at the surface only when the mean temperature of the troposphere below changes sufficiently in the same sense. Evidently, however, a change of pressure at the surface is not, necessarily, accompanied by any change at the base of the stratosphere, provided the temperature of the troposphere is altered in the opposite sense. But while changes of pressure can occur at the surface without changes in the stratosphere, they evidently are very exceptional.

The cyclones and anticyclones, therefore, that must occur in the stratosphere, presumably occur, in large measure at least, as extensions of those in the troposphere. However, it seems likely that some occur there independently, or rather, start there, since, as just explained, a change of pressure in the stratosphere all but certainly will lead to a decidedly greater change of the same sign at the surface of the earth. It may be, therefore, that many a breach in the dynamical wall between warm and cold winds is made—many a surface cyclone initiated—by some change of pressure begun in the stratosphere. Perhaps slight pressure changes, initiated in the upper atmosphere, may also account for those surface changes, occasionally decided, and even extensive surges, for which one cannot find an adequate cause—that just "drop from the blue," as we say.

Changes in the atmospheric pressure, at any place on the surface of the earth, obviously are due, almost wholly, to corresponding variations in the mass of air in a vertical column above that place. Hence investigations of the processes in the free air that lead to such local changes of mass are of importance to the elucidation of the genesis, structure, and mechanism of cyclones and anticyclones. The problem is a difficult one, and the necessary observational data very limited; however, progress has been made toward its solution by Rossby,[1] Haurwitz,[2] and others.

ANTICYCLONES

Anticyclones, or "highs," are divisible, with respect to their genesis, into three classes: (1) mechanical: (*a*), permanent, and (*b*), migratory; (2) radiational: (*a*) permanent, and (*b*) transitory; (3) thermal.

In this classification the relative "high" that obtains over an entire hemisphere during its winter, and also those seasonal highs of continental (during winter) and oceanic (during summer) extent, have all been excluded. Like the lows of similar great size, they only modify, somewhat, the course of the general circulation, and give direction to monsoon winds.

Mechanical. *Permanent.*—Since the surface of the ocean is a gravitational equipotential surface, it follows that west winds, by virtue of

[1] ROSSBY, C. G., *Beitr. z. Phys. Atm.*, **13**; 163, 1927.

[2] HAURWITZ, B., *Veröff. Geophysikal. Inst. Univ. Leipzig*, (2), Bd. 3, Heft 5, 1927.

their excess centrifugal force, will tend to climb up the bulge of the earth toward the equator; and east winds, because of deficiency in centrifugal force, will tend to slide down this bulge toward the nearest pole. Hence along the borders, between trade winds and the west winds of adjacent higher latitudes, the atmosphere must be subject to a mechanical squeeze. In other words, mechanically produced high-pressure belts tend to encircle the earth at about latitudes 30° to 35° N. and S., as shown in Fig. 62. They cannot, however, be fully developed and persistent all the way around, since they then would be barriers across which interzonal circulation, the very thing upon which they depend, could not occur. Necessarily, therefore, they are broken down into segments with tropical winds blowing poleward around their western ends and polar winds going equatorward around their eastern ends—at any rate, over the oceans, where surface friction is least, temperature nearly constant, and the winds strongest. Over land areas, owing to turbulence, convection, and high surface temperatures, these belts are manifest only at considerable elevations. However, the ocean segments often do encroach to some extent onto land areas. Indeed, it seems probable that the high-pressure, droughty weather that occasionally prevails over the southern United States, and even much of the Mississippi valley, frequently is due, in part at least, to such an encroachment, incident to the poleward summer shift of the northern high-pressure belt.

Migratory.—The migratory anticyclone referred to here is the common one of middle latitudes. The directions of its system of winds, but in no sense the complete paths of the air particles, are given by synoptic charts. These directions are spirally outward, clockwise in the northern hemisphere, counter-clockwise in the southern. Hence the relation of anticyclonic wind velocity to horizontal pressure gradient is given by the equation

$$\frac{dp}{dn} = \rho v \left(2\omega \sin \varphi - \frac{v}{r} \right),$$

in which r is the radius of curvature, nearly, of the wind path at the place considered, and the other symbols have the usual significance as previously given. From the negative sign it appears that for a given radius of curvature the possible wind velocity in a "high" is strictly limited, whatever the pressure gradient.

Velocity and Path of Travel.—The velocity and normal path of the migrating anticyclone are by no means as well known as those of the cyclone, except, perhaps, through the studies of Bowie and Weightman[1] in respect to those that cross the United States. However, the size, frequency, and velocity of travel of anticyclones are all, roughly, the

[1] *M. W. R. Supplement*, 4, 1917.

same as those of similarly located cyclones. Furthermore, their most frequented paths begin at high latitudes and run eastward to much lower.

Wind Velocity.—The actual velocity of the wind in the different quadrants of an anticyclone, and at different elevations, is given in the

ANTICYCLONIC WIND VELOCITY IN METERS PER SECOND AND (MILES PER HOUR)

Altitude		Surface 122 m.	500 m.	1000 m.	1500 m.	2000 m.	2500 m.	3000 m.	3500 m.	4000 m.
South quadrant	Winter	4.43 (9.9)	8.48 (19.0)	8.82 (19.7)	8.68 (19.4)	8.60 (19.2)	8.92 (19.9)	9.71 (21.7)	10.14 (22.7)	10.97 (24.5)
	Summer	3.92 (8.7)	6.19 (13.9)	6.25 (14.0)	6.36 (14.2)	6.17 (13.8)	5.97 (13.3)	6.19 (13.9)	7.08 (15.9)	7.83 (17.5)
	Year	4.16 (9.3)	7.32 (16.4)	7.52 (16.8)	7.51 (16.8)	7.38 (16.5)	7.44 (16.7)	7.94 (17.8)	8.60 (19.2)	9.39 (21.0)
West quadrant	Winter	3.93 (8.8)	7.60 (17.0)	7.19 (16.1)	7.35 (16.4)	7.23 (16.2)	7.21 (16.1)	7.57 (16.9)	7.75 (17.3)	8.11 (17.9)
	Summer	3.39 (7.6)	5.26 (11.8)	5.41 (12.1)	5.18 (11.6)	5.28 (11.8)	5.39 (12.1)	5.20 (11.6)	4.74 (10.6)	5.04 (11.3)
	Year	3.74 (8.4)	6.51 (14.5)	6.38 (14.3)	6.35 (14.2)	6.34 (14.2)	6.38 (14.3)	6.46 (14.4)	6.32 (14.1)	6.65 (14.9)
North quadrant	Winter	4.21 (9.4)	9.69 (21.7)	9.54 (21.4)	9.78 (21.9)	10.19 (22.8)	10.69 (23.9)	11.59 (25.9)	12.29 (27.5)	14.43 (32.3)
	Summer	4.05 (9.0)	7.01 (15.7)	7.68 (17.2)	8.41 (18.8)	8.85 (19.8)	9.51 (21.3)	10.04 (22.5)	10.68 (23.9)	11.45 (25.6)
	Year	4.13 (9.3)	8.35 (18.7)	8.61 (19.2)	9.09 (20.4)	9.51 (21.3)	10.09 (22.6)	10.80 (24.2)	11.47 (25.6)	12.92 (28.9)
East quadrant	Winter	4.29 (9.6)	8.24 (18.4)	8.83 (19.8)	9.56 (21.4)	10.92 (24.4)	12.44 (27.8)	13.52 (30.2)	14.02 (31.3)	15.68 (35.1)
	Summer	3.92 (8.7)	5.88 (13.2)	6.42 (14.3)	6.55 (14.6)	6.98 (15.6)	7.54 (16.9)	7.31 (16.3)	7.83 (17.5)	8.28 (18.5)
	Year	4.06 (9.1)	7.01 (15.7)	7.57 (16.9)	8.00 (17.9)	8.89 (19.9)	9.93 (22.2)	10.35 (23.2)	10.86 (24.3)	11.91 (26.6)

table herewith by Peppler,[1] based on a large number of observations made during 1903–1909, at Lindenburg, latitude 52° 10′ N., longitude 14° 15′ E. The corresponding winds of the United States, east of the Rocky Mountains, are shown in Figs. 58 to 61, kindly supplied by the Aerological Division of the U. S. Weather Bureau. Greater details on this subject have been published by L. T. Samuels.[2]

Origin, Course, and End of the Migratory Anticyclone.—As explained under the theory of the cyclone, a break in the dynamical barrier between polar and tropical winds is accompanied by a vast flow of cold air, from

[1] *Beitr. Physik freien Atmosphäre*, **4**; 95, 1911.
[2] *M. W. R.*, **54**; 195, 1926.

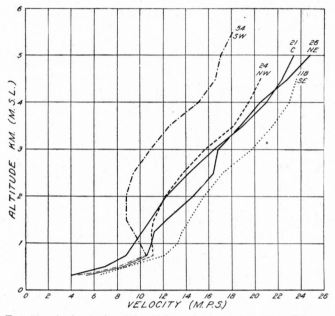

Fig. 58.—Anticyclonic wind velocity, winter, northern United States.

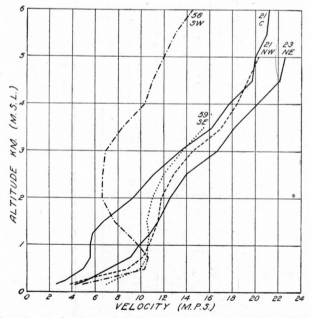

Fig. 59.—Anticyclonic wind velocity, winter, southern United States.

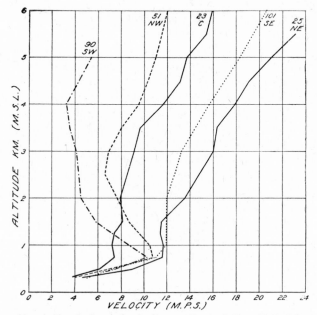

FIG. 60.—Anticyclonic wind velocity, summer, northern United States.

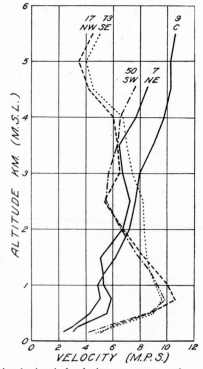

FIG. 61.—Anticyclonic wind velocity, summer, southern United States.

higher to lower latitudes. To some extent, this flow is of the drainage type, as evidenced by the abrupt increase of pressure along the polar, or cold, front, in which the motion is partly in response to gravity and not wholly to horizontal pressure gradient and earth rotation. The front, or east, portion of this cold air, whether from beyond a polar circle or from frigid land areas, such as Siberia, or northern North America, in winter, constitutes the rear half of the cyclone. The more westerly part of the cold current, however, is but little affected by the low pressure of the cyclonic swirl, and therefore tends more to lag behind—to pull away from the cyclone and become a wind of a different system. The westerly winds thus underrun are, in a measure, checked in their course as they rise over the intruding cold air, and to that extent add to the local increase of pressure already begun by the fall of temperature. An anticyclone thus formed, presumably, would move forward with, but to the rear of, the cyclone with which it initially began, so long as it was well connected with the reservoir of cold air pouring through the moving breach in the dynamic partition. After a time, however, this connection would fail owing (a) to partial drainage of the basin, or shift of the reservoir itself, in the sense of location of the cold air; (b) great distance of the intruded air which lags behind from the forward-driving breach; (c) separation by topographical barrier, or otherwise. If the cyclone should become rather early occluded, however, practically all the outpouring cold air would form a single, relatively large, anticyclone. In either case the anticyclone soon would become occluded, as distinctly as the cyclone is when shut off from access to warm air. It then would move on, in general, eastward and equatorward under the urge of the over-running westerlies and its own momentum, modified, of course, by the surrounding distribution of pressure. In most cases it would be weathered away, as it were, by warm winds, and heated up by the surface —and slightly by compression—until it finally disappeared as a temporary local intensification in the neighboring belt of high pressure, or a fading atmospheric swell over a tropical sea. But occasionally, and especially when favored by a well developed low to poleward, it presumably would skirt the belt of high pressure, or travel as a spur to this ridge, to its eastern end, and, thence, onto and across the neighboring land—probably there reinforced—to the ocean beyond.

This is substantially the way the migrating anticyclone does behave. We, therefore, believe (positive proof, whether by sufficient observation or by mathematical analysis, is lacking) that in many cases both a cyclone and an anticyclone simultaneously develop with, and owing to, the same initial break in the dynamical partition between polar air, on the one side, and equatorial, on the other; that, often, they grow greatly in size and become widely separated; that, occasionally, the cyclone soon is suppressed, leaving only a well-developed anticyclone; and that, in any case, each is ultimately occluded and then rapidly brought to the temperature of its new environment and wholly smoothed away.

Radiational. *Permanent.*—There are two extensive regions, Antarctica and Greenland, where the barometric pressure always is high. At each place the high pressure appears to be the result of the very low prevailing temperatures, which in turn are due, in part, to the great elevations, and, in part, to the free and abundant radiation from the snow surface through the comparatively clear skies, kept generally free from clouds by the descent of the upper air induced and maintained by the vigorous fallwinds. That surface radiation is an essential factor in establishing and maintaining these low temperatures is obvious from the fact that air cannot flow downhill, as it does in these regions, unless it has a greater density, and, therefore, lower temperature, than the adjacent atmosphere of the same level. It is also obvious from the prevailing and excessive surface temperature inversions, in which, and because of which, those ice fogs, that doubtless furnish much of the interior precipitation, are so common.

It will be well to remember, in this connection, that snow, in addition to reflecting about 70 per cent of the incident solar radiation,[1] is also a good emitter of those long wave-length $(12–30\mu)$ radiations appropriate to its temperature. In this way the low temperatures are maintained, not only during winter when air circulation and, to some extent, cooling ice supply the only available heat, but, also, during the long-continued insolation of summer.

The air drainage thus produced is manifest in those strong and persistent southeast, or anticyclonic, winds that characterize the climates of the border and all explored portions of Antarctica, except, of course, near the pole, and, presumably, therefore, of the whole continent. Similar, though less vigorous, anticyclonic winds also prevail over and around Greenland. Each of these great areas, but especially Antarctica, by virtue of its strong and continuous refrigeration, obviously influences the atmospheric circulation of its respective region. If there were no such extensive high and snow-covered areas in the polar regions, it is clear that our general circulation would be less vigorous and, doubtless, different in many places.

Transitory.—During winter, elevated snow-covered regions often become very cold and thus build "highs" similar to those of Greenland and Antarctica, though, usually, much smaller in extent, as well as only temporary. Occasionally, these give rise to strong and cold surface winds, especially when the existing gradient is accentuated by the passage of a well-developed cyclone along lower latitudes. Examples of such winds are the mistral of the Rhone Valley and the bora of the Adriatic and Black Seas. The Texas norther and the blizzard of the Great

---

[1] Abbot and Aldrich, *Proc. Nat. Acad. Sci.*, **2**; 335, 1916.

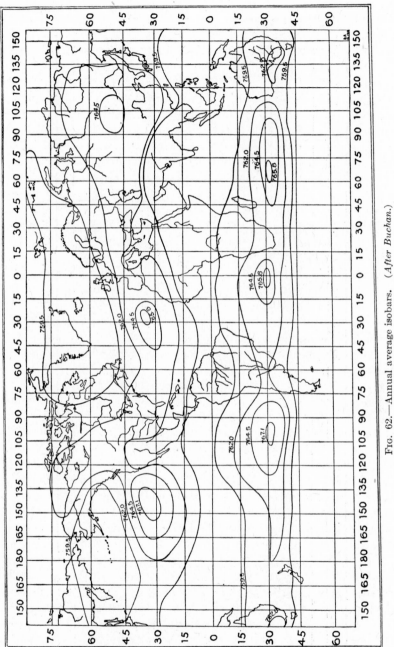

Fig. 62.—Annual average isobars. (*After Buchan.*)

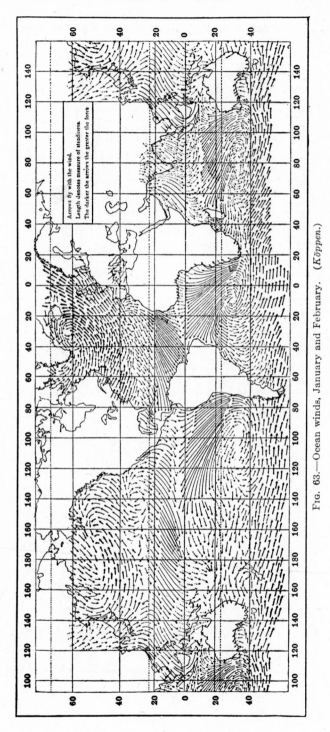

Arrows fly with the wind.
Length denotes measure of steadiness.
The darker the arrows the greater the force

Fig. 63.—Ocean winds, January and February. (*Köppen.*)

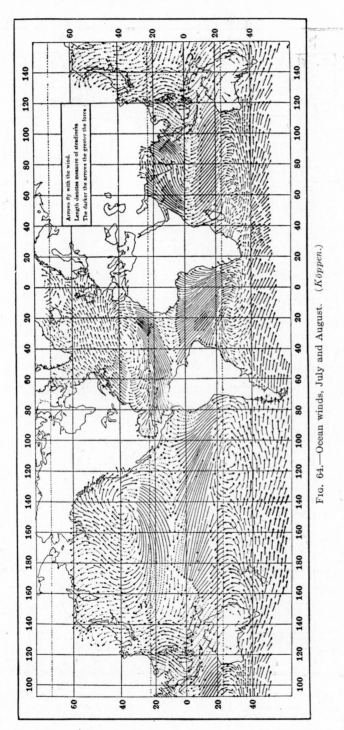

Arrows fly with the wind.
Length denotes measure of steadiness.
The darker the arrows the greater the force

FIG. 64.—Ocean winds, July and August. (Köppen.)

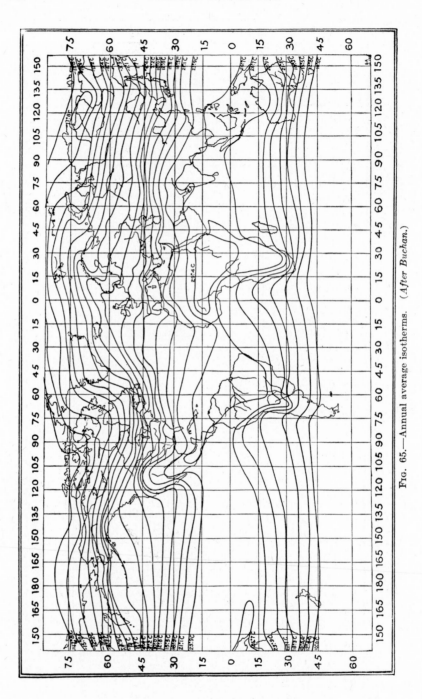

Fig. 65.—Annual average isotherms.   (After Buchan.)

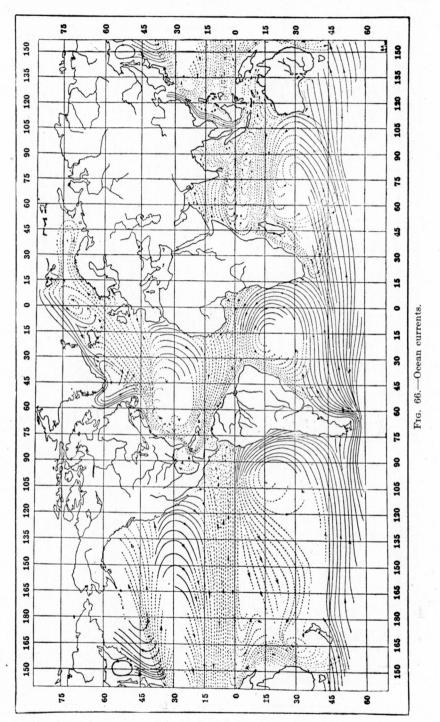

FIG. 66.—Ocean currents.

Fig. 67.—Ocean currents, annual average isotherms and annual average isobars.

Plains seem to be other and important examples of the drainage of transitory radiational anticyclones. The well-known violent fallwind of the coast of Norway appears to have a similar origin, as indeed have innumerable other drainage winds in all mountainous and high plateau regions outside the tropics.

Thermal. *Semipermanent.*—As is well known, there are five semi-permanent "highs," all of which occur on the oceans: Two, as Fig. 62 shows, about 35° north of the equator and three about 32° south of it. Two are on the Pacific Ocean—one west of southern California, the other off the coast of Chile; two on the Atlantic Ocean—near the Azores (known as the Azores "high") and off the coast of southern Africa; and one on the Indian Ocean, about halfway between Africa and Australia. A sixth oceanic "high" of this same class, but far less persistent than any of the above, often develops, especially during winter, in the region of the Bermudas.

Obviously there must be a close relation between the intensities and locations of these highs and the directions and velocities of the surrounding winds, even to great distances, as shown by Figs. 63 and 64. Hence it is meteorologically important to form some conception in regard to their origin.

It will be seen from Fig. 62 that all these "highs" or centers of maximum pressure occur along the high-pressure belts, and from Fig. 65 that they occur at those places along these belts where the temperature of the air is low for that latitude; that is, where the isotherms are deflected equatorward. At these places, then, there are two causes of high pressure: (*a*) the mechanical pressure, that produces the high-pressure belts, as already explained, and (*b*) a relatively low surface temperature, which allows the upper air to cool, somewhat, and, correspondingly, contract.

It is known, from sounding balloon records, that the temperature of the atmosphere even to great heights follows more or less closely any long-continued temperature changes of the surface. Hence, one might reasonably expect the atmosphere over the cold regions, as shown by Fig. 65, to be colder at every level than that of the surrounding atmosphere over warmer regions. A change of 1° C. throughout would change the pressure by 2 mm. or more. Hence, since the regions in question, according to Buchan's charts, are from 1° to 3° C. colder than those of the same latitude east or west, it appears that the pressure maxima of 2 mm. to 6 mm. probably are due to the continuous relatively low surface temperatures. In this case the "high" appears to be due to the cooling of the superincumbent atmosphere to that temperature at which its radiation is in substantial equilibrium with the minimum radiation from below.

But what is the cause of the local low surface temperatures? Referring to Fig. 66, it will be seen that there are five different places, and only five, where a distinctly cold ocean current crosses a belt of high pressure, and that every one of these is associated with a region of maximum pressure. Neither is there a semipermanent "high" anywhere else on the oceans. Wherever, then, the mechanical effect that produces a belt of high pressure is reinforced by thermal contraction due to cold water, there, and only there, as illustrated by Fig. 67, are found a maximum of atmospheric pressure and the center of a semipermanent anticyclone. During winter, there is also a slight minimum temperature along the North Atlantic high-pressure belt, near Bermuda, and a similar one along the South Pacific belt, just east of New Zealand; and at each place a corresponding tendency to the maintenance of an anticyclone.

One obvious effect of all these semipermanent highs is the location of branches or channels of interzonal circulation, analogous to those of the cyclones and anticyclones of higher latitudes. Thus, much tropical atmosphere, in addition to that carried by the counter trades, reaches middle latitudes by flowing around and to the west of the semipermanent "highs." From here, the next stage in the general circulation takes the air to still higher latitudes, and even to polar regions, around and to the east either of the semipermanent "lows" or of the migratory cyclones. In its return it passes to the west of the "lows" or east of the traveling "highs," and finally around and to the east of the semipermanent "highs." These, however, are only general channels, and, presumably, average routes, upon which are superimposed innumerable and ever-changing irregularities.

Identifying an Air Mass.—Since the weather changes at any particular place are caused largely by the advections to it and migrations across it of discrete masses of air and by the interplay between those of marked temperature and humidity contrasts, obviously a knowledge of the conditions of these masses, of their movements, and of the locations of their fronts or progressing borders could be used—and it is—as an excellent aid in forecasting the coming weather. In fact, this type of air-mass analysis, first practiced in Norway for the purpose stated, by J. Bjerknes and his colleagues, is now so used to a greater or less extent by all meteorological services, and increasingly with the extension of free-air data. To distinguish one air mass (body of air from a particular general region) from another and keep track of its advancing front, those conditions commonly are observed that change so slowly as to be relatively conservative and that also can be measured readily and accurately. As a rule, this restricts one to some sort of temperature and humidity measurements. Of the latter, specific humidity, and it alone, is useful in this connection, since it, and only it, is independent of temperature, pressure, and volume, and therefore constant so long as the water vapor is neither increased by evaporation nor decreased by condensation.

The potential temperature of the air is another condition, or potential condition, that commonly changes very slowly and hence might be used as an air-mass voucher. A still better criterion, one that varies more slowly, being unaffected by cloud dissipation, or formation, from the contained vapor, is the equivalent potential temperature (see Chap. II).

Historical.—The association of type of weather and weather changes with separate, moving masses of diverse air and their interaction, one on the other, traces back, though less and less distinctly, through many centuries. Homer is credited by Gold[1] with recognizing a warm front and its effect on precipitation fully 3000 years ago, and 350 years B.C. Aristotle noted that current weather depends largely on the condition, warm or cold, of the source region of the accompanying wind. More than a century ago, Luke Howard, in his "Climate of London," spoke of northerly and southerly winds blowing alongside each other, with the colder wedging in under the warmer and the warmer gliding up over the colder and giving extensive and continued rains. In 1852, Blasius spoke of an advancing cold, polar wind underrunning a warm, nearly saturated tropical wind and pushing it up with the production of cumulus clouds and precipitation. Helmholtz, Margules, and, especially, V. Bjerknes developed the mathematical theory of "fronts" and their effects. Shaw and Lempfert[2] furnished the observational basis for our present concept of the extratropical cyclone; Shaw[3] gave a clear notion of its general structure; and J. Bjerknes and H. Solberg began, in 1918, its practical use, now nearly universal, in weather forecasting.

[1] *Quart. J. Roy. Meteorol. Soc.*, **61**; 108, 1935.
[2] Life History of Surface Air Currents, *M. O.*, **174**; 1906.
[3] "Forecasting Weather," 1911.

CHAPTER XII

ATMOSPHERIC CIRCULATION (*Continued*)

FORCED WINDS

Although, in greater or less measure, all winds are interdependent, only a relatively small number obviously are generated and maintained by other, and coexisting, winds. Among these are eddy winds, Maloja winds, foehn or chinook winds, and, presumably, the winds of the tornado and waterspout.

Eddies.—Wherever the wind blows across a steep-sided hill or mountain, eddies are likely to be formed, especially on the lee side. In such cases, the direction of the surface wind is approximately opposite to that of the general or prevailing wind, with a calm between them.

Evidently we may consider a steady wind to consist of tubes of flow, in each of which, between fixed cross sections, the quantity of air and its energy remain constant. Furthermore, since thoroughly mixing air brings it to a constant potential temperature, or state of neutral equilibrium, it is clear that there is neither gain nor loss of gravitational energy in these tubes, whatever their inclination. Hence, the total energy is the volume energy, pv, in which p is the pressure and v the volume, and velocity energy $\frac{1}{2}mu^2$ where m is the mass and u its velocity, at the given place along the tube. That is, along each tube, hence, any number of them,

$$pv + \frac{1}{2}mu^2 = \text{a constant}$$

or, dividing by v,

$$p + \frac{1}{2}\rho u^2 = \text{a constant}.$$

Now, experiment shows that the product of the density of air, or other fluid, by the square of its velocity, is greatest where, or close to where, it flows past an obstruction. That is, at this place ρu^2 is a maximum, and therefore p is a minimum.

Hence the atmospheric pressure is reduced, near the crest, on the lee side, of a mountain across which a strong wind is blowing. This reduction of pressure causes air, already in neutral equilibrium, to flow gently up the lee side—a return or eddy wind—and there into the adjacent wind tube, thus maintaining the eddy.

For the practical purpose of the weather forecaster, wind eddies have but little significance, except in one important particular. He must exclude from his forecasting data all reports of wind direction obtained

216

at places where eddies are likely to prevail. Such eddies, however, may be of great importance to the aviator, since they produce, on their forward sides, troublesome down currents and also shallow surface wind which, because oppositely directed to the winds, less, perhaps, than 100 meters above, may render landing at such places difficult or even very dangerous.

Maloja Wind.—The "Maloja" wind, named after the Maloja pass in Switzerland, below which, and for some distance along the valley of the Inn, it is well defined, is only a reverse valley breeze—reverse because such convectional tendency as the insolational heating of the valley in question may produce is more than counteracted by the similar heating of a suitable, and suitably situated, neighboring region. It is the controlling pressure distribution due to this latter heating that locates the updraft and induces the down-valley Maloja wind.

Similarly, the flooding of a basin by gravity winds often produces a forced breeze up a narrow pass, where ordinarily a downcurrent would be expected.

Foehn, Chinook.—The foehn, or chinook, as it generally is called in North America, is a warm, dry wind blowing down a mountain side onto the valleys and plains beyond. It differs from the typical fallwind in being warm, level for level, and not cold, as is the latter, in comparison with the air of surrounding regions. It has been elaborately studied, as is evident from J. Küttner's[1] lengthy article on it, with numerous citations of original literature.

Any system of winds, whether of trade, cyclonic, or other origin, extending to, or near to, the surface and blowing more or less normally across a mountain ridge, necessarily induces upcurrents, dynamically cooled, on the windward side and downcurrents, adiabatically heated, on the lee side, except along the under portions of such eddies as may be produced, where the directions and consequent temperature changes are just the reverse. Therefore:

1. Foehns occur in all seasons.

2. The relative humidity of the foehn is always low.

3. The rise in temperature is greatest when the original vertical temperature gradient is least; hence, greatest, other things being equal, (a) when the upper air is warmest—that is, when there has been precipitation to the windward; (b) when the surface air is coldest—that is, when there has been free night radiation (clear skies) on the lee side; and (c) during winter, when the vertical temperature gradient through the first several hundred meters may be only 4° C., say, per kilometer, instead of the usual 7° to 8° C. of summer.

The inertia of the wind, crossing the mountain, tends to carry it on well above the valley, or plain, beyond, but its drag on the lower

[1] *Phys. der frei. Atmos.*, **25**; 251, 1939.

air, due to viscosity, deflects it downward. Because of this deflection a foehn wind often strikes on the lower slopes, or adjacent region, with great violence, from which, and mainly because of its dynamical heating, it rebounds to higher levels. Along a belt, therefore, well down the mountain, or even a little beyond it, the surface wind may be exceedingly turbulent and violent, while both farther away and also nearer, or on the higher slopes, it is comparatively light. Furthermore, owing to changes in the general direction of the crossing current, or in its strength, or both, the wind belt may shift toward or from, or up or down, the mountain, or even vanish entirely.

During its earlier stages a foehn is often accompanied by a crest cloud, by dissolving scud drawn down out of this cloud, and by a cumulus roll over the rebounding wind; and, a little later, by general precipitation.

Another interesting phenomenon of the foehn is the transmission of sounds from the windward to the leeward side of a mountain, and often miles away, where ordinarily they are not heard at all. The explanation is obvious. The wind, which blows roughly parallel to the slopes, increases rapidly with distance from the surface; hence the sound wave, because it is carried forward in the faster layers more speedily than in the slower, crosses the crest in an approximately vertical position, and then roughly converges, or focuses onto places some distance to the leeward.

Since winds of this origin often are swift, and their dynamical heating pronounced, it follows that under favorable circumstances a very strong foehn may even develop a secondary "low"—on the same side of the mountain, of course, as the center of the primary one.

Tornado.—The tornado, or "twister" of the American prairies, may be defined as a slightly funnel-shaped, hollow, circular column of upward-spiraling winds of destructive velocity. It is the most violent, least extensive, and most sharply defined of all storms.

During the 17 years, 1916–1932, there were, in the United States, 2108 tornadoes that took 4760 lives and destroyed $42,700,000 worth of property.

Some of the normal, but not all of them invariable, circumstances of place and meteorological conditions connected with the occurrence of tornadoes are the following:

1. *Geographic Location.*—Tornadoes occur most frequently in central and southeastern United States, chiefly; next, perhaps, in southern Australia, though Griffith Taylor says, in his "Australian Meteorology," "tornadoes are not common in Australia"; and occasionally in several other parts of the world, except, in general, the tropical regions. The so-called tornado of tropical west Africa appears to be a violent thunderstorm of the squall type. The waterspout is relatively mild, and often, if not usually, of different origin.

2. *Meteorological Location.*—Southeastern section, or, more exactly, east of the wind-shift line, of a cyclone, of moderate to decided intensity.

3. *Kind of Cyclone.*—The trough or V shaped, the kind productive of secondary cyclones, is very favorable, especially when the V protrusion points southward, or, more particularly, southwestward. However, tornadoes occur also when this protrusion of the isobars is not conspicuous, if, indeed, present at all, at the surface of the earth.

4. *Other Pressure Distribution.*—A moderate anticyclone to the rear, that is, west or northwest (southwest in the southern hemisphere) of the cyclone, appears to be an invariable condition; but even if this pressure distribution is essential, as we believe it is, to the genesis of the tornado there is no proof of it from statistical evidence alone, since normally the extratropical cyclone has an anticyclone to its rear.

5. *Surface Pressure Gradient in Region of Tornado.*—Usually moderate to steep in comparison with the average cyclone.

6. *Horizontal Temperature Gradient.*—Usually steep along a portion of the border between cyclone and anticyclone.

7. *Previous Wind.*—Moderate to fresh, southerly, often southwest, in the northern hemisphere, similarly in the southern.

8. *Following Wind.*—Moderate to fresh, northerly, often northwest, in the northern hemisphere, similarly in the southern.

9. *Previous Temperature.*—At 8 a.m. 70° or over and increasing.

10. *Following Temperature.*—Distinctly lower than just before the storm.

11. *Previous Humidity.*—Excessive—making the air, at its high temperature, sultry and oppressive, from hours to even days before.

12. *Clouds.*—Heavy cumulonimbus, from which a funnel-shaped cloud depends. Sometimes this cumulus is isolated and very towering, but, when not isolated, often preceded briefly to an hour or longer by mammatocumuli.

13. *Precipitation.*—Rain and, usually, hail, 10 to 30 minutes before; light precipitation at instant of storm (funnel cloud often clearly seen and occasionally photographed); deluge of rain, mixed at times with small hail, shortly after.

14. *Lightning.*—Nearly, or quite, invariably lightning accompanies the tornado, but seldom, if at all, occurs in the funnel cloud.

15. *Sounds.*—There always is a loud rumbling or roaring noise while the whirling pendant cloud is in touch with, or even closely approaches, the earth.

16. *Direction of Tornado Wind.*—Spirally upward around a traveling axis, and in the same sense as the accompanying cyclone—counterclockwise in the northern hemisphere.

17. *Horizontal Velocity of Wind in Tornado.*—Unmeasured, but destructively great.

18. *Vertical Velocity of Wind in Tornado.*—Also unmeasured, but sufficient to carry up pieces of lumber and other objects of considerable weight—say 100 to 200 miles per hour.

19. *Location of Initial and Sustaining Whirl.*—Above, probably close above, the general cloud base.

20. *Velocity of Storm Travel.*—Usually 25 to 40 miles per hour.

21. *Length of Path.*—Anything up to possibly 300 miles, usually 20 to 40 miles.

22. *Direction of Travel.*—Roughly, parallel to travel of the center of the general, or cyclonic, storm, hence usually northeastward in the northern hemisphere, southeastward in the southern.

23. *Width of Storm.*—Anything from 40 to 50 feet up to, rarely, a mile or even more, but averaging around 1000 feet. Many are only 500 to 600 feet across and others, as stated, even much less.

24. *Number.*—Usually several, often in groups, in connection with the same low-pressure system, and on the same day.

25. *Time of Year.*—Mainly spring, and early to midsummer, but occasionally also at other seasons.

26. *Time of Day.*—Usually midafternoon, or 3 to 5 p.m.

All the foregoing meteorological conditions are inferred from observations at the surface of the earth, and not in the free air 1 or 2 kilometers above the surface, where the tornado seems to have its origin. Data from this obviously desirable upper level appear to be very scanty. However, through the kind assistance of the Climatological and the Aerological divisions of the United States Weather Bureau, twenty-six cases were found where observations by sounding balloon or kite, or both, were made less, to much less, than 6 hours from the time of and nearer—some far closer—than 100 miles from, a tornado. These observations indicate (they are too few to prove anything) that when tornadoes occur the wind, whatever its value at the surface, is strong (around 20 to 25 meters per second or, say, 50 miles per hour) at the height of 1 to 2 kilometers. In some cases the direction of the wind is nearly constant throughout at least the lower 2 kilometers, the approximate depth explored. Sometimes it backs, turns counter-clockwise, perhaps 30°, but usually veers at this height, roughly 45°.

Mid-air temperature inversions appear to be quite common and the lapse rates next above them very rapid, often nearly, or quite, of adiabatic value. In short, so far as one can infer from these few observations, the atmosphere in the neighborhood of a tornado seems to be unusually stratified, and tending to become unstable at one or more levels.

As implied, several of the above circumstances and meteorological conditions are only usually, and not invariably, associated with the tornado, nor perhaps are they all that have any importance in respect to its genesis and maintenance. Nevertheless, they are among the more conspicuous and sufficient, it would seem, to restrict explanations to those that contain elements, at least, of the truth.

a. Since the linear velocity in whirls frictionally created between passing currents, whether liquid or gaseous, cannot exceed that of these currents relative to each other, it follows that the tornado, whose winds far surpass this limiting value, is generated in some way that is not purely mechanical.

b. The only other way by which vortical motion is produced, naturally, in the atmosphere, is that of drawing closer together, through vertical convection, masses of air, the algebraic sum of whose angular momenta, about the center of that convection, is different from zero; whether positive, rotation in one sense, or negative, with opposite rotation. Here the principle of conservation of angular momentum, or conservation of areas, is operative, by virtue of which the linear velocity, except as reduced by friction, so increases as the distance from the center decreases that the product of this distance and the velocity is a constant.

In this way, and in no other, persistent whirls in the air of great linear velocity can, and do, occur naturally where the interference, frictional and turbulent, is quite small. That is, in the free air, from where they may, and often do, feed down to the surface.

c. The production of a violent whirl in the air, through the conservation of angular momentum, requires (1) a central or localized vertical convection at the level at which the whirl begins; and (2) that the currents drawn into the ascending column have initially either different directions, or different speeds if originally in the same direction. Local convection does not produce rotation in still air, nor in wind that has the same direction and speed throughout except, in each case, to the slight extent caused by the rotation of the earth. The ordinary dust whirl is induced by convection over a surface, across which the flow of air is so disturbed as to miss the center of convection and start a spin. This spin may be in either sense, clockwise or the contrary, from which it follows, as also from other considerations, that the dust whirl and the tornado, which always turns in the same sense, are radically different in origin.

d. Kite, pilot balloon, and cloud observations all show that the winds 1 or 2 kilometers above the surface are moderately swift, in the neighborhood of a tornado, and increased over the surface winds more than commonly is the case at that level. These observations also indicate that the rapid velocity increase frequently, at least, begins at some intermediate level where a greater or less change in direction also usually occurs.

We infer, therefore, that there are adjacent, presumably superjacent, currents of air of different sources where and whenever tornadoes are likely to occur.

e. From the rather common occurrence of the mammatocumulus cloud shortly before the development of a tornado, it would seem that, at the level at which this storm originates, there is a superjacent wind, cold enough to be unstable with reference to the air just below it. From this fact, and from the approximate to full adiabatic lapse rates that have been found at such times at the cloud level, we infer that on these occasions vigorous convection might be expected—started by gravity instability, and intensified by vapor condensation. Furthermore, from the lightning that accompanies the tornado, we are sure that there, then, is strong convection within the clouds, and, from the hail that so frequently falls well to the front of a tornado, it is evident that the convection is up to great heights and into strong winds.

Now, the southerly winds over the lower and mid-Mississippi Valley, especially, often have rather small lapse rates, very much less than the adiabatic, and, therefore, are comparatively stable, or difficult to upset convectionally. Over such lower air an upper wind might blow, sinking down only to that level at which its adiabatic warming brings it to the temperature of the under air at that same height. Presumably, then, in this region the mid-level winds of the southeastern portion of an anticyclone to the west or northwest may flow out over a lower stratum of southerly winds belonging to the adjacent cyclone. In this case there would be a cold front, or squall line, in mid air, a kilometer, perhaps, above the surface, with a shift of wind direction similar to that which, under otherwise like circumstances, occurs at the ground when the anticyclonic air extends to the surface, as it usually does.

When the cold front is along the ground the slope of the under surface of the anticyclonic wedge, in the direction normal to this front, is very gentle—a rise of 1 or 2 kilometers, say, in 100. This condition is due largely to the fact that the velocity of the air near the surface is much less than that at a considerable height, owing, of course, to turbulence and surface drag. Along the mid-air cold front, however, the slope between the two wind systems, the cyclonic and the anticyclonic, presumably is much steeper, as there is no excessive drag at a strata interface.

If now, a cold front should occur, as occasionally one does,[1] some distance above the surface of the earth, it is probable that local convections would develop here and there along it, much as, under similar circumstances, they do along the squall line. Owing, however, to the steeper ascent of the interface between the two wind systems there would be this difference: Convection from the ground, the usual case, would be of overrun and entrapped, or, more commonly, of forward-driven, masses of the warmer and humid cyclonic air, the first up *through* and the second out in front of the anticyclonic air above, and would not in either case produce much vorticity no matter how different the directions of the

[1] LICHTBLAU, S., *M. W. R.*, **64**; 414, 1936.

two systems of winds. On the other hand, local convection on a mid-air cold front could be *between* the two wind systems (their interface being steep, as explained) and consist of roughly equal parts from each.

This convection would produce rotation at cloud level, at least in those cases in which the cyclonic wind had a strong southerly component and the anticyclonic, at the same height, a considerable northerly component. Such winds, if both are being carried bodily with the same velocity, as may be the case, eastward, or, for that matter, along any other course (the principle is general), might differ in direction over the surface of the earth, that is, as seen from the surface of the earth, by almost any angle from 0° to 180°, as determined by the values of their north-south and east-west components, and yet, *with reference to each other, have exactly opposite directions*—be flowing beside and past each other at the same level. In this case they would tend to develop swirls along their more or less vertical interface, of the nature of minature secondary cyclones, after the fashion of the greater cyclones along any polar "front." In either case, that is, whether convection were of the squall-line type or started by a swirl like a miniature cyclone, the heat liberated by the incident condensation would increase the convection and consequent spin. This spin, in turn, would drag in the air from lower and lower levels until the surface of the earth was reached. Furthermore, since the rotation of the earth requires the southerly wind to lie east of the northerly, this spin has always to be counter-clockwise in the Northern Hemisphere and clockwise in the southern.

Where the two streams, cyclonic and anticyclonic, are drawn together, presumably at or about the cloud level, the velocity of the whirling wind tends to follow the law of the conservation of areas, or to be inversely proportional to the radius of curvature. At lower levels, however, where the spin is the result of a drag from above, the decrease of velocity with increase of radius appears to be much more rapid. Indeed the path of destruction shows so little shading off that generally it is described as being sharply defined, a condition that proves the wind velocity to drop off exceedingly rapidly with increase of distance beyond this boundary.

A familiar detail of the tornado is its pendent, funnel-shaped cloud, caused, as is well known, by the dynamical or expansional cooling of the air under the decreased pressure within the vortex. This decrease of pressure causes houses, in a measure, to burst open as the tornado passes over them. However, it is not very great, probably of the order of one-tenth of an atmosphere, the value observed in one particular case,[1] as is readily computed from the spin of the vortex and the rapid decrease of velocity beyond the path of destruction.

But the pressure inside the vortex tube is less than that on the outside, and how that difference can persist—why the tube does not quickly fill

[1] BAIER, J., *M. W. R.*, **24**; 332, 1896.

and the rotation dissipate in eddy turbulence—needs to be explained. Of course the whirling wall furnishes a dynamical partition across which air cannot flow into the low pressure space; but the tornado funnel is not a closed vortex with a whirling partition shielding every point. It is openended, above all the time, and below, also, at first. Assume, then, a spin in the free air. Its axis will be roughly vertical, since the air feeding it necessarily flows in, approximately, horizontally. The upward push on the ascending air above the center of the whirl will be partially, but not wholly, balanced by the decreases of pressure, beneath it and over it, incident to the gyration. Above the level at which the initially rotating air is evicted, other air will flow in, because of the low pressure at the center, and by its consequent spin sustain, in large part, the diminished pressure below. This effectually closes the upper end of the tube, but leaves the lower quite open. Hence, air flows into the lower end, owing to the decreased pressure immediately above it, and in so doing acquires acceleration, and, therefore, reaction, thus becoming an inertia plug, as it were, that prevents immediate filling. This inflowing air is spun around by the gyration above and finally evicted from the upper portion of the column. But, always, there is a flow into the lower end, so long as it is in the free air, as well as toward and spirally up about the axis. Hence, if the initial or sustaining, rotation is both violent and persistent, the vortex burrows lower and lower until it reaches the surface. In this final state the low pressure within the tube is sustained by a dynamical wall on the sides, a combination gravity and dynamical cap above, and the earth beneath.

The above, or something more or less like it, appears to be the physical explanation of the origin of the tornado. But if so, why, then, one asks, are tornadoes so much more frequent in the central Mississippi Valley than elsewhere, and why most frequent there in the spring of the year? Because there, and especially at that season, certain of the conditions listed above are best developed and most frequent; such as very humid southerly winds (having come from over the Gulf of Mexico); a strongly encroaching anticyclone to the west or northwest, and the formation of a mid-air cold front. Why, also, one further asks, does the tornado rarely occur in tropical countries? Because, as explained above, it is a joint product of cyclone and anticyclone, one of which, the anticyclone, is, there, practically unknown.

A complete discussion of the tornado, obviously, would involve the liberal use of vortex equations. But the data necessary to such a discussion are not available, nor is the theory of the vortex in viscous fluids sufficiently developed to be readily applicable to this case.

Waterspout.—When a tornado goes to sea it becomes a waterspout and when a waterspout runs ashore it becomes, if violent, a tornado; if of small dimensions and not severe, probably just a whirlwind—the nomenclature is not fixed. In many cases the waterspout, or whirlwind at sea strong enough to produce a cloud column, evidently is produced in exactly the same way as the tornado; that is, by the convectional drawing together of oppositely flowing currents along a windshift line, or cold front, in the free air, where they frequently occur in families. Among the more favorable places for the formation of sea tornadoes are: Off the east coast of the United States, at the time of an encroaching cold wave; off the coast of China and Japan, under similar conditions; and the Gulf of Mexico. Waterspouts thus produced should rotate counterclockwise in the northern hemisphere and clockwise in the southern. Many spouts, however, rotate in the opposite sense and must, therefore, be formed by the convectional inflow of winds of anticyclonic movement with reference to each other. Now, both this movement and the cyclonic occur, and with about equal frequency, in the conflicting winds off the westernmost coast of Africa just north of the equator, along the west coast of Central America and southern Mexico, and in the wake of island peaks; and in all such places the spout of either rotation is common, owing to the instabilities occurring there in the atmosphere and the resulting convections. Such spouts are conical, with point downward, because the temperature decreases, and the dew point is neared, both with increase of height and approach to the center of the whirl.

The fair-weather spout, whether at sea or over a lake, usually is solitary, or at least sporadic, and has an entirely different origin. It starts from the surface and grows upward, substantially as the dust whirl, and not aloft, as do all tornadoes and most waterspouts. As is well known, a superheated surface layer of air leads to a dust whirl wherever it rises locally over land. Similarly, a quiet superheated layer of air over water would also produce, here and there, rising, rotating columns, of which an occasional one might be of waterspout size. But, the surface air over water does not become appreciably superheated, except where cold air has drifted in, a phenomenon at least rare over tropical oceans. When both the atmosphere and the water are quite warm, however, the lower layer of air becomes very humid, and that is just as effective in inducing convection as increase of temperature. For instance, a lapse rate of 1° C. per 140 meters would give, so far as temperature is concerned, a very stable atmosphere; but if at the same time the vapor lapse in the lower air should be 2 mm. pressure per 100 meters, the thermal stability would be more than neutralized by the vapor instability for temperatures of 15° C. and over. Clearly, then, high humidity of the surface, as well as high temperature, can induce local rotating columns of ascending air. Furthermore, such a column, being highly humid, might well lead to the production of a cumulus cloud at its top, and even a thundershower, precisely as occasionally does occur in connection with the fair weather waterspout.

The waterspout appears to be a hollow tube because, so far as cloud is concerned, the only visible material present, it is hollow. The droplets do not form until the decrease of pressure, through its cooling effect, is sufficient, as determined by the humidity, and, when formed, are kept away from the center of the vortex by their "centrifugal force." Hence the spout is both hollow and of limited cross section.

A few double-walled waterspouts have been reported, indicating, possibly, the presence of two sets of condensation nuclei, one more hygroscopic than the other.

CHAPTER XIII

ATMOSPHERIC CIRCULATION (*Continued*)

WINDS ADVERSE TO AVIATION

Several local winds, to which but little attention formerly was given, so little indeed that some of them are without special names, are now important through the art of aviation. These are here grouped together, however different in origin and type they may be, for the convenience of any one who may have occasion to consider them.

General Statement.—Every aviator experiences, in the course of his flights, many abrupt drops and numerous more or less severe jolts. The cause of the first—the sudden drops—he has grouped together and called "holes in the air," "air pockets," and the like, while to the latter he has given such names as "bumps," "dunts," etc. There are, of course, no holes, in the ordinary sense of the term, in the atmosphere— no vacuous regions—but at various places in the atmosphere there are, occasionally, conditions which, so far as flying is concerned, are very like unto holes. Neither is the air ever "full of bumps," in the sense of spots of abnormal density, but often it is turbulent in such manner as to render flying rough and uncomfortable. Both sets of atmospheric movements, those that produce appreciable drops and those that cause jolts, are indeed real; and the former, because of their general interest and practical importance, will be considered in some detail. The latter, being of little importance, will be mentioned only incidentally. Furthermore, there are no "pockets of noxious gas." No single gas, and no other likely mixture of gases, has, at ordinary temperatures and pressures, the same density as atmospheric air. Therefore, a pocket of foreign gas, in the atmosphere, would almost certainly either bob up like a balloon, or sink like a stone in water. It is possible, of course, as will be explained a little later, to run into columns of rising air that may contain objectionable gases and odors, but these columns are quite different from anything likely to be suggested by the expression "pocket of gas."

The above are some of the things that, fortunately, do not exist. The following, however, are some that do exist, and that produce sudden drops; usually small, so as to give only a negligible bump, but occasionally great enough to involve, when near the surface, an element of danger. For clearness and simplicity these several kinds of air movements will be provisionally classified under terms suggested by water analogies.

Air Fountains.—A mass of air rises, or falls, according as its density is less, or greater, respectively, than that of the surrounding atmosphere, just as, and for the same reason that, a cork bobs up in water and a stone goes down. Hence, any body of air is driven up whenever it is warmer and therefore lighter (less dense) than the surrounding air at the same level; and as the atmosphere is heated, mainly, through contact with the surface of the earth, which in turn has been heated by sunshine, it follows that these convection currents, or vertical uprushes, are most numerous during calm summer afternoons.

The turbulence of some of these rising masses is evident from the numerous rolls and billows of the large cumulus clouds they produce, within, and immediately beneath, which the air is always rough, however smooth it may be either above or considerably below; and it is obvious that the same sort of turbulence, probably on a smaller scale, occurs near the tops of such columns, also, as do not rise to the cloud level. Further, when the air is exceptionally quiet, a rising column may be rather sharply separated from the surrounding quiescent atmosphere, as has often been reported by aviators, and as evidenced by the closely-adhering tall pillars of smoke occasionally seen to rise from chimneys.

The velocity of ascent of such fountains of air, whether continuous, as in the dust whirl, or only intermittent, is at times surprisingly great. Measurements on pilot balloons, and also measurements taken in manned balloons, have shown vertical velocities, both up and down, of more than 3 meters per second (600 feet per minute). The soaring of large birds is a further proof of an upward velocity of the same order of magnitude, while the formation, in cumulus clouds, of hailstones of various sizes shows that uprushes of 10 to 12 meters per second (2000 to 2400 feet per minute), and occasionally much greater, not merely may, but actually do, occur.

There are, then, "air fountains" of considerable velocity whose sides, at times and places, are almost as sharply separated from the surrounding atmosphere as are the sides of a fountain of water, and it is altogether possible for the swiftest of these to produce effects on an aeroplane more or less disconcerting to the pilot. The trouble may occur:

1. On grazing the column, with one wing of the machine in the rising and the other in the non-rising air; a condition that interferes with lateral stability, and produces a sudden shock both on entering the column and on leaving it.

2. On plunging squarely into the column; thus suddenly increasing the angle of attack, the pressure on the wings, and the angle of ascent.

3. On abruptly emerging from the column; thereby causing a sudden decrease in the angle of attack and also abruptly losing the supporting force of the rising mass of air.

4. As a result of rotation, if rapid, as it sometimes is, of the rising air.

That flying with one wing in the column and the other out must interfere with lateral stability and possibly cause a drop is obvious, but the effects of plunging squarely into, or out of, the column require a little further consideration, as does also the effect of rotation.

Let an aeroplane that is flying horizontally pass from quiescent air squarely into a rising column. The front of the machine may be lifted, as it enters the column, a little faster than the rear. If so, and, in any case, owing to the upward trend of the air, the angle of attack—that is, the angle which the plane of the wing, or plane of the wing chords, makes with the apparent wind direction—will be slightly increased. This will carry the machine to higher levels, which, of itself, is not important. If, however, the angle of attack is so changed by the pilot as to keep the machine while in the rising column at a constant level, and if, with this new adjustment, the rising column is abruptly left, a corresponding descent must begin. But even this is not necessarily harmful. Probably the real danger under such circumstances arises from *overadjustments* by the novice in his hasty attempt to correct for the abrupt changes, instead of letting his ship mainly ride out the inequalities.

If the rising column is in fairly rapid rotation (tornadoes are excluded —they can be seen and must be avoided), as sometimes is the case, disturbances may be produced in several ways. If the column is entered on its approaching side, the head-on wind may so decrease the velocity of the plane with reference to the surrounding air that on emerging there necessarily must be a greater or less drop, as explained below under the caption "wind layers." On the other hand, if entered on the receding side there will be a tendency to drop within the column, which may, or may not, be fully compensated for by the vertical component of the wind. Finally, such a rotating column, especially, perhaps, if crossed near its outer boundary, may quickly change the orientation of the plane, and, therefore, the action on it of the surrounding air.

None of these conditions, however, except when encountered near the surface of the earth, is likely to involve any appreciable element of danger to the skilled aviator. But this does not justify ignoring them— no beginner is skilful, and all must start from, and return to, the surface.

Rising columns, of the nature just described, occur most frequently during clear summer days and over barren ground. They also occur, even to surprising altitudes, over roads, sandspits, and other places of similar contrast to the surrounding areas. Isolated hills, especially short or conical ones, should be avoided on low flights during warm, still days, for on such occasions their sides are certain to be warmer than the adjacent atmosphere at the same level, and hence act like so many chimneys in producing updrafts. Rising air columns occur less frequently, and are less vigorous, over water, and over level green vegetation, than elsewhere. They are also less frequent during the early forenoon than in the hotter portion of the day, and are practically absent before sunrise and at such times as the sky is wholly covered with clouds.

Although, as just explained, rising currents are certain to be more or less turbulent and "bumpy," they, nevertheless, are great aids to climbing. Hence, the experienced aviator often deliberately gets into them, as do soaring birds, when making a quick ascent.

Air Sinks.—The air sink, obviously, is the counterpart of the air fountain, and is most likely to occur at the same time. Indeed, it is certain to occur over a small pond, lake, or clump of trees in the midst of a hot and rather barren region. These cooler spots localize the return or down branches of the convection currents, and generally should be avoided by the aviator when flying at low levels. Similarly, on calm, clear summer days, down currents nearly always obtain at short distances off-shore, over rivers, and along the edges of forests. This type of down current, however, rarely is swift, except in connection with thunderstorms, and, therefore, while it may render flying difficult, or even impossible with a slow machine, it seldom involves much danger.

Air Cataracts.—The air cataract is caused by the flow of a dense, or, what comes to the same thing, a heavily laden surface layer of air up to, and then over, a precipice, much as a waterfall is formed. Such cataracts are most frequent among the barren mountains of high latitudes. The cold surface winds catch up, and become weighted with, great quantities of dry snow, and then, because of both this extra weight and their high density, often rush down the lee sides of steep mountains with the roar and the force of a hurricane. But the violence of such winds clearly is all on the lee side and of shallow depth. Hence, where such conditions prevail, the aviator should keep well above the drifting snow or other aerial ballast, and, if possible, strictly avoid any attempt to land within the cataract itself.

Cloud Currents.—It frequently happens that a stratum of broken or detached clouds, especially of the cumulus type, is a region of turbulent currents, however quiet the air at both lower and higher levels. In the case of cumuli, at least, the currents within the clouds are upward, and those in the open spaces, therefore, generally downward. Also each branch of this circulation is more or less turbulent. Hence, while passing through such a cloud layer the aviator is likely to encounter comparatively rough flying, though, owing to the height, of very little danger.

Aerial Cascades.—The term "aerial cascade" may, with some propriety, be applied to the wind as it sweeps down the lee of a hill or mountain. Ordinarily, it does not come very near the ground, where, indeed, there frequently is a countercurrent, but remains at a considerable elevation. Other things being equal, it is always most pronounced when the wind is at right angles to the direction of the ridge and when the mountain is rather high and steep. The swift downward sweep of the air when the wind is strong may carry a passing aeroplane with it, and lead observers, if not the pilot, to fancy that a hole has been encountered, where, of course, there is nothing of the kind. Indeed, such cascades should be entirely harmless so long as the aviator keeps his machine well above the surface and thus out of the treacherous eddies presently to be discussed.

Wind Layers.—For one reason or another, it often happens that adjacent layers of air differ abruptly from each other in temperature, humidity, and density, and, therefore, as explained by Helmholtz, may, and often do, glide over each other in much the same manner that air flows over water, and with the same general wave-producing effect. These air waves are *seen* only when the humidity at the interface is such that the slight difference in temperature between the crests and troughs is sufficient to keep the one cloud capped and the other free from condensation. In short, the humidity condition must be just right. Clearly then, though such clouds often occur in beautiful parallel rows (Fig. 94), adjacent wind strata of different velocities, and their consequent air billows, must be of far more frequent occurrence.

Consider now the effect on an aeroplane as it passes from one such layer into another. For the sake of illustration, let the propeller be at rest and the machine be making a straightaway glide to earth, and let it suddenly pass into a lower layer of air moving in the same horizontal direction as the machine and with the same velocity. This, of course, is an extreme case, but it is by no means an impossible one. Instantly on entering the lower layer, under the conditions just described, all dynamical support must cease, and with it all power of guidance. A fall, for at least a considerable distance, is absolutely inevitable, and if near the earth, perhaps a disastrous one. To all intents and purposes, a "hole" has been run into.

The reason for the fall will be understood when it is recalled that the pressure of any ordinary wind is very nearly proportional to the square of its velocity with respect to the thing against which it is blowing. Hence, for a given inclination of the wings the lift on the aeroplane is approximately proportional to the square of the velocity of the machine with reference, *not* to the ground, but to the *air* in which it happens to be at the instant under consideration. If, then, it glides, with propellers at rest, into a wind stratum that is blowing in the same horizontal direction and with the same velocity, it is in exactly the condition it would be if dropped from rest at the top of a monument in still air. It inevitably must fall unless inherent stability, or skill of the pilot, brings about a new glide after additional velocity has been acquired as the result of a considerable drop.

Of course such an extreme case must be of rare occurrence, but cases less extreme are met with frequently. On passing into a current where the velocity of the wind is more nearly that of the aeroplane, and in the same direction, part of the supporting force is instantly lost, and a corresponding drop or dive becomes at once inevitable. Ordinarily, however, this is a matter of small consequence, for the relative speed necessary to support is soon reacquired, especially if the engine is in full operation. Occasionally, though, the loss in support may be large, and occur so near the ground as to be more or less dangerous.

If the new wind layer is against, and not with, the machine, an increase instead of a decrease in the sustaining force is the result, and little occurs beyond a mere change in the horizontal speed with reference to the ground, and a slowing up of the rate of descent.

All the above discussion of the effect of wind layers on aeroplanes is on the assumption that they flow in parallel directions. Ordinarily however, they flow more or less across each other. Hence the aviator, on passing out of one of them into the other, as a rule, has to contend with more than a disconcertingly abrupt change in the supporting force. That is, on crossing the interface between wind sheets, an aviator, in addition to suffering a partial loss of support, usually has to contend with the turmoil of a choppy aerial sea in which "bumps," at least, seem to abound everywhere.

Wind strata, within ordinary flying levels, are most frequent during weather changes, especially as fine weather is giving way to stormy. On such occasions, then, one should be on the watch for these strata, even to the extent of making test soundings for them with pilot balloons. It is also well, at such times, to avoid making great changes in altitude, because, since wind strata remain, roughly, parallel to the surface of the earth, the greater the change in altitude, the greater the risk of passing from one stratum to another and thereby encountering at least a "bump," and, perhaps, a "hole." Also, to avoid the possibility of losing support, when too low to dive, and for other good reasons, landings and launchings should be made, if practicable, squarely in the face of the *surface* wind.

Wind Billows.—It was stated, above, that when one layer of air runs over another of different density, billows are set up between them, as is often shown by windrow clouds. However, the warning clouds are comparatively seldom present; hence, even the cautious aviator may, with no evidence of danger before him, take the very level of the air billows themselves, and before getting safely above or below them, encounter one or more sudden changes in wind velocity and direction due, in part, to the eddylike or rolling motion within the waves, with chances in each case of being suddenly deprived of a large portion of the requisite sustaining force. There may be perfect safety in either layer, but, unless headed just right, there necessarily is some risk in going from one to the other. Hence, flying at the billow level, since it would necessitate frequent transitions of this nature, should be avoided.

When the billows are within 300 meters, say, or less, of the earth (often the case during winter owing to the occurrence then of cold surface air with warmer air above) they are apt to be very turbulent, just as, and for much the same reason that, waves in shallow water are turbulent. For this reason, presumably, winter flying sometimes is surprisingly rough—the air very "bumpy." Fortunately, however, it is easy to determine by the aid of a suitable station barograph whether or not billows are prevalent in the low atmosphere, since they produce frequent (5 to 12 per hour, roughly) pressure changes, usually of 0.1 mm. to 0.3 mm. at the surface, as shown by Fig. 69.

Wind Gusts.—Near the surface of the earth the wind is always in a turmoil, owing to friction, and to obstacles of all kinds that interfere with the free flow of the lower layers of the atmosphere and thereby allow the next higher layers to plunge forward in irregular fits, swirls, and gusts with all sorts of irregular velocities and in every direction. Indeed, the actual velocity of the wind near the surface of the earth often, and abruptly, varies from second to second by more than its full average value, and the greater the average velocity, the greater, in approximately the same ratio, are the irregularities or differences in the successive momentary velocities. This is well shown by pressure-tube traces, of which Fig. 42 is a fine example.

Clearly, the lift on an aeroplane flying either with or against a gusty wind is correspondingly erratic, and may vary between such wide limits that the aviator will find himself in a veritable nest of "holes" out of which it is difficult to rise, at least with a slow machine, and sometimes dangerous to try. As the turmoil due to the horizontal winds rapidly decreases, however, with increase of elevation, and as the aviator's safety depends upon steady air conditions, or upon the velocity of his machine, with reference to the atmosphere, and not with reference to the ground, it is obvious that the windier it is, the higher, in general, the minimum level at which he should fly.

Probably, however, the chief disturbance due to gusty wind—excessive tipping and consequent side slipping—occurs, not during straightaway flying, to which the above discussion applies, but as the aviator turns at low levels, from flying against the gusts, to flying with them. This is not owing to change in direction, since the velocity of an aeroplane with reference to the air, and therefore the sustaining force, is wholly independent of the velocity of either with reference to any third object, the surface of the earth, for instance. It may be, and presumably usually is, caused as follows: The aviator starts turning, suppose, while in, and facing, a relatively slow-moving portion of air. On banking, the plane is tipped with its under side more or less against the wind, whereupon the *higher* wing often runs into, or for brief intervals is caught by, a much swifter current than that into which the lower wing dips. Numerical values are not at hand, but the phenomenon of overrunning gusts is familiar from the action of winds on isolated tall trees. This obviously increases the tip, and, in extreme cases, sufficiently to induce a dangerous side slip.

On the other hand, when turning from flying with to flying against the wind, the higher wing catches the increased impact on its upper side. Hence, in this case, the result is merely a temporary flattening of the bank, and a consequent skid of but little danger.

Gusts that envelop the whole of an aeroplane while turning obviously affect the lift, as above explained, and even so, to some extent, when the path of the wind is at right angles to the course of the plane, but in this latter case seldom sufficiently to be of much importance.

Wind Eddies.—Just as eddies and whirls exist in every stream of water, from tiny rills to the great rivers and even the ocean currents, wherever the banks are such as greatly to change the direction of flow, and wherever there is a pocket of considerable depth and extent on either side, and as similar eddies, but with horizontal instead of vertical axes, occur at the bottoms of streams where they flow over ledges that produce abrupt changes in the levels of their beds, so, too, and for the same general reasons, horizontal eddies occur in the atmosphere with rotation proportional, roughly, to the strength of the wind. These are most pronounced on the lee sides of cuts, cliffs, and steep mountains, but often occur also, to a less extent, on the windward sides of such places.

The air at the top and bottom of such whirls is moving in diametrically opposite directions—at the top with the parent or prevailing wind, at the bottom against it—and since they are close to the earth they may, therefore, as explained under "wind layers," be the source of decided danger. There may be some danger also at the forward side of the eddy where the downward motion is greatest.

When the wind is blowing strongly, landings should not be made, if at all avoidable, on the lee sides of, and close to, steep mountains, hills, bluffs, or even large buildings; for these are the favorite haunts, as just explained, of treacherous vortices. The whirl is best avoided by landing in an open place some distance from bluffs and large obstructions, or, if the obstruction is a hill, on the top of the hill itself. If a landing to one side is necessary, however, and the aviator has a choice of sides, other things being equal, he should take the *windward* and not the *lee* side. Finally, if a landing close to the lee side be compulsory he should, if possible, head up the hill with *sufficient velocity* to offset any probable loss of support due to an eddy current in the same direction. He could, of course, avoid loss of velocity with reference to the air, and hence loss of support, by heading along the hill—that is, along the axis of the vortex —but this gain would be at the expense of the dangers incident to landing in a side or cross wind. His only other alternative, heading down the hill, might be correct so far as the direction of the surface wind is concerned, but it probably would entail a long run on the ground and its consequent danger.

Eddies of a very different type, relatively small and so turbulent as to have no well-defined axis of rotation, are formed, as is well known, by a flow of strong winds past the side or corner of a building, steep cliff, and the like. In reality, such disturbances are, perhaps, more of the "breaker" type, presently to be discussed, than like smoothly-flowing vortices, and should be avoided whenever the wind is above a light breeze.

Air Torrents.—Just as water torrents are due to drainage down steep slopes, so, too, gravity winds strong enough to be called "air torrents" owe their origin to drainage down steep, narrow valleys. Whenever the surface of the earth begins to cool through radiation, or otherwise, the air in contact with it becomes correspondingly chilled and, because of its increased density, flows away to lower levels except when held in check, or even driven up, by opposing winds. Hence, when the weather is clear, and there is no counter wind, there is certain to be air drainage down almost any steep valley during the late afternoon and most of the night. When several such valleys run into a common one, like so many tributaries to a stream, and especially when the upper reaches contain snow, and the whole section is devoid of forest, the aerial river is likely to become torrential in nature along the lower reaches of the drainage channel.

A flying machine attempting to land in the mouth of such a valley after the air drainage is well begun is in danger of going from relatively quiet air into an atmosphere that is moving with considerable velocity, at times amounting almost to a gale. If one must land at such a place and time, he should head up the valley so as to face the wind. If he heads down the valley and thereby runs with the wind, he will, on passing into the swift air, lose his support, or much of it, for reasons already explained, and correspondingly drop.

Air Breakers.—The term "air breakers" is used here in analogy with water breakers as a general name for the rolling, dashing, and choppy winds that accompany thunderstorm conditions. They often are of such violence, up, down, and sideways, in any and every direction, that an aeroplane in their grasp is likely to have as uncontrolled and disastrous a landing as would be the case in an actual hole of the worst kind.

Fortunately, "air breakers" usually give abundant and noisy warnings, and hence the cautious aviator seldom need be, and, as a matter of fact, seldom is, caught in so dangerous a situation. However, more than one disaster is attributable to just such turbulent winds as these— air breakers.

This class of winds must be avoided also by the balloon when near the surface, and should be even when high up. Indeed the heaviest going in the cruise of a dirigible normally occurs when crossing a squall line—that windshift line, or cold front, that is a feature of every well developed extratropical cyclone—for here thunderstorm convections prevail, always rough, and sometimes dangerous. And these sudden disturbances may be encountered without warning, for often there is no thunder or lightning, and rarely not even a cloud, to give timely signals. Evidently, therefore, the squall line should be crossed only when necessary and then at as great a height as practicable so as to override possibly the whole of the disturbance or, at least, a part of it.

Classification.—The above eleven types of atmospheric conditions may conveniently be divided into two groups with respect to the method by which they force an aeroplane to drop.

1. *The Vertical Group.*—All those conditions of the atmosphere, such as air fountains, sinks, cataracts, cloud currents, cascades, breakers (in places), and eddies (forward side), that, in spite of full speed ahead with reference to the *air*, make it difficult or impossible for the aviator to maintain his level, belong to a common class and depend for their effect upon a vertical component, up or down, in the motion of the atmosphere itself. Whenever the aviator, without change of the angle of attack and with a full wind in his face, finds his machine rapidly sinking, and not ice coated, he may be sure that he has run into some sort of a down current. Ordinarily, however, assuming that he is not in the grasp of storm breakers, this condition, bad as it may seem, is of but little danger. The wind cannot blow into the ground, and therefore any down current, however vigorous, must somewhere become a horizontal current in which the aviator may fly away, or land, as he chooses.

2. *The Horizontal Group.*—This group includes all those atmospheric conditions—wind layers, billows, gusts, eddies (central portions), torrents, breakers (in places), and the like—that in spite of full speed ahead with reference to the ground deprive an aeroplane of a portion, at least, of its dynamical support. When this loss of support, due to a running of the wind more or less with the machine, is small, and the elevation sufficient there is but little danger, but on the other hand when the loss is relatively large, especially if near the ground, the chance of a fall is correspondingly great.

CHAPTER XIV

BAROMETRIC FLUCTUATIONS

The pressure of the atmosphere undergoes changes that may be classified as seasonal, regional, storm, "ripple," diurnal, semidiurnal, and tidal. Most of these have already briefly been referred to, but they deserve further and separate consideration.

Seasonal Pressure Changes.—Since the atmosphere both expands and becomes more humid with increase of temperature, and, when cooled, contracts and also loses moisture, it follows that the resulting circulation (due to gravity) decreases the mass of air, and, therefore, its pressure over places at, or near, sea level in any warming region; and increases it, and its pressure at similar levels over cooling regions. Hence, in general, the normal reading of the barometer at sea level is greater during winter than summer. It is not much greater, however—perhaps 3 millimeters on the average—since the viscosity of the atmosphere is too small to enable it to maintain any considerable pressure gradient. This means that about 1 part in 500 of the whole atmosphere, or, roughly, 11×10^{12} tons of air, accumulates across the equator every 6 months in consequence of a seasonal drift; the amount that actually crosses is much greater, since the exchange is a continuous process. At places of high elevation the average actual (not reduced) pressure is *less* during winter than summer, because of the increased density, during the colder season, of the lower air.

The approximate level at which January and July pressures, say, are equal may be computed as follows:

Let the sea-level pressures differ by 2.5 mm. and let the January temperature of the lower air be 20° C. colder than that of July. The pressure difference represents a stratum of the lower air about 27 meters thick, while the temperature difference is, roughly, 0.075 of the absolute temperature. Hence, under the above conditions, the height h at which the January and July pressures are the same is given approximately by the equation:

$$h = \frac{27 \text{ meters}}{0.075} = 360 \text{ meters.}$$

In addition to this seasonal pressure change over the whole of the northern and southern hemispheres, complicated to some extent by local conditions and the shifting of the belts of high pressure, there also are similar, but greater, pressure changes between the continents (high in winter, low in summer) and oceans (high in summer, low in winter) of each hemisphere itself. This pressure swing between continent and ocean is due to the fact that the summer temperature of the land is much higher and its winter temperature much lower than that of the water.

237

Regional Pressure Changes.—The great semipermanent lows and highs often shift, more or less, from their normal positions. These displacements may be in any direction (more frequent in some than in others) and may last for any length of time, from a day or two to a fortnight or even longer. Such pressure changes, whatever their immediate cause, obviously, are not seasonal, since they occur at all times of the year. Neither are they of the migratory storm type, though themselves contributing to the genesis and development of storms and of great importance in the control of storm courses.

Pressure Surge.—This is an approximately equal, and, roughly, simultaneous change of pressure over an extensive area, often covering both a cyclone and an anticyclone; of unknown origin, and only occasionally conspicuous.

Storm Pressure Changes.—The progressive travel of cyclones and anticyclones, or, rather, of cyclonic and anticyclonic conditions, neces-

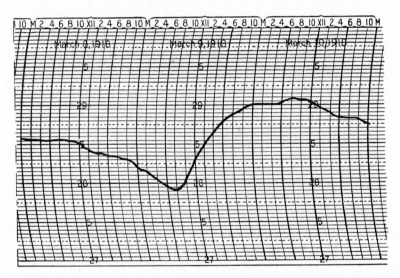

Fɪɢ. 68.—Pressure changes (inches) cyclone to anticyclone, Drexel, Nebraska, altitude 396 meters.

sarily implies a regular order of pressure changes, through a range often amounting to 25 mm. or more, at each point along the storm path (Fig. 68). This type of change, frequent in extratropical regions at all times of the year, seldom lasts longer than 24 to 36 hours, and averages, perhaps, about 18 hours.

A secondary pressure change, due to the rapid rotation of a tornado or a waterspout, very intense but exceedingly brief—averaging less than 1 minute—occasionally develops under special conditions.

Perhaps, too, the pulsatory irregularities of the barometer during a thunderstorm should also be included here. Their origin, however, is entirely different.

Barometric "Ripples."—Small pressure changes, amplitude usually 0.1 to 0.3 mm. and period of 5 to 10 minutes (Fig. 69) (the regularly spaced vertical lines along the trace are hour marks), and continuing for hours, or even days, together, are very common during cold weather. As first demonstrated by Helmholtz,[1] whenever layers of air that differ in density at their interface flow over each other, long billows, analogous

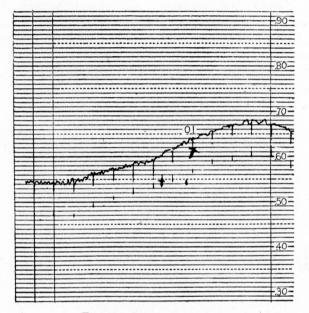

Fig. 69.—Barometric ripples.

to gravity water waves, are produced which conform approximately to the equation,

$$d_1(u - V)^2 + d_2(V - v)^2 = \frac{g\lambda(d_2 - d_1)}{2\pi}$$

in which V is the velocity of wave propagation, d_1 and d_2 the densities of the layers whose velocities are u and v, respectively, g the gravity acceleration, and λ the wave length. If, now, the surface layer is colder than the next above, as it often is during winter, and rather shallow, 100 to 500 meters thick, say, the passage of the air billows, like the passage of waves in shallow water, necessarily produces greater or less corresponding changes in the pressure on the bottom—changes that appear as a series of

[1] *Sitzb. kgl. preuss. Akad. Berlin*, p. 761, 1889; p. 853, 1890. Translated by Cleveland Abbe, "Mechanics of the Earth's Atmosphere," Smithsonian Institution, 1891.

ripples in the record of a sensitive barograph. Furthermore, such shallow air billows, like shallow water waves, doubtless are turbulent—a condition that accounts, presumably, for the surprisingly rough flying the aviator often experiences during winter at low levels—300 meters and less.

During summer, when air billows rarely form near the surface, though frequently at greater altitudes, especially that of the cirrus cloud, neither barometric ripples nor shallow turbulences, of the kind just mentioned, often occur. This, doubtless, is because wave disturbances in air, as in water, do not penetrate far beneath the wave level.

Diurnal, Semidiurnal, and Terdiurnal Pressure Changes.—It has been known, now, for two and a half centuries, that there are more or less regular daily variations in the height of the barometer, culminating in two maxima and two minima during the course of 24 hours. The phenomenon in question is well illustrated by Fig. 70, a direct copy of a

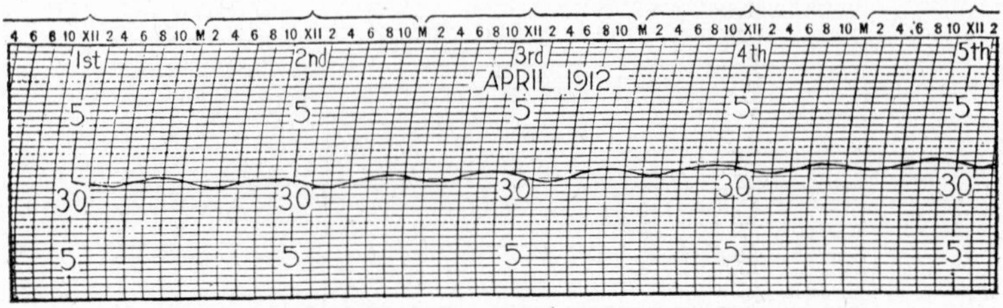

FIG. 70.—Barogram (pressure in inches), Grand Turk Island, West Indies.

barograph trace, obtained Apr. 1 to 5, 1912, on Grand Turk Island, latitude 21° 21' N., longitude 70° 7' W. It is further illustrated, and shown to persist through all the seasons, by Fig. 71, which gives, from hourly values, the actual average daily pressure curve for each month, and, also, for the entire year, as observed at Key West, latitude 24° 33' N., longitude 81° 48' W., during the 14 years, 1891–1904. The actual values are given in the accompanying table.

Probably the earliest observations of these rhythmical daily changes in the atmospheric pressure were made by Doctor Beal[1] during the years 1664–1665, and therefore very soon after the invention, 1643, of the mercurial barometer. Since Beal's discovery, the same observation has been made and puzzled over at every station at which pressure records were kept and studied, but without success in finding for it the complete physical explanation. In speaking of the diurnal and semidiurnal variations of the barometer, Lord Rayleigh[2] says:

The relative magnitude of the latter [semidiurnal variation], as observed at most parts of the earth's surface, is still a mystery, all the attempted explanations being illusory.

[1] *Phil. Trans.*, **9**; 153, 1666.
[2] *Phil. Mag.*, **29**; 179, 1890.

AVERAGE HOURLY READINGS OF THE BAROMETER, 1891–1904, AT KEY WEST, LATITUDE 24° 33′ N., LONGITUDE 81° 48′ W., ELEVATION, 7 METERS

75th Meridian time	January	February	March	April	May	June	July	August	September	October	November	December	Year
Average	764.40	764.08	763.55	762.90	761.58	761.80	763.10	762.20	760.90	760.38	763.05	764.34	762.69
1 a.m.	+.07	+.15	+.17	+.15	+.12	+.02	+.12	+.15	+.14	+.02	+.05	+.05	+.10
2 a.m.	−.11	−.05	−.10	−.14	−.14	−.14	−.14	−.10	−.10	−.21	−.16	−.11	−.13
3 a.m.	−.27	−.30	−.38	−.39	−.34	−.38	−.34	−.30	−.35	−.39	−.34	−.31	−.34
4 a.m.	−.37	−.41	−.48	−.45	−.37	−.41	−.39	−.40	−.42	−.46	−.39	−.38	−.41
5 a.m.	−.39	−.38	−.43	−.34	−.29	−.34	−.34	−.35	−.35	−.34	−.36	−.38	−.36
6 a.m.	−.29	−.20	−.20	−.11	−.06	−.13	−.19	−.15	−.15	−.13	−.16	−.26	−.15
7 a.m.	+.02	+.13	+.12	+.25	+.27	+.17	+.10	+.15	+.19	+.20	+.17	+.08	+.15
8 a.m.	+.40	+.46	+.31	+.50	+.50	+.45	+.32	+.34	+.44	+.50	+.52	+.43	+.43
9 a.m.	+.83	+.82	+.74	+.72	+.65	+.58	+.50	+.54	+.67	+.78	+.83	+.84	+.71
10 a.m.	+1.10	+1.05	+.87	+.82	+.70	+.63	+.57	+.66	+.80	+.88	+.96	+1.04	+.83
11 a.m.	+.98	+1.05	+.89	+.82	+.67	+.65	+.62	+.69	+.77	+.78	+.83	+.81	+.81
Noon	+.54	+.71	+.68	+.62	+.55	+.55	+.52	+.56	+.56	+.42	+.45	+.50	+.56
1 p.m.	−.08	+.18	+.23	+.32	+.29	+.29	+.30	+.31	+.24	−.05	−.11	−.16	−.15
2 p.m.	−.57	−.33	−.20	−.06	−.06	+.00	+.05	−.02	−.20	−.46	−.51	−.59	−.26
3 p.m.	−.80	−.68	−.56	−.50	−.44	−.33	−.31	−.40	−.60	−.72	−.77	−.77	−.56
4 p.m.	−.83	−.86	−.84	−.80	−.75	−.59	−.59	−.71	−.86	−.85	−.87	−.84	−.79
5 p.m.	−.73	−.83	−.89	−.90	−.88	−.74	−.72	−.79	−.86	−.77	−.75	−.74	−.79
6 p.m.	−.57	−.71	−.76	−.85	−.85	−.69	−.65	−.71	−.71	−.59	−.54	−.53	−.69
7 p.m.	−.34	−.48	−.50	−.60	−.60	−.41	−.41	−.45	−.42	−.31	−.26	−.26	−.41
8 p.m.	−.01	−.15	−.18	−.21	−.22	−.08	−.11	−.12	−.05	−.07	−.10	−.05	−.08
9 p.m.	+.19	+.10	+.12	+.12	+.04	+.15	+.12	+.15	+.24	+.32	+.30	+.28	+.17
10 p.m.	+.32	+.26	+.36	+.32	+.27	+.33	+.30	+.34	+.39	+.42	+.40	+.38	+.36
11 p.m.	+.32	+.34	+.41	+.37	+.34	+.40	+.35	+.39	+.39	+.40	+.40	+.38	+.38
Midnight.	+.22	+.26	+.33	+.30	+.27	+.30	+.30	+.28	+.29	+.25	+.25	+.23	+.27

At present the situation is both better and worse. Great progress has been made in the theory of the semidiurnal wave, but it still is far from perfect and, besides, we now are aware of a curious terdiurnal wave, and even suspect a quartodiurnal.

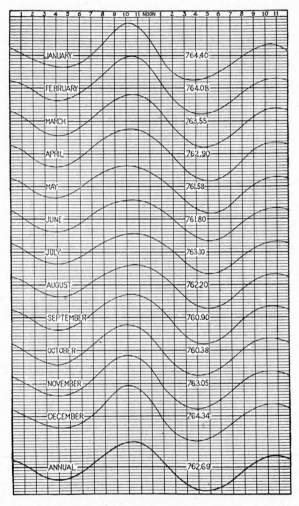

Fig. 71.—Average daily barometric curves, Key West, Florida.

Obviously, the average hourly pressures, for a decade or longer, at any given place, are practically free from storm and other irregular effects, but contain all diurnal and shorter period disturbances that may exist. On being analyzed, these actual data show two well-defined sine curves, a diurnal and a semidiurnal, as illustrated by Fig. 72,[1] each

[1] BENNETT, *Monthly Weather Review*, **34**; 528, 1906.

of which requires a special explanation. Higher harmonics of small amplitude also have been found.

Diurnal Pressure Changes.—There are two classes of well-defined, 24-hour pressure changes. One obtains at places of considerable elevation and is marked by a barometric maximum during the warmest hours and minimum during the coldest. The other applies to low, especially sea level, stations and is the reverse of the above, the maximum occurring during the coldest hours and the minimum during the warmest.

The first class of changes just mentioned, the one that concerns elevated stations, is due, essentially, to volume expansion and contraction of the atmosphere caused by heating and cooling respectively. Thus, the lower atmosphere over that side of the earth which is exposed to insolation becomes more or less heated, and, therefore, because of the resulting

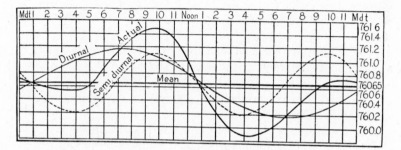

Fig. 72.—Average daily barometric curve and its components, Washington, D. C. (*After W. J. Bennett.*)

expansion, its center of mass is correspondingly raised. Conversely, during the night the atmosphere cools and contracts and the center of mass is proportionately lowered. Hence, so far as this effect alone is concerned, a mountain station, 1000 meters, say, above sea level, will have the greatest mass of air above it when the atmosphere below is warmest, or most expanded, and the least when the lower atmosphere is coldest, or most contracted—that is to say, this effect tends to produce, at such stations, barometric maxima during afternoons, and minima about dawn.

There is, however, another effect resulting from the volume expansion and contraction of the atmosphere to consider; namely, its lateral flow. To this, mainly, is due that daily barometric swing at sea level, as shown by harmonic analysis; the early evening minimum and the early morning maximum, that is, the reverse of the high-level oscillation.

The expansion and consequent vertical rise of the air on the warming side of the earth, together with the simultaneous contraction and fall of the atmosphere on the cooling side, establishes a pressure gradient at *all* levels of the atmosphere, directed from the warmer toward the cooler regions, a gradient that obviously causes the well-known heliotropic wind—the wind that turns with the sun—and, thus, leads to maximum pressures at the coldest places, and minimum pressures at the warmest. But, as these regions are along meridians, roughly, 10 hours, or 150° apart, and perpetually move around the earth at the rate of one revolution every 24 hours, there must be a corresponding perpetual flow of air, or change of flow, as above described, in a ceaseless effort to establish an equilibrium which, since the disturbance is continuous, can never be attained.

Semidiurnal Pressure Changes.—Both the actual barometric records and their harmonic analyses show conspicuous 12-hour cyclic changes that culminate in maxima and minima at approximately 10 a.m. and 10 p.m., and 4 a.m. and 4 p.m., respectively—the exact hour, in each case, depending somewhat upon season, elevation, and, presumably, weather conditions.

Some of the observed facts in regard to this 12-hour cyclic change of pressure are:[1]

a. The amplitude, when other things are substantially equal, varies with place, approximately, as the cube of the cosine of the latitude, and is uncertain beyond 60°.

b. The amplitude is, everywhere, greatest on equinoxes; and, everywhere, least on solstices.

c. The amplitude is greater at perihelion than at aphelion.

d. The amplitude is about the same at night as by day.

e. The amplitude is practically independent of the state of the sky, while that of the diurnal is much greater on clear days than cloudy.

f. The amplitude is about the same over land as over water, while that of the diurnal is greatest over land.

g. Over the tropical Pacific Ocean the forenoon barometric maximum is about 1 mm. above, and the afternoon minimum 1 mm. below, the general average pressure. This pressure swing should produce a simultaneous range in temperature of about 0.8° C.

Obviously, other things being equal, both the daily change in temperature, and the resulting change in convection, are greater in the tropics than elsewhere; greater at perihelion than at aphelion; and greatest when the time of heating and the time of cooling (day and night) are equal, and least when these are most unequal or at the times of solstice. Hence, all the above facts of observation strongly favor, if they do not compel, the conclusion that the daily cyclic pressure changes

---

[1] Angot, "Étude sur la marche diurne du baromètre," *Ann. Bureau Central Météorol.*, 1887.

Hann, "Untersuchungen über die tägliche Oscillation des Barometers," *Denkschriften der Wiener Akademie*, Bd. 55, 1889.

Hann, *Meteorol. Zeit.*, **15**; 361, 1898.

Chapman, *Quart. J., Roy. Met. Soc.*, **50**; 165, 1924.

Bartels, *Zeit. Geophysik*, **4**; 1, 1928.

are somehow results of daily temperature changes. There are, however, a number of other causes of slight pressure changes,[1] but apparently only the following have any appreciable value:

1. *Horizontal Flow of the Atmosphere from the Regions Where It Is Most Expanded toward Those Where It Is Most Contracted.*—The exact hour at which the atmosphere is warmest, and most expanded, depends upon a variety of circumstances, but on the average it is approximately at 4 p. m. Hence, in general, at about this time the amount of air overhead, counting from sea level, should be least, and, therefore, at this hour a sea-level barometer should have its lowest reading. On the other hand, lowest temperatures and maximum contractions obtain soon after dawn, or shortly before 6 a.m. throughout the year, near the equator, and everywhere at the time of equinox.

The 24-hour swing of the barometer, therefore, does not appear to be of even period, but, rather, of intervals that are to each other, roughly, as 5 to 7. To be sure, the barometer is lower at six o'clock in the afternoon than at the same hour of the morning, and, hence, one may assume an even period 24-hour swing, with a morning six o'clock maximum and evening six o'clock minimum, and partially correct this regular curve (the correction is never perfect) by the superposition of one or more additional sine curves of convenient periods. But, this approximation to the true curve does not prove the existence of actual forces with the periods assumed.

It appears, then, that the physical causes of the 24-hour component of the diurnal pressure changes are such as to give a morning maximum at about six o'clock and an afternoon minimum at about four o'clock. The above causes of pressure change, however, do not account for either of the ten o'clock maxima.

2. *Interference by Vertical Convection with Free Horizontal Flow.*— It was long ago suggested, by Abbe,[2] that convectional interference is the principal cause of the forenoon maximum pressure. Presumably, it is at least a contributing factor.

Let the mass m of air be near the ground and have the horizontal velocity v, and let the larger mass M be at a higher elevation and have the greater velocity V in the same direction. If, now, these two masses should mingle in such manner as to be free from all disturbance, except their own mutual interference, the resulting final velocity U in the same direction, would be given by the equation

$$U = \frac{mv + MV}{m + M},$$

and there obviously would be no check in the total flow—no damming up and consequent increase of pressure. But this simple mixing of the

---

[1] HUMPHREYS, *Bull. Mt. Weather Observatory*, **5**; 132, 1912.

[2] "Preparatory Studies," pp. 8 and 56, 1890.

two masses is by no means all that happens in the case of vertical convection. The rise of the mass m is simultaneously accompanied by an equivalent descent of air from a higher level, which, in turn, loses velocity, directly or indirectly, by surface friction. If the falling mass is also m, and if its velocity is reduced by friction to v, then from a single interchange, due to vertical convection, the total momentum becomes

$$2mv + (M - m)V$$

and the total flow is reduced by the amount

$$m(V - v).$$

But, as this is for a single interchange, it is obvious that the more active vertical convection becomes, the greater will be its interference with the flow of the atmosphere, the more the winds will be dammed up, and the higher the barometric pressure. As convection increases, reaches a maximum, and then decreases, so, too, will the resulting interference go through the same changes.

Now, the general movement of the atmosphere is from east to west within the tropics and from west to east at higher latitudes. Therefore, in either case, such damming up of the air as vertical convection may produce will be essentially along meridians, and thus a function of the time of day. But, in general, convection increases most rapidly during the forenoon, say, eight to nine o'clock, is most active at ten to eleven o'clock, and reaches its greatest elevation about four o'clock in the afternoon. Hence, the damming up of the atmosphere, due to vertical convection, and the resulting increase of barometric pressure must increase most rapidly during the forenoon, and come to a maximum about ten o'clock. After this, the convectional interference decreases, while at the same time the amount of air in a vertical column of fixed cross-section diminishes, as a result of expansion and overflow; until, at about four o'clock in the afternoon, the barometric pressure, as already explained, has reached a minimum.

To form some idea of the magnitude of the barometric change due to convectional turbulence, consider the atmosphere between two parallels of latitude near the equator. This limited quantity may be regarded as a stream flowing around the earth, having its minimum velocity and maximum depth where convectional interference is greatest, and maximum velocity with minimum depth where convection is absent. And, since the linear velocity of a point on the equator is approximately 1670 kilometers per hour, while, during the forenoon, the rate of increase of the barometric pressure at the same place is, roughly, 0.2 mm. per hour, it follows that a damming up, or check in the flow, of the given stream, at the rate of 0.44 kilometer per hour would be sufficient of itself to account for the observed rise in the barometer. But, if the average velocity of the wind, or flow of the stream in question, is 10 meters per second, which it may well be, the rate of decrease in velocity requisite for the given rate of pressure increase could be produced by having only 1 part in 80 of the whole superincumbent atmosphere brought to rest per hour; or the equivalent thereof, an amount that perhaps is reasonable. At any rate, the assumed velocity decrease is of the same order of magnitude as that observed to take place during, and as the result of, diurnal convection, and presumably is a factor in the production of the pressure increase.

Summing up the effects of all the above causes of barometric changes, it appears:

a. That the afternoon minimum is caused, essentially, by overflow from the region where the atmosphere is warmest, or, better, perhaps, from the meridian along which the temperature increase has been greatest, toward that meridian along which there has been the greatest decrease in temperature.

b. That vertical convection interferes with the free horizontal flow of the atmosphere and to that extent dams it up, and correspondingly increases the barometric pressure; also, that the time of this interference agrees with the forenoon changes of the barometer, and that its magnitude is of sufficient order to account for, certainly, an appreciable portion of the forenoon barometric maximum.

Both the afternoon barometric minimum and the forenoon maximum, therefore, are to be regarded as effects, in part at least, of temperature increase; the minimum as due to expansion and consequent overflow; the maximum as caused by vertical convection and consequent interference with the free circulation of the atmosphere.

The forced afternoon minimum would occur in an otherwise stagnant atmosphere, and substantially as at present; but not so with the forced forenoon maximum, since the interference, or damming effect, depends upon a flow, or circulation, of the atmosphere, parallel, roughly, to the equator.

It remains, now, to account for the night ten o'clock maximum and four o'clock minimum.

3. *Natural or Free Vibration of the Atmosphere as a Whole.*—This subject has been discussed by several mathematical physicists of great eminence, Margules,[1] Lamb,[2] Chapman,[3] Bartels,[3] and others[4]; and all agree that the fundamental period of the free oscillation of the atmosphere as a whole is about 12 mean solar hours.

[1] *Wien. Sitz. Ber. Kk. Wiss.*, **99**; 204, 1890; **101**; 597, 1892; **102**; 11 and 1369, 1893.

[2] *Proc. Roy. Soc.*, **84**; 551, 1911.

[3] *Loc. cit.*

[4] Chapman, Pramanik, and Topping, *Beiträge Geophys.*, **33**; 246, 1931; Marchi, L. de, *Com. Naz. Ital. Geod. e Geofis., Boll.* 9–10; Pekeris, C. L., *Proc. Roy. Soc.*, **158**; 650, 1937.

Hence any cause of pressure change, having a period approximately semidiurnal in length, would, if of sufficient magnitude and proper phase, account for the 12-hour barometric swing. Such a cause, many believe, is in the semidiurnal harmonic of the daily temperature curve. Perhaps so, but, as just stated, all that is needed is a pressure impulse of the same period and phase as that of the free vibration of the atmosphere as a whole. And this is furnished by the forced forenoon barometric maximum, in conjunction with the forced afternoon barometric minimum. 6 hours later, at the same place, supplemented by the amplified (through synchronism) solar atmospheric tide.

The course of events, at each locality, appears to be substantially as follows:

1. A forced forenoon compression of the atmosphere, followed by its equally forced afternoon expansion, the two together forming one complete barometric wave, with a ten o'clock maximum and a four o'clock minimum, in harmony with the free vibration of the entire atmospheric shell, supplemented by solar tides.

2. Nondisturbance through the night, or during the time of a single free vibration, except by tidal action.

3. Repetition the following day of the forced disturbances in synchronism with, and, therefore, at such time as to reënforce, the free vibrations.

The series of disturbances is continuous, forced by day and free, excepting tidal action, by night, but the resulting amplitudes of the barometric changes are limited, through friction and through the absence of perfect synchronism, to comparatively small values. Each point upon the atmospheric shell receives at every alternate swing, in addition to tidal pull, a forced impulse of thermal origin in phase with the free vibration, and, therefore, at such time and in such manner as indefinitely to maintain the vibrations of the atmosphere as a whole. In short, the semidiurnal swing of the barometer is a result of merely fortuitous circumstances—of the fact that the mass of the atmosphere happens to be such that the period of its free vibration is, approximately, just one-half that of the earth's rotation.

Terdiurnal Pressure Changes.—An 8-hour pressure change, corresponding to a harmonic of the 24-hour temperature curve, has been found. It does not occur at, or near, the equator; has its maximum amplitude, about 0.15 mm. around latitude 30°. It lies along meridians, but is in opposite phase in the northern hemisphere to that in the southern; and changes phase, for any given hour, from winter to summer. During winter its first maximum pressure occurs about 2 a.m.

Tidal Pressure Changes.—The theory of atmospheric tides is too tedious to include here, especially as it is easily accessible[1] to all who may

[1] LAMB, "Hydrodynamics"; BARTELS, *loc. cit.*

have any occasion to look it up. According to this theory the barometric amplitudes in equatorial regions, due to the gravitational action of the sun and the moon, should be about 0.0109 mm. (except if, and as, amplified through free period synchronism) and 0.025 mm., respectively, and rapidly decrease with increase of latitude. These, of course, are not

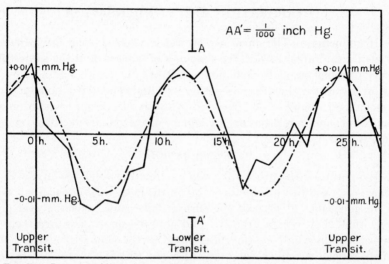

Fig. 73.—Lunar semidiurnal atmospheric tide at Greenwich, England, 1854–1917.

easily disentangled from the numerous other barometric changes. Nevertheless, efforts to do so have been made, and, apparently, with fair success; notably, by Chapman,[1] whose results from the Greenwich data of 1854–1917 are shown in Fig. 73, and more recently by others.

[1] *Quart. J. Roy. Meteorol. Soc.*, **44**; 271, 1918; **45**; 113, 1919; *Mem. Roy. Meteorol. Soc.*, **4**; No. 33, 1932; *Proc. Roy. Soc.*, **151**; 105, 1935; *Trans. Intern. Geodet. and Geophys. Union*, Washington meeting, 1939.

CHAPTER XV

EVAPORATION AND CONDENSATION

Introduction.—The presence of water vapor in the atmosphere is of such vital importance in the economy of Nature, and the source of so many phenomena, as to demand a study of, among other things: evaporation, by which the vapor is gotten into and rendered a portion of the atmosphere, mainly from free surfaces, but also from vegetation and damp soil; and condensation, by which, in various forms, it is removed from the air.

EVAPORATION

Evaporation, the process by which a liquid or solid becomes a vapor, or gas, is a result of the kinetic energy of the individual molecules. Some of the molecules at or near the surface have such velocities and directions that they escape from it, and thus become an integral part of the surrounding gas or atmosphere; and as the chance of escape, other things remaining equal, increases with the velocity, it follows (a) that the average kinetic energy of the escaping molecules is greater than that of the remaining ones, or that evaporation decreases the temperature of a liquid, say, and (b) that the rate of evaporation increases with increase of temperature.

Just as the kinetic energy of some of the molecules of a liquid carries them into the adjacent space, so, too, the kinetic energy of some of the molecules of the gaseous phase causes them to penetrate into, and thus become a part of, the liquid. In reality, therefore, evaporation from, and condensation onto, the surface of a liquid, though necessarily taking place by discrete molecular units, practically are continuous processes whose ratio may have any value whatever. As popularly used, however, and even as very commonly used scientifically, the term "evaporation" refers to the net loss of a liquid or solid, and "condensation" to its net gain; so that, in this sense, both are said to be zero when, as a matter of fact, they are only equal to each other.

In the sense of net loss, which admits of accurate measurement, evaporation has been the subject of numerous investigations. Vegetation, soil, and the free water surface, each offers its own peculiar and numerous evaporation problems. In what follows, however, only the free surface will be considered.

Evaporation into Still Air: *a. From Tubes.*—The rate of loss of a liquid, by evaporation and diffusion, through a tube of fixed length and constant cross-section into a still atmosphere, has been carefully studied by Stefan.[1] Obviously, when a steady state has been attained, the rate at which the vapor escapes per unit area of the cross-section of the tube is constant, directly proportional to the driving force and inversely proportional to the resistance. These in turn are proportional, respectively, to the pressure gradient of the vapor along the tube and the partial pressure of the foreign gas at the same place. In symbols,

$$v = -\frac{k}{P-p}\frac{dp}{dn} = k\frac{d}{dn}\log(P-p),$$

in which v is the volume at $0°$ C. and 760 mm. pressure of the vapor that escapes per second per unit area of the cross-section of the tube, P the total pressure, a constant, dp/dn the vapor pressure gradient along the tube at and normal to the cross-section at which the partial pressure due to the vapor is p, and k the coefficient of diffusion, whose value depends upon the nature of the vapor and the gas through which it is passing, and their temperature.

But as a steady state is assumed, it follows that both the rate of flow and the coefficient of diffusion k are independent of the distance n along the tube above the liquid surface. Hence,

$$V = \frac{kA}{h}\log\frac{P-p''}{P-p'}$$

in which V is the rate of total evaporation, A the area of the cross-section of the tube, h its height, or the distance of its top (tube supposed vertical) above the liquid, p'' and p' the partial pressures of the vapor at the free end and evaporating surface, respectively.

All the terms in this equation except k may easily be measured, and thus k itself evaluated. But with k known, the rate of evaporation of the same liquid (water, say) from a circular tube or well of any given cross-section and length, provided the length is equal to or greater than the diameter, may be computed from the total gas pressure and the vapor pressures at the surface of the liquid and top of the tube.

b. From Flush Circular Areas.—The rate of evaporation into still air from a circular tank or pond filled flush with a relatively extensive plane, which itself neither absorbs nor gives off any vapor, has also been found by Stefan[2] susceptible of complete analysis.

From the general equation

$$v = -\frac{k}{P-p}\frac{dp}{dn}$$

it follows that

$$v = -k\frac{d}{dn}\log\frac{P-p_o}{P-p}$$

[1] *Sitzb. Akad. Wiss. Wien.* **68**; 385–423, 1873.
[2] *Sitzb. Akad. Wiss., Wien,* **73**; 943–954, 1881.

in which p_o is the constant partial pressure of the vapor, during a steady state, at a given point. Hence if

$$u = \log \frac{P - p_o}{P - p}$$

$$v = -k\frac{du}{dn}.$$

But, this is identical with the equation for the force in an electrostatic field when u is the potential, and v/k the electric intensity, at any point; hence, the value of u at any point is the same as the electric potential would be at that point if the water surface were a conductor at potential u_1 where

$$u_1 = \log \frac{P - p_o}{P - p_1},$$

in which p_o is the vapor pressure of the free air at a great distance from the evaporating surface and p_1 its pressure at the surface, or saturation pressure at the surface temperature. Now if σ be the density of the surface charge on a conductor, then just outside the conductor

$$-\frac{du}{dn} = 4\pi\sigma,$$

and integrating over the surface we have for the quantity corresponding to the total diffusion

$$V = 4\pi kE = 4\pi kCu_1,$$

E being the total charge and C the capacitance. In the case of a circular disk of radius a, $C = 2a/\pi$, and, hence, the total diffusion, from *one* side only of the plate, will be

$$V = 2\pi kCu_1$$

$$= 4ak \log \frac{P - p_o}{P - p_1}.$$

If p_o and p_1 are both small in comparison to P,

$$V = 4ak\,\frac{(p_1 - p_o)}{P}, \text{ nearly.}$$

The real importance of this equation is its proof that evaporation, under the restricted conditions assumed, is proportional to the *diameter* (or other linear dimension) of the evaporating surface and *not*, as one might suppose, to its area. Obviously, therefore, evaporation in the open, under ordinary conditions, cannot be directly proportional, as often assumed, to the area involved.

c. From Elliptical Areas.—Evaporation from an elliptical surface is slightly faster than from a circular one of equal area, but the difference is small until the major axis of the ellipse becomes several times longer than the minor; being only 1.11 times as fast when the ratio of the axes is 1 to

4. Hence, when the axes do not greatly differ, a close approximation to the rate of evaporation from an elliptical surface is given by the equation

$$V = 4\sqrt{ab} \, k \log \frac{P - p_o}{P - p_1},$$

or, when p_o and p_1 are small with reference to P,

$$V = 4\sqrt{ab} \, k \frac{P_1 - p_o}{P}.$$

No exact mathematical expression has yet been obtained for the rate of evaporation into still air from surfaces of any other outline than the above—circle and ellipse.

Evaporation into a Steady Horizontal Wind.—Significant progress towards the complete solution of this difficult problem has been made by Jeffreys,[1] whose discussion of it is substantially as follows: Let ρ be the density of the atmosphere at any point and D the fraction of this density due to water vapor; let the wind be in the direction x parallel to the evaporating surface, and let its velocity at some distance above this surface be u. The components v and w of the wind velocity in the directions y and z, respectively (z being normal to the surface and y at right angles to both x and z) are, therefore, both zero. For moderate winds, the velocity of the air may be assumed to increase rapidly through a thin shearing layer from zero at the surface to perhaps half value, $u/2$, a millimeter or so above it. Through this same layer the vapor density will rapidly decrease, if the general air is comparatively dry, from saturation at the surface, where $D = D_0$, say, to some decidedly less value. Beyond this layer the transfer of water vapor, of heat, and of momentum, are all owing essentially to turbulence, as fully explained by Taylor,[2] and the coefficient k of this "eddy diffusion" is practically independent of position.

Therefore, in analogy to heat conduction, molecular diffusion, etc.,

$$\frac{dD}{dt} = \frac{\partial}{\partial x}\left(k\frac{\partial D}{\partial x}\right) + \frac{\partial}{\partial y}\left(k\frac{\partial D}{\partial y}\right) + \frac{\partial}{\partial z}\left(k\frac{\partial D}{\partial z}\right).$$

Also

$$\frac{dD}{dt} = \frac{\partial D}{\partial t} + u\frac{\partial D}{\partial x} + v\frac{\partial D}{\partial y} + w\frac{\partial D}{\partial z}.$$

Hence, as the density gradient changes only with elevation ($v = w = o$), and as k is constant, it follows that, when a steady state has been attained,

$$u\frac{\partial D}{\partial x} = k\frac{\partial^2 D}{\partial z^2},$$

[1] *Phil. Mag.*, **35**; 273, 1918.
[2] *Phil. Trans. Roy. Soc.*, **215**; I, 1915.

or, putting $k/u = h^2$, a constant, that

$$\frac{\partial D}{\partial x} = h^2 \frac{\partial^2 D}{\partial z^2}.$$

An integral of this equation is[1]

$$D = D_0 \left(1 - \frac{2}{\sqrt{\pi}} \int_0^q e^{-q^2}\, dq \right),$$

in which

$$q = \frac{z}{2h\sqrt{x}}.$$

Let the oncoming air be absolutely dry and take the origin at the windward edge of the liquid surface. Then

$$D = 0, \text{ when } x \text{ is negative.}$$

Hence, at the surface, where $z = 0$,

$$\frac{\partial D}{\partial z} = \frac{D_0}{h\sqrt{\pi x}}.$$

Therefore, the rate of evaporation is

$$k\rho \frac{\partial D}{\partial z} = \rho D_0 \sqrt{\frac{ku}{\pi x}} \text{ per unit area,}$$

and, for a strip of width dy, extending from $x = 0$ to $x = x$

$$\rho D_0 dy \int_0^x \left(\frac{ku}{\pi x}\right)^{1/2} dx = 2\rho D_0 \left(\frac{kux}{\pi}\right)^{1/2} dy.$$

If, now, the length of the strip from margin to margin be l, neglecting end corrections due to sidewise diffusion, the rate of total evaporation is given by the integral over the whole area,

$$2\rho D_0 \left(\frac{ku}{\pi}\right)^{1/2} \int l^{1/2} dy,$$

with the lower limit, corresponding to $x = 0$, along the windward edge.

In the case, therefore, of free, unruffled liquid surfaces of medium dimensions, roughly, 20 centimeters to 500 meters across,[2] it appears, in the case of "eddy diffusion:"

1. That the rate of evaporation is proportional to the square root of the wind velocity.

2. That the rates of total evaporation from surfaces of the same shape and same orientation to the wind are to each other as the three-quarter powers of their respective areas.

---

[1] Van Orstrand and Dewey, *Professional Paper* 95-G, U. S. Geological Survey, 1915.

[2] Jeffreys, *loc. cit.*

If, for instance, the surface is a circle of radius a, the rate of evaporation from it is, reckoning from the diameter $x = 0$ and doubling,

$$3.95\rho D_0(kua^3)^{\frac{1}{2}};$$

which accords with the observations of Thomas and Ferguson.[1]

The equation, therefore, that expresses the rate of total evaporation from a given surface by "eddy diffusion" is very different from the corresponding equation when the diffusion is wholly molecular, nor are they reducible the one to the other. The first applies, approximately, at least, when there is an appreciable wind of the kind specified, namely, steady and strictly horizontal; the second, only when the air is absolutely quiet. The problem, however, of evaporation into imperceptible to very light winds is more difficult, and, as yet, unsolved.

A problem somewhat analogous to the above is that of finding the state of humidity of the atmosphere at any time after starting, in a given condition, over an extensive body of water. We may, for example, assume the air, as it crosses the shore, to have the same absolute humidity through, say, the first 1 or 2 kilometers, and uniform eddy diffusion—assumptions that usually, roughly, accord with the facts. Evidently this problem is identical with that of the flow of heat along an infinite, homogeneous, straight rod of constant cross-section and insulated sides, when a given section normal to the axis is kept at a fixed, and relatively high, temperature.

Hence, giving the symbols the same meaning as above, our fundamental equation is

$$\frac{\partial D}{\partial x} = \frac{k}{u} \frac{\partial^2 D}{\partial z^2}.$$

This is to be solved with the conditions (1) that when x and t are zero, *i.e.*, as the air crosses the shore, D has the same, and given, value at all heights, and (2) that the rate of vertical flux of water vapor at the surface $z = 0$ is the rate of evaporation per unit area.

The numerical solutions of the problem under given conditions of initial humidity, wind velocity, and decrease of temperature with increase of height, are tedious. However, several such solutions, with all the essential details, are given in an important paper by Giblett,[2] which should be consulted by anyone interested in this subject. O. G. Smith[3] has discussed the theory of evaporation when u and k of the above equations are not constant. See also papers by F. Graham Millar,[4] H. U. Sverdrup,[5] and C. W. Thornthwaite[6] on this subject.

[1] *Phil. Mag.*, **34**; 308, 1917.

[2] *Proc. Roy. Soc.*, **99**; 472, 1921.

[3] *Proc. Roy. Soc.*, **146**; 712, 1934.

[4] *Can. Meteorol. Mem.*, **1**; No. 2, 1937.

[5] *Ann. Hydro. und Mar. Meteorol.*, 1936, p. 41. *J. Marine Research*, **1**; 3, 1937.

[6] *M. W. R.*, **67**; 4, 1939.

The upper air, as everyone knows, frequently loses vast amounts of its humidity through condensation and precipitation. Hence, turbulence not only carries water vapor up, and completely out of the atmosphere (condensed and falling back as rain or snow), but also brings down relatively dry air and thereby makes evaporation, in general, an endless process—the primal half in the ceaseless round of humidification below and desiccation above.

Evaporation in the Open.—Several hundred papers,[1] many of them giving the results of elaborate investigations, have been published on the evaporation of water from free surfaces, vegetation, and soil, and, while no equation has been found that expresses, in terms of easily measurable quantities, the rates of evaporation in the open, nevertheless several factors that control these rates have been discovered and, more or less approximately, evaluated. In the case of free, clean surfaces, the principal factors are:

a. Salinity.—It has, repeatedly, been observed that the evaporation of salt solutions decreases with increase of concentration, and that sea water evaporates approximately 5 per cent less rapidly than fresh water under the same conditions.

b. Dryness of the Air.—Many observations have shown that, to at least a first approximation, the rate of evaporation is directly proportional, other things being equal, to the difference in temperature indicated by the wet and dry bulb thermometers of a whirled psychrometer. According to the psychrometric formula developed by Apjohn, Maxwell, Stefan, and others,

$$p_1 - p_0 = AB(t_0 - t_1),$$

in which t_0 is the temperature and p_0 the vapor pressure of the free air, t_1 the temperature of the wet bulb (and surface of evaporating liquid), p_1 the saturation vapor pressure at temperature t_1, B the barometric pressure, and A a constant, provided ventilation is sufficient. But, evaporation is proportional to the ratio of vapor pressure gradient to total pressure; that is,

$$V = k\frac{p_1 - p_0}{B}.$$

Hence, other things being equal,

$$V = C(t_0 - t_1), \text{approximately.}$$

But $t_0 - t_1$ increases with the dryness, and hence so does evaporation.

c. Velocity of the Wind.—All observers agree that evaporation increases with wind velocity, presumably through increase, by the action of eddy

[1] LIVINGSTON, "An Annotated Bibliography of Evaporation," *M. W. R.*, June, September, and November, 1908, and February, March, April, May, and June, 1909.

diffusion, of the vapor pressure gradient near the surface. As above explained, it is now known that in the case of a strictly horizontal and steady wind, evaporation from an area of medium size is proportional to the square root of the wind velocity. But, in general, these conditions are not fulfilled in nature. The wind usually has a variable vertical component, and, besides, is irregular in strength and direction. There is not, therefore, any constant relation of evaporation to the *average horizontal* component of wind velocity—the value usually measured.

d. Barometric Pressure.—Since the presence of any gas retards the diffusion of other gas molecules, whether of the same or different nature, it follows that, when the vapor tension is comparatively small, evaporation must vary inversely, nearly, as the total barometric pressure, if temperature is constant.

e. Area of Surface.—Obviously the total amount of water evaporated must increase with the area of the evaporating surface, but not necessarily at the same rate. In fact, as already explained, if the evaporation is from a circular area into still air, it increases as the square root of the area; and as the three-fourth power of the area in the case of a strictly horizontal wind. Under outdoor conditions, however, it is much more nearly, though probably by no means exactly, proportional to the first power of the surface.

f. Temperature of the Water.—Evaporation increases rapidly with the temperature of the water, roughly in proportion to the saturation pressure at that temperature, provided the general humidity of the air is low. When, however, the water surface is colder than the dew-point temperature of the air, the evaporation becomes negative; that is, condensation occurs. When the air is colder than the water surface, evaporation may continue into it after saturation has been reached and, thereby, produce fog, the process being one of distillation and condensation.

Even when the water is frozen, it still continues, slowly, to evaporate (sublime) whenever the air is sufficiently dry, but the laws governing this sublimation are not well known.

Energy Equations of Evaporation.—Evaporation obviously can be evaluated from energy measurements, as developed by N. W. Cummings[1] and others and summarized by G. F. McEwen.[2] Clearly, as they state, if, in a particular time, evaporation occurs to the depth of E centimeters while, in the same time, per square centimeter of surface, the calories absorbed from radiation are I; emitted, B; used in warming the water, S; lost by conduction to the air, K; lost by conduction to the ground, by runoff, and otherwise, C, then

$$E = \frac{I - B - S - K - C}{L}$$

[1] *Bull. Nat. Research Council,* **68**; 47, 1929.
[2] *Bull. Scripps Inst. Oceanog., Tech. Series,* **2**; 501, 1930.

in which L is the latent heat of vaporization of a gram of water at the temperature of the evaporating surface. If R is the ratio of the sensible heat K carried off by the air to the latent heat LE removed by evaporation, then

$$E = \frac{I - B - S - C}{L(1 + R)}.$$

An approximate value of R, in terms of measurable quantities, was found by I. S. Bowen[1] in the form

$$R = 0.46\left(\frac{T_w - T_a}{P_w - P_a}\right)\frac{P}{760}$$

in which T_w is the temperature of the water surface and T_a that of the air, P_w is the saturation vapor pressure at the temperature T_w, P_a is the current vapor pressure and P, the current atmospheric pressure—temperatures in centigrade and pressures in terms of millimeters of mercury.

The value of R necessarily varies with conditions, and so, too, greatly, does that of each of the other terms I, B, S, and C; nor, in many cases, can these values be better than very roughly determined. Nevertheless, the first two of these energy equations are entirely rational and therefore merit extensive use, especially in relation to large bodies of open water where direct measurement of evaporation is impossible or unreliable.

Empirical Evaporation Equations.—Various equations, each at least partially empirical, have been devised to fit evaporation data obtained under special conditions. But the "constants" of these equations, generally, are not constant under other circumstances. Indeed, it may be that no simple equation of this kind, applicable to a wide range of conditions, is possible, and that, therefore, the most expeditious way to obtain useful evaporation data would be to note the daily, monthly, annual, etc., loss from standard exposures in each climatic region, and, wherever practical, to supplement such data by similar observations on lakes, ponds, and reservoirs. Controlled wind-tunnel experiments would also be interesting and useful.

One of the earliest experimenters to make a careful study of evaporation was John Dalton,[2] who says:

1. Some fluids evaporate much more quickly than others.
2. The quantity evaporated is in direct proportion to the surface exposed, all other circumstances alike.
3. An increase of temperature in the liquid is attended with an increase of evaporation, not directly proportionable.
4. Evaporation is greater where there is a stream of air than where the air is stagnant.

[1] *Phys. Rev.*, **27**; 779, 1926.
[2] *Mem. Manchester Lit. Phil. Soc.*, **5**; 574, read October, 1801.

5. Evaporation from water is greater the less the humidity previously existing in the atmosphere, all other circumstances the same.

All these are important observations, but they do not fully justify the so-called Dalton equation which Dalton himself apparently never wrote.

Weilenmann and Stelling, working independently and at different places, obtained evaporation equations of the general form[1]

$$\frac{dn}{dt} = (cb + kw)(p_s - p_0)$$

in which c and k are constants, b the barometric pressure, w the wind velocity, p_s the saturation vapor pressure at the temperature of the water surface, and p_0 the actual vapor pressure in the free air at some distance from the water.

Fitzgerald[2] finds the rate of evaporation E in inches per hour given approximately by the equation

$$E = \frac{(p_s - p_0)\left(1 + \dfrac{w}{2}\right)}{60}$$

in which p_s and p_0 have the meanings, respectively, given above, and w is the average wind velocity in miles per hour.

Various other equations have been found or proposed, but they either contain unevaluated functions, or else were constructed to fit a special set of observations. The multiplicity of such equations, each of but limited use, emphasizes the difficulty of the evaporation problem, if not even the impossibility of finding for it a practical, universal equation.

CONDENSATION

Condensation, the process by which a vapor is reduced to a liquid or solid, is induced by: (*a*) reduction of temperature, volume remaining constant; (*b*) reduction of volume, temperature remaining constant; (*c*) a combination of temperature and volume changes that jointly reduce the total vapor capacity. In the open, water vapor is condensed: (1) by contact cooling; (2) by radiational cooling; (3) by the mixture of masses of air of unequal temperatures; (4) by expansional or dynamic cooling due to vertical convection, or, occasionally, other causes, especially rotation, as in tornado and waterspout funnels. The causes of vertical convection are: (*a*) unequal temperatures at the same level of neighboring masses of air, the warmer, hence lighter, being pushed up

[1] HANN and SÜRING, "Lehrbuch der Meteorologie," 4th Ed., p. 227.
[2] *Trans. Am. Soc. Civ. Eng.*, **15**; 581–645, 1886.

by the colder; (*b*) the flow of air up mountain slopes; (*c*) the flow of warm air up a slope of cold air; (*d*) the flow of cold air under warm air; (*e*) the entrapping of masses of warm air by overflowing cold air; (*f*) the convergence of air currents.

In what follows, except as stated to the contrary, condensation is expected to occur only, and always, when saturation, as in the presence of a flat surface of pure water, is passed; neither hastened by the presence of highly hygroscopic substances nor delayed by the absence of suitable nuclei.

Condensation Due to Contact Cooling.—During clear nights, the surface of the earth, including vegetation and other objects, loses much heat by radiation, and, thus, both it and the air in contact with it are reduced to lower temperatures, obviously more pronounced the gentler the winds. After the dew point has been reached all further loss of heat, producing, now, a much smaller proportionate decrease of temperature, results in the deposition, respectively, of dew and hoarfrost at temperatures above and below freezing. Similarly, relatively warm, moist air moving over a snow bank, for instance, may deposit some of its moisture. Likewise, warm, humid winds blowing into cold regions, as, for instance, tropical maritime air into high latitudes, give cloud, fog, and light rain.

In any typical case of surface cooling the deposition of dew, say, is caused partly by temperature reduction and partly by decrease of volume. Let the air, saturated at the absolute temperature T_0, be cooled, without change of volume, to T_1, and let the water vapor per unit saturated volume at these temperatures be w_0 and w_1, respectively. Then the quantity of water $w_0 - w_1$ will be deposited per unit volume as a result of cooling alone, while if the pressure remains constant, as it does, approximately, the volume will be reduced in the proportion

$$\frac{V_0}{V_1} = \frac{T_0}{T_1}$$

and an additional quantity of water

$$w_1\frac{T_0 - T_1}{T_0}$$

deposited per unit volume at temperature T_0. Hence the quantity q of water deposited per original unit volume due to both processes combined, decrease of temperature and decrease of volume, is given by the equation

$$q = w_0 - w_1\frac{T_1}{T_0}.$$

Condensation Due to Radiation.—In the main, this is just the formation of dew and frost on objects that themselves have cooled by radiation. Such cooling of the free air normally leads to its sinking, thereby becoming warmer and dryer than it was before it cooled. However, this sinking might be arrested at the upper surface of an underlying mass of relatively cold air and a stratus cloud thereby formed at that level.

Condensation Due to Mixing.—Since the amount of water vapor per saturated unit volume decreases with temperature more rapidly than the absolute temperature itself, at least through the range of atmos-

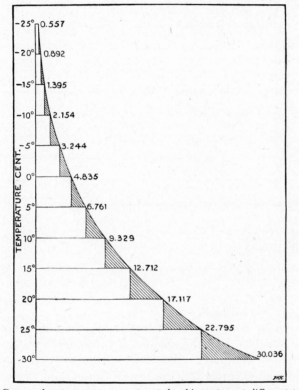

Fig. 74.—Grams of water vapor per saturated cubic meter, at different temperatures. Bases of shaded portions proportional to precipitations per 5° C. cooling from the temperatures indicated.

pheric temperatures (Fig. 74), it follows that the mixture of two saturated masses of air of unequal temperatures must produce some precipitation. The amount of precipitation induced in this manner, however, is surprisingly small; indeed, it seldom can be sufficient to produce more than a light cloud or fog. If the resulting temperature were the proportionate mean of the known temperatures of the quantities of air mixed, the amount of precipitation could easily be computed from the initial humidities. But the latent heat of the condensation prevents this simple relation from obtaining, so that the actual amount of precipitation can better be determined graphically than by direct calculation.[1] To this end use a humidity temperature curve, such as Fig. 75, drawn to scale. For example, let equal masses of saturated air at 0° and 20° C. be mixed at normal pressure—certainly an extreme case. As a first approximation it may be assumed that the final temperature is 10° C., and, since there are 3.75, 7.52, and 14.34 grams of water vapor per 1000 grams of saturated

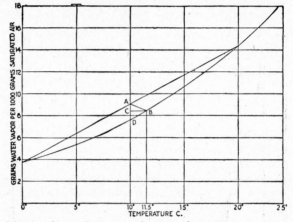

FIG. 75.—Precipitation due to the mixing of saturated equal masses of warm and cold air.

air at normal pressure and 0°, 10°, and 20° C., respectively, the precipitation per 1000 grams of the mixed air would seem to be

$$\frac{3.75 + 14.34}{2} - 7.52 = 1.53 \text{ grams,}$$

represented by AD in the figure.

But the latent heat of condensation causes the final temperature to be above the average, and the amount of precipitated water, therefore, less than that just computed. But since the latent heat of vaporization at 10° C. is approximately 591 calories per gram, and the specific heat of the air at constant pressure about 0.24, it follows that the warming of the air will be at the rate of 2.46° C., nearly, per gram of water vapor condensed per 1000 grams of air. Hence a second approximation to the final temperature and condensation is found by drawing from A a line in such direction that it shall indicate a change of 2.46° C. per gram of condensate, and prolonging it until it meets the humidity temperature curve in B. This second approximation gives 11.615° C. very closely, instead of 10° C., as the temperature of the mixture, and 0.657 gram, instead of 1.53 grams, as the amount of condensation per 1000 grams of air, a quantity which, as the figure shows, would be less than that condensed by cooling the warmer 1° C.

[1] HANN and SÜRING, "Lehrbuch der Meteorologie," 4th Ed., p. 262.

Obviously, similar graphical solutions may easily be made for mixtures of unequal masses of air, for unsaturated air, for other pressures, and for other temperatures; though for temperatures slightly below 0° C. a greater latent heat of vaporization, approximately 680, must be used.

Since 1000 grams of saturated air at 10° C. and normal pressure occupies very approximately $25\!/\!31$ cubic meter, it follows that the condensation above described is about 0.8 gram per cubic meter, a quantity capable of producing only a light cloud through which objects would be visible to a distance of about 70 meters.[1] Further, assuming the diameter of each cloud particle to be 0.033 mm., Wagner's average value, it follows that the condensation in question could produce only about 43 such fog particles per cubic centimeter.

Even if such a cloud were 1 kilometer thick and all its droplets should be brought down, they would produce a water layer only 0.08 cm. deep. Obviously, therefore, the mere mixing of masses of humid air at different temperatures cannot produce any appreciable precipitation in the form of rain or snow.

Condensation Due to Dynamic Cooling.—Dynamic cooling incident to vertical convection is, by far, the most effective method of inducing precipitation, but even when the convection is adiabatic it is not immediately obvious, from the initial temperature, humidity, and pressure, just how much water will be precipitated as the result of a given increase of altitude, nor even for a given decrease of temperature. This is because the rate of cooling with elevation is affected by the latent heat of vaporization, and the amount of condensation, in turn, decreased by the increase of volume, which itself is a function of the temperature and pressure. The problem is further complicated, on passing to temperatures below 0° C., by the latent heat of fusion and by the abrupt considerable change in the heat of vaporization.

It, therefore, will be convenient to consider independently four possible stages in the dynamic cooling of a quantity of moist air: (*a*) the unsaturated; (*b*) the saturated at temperatures above 0° C.; (*c*) the freezing; and (*d*) the saturated at temperatures below 0° C.

This subject has been studied by several investigators, especially Hann,[2] Guldberg and Mohn,[3] Hertz,[4] Neuhoff,[5] and Fjeldstad.[6] Neuhoff's paper has been used as the basis of the following brief discussion.

---

[1] WAGNER, *Sitzb. Akad. Wiss. Wien,* **117**; 1290, 1908.

[2] *Met. Zeit.,* **9**; 321, 337, 1874.

[3] "Études sur les Mouvements de l'Atmosphère," Part I, Christiania, 1876, revised 1883; translation by ABBE, "Mechanics of the Earth's Atmosphere," Smithsonian Institution, 1910.

[4] *Met. Zeit.,* **1**; 421, 1884; translation by ABBE, "Mechanics of the Earth's Atmosphere," Smithsonian Institution, 1891.

[5] *K. Prus. Meteor. Inst.,* **1**; 271, 1900; translated by ABBE, "Mechanics of the Earth's Atmosphere," Smithsonian Institution, 1910.

[6] *Geophys. Pub.* III, No. 13, Oslo, 1925.

Dry (Unsaturated) Stage.—Let the humidity be such that the mass ratio of dry air to water vapor is $1:w$. Then the number of calories dQ necessary to change temperature of $1 + w$ grams of this atmosphere by dT and its volume by dV is given by the equation

$$dQ = (C_v + wC_v')dT + ApdV,$$

in which C_v and C_v' are the specific heats at constant volume, respectively, of dry air and *unsaturated* water vapor, A the reciprocal of the mechanical equivalent of heat, and p the pressure.

But, for n grams,

$$pV = nRT,$$

in which R is the well-known gas constant and T the absolute temperature, numerically, $273 +$ reading of centigrade thermometer. Hence,

$$dQ = (C_v + wC_v')dT + (R + wR')AT\frac{dV}{V}.$$

Since pressures in the open air are easily measured, while volumes are not, it will be more convenient to have this equation expressed in terms of the former. This may be done by substitutions from the equations

$$pdV + Vdp = RdT$$

and

$$C_v = C_p - AR,$$

in which C_p is the specific heat at constant pressure.

If the convection is adiabatic, that is, if

$$dQ = 0,$$

these substitutes give the equation

$$(C_p + wC_p')\frac{dT}{T} = A(R + wR')\frac{dp}{p},$$

or, by integration,

$$(C_p + wC_p') \log \frac{T}{T_0} = A(R + wR') \log \frac{p}{p_0},$$

or, more simply,

$$\log \frac{p}{p_0} = K \log \frac{T}{T_0}, \quad K = \text{a constant,}$$

in which p_0 and T_0 are, respectively, the initial surface pressure and temperature.

Obviously this equation is applicable only until saturation is attained.

Let e_0 and e be, respectively, the initial and saturation vapor pressures corresponding to the total pressures p_0 and p, and absolute temperatures T_0 and T.

Then, since $e/p = $ constant,

$$\log \frac{e}{e_0} = K \log \frac{T}{T_0}$$

and

$$\log e - K \log T = \log e_0 - K \log T_0 = C, \text{ a constant.}$$

If e_0 and T_0 are both known, C is also known, and since saturation vapor pressure depends upon temperature alone, and is known through a wide temperature range, it is obvious that both $\log e$ and $K \log T$ may be tabulated for many values of T, and that with such a table it is easy to pick out that value of T which gives the equation

$$\log e - K \log T = C,$$

the equation that determines the limit of the nonsaturated or dry stage.

If the convection has been adiabatic it is obvious, since the decrease of temperature is 1° C. per 100 meters rise, that the height h of the dry stage is given by the equation

$$h = 100(T_0 - T) \text{ meters, approximately.}$$

A crude estimate of the saturation, or cloud, height may also be made from the current temperature T_0 and dew point T_d. Thus, when owing to convection

$$T_0 - T = 1° \text{ C.,}$$

the new volume is, roughly, one part in 80 larger than it would be under the initial pressure. But this increase in volume lowers the dew point 0.2° C., roughly, for average temperatures, as shown by vapor-saturation tables.

Hence,

$$T_0 - T_d = \tfrac{4}{5}(T_0 - T), \text{ roughly,}$$

and

$$h = 125(T_0 - T_d) \text{ meters, roughly.}$$

It should be distinctly noted that, in general, vertical convection does not follow a fixed plumb line. In cyclonic areas, for instance, the horizontal travel of the air, doubtless, often is hundreds of times the vertical. Hence, in the quadrant of such a region, where the clouds are from lower latitudes, the vertical temperature gradient at any given place is likely to indicate a greater departure from adiabatic expansion than actually has occurred. This, as explained, is because the proper P_0 and T_0 to use in the above equations are those that obtained when, and where, the mass of air in question started to rise, and not those at the surface beneath its position at the time for which the equations are given, if there has been no change due to radiation and absorption.

Under such circumstances the true values of p_0 and T_0 are not accurately known, but that does not affect the validity of the above discussion; it only emphasizes the complexity of the problem as frequently presented in nature.

Rain (Saturated, Unfrozen) Stage.—After saturation has been attained any further convectional cooling leads to precipitation. It will be assumed that this water is carried along with the ascending current (never strictly true, and less nearly so as the drops grow in size), thus leaving the process adiabatic and reversible, and that the volume of the liquid water is negligible in comparison to the space from which it was condensed.

Let p be the total pressure, made up of the two partial pressures air pressure p' and saturated water-vapor pressure e, a function of the temperature alone, and let the mass ratio of air to total water, condensed and uncondensed, be $1:w$. Then

$$p = p' + e = \frac{RT}{V} + e.$$

As before, the quantity of heat necessary to change the temperature of 1 gram of air by an amount dT and its volume by dV is

$$dQ' = C_v dT + ART\frac{dV}{V}.$$

Let w' be the grams of uncondensed water vapor per gram of dry air. Then $w - w'$ is the corresponding number of grams of liquid water. Hence, the heat necessary to bring about the temperature change dT and the vapor change dw' is

$$dQ'' = w's_2 dT + (w - w')s_1 dT + Ldw',$$

in which s_2 is the specific heat of *saturated* water vapor (that is, its specific heat when the volume so changes with the temperature as to maintain saturation and avoid condensation—a negative quantity), s_1 the specific heat of water, and L the latent heat of vaporization.

Now

$$\frac{dQ''}{T} = \frac{w's_2 + (w - w')s_1}{T}dT + \frac{L}{T}dw' = d\varphi,$$

φ being entropy; but $d\varphi$ is a perfect differential (see "Entropy and Potential Temperature," Chap. II), and, therefore, from the properties of a perfect differential,

$$\frac{\partial}{\partial w'}\left(\frac{s_1(w - w') + s_2 w'}{T}\right) = \frac{\partial}{\partial T}\left(\frac{L}{T}\right),$$

and

$$(s_2 - s_1) = T\frac{\partial}{\partial T}\left(\frac{L}{T}\right).$$

Hence,

$$dQ'' = ws_1 dT + T \frac{\partial}{\partial T}\left(\frac{Lw'}{T}\right)dT,$$

and

$$dQ = \left(C_v dT + ART\frac{dV}{V}\right) + T\frac{\partial}{\partial T}\left(\frac{Lw'}{T}\right)dT + ws_1 dT.$$

$$= \left(C_p dT - ART\frac{dp'}{p'}\right) + T\frac{\partial}{\partial T}\left(\frac{Lw'}{T}\right)dT + ws_1 dT.$$

Hence, since the process is adiabatic,

$$(C_p + ws_1)\frac{dT}{T} + \frac{\partial}{\partial T}\left(\frac{Lw'}{T}\right)dT = AR\frac{dp'}{p'}.$$

By integration, using the subscript 0 for initial conditions,

$$\log \frac{p'}{p_0'} = \frac{C_p + ws_1}{AR}\log\frac{T}{T_0} + \frac{M}{AR}\left(\frac{Lw'}{T} - \frac{L_0 w_0'}{T_0}\right),$$

in which M is the modulus of the system of logarithms used.
But

$$w' = \frac{Re}{R'p'}.$$

Therefore,

$$\log\frac{p'}{p_0'} = \frac{C_p + ws_1}{AR}\log\frac{T}{T_0} + \frac{M}{AR'}\left(\frac{eL}{p'T} - \frac{e_0 L_0}{p_0'T_0}\right) = b\log\frac{T}{T_0} + \left(\frac{a}{p'} - \frac{a_0}{p_0'}\right),$$

in which b, a, and a_0 obviously are determinable numerical quantities for given values of w, T, and T_0.
Hence

$$\log p' - \frac{a}{p'T} - b\log T = \log p_0' - \frac{a_0}{p_0'T_0} - b\log T_0 = \text{a constant}.$$

From this equation a table may be constructed giving the relation between p' and T, and also, since e is known through a wide range of temperatures, between p and T. The value of w', or grams of water per gram of dry air, is given for any temperature by the equation

$$w' = \frac{Re}{R'p'},$$

and the condensed water w'' per gram of dry air by the equation

$$w'' = w - \frac{Re}{R'p'}.$$

Hail (Freezing) Stage.—Further lowering of the pressure beyond that at which the temperature reaches 0° C. causes, so long as there is any liquid water present, both freezing and evaporation. The latent heat of fusion keeps the temperature constant, while the increase of volume under the reduced pressure increases the vapor capacity and thus leads to evaporation.

To each gram of dry air let there be w, w', and w'' grams, respectively, of water in all forms, vapor, and ice. Then, as there is no change of temperature through this stage,

$$dQ = ART_0\frac{dV}{V} + Ldw' - Fdw'',$$

in which F is the latent heat of fusion, and T_0 the absolute temperature at 0° C. The negative sign is used because the heat of fusion is added, or becomes sensitive with freezing; that is, with decrease of pressure and increase of volume.

Assuming the process adiabatic, dividing by T, as before, and integrating, the above equation reduces to

$$\frac{AR}{M} \log \frac{V_1}{V_0} + \frac{L}{T_0}(w_1' - w_0') - \frac{F}{T_0}(w_1'' - w_0'') = 0.$$

Let the subscript 0 indicate the condition when the temperature reaches 0° C. with no ice, and subscript 1 the condition when all the water is just frozen. As the temperature is constant, e will be the same at the beginning and end of the freezing process. At the end of the freezing $w_1'' = w - w_1'$.

Also,

$$\frac{V_1}{V_0} = \frac{p_0'}{p_1'}; \ w_0' = \frac{R}{R'}\frac{e}{p_0 - e}; \ w_1' = \frac{R}{R'}\frac{e}{p_1 - e}; \text{ and } w_0'' = 0.$$

Hence

$$\log p_1' - \frac{e}{p_1'}\frac{M(L + F)}{AR'T_0} = \log p_0' - \frac{e}{p_0'}\frac{M}{AR'}\frac{L}{T_0} - w\frac{M}{AR}\frac{F}{T_0}.$$

This equation gives, in terms of known quantities, the relation between the partial pressures of the air at the beginning and end of the "hail stage," and, therefore, the depth of this stage, obviously determined by the amount of water to be frozen, which, in turn, depends on the original temperature and humidity.

Snow (Frozen) Stage.—At temperatures below 0° C., there will be present in the air only ice and enough water vapor to produce saturation. Hence the discussion applicable to this stage is identical with that for the "rain stage," though two of the constants, specific heat and latent heat, will be different. The specific heat is now of ice, roughly one-half that of water, while the total latent heat is due to two distinct processes, fusion and vaporization. The equation, therefore, applicable to the snow stage is

$$\log \frac{p'}{p_0'} = \frac{C_p + ws_i}{AR} \log \frac{T}{T_0} + \frac{M}{AR'}\left(\frac{e(L+F)}{p'T} - \frac{e_0(L_0+F_0)}{p_0'T_0}\right),$$

in which s_i is the specific heat of ice, and the other terms have the meanings previously given.

It will be interesting to note that the form of the adiabatic equation is:

1. For the dry stage,

$$\log p - a \log T = C, \text{ a constant.}$$

2. For a condensation stage,

$$\log p' - \frac{b}{p'T} - a \log T = K, \text{ a constant,}$$

in which a and b are numerical coefficients, p the total pressure, and p' the partial air pressure.

The short hail or freezing stage is distinct from either of the others, though it may be represented approximately by an equation of the second or condensation type.

"Pseudoadiabatic" Convection.—Adiabatic expansion of the atmosphere obviously implies that all cloud particles, raindrops, and snowflakes are carried along with the identical mass of air out of which they were condensed. This condition cannot rigorously obtain in Nature at any level; neither do all the products of condensation, especially the smaller droplets, rapidly fall away immediately they are formed. Hence the actual process, if conduction, radiation, and absorption were negligible, would lie somewhere between the adiabatic, with all condensation products retained, and that special type of the nonadiabatic which Neuhoff and others have called pseudoadiabatic, where all such products are immediately removed, probably much nearer the latter than the former.

To reduce adiabatic to "pseudoadiabatic" equations it evidently is only necessary to drop the water and ice terms. This, of course, automatically excludes the hail stage—it eliminates all water, and, therefore, renders freezing impossible. Nevertheless, the differences between the temperatures and pressures given by the two processes, generally, are small.

For convenience of intercomparison, the two sets of equations, adiabatic and "pseudoadiabatic," are here grouped together.

Dry stage $\begin{cases}\text{Adiabatic, } \log \dfrac{p}{p_0} = \dfrac{C_p + wC_p'}{A(R + wR')} \log \dfrac{T}{T_0} \\ \text{"Pseudoadiabatic," does not exist, there having been no condensation.}\end{cases}$

Rain stage $\begin{cases}\text{Adiabatic, } \log \dfrac{p'}{p_0'} = \dfrac{C_p + ws_1}{AR} \log \dfrac{T}{T_0} + \dfrac{M}{AR'}\left(\dfrac{eL}{p'T} - \dfrac{e_0L_0}{p_0'T_0}\right) \\ \text{"Pseudoadiabatic," } \log \dfrac{p'}{p_0'} = \dfrac{C_p}{AR} \log \dfrac{T}{T_0} + \dfrac{M}{AR'}\left(\dfrac{eL}{p'T} - \dfrac{e_0L_0}{p_0'T_0}\right), \text{ nearly.}\end{cases}$

Hail stage $\begin{cases} \text{Adiabatic, } \log \dfrac{p_1'}{p_0'} = \dfrac{M}{AR'T_0}\left(\dfrac{e}{p_1}(L+F) - \dfrac{e}{p_0}L - \dfrac{R'}{R}wF\right) \\ \text{``Pseudoadiabatic,'' does not exist, there being no water and, therefore,} \\ \quad \text{no freezing.} \end{cases}$

Snow stage $\begin{cases} \text{Adiabatic, } \log \dfrac{p'}{p_0'} = \dfrac{C_p + ws_i}{AR} \log \dfrac{T}{T_0} + \dfrac{M}{AR'}\left(\dfrac{e(L+F)}{p'T} - \dfrac{e_0(L_0+F_0)}{p_0'T_0}\right) \\ \text{``Pseudoadiabatic,'' } \log \dfrac{p'}{p_0'} = \dfrac{C_p}{AR} \log \dfrac{T}{T_0} + \dfrac{M}{AR'}\left(\dfrac{e(L+F)}{p'T} - \dfrac{e_0(L_0+F_0)}{p_0'T_0}\right), \end{cases}$

nearly.

It will also be convenient to have listed the several constants of these equations, and their numerical values. If the unit of heat is 1 calorie, the heat necessary to raise the temperature of 1 gram of water from 0° to 1° C., the values of these constants are:

$$A = \frac{1}{4.185 \times 10^7} \text{ ergs, nearly.}$$

$F = 80$ calories, about.

$L = 600$ calories, approximately.

$M = 0.43429448$, for base 10.

$T = 273 +$ reading of centigrade thermometer.

$R = 28.71 \times 10^5$ ergs per gram 1° C., nearly.

$R' = 46.42 \times 10^5$ ergs per gram 1° C., closely.

$C_p = 0.240$, about.

$C_p' = 0.46$, roughly.

$s_1 = 1$, closely.

$s_i = 0.5$, approximately.

With these values various tables may be constructed for convenient use of the formulas, as has been done by Neuhoff[1] and Fjeldstad.[1] Proper hypsometric formulas give the elevations above sea level corresponding to different conditions of the atmosphere with respect to temperature, pressure, and humidity. Hence, it is possible to construct diagrams more or less accurately embodying all such calculations. Figure 76, copied from Neuhoff's paper, is an especially good adiabatic diagram of this kind, of which there are several modifications.

As is obvious from inspection, this diagram applies to all altitudes from 0 (sea level) to 7000 meters, and from −30° to +30° C. The temperature and altitude differences are equally spaced, and the pressure differences, therefore, unequally, in respect to both the other terms. It is assumed that the adiabatic cooling of nonsaturated air is at the rate of 1° C. per 100 meters increase of elevation, an approximately correct value; hence the dry adiabats, given in full lines for intervals of 10° C., are straight diagonals, while the saturation adiabats, represented by dot and dash, are considerably curved. The saturation moisture content, in terms of grams of water vapor per kilogram of dry air, is given by the broken lines.

Interpolations are readily made on the diagram, and approximate values easily obtained, by always starting from the intersection of the

[1] Loc. cit.

given temperature and pressure coordinates. For example, let the temperature be 20° C., the barometer reading 760 mm., and the relative humidity 55 per cent. Since, as the diagram shows, saturation at the given temperature and pressure would require about 14.6 grams of water vapor per 1000 grams of dry air, it follows that under the assumed conditions only about 8 grams would be present. Hence the temperature, pressure, and altitude of such a mass of air, rising adiabatically, are

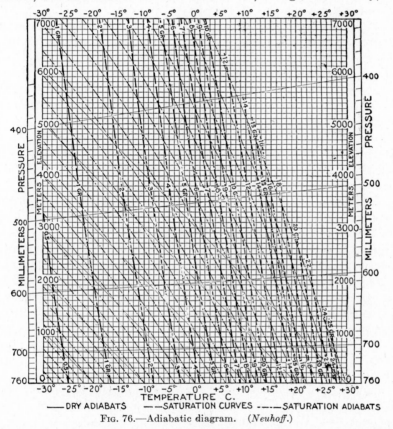

—— DRY ADIABATS   — —SATURATION CURVES ·—·—SATURATION ADIABATS

Fig. 76.—Adiabatic diagram. (*Neuhoff.*)

given, through the first convective stage, by that dry adiabat that starts at the intersection of the initial temperature and pressure ordinates, 20° C. and 760 mm. The first stage terminates when saturation is attained, and therefore, in the present case, at the intersection of the given adiabat with the 8-gram humidity curve at an elevation, as inspection shows, of rather more than 1100 meters, and where the pressure corresponds to a barometric reading of about 665 mm. From this level up the conditions of the rising mass of air are given by a saturation adiabat, according to which the temperature will have fallen to 0° C. and the humidity to about 5.25 grams at an elevation of approximately 2700 meters. The humidity decrease, 2.75 grams per 1000 grams of dry air, is the amount precipitated as water in the form of cloud particles and raindrops. If all this water is carried along, its latent heat of fusion will maintain the temperature at 0° C. through an additional rise of about 80 meters, but, as much of this water obviously must drop out, it follows that the actual conditions, presumably, are rather better represented by omitting the "hail stage," or by a continuous, rather than a broken, adiabat.

While this diagram gives, approximately, the relations between temperature, pressure, humidity, and altitude that obtain in regions of strong vertical convection, it does not closely represent them as they normally exist at other places. This is due partly to the horizontal component of air movement, as above explained, and partly to that constant emission and absorption of radiation that always precludes the existence in the atmosphere of strictly adiabatic conditions.

It is interesting to note that, as shown by the diagram, dry air has but one, and the same, adiabatic gradient under all conditions, while that of saturated air varies with both temperature and pressure and, therefore, its possible gradients are infinite in number.

Tephigram, or T **(temperature)**—φ **(entropy)-gram.**—The thermodynamical state of the atmosphere may, of course, be expressed in the form of any one of a number of related diagrams, of which Fig. 76 is one of the best. However, in considering the distribution of energy per unit mass of dry air, say, and amount short of the equilibrium requirement (degree of stability), or quantity available for convection or other effects, it is convenient, as developed by Sir Napier Shaw and his colleagues, to plot values on a temperature-entropy diagram, based on the equation (see Chap. II)

$$\varphi = C_p \log \theta + \text{constant},$$

in which C_p is expressed in joules per degree per unit mass of dry air.

Figure 77 is a tephigram (the heavy line) of a balloon sounding made at Groesbeck, Texas, noon, Oct. 15, 1927. The abscissas are the actual temperatures of the air counted from $-273°$ C., or on what Sir Napier calls the tercentesimal scale, and the ordinates are the potential temperatures on the same scale with one bar, or 10^6 dynes per square centimeter, as the base pressure. The spacing of the ordinates is logarithmic, to reduce to a minimum the computations required by the entropy equation. The curved full lines are pseudoadiabats, and, therefore, irreversible for saturated air. Dry adiabats are *horizontal*. The curved broken lines indicate pressure of saturated air in terms of millibars or 10^3 dynes per square centimeter. The dotted lines indicate the number of grams of water vapor necessary to saturate 1 kilogram of dry air. The entropy is counted from 100°, same scale. All the above is the prepared base on which the actual state of the atmosphere, at a given time and place, as shown by observations, may be graphically represented.

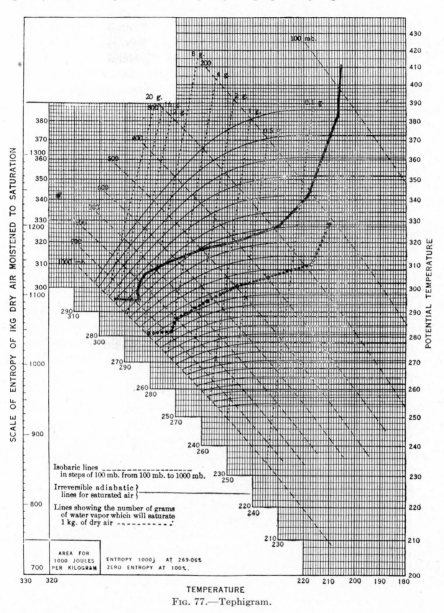

FIG. 77.—Tephigram.

Dry air is stable wherever the graph slopes up, on the way to lower pressure; unstable where it slopes down. Saturated air is stable only where the slope of the graph is steeper than the pseudoadiabat; where it

is less steep, saturated air may spontaneously rise.   The area enclosed
by a pseudoadiabat, and the graph between any starting point and
their next point of intersection, is proportional to the degree of instability, or energy per unit mass of saturated air available for convection
from the lower to the higher of the two given levels (greater and less
pressures), when the graph lies below the pseudoadiabat; and when it
lies above, to the degree of stability, or energy per unit mass of saturated air at the lower level needed to bring it into equilibrium with that
at the upper; similarly, for the area enclosed between the graph and a
dry adiabat.

If the humidity is known, that, also, can be added to the graph by a
dot, say, on each isobaric curve at the dew-point temperature, and the
chart thus made applicable to air in any state.   This adds much information: for instance, the quantity line (dotted) through any point on
the dew-point graph (heavy dotted line) intersects the adiabat through
the corresponding point of the tephigram at that height (pressure) at
which air, rising adiabatically from the given lower level, would become
saturated and begin to form cloud.

These are not all the uses of the tephigram, but enough to illustrate
the great amount of information it contains in a most compact and
legible form.

Principal Forms of Condensation.—Condensation assumes many
forms, of which the chief are: (*a*) *free drops*, varying in size all the way
from the fog or cloud particle up to the largest raindrop, or from 0.03
mm., roughly, to about 5 mm. in diameter; (*b*) *dew*, water that has
condensed on objects that by any process have attained a temperature
below the current dew point of the air immediately in contact with the
bedewed objects.   The cooling necessary to the formation of dew usually
results from loss of heat by radiation; (*c*) *frost*, a light, feathery deposit
of ice caused by the same process that produces dew, but occurring
when the temperatures of the objects on which it forms are below freezing;
(*d*) *rime*, a frost-like deposit of ice, often several inches deep on the
windward sides of exposed objects.   It is formed from impinging undercooled fog particles, and, hence, grows straight into the wind; (*e*) *glaze*
(ice storm), a coating of clear, smooth ice on the ground, trees, etc.,
including even aeroplanes.   It generally is caused by the falling of rain
on cold (below freezing) surfaces; (*f*) *snow*, tabular and columnar particles of ice formed in the free air at temperatures below freezing.   All are
hexagonal in type but of endless variety in detail—many exquisitely
beautiful; (*g*) *sleet*, ice pellets, mere frozen raindrops (or largely melted
snowflakes refrozen)—frozen during the fall of the precipitation through
a cold layer of air near the surface of the earth—that rattle when they
strike a window, for instance; (*h*) *hail*, lumps of ice more or less irregular
in outline and generally consisting of concentric layers of clearish ice and

compact snow. It occurs only in connection with thunderstorms and may be of any size up to that, at least, of a baseball or large orange, such as fell in considerable quantities at Annapolis and other points in Maryland on June 22, 1915.[1] Indeed, much larger stones have occasionally been reported and presumably have occurred. At any rate, in some instances, stock in the fields have been killed by blows from hailstones of unusual size.

Other forms of precipitation that should, perhaps, be mentioned are: *graupel*, soft snow pellets; *mist*, a thin fog of relatively large particles; and *drizzle*, a light rain of very small drops.

How Raindrops Are Formed.—As already explained, the amount of condensation resulting from given temperature and pressure changes can easily be computed, but this is not sufficient to account for the formation of ordinary raindrops. The difficulty lies in the fact that the number of nuclei per unit volume of the air (hundreds, or thousands, usually, per cubic centimeter) is so great that the condensation of even all the water vapor present would produce nothing larger than minute fog particles.

It is natural, of course, to suppose that some of the droplets in any cloud are relatively large, and that all of this kind that happen to be in the upper portion will, on falling, grow by collision into full-sized raindrops. But this simple assumption is beset with several difficulties. In the first place, nothing of the kind occurs, at least not to any appreciable extent, in a fog, or even in the average cloud. In fact, clouds may continuously cover the sky for days without yielding any rain whatever. Secondly, it is far from obvious that the droplets will coalesce, as assumed, on collision. Indeed, if they are not electrified, it is highly probable that, on the contrary, they will rebound from each other, as do the drops of a spraying jet of water,[2] due, presumably, to the air film between them. Finally, whether one considers a dense sea fog, diameter of particle 10μ, 1200 particles per cubic centimeter,[3] or a cloud, diameter of particle 33μ, 120 particles per cubic centimeter,[4] a little calculation shows that not enough water could, on the average, be accumulated by simple collisions, in the manner assumed, to produce medium-sized raindrops. Since the gain in volume is equal to the catch, or $4\pi r^2 dr = \pi r^2 a dh$, in which dh is the distance fallen and a the fraction of the total space actually occupied by water, therefore, a particle falling 1 kilometer through a cloud containing 2 grams of liquid water per cubic meter would grow to a drop only 1 mm. in diameter.

[1] FASSIG, *Monthly Weather Review*, September, 1915.

[2] LORD RAYLEIGH, *Proc. Roy. Soc.*, **28**; 406, 1879.

[3] WELLS and THURAS, *U. S. Coast. Guard, Bull.* 5, 1916.

[4] WAGNER, *Sitzb. Akad. Wiss. Wien*, **117**; 1281, 1908; BRAAK, K. *Magn. Met. Obs. Verh.*, No. 10, Batavia. 1922.

A factor in the growth of drops that needs to be examined is the relation of the saturation vapor pressure to their size, by virtue of which the larger tend to increase at the expense of the smaller. From the equation (see page 12)

$$\Delta p = \frac{2T\rho_v}{R(\rho_w - \rho_v)}$$

it appears that at 10° C. the excess pressure above that of normal saturation about fog droplets of diameter 10μ is 2.80 dynes per square centimeter. Now, at 10° C. saturation pressure balances a column of mercury 9.21 millimeters high; hence at 10° C. the ratio of the excess pressure about droplets of 10μ diameter to normal saturation pressure is, approximately, 1 to 4400; nor is this ratio greatly different at other ordinary temperatures.

Obviously, therefore, the growth of the larger drops at the expense of the smaller, as a result of the difference between their saturation pressures, is entirely negligible.

Another factor is the difference between the temperature of the relatively cool falling drop and that of the adjacent atmosphere. But the amount of condensation thus induced is very small, owing to the large value of the latent heat of vaporization.

The difficulties, then, that have to be considered in an attempt to explain the formation of raindrops seem to be as follows:

a. Drops large enough to fall at an appreciable rate—drops upon which any subsequent coalescence and resulting rain must depend—do not form in the average cloud.

This merely amounts to saying that such formation occurs only in rain clouds—that is, in clouds formed essentially by vertical convection. But how can convection produce drops of the necessary drizzle size in view of the hundreds, or, usually, thousands of nuclei per cubic centimeter? This seemingly insuperable difficulty is overcome (for it does rain), presumably, in the following manner: All droplets, of whatever size, are actually falling in respect to the air in which they happen to be. Hence, the rising air leaves more and more of its own nuclei behind as the droplets are abandoned—passes on as progressively filtered air— and thus contributes its subsequent condensation to only the fewer and fewer particles that exist along its upward path. Not only do the droplets fall out of the air in which they were formed, but they also aid in filtering the next portions of the rising column; and so on, continuously. In this way, the droplets well up within a cloud that is formed by vertical convection eventually become relatively few, and, therefore, grow comparatively large as a result of the continuous condensation onto them.

b. Water drops commonly do not unite on collision, but rebound, as shown by the scattering of a jet.

This difficulty is met by the fact that, when slightly electrified, drops do unite on collision,[1] together with the further fact that rain is always more or less electrified.

c. A cloud particle in passing straight down through a cloud from top to bottom would not, on the average, touch enough other particles to form, by union with them, a medium-sized drop.

But this is not important since rains are caused by rising air through which drops cannot approach the earth until they have grown beyond a certain size, which increases with the upward velocity. Besides, the variations in this velocity produce repeated rises and falls of drops of the appropriate sizes, until growth through coalescence, or condensation, or both, sufficient for their final fall does occur.

The rain process may, therefore, conveniently be divided into the following stages:

1. Vertical convection and the consequent formation of innumerable cloud particles about the condensation nuclei immediately after the dew point is passed, or, in the case of the more hygroscopic nuclei, before it is reached.

2. The continued rise of the saturated air, but, now, in a progressively filtered condition, as more and more cloud particles are abandoned.

3. Continuous condensation on the fewer and fewer droplets that remain in the "filtered" air, and their consequent growth to appreciable size, accelerated, presumably, by coalescence, though at what stage this phenomenon becomes important is not known.

4. The growth of the small drops by further condensation and, especially, by coalescence with other drops (all, on the average, being more or less electrified) during their fall through the cloud and to the earth.

In short, the rising air automatically filters itself immediately it passes the dew point; the remaining water vapor condenses on relatively few nuclei (transported cloud particles) and thus produces droplets of appreciable or drizzle size; these, being electrified, unite on collision and form raindrops.

Persistent vertical convection does not occur in fogs, or in the average cloud. Hence they exhibit neither progressive filtering nor continuous condensation. Drops of appreciable size do not, therefore, form within them, nor does rain fall from them.

The Mass Grouping of Raindrops.—Defant[2] found that the more than 10,000 raindrops he measured grouped themselves chiefly about the mass ratios 1:2:4:8: . . . . This he accounted for on the assumption that, on coming in contact with each other, drops of the same size

---

[1] LORD, RAYLEIGH, *loc. cit.*

[2] *Sitzb. Akad. Wiss. Wien,* **114**; 585, 1905. Also, WIEDERDORFER, ERICH, *Met. Zeit.,* **49**; 1, 1932.

are more likely to unite than are drops of unequal size. There appears, however, to be no justification for this assumption.

Schmidt[1] attributes this grouping to hydrodynamic forces which, whether adequate or not, certainly act in the right direction. His argument is substantially as follows: Drops falling side by side through the atmosphere, or other fluid, are pushed toward each other in accordance with Bernouilli's principle. Now, drops of the same, or nearly the same, size are far more likely to keep up with each other long enough to be forced together than are drops of unequal size; the larger, because of their greater velocity, quickly leave the smaller behind, except when their proximity is very close to actual contact.

Let, then, two drops of the same size, radius R, be falling side by side, with the uniform, or terminal, velocity v, and let the distance between their centers be $2x$. The force F on each towards the other is[2]

$$F = -\frac{3}{16}\sigma\pi v^2\frac{R^6}{x^4},$$

in which σ is the density of the adjacent air.

Substituting for F its value $\frac{4}{3}\pi R^3\frac{d^2x}{dt^2}$, multiplying through by $2\frac{dx}{dt}$, dividing by dt, and integrating, we get

$$\int_0^{\frac{dx}{dt}} 2\left(\frac{dx}{dt}\right)d\left(\frac{dx}{dt}\right) = -2k\int_a^x \frac{dx}{x^4},$$

in which

$$k = \frac{9}{64}\sigma v^2 R^3;$$

or

$$\left(\frac{dx}{dt}\right)^2 = \frac{2k}{3}\left(\frac{1}{x^3} - \frac{1}{a^3}\right).$$

Hence, integrating from zero to a, we get for the time required to effect collision

$$T = \frac{3.27}{v\sqrt{\sigma R^3}}\int_0^a \frac{dx}{\sqrt{\frac{1}{x^3} - \frac{1}{a^3}}} = \frac{3.27}{v}\sqrt{\frac{a^5}{\sigma R^3}}\int_0^1 \frac{dy}{\sqrt{\frac{1}{y^3} - 1}}.$$

But

$$\int_0^1 \frac{dy}{\sqrt{\frac{1}{y^3} - 1}} = 0.74683.$$

---

[1] *Met. Zeit.*, **25**; 496, 1908.
[2] WIEN, "Lehrbuch der Hydrodynamik," p. 156.

Hence, where $\sigma = 0.001150$, its average value at about 750 meters above sea level, the distance D of fall during the time T the drops are being pushed into contact is given by the equation

$$D = vT = 72a\sqrt{\left(\frac{a}{R}\right)^3}\ cm.$$

The following table, computed by this formula, gives the values of D in *meters* for the assumed values of a and of R in centimeters. Where R is a considerable fraction of a the computed value of D is too great.

DISTANCE OF FALL OF RAINDROPS BEFORE COLLISION

a \ R	0.01	0.02	0.05	0.1	0.2
0.1	2.3	0.8	0.2	0.07	0.03
0.5	127	45	11.4	4.0	1.4
1.0	.....	255	64	23	8.0
2.0	.....	.....	364	129	46

All the above assumes, of course, a dominant initial unit. This, we may suppose, is that which is just large enough to overcome the lift of the rising air at, or near, the cloud level. However, Köhler[1] finds the same relation for fog droplets.

Velocity of Fall of Raindrops.—If the diameter of the drop is very small, 0.1 mm. or less, its approximate steady, or terminal, velocity of fall can be computed by Stokes' well-known equation[2]

$$V = \frac{2}{9}gr^2\frac{(\sigma - \rho)}{\mu},$$

in which V is the velocity in centimeters per second, g the value, in c.g.s. units, of gravity acceleration, r the radius of the drop in centimeters, σ the density of the drop, ρ the density of the air, and μ its viscosity.

The equations of fall in the case of raindrops of average and larger sizes, 1 to 5 mm. diameter, are, however, very different, and little more than empirical.[3] Several of the more important velocities, and sufficient for approximate interpolations, are given below in the table of Precipitation Values. The maximum velocity, in air of normal density (velocity proportional, nearly, to square root of density), at which the larger drops break up is about 8 meters per second.

Intensity of Precipitation.—The intensity, or rate, of rainfall varies from zero up to several inches per hour, and, like the strength of the

[1] *Geofys. Pub.*, Vol. V, No. 1, Oslo, 1927.
[2] *Phys. Math. Papers*, **3**; 59.
[3] LIZNAR, *Met. Zeit.*, **31**; 339, 1914.

wind, has been popularly divided into several more or less definite grades. Most of these, together with other roughly average values they imply, are given in the accompanying table.

PRECIPITATION VALUES
(Air density as at 0° C. and 740 mm. pressure)

Popular name	Precipitation intensity, millimeters per hour	Diameter of drop, millimeters	Velocity of fall, meters per second	Milligrams of liquid water per cubic meter of air	Height of cloud above surface, meters
Clear............	0.00	....	.....	0.00	
Fog.............	Trace	0.01	0.003	6.0	0
Mist............	0.05	0.1	0.25	55.5	100
Drizzle..........	0.25	0.2	0.75	92.6	200
Light rain........	1.00	0.45	2.00	138.9	600
Moderate rain.....	4.00	1.0	4.00	277.8	600
Heavy rain........	15.00	1.5	5.00	833.3	1000
Excessive rain....	40.00	2.1	6.00	1851.9	1200
Cloudburst........	100 to 1000?	3.0	7.00	4000 to 35000?	1200
....	......	5.0	8.00		

Why the Atmosphere Generally Is Unsaturated.—It may, perhaps, seem strange that, in spite of the continuous and rapid evaporation from nearly all parts of the earth's surface, the atmosphere as a whole never becomes even approximately saturated. This condition, however, is a necessary result of vertical convection. Obviously, whatever the temperature and relative humidity of a given mass of air at any point of its convectional route, its specific humidity is less then, in general, than when its ascent began, by the amount of rain or snow already abandoned by it. That is, on the average, air in a convection circuit descends to the earth drier than when it previously ascended from it. In short, convection, because it induces abundant precipitation, is, therefore, a most efficient drying process; and, because comparatively little precipitation is produced in any other way, convection alone prevents the atmosphere from becoming and remaining intolerably humid.

Summer and Winter Precipitation.—Vertical convection, essential, as above explained, to all considerable condensation, results from three distinct causes: (*a*) superadiabatic temperature gradients, due often to surface heating; (*b*) converging winds, as in the front half of cyclones; and (*c*) forced rise from (1) flow over land elevations and barriers of cold air, especially along the warm front, (2) underrunning of cooler winds, as along the polar front. The first, or thunderstorm, type of convection causes much of the summer precipitation of temperate regions, as, also, nearly all the rain of the tropics, while, due to cold air, the second and all the third, or cyclonic, convections produce by far the greater part of winter precipitation; except, perhaps, that which occurs along the windward sides of the most favorably situated land barriers. Also, during the colder season, precipitation usually occurs lower down the barrier slope, and may be induced by feebler cyclones, or other storms, than in the warmer. This is owing, in part, to the fact that, generally, there is less difference between the actual and dew-point temperatures during winter than during summer (a condition determined by the great seasonal temperature changes of continents with reference to the ocean), and, therefore, a less convection is required in the first case than in the second to induce condensation; and, due partly to the greater rate of decrease of temperature with increase of latitude while the days are short than while they are long—a condition that favors winter precipitation, by causing a greater fall of temperature during the winter season than any other, for a given travel of the wind on the front or rainy side of a cyclone. That is, usually a less vertical convection and a less horizontal travel of the air—a feebler storm—suffices to induce precipitation during winter than during summer.

The contrasts, then, between summer and winter precipitation are manifold. The more important differences are listed in the following table:

CONTRAST BETWEEN SUMMER AND WINTER PRECIPITATION

	Summer	Winter
Rain	Usually	Often
Snow	Never	Frequent
Hail (ice lumps)	Occasionally	Never
Sleet (frozen rain)	Never	Occasionally
On barrier	High	Low, and up
Type of storm	Thunderstorm frequently	Cyclone
Strength of convection	Strong, generally essential	Feebler, often sufficient
Intensity of cyclone	Decided, usually essential	Slight, often sufficient

Summer Daytime and Nighttime Precipitation in the United States.— This restriction to season and locality is entirely owing to the excellence of the corresponding data,[1] for the principles involved are the same everywhere.

In most, if not all, parts of the United States, as, also, nearly everywhere else, the day and night distribution of summer rainfall is largely determined by the corresponding distribution of the thunderstorm, or strong vertical convection of tolerably humid air.

In the southeastern portion of the United States where the prevailing summer winds are southerly, humid, and gentle, the larger part of the

[1] KINCER, *Monthly Weather Review*, 44; 628, 1916.

rainfall of this season is owing to heat thunderstorms, that is, local showers, resulting from convection induced by strong surface heating, and, therefore, most frequent in the early afternoon.

Similarly, throughout much of the Rocky Mountain and Plateau regions, especially about the chimney-acting peaks, and other places favorable to strong updrafts, cumuli and the resulting precipitation are most frequent, during summer, in the afternoon, and least at night.

Through the northeastern portion of this country, the typical heat thunderstorm is of secondary importance. Nevertheless, its occurrence there appears, still, to be often enough to account for the slight excess, in that region, of the daytime over the nighttime precipitation.

In the lower Michigan peninsula, on the other hand, precipitation is most abundant by night. Here, as elsewhere, rain, at any given place and time, is due to clouds that had their inception to the windward. In general, therefore, the rains of the peninsula in question are from clouds that either originated above, or crossed over, Lake Michigan. Now, during summer, the land areas about this lake, as, in general, about all lakes, commonly are warmer than the surface of the water, through the day, and cooler at night. Hence, convection over the lake and, consequently, the cloudiness and precipitation to the near east, that is, over the lower peninsula, are greatest at night, as they are also over the oceans and along their leeward coasts.

The extreme southwestern portion of the United States appears, also, to get most of its summer rain at night. Here the air that rises during the day, being over hot, desert regions, is too dry, except rarely, to yield any considerable precipitation. Furthermore, any daytime rain that may fall as the result of a local convection must be from a high cumulus and through more or less dry air. Hence the daytime catch in this region is reduced, often greatly, by evaporation in mid-air.

The nighttime catch, presumably, is greater than that of the daytime, as indicated by the rather scanty data, because (a) when the wind at the cumulus level is from the general direction of the Gulf of California, the night rains, obviously, must predominate, owing to the fact that the ascending night air, being over the gulf, is humid in comparison with the daytime convective columns that rise from the desert; and (b) the percentage of the rain lost by evaporation, while falling, is less at night than through the day, owing to the lower level of the night clouds, and the greater relative humidity of the air at that time.

Finally, summer precipitation is greater at night than during the day over a large area that is centered, roughly, in eastern Nebraska. The maximum hourly catch occurs about midnight and the maximum frequency an hour or two later.

Cold anticyclones, cold because of their considerable southward travel over land, frequently enter the United States by way of Montana, or anywhere east to and including the Great Lakes—anticyclones that "break" the "hot waves" of the Mississippi, Missouri, and Ohio valleys. On such occasions, thunderstorms are frequent in the region under consideration (*a*) when, in conjunction with an anticyclone over Montana, say, the pressure is high over the eastern and southeastern portions of the United States, and, consequently, a north-south or northeast-southwest "trough" of low pressure lies over eastern Nebraska and adjacent regions; (*b*) when there is a low, or cyclone, in the southwest, over New Mexico, for instance, and a cold anticyclone centered just north of the Great Lakes.

Under each of these, and similar, conditions, eastern Nebraska and the adjacent regions are likely, during summer, to be quite warm, and the surface pressure more or less below normal. At 1-kilometer elevation, however, and for some distance above that level, the pressure over the heated region may, during the daytime, be approximately equal (owing to expansion of the air below) to that over the anticyclone, and, hence, the winds at that level correspondingly gentle.

At night, the warmer region normally loses heat more rapidly than the cooler, and, hence, the pressure at any considerable elevation above the former tends to fall below that of the latter at the same level. This, in turn, allows the cooler air, here and there, to overflow the warmer, and, thereby, establish that convectional instability essential to the genesis of the thunderstorm.

Presumably, then, the above is at least a part of the reason why, in the central portion of the United States, the thunderstorm is more frequent and the summer precipitation more abundant during the night than in the daytime.

CHAPTER XVI

FOGS AND CLOUDS

The deposition of dew, the forming of hoarfrost, and the sweating of ice pitchers, all examples of surface condensation, show that atmospheric moisture promptly condenses upon any object whose temperature is below the dew point. Similarly, volume condensation takes place in the form of a fog, or cloud, of innumerable droplets, or ice spicules, throughout the body of ordinary air, whenever, by expansion or otherwise, it is sufficiently cooled. But this is not equally true of all air. Thus, while the first considerable rapid expansion, and, therefore, decided volume cooling, of humid air in a receiver, if recently admitted unfiltered, is quite certain to produce a miniature cloud, subsequent expansions of the same air produce fewer and fewer fog particles. If the old air is removed, and unfiltered, fresh air admitted, the condensations again occur as before; but if the fresh air enters through an efficient filter, such as a plug of cotton wool a few centimeters long, condensation remains as difficult as in the exhausted air. The admission, however, of a little smoke restores to the exhausted, and confers upon the filtered, air full powers of condensation.

Obviously, then, cloud droplets form about nuclei that cannot easily pass through mechanical filters of fine texture, and microscopic examinations of the residue left, on the evaporation of these droplets, have shown the nuclei to consist in large measure of dust particles, both mineral and organic. Hygroscopic gases, such as the oxides of sulphur and of nitrogen, also act as condensation nuclei; but, ordinarily there is abundant hygroscopic dust in the atmosphere (thousands of particles per cubic centimeter) to provide for all precipitation. It is often urged that free electrons in the air also act as nuclei about which water vapor condenses, but, since this type of condensation requires about a fourfold supersaturation, its occurrence in the open seems extremely improbable. Indeed, the first part, at least, of the condensation must occur on the more hygroscopic particles, such as those of sea salt, and even before normal saturation is reached. The drops thus formed, mechanically wash out, in great measure, the nonhygroscopic dust.

As stated, volume condensation may be induced in the atmosphere by any cooling process: whether by radiation, as on clear nights; by mixing warmer with colder masses of air; by the flow of relatively warm air over cold surfaces, as in the case of winter south winds (northern hemisphere); or by expansion, owing either to convection or barometric depression. But the extent of the condensation, the kind and amount of precipitation from it, and its general appearance, according to which, chiefly, it is classified, depend largely on which cooling process is involved.

Distinction between Fog and Cloud.—Volume condensation is divided primarily into fog and cloud, but a sharp distinction between them, that would enable one always to say which is which, is not possible. In general, however, a fog differs from a cloud only in its location. Both are owing, as explained, to the cooling of the atmosphere to a temperature below its dew point, but in the case of the cloud this cooling usually results from vertical convection, and, hence, the cloud is nearly always separated from the earth, except on mountain tops. Fog, on the other hand, is induced by relatively low temperatures at, and near, the surface, and, commonly, itself extends quite to the surface, at least during the stage of its development. In short, fog consists of water droplets, or ice spicules, condensed from, and floating in, the air near the surface; cloud, of water droplets, or ice spicules, condensed from, and floating in, the air well above the surface. Fog is a cloud on the earth; cloud a fog in the sky.

FOGS

According to the conditions under which they are formed, fogs may be divided into two general classes—radiation fogs and advection fogs.

Radiation Fog.—Fog is likely to form along rivers and creeks and even in cleared mountain valleys during any still, cloudless night of summer and especially, autumn. In the course of a calm, warm day and earlier portion, at least, of the night, much water is evaporated into the lower atmosphere of such regions, where, in large part, it remains as long as there are no winds. Hence this air, because it is humid, and the adjacent surface of the earth lose heat rapidly during the night by radiation to the clear sky. In many cases they cool, in the end, to a temperature below the dew point, and thus induce a greater or less volume condensation, on the always-present dust motes, that results in a correspondingly dense fog (Fig. 78). Such fog, however, is not likely to occur during cloudy nights, because the air seldom, then, cools sufficiently; nor during high winds, since they dissipate the moisture, and, also, through turbulence, prevent the formation of excessively cold aerial lakes; nor in absolutely calm air, since the droplets then would fall out as fast as formed.

The distinctive factor, in the formation of this type of fog, is the free radiation of the ground and the lower air by which the latter is sufficiently cooled to induce condensation. Hence, fogs formed in this manner are properly termed "radiation fogs," sometimes also called "land fogs" and "summer fogs."

A frequent incidental phenomenon, in connection with fogs of this class, is their accelerated growth well after daybreak, which occasionally continues until after sun up, when radiation gain exceeds the corresponding loss. It has been suggested that this phenomenon is due to hygroscopic compounds formed in the air by insolation, either direct or diffused; but there is, as yet, no proof that these compounds are more than a contributing factor, perhaps an entirely negligible one, to the observed result. Another factor that, at times and places, may be of some importance, is the soot and hygroscopic compounds discharged into the foggy air from numerous breakfast fires. Usually, however, the sole appreci-

Fig. 78.—Radiation fog, Loudon Valley, Virginia. (*A. J. Weed, photographer.*)

able cause is the gradual onset of convectional disturbances in the quiescent valley air incident to the insolational warming of the mountain tops and sides. This mixes the cool surface layer with that next above and, thereby, often increases the fog depth. Furthermore, it drags the river of fog up the valley walls, and thus also increases its width. However, before either process has gone very far, evaporation becomes manifest, and, generally, within an hour or two, the fog has totally vanished.

Advection Fog.—Whenever warm, humid air drifts over a cold surface, its temperature is reduced throughout the lower turbulent layers by conduction to that surface, and by mixture with remaining portions of the previous cold air and a correspondingly dense fog produced. Hence fog often occurs, during winter, in the front portion of a weak cyclone; also, whenever air drifts from warm water to cold—from the Gulf Stream, for instance, to the Labrador Current; and, wherever gentle ocean winds blow over snow-covered land—circumstances that justify the terms "winter fog" and "sea fog" (drifting on shore in places, and even some distance inland (Fig. 79)). Similarly, a cold wind drifting or spreading under, and through, a body of warm, humid air, also produces a fog, though usually a comparatively light one. This explains the fog that frequently forms, during winter, along the front of a "high," and the thin fog that occasionally is seen over lakes, on frosty autumn mornings, when the water appears to be steaming—actually evaporating

Fig. 79.—Advection fog, seen from Mount Wilson, California. (*F. Ellerman, photographer.*)

into air already saturated, and, thus, inducing condensation. It also explains the frequent occurrence of "frost smoke" on polar seas. Fog at sea, of various densities, must often occur while the humidity still is distinctly below that of saturation, owing to the presence of the highly hygroscopic sea-salt "dust."

If the wind is strong, the turbulence extends through a comparatively deep layer. Hence, in the case of warm air drifting over a cold surface, if the movement is rapid, the total duration of contact between any portion of the air and that surface is likely to be so brief that but little cooling can take place, and no fog can be formed. Similarly, it usually happens, also, that fog does not form when the cold wind, blowing over a warm, humid region, is even moderately strong. Here, the turbulence mixes the excessive moisture, near the surface, through so large a volume that saturation, commonly, is not closely approached nor, therefore, is any trace of fog produced.

From the above, it appears that all fogs that result from the drifting of warm, humid air over cold surfaces, as, also, those that are caused by the flow of cold air over warm, humid regions, are but effects of temperature changes induced by the horizontal transportation of air; hence, the proposed general name, "advection fog," is applicable, also, to fogs that have merely drifted in from some other place, as from sea onto land. The term advection is preferred to convection, because the latter is practically restricted, in meteorological usage, to a change of level; whereas, in the case under consideration only horizontal movements are concerned. The contradistinction, therefore, between "advection fog" and "convection cloud" is obvious, and, presumably, worth while.

Far longer discussions of fog than are here practicable have been published by H. C. Willett[1] and S. Petterssen[2] whose monographs should be consulted by all who are interested in that phenomenon.

CLOUDS

The cooling of the atmosphere by which cloud condensation is induced is, perhaps, most frequently caused by vertical convection, either thermal or forced, including eddy convection; often, presumably, by the mixing of winds of different temperatures; occasionally, by pressure changes, elevation remaining the same; occasionally, also, by radiation; and, rarely, in the case of very thin clouds, by diffusion and conduction.

Radiation, though productive of many fogs, is excluded from the list of principal cloud-forming processes for the reason that, as explained elsewhere, any mass of free air that cools in position, as it must, whenever its radiation exceeds its absorption, immediately gains in density and falls to a lower level where, when equilibrium is reached, it actually is *warmer* than it was before the cooling began, and its relative humidity, therefore, lower. Hence, it seems that radiation could produce clouds only when equally active, or nearly so, over an extensive layer of practically saturated air, or when the lower air is exceptionally cold and dense. If radiation is unequally distributed it tends to evaporate clouds rather than to produce them.

Classification.—It is not practicable, however desirable, to classify clouds according to their causes, as in the case of fogs, for it often happens that the exact cause is not obvious. Hence, other bases of classification have been adopted, especially form or appearance, activity, and position. Most, but not all, clouds belong to one or other of the four distinct

[1] *M. W. R.*, **56**; 435–468, 1928.
[2] *Geof. Pub.* **12**, No. 10, Oslo, 1939.

types, *cirrus, stratus, cumulus, nimbus,* including their alto, fracto, and combination forms; altostratus, altocumulus; fractostratus, fracto-cumulus; cirrostratus, cirrocumulus, stratocumulus, cumulonimbus.

The following names and descriptions of the major cloud forms are essentially the same as those proposed by the International Cloud Commission and now in general use.

Cirrus (Ci.).—The name cirrus, literally a curl, or ringlet, has been given to those fibrous white clouds that resemble great wisps of hair (mares' tails), giant curling plumes (feather clouds), tangled skeins, and

Fig. 80.—Cirrus.   (*F. Ellerman, photographer.*)

various other things (Figs. 80 and 81). Though on occasions cirri form at low levels, especially in polar regions, normally they are the highest (save the two rare forms in the stratosphere), often 10 to 12 kilometers above the earth in middle latitudes and still higher in tropical regions, the most tenuous, and among the most familiar of all clouds.

Since cirri usually run far ahead of the rainy portions of a cyclonic area, often even well into the preceding anticyclone, and grow denser as the storm approaches, it is obvious that they frequently result from cyclonic convections that extend nearly or quite to the stratosphere, where, and for some distance below which, the rising air is carried forward much faster than the storm center. But they, also, are fairly common as isolated clouds in the midst of "highs," due, presumably, to a mechanical, or bodily, lifting of the upper air of these regions, or overrunning of air in the general circulation, and, consequently, dynamical cooling, not only of the stratosphere, as abundantly shown by the records of sounding balloons, but, also, of the topmost portion of the troposphere where cirri usually form.

It has been suggested that cirri often are caused by cooling in place by radiation, but, as already explained, this appears to be improbable for clouds so broken and discontinuous. On the contrary, however, it seems likely that through free radiation and cooling at night they often sink to lower levels, get *warmer*, and evaporate. Thermal and

Fig. 81.—Cirrus. (*F. Ellerman, photographer.*)

mechanical convection, therefore, the first prevailing in tropical regions, and both, presumably, in extratropical, appear to be the only abundant causes of cirri.

The excessively low temperatures at which cirri are formed, generally $-30°$ to $-50°$ C., necessitate their being tenuous (at such temperatures there is but little water vapor to condense) and practically insure (exceptions have been reported[1]) that they shall consist of ice needles, or, in some cases, of small snowflakes. The fibrous and feathery structures of the highest cirri may perhaps be explained as follows: Since diffusion is a very slow process, it is clear that moisture is carried into the upper atmosphere, mainly, by vertical convection, and, as this often occurs

[1] Simpson, *Quart. J. Roy. Meteorol. Soc.*, **38**; 291, 1912.

sporadically, it appears that through the increase of winds with elevation, the rising and generally humid air is likely to be drawn out into long threads and bands, and to float away in filaments at the convective limit, just as, during the early hours of calm autumn mornings, chimney smoke in mountain valleys often is drawn out into streaks and ribbons at or near the inversion level.

Any cloud, therefore, produced in this fibrously humid air obviously itself must have the same general structure—a common structure of cirrus clouds. Through local convection, however, and abrupt changes in velocity at the upper surface of these clouds, the air currents to which

Fig. 82.—Cirrostratus, and advection fog, seen from Mount Wilson, California. (*F. Ellerman, photographer.*)

they are due, presumably, often are deflected into curves of changing radii. Hence, perhaps, the curved or plumed cirrus. Mare's tails are streaks of snow falling from, and generally trailing behind, small alto- or cirrocumuli, the cloudlet itself drawn out, often to complete exhaustion, by increase of wind velocity with altitude. They often are curved by changes with level of wind direction.

Cirrostratus (Cist.).—When cirrus clouds thicken, as they usually do on the approach of a cyclonic storm, they gradually merge into a broad cloud layer, having the appearance of a more or less continuous white veil of uneven and often fibrous texture (Fig. 82), to which the name cirrostratus has been given. Its altitude is nearly that of the cirrus, of which, indeed, it is only a dense and extensive form, though its under surface is not so high.   Like its forerunner, the thinner cirrus, it also consists of ice crystals, as is evident from the various types of halos it forms about the sun and moon.

The origin of these clouds is substantially the same as that of the cirrus; that is, convection, which, in turn, may be caused by general expansion of the air below, or by convergence of winds, such as occurs in the cyclone.   Frequently, as explained above, the cirrostratus is only the higher and swifter portion of the cyclonic cloud system, the result of forced convection to great altitudes.

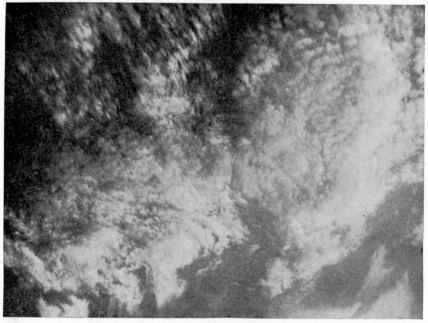

Fig. 83.—Cirrocumuli.   (*F. Ellerman, photographer.*)

Cirrocumulus (**Cicu.**).—Cirrocumuli are small, fleecy cumulus clouds, generally 6 to 7 kilometers above the surface; that is, in the lower cirrus region.   They usually occur in large numbers, producing an effect sometimes described as "curdled sky"; frequently, also, in groups and rows that remind one of the patterns (not the scales) on the backs of mackerel.   Hence the expression "mackerel-back sky," commonly abbreviated to "mackerel sky" (Fig. 83).

Their origin obviously is due, chiefly, to a single cause—local vertical convections, induced perhaps by an overrunning cold, or underflowing warm, layer of air, or by the lift or drop of a thin cloud sheet, itself changing temperature according to the wet adiabatic rate and the clear air according to the dry.   When an unstable fluid sheet is thin, it breaks up into numerous convectional regions, the theory of which, for liquids, has been developed by Lord Rayleigh[1]; a theory that, if extended to include gases, especially when subjected to shearing stresses, might also, as Brunt[2] has suggested, account for the formation of all layers of closely set, but essentially isolated, clouds, such as cirrocumuli, some forms of altocumuli, and the mammatocumuli.

To each convective rise of the air there evidently must be an equivalent descent, and, if the heating maxima are numerous, the minima between must also be numerous, thus producing many rising currents, each with its small cumulus surrounded by descending air and relatively

Fig. 84.—Altostratus, and advection fog, seen from Mount Wilson, California. (*F. Ellerman, photographer.*)

clear sky. Through precipitation and turbulence, the cirrocumulus often develops into a cirrostratus, or altostratus.

Altostratus (Ast.).—The altostratus is a thick, grayish cloud veil (Fig. 84), at times compact and fibrous in structure, and, again, thinner, like a heavy cirrostratus, through which the sun or moon may dimly be seen. Its average elevation (under surface) is about 4 kilometers. It may result from the forward running of air forced up in the storm area of a cyclone, from the spreading tops of cumuli, from the flow of warmer over colder air, from falling precipitation out of alto- and cirrocumuli, or from the mere radiational cooling, in place, of a layer of relatively humid air—humid from the evaporation of altocumuli, perhaps.

[1] *Phil. Mag.*, **32**; 529, 1916.
[2] *Meterological Mag.*, **60**; 1, 1925; *Quart. J. Roy. Meteorol. Soc.*, **63**; 277, 1937.

Altocumulus (Acu.).—The name altocumulus has been given to those detached, fleecy clouds, with shaded portions (Fig. 85), often occurring in closely packed groups and rows, that resemble enlarged cirrocumuli, and, doubtless, are formed in much the same way. The moisture involved, especially during fair weather, seems often to be furnished by previously evaporated cumuli. Their average altitude is approximately that of the altostratus, that is, 4 kilometers. Indeed, detached portions of forming or evaporating altostratus, also, are generally called altocumuli, the more exact term, fractoaltostratus, not being in use.

Fig. 85.—Altocumulus.   (*A. J. Weed, photographer.*)

Stratocumulus (Stcu.).—Stratocumuli are large rolls of dark cloud, more or less connected with thinner clouds, which, together, cover nearly, or quite, the entire sky (Fig. 86). Their bases are flat and at about the same height, generally 1.5 to 2 kilometers. They are formed by vertical convection, as is obvious from their rounded tops and flat bases at approximately the same level—the common saturation level. Their shallow depth and broad expanse are due, presumably, to an overlying layer of small, or even inverted, temperature gradient through which rising air cannot easily penetrate. This name is also given to a stratus of irregular density, and, thus, to all that entire range of clouds between the uniform stratus and the discrete cumuli.

Nimbostratus (Nbst.).—The nimbostratus, formerly called nimbus, is any thick, extensive layer of formless cloud from which rain or snow

Fig. 86.—Stratocumulus, Washington, D. C. (*W. J. Humphreys, photographer.*)

Fig. 87.—Nimbostratus, Ashland, Kentucky. (*W. J. Humphreys, photographer.*)

is falling or seemingly on the point of falling (Fig. 87). The average altitude of its undersurface is of the order of 1 kilometer. It is produced

FIG. 88.—Cumulus, near Gap Mills, West Virginia. (*L. W. Humphreys, photographer.*)

FIG. 89.—Cumulus, (becoming cumulonimbus) seen near Mount Wilson, California. (*F. Ellerman, photographer.*)

chiefly by some type of forced convection: the upward deflection of winds by land or by cold atmospheric barriers, as along the warm front of the cyclone, and the underrunning of warmer by colder air. In part, however, the cooling and consequent condensation often is owing to the mixing of cold air with warm, and to the transfer of warm air to a colder

Fig. 90.—Cumulus cloud formed by convection over fire on Sister Elsie Peak, California, Sept. 13, 1913. (*O. H. Lawrence, photographer.*)

region, where it is cooled by contact, by mixing with cooler air, and by excess of radiation loss over radiation gain.

Fractonimbus (Frnb.).—The fractonimbus, popularly known as *scud*, is that low, detached cloud fragment, too thin and fog-like to produce rain, that, occasionally, is seen drifting rapidly beneath a heavy nimbostratus at an average elevation of probably not more than 100 to 300 meters. It may rise, like steam, during, or following, rainfall on a warm surface, especially in valleys and on the sides of mountains (where it is often called fog) which it ascends. It is also caused by forced convection over cliffs or other obstacles.

Cumulus (Cu.).—The cumulus (Figs. 88 and 89) often 'called "woolpack," is a dense, detached cloud with a rapidly changing cauliflower head and flat base at the saturation level of rising air. Its illuminated portions are snow white, while the shaded parts are usually dark. Its

Fig. 91.—Cumulus over island—Krakatao. (*E. E. Barnard, photographer.*)

border is sharply defined and, when near the sun, very bright. The average altitude of the base is about 1.5 kilometers, and of the top rather more than 2 kilometers.

Cumuli are produced entirely by vertical convection induced by temperature differences—even fires, sometimes, cause them (Fig. 90). Hence they are always frequent in tropical regions, and also over continents at higher latitudes during summer. For the same reason, they occur over land most numerously of afternoons, and at sea late in the night. At times rather low cumuli form a sort of coastal fringe along the locus of upward convection, that is, a short way out over the sea at night, and a few miles inland during the day—attendants of the land breeze and the sea breeze, respectively. They often occur over reefs and islands (Fig. 91) whose presence, frequently, is thus revealed while they themselves are still below the horizon. Occasionally they even parallel a large river on either side where there is rising air over the hills and bottoms, and sinking air over the cooler water. Further, since vertical convection depends only on the establishment of a proper vertical temperature gradient, it follows that cumuli may also form at high latitudes over the warmer portions of the ocean, or, indeed, wherever there is a sufficient temperature contrast between the surface and overlying air to induce marked upward currents.

Fractocumulus (Frcu.).—During the initial stages, especially, of their development, cumuli often are small, and appear tattered and torn

Fig. 92.—Cumulus and fractocumulus, in Monroe County, West Virginia, Peters Mountain to left. (*L. W. Humphreys, photographer.*)

like detached and dissolving masses of fog (Fig. 92). While in this condition such clouds are often called fractocumuli.

Cumulonimbus (Cunb.).—The cumulonimbus (Fig. 93), a necessary accompaniment of every thunderstorm, is, as its name implies, a cumulus cloud from which rain is falling. It is very turbulent and much the deepest of all clouds, being usually anywhere from 1 to 4 or 5 kilometers thick—occasionally even 10 or more, especially in the tropics. Its times and places of occurrence and mode of formation are the same as those of the cumulus.

Stratus (St.).—The stratus is a low, fog-like cloud of wide extent, often merging into a nimbostratus, and, again, clearing away like lifted fog. Its average altitude is between 0.5 and 1 kilometer. It seems, often, to result from forced convection due to the underrunning of cold

Fig. 93.—Cumulonimbus, near Pensacola, Florida.

Fig. 94.—Billow cloud, a variety of altocumulus.   (*A. J. Henry, photographer.*)

air, and, also, perhaps, to the mixing of humid layers of different temperatures. In some cases, that of the "velo" cloud, for instance, in southern California, it is only sea fog drifting over relatively warm land.

SPECIAL CLOUD FORMS

Although it might seem that the above cloud types, including their numerous gradations and transitions, are exhaustive, there, nevertheless, are several occasional forms sufficiently distinct to justify individual names and special descriptions.

Fig. 95.—Lenticular cloud, over Mount Rainier. (*O. P. Anderson, photographer.*)

Billow Cloud.—Billow clouds (Fig. 94), also called windrow clouds and wave clouds, occur in series of approximately regularly spaced bands, generally with intervening strips of clear sky. They usually form in the lower cirrus region, that is, at elevations of 6 to 8 kilometers, but may occur at any level from the surface—fogs are occasionally billowed—up to that of the highest cirrus. They appear to be caused by local convections out of a thin layer of cloud into slightly faster air above, by which the cloud columns are thrown into horizontal rolls normal to the direction of the wind.[1]

Lenticular Cloud.—The lenticular cloud (Figs. 95 and 96) is stationary and marks the cool crest of an air billow commonly induced by a

[1] Brunt, D., *Quart. J. Roy. Meterol. Soc.*, **63**; 277, 1937.

mountain peak, or range, or other surface irregularity. It grows from the windward edge by increase of condensation and thins toward the

Fig. 96.—Lenticular cloud, stratus lenticularis. (*F. Ellerman, photographer.*)

leeward by progressive evaporation. It, therefore, is thickest in the middle and thins to nothing on the sides; hence, its name.

Fig. 97.—Crest cloud, windward side, seen from the Pali, near Honolulu. (*A. M. Hamrick, photographer.*)

Crest Cloud.—The crest cloud (Figs. 98 and 98) is formed by the upward deflection of the wind by a long mountain ridge. It usually covers the higher slopes, as well as the top, and, though called cloud by people in the valleys below, is likely to be termed fog by anyone actually in it. Occasionally condensation occurs only along the upper reaches of the deflected winds, in which case it forms a lenticular cloud above, and to the leeward of, the mountain ridge.

In either case, the individual droplets are quickly evaporated, and the cloud form preserved, only through continuous condensation from renewed air. It is permanent in the same sense that a cataract is permanent through the continuous supply of water by the stream above.

Banner Cloud.—The banner cloud (Fig. 99), as its name implies, resembles a great white flag floating from a high mountain peak. In

Fig. 98.—Crest cloud, lee side, seen from Honolulu. (*A. M. Hamrick, photographer.*)

strong winds the pressure to the immediate leeward of such a peak is, more or less, reduced, and the resulting low temperature, intensified by the mountain surface, appears to be the cause of this singular cloud that, though continuously evaporating, as constantly re-forms in the turbulent wake.

Scarf Cloud.—It occasionally happens that, as a cumulus rises rapidly and to great heights, a thin, cirrus-like cloud, convex upward, forms above the topmost billow and, at first, entirely detached from it. Then, if convection progresses, and it usually does, the flossy cloud becomes more extensive and rests on the thunder head, or heads. A little later it mantles the shoulders, the heads being free (Fig. 100), and may even drape the sides of the towering cumulus. In all stages, it resembles a great silken scarf; hence, the name. It often is called false cirrus, but that term is now, and better, applied to a different formation. It has also been called cap cloud, but this is confusing,

because the same term has long been applied, loosely, to any cloud that
hovers above, or, especially, rests upon, a mountain peak; and, besides,
the cap analogy applies only to the early stages.

Fig. 99.—Banner cloud, Mount Assiniboine, near Banff, Canada. (*C. D. Walcott,
photographer.*)

It is caused by the elevation and consequent expansion and cooling
of the air immediately, and to some distance above, the rising mass of
the cumulus. Generally, this expansion of the superincumbent atmos-

phere produces no visible effect, but, occasionally there exists a thin stratum of nearly saturated air in which an altostratus might form, or, indeed, later does form, and when this is lifted by the rising cumulus it immediately develops a local cirrus-like cloud. But, if the saturated layer is thin, as it often is, the cumulus head may, easily, rise quite above it into drier air, leaving the filmy cloud at practically its original level, the level of the humid stratum, or completely absorbing it.

False Cirrus.—The name "false cirrus" formerly was applied, indifferently, to the scarf cloud, just described, and to those gray locks,

Fig. 100.—Scarf cloud. (*W. A. Bentley, photographer.*)

to speak figuratively, combed out from old thunder heads by the upper winds. At present, however, the term, usually, is restricted to the latter phenomenon. *Tonitrocirrus*, that is, thunder cirrus, is a better name.

Although the lower atmosphere, up to at least 3 or 4 kilometers, generally, is comparatively calm whenever cumuli are most conspicuous, it, nevertheless, occasionally happens that the highest thunder heads reach into a stratum of much greater velocity in which, therefore, the topmost portions of the cloud are drawn out into wispy bands and fibers of snow crystals—a truly cirrus cloud whose peculiar origin is, perhaps, its only claim to the special name "false cirrus." The same name is also applied to the thinner edges of the *anvil cloud*, or spreading top of a cumulonimbus.

Mammatocumulus.—The mammatocumulus, sometimes called pocky-cloud, festoon-cloud, "rain balls," sack-cloud, or other similar name, is essentially a reversed cumulus (Fig. 101). It occurs, generally, in an altostratus or cumulostratus cloud, and seldom except in connection with a severe thunderstorm.

As is well known, ice, in the form of hail and snow, often occurs in the upper portions of large cumuli. If, now, this snow, say, is drifted out just above an altostratus cloud, it is obvious that the cooled layer will descend at many different places, and that at each such place there

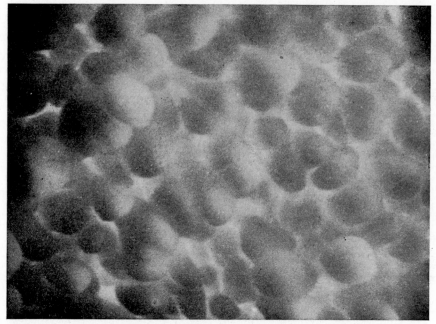

Fig. 101.—Mammatocumulus. (*L. C. Twyford, photographer.*)

will be produced a sag, or pendulous bulge, in the cloud base, and, of course, a lift or rise wherever the countercurrent obtains, thus producing the festooned appearance characteristic of this rather unusual cloud. Evidently, too, as explained under *cirrocumulus*, a cloud sheet can be rendered unstable and distorted into mammatocumuli, by being elevated over a wide area from below or depressed from above, since its temperature then would change slowly, following the wet adiabat, whereas that of the dry air above and below would change more rapidly.

Tornado or Funnel Cloud.—The tornado cloud (Fig. 102) is only a funnel-shaped extension of, generally, if not quite always, a cumulonimbus. It is produced by the expansional cooling incident to the rapid rotation of the atmosphere in which it appears.

Nacreous Cloud.—On rare occasions, and in rather high latitudes, a thin iridescent cloud, resembling cirrostratus, has been seen at the height of about 25 kilometers.[1] The material and method of formation of this cloud are both unknown. One might suspect, however, that it consists of extremely minute water droplets formed in the ascending branch of the general circulation in the stratosphere.

Noctilucent Cloud.—Very rarely a cirrus-like, silvery cloud has been seen at the great height of 82 kilometers; at night only—hence the name

Fig. 102.—Tornado cloud, Antler, North Dakota. (*W. H. Wegner, photographer.*)

noctilucent—and where and when it still is in sunshine. It possibly may consist of ice crystals.[2]

CLOUD HEIGHTS

Relation to Humidity.—The heights of clouds have been measured by several obvious methods of triangulation, and, from the data thus obtained, it appears, as one might infer *a priori*, that whatever condition tends to increase the relative humidity tends, also, to lower the cloud levels, since the greater this humidity, the less the amount of convectional cooling essential to condensation. Hence, in general, each type of cloud is lower in winter than summer, lower over humid

[1] Störmer, Carl, *Nature*, **145**; 221, 1940.

[2] Humphreys, W. J., *M. W. R.*, **61**; 228, 1933.

than over desert regions, lower over oceans than continents, and lower with increase of latitude.

AVERAGE CLOUD HEIGHTS IN KILOMETERS

Station	Ci.	Ci.-St.	Ci.-Cu.	A.-St.	A.-Cu.	St.-Cu.	Nb.	Cu.-Nb. top	Cu. top	Cu. base	Fr.-Cu.	St.
1. Summer, chiefly April to September												
Bossekop, 70° N	8.32	6.61	5.35	4.65	3.42	1.34	0.98	3.96	2.16	1.32	....	0.66
Pavlovsk, 60° N	8.81	8.09	4.60	....	3.05	1.85	....	4.68	2.41	1.64	2.15	0.84
Upsala, 60° N	8.18	6.36	6.45	2.77	3.95	1.77	1.20	3.97	2.00	1.45	1.83	
Potsdam, 52½° N	9.05	8.08	5.89	3.29	3.63	2.16	1.79	3.99	2.10	1.44	1.71	0.68
Trappes, 49° N	8.94	7.85	5.83	3.79	3.68	1.82	1.08	5.48	2.16	...	1.40	0.94
Toronto, 43½° N	10.90	8.94	8.88	4.24	3.52	2.06	....	....	1.70			
Blue Hill, 42° N	9.52	10.10	6.67	6.25	3.76	1.16	1.19	9.03	2.90	1.78	....	0.51
Washington, 39° N	10.36	10.62	8.83	5.77	5.03	2.87	1.93	4.96	(2.45)	1.18	....	0.84
Allahabad, 25½° N	10.76	....	11.28	....	4.50	....	0.84	....	1.76			
Manila, 14½° N	11.13	12.97	6.82	4.30	5.71	1.90	1.38	6.45	1.84		....	1.06
Batavia (year), 6° S	11.49	10.59	6.30	....	5.40	....	....	....	1.74		....	0.70
2. Winter, chiefly October to March												
Pavlovsk	8.74	7.09	5.98	....	3.17	1.50	....	....	1.60	1.12	....	1.00
Upsala	6.98	5.46	6.13	4.09	4.15	1.96	0.99	5.18	1.52	0.71	1.22	0.51
Potsdam	8.07	7.65	5.41	2.99	3.35	1.42	1.28	4.74	1.74	0.99	1.02	0.61
Trappes	8.51	5.85	5.63	3.82	4.27	1.61	1.05	3.85	2.37	....	1.43	
Toronto	9.98	8.53	8.25	4.18	2.50	1.54	....	....	1.33			
Blue Hill	8.61	8.89	6.16	4.57	3.66	1.60	0.65	....	1.62	1.54	....	0.61
Washington	9.51	9.53	7.41	4.80	3.82	2.40	1.80	3.73	2.28	1.20	....	1.13
Manila	10.63	11.64	6.42	3.90	4.64	2.32	1.49	3.14	1.82			

The table on this page, copied from Hann and Süring's "Lehrbuch der Meteorologie," gives the average summer and winter heights of clouds at places of widely different latitudes.

Levels of Maximum Cloudiness.—When the frequency of clouds is tabulated with reference to elevation, maxima and minima are found with the layers to which they obtain, growing thicker with decrease of latitude. This phenomenon, as a whole, is interesting, but it will be necessary, in discussing it, to consider the different levels separately, since each has its own explanation.

Fog Level.—As already explained, fogs, whether caused by radiation or advection, are surface phenomena, seldom more than 100 to 200 meters thick, although, occasionally, reaching much greater heights, merging, perhaps, with clouds above. Hence, the surface of the earth, because of the fogs that form upon it, is, itself, a level of maximum condensation or maximum "cloudiness."

Cumulus Level.—Since the cumulus and the cyclone nimbus both are due to vertical convection—the first thermal, the second forced—it is obvious that the base of each occurs, approximately, at the saturation level; that is, the level at which a mass of air, rising from the surface, will have cooled to its dew point. Clearly, too, clouds cannot form at a lower level, the air there being unsaturated, and, even if drifted in, they would evaporate. Further, ordinary thermal convection usually does not extend to much higher altitudes, because the cooling of the rising mass through expansion and evaporation (the outer portions, at least, of the cloud evaporate) quickly brings it to, or below, the temperature of the surrounding air at the same level, except in the case of the largest cumuli, in which the amount of evaporation is very small in comparison to the total condensation. Hence, foul weather cumuli and the lower cyclone clouds mark a second level of maximum cloudiness, commonly 1 to 2 kilometers above the surface.

Altocumulus Level.—During fair, calm, summer weather vertical convection is very strong, but, as the relative humidity is low, the resulting clouds are sufficiently high to furnish, on evaporation, much of the moisture that later often condenses into the altostratus or altocumulus. Hence the altocumulus, 3.5 to 4 kilometers above the surface, marks another level of decided maximum cloudiness.

Cirrostratus Level.—Since the different types of cirrus formed in the region of a cyclone (the cirrostratus being, perhaps, the most frequent) are spread far in advance of the storm, itself, by the swift upper winds, it follows that they also mark a level of maximum cloud frequency, by virtue of the area covered.

Cirrus Level.—During fair weather thin cirri often occur, as already explained, at, or near, the top of the troposphere, due, probably, to that marked cooling of the upper atmosphere characteristic of "highs," and, as these are the highest of all ordinary clouds, it is obvious that they also denote a level of maximum cloudiness, one whose average elevation in middle latitudes is about 10 kilometers.

Nacreous Level.—A rare iridescent cloud occurs at this level, 25 kilometers above the surface.

Noctilucent Level.—The rarest of all clouds occurs at this height, 82 kilometers.

Regions of Minimum Cloudiness.—Between the levels of maximum cloudiness there, obviously, must be regions of minimum condensation. These are:

Scud Region.—Since one level of maximum cloud formation, including fog, is at the surface of the earth, and the next at an elevation of approximately 1.5 kilometers, the average base height of the cumulus, it follows that the intervening region is one of minimum cloudiness, the absolute minimum being just above the highest fog. The name "scud region" might be appropriate to this space, since "scud" is, perhaps, the only cloud that occurs in it.

Intercumulus Region.—The intercumulus region of minimum condensation lies, as the name suggests, between the cumulus and altocumulus levels of maximum cloudiness. Its elevation is, roughly, 2.5 to 3.5 kilometers.

Altostratus Region.—As the altocumulus and the cirrostratus mark adjacent levels of maximum cloudiness at the heights of about 4 and 8 kilometers respectively, it follows, as above, that the region between, at the heights of 4.5 to 6 kilometers, especially the higher altostratus region, must be one of minimum cloudiness. And this it is, because (*a*) it is above the level of diurnal convection and therefore of most cumulus clouds; (*b*) the clouds of intermediate level formed in cyclonic areas are not blown forward so rapidly nor, therefore, over such wide areas as are the cirri; and (*c*) the atmosphere at this level in anticyclones is nearly always dry, apparently dynamically warmed, and, therefore, non-cloud-forming.

Intercirrus Region.—Since the cirrus region furnishes two adjacent levels of maximum cloudiness, a foul (cyclonic) and a fair weather type, whose elevations are about 8 and 10 kilometers, respectively, it follows that an intercirrus region of minimum cloudiness must lie between them at any elevation of, say, 8.5 to 9.5 kilometers.

Stratosphere Region.—Obviously water vapor is not carried by convection, above the troposphere. Neither can it accumulate, by diffusion, in the lowest portion of the stratosphere, to a density greater than that of saturation at the minimum temperatures of this level, incident to the passage of anticyclones; and even this low density must rapidly decrease, under the influence of gravity, with increase of elevation. Hence, there being but little water vapor present, and the relative humidity being very low, clouds normally cannot form in the stratosphere; that is, beyond an elevation of about 11 kilometers in middle latitudes.

There are, then, five principal levels of maximum cloudiness in the troposphere.

1. Fog level, surface of the earth or water.
2. Cumulus level, height above surface about 1.5 kilometers.
3. Altocumulus level, height above surface about 4 kilometers.
4. Cirrostratus level, height above surface about 8 kilometers.
5. Cirrus level, height above surface about 10 kilometers.

There also are five regions of minimum condensation in the troposphere.

1. Scud region, 100 to 300 meters elevation.
2. Intercumulus region, 2.5 to 3.5 kilometers elevation, roughly.
3. Altostratus region, 4.5 to 6 kilometers elevation, roughly.
4. Intercirrus region, 8.5 to 9.5 kilometers elevation, roughly.
5. Isothermal region, beyond 11 kilometers elevation.

Cloud Depth or Thickness.—It is known that the thickness of clouds varies from the 8 to 10 kilometers of the most towering cumulus, usually associated with a violent hailstorm, down to that of a vanishingly thin cirrus. Systematic measurements of cloud thickness, however, have not been numerous. The best, perhaps, were made at Potsdam and are given in the following table copied from Hann and Süring's "Lehrbuch der Meteorologie:"

CLOUD THICKNESS

Cloud		A.-St.	A.-Cu.	St.-Cu.	Nb.	Cu.-Nb.	Cu.	Fr.-Cu.
Depth in meters	Average........	510	194	353	(590)	2070	669	214
	Maximum.......	1310	370	1265	1240	>4600	2230	430
	Minimum........	105	50	50	160	340	90	70
Number of observations....		6	18	18	16	21	22	26

Cloud Velocities.—The velocity of a cloud is usually the velocity of the air in which it floats, except in the case of a stationary type—crest cloud, banner cloud, etc.—or a billow cloud. With these exceptions, it, therefore, is approximately the gradient velocity at the cloud level, which varies with altitude, latitude, temperature, and pressure distribution.

Average values, observed at certain places, are given in the following table, also copied from Hann and Süring's "Lehrbuch der Meteorologie:"

AVERAGE WIND VELOCITY IN METERS PER SECOND

	Ci.	Ci.-St.	Ci.-Cu.	A.-St.	A.-Cu.	St.-Cu.	Nb.	Cu.-Nb. top	Cu. top	Cu. base	Fr.-Cu.	St.
				1. Summer, chiefly April to September								
Bossekop, 70° N...........	18	18	11	13	11	5	6	..	7	7	..	7
Upsala, 60° N.............	20	(39)	17	5	12	7	7	..	7	6	8	
Potsdam, 52½° N.........	22	24	13	11	10	9	11	9	8	6	7	7
Trappes, 49° N............	23	23	23	15	13	9	10	14	10	9	8	10
Blue Hill, 42° N...........	30	30	18	25	13	10	14	22	13	9	..	6
Washington, 39° N........	30	27	23	18	16	10	8	15	7	....	..	6
Manila, 14½° N...........	13	16	3	..	11	4	..	..	..	....	..	
Batavia (year), 6° S........	12	19	3	..	6	6	..	..	4	....	..	1
				2. Winter, chiefly October to March								
Upsala..................	23	13	18	..	13	12	6	18	12	....	12	
Potsdam.................	28	20	24	16	16	12	13	28	10	(14)	12	10
Trappes.................	23	19	27	18	14	11	16	..	12	12	11	10
Blue Hill................	37	41	36	25	24	13	13	..	..	15	..	10
Washington..............	35	30	33	21	21	15	12	21	11	....	..	10
Manila..................	13	16	3	19	4	8	6	..	..	....	..	

CHAPTER XVII

THE THUNDERSTORM

Introduction.—A thunderstorm, as its name implies, is a storm characterized by thunder and lightning, just as a dust storm is characterized by a great quantity of flying dust. But the dust is never in any sense the cause of the storm that carries it along, nor, so far as is known, does either thunder or lightning have any influence on the course—genesis, development, and termination—of even those storms of which they form, in some respects, the most important features. No matter how impressive or how terrifying these phenomena may be, they never are anything more than mere incidents to, or products of, the peculiar storms they accompany. In short, they are never in any sense either storm-originating or storm-controlling, factors.

Origin of Thunderstorm Electricity.—Many have supposed that, whatever the genesis of the thunderstorm, the lightning, at least, is a product, or manifestation, of the free electricity always present in the atmosphere—normal atmospheric electricity. Observations, however (discussed later), seem definitely to exclude this assumption. Thus, while the difference in electrical potential between the surface of the earth and a point at constant elevation is, roughly, the same at all parts of the world, the number and intensity of thunderstorms vary greatly from place to place. Further, while the potential gradient at any given place is greatest in winter, the number of thunderstorms is most frequent in summer; and while the gradient in the lower layer of the atmosphere, at many places, usually is greatest from eight to ten o'clock, both morning and evening, and least at 2 to 3 p.m. and 3 to 4 a.m., no closely analogous relations hold for the thunderstorm.

But how, then, is the great amount of electricity incident to a thunderstorm generated? Of the various attempts to answer this question, only the Elster and Geitel influence theory,[1] the Simpson rupture theory,[2] and the Wilson capture theory[3] have received much attention, and of these only the latter two still survive.

Obviously, the tops and bottoms of raindrops are charged, oppositely, by the electric field of the earth. Hence, any much smaller drops,

---

[1] *Ann. Phys.*, **25**; 121, 1885; *Phys. Zeit.*, p. 455, 1916 (contains other references).

[2] *Mem.*, Indian Meteorol. Dept., Simla, **20**; pt. 8, 1910; *Phil. Mag.* **30**; 1, 1915; *Proc. Roy. Soc.* **114**; 376, 1927. See also LENARD, *Ann. Phys.*, **65**; 629, 1921, and NOLAN and ENRIGHT, *Sci. Proc. Roy. Dublin Soc.*, **17**; No. 1, 1922; SCRASE, F. J., *Geophys. Mem.*, 75, 1933.

[3] *J. Franklin Inst.*, **208**; 1, 1929.

blown against the undersides of the larger by an updraft, such as exists in the cumulonimbus cloud, must, thereby, acquire positive or negative charges, according as the earth beneath is negative or positive, rebound (assumed by the theory), and be carried by the ascending air to higher levels. In this manner, analogous to the action of an influence machine, the potential of the original field is supposed to be gradually increased to lightning values. However, the assumption that the large and small drops come into electrical contact with each other, without flowing together, has not been justified—rather the contrary—by experiment.[1] Hence, the influence theory of the origin of lightning appears to be disproved. The rupture theory, on the other hand, is supported by careful experiments and numerous observations. The first, and most extensive, series of these observations was made by Simpson[2] at Simla, India, at an elevation of about 7000 feet above sea level, and covered all of the monsoon seasons, roughly, Apr. 15 to Sept. 15, of 1908 and 1909. He also made observations of the electrical conditions of the snow, at Simla, during the winter of 1908–1909.

A tipping-bucket rain gage gave an automatic, continuous record of the rate and time of rainfall, while a Benndorf[3] self-registering electrometer marked the sign and potential of the charge acquired during each 2-minute interval. A second Benndorf electrometer recorded the potential gradients near the earth, and a coherer, of the type then used in radiotelegraphy, registered the occurrence of each lightning discharge. These records show that:

1. The electricity brought down by the rain was sometimes positive and sometimes negative.

2. The total quantity of positive electricity brought down by the rain was 3.2 times greater than the total quantity of negative electricity.

3. The period during which positively charged rain fell was 2.5 times longer than the period during which negatively charged rain fell.

4. Treating charged rain as equivalent to a vertical current of electricity, the current densities were, generally, smaller than 4×10^{-15} amperes per square centimeter; but, on a few occasions, greater current densities, both positive and negative, were recorded.

5. Negative currents occurred less frequently than positive currents, and the greater the current density the greater the preponderance of the positive currents.

6. The charge carried by the rain was, generally, less than 6 electrostatic units per cubic centimeter of water, but larger charges were occasionally recorded, and in one exceptional storm (May 13, 1908) the negative charge exceeded 19 electrostatic units per cubic centimeter.

[1] SCHUMANN, T. E. W., *Phys. Rev.*, **26**; 105, 1925; GOTT, J. P., *Proc. Roy. Soc.*, **151**; 665, 1935.

[2] *Loc. cit.*

[3] *Physik. Z.*, Leipzig, **7**; 98, 1906.

7. As stated in paragraph (3) above, positive electricity was recorded more frequently than negative, but the excess was the less marked the higher the charge on the rain.

8. With all rates of rainfall, positively charged rain occurred more frequently than negatively charged rain, and the relative frequency of positively charged rain increased rapidly with increased rate of rainfall. With rainfall of less than about 1 millimeter in 2 minutes, positively charged rain occurred twice as often as negatively charged rain, while with greater intensities it occurred fourteen times as often.

9. When the rain was falling at a less rate than about 0.6 millimeter in 2 minutes, the charge per cubic centimeter of water decreased as the intensity of the rain increased.

10. With rainfall of greater intensity than about 0.6 millimeter in 2 minutes the positive charge carried per cubic centimeter of water was independent of the rate of rainfall, while the negative charge carried decreased as the rate of rainfall increased.

11. During periods of rainfall the potential gradient was more often negative than positive, but there were no clear indications of a relationship between the sign of the charge and the sign of the potential gradient.

12. The data do not suggest that the negative electricity occurs more frequently during any particular period of a storm than during any other.

Concerning his observations on the electrification of snow Simpson says:

So far as can be judged from the few measurements made during the winter of 1908–1909, it would appear that:

1. More positive than negative electricity is brought down by snow in the proportion of about 3.6 to 1.

2. Positively charged snow falls more often than negatively charged.

3. The vertical electric currents during snowstorms are, on the average, larger than during rainfall.

While these observations were being secured a number of well-devised experiments were made to determine the electrical effects of each obvious process that occurs in the thunderstorm. All but one gave negative results. This one, however, the tearing of spray from distilled water drops by an air blast, showed:

1. That breaking of drops of water is accompanied by the production of both positive and negative ions.

2. That three times as many negative ions as positive ions are released [thus leaving the drops charged positively].

The source of the charges thus obtained appears to be an electrical double layer due to complex water molecules—negative outer shell, giving most of the spray, and positive interior.[1] Furthermore, John Zeleny[2] showed that the amount of electrification so produced by a given

---

[1] LENARD, P., *Ann. Phys.*, **47**; 463, 1915.

[2] *Phys. Rev.* **44**; 837, 1933.

air blast rapidly increases with the temperature of the ruptured drops, a phenomenon that must contribute to the increase of lightning with increase of temperature.

Now, a strong upward current of air is one of the most conspicuous features of the thunderstorm. It is always evident in the turbulent cauliflower heads of the cumulus cloud, the parent, presumably, of all thunderstorms. Besides, its inference is compelled by the occurrence of hail, a frequent thunderstorm phenomenon, whose formation requires the carrying of raindrops and the growing hailstones, repeatedly, to cold, and, therefore, high, altitudes. And, from the existence of hail, it is further inferred that an updraft of at least 8 meters per second must often occur within the body of the storm, since, as experiment shows,[1] air of normal density must have, approximately, this upward velocity to support the larger drops, those of 4 mm. or more in diameter, and, because of its greater weight, even a stronger updraft to support the average hailstone. Indeed, accelerations several fold that due to gravity have been experienced in airplanes caught in thunderstorms.

Experiment also shows[1] that raindrops, of whatever size, cannot fall through air of normal density whose upward velocity is greater than about 8 meters per second, nor themselves fall with greater velocity through still air; that drops large enough, 4.5 mm. in diameter and up, if kept intact, to attain through the action of gravity a greater velocity than 8 meters per second with reference to the air, whether still or in motion, are so blown to pieces that the increased ratio of supporting area to total mass causes the resulting spray to be carried aloft, or, at least, left behind, together with, of course, all the original smaller drops. Above sea level this limiting velocity is greater. It is given approximately by equating the weight of the drop $\frac{4}{3}\pi r^3 g(\rho - \sigma)$ to the supporting force, $k\pi r^2 \sigma v^2$, roughly, in which r is the radius of the drop ρ its density, σ the density of the air, v the velocity in question, and g the gravitational acceleration. Or, while the drop falls the distance $2r$, its gravity potential energy decreases by $\frac{4}{3}\pi r^3(\rho - \sigma)2rg$, and kinetic energy is given to an equal volume of air to the amount $\frac{4}{3}\pi r^3 \sigma v^2/2$. Hence, since the sum of the two forms of energy is constant, $v = 2\sqrt{\rho r g/\sigma}$, nearly, as σ is small in comparison with ρ. Hence the limiting velocity increases in practically the same ratio that the square root of the density of the air decreases. Thus, at an elevation of 3 kilometers above sea level, where the barometric pressure is about 520 mm. and the temperature, say, 15° C. lower than at the surface, the limiting velocity is approximately 9.4 meters per second, instead of 8, the value for normal density, or density at 0° C. and 760 mm. pressure. Clearly, then, the updrafts within a cumulus cloud, frequently, must be strong, and, therefore, break up, at about the same level, that of maximum rain accumulation,

[1] LENARD, P., *Met. Zeit.*, **21**; 249, 1904.

innumerable drops which, through coalescence, have grown beyond the critical size, and, thereby, according to Simpson's experiments, produce electrical separation within the cloud itself. Obviously, under the turmoil of a thunderstorm, such drops may be forced through the cycle of union (facilitated by any charges they may carry) and division, of coalescence and disruption, from one to many times, with the formation on each, at every disruption, again *according to experiment*, of a correspondingly increased electrical charge. The turmoil compels mechanical contact between the drops, whereupon the disruptive equalization of their electrical potential breaks down their surface tensions and insures coalescence. Hence, once started, the electricity of a thunderstorm rapidly grows to a considerable maximum.

After a time, the larger drops reach, here and there, places below which the updraft is small—the air cannot be rushing up everywhere—and then fall as positively charged rain, because of the processes just explained. The negative ions, in the meantime are carried up into the higher portions of the cumulus, where they unite with the cloud particles, and, thereby, facilitate their coalescence into negatively charged drops. Hence, the heavy rain of a thunderstorm should be positively charged, as it almost always is, and the gentler portions negatively charged, which, also, very frequently, is the case.

According to Simpson's theory, it would seem that where convection is most vigorous, and electric separation most active, the cloud must be negative above and positive below. But, exactly the opposite polarity, positive thereabove and negative below, has been indicated in most cases observed by C. T. R. Wilson,[1] Schonland and Craib,[2] and Wormell.[3]

This electrical state of the cloud seems most easily accounted for by Wilson's theory[4] that a raindrop with a positive charge on its lower half and negative on the upper (as it would have in the normal electrical field of the earth) falling through a space filled with slow-moving positive and negative ions, such as charged nuclei and cloud particles, must capture many of the negative class and few, if any, of the positive and therefore accumulate a negative charge. In this way more and more positive ions, supplied in part, at least, by the fresh ascending air, are carried to the upper portion of the cloud, and more and more of the negative are gathered on the larger drops below, until the increasing difference in potential causes a strain-releasing discharge, whereupon the same phenomena of charge and discharge occur over and over again as long as the vigorous convection and heavy rainfall continue.

[1] *Proc. Roy. Soc.*, **92**; 555, 1916.
[2] *Proc. Roy. Soc.*, **114**; 229, 1927.
[3] *Proc. Roy. Soc.*, **115**; 443, 1927; **127**; 567, 1930.
[4] *J. Franklin Inst.*, **208**; 1, 1929.

How ions can be supplied fast enough to induce two or three lightning discharges per minute, a common rate in vigorous thunderstorms, is not obvious. Many are furnished, as explained, by the fresh ascending air, but it does not seem probable that these alone can furnish all the electricity carried by the observed discharges. Suppose, to be liberal, that there are 630 electrons per cubic centimeter of the incoming air available for the electrification of the drops; then it would take about 2×10^{11} cubic meters of this air to afford one normal discharge of 20 coulombs. And, if the air ascended 200 meters between discharges, the cross-section of the ascending column would need to be 1000 square kilometers, a preposterous value. It seems, therefore, that in any case the cloud must somehow furnish most of its own ionization and electrical separation, and furnish it at a faster rate than the frequency of the discharges would indicate, to make good the heavy leakage evidenced by the rates of increase of voltage after each stroke—rapid at first, then slower and slower to the next rupture value. As soon as the electrical gradient within the cloud has reached 5000 volts per centimeter, or thereabouts, the water drops present are pulled out into discharging and disrupting filaments[1] that supply vast quantities of ions. Also, the mechanical rupture of the drops by the vigorously ascending air produces ionization, as explained above.

Simpson and Scrase[2] examined the electrification of many thunderstorm clouds with instruments carried through them by small balloons and found that, in general, these clouds are electrified positively near the top, where frequently there is snow, and often, also, in a limited region near the base, where the uprush of the incoming air is vigorous, and negatively everywhere else.

This observed distribution of electricity in the cumulonimbus cloud may seem to contravene the drop-rupture theory of its origin, whereas in reality it rather strongly supports it because the rapidly ascending air of a vigorous thunderstorm must carry most of the raindrops, temporarily, and in the manner presently explained, to high levels, as indicated by the frequent occurrence of hail, where commonly, therefore, the most abundant electrical separation must occur, the larger drops being charged positively and the negative charges carried away with the circulating air— up, sidewise, and down, over and through the cloud. This downflow of air over the evaporating, hence cooling, surface of a cumulus cloud is well known to aviators, and presumably is the cause of the drooping of its edges and concavity of its base. The positively charged drops fall out wherever the velocity of ascent of the air is insufficient to sustain them. In the course of their fall they may collect enough negative electricity to neutralize, or even more than neutralize, their initial charges.

---

[1] Macky, W. A. *Proc. Roy. Soc.*, **133**; 565, 1931.
[2] *Proc. Roy. Soc.*, **161**; 352, 1937.

Nevertheless, all the while, most of the positive electricity will be with and on the accumulated water, well up in the column of ascending air. At any rate, and whatever the details, the one essential to the formation of the giant cumulus cloud, namely, the rapid uprush of moist air, is also the one essential to the generation of the electricity of thunderstorms. Hence, the reason why lightning seldom occurs, except in connection with a cumulus cloud, is understandable and obvious. It is, simply, because the electrifying process of splashing is vigorously active in this cloud and nearly absent in others.

The occasional lightning in connection with snowstorms, dust storms and volcanic eruptions, may, in each case, be due to the fact that the collision of solid particles produces electrification.[1]

Violent Motions of Cumulus Clouds.—From observations, and from the graphic descriptions of the few balloonists and aviators who have experienced the trying ordeal of passing through the heart of a thunderstorm, it is known that there is violent vertical motion and much turbulence in the middle of a large cumulus cloud; a fact which, so far as it relates to the theory, alone, of the thunderstorm, it would be sufficient to accept, without inquiring into its cause. However, to render the discussion more nearly complete, it perhaps is worth while, since it is a moot question, to inquire what the probable cause of the violent motions in large cumulus clouds really is—motions which, in the magnitude of their vertical components and degree of turmoil, are never exhibited by clouds of any other type, nor met with elsewhere by either kites or balloons of any kind, manned, sounding, or pilot.

It has been shown by von Bezold[2] that sudden condensation from a state of supersaturation, and also sudden congelation of undercooled cloud droplets, would, as a result of the heat thus liberated, cause an equally sudden expansion of the atmosphere, and, thereby turbulent motions analogous to those observed in large cumuli. However, as von Bezold himself points out, it is not evident how either the condensation or the freezing could suddenly take place throughout a cloud volume great enough to produce the observed effects. Besides, these eruptive turmoils, whatever their genesis, undoubtedly originate and run their course in regions already filled with cloud particles in the presence of which no appreciable degree of supersaturation can occur. Hence, the rapid uprush and the violent turbulence in question, obviously, must have some other cause, which, indeed, is mainly provided by the difference between the actual temperature gradient of the surrounding atmosphere and the adiabatic temperature gradient of the saturated air within the cloud itself. The buoyancy of the air within the cloud is further increased by the excess of its vapor density over that of the adjacent outer space,

[1] RUDGE, *Proc. Roy. Soc.*, **A90**; 256, 1914.
[2] *Sitzb. kgl. preuss. Akad. Wiss.*, **8**; 279–309, Berlin, 1892.

but this is partially to wholly, or, at places, even more than wholly, offset by the weight of the liquid water present per unit volume. It will be convenient, therefore, and sufficient for a first approximation, to consider only the temperature effect.

Let the surface temperature be 30° C., pressure 760 mm., and assume the dew point to be 18° C. Now, the adiabatic decrease of temperature of non-saturated air is about 1° C. per 100 meters increase in elevation, and, therefore, under the assumed conditions, vertical convection of the surface air causes condensation to begin at an elevation of approximately 1.5 kilometers—allowing for the increase of volume per unit mass of vapor. From this level, however, so long as the cloud particles are carried up with the rising air, the rate of temperature decrease for at least 2 kilometers is much less—at first, about one-half the previous rate, and appreciably less than that of the surrounding clear air. After a considerable rise above the level of initial condensation, ½ kilometer, say, the rain drops have so increased in size as to lag behind the upward current and even to drop out, while at the same time the amount of moisture, condensed per degree fall of temperature, grows rapidly less, as shown by the saturation adiabats of Fig. 76. Hence, for both reasons —because the heat of the water is no longer available to the air from which it was condensed, the drops having been left behind, and because a decreasing amount of latent heat is to be had from further condensation, there being less and less precipitation per degree cooling—the rate of temperature decrease again approaches the adiabatic gradient of dry air, or 1° C. per 100 meters change of elevation.

Obviously, then, for some distance above the level at which condensation begins to set free its latent heat, the temperature of the rising mass of moist air departs farther and farther from the temperature of the surrounding atmosphere, at the same level, and, therefore, its buoyancy for a time as steadily increases. But, of course, as explained above, this increase of buoyancy does not continue to any great altitude.

In the lower atmosphere, continuous and progressive convection builds up the adiabatic gradient so gradually that no great difference, between the temperature of the rising column and that of the adjacent atmosphere, is anywhere possible. Hence, under ordinary conditions, the uprush in this region is never violent. But, whenever the vertical movement of the air brings about a considerable condensation it follows, as above explained, that there is likely to be an increase in its buoyancy, and, hence, a more or less rapid upward movement of the central portion, like air up a heated chimney, and for the same reason, together with, because of viscosity, a rolling and turbulent motion of the sides, of the type so often seen in towering cumulus clouds. Obviously, too, the uprushing column of air must continue to gain in velocity so long as its temperature is greater, or density less, than that of the surrounding atmosphere, except as modified by viscosity, and, therefore, have its greatest velocity near the level at which these two temperatures are the same. Hence, the rising column must ascend somewhat beyond its point of equilibrium, and then, because slightly undercooled, correspondingly drop back.

Figure 103, based upon approximately average conditions, illustrates the points just explained. The elevation is in kilometers and the temperature in degrees Centigrade.

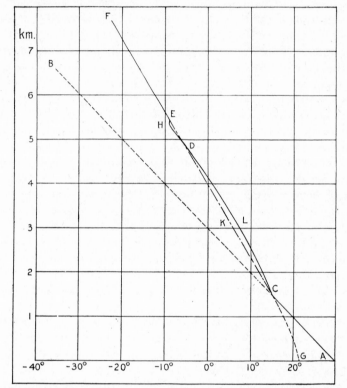

Fig. 103.—Temperature gradients within (*CLD*) and without (*CKD*) cumulus clouds.

AB is the adiabatic temperature gradient for nonsaturated air, about 1° C. per 100 meters change in elevation. *GCKDEF* is the supposed temperature gradient before convection begins, or a decrease, in accordance with observations, of 6° C., about, per kilometer increase in elevation, except near the surface, where the temperature decrease, before convection has begun, ordinarily is less rapid, and at elevations between 5 kilometers, roughly, and the isothermal level, where it is more rapid.

As convection sets in, the temperature decrease near the surface soon approximates the adiabatic gradient for dry air, and this condition extends gradually to greater altitudes, till, in the given case, condensation begins at the level *C*, or where the temperature is 15° C. Here the temperature decrease, under the assumed conditions, suddenly changes from 10° C. per kilometer increase of elevation to rather less than half that amount, but slowly increases with increase of altitude and consequent decrease of temperature. At some level, as *L*, the temperature difference between the rising and the adjacent air is a maximum. At *D* the temperature of the rising air is the same as that of the air adjacent, but its momentum presumably carries it on to some such level as *H*. Within the rising column, then, the temperature gradient is given approximately by the curve *ACLDHE*, while that of the surrounding air is substantially as shown by the curve *ACKDEF*.

The cause, therefore, of the violent uprush and turbulent condition within large cumulus clouds, is the difference between the temperature of the inner or warmer portions of the cloud itself and that of the surrounding atmosphere, at the same level, as indicated by their respective temperature gradients *CLD* and *CKD*. Clearly, too, while some air must flow into the condensation column all along its length, the greatest pressure difference, and therefore the greatest inflow, obviously, is at its base. After the rain has set in, however, this basal inflow is from immediately in front of the storm, and necessarily so, as will be explained later.

Let the mean temperature *T* from *C* to *D*, be 280° Abs. and the mean difference of temperature ΔT, between cloud and adjacent free air, be 0.6° C.; then the maximum velocity *V* of ascent is at *D* and is given by the equation $V^2 = 2ah$, in which the acceleration $a = g\Delta T/T$, and $h = 3.5$ kilometers. Hence $V = 12$ meters per second, approximately. Well up in a thunderstorm cloud the velocity of ascent often is much greater than that here computed, as evidenced by large hailstones and attested by aviators.

The approximate difference in level between *D* and *H*, or the height to which the momentum of the ascending column will force it to rise after it has cooled to the temperature of the surrounding air, may easily be computed in terms of the vertical velocity at *D* and the difference between the temperature gradients of the rising and the non-rising masses of air. Let the vertical velocity of the rising column be *V* centimeters per second at *D*; let the average absolute temperature between *D* and *H* be *T*; and let the difference between the temperature of the rising air and the surrounding air change uniformly at the rate δT per centimeter change of elevation.

Obviously the kinetic energy of the rising air at *D* will be used up in lifting it to some greater elevation. But the weight of a mass *m* of this air is not *mg* (*g* being gravity acceleration), which it would be *in vacuo*, but $mg\left(\dfrac{\rho - \sigma}{\rho}\right)$, in which ρ is the density of the air in question and σ the density of the surrounding air. Thus at *h* centimeters above *D*, $\rho - \sigma = (h\delta T)\rho/T$, approximately, and therefore the weight of the mass

m at this level is $mg\dfrac{h\delta T}{T}$, approximately. Hence the work in lifting the mass m through this altitude h is its average weight, $mgh\delta T/2T$, multiplied by the distance h.

Hence,

$$\frac{1}{2}mV^2 = mgx^2\frac{\delta T}{2T} \text{ or } x^2 = \frac{V^2T}{g\delta T}$$

in which x, directly proportional to V, is the height in centimeters to which the air will rise above D, neglecting viscosity.

Since the height of the barometer at an elevation of 5 kilometers above sea level is, roughly, 400 mm., and since the supporting force of an updraft is proportional to the product of its density by the square of its velocity, it follows that the vertical velocity in meters per second, necessary to support the largest drops at this elevation, is given by the equation

$$V = v\sqrt{\frac{760 \times 265}{400 \times 295}},$$

265 and 295 bring the degrees, absolute temperatures, at the levels of 440 and 760 mm. pressure, respectively, and v the required velocity at normal density. But, as above explained, $v = 8$ meters per second, about, and, therefore, $V = 10.5$ meters per second, approximately.

Hence the above assumption that the vertical velocity at D is 12 meters per second appears to be conservative.

Viscosity between the rising and the adjacent air prevents the actual height attained from being equal to the above theoretical value; nevertheless, the maximum elevation, or what might be called the "momentum level" often, especially in the case of the largest and most active cumulus clouds, is much greater than the equilibrium level.

Convectional Instability.—Rapid vertical convection of humid air, as we have seen, is essential to the production of the cumulus cloud and, therefore, to the generation of the thunderstorm. Hence it is essential to consider the conditions under which the vertical temperature gradient, necessary to this convection, can be established. These are:

1. Strong surface heating, especially in regions of light winds; a frequent occurrence. The condition that the winds be light is essential to only the local or heat thunderstorm, and essential to it simply because winds, by thoroughly mixing the air, prevent the formation of isolated rising columns, the progenitors of this particular type of storm.

2. The overrunning of one layer of air by another at a temperature sufficiently lower to induce convection. This apparently is the cause of some thunderstorms, especially in the warm sector, or interfrontal region of a cyclone.

3. The underrunning and consequent uplift of a saturated layer of air by a denser layer; a frequent occurrence along a "squall line" or "cold front" and therefore the cause of many thunderstorms.

Here the underrunning air lifts both the saturated layer and the superincumbent unsaturated layer, and thereby forces each to cool adiabatically. But as both layers are lifted equally, while, because of the latent heat of condensation, the saturated layer cools much slower than the dry, it follows that a sufficient mechanical lift of a saturated layer of air would establish, between it and the nonsaturated layer above, a superadiabatic temperature gradient, and, thereby, produce local convection, cumulus clouds, and, often, a thunderstorm. Indeed, condensation begun in conditionally unstable air, that is, air whose lapse rate is between the adiabatic lapse rates of dry and saturated air, respectively, often so grows as to produce a large cumulus cloud and a thunderstorm.

4. The ascent of warm, humid air up a sloping obstacle—a mountain or an intercepting mass of cool air, such as characterizes the "warm front."

Periodic Recurrence of Thunderstorms.—While thunderstorms may develop at any hour of any day, they, nevertheless, have three distinct periods of maximum occurrence: (a) daily, (b) yearly, and (c) irregularly cyclic. Each maximum depends upon the simple facts that the more humid the air, and the more rapid the local vertical convections, the more frequent, and also the more intense, the thunderstorms, for the obvious reason that it is rapid vertical convection of humid air that produces them.

Daily Land Period.—Vertical convection of the atmosphere over land areas reaches its greatest altitudes and thereby produces the heaviest condensation and largest cumulus clouds when the surface is most heated; that is, during afternoons. Hence, the hours of maximum frequency of inland, or continental, thunderstorms are, in most places, 2 to 4 p.m. In the central portion of the United States, one of the exceptional places, they are most frequent at night.

Daily Ocean Period.—Because of the great amount of heat rendered latent by evaporation, because of the considerable depth to which the sea is penetrated by solar radiation, and because of the high specific heat of water, the surface temperature of the ocean increases but little during the day, and, because of convection, or the sinking, of any surface water that has appreciably cooled, and the bringing of the warmest water always to the top, it decreases but slightly at night. Indeed, the diurnal temperature range of the ocean surface, usually, is but a small fraction of 1° C., while that of the atmosphere at from 500 to 1000 meters elevation is several fold as great.[1] Hence those temperature gradients over

[1] BRAAK, *Beitr. Physik Atmosph.*, **6**; 141, Leipzig, 1914.

the ocean that are favorable to rapid vertical convection are most frequent during the early morning hours, and therefore the maximum of ocean thunderstorms usually occurs between midnight and 4 a.m.

Yearly Land Period.—Just as inland thunderstorms are most frequent during the hottest hours of the day, so, too, and for the same reason, they are, in general, most frequent over the land during the hottest months of the year; or, rather, during those months when the amount of surface heating, and, therefore, the vertical temperature gradient, is a maximum. This will be better understood by reference to the winter and summer temperatures of Figs. 16 and 16a.

That this important difference between the temperature gradients of winter and summer is general, and not peculiar to particular localities, is obvious from the fact that during summer the surface of the earth gradually grows warmer, and, therefore, induces correspondingly frequent and vigorous convection; while during winter, it as steadily becomes colder, and, therefore, only occasionally, at the times of temporary warming, induces convections strong enough to form large and well-defined cumulus clouds.

From these several considerations it is evident that:

a. Winter convections cannot, in general, rise to nearly so great altitudes nor with such velocity as those of summer.

b. The absolute humidity of summer air may, at times, be greatly in excess of that of winter.

c. The winter snow level usually is much below that of summer.

Hence, thunderstorms, since they depend, as explained, upon the action of strong vertical convection on an abundance of *rain* drops, necessarily occur most frequently during the warmer seasons, and only occasionally during the colder months. In middle latitudes, where there are no late spring snows to hold back the temperatures, the month of maximum frequency is June. In higher latitudes, where strong surface heating is more or less delayed, the maximum occurs in July or even August.

Yearly Ocean Period.—Over the oceans, on the other hand, temperature gradients favorable to the genesis of thunderstorms, and, therefore, the storms themselves, occur most frequently during winter and least frequently during summer. This is because the temperature of the air at some distance above the surface, being largely what it was when it left the windward continent, greatly changes from season to season, while that of the water, and, of course, the air in contact with it, changes relatively but little through the year; hence, over the oceans, the average decrease of temperature with increase of elevation is least, and, therefore, thunderstorms fewest, in summer, and greatest, with such storms most numerous, in winter.

Cyclic Land Period.—Since thunderstorms are accompanied by rain, and since over land they are most numerous during summer, it would appear that they must occur most frequently either in warm or in wet years and least frequently in cold or in dry years. Further, if it should happen, as it probably does, that, for the earth as a whole, warm years are also wet years, being, presumably, the years of maximum evaporation, and dry years cold years, it would appear logically certain that, for the entire world, the maxima numbers of thunderstorms must belong to the years that are wet and warm, and the minima to those that are cold and dry.

A complete statistical examination of these statements is not possible, owing to the fact that meteorological data are available for only portions of the earth's surface and not for the whole of it. Nevertheless, well-nigh conclusive data do exist. The annual rainfall, for instance, to the leeward of a large body of water, obviously must bear the same relation to the

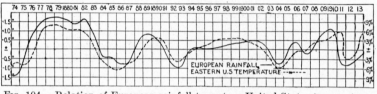

Fig. 104.—Relation of European rainfall to eastern United States temperature.

annual average windward temperature that the total annual precipitation over the entire world does to the annual average world temperature. In each case the amount of evaporation or amount of water vapor taken into the atmosphere, and, therefore, the amount of subsequent precipitation, clearly must increase and decrease with the temperature if the other conditions, especially the wind velocity, are the same. Support of this deduction appears to be furnished by Fig. 104, even though it must be more or less affected by other factors, in which the full line represents the smoothed annual European precipitation,[1] and the dotted line smoothed annual average temperatures over the eastern United States. Later data, down to 1921, show the same relation. Obviously the warmer the air as it leaves America, the greater the moisture it takes up in its passage across the Atlantic; and, therefore, the greater its supply of humidity on reaching Europe and the heavier the subsequent precipitation. Clearly, too, the same relations must apply to the entire earth that so obviously should, and so demonstrably do, hold for the North Atlantic and its adjacent continents.

Beyond a reasonable doubt, therefore, for the world as a whole, warm years are wet and cold ones are dry. Hence, as above stated, it is

---

[1] HELLMANN, "Die Niederschläge in den Norddeutschen Stromgebieten," **1**; 336–337, Berlin, 1906 and elsewhere.

practically certain that the maxima of thunderstorms occur during years
that are wet, or warm—for the two are identical—and the minima during
years that are dry or cold. A partial and, so far as it goes, a confirmatory
statistical test of this conclusion is given by Fig. 105. The lower group
of curves is based on an exhaustive study by Dr. van Gulik,[1] of thunderstorms and lightning injuries in Holland. The continuous zigzag line
gives the actual number of thunderstorm days, and the continuous
curved line the same numbers smoothed. The broken lines give, respectively, the actual and the smoothed values of the annual average precipitation. The upper curve represents the variations in the smoothed
number of destructive thunderstorms[2] (number of thunderstorm days not
readily available) in Germany.

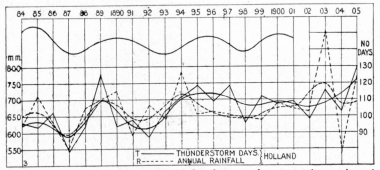

Fig. 105.—Relation of annual number of thunderstorm days to total annual precipitation—Holland. The uppermost wavy curve shows the variation in the smoothed number
of destructive thunderstorms in Germany.

The original data on which this last curve is based, indicate a continuous and rapid increase of thunderstorm destructiveness throughout
the period studied, 1854–1901. Presumably, however, this increase is
real only to the extent that the country has become more densely popu-
lated and more thickly studded with destructible property. Since
thunderstorms are caused by rapid vertical convection and heavy condensation, and since the temperature of the air upon which these in
turn depend has not, on the decade average, very much changed since
reliable records began, at least a hundred years ago, there clearly is
no logical reason for believing that the decade average either of the
frequency or the intensity of the storms themselves has greatly changed
during that time. At any rate, this element, that is, the rapid increase
suggested by insurance data, has been omitted from the curve and only
the fluctuation factor retained.

It will be noticed that the curve of thunderstorm frequency for
all Holland closely parallels the curve of thunderstorm injury in all

[1] *Met. Zeit.*, 25; 108, Braunschweig, 1908.

[2] STEFFENS, OTTO, *Ztschr. gesamte Versicherungswiss.*, 4; pt. 4, Berlin, 1904. (Also
Diss.-Berlin, 1904.)

Germany. Hence it seems safe to infer that the frequency of thunder-storms varies much the same way over both countries, and, presumably, also, over many other portions of Europe; that is, roughly, as the rain-fall varies, or, considering the world as a whole, roughly, as the tem-perature varies.

Additional statistical evidence of the relation between the annual number of thunderstorm days and the total annual precipitation, kindly furnished by P. C. Day, formerly in charge of the Climatological Division of the Weather Bureau, is shown by Fig. 106, in which the upper line gives, in millimeters, the smoothed annual precipitation of 127 stations

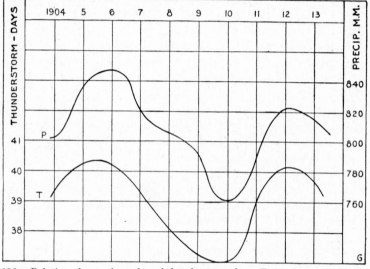

Fig. 106.—Relation of annual number of thunderstorm days, *T*, to total precipitation, *P*—
United States.

scattered over the whole of the United States, and the lower line the smoothed average annual number of thunderstorm days at these same stations. It was thought at first that this relation might differ greatly for those portions of the United States whose climates are radically dis-similar, and for this reason the stations east of the one-hundredth merid-ian, provisionally, were classed separately from those west of it; but the results for the two sections, being substantially alike, show that, for this purpose, their division is entirely unnecessary.

As will be seen from the figure, the earliest statistics used are those of 1904. This is because the annual number of such days reported rapidly decreases from 1904 back to about 1890. Indeed, the annual number of thunderstorm days reported per station since 1903 is almost double the annual number per station (practically the same stations) from 1880 to 1890. The transition from the smaller to the larger number was due in great measure, doubtless, to an alteration in station regulations equivalent to changing the official definition of a thunderstorm from "thunder *with* rain" to "thunder *with* or *without* rain."[1] This, however, does not account for the fact that from 1890 to 1904 the average annual number of thunderstorm days reported per station increased, at a nearly constant rate, almost 100 per cent. Either the storms did so increase, which from the fact that there have been no corresponding temperature changes seems incredible, or else there was, on the average, an increase of attention given to this particular phenomenon. At any rate, so continuous and so great an increase in the average number of thunderstorm days cannot be accepted without abundant confirmation, and, for this reason, the earlier thunderstorm records, provisionally, have been rejected. This average number still (1939) remains substantially constant, as one might expect it to; also, the number of thunderstorm days and the annual precipitation still run, roughly, together.

Obviously, a much closer relation between the number of thunderstorm days and total precipitation would hold for some months and seasons than for others, but no such subgrouping of the data has been made, though, presumably, it would give interesting results. The whole purpose of this portion of the study was to arrive at some definite idea in regard to the cyclic change of thunderstorm frequency, to see with what other meteorological phenomena this change is associated, and, if possible, to determine its cause.

Now, it is well known that the average temperature of the world, as a whole, follows, in general, the sun-spot changes, in the sense that the greater the number of spots the lower the temperature, and the smaller the number of spots the higher the temperature. This regular relation, however, often is greatly modified[2] by the presence, in the high atmosphere, of fine volcanic dust, one invariable effect of which is a lower average temperature. Coarse dust produces the opposite effect. Hence, the warm and the cold periods are irregularly cyclic, and also irregular in intensity. Hence, also, the annual amount of precipitation, the frequency of thunderstorms, and many other phenomena, must perforce undergo exactly the same irregular cyclic variation.

As already stated, the statistical evidence bearing on these conclusions neither is, nor can be, complete, but the deductions are so obvious and the statistical data already examined so confirmatory that but little doubt can exist of their general accuracy.

Cyclic Ocean Period.—The record of thunderstorms over the ocean is not sufficiently full to justify any conclusions in regard to their cyclic changes. Possibly, as in the yearly and the daily periods, the ocean cyclic period may be just the reverse of that of the land, but this is not certain.

---

[1] *Monthly Weather Review*, **43**; 322, 1915.

[2] HUMPHREYS, W. J., *Bull. Mount Weather Observatory*, **6**; 1, Washington, 1913. Also in Part IV of this book.

Geographic Distribution.—The geographic distribution of the thunderstorm may safely be inferred from the fact that it is caused by the strong vertical convection of humid air. From the nature of its formation

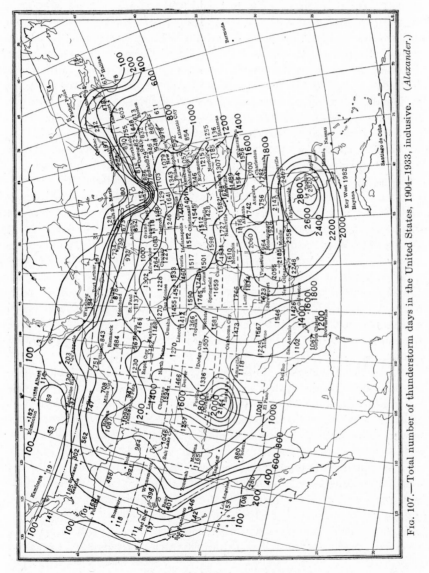

Fig. 107.—Total number of thunderstorm days in the United States, 1904–1933, inclusive. (*Alexander.*)

one would assume—and the assumption is supported by observation[1]—that the thunderstorm must be rare beyond either polar circle, especially over Greenland and over the Antarctic continent; rare over great desert regions wherever situated; rare over the trade belts of the oceans, and,

[1] Brooks, C. E. P., *Geophys. Mem.*, **24**; 1925.

on the other hand, increasingly abundant with increase of temperature and humidity, and, therefore, in general, most abundant in the more rainy portions of the equatorial regions. The east coast of South America, from Pernambuco to Bahia, is said to be an exception.

An interesting and instructive example of the annual geographic distribution of thunderstorms is given by Fig. 107, copied from a statistical study of this subject by W. H. Alexander.[1] Although this example, based on a 30-year (1904–1933) average, refers only to the United States and southern Canada, it, nevertheless, shows the great influence of humidity, latitude, and topography, on thunderstorm frequency.

One of the most striking facts shown by this map is the, relatively, unusual occurrence of this phenomenon along and near the Pacific Coast. Thunderstorms are rare over the littoral and adjacent waters, owing to the practical absence there of strong convection, and rare, also, over the near-by valleys, because here the incoming winds from the ocean normally are too dry, incident to their initial low temperatures, to permit the formation of abundant cumuli at moderate levels, and the lapse rate is commonly too small (upper air too warm) to allow that depth of convection necessary to generate them at high levels.

Frequency of Thunderstorms and of Lightning.—The frequency of thunderstorms varies from less than once a decade, in much of the polar regions, to twice a week, even daily for a season, in many of the warmer and more humid portions of the earth. C. E. P. Brooks[2] has estimated that there are about 44,000 thunderstorms per day, 1800 simultaneously at any time, and 100 flashes of lightning every second.

As we shall see later, these discharges must be the equivalent of a continuous current of the order of 2000 amperes. If the potential difference is 100,000,000 volts,[3] the lightning of the world represents a continuous transfer of energy at the rate, roughly, of 268,000,000 horsepower, or 2 horsepower for every man, woman, and child in the United States and its possessions.

Pressure and Temperature Distribution.—In illustrating the occurrence of thunderstorms, with reference to the disposition of isobars and isotherms, or the distribution of atmospheric pressure and temperature, typical weather maps of the United States[4] (Figs. 108 to 122), have been used, not because the thunderstorms of this country are different in any essential particular from those of other countries, but chiefly as a matter

---

[1] *Monthly Weather Review*, **63**; 157, 1935.

[2] *M. O. 254d*, London, 1925.

[3] Peek, *J. Franklin Inst.*, **199**; 141, 1925.

[4] The author wishes to acknowledge the kind cooperation of the official forecasters of the U. S. Weather Bureau in selecting maps typical of thunderstorm conditions in the United States.

of convenience in making the drawings. To facilitate their study, each of the several types discussed is illustrated with three consecutive maps. The first shows the 12-hour antecedent conditions, the second the partic-

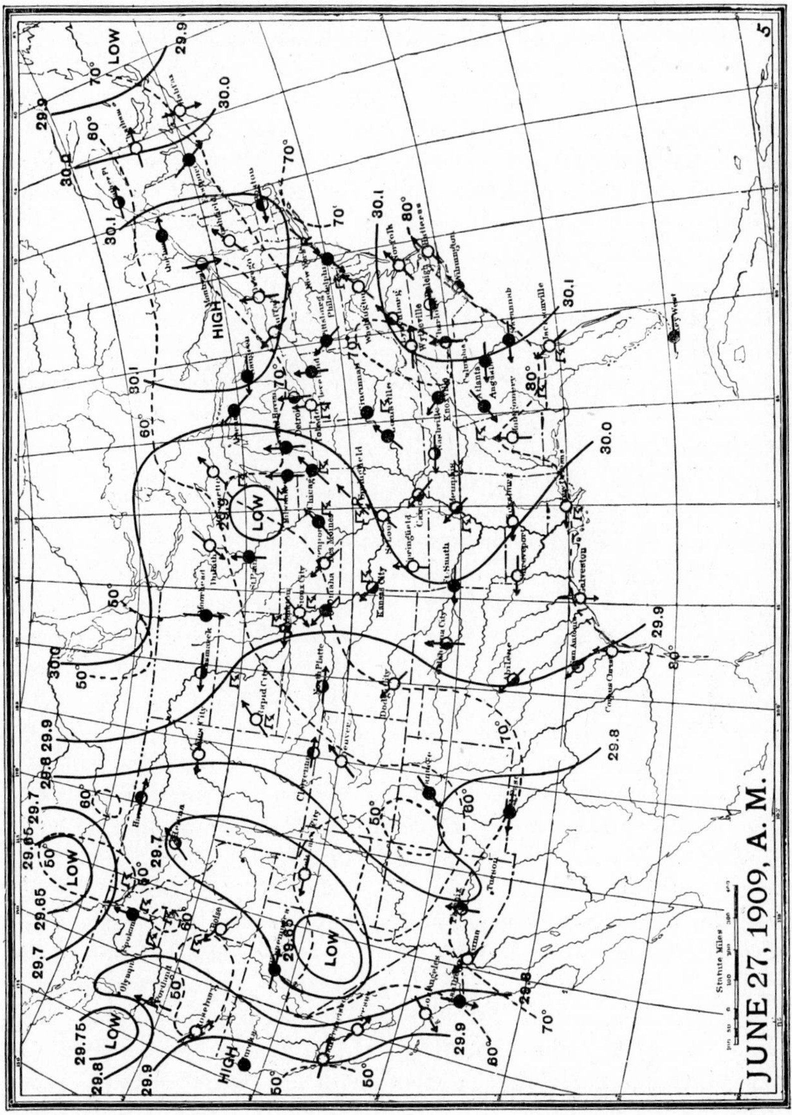

FIG. 108.—Weather map, 8 a.m., June 27, 1909, typical conditions at beginning of "heat" thunderstorms: O, clear; ☉, partly cloudy; O, cloudy; R, rain; K, thunderstorm.

ular pressure-temperature distribution in question, and the third the 12-hour subsequent conditions.

In these figures, the isobars, in corrected inches of mercury as read on the barometer and reduced to sea level, and the isotherms in Fahrenheit degrees, are marked by full and dotted lines respectively. The

legend "low" is written over a region from which, for some distance in
every horizontal direction, the pressure increases.   Similarly, the legend
"high" applies to a region from which, in every horizontal direction,
the pressure decreases.   The arrows, as is customary on such maps, fly

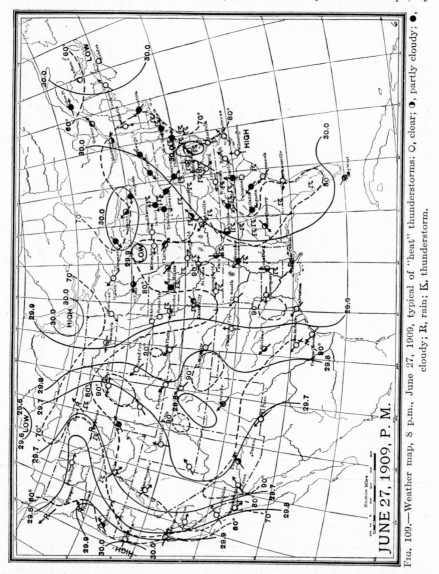

Fig. 109.—Weather map, 8 p.m., June 27, 1909, typical of "heat" thunderstorms: O, clear; ◐, partly cloudy; ●, cloudy; R, rain; K, thunderstorm.

with the wind, while the state of the weather is indicated by the usual
U. S. Weather Bureau symbols.   All refer to the time of observation,
except that of the thunderstorm, which covers the previous 12 hours.
As originally drawn, fronts were not indicated on these maps though

they were mentally noted as wind-shift lines by the forecasters, and they are not added now because their approximate locations are obvious and, also, because the discussion here is of the distributions of isotherms and isobars only, as related to the occurrence of thunderstorms.

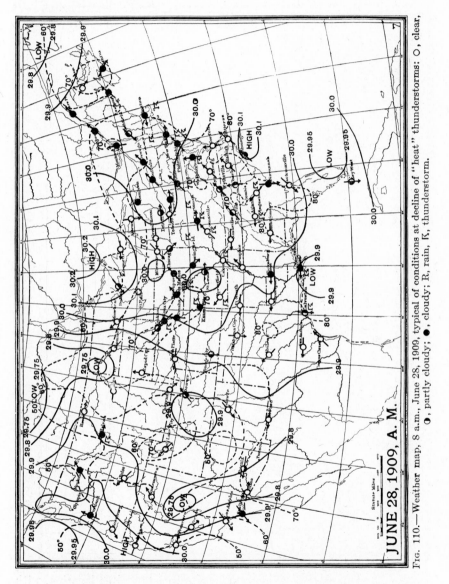

FIG. 110.—Weather map, 8 a.m., June 28, 1909, typical of conditions at decline of "heat" thunderstorms: O, clear, ◑, partly cloudy; ●, cloudy; R, rain, K, thunderstorm.

JUNE 28, 1909, A. M.

A full discussion of all the data, both surface and free-air, available for the prediction of thunderstorms and how to use this data, would be valuable, but its place is in a comprehensive work on forecasting—subject

to frequent revision to keep up with the development of synoptic practice
—not here.

Obviously, the key to the geographic distribution of thunderstorms,
that is, the distribution of conditions likely to induce strong vertical

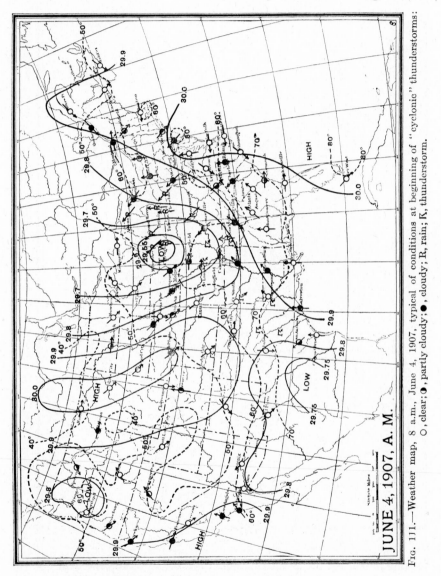

Fig. 111.—Weather map, 8 a.m., June 4, 1907, typical of conditions at beginning of "cyclonic" thunderstorms: O, clear; ◑, partly cloudy; ●, cloudy; R, rain; K, thunderstorm.

JUNE 4, 1907, A. M.

convection of humid air, is also the key to their probable location, with
reference to any given system of isotherms and isobars, or distribution of
atmospheric temperature and pressure. From this standpoint the places
of their most frequent occurrence are:

a. Regions of high temperature and widely extended nearly uniform pressure (see Figs. 108, 109, and 110).

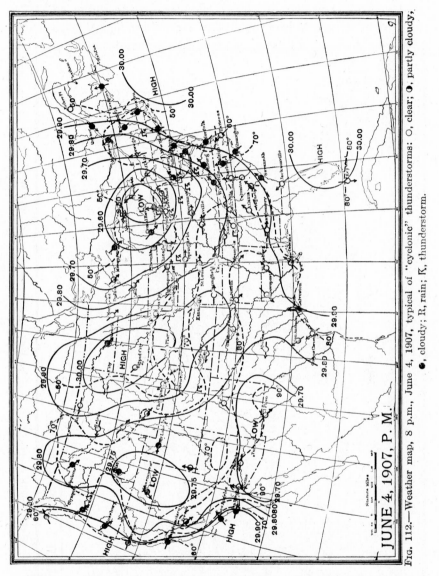

Fig. 112.—Weather map, 8 p.m., June 4, 1907, typical of "cyclonic" thunderstorms: O, clear; ◑, partly cloudy; ●, cloudy; R, rain; K, thunderstorm.

The conditions are still more favorable to the genesis of thunderstorms when the air is humid and the pressure, partly because of the humidity, slightly below normal, or, at most, but little above normal.

When the pressure is approximately uniform the winds are light, and, therefore, the turbulence and general mixing of the lower air practically negligible, hence, every opportunity is given for the surface air to become strongly heated, and, thereby, finally, to establish vigorous local convections, with their consequent thunderstorms. Such storms, always favored by the drafts up the sides of mountain ranges, and, particularly, by those up steep mountain peaks and strongly heated valleys, are, of

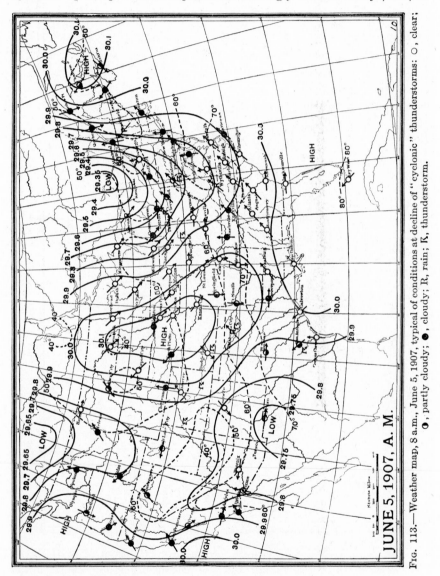

Fig. 113.—Weather map, 8 a.m., June 5, 1907, typical of conditions at decline of "cyclonic" thunderstorms: ○, clear; ◑, partly cloudy; ●, cloudy; R, rain; K, thunderstorm.

JUNE 5, 1907, A. M.

course, most frequent of summer afternoons, and are especially liable to occur at the end of 2 or 3 days of unusually warm weather, when the lower air has become so heated that convection extends to relatively great altitudes. They develop, here and there, sporadically, hence, the name "local" thunderstorms; last, as a rule, only an hour or two, and travel but a short distance—those that form over mountain peaks often do not travel at all. They also, frequently, are referred to as "heat" thunderstorms, from the fact that, under the given conditions, the

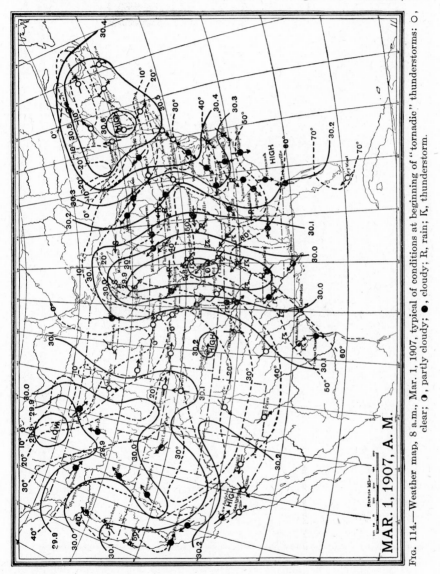

FIG. 114.—Weather map, 8 a.m., Mar. 1, 1907, typical of conditions at beginning of "tornadic" thunderstorms: O, clear; ☉, partly cloudy; ●, cloudy; R, rain; K, thunderstorm.

necessary initial convection is essentially, if not wholly, due to surface heating.

Local or heat thunderstorms seldom are especially violent and dangerous, and fortunately so, since they are exceedingly numerous, constituting, as they do, well nigh the only type of thunderstorm in the tropics, and also, perhaps, the most common type in the warmer portions of the temperate zones.

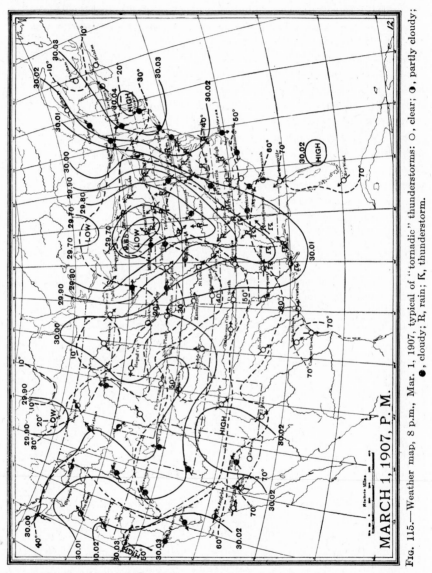

FIG. 115.—Weather map, 8 p.m., Mar. 1, 1907, typical of "tornadic" thunderstorms: O, clear; ☉, partly cloudy; ●, cloudy; R, rain; K, thunderstorm.

b. The southeast quadrant (northeast, in the Southern Hemisphere), or less frequently, the southwest (northwest, in the Southern Hemisphere), of a regularly formed low, or typical cyclonic storm (see Figs. 111, 112, and 113).

In this case, the temperature gradient, essential to a rapid vertical convection, is not produced chiefly by surface heating, as it is during the genesis of "heat" thunderstorms, but, commonly, from the heat of condensation in humid southerly winds as they rise over colder air in their course. Some thunderstorms, however, in this warm sector, or interfrontal region, appear to be, and presumably are, owing to the more or less crossed directions of the under- and overcurrents of air, the under being directed spirally inward toward the region of lowest pressure, and the over tending to follow the isobars. The surface air of the quadrant in question, therefore, normally flows from lower and warmer latitudes, while, with increasing altitude, the winds come more and more nearly from the west, or even northwest. This crossing of the air currents, then, the lower coming from warmer sections and the upper from regions not so much warmer—possibly even colder—progressively increases the vertical temperature gradient, or rate of temperature decrease with increase of altitude, and, therefore doubtless often is the determining cause of rapid vertical convection, production usually of only a shower, but occasionally of a thunderstorm. Thunderstorms may occur in this region, also, incident to the convergence of warm, humid winds on their spiral course toward the low-pressure center.

This particular type, formerly known as the "cyclonic" thunderstorm, now commonly is called the "warm-front" thunderstorm. However, there really are two classes here, the strictly "warm-front" type induced by the flow of humid air up a sloping mass of colder air and the "interfrontal" type due to increase of lapse rate incident to certain cross-currents.

Frontal thunderstorms, both cold and warm, are almost wholly confined to the temperate and higher zones, for the simple reason that tropical cyclones, themselves of infrequent occurrence, seldom can have the necessary temperature contrast between its winds of different directions, since all come from equally warm regions. Nevertheless, thunderstorms do occur in connection with many, perhaps nearly all, tropical cyclones. They occur, however, either incidentally during the development of such disturbances or else, later, along their borders and not, or but rarely, within the body of strong winds, and belong, therefore, to the "heat" variety rather than to the "cyclonic," or "warm front" type.

c. The barometric valley between the branches of a distorted or V-shaped cyclonic isobar (see Figs. 114, 115, and 116).

The eastern portion of this region is occupied by warm tropical winds of moderate strength, and the western by cold polar winds—usually southwesterly and northwesterly, respectively (in the northern hemisphere), a few hundred meters above the surface. Along the boundary between these two systems, a marked change in wind direction rapidly occurs. Hence, the intersection of this boundary with the surface of the

earth has long been known as the "wind-shift line." It also is called
the "squall line" and "cold front," the designation now chiefly used.

When the interface between the warm and cold winds is but slightly
inclined to the surface of the earth, with the colder system above and

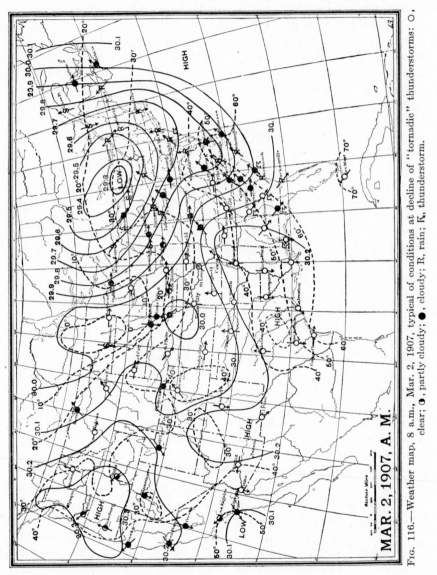

Fig. 116.—Weather map, 8 a.m., Mar. 2, 1907, typical of conditions at decline of "tornadic" thunderstorms: O, clear; ☉, partly cloudy; ●, cloudy; R, rain; K, thunderstorm.

MAR. 2, 1907, A. M.

driving forward, as normally is the case, masses of the lower, and commonly humid air may, here and there, become entrapped and then forced
upward as individual columns or, commonly, forced forward and then
up in front of the cold nose. Many of these develop cumuli of sufficient

magnitude to start thunderstorms of widely varying size and intensity. When the interface is steeply inclined, however, as it seems occasionally to be, especially in mid-air, when the difference in temperature between the two systems of winds, or air masses, is not great, convection can occur

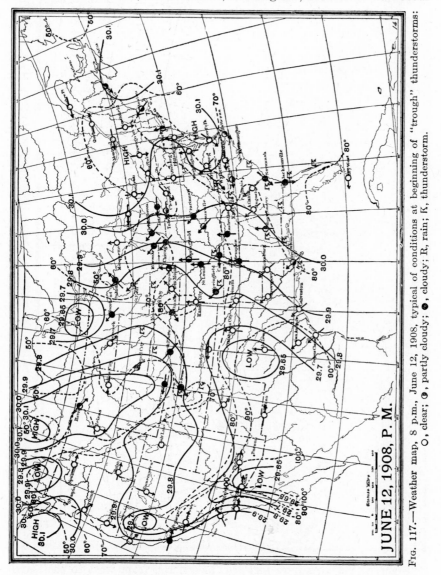

JUNE 12, 1908, P. M.

FIG. 117.—Weather map, 8 p.m., June 12, 1908, typical of conditions at beginning of "trough" thunderstorms: O, clear; ◑, partly cloudy; ◉, cloudy; R, rain; K, thunderstorm.

locally along this junction, and create a vortex at each such place by dragging air from both systems towards a common center. The more violent of these vertical atmospheric whirls, accompanied by thunder and rain and extending down to the surface of the earth, are, of course, tornadoes, or, in some cases, water spouts. Thunderstorms generated in the region under discussion, that is, along a cold front, now usually are called "cold-front" thunderstorms.

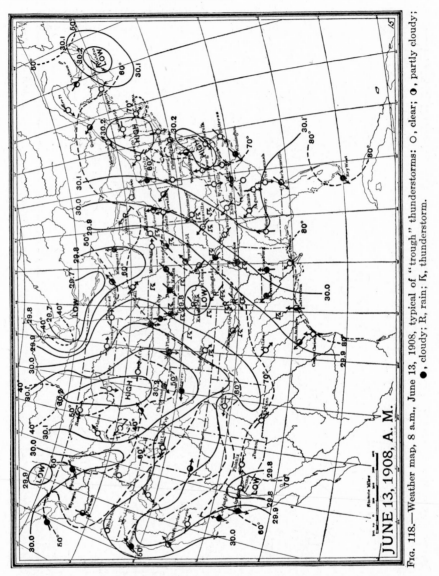

Fig. 118.—Weather map, 8 a.m., June 13, 1908, typical of "trough" thunderstorms: O, clear; ☉, partly cloudy; ●, cloudy; R, rain; K, thunderstorm.

Since a cyclone moves forward, in general, from west to east, and maintains for many hours, approximately, the same form and nature, it follows that its valley of low pressure, if, as in this case, there be one, and, therefore, the line of thunderstorms, must also travel with it in the same general direction and with approximately the same velocity.

Furthermore, as the wind-shift line runs southerly from the center of low pressure, it follows that its accompanying thunderstorms always move abreast, and not in file.

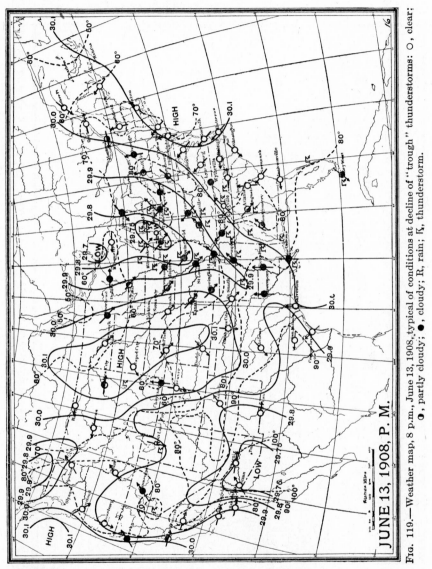

FIG. 119.—Weather map, 8 p.m., June 13, 1908, typical of conditions at decline of "trough" thunderstorms: O, clear; ◑, partly cloudy; ●, cloudy; R, rain; K, thunderstorm.

d. The region covered by a low-pressure trough between adjacent high-pressure areas (Figs. 117, 118, and 119).

Along the adjacent borders of two neighboring anticyclones—that is, along the barometric trough between them—the surface winds from one side are more or less directly opposed to those of the other, each flowing spirally outward from the region of higher pressure. Hence, because of the under- and overrunning, as previously explained, and the resulting temperature gradients, this also is a region of frequent thunderstorms. Here, too, a number of more or less independent storms may exist simul-

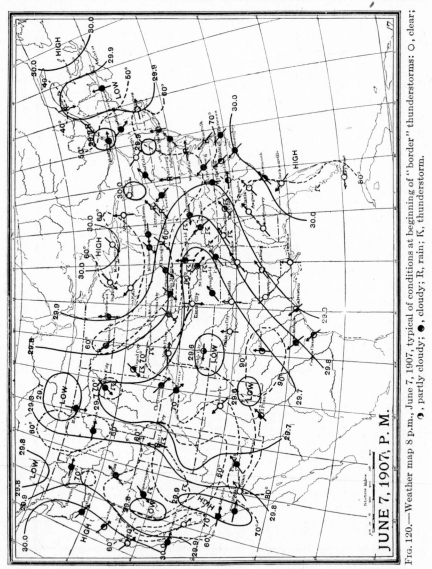

Fig. 120.—Weather map 8 p.m., June 7, 1907, typical of conditions at beginning of "border" thunderstorms: O, clear; ◑, partly cloudy; ◐, cloudy; R, rain; K, thunderstorm.

JUNE 7, 1907, P. M.

taneously along the same line, and advance abreast for considerable distances across the country.

As shown by Fig. 119, this region may be regarded as that of a very elongated V-shaped depression with the wind-shift line following the lowest part of the barometric valley. Hence, this thunderstorm, also, belongs to the "wind-shift," "squall line," or "cold-front" type.

e. The east-west boundary between warm and cold waves (see Figs. 120, 121, and 122), or along an east-west trough of low pressure.

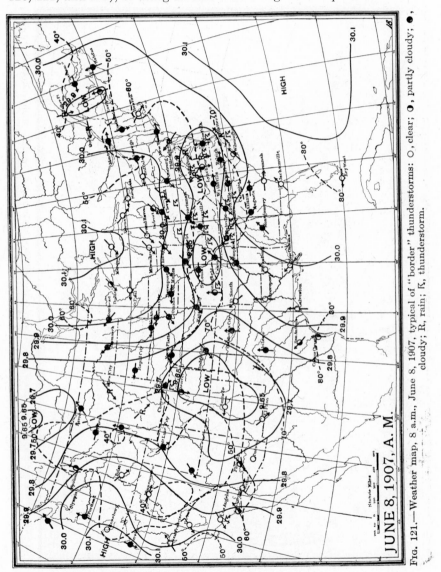

FIG. 121.—Weather map, 8 a.m., June 8, 1907, typical of "border" thunderstorms: O, clear; ⊙, partly cloudy; ●, cloudy; R, rain; K, thunderstorm.

At such a boundary, the direction of flow of the warm, humid layers of air is more or less opposite, as shown on the maps, to that of the colder ones; therefore, it must frequently happen that at irregular intervals along it, lower air, coming from the cold area, underruns a section of sur-

face air belonging to the warm region.　Now, wherever this underrunning
on the part of the cold air, does occur, the lifted warm air normally is
sufficiently cooled by expansion, incident to decrease of pressure, to start

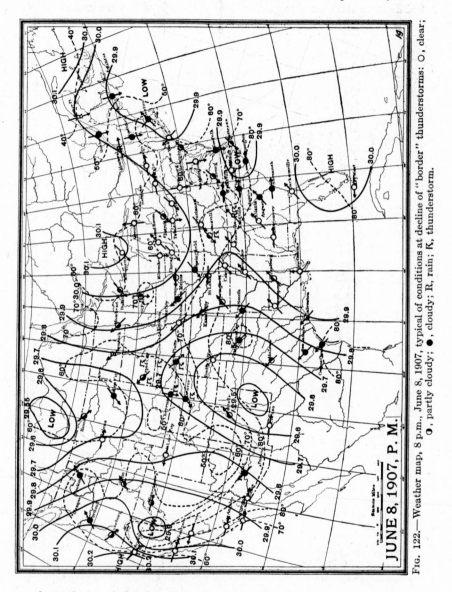

Fig. 122.—Weather map, 8 p.m., June 8, 1907, typical of conditions at decline of "border" thunderstorms: O, clear; ◐, partly cloudy; ●, cloudy; R, rain; K, thunderstorm.

JUNE 8, 1907, P. M.

condensation and develop into an active thunderstorm, for this is but a
special case of the squall line or cold front.　Hence, as stated, the east-
west boundary between warm and cold waves is another place favorable to
the genesis of the thunderstorm.

Although the above division of weather maps, into several classes favorable to the occurrence of thunderstorms, may be, generally, satisfactory to some practical meteorologists, many others, no doubt, will prefer some other classification. Very well; let everyone select types and subtypes, whether few or many, according to his own experience. The maps may be assorted in many ways, but so far as the cause of the storm is concerned, the classes are very few: *Heat* thunderstorms, due to marked increase of surface temperature; *cyclonic* or, commonly, *warm front*, induced commonly by the flow of warm air up over obstructing cold air, sometimes by the convergence of warm currents in the front portion of the cyclone, and occasionally by the crossing of surface and free-air currents; and *squall* or *cold front*, caused by the underrunning, or by the forceful forward drive of cold air, or, occasionally, perhaps, by the entrapping of warm humid air by colder winds of a different system.

Thunderstorm Winds.—Shortly, say 20 minutes or so, before the rain of a thunderstorm reaches a given locality the wind at that place, generally light, begins to die down to an approximate calm and to change its direction. At first, it usually is from the south or southwest in the northern hemisphere; from the north or northwest in the southern, and, in both, more or less directly, across the path of the storm itself. When the change is complete, it blows for a few minutes, rather gently, directly toward the nearest portion of the storm front, and, finally, as the rain is almost at hand, abruptly, and in rather violent gusts, away from the storm, and, because it has come from above, as will be explained later, in about the direction that the storm is traveling, a direction that, in most cases, differs appreciably from that of the original surface wind. Usually, this violent gusty wind lasts through only the earlier portion of the disturbance and then is gradually, but rather quickly, succeeded by a comparatively gentle wind, that, though following the storm at first, frequently, after an hour or so, blows in the same general direction as the original surface wind.

The cause of the thunderstorm winds needs to be carefully considered if one would understand at all clearly the mechanism of the storm itself.

As already explained, this type of storm owes its origin to that vertical convection which results from a superadiabatic temperature gradient. It is this gradient, no matter how established, whether by simple surface heating or by the over- and underrunning of layers of air of widely different temperatures, that permits, or rather forces, the production of the cumulus cloud in which, and by the motions of which the electricity that characterizes the thunderstorm is generated.

Nevertheless, as everyone knows, the passage of a cumulus cloud overhead, however large, so long as no rain is falling from it, does not greatly affect the direction and magnitude of the surface wind—does

not bring on any of the familiar gusts and other thunderstorm phenomena. Hence, somehow or other, the rain is an important factor, both
in starting and in maintaining the winds in question, for they do not
exist before the rain begins nor continue after it has ceased. On the
other hand, it cannot be assumed that the rain is the whole cause of
these winds, for they do not accompany other, and ordinary, showers,
however heavy the downpour may be.

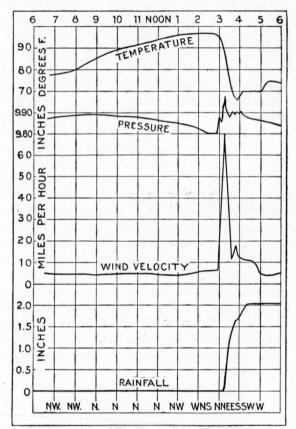

Fɪɢ. 123.—Course of meteorological elements on a thunderstorm day.   (Washington, D. C.,
July 30, 1913.)

The actual course of events, illustrated by Fig. 123 taken from the
records obtained at Washington, D. C., during the passage of the notable
thunderstorm of July 30, 1913, seems to be about as follows:

First.—An approximately adiabatic temperature gradient, presumably, is established over a wide area, roughly, up to the base level
of the cumulus clouds, all of which, because of a practically common
temperature and common humidity over the whole region, must have,
substantially, the same base level, and, therefore, often appear *en échelon,*

as shown in Fig. 124. But while the uprising branches of the existing convection currents, due to superadiabatic gradients, may be localized and, here and there, rather rapid, the return or compensating down-

Fig. 124.—Cumuli *en échelon*, Loudon Valley, Virginia. (*E. B. Calvert, photographer.*)

flow is relatively widespread and correspondingly gentle. The condition essential to a local and rapid downflow, that is, a local decided cooling at a high altitude, does not exist, and, therefore, the counterpart to the upward current is nowhere conspicuous.

Second.—The convections in the cumuli are accelerated by virtue of the latent heat of vaporization set free in them, and thus one or more of them rapidly developed. In some cases, great size and remarkable altitudes are attained, as illustrated by Fig. 125.

Third.—After a time, as a result of the abundant condensation induced by the convectional cooling, rain is formed at a considerable altitude where, of course, the air is quite cold, in fact so cold that often hail is produced. Now this cold rain, or rain and hail, as it falls, and as long as it falls, chills the air from the level of its formation all the way to the earth, partly as a result of its initial low temperature and partly because of the evaporation that takes place during its fall. Hence,

Fig. 125.—Towering cumulus, west end of Java.   (*E. E. Barnard, photographer.*)

this continuously chilled column of air, partly because of the frictional drag of the rain, but mainly because of the increase, due to this chilling, of its own density, immediately, and necessarily, becomes a concentrated and vigorous return branch of the vertical circulation. In fact, it (or gravity acting through it) becomes the sustaining cause of the storm's circulation. At the same time, because of the downward blow and because of the retardation of the winds by surface friction, the barometric pressure is abruptly increased, as will be explained later.

It will be worth while to consider some of these statements a little more closely, and to test them with possible numerical values.

Omitting, as one may, the effects of radiation, there seem to be but three possible ways by which the cooling of a thunderstorm may be obtained: (*a*) by the descent of originally potentially cold air; (*b*) by

chilling the air with the cold rain; (c) by evaporation. Each of these will
be considered separately.

a. Obviously no portion of the upper air could maintain its position
if, potentially, even slightly colder than that near the surface, that is, so
cold that, even after warming up adiabatically in a fall to the surface,
it still would be colder than the air displaced. If at all, potentially,
colder, it would fall until it, itself, became the surface air. Hence
the great decrease in temperature that comes with a thunderstorm
is not the result of the descent of a layer of air originally potentially
cold, for, as explained, an upper layer sufficiently cold to give, after its
descent, the actual cooling, could not exist. Again, any descending
air must come from either below the under surface of the cloud, or from
above this level. If from below, then, because of adiabatic heating
during its descent through air which, as above explained, has practically
the adiabatic temperature gradient, it must reach the earth at substantially the original surface temperature. If from above, it would, as is
obvious from Fig. 103, reach the earth even warmer than the original
surface temperature. Hence, looked at in any way, case (*a*) clearly
is inadmissible.

The above statements may, possibly, seem to contravene the explanation that some thunderstorms may originate in the establishment, by
cross-currents, or by entrapment of superadiabatic temperature gradients.
In reality, however, they are in harmony with that explanation which is
based on the fact that such gradients cannot be maintained, but must at
once cause vertical convection. Besides, such mechanically established
gradients could merely initiate but not, as we shall see, maintain the
storm.

b. Let the under surface of the thunderstorm cloud be 1500 meters
above the earth, and the column of air, cooled by the cold rain and its
evaporation, 2000 meters high. Let the surface temperature be 30° C.,
and the temperature gradient, before the storm begins, adiabatic up
to the undercloud level, and let there be a 2-cm. rainfall.

Now at the temperature assumed, a column of air 2000 meters high
whose cross-section is 1 square cm., and whose base is at sea level, weighs,
roughly, 210 grams, and its heat capacity, therefore, is approximately
that of 50 grams of water. At the top of this column the temperature
can be, at most, only about 20° C. lower than at the bottom, corresponding to the adiabatic or maximum temperature gradient, and if the rain
leaves the top at this temperature but reaches the earth 7° C. colder
than the surface air before the storm (temperatures that seem at least to
be of the correct order), it will have been warmed 13° C. during its fall,
and the air column, at the expense of whose heat this warming was
produced, cooled, on the average, about 0.5° C. But, as a matter of fact,
the air usually is cooled 5° to 10° C. Hence, while the temperature

of the air, necessarily, is reduced to some extent by mere heat conduction to the cold rain, much the greater portion of the cooling clearly must have some other origin. Further, since (a) is inadmissible and (b) only a minor contributing factor, it follows, by exclusion, that of the three obvious causes, only evaporation is left to account for much the greater portion of the cooling. Consider, then, whether evaporation really can produce the effects observed.

(c) It is a common thing, in semiarid regions, to see a heavy shower, even a thundershower, leave the base of a cloud and yet fail utterly to reach the surface of the earth. Also in the case of a heat thunderstorm, around which the air is the same in every direction, the absolute humidity increases with the onset of the rain. Hence, it appears quite certain that, in the average thunderstorm, a considerable portion of the rain that leaves the cloud may evaporate before it reaches the ground, and, therefore, that the temperature decrease of the atmosphere may be largely owing to this fact. But if so, why, then, one properly might ask, does not an equally great temperature drop accompany all heavy rains?

The answer is obvious: It is because, as a rule, the temperature is higher, the relative humidity lower, and the temperature gradient more nearly adiabatic, during a thunderstorm than at the time of an ordinary rain. Other rains, those that are accompanied by long horizontal, and slow, rather than rapid, upward movements of the air, begin only when the humidity is so high that but little evaporation and, therefore, but little cooling from this source can take place. In such rains, there is nothing that can greatly increase the density of the air locally and, consequently, there is no rapidly descending current or wind. Thunderstorms, on the other hand, are developed by strong vertical convection which establishes a nearly adiabatic gradient and when the relative humidity, in the case of the heat thunderstorm, at least, is low, 50 per cent, say. Evaporation into this air, as soon as the rain has begun, obviously must be rapid, with the consequent cooling and increase of density correspondingly great. Hence, since the temperature gradient was already nearly adiabatic, a strong downward current, necessarily, is established in the midst of the falling and evaporating rain. Further, whatever the type of thunderstorm, the descending air, which can be no more than saturated at the base of the cloud, dynamically warms so rapidly that evaporation into it can not keep pace with its water capacity. That is, evaporation which takes place all the way from cloud to earth, by rendering the air locally cool and dense, causes it to fall, while this fall, in turn, through dynamical heating, maintains the evaporation. Hence the downrush of the air must continue so long as there is an abundant supply of local rain, and cease when the rain becomes light.

It will be instructive, now, to return to the numerical values and compute a probable magnitude of the cooling due to evaporation. As before, let a 2-cm. rain leave the cloud, but let one-fourth of the rain that started, or $\frac{1}{2}$ cm., be evaporated. This would consume 303 heat units, from an air column 2000 meters high, whose heat capacity is that of only 50 c.c. of water. Hence, as a result of evaporation alone, the temperature of the air column would be lowered on the average by about 6° C. Evaporation, therefore, appears to be both necessary and sufficient to produce all, or nearly all, the cooling of a thunderstorm.

But what is the effect of this evaporation on the density of the atmosphere? Since the molecular weight of water is 18, while the average molecular weight of air is approximately 28.9, it follows that the amount of evaporation, above assumed, would decrease the density of the atmosphere by, roughly, 1 part in 1000. On the other hand, a decrease in temperature of 6° C., that would be produced by the evaporation assumed, would increase it by about 1 part in 50. Hence the resultant of these two opposing effects is substantially that of the second alone; that is, a distinct increase in density, and a consequent downrush of cold air.

Doubtless, as already implied, the evaporation of thunderstorm rain, and, therefore, the drop in temperature and the consequent fractional gain in density, all increase with decrease of elevation. In some measure, however, this effect is counteracted by the higher temperatures of the lower layers—the higher the absolute temperature the less, proportionately, the change of density per degree change of temperature. But, no matter how nor to what extent the details may vary, it seems quite certain that the cold rain of a thunderstorm and its evaporation, together, must establish a local downrush of cold air, an observed important and characteristic phenomenon, really the immediate cause of the vigorous circulation, whose rational explanation has been attempted in the past few paragraphs.

As the column, or sheet, of cold air flows down, it maintains in great measure its original horizontal velocity and, therefore, on reaching the earth, rushes forward in the direction of the storm movement, underrunning and buoying up the adjacent warm air. And this condition, largely due, as explained, to condensation and evaporation, once established, necessarily is self-perpetuating, so long as the general temperature gradient, humidity, and wind direction are favorable. It must be remembered, however, that thunderstorm convection, rising air just in front of, and descending air with, the rain, does not occur in a closed circuit, for the air that goes up does not return nor does the air that comes down immediately go up again; there simply is an interchange between the surface air in front of the storm and the upper air in its rear. The travel of the storm, by keeping up with the underrunning cold current, just as effectually maintains the temperature contrasts essential to this open-circuit convection as does continuous heating, on one side, and cooling on the other, maintain the temperature contrast essential to a closed-circuit convection.

The movements of the warm air in front of the rain, the lull, the inflow, and the updraft, resemble somewhat those of a horizontal cylinder resting on the earth where the air is quiet and rolling forward with the speed of the storm. Similarly, the cold air, in its descent and forward rush, together with the updraft of warm air, also resembles a horizontal cylinder, but one sliding on the earth and turning in the opposite direction from that of the forward-rolling, or all-warm, cylinder. In neither case, however, is the analogy complete, for, as above explained, the air that goes up remains aloft, while the cold air that comes down is kept, by its greater density, to the lower levels. The condition of flow persists, as do cataracts and crestclouds (clouds along mountain crests), but here, too, as in their case, the material involved is ever renewed.

Another thunderstorm phenomenon, not, however, shown in Fig. 123, is the increase in all cases of the relative humidity, and of the absolute humidity, also, in the case of the heat thunderstorm, with the onset of the rain. The cold-front storm, on the other hand, generally is accompanied with a decrease of the absolute humidity owing to the dryness of the incoming cool air.

The Squall Cloud.—Between the uprising sheet of warm air and the adjacent descending sheet of cold air, horizontal vortices are sure to be formed, in which the two currents are more or less mixed. The lower of these vortices can only be *inferred*, as a necessary consequence of the opposite directions of flow of the adjacent sheets of warm and cold air, for there is nothing to render them visible. Neither can any vortices, that may exist within the cloud, be seen. Near the front lower edge of the cumulonimbus system, however, and immediately in front of the sheet of rain, or rain and hail, the rising air has so nearly reached its dew point that the somewhat lower temperature produced by the admixture of the descending cold air is sufficient to produce in it a light fog-like condensation, which, of course, renders any detached vortex at this position quite visible.

This squall cloud, in which the direction of motion on top is against the storm, may be regarded as a third horizontal thunderstorm cylinder, much smaller but more nearly complete than either of the others.

Schematic Illustrations.—The above conceptions of the mechanism of a thunderstorm can, perhaps, be made a little clearer with the aid of illustrations. Figure 126, a schematic representation of a thunderstorm in the making, gives the boundary of a large cumulus cloud from which rain has not yet begun to fall, and the stream lines of atmospheric flow into it. When the cloud is stationary and there is no surface wind, the updraft, obviously, will be more or less symmetrical about a vertical through its center, but when it has an appreciable velocity, as indicated in the figure, it is equally obvious that most, often nearly all, of the air entering the cloud will do so through its front undersurface. At this stage there will be no concentrated, or local, downcurrent, only counter-settling of the air round about, because, as previously explained, the air cataract requires strong local cooling, and this, in turn, calls for local rain.

Figure 127 schematically represents a well-developed thunderstorm in progress. The rain, often mixed with hail, cools the air through which

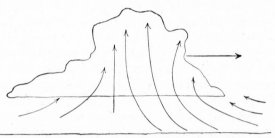

Fɪɢ. 126.—Principal air movements in the development of a cumulus cloud.

it falls, both by conduction and evaporation, the hail also by fusion, and as the temperature gradient, over a considerable area, already was closely adiabatic, it follows that the actual temperatures within the rain column must be lower than those of the surrounding air at cor-responding levels, all the way from the surface of the earth to within the cloud, that is, throughout, and a little beyond, the nonsaturated or

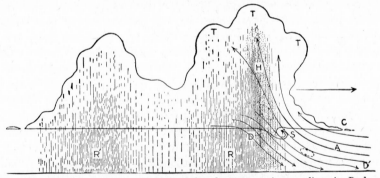

Fɪɢ. 127.—Ideal cross-section of a typical thunderstorm. *A*, ascending air; *D*, descend-air; *C*, storm collar; *S*, roll scud; *D'*, wind gust; *H*, hail; *T*, thunderheads; *R*, primary rain; *R'*, secondary rain.

evaporating region. As soon, then, as this column, or sheet, of air is sufficiently cooled, it flows down and forward and all the atmospheric movements peculiar to the thunderstorm are established, substantially, as represented.

Referring to the figure: The warm ascending air is in the region *A*; the cold descending air at *D*; the dust cloud (in dry weather) at *D'*; the squall cloud at *S*; the storm collar at *C*; the thunderheads at *T*; the hail at H; the primary rain, due to initial convection, at R; and the secondary rain at R'. This latter phenomenon, the secondary rain, is a thing of frequent occurrence and often is due, as indicated in the figure, to the coalescence and quiet settling of drops from an abandoned portion of the cumulus in which, and below which, winds and convection are no longer active.

The thunderstorm is also frequently accompanied by false cirri, occasionally by scarf clouds and, even, though rarely, by mamato-cumuli; but, as none of these is essential to it, all, therefore, are omitted from the above schematic illustration.

Thunderstorm Pressures.—Before the onset of a thunderstorm there usually, if not always, is a distinct fall in the barometer. At times, this fall is extended over several hours, but, whether the period be long or short, the rate of fall usually is greatest at the near approach of the storm. Just as the storm breaks, however, the pressure rises very rapidly, usually from 1 to 2 millimeters, fluctuates irregularly, and finally, as the storm passes, again becomes rather steady but, generally, at a somewhat higher pressure than prevailed before the rain began.

The cause of these pressure changes is rather complex. The decrease in the absolute water vapor of the air as a whole, measured by the condensation, and the decrease in the temperature of the lower air—perhaps more than offset by the latent heat set free in the upper—both tend to increase the atmospheric pressure, and each contributes its share to the final result. Both these effects, however, are comparatively permanent, and while they, and the passing anticyclone, in the case of the squall storm, may be mainly responsible for the increase of pressure after the storm has gone by, they probably are not the chief factors in the production of the initial, and quickly produced, pressure maximum. Here at least two factors, one obvious, the other inconspicuous, are involved. These are: (*a*) the rapid downrush of air, and (*b*) the interference to horizontal flow caused by the vertical circulation.

The downrush of air clearly produces a vertically directed pressure on the surface of the earth, in the same manner that a horizontal flow produces a horizontally directed pressure against the side of a house. But a pressure equal to that given by 2 mm. of mercury, a pressure increase frequently reached in a thunderstorm, would mean about 2.72 grams per square centimeter, or 27.2 kilograms per square meter, and require a wind velocity of, roughly, 60 kilometers per hour or 17 meters per second. Now, the velocity of the downrush of air in a thunderstorm is not at all accurately known, but while at times probably very considerable, the above value of 17 meters per second seems to be excessive; in fact, its average value may not be even half so great. If in reality it is not, then, since the pressure of a wind varies as the square of its velocity, it follows that less than one-fourth of the actual pressure increase can be caused in this way. Hence, it would seem that there, probably, is at least one other pressure factor, and, indeed, such a factor obviously exists in the check to the horizontal flow caused by vertical convection.

To make this point clear: Assume two layers of air, an upper and a lower, flowing parallel to each other. Let their respective masses per unit length in the direction of their horizontal movement be M and m, and their velocities V and v. Now, if, through convection, say, the whole, or any portion, of the lower layer is carried aloft, it must be replaced below by an equal amount of the upper air.

Let the whole of the lower layer be carried up. To produce the rainfall above assumed, 2 cm., this layer would have to be at least 1 kilometer deep; but, no matter what its depth, if it should merely change places with the upper air, there, obviously, could be no effect on the flow nor on the height of the barometer. Even if the different layers should mingle and assume a common velocity V', the rate of flow would still remain unchanged, in accordance with the law of the conservation of linear momentum, and the barometer reading unaltered.

In symbols we would have the equation

$$MV + mv = (M + m)V'.$$

Hence, neither interchange nor mingling of the two air currents, upper and lower, can change the vertical mass of the atmosphere, nor, therefore, the surface pressure. But, then, in the case of atmospheric convection there is something more than simple mingling of two air currents, and the linear momentum does not, in general, remain constant. The increased surface velocity following convection, a phenomenon very marked in the case of a thunderstorm, causes an increased frictional drag, and, therefore, a greater or less decrease in the total flow. Suppose this amounts to the equivalent of reducing the velocity of a layer of air only 25 meters thick from V to v, and let $V = 5v$. That is, the equivalent of the one-three-hundred-and-twentieth part of the atmosphere having its flow reduced to one-fifth its former value. This would reduce the total flow of the atmosphere by about 1 part in 400, and, thereby, increase the barometric reading by nearly 2 millimeters.

It would seem, then, that the friction of the thunderstorm gust on the surface of the earth, through the consequent decrease in the total linear momentum of the atmosphere and, therefore, its total flow, must be an important contributing cause of the rapid and marked increase of the barometric pressure that accompanies the onset of a heavy thunderstorm.

To sum up: The chief factors contributing to the increase of the barometric pressure during a thunderstorm appear to be, possibly in the order of their magnitude: (*a*) decrease of horizontal flow, due to surface friction; (*b*) vertical wind pressure, due to descending air; (*c*) decrease in total humidity, due to precipitation; (*d*) lower temperature, due largely to evaporation—probably more than offset by the heat of condensation.

Thunderstorm Temperatures.—Before the onset of the storm, the temperature commonly is high, but it begins rapidly to fall with the first outward gust and soon drops often as much as 5° C. to 10° C., because, as already explained, this gust is a portion of the descending air cooled by the cold rain and by its evaporation. As the storm passes, the temperature generally recovers somewhat, though it seldom regains its original value—never when the disturbance is of the cold-front type, that is, induced by the advection of cooler air.

Thunderstorm Humidity.—As previously explained, heavy rain, at least up in the clouds, and, therefore, much humidity, and a temperature contrast sufficient to produce rapid vertical convection are essential to the genesis of a thunderstorm. Hence, during the early forenoon of a day favorable to the development of *heat* thunderstorms both the absolute and relative humidity are likely to be high. Just before the storm, however, when the temperature has greatly increased, though the absolute humidity still is high, the relative humidity is likely to be rather low. On the other hand, during and immediately after the storm, the relative humidity is high, owing to both evaporation and decrease of temperature, and the absolute humidity increased. With the passage of the squall, or cold-front, thunderstorm, the absolute humidity decreases, owing to the comparative dryness of the oncoming air. The warm-front thunderstorm, on the other hand, is accompanied by but little to no changes in the humidity.

"Rain-gush."—It frequently has been noted that the rainfall is greatest after heavy claps of thunder, a fact that appears to have given much comfort and great encouragement to those who maintain the efficacy of mere noise to produce precipitation—to jostle cloud particles together into raindrops. The correct explanation, however, of this phenomenon seems obvious: The violent turmoil and spasmodic movements within a large cumulus, or thunderstorm, cloud cause similar irregularities in the condensation and resulting number of raindrops at any given level. These, in turn, as broken by the air currents, give local excess of electrification and of electric discharge, or lightning flash. We have, then, starting toward the earth at the same time and from practically the same level, mass, sound, and light. The light travels with the greatest velocity, about 300,000 kilometers per second, and, therefore, the lightning flash is seen before the thunder is heard—its velocity being, roughly, only 330 meters per second—while the rain, with a maximum velocity of 8 to 10 meters per second with reference to the air, reaches the earth still later. In fact, it is the excessive condensation, or rain formation, up in the cumulus cloud that causes the vivid lightning and the heavy thunder. According only to the order in which their several velocities cause them to reach the surface of the earth, it might appear, and has often been so interpreted, that lightning, the first perceived, is the cause of thunder, which, indeed, it is; and that heavy thunder, the next in order, is the cause of excessive rain, which most certainly it is not.

Thunderstorm Velocity.—The velocity of the thunderstorm is nearly the velocity of the atmosphere in which the bulk of the cumulus cloud happens to be located. Hence, as the wind at this level is faster by night than by day, and faster over the ocean than over land, it follows that exactly the same relations hold for the thunderstorm, namely, that it travels faster over water than over land, and faster by night than by day. The actual velocity of the thunderstorm, of course, varies greatly, but its average velocity in Europe is 30 to 50 kilometers per hour; in the United States, 50 to 65.

Hail.—Hail, consisting of lumps of roughly concentric layers of compact snow and solid ice, is a conspicuous and well-known phenomenon that occurs in the front portion of most severe extratropical thunderstorms, especially in early summer. But in what part of the cloud it is formed, and by what process the layers of ice and snow are built up are facts that, far from being obvious, become clear only when the mechanism of the storm itself is understood.

As before, let the surface temperature be 30° C. and the relative humidity 50 per cent, or the dew point 18° C., nearly. Under these conditions saturation will obtain, and, therefore, cloud formation begin, when the surface air has risen to an elevation of approximately 1.5 kilometers. Immediately above this level, the latent heat of condensation reduces the rate of temperature decrease with elevation to about one-half its former value, nor does this rate rapidly increase with further gain of height. Hence, in mid-latitudes, where the above assumptions correspond in general to average thunderstorm conditions, it is only beyond the 4-kilometer level that freezing temperatures are reached, and where hail, therefore, can form. In the tropics and, after mid-summer, in the warmer portions of the temperate regions, where the freezing level is very high, hail seldom occurs. Generally, either it is not formed at all, owing to insufficient cloud height, or, if formed, melts while falling from its initial great height and reaches the ground as extra large raindrops.

The process by which the nucleus of the hailstone is formed, and its layer upon layer of snow and ice built up, seems to be as follows: Such drops of rain as the strong updraft within the cloud blows into the region of freezing temperatures quickly congeal and also gather coatings of snow and frost. After a time, each incipient hailstone gets into a weaker updraft, for this is always irregular and puffy, or else tumbles to the edge of the ascending column. In either case, it then falls back into the region of liquid drops, where it gathers a layer of water, a portion of which, at once, is frozen by the low temperature of the kernel. But again it meets an upward gust, or falls back where the ascending draft is stronger, and again the cyclic journey from realm of rain to region of snow is begun; and each time—there may be several—the journey is completed, a new layer of ice and a fresh layer of snow are added. In general, the size of the hailstones will be roughly proportional to the strength of the convection current, but since their weights vary approximately (they are not homogeneous) as the cubes of their diameters, while the supporting force of the upward air current varies, also approximately, as only the square of their diameters, it follows that a limiting size is quickly reached. Evidently, too, from the fact that a strong convection current is essential to its formation, hail can occur only where this convection exists; that is, in the *front* portion of a heavy to violent thunderstorm, and high up where the air is very cold.

The velocity of the uprush necessary to support the hailstone is surprisingly great. From the measured drag of wind on spheres it seems that to sustain a stone 1 inch in diameter, density 0.8, the vertical velocity of the air 5 kilometers above sea level would have to be at least 59 miles per hour; and 116 miles per hour if the stone were 3 inches in diameter,[1] a size that is by no means rare, nor even the largest known. Evidently, therefore, hail storms, and, in fact, all thunderstorms should be avoided by aircraft of every type. The "glider," however, sometimes is deliberately taken into the uprushing air in the forepart of a thunderstorm, but at best this is a dangerous stunt.

Most hailstones of whatever size are roughly spherical; some are spheroidal, prolate, or oblate; some are pear-shaped on reaching the earth, owing, presumably, to being melted, during their fall, into a streamline shape—blunt in front and tapering to the rear; a few are discoidal, due, possibly, to a spinning motion induced by rolling down the outside of a rising column; a very few are hexagonal plates, as though giant snow crystals of the simplest form. Some are rough and lumpy or even jagged; others are smooth, at least after falling.

---

[1] HUMPHREYS, W. J., *M. W. R.*, **56**; 314, 1928; BILHAM, E. G., and RELF, E. F., *Quart. J. Roy. Meteorol. Soc.*, **63**; 149, 1937.

CHAPTER XVIII

LIGHTNING

Introduction.—About the middle of the eighteenth century, Franklin, and others, clearly demonstrated that the lightning of a thunderstorm and the discharge of an ordinary electric machine are identical in nature, and thereby established the fact that many of the properties of the former may logically be inferred from laboratory experiments with the latter. There is, however, one important difference between the two phenomena that does not seem always to be kept in mind; namely, the distribution of the charge. In the one case, that of the laboratory experiment, the charge commonly exists almost wholly on the surface of the apparatus used, while in the other, that of the thunderstorm, it is irregularly distributed throughout the great non-conducting cloud

Fig. 128.—Growth of an electric spark discharge. (*Walter.*)

volume. Hence, the two discharges, lightning and laboratory sparks, necessarily differ from each other in important details. Nevertheless, in each case, the atmosphere must be ionized before the discharge can take place freely, and this condition seems, at times at least, to establish itself progressospasmodically. That is, a small initial discharge, losing itself in a terminal brush, is rapidly followed by another and another, each losing itself in a manner similar to the first, until a path from pole to pole is sufficiently ionized to permit of a free electric flow and quick exhaustion of the remaining charge. Figure 128, copied from a photograph by Walter,[1] taken on a rapidly moving plate, shows, as many others since have found, how a laboratory spark spasmodically (doubtless influenced by the period of electrical oscillation) ionizes the air from either pole, and thus progressively extends, mainly from the positive pole, and finally closes, the conducting path of complete discharge. T. E. Allibon and G. M. Meek[2] find that sparks have a simple or stepped leader from

[1] *Ann. Phys. Chem.*, **68**; 776, Leipzig, 1899.

[2] *Nature*, **140**; 804, 1937; *Proc. Roy. Soc.*, **166**; 97, 1938; **169**; 246, 1938.

either the positive or the negative pole and a heavier return stroke.   The
leader of the first discharge has branched branches, all in the direction
of the leader.   The velocities of the negative leader, the positive leader,
and the return stroke are, respectively, about 10^6 cm./sec.; 10^7 cm./sec.;
and too great to measure.   There appears, also, to be good evidence
that lightning often, if not always, behaves in a manner generally similar
to that of the electric spark, though, perhaps, radically different in
certain details.   In the case of lightning between cloud and earth,
there are, according to J. M. Meek,[1] first, a faint pilot discharge from the
negative pole, or base of the cloud, if that be negative, as it commonly is,
that travels toward the earth at the uniform speed of about 2×10^7
cm./sec., ionizing the air as it goes, and, simultaneously with the pilot,
a series of leader discharges that follow along the same path, but with
the greater speed of approximately 2×10^9 cm./sec., each pausing
0.00005 sec., or thereabouts, on catching up with the slower pilot, until
it can forge ahead 10 meters or so.   At the same time, shorter positive
leaders reach up from the ground until at last negative leader and
positive complete the path between cloud and ground, whereupon there is
a violent rush of a positive discharge up the ionized trunk and out its
branches at the very high speed of roughly 10^9 to 10^{10} cm./sec., becoming
feebler with the distance traveled.

In the subsequent discharges, if there are any, along this path,
now without branches, there are only the negative leader, all the way
from the cloud to the ground, and the positive return.   Discharges from
cloud to cloud and discharges that are lost in the free air have both pilots
and leaders but no return discharge.

Clearly, if the preceding explanation of the mechanism of the lightning
discharge is correct, it never can be alternating, that is, it cannot surge
back and forth several to many times at equal brief intervals.

Lightning does not oscillate, but often is pulsatory, as is obvious from
the flicker of sheet lightning, described below, discharge after discharge
taking place in the same direction and along the same path.   Occasionally
these sequent discharges extend to unequal distances, the latter especially
becoming feebler and shorter, as shown in Fig. 129, thereby in their decay
inversely simulating the growth or progressive development of a freely
oscillating laboratory discharge.   Being pulsatory, however, or consisting of a group of unidirectional discharges, is an entirely different
thing from being oscillatory, that is, consisting of an equally spaced series,
the units of which are alternately in opposite directions.

It will be convenient, in discussing the facts about lightning, to
classify the discharges according to their general appearance.

Streak Lightning.—When the storm is close by, the lightning discharge invariably appears to the unaided eye as one or more vivid lines

[1] *Phys. Rev.*, **55**; 972, 1939.

or streaks; invariably sinuous, because, electrically, the atmosphere is always heterogeneous or unequally ionized, and the directive force constantly changing during, and because of, the discharge itself. Often there is one main trunk with a number of branches, all occurring in exceedingly quick succession and only at step termini,[1] while at other times there are two or more simultaneous though locally disconnected streaks. Frequently the discharge continues flickeringly (on rare occasions steady, like a white-hot wire) during a perceptible time—even a full second, or longer.

But all these phenomena are best studied by means of the camera, and have been so studied by several persons, among whom Walter, of Hamburg; Larsen, of Chicago; Steadworthy, of Toronto, and Schonland,

FIG. 129.—Streak lightning (sequent discharges), rotating camera. (*Larsen.*)

of Cape Town, have been especially persistent and successful. Stationary cameras, revolving cameras, stereoscopic cameras, cameras with revolving plates, and cameras with spectrographic attachments have all been used, separately and jointly, and the results have abundantly justified the time and the labor devoted to the work.

Figure 130, copied by permission from one of Walter's negatives, shows the ordinary tracery of a lightning discharge when photographed with a stationary camera. It is only a permanent record of the appearance of the lightning to the unaided eye. Figure 131, however, also copied by Walter's kind permission from one of his photographs, is a

[1] McEachron, K. B., and McMorris, W. A., *Gen. Elec. Rev.*, October, 1936; Schonland, B. F. J., Malan, D. J., and Collans, H., *Proc. Roy. Soc.*, **152**; 595, 1935; **162**; 175, 1937. Schonland, B. F. J., *Proc. Roy. Soc.*, **164**; 132, 1938; Schonland, B. F. J., and Hodges, D. B., *Proc. Roy. Soc.*, **166**; 56, 1938. Whipple, F. J. W., *Nature*, **141**; 143, 1938.

record of the same discharge obtained with a rotating camera. It will be noted that the more nearly vertical discharge occurred but once, or was single; that this discharge was quickly followed by a second along the same path to about one-fourth of the way to the earth, where it branched off on a new course; that the second discharge was followed, in turn, at short but irregular intervals by a whole series of sequent discharges; that most of the discharges appeared as narrow, intensely luminous streaks, and that one of the sequent discharges appeared, not to the eye, but on the plate of the rotating camera, as a broad band or

Fig. 130.—Streak lightning, stationary camera; companion to Fig. 131. (*Walter.*)

ribbon. On close inspection it will be obvious that the warp of this plaid-like ribbon is due to irregularities in the more or less continuous discharge, and the woof to, roughly, end-on and therefore brighter portions of the streak. Another point, particularly worthy of attention, is the fact that while the first and second discharges have several side branches the following ones remain entire from end to end and are nowhere subdivided.

Figure 129, taken from a photograph obtained by Larsen, of Chicago, and kindly lent for use here by the Smithsonian Institution, shows another series of sequent discharges similar to those of Fig. 131, except that in this case there was no ribbon discharge. The time of the whole discharge, as calculated by Larsen, was 0.315 second. Here, too, side branches occur with the first, but only the first, discharge. This, however, is not an invariable rule, for, occasionally, as illustrated by Fig. 132, copied from a published photograph by Walter, the side branches persist through two or three of the first successive discharges, but not

Fig. 131.—Streak lightning (sequent discharges), rotating camera; companion to Fig. 130. (*Walter.*)

through all. In such case, each tributary, when repeated, follows, as does the main stream, its own original channel.

The phenomenon of sequent discharges, all along the same path, and the disappearance of the side branches with, or quickly after, the first discharge, both seem reasonably clear. The first discharge, however produced, obviously takes place against very great resistance, and, therefore, under conditions the most favorable for the occurrence of side branches, or ramifications. But the discharge itself leaves the air along its path temporarily highly ionized, puts a temporary line conductor, with here and there a poorer conducting branch, in the atmosphere. This conductor is not only temporary (half the ions are reunited in about 0.15 second, the air being dusty[1]) but also so extremely fragile as to be liable to rupture, by the violent disturbances; both explosive and of other types to be discussed later, it, itself, creates in the atmosphere. Because, partly, perhaps, of just such interruptions, but especially because of the volume distribution of the electricity which, requiring diffusion for neutralization, prevents a sudden and complete discharge,[2] the actual discharge is divided into a number of partials that occur sequently. Obviously, the later discharges, if they occur quickly, must follow the

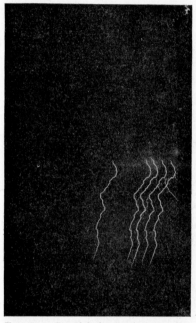

conducting and, therefore, original discharge path. Besides, in the subsequent discharges, the original side branches will be quickly abandoned because of their greater resistance, or, what comes to the same thing, because of the more abundant ionization and consequent higher conductivity of the path of heaviest discharge.

This leaves to be explained the genesis of the initial discharge, the least understood, perhaps, of all the many thunderstorm phenomena. Judging from the voltages required to produce laboratory sparks, roughly 30,000 volts per centimeter, it is not obvious how such tremendous potential differences can be established between clouds, or between a cloud and the earth, as would seem to be necessary to produce a discharge kilometers in length, as frequently occurs. Indeed, a fatal objection to the assumption

Fig. 132.—Streak lightning (sequent discharges), rotating camera. (*Walter.*)

of such high voltage is the effect it would have on the velocity of fall, and consequent size of the electrified raindrops. According to Simpson,[3] thunderstorm rain often carries as much as 6 electrostatic units of electricity per cubic centimeter, and occasionally even more. Hence 30,000 volts per centimeter would produce an electric force on such rain roughly six-tenths that due to gravity and, therefore, either retard its fall, if directed upward, or, if directed downward, give it a velocity that would quickly break it into smaller drops. But

[1] RUTHERFORD, *Phil. Mag.*, **44**; 430, 1897.

[2] SIMPSON, G. C., *Inst. Elec. Engineers*, **67**; 1269, 1929.

[3] *Mem. Ind. Meteorol. Dept.*, Simla, **20**; Pt. 2, 149–150, 1910.

thunderstorm rain does not consist, essentially, of smaller drops. On the contrary, as casual observation leads one to believe and as measurements have shown,[1] raindrops average larger (1 to 6 mm. in diameter) during a thunderstorm than at any other time. Their velocity of fall, therefore, cannot be excessive, nor indeed does it ever appear to be greatly different from that of ordinary rain. Hence electrical gradients, of the order above assumed, do not exist between clouds and the earth. Indeed, F. W. Peek,[2] from the voltages induced on electric wires during a thunderstorm, finds that the average lightning gradient along the path of discharge is of the order of 3000 volts per centimeter, a value that obviates the difficulty just mentioned. At places, however, the gradient may be much steeper. Wilson[3] and Macky[4] find 10,000 volts per centimeter sufficient to cause a discharge within a cloud.

Obviously the potential of individual drops may grow in either of two ways: (a) by the union of similarly charged smaller drops into larger ones, in which case, since capacitance is directly proportioned to the radius, and the charge, after coalescence, to the volume (if droplets had equal size and charges), the potentials of the resultant drops, that is, their charges divided by their capacities, must be proportional to the squares of their radii, and, therefore, rapidly increase with coalescence and growth of size; (b) by evaporation of however charged drops. Here the charges remain constant and, therefore, the potential of each individual drop, being inversely proportional to its radius, obviously must become larger as the drop itself evaporates and gets smaller. In each case the tendency of the separate drops to discharge is increased, and the general ionization, perhaps, somewhat correspondingly increased; but the potential difference between the earth and the cloud as a whole is unchanged. At present, therefore, one can do little more than speculate on the subject of the primary lightning discharge, but even that much may be worth while, since it helps one to remember the facts.

As already explained, the electrical separation within a thunderstorm cloud is such as to place a heavily charged layer (lower portion of the cloud) between the earth and a much higher oppositely charged, layer (upper portion of the cloud). Hence the discharges, or lightning, from the intermediate layer may be to either the portion above, in some cases even an entirely different cloud, or the earth below. Further, through the sustaining influence and turbulence of the uprushing air there must be formed, at times and places, practically continuous sheets and streams of water, of course, heavily charged and at high potential, and also layers and streaks of highly ionized air. That is, electrically

[1] BENTLEY, *Monthly Weather Review*, **32**; 453, 1904.
[2] *J. Franklin Inst.*, **197**; 40, 1924.
[3] *J. Franklin Inst.*, **208**; 1, 1929.
[4] *Proc. Roy. Soc.*, **133**; 565, 1931.

speaking, heavily charged conducting sheets and rods, whether of coalesced drops or of ionized air, are over and over, so long as the storm lasts, momentarily placed here and there within the charged mass of the storm cloud.

Consider, then, what might be expected as the result of this peculiar disposition of charges and conductors, the result, namely, of the existence of a heavily surface-charged vertical conductor in a strongly volume-charged horizontal layer, or region, above and below which there are steep potential gradients to charged parallel surfaces.

The conductor will be at the same potential throughout, and, therefore, the maxima of potential gradients normal to it will be at its ends, where, if these gradients are steep enough, and the longer the conductor the steeper the gradients, brush discharges will take place, mainly from the positive end—really of close-by negative ions onto the positive end. Assume, then, that a brush discharge does take place and that there is a supply of ions flowing into the conductor from the region through which it is burrowing to make good the loss. The brush and the line of its most vigorous ionization, other things being equal, necessarily will be directed along the steepest potential gradient, or directly toward the surface of opposite charge. But this very ionization automatically increases the length of the conductor, for a path of highly ionized air is a conductor, and as the length of the conductor grows, so, too, does the steepness of the potential gradient at its forward, or terminal, end, and as the steepness of this gradient increases, the more vigorous the discharge, always assuming an abundant ion supply and united not ramified path. Hence, a spark once started within a thunderstorm cloud has a good chance, by making its own conductor as it goes, of growing geometrically into a lightning flash of large dimensions. Of course, when the charge is small, the lightning is feeble and soon dissipated. In an exactly similar way discharges may start from objects on the earth, particularly to a negative cloud, but this type is quite unusual.[1]

That the discharge actually does burrow, or, rather, hop, skip, and jump its way through the atmosphere in some such manner as that indicated is well known from photographs of it on rapidly moving films or plates.

Rocket Lightning.—Many persons have observed what, at least, seemed to be a progressive growth in the length of a streak of lightning. In some cases[2] this growth, or progression, has appeared so slow as actually to suggest the flight of a rocket, hence the name.

At first one might feel disposed to regard the phenomenon in question as illusory, but it has been too definitely described, and too frequently observed, to justify such summary dismissal. Naturally, in the course

[1] *Proc. Roy. Soc.* **111**; 56, 1926.

[2] Everett, *Nature*, **68**; 599, 1903; Simpson, *Proc. Roy. Soc.* **111**; 66, 1924.

of thousands of lightning discharges, many degrees of ionization, availability of electric charge, and slopes of potential gradient are encountered. Ordinarily, the growth of the discharge, doubtless, is in a geometric ratio and the progress of its end exceedingly swift, but it seems possible for the conditions to be such that the discharge can barely more than sustain itself, in which case the movement of the flash terminal may, possibly, be relatively slow, and the appearance of a rocket therefore roughly imitated.

Ball Lightning.—Curious luminous balls or masses, of which C. de Jans[1] and Walther Brand[2] have given the fullest accounts, have, time and again, been reported among the phenomena observed during a thunderstorm. Most of them appear to have lasted only a second or two and to have been seen at close range, some even passing through a house, but they have also seemed to fall, as would a stone,[3] like a meteor, from the storm cloud, and along the approximate path of both previous and subsequent lightning flashes. Others appeared to start from a cloud and then quickly return, and so on through an endless variety of places and conditions.

Doubtless most reported cases of ball lightning, if not all, are entirely spurious,[4] being mostly either fixed or wandering brush discharges or else nothing other than optical illusions, due, presumably, to persistence of vision.

Sheet Lightning.—When a distant thundercloud is observed at night, one is quite certain to see in it beautiful illuminations, appearing like great sheets of flame, that usually wander, flicker and glow in exactly the same manner as does streak lightning, often for well nigh a whole second, and, occasionally, even longer. In the daytime and in full sunlight, the phenomenon, when seen at all, appears like a sudden sheen that travels and spreads, here and there, over the surface of the cloud. Certainly in most cases, so far as definitely known in all cases, this is only reflection from the body of the cloud of streak lightning in other and invisible portions. Often a blurred, yellowish streak is seen through the thinner portions of the intervening cloud. Occasionally, too, the cloud is wholly cleared in places where, of course, the discharge, usually, is white and dazzling. Conceivably a brush, or coronal, discharge may take place from the upper surface of a thunderstorm cloud, but one would expect this to be either a faint continuous glow (one remarkable concentrated glow has been reported[5]) or else a momentary flash coincident with a discharge from the lower portion of the cloud to earth,

---

[1] *Ciel et terre*, **31**; 499, 1910.

[2] *Der Kugelblitz*, Hamburg, 1923.

[3] Violle, *Comptes rendus*, **132**; 1537, Paris, 1901.

[4] Humphreys, W. J., *Proc. Amer. Phil. Soc.*, **76**; 613, 1936.

[5] Laurenson, M. D., *Meteorol. Mag.*, **71**; 134, 1936.

or to some other cloud. But, as already stated, only reflection is definitely known to be the cause of sheet lightning. Coronal effects seem occasionally to occur, but that they ever are the cause of the phenomenon in question has never clearly been established and appears very doubtful. It has often been asserted, too, that there is a radical difference between the spectra of streak and sheet lightning, but even this appears never to have been photographically, or otherwise definitely established.

Beaded Lightning.—Many photographs, showing streaks of light broken into more or less evenly spaced dashes, have been obtained and reported as records of beaded lightning. Without exception, however, these seem certainly to be nothing other than photographs of alternating-current electric lights, taken with the camera in motion. On the other hand, it occasionally happens that a reliable observer reports that he has actually seen a discontinuous or beaded streak of lightning. Thus Prof. O. J. Ferguson, of the University of Nebraska (Department of Electric Engineering), says:[1]

In the spring of 1914 a violent thunderstorm swept over Lincoln at about nine o'clock at night. There were numerous vivid lightning displays. One of these discharges occurring in the storm front originated at an elevation of about 45° from my viewpoint and struck almost vertically downward. I was watching the storm from the window of a dark room, and the flash occurred directly in front of me. It was a direct stroke of chain or streak lightning.

However, in dying away, it took probably a full second to disappear; it broke up, seemingly, into detached portions, short and numerous. In fact, it gave a bead-like effect, and it would be very easy for one to have retained the latter impression and to have called the stroke bead lightning.

In explanation of this phenomenon I would suggest that each bead probably represents the "end on" view of the irregular portions of the lightning path, and that they remained luminous during the subsequent lesser discharges, while the intermediate sections became nonluminous, because viewed from the side.

The explanation offered by Prof. Ferguson and illustrated by Fig. 131, doubtless, is entirely correct. Hence, beaded or pearl lightning must be accepted as a real, though unusual, phenomenon, which probably would be more often seen if definitely watched for. Indeed, by close observation, the author has several times had that pleasure.

Return Lightning.—This is commonly referred to as the return shock, and is only that relatively small electrical discharge which takes place here and there from objects on the surface of the earth coincidently with lightning flashes, and as a result of the suddenly changed electrical strain. This discharge is always small in comparison with the main lightning flash, but at times is sufficient to induce explosions, to start fires and, even, to take life.

[1] *J. Franklin Inst.*, **179**; 253, 1915.

Dark Lightning.—When a photographic plate is exposed to a succession of lightning flashes, it occasionally happens that one or more of the earlier streak images, on development, exhibits the "Clayden effect," that is, appears completely reversed, while the others show no such tendency. Obviously, then, on prints from such a negative the reversed streaks must appear as dark lines (Fig. 133), and for that reason the lightning flashes that produced them have been called "dark lightning." There is, of course, no such thing as dark lightning, since the only invisible radiation to which the ordinary photographic plate is sensitive is the ultraviolet, which cannot be excited by electric discharges in the atmosphere without, at the same time, producing visible radiation. Never-

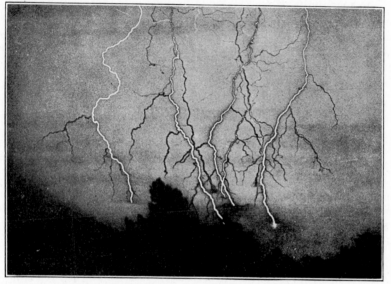

Fig. 133.—Dark lightning. (*F. Ellerman, photographer.*)

theless, the photographic phenomenon that gives rise to the name "dark lightning," is real, interesting, and reproducible, at will, in the laboratory.[1]

Duration.—The duration of the lightning discharge is exceedingly variable, ranging from a few microseconds for a single flash, to even a full second or more, for a multiple flash consisting of a series of sequent discharges. In one case a duration of 15 to 20 seconds was reported.[2] On rare occasions a discharge of long duration appears *to the eye* to be steady like a glowing solid. Flashes that last as long as a few tenths or even a few hundredths of a second are almost certainly multiple, consisting of a succession of apparently individual discharges occurring at unequal intervals. Occasionally a practically continuous discharge of

[1] Wood, *Science,* **10**; 717, 1899.

[2] *Nature,* **53**; 272, 1936.

varying intensity, but all the time strong enough to produce luminosity, lasts a few hundredths of a second.

It must be remembered that the duration of even a single discharge and the length of time to complete the circuit, or ionize a path, from cloud to earth, say, are entirely different things. The latter seems usually (rocket lightning may furnish an exception) to be of exceedingly short duration, while the former depends upon the supply of electricity and the ohmic resistance directly, and upon the potential difference inversely.

Length of Streak.—The total length of a streak of lightning varies greatly. Indeed, the brush discharge so gradually merges into the spark and the spark into an unmistakable thunderbolt, that it is not possible, sharply, to distinguish between them, nor, therefore, to set a minimum limit to the length of a lightning path. When the discharge is from cloud to earth the length of the path is seldom more than 2 to 3 kilometers; in the case of low-lying clouds, even much less, especially when they envelop a mountain peak.

On the other hand, when the discharge is from cloud to cloud the path, generally, is far more tortuous and its total length much greater, amounting at times to 10, 15, and even 20 kilometers.

Discharge, Where to Where?—As already explained, lightning discharges may be between cloud and earth, between one part and another of the same cloud, or between cloud and cloud. But, since the great amount of electrical separation, without which the lightning could not occur, takes place within the rain cloud, it follows that this is also likely to be the seat of the steepest potential gradients. Hence, it would appear that lightning must occur most frequently between the lower and the upper portions of the same cloud, and this is fully supported by observations. The next in frequency, especially in mountainous regions, is the discharge between cloud (lower portion) and earth, and the least frequent of all, ordinarily, that which takes place between two entirely independent, or disconnected, clouds.

Since the electricity of the thunderstorm, obviously, is generated within the cumulus cloud, and there mechanically separated into upper and lower layers, it may not at first be clear how discharges can take place to earth at all. Of course, there will be some lines of force between the earth and each cloud charge, but these must be relatively few so long as the charges are equal and approximately superimposed, and the resulting dielectric strain correspondingly feeble. Rain, however, commonly brings down more electricity of one sign than the other, and, thus, promotes cloud-to-earth discharges. Also, as the upper charge is carried higher, and especially as it is drifted away from the lower, by the winds into which it projects, the lines of force between cloud and earth become more and more numerous, and the strain progressively greater, until suddenly relieved by the lightning's disruptive flash.

It would seem, therefore, that a marked difference between the wind velocities at the upper and lower storm levels would be especially favorable to frequency of cloud-to-earth discharges. Hence, one would infer that heat thunderstorms, since they occur only when the general winds are light, are less dangerous—less likely to be accompanied by cloud-to-earth lightning—than those (presumably every other type) in which the wind velocity increases more rapidly with elevation. And, from this, one would further infer that tropical thunderstorms, since they commonly belong to the heat variety, are less dangerous than storms of equal electrical intensity of middle and higher latitudes, where the other, or cross-current, varieties prevail.

Unfortunately, data are not at hand by which these deductions may be tested statistically. They are, however, in accord with the general impression[1] that thunderstorms are more dangerous in England than in India.

Discharges Direct, Not Alternating.—Years ago, someone, for some reason or other, or for no reason, made the statement that the lightning flash is alternating and of high frequency, like the discharge of a Leyden jar; and, forthwith, despite the fact that all evidence is to the contrary, it became a favorite dogma of the textbook, passed on unquestioned from author to author and handed down inviolate from edition to edition. True, often there are a number of successive discharges in a fraction of a second, as shown by photographs taken with a revolving camera, or equivalent analyzing device, but these not only are along the same path, but also in the same direction. This is obvious from the fact that side branches, whose trend with reference to the main trunk gives the direction of discharge, persisting as in Fig. 132, through two or more partial or sequent discharges, always follow the same paths. It is also proved by the direct evidence of the oscillograph.[2] In the case of each separate discharge, also, the direction seems constant; it may vary in strength, or pulsate, but, apparently, it does not alternate.

There are several reasons for concluding that lightning discharges, both single and multiple, are direct and not alternating, of which the following cover a wide range and probably are the best:

a. Lightning operates telegraph instruments. If the discharge were alternating, it would not do so, unless very heavily damped.

b. At times it reverses the polarity of dynamos. This requires either a direct current, or an alternating one so damped as to be quasidirect.

c. The oscillograph[3] shows each surge or pulsation, as well as the whole flash, to be unidirectional.

d. The rotating camera affords strong evidence that a lightning discharge between a cloud and the earth consists of a surge of electricity of

[1] BONACINA, *Metrl. Mag.*, **49**; 114 and 164, 1914.

[2] DeBLOIS, *Proc. Amer. Inst. Elec. Eng.*, **33**; 563, 1914.

[3] DE BLOIS, *loc. cit.*; NORINDER, H., *Elec. World*, **83**; 223, 1924.

one sign from the cloud to the earth, followed immediately by a surge of electricity of the opposite sign from the earth back along the same course, growing feebler with distance from the earth. Similarly, a discharge from cloud to cloud, or cloud to free air, appears to consist of but a single surge, growing feebler with increase of distance from the source.

e. The relative values of the ohmic resistance, the self-induction, and the capacitance, in the case of a lightning discharge, appear usually, if not always, to be such as to forbid the possibility of oscillations.

The last of these reasons, *e*, may be developed as follows:

From the equation of a condenser discharge,

$$L\frac{d^2Q}{dt^2} + R\frac{dQ}{dt} + \frac{Q}{C} = 0,$$

it may be shown[1] that whenever the product of the capacitance by the square of the resistance is greater than four times the self-induction, or, in symbols, that whenever

$$CR^2 > 4L$$

oscillations are impossible. Undoubtedly, all these terms vary greatly in the case of lightning discharges, but R, presumably, is always sufficiently large to maintain the above inequality and, therefore, absolutely, to prevent oscillations, even if the cloud were a conductor.

To illustrate with, perhaps a typical case, assume a cloud whose under surface is circular, with a radius of 3 kilometers, and whose height above the ground is 1 kilometer, and let there be a discharge from the center of the cloud base straight to the earth: Find a probable value, on the assumption that the cloud is a conductor, for the self-induction and capacitance, and from these the limiting value of the resistance to prevent oscillations, or the value of R in the equation

$$CR^2 = 4L.$$

To find L we have the fact that the coefficient of self-induction is numerically equal to twice the energy in the magnetic field per unit current in the circuit, and the further fact that per unit volume this energy is numerically equal to $\mu H^2/8\pi$, in which H is the magnetic force and μ the magnetic permeability of the medium. Let a be the radius of the lightning path and assume the current density in it to be uniform. Let b be the equivalent radius of the cylinder, concentric with the lightning path, along which the return or displacement current flows. In this case, μ being unity, the energy W of the magnetic field

---

[1] Thomson, J. J., "Elements of Electricity and Magnetism," § Discharge of a Leyden Jar.

per unit current and per centimeter length of the discharge is given by the equation

$$W = \log \frac{b}{a} + \frac{1}{4}.$$

Let $b = 2$ kilometers and $a = 5$ centimeters. Then $W = \log_e 4 \times 10^4$ $+ \frac{1}{4} = 11$, approximately. Hence, the energy of the magnetic field per unit current for the whole length, 1 kilometer of the flash is represented by the equation

$$W10^5 = 11 \times 10^5,$$

and the self-induction $= 22 \times 10^5 = 22 \times 10^{-4}$ henry.

To find C, assume a uniform field between the cloud and the earth. As a matter of fact, this field is not uniform, and the calculated value of C, based upon the above assumption, is somewhat less than its actual value, but not greatly less. Assuming, then, a uniform field we have

$$C = \frac{A}{4\pi d} = \frac{\pi 9 \times 10^{10}}{4\pi \times 10^5} = 225 \times 10^3 = 25 \times 10^{-8} \text{ farad, about.}$$

Hence, by substitution in the equation

$$CR^2 = 4L,$$

it appears that

$$R = 190 \text{ ohms per kilometer, approximately.}$$

Neither a, the radius of the lightning path, nor b, the equivalent radius of the return current, is accurately known, but from the obviously large amount of suddenly expanded air necessary to produce the atmospheric disturbances incident to thunder, and from the fact that the current density is about 10 amperes per square millimeter of the cross-section of the discharge path,[1] it would seem that 1 centimeter would be the minimum value for a. Also, from the size of thunder clouds, it appears that 10 kilometers would be the maximum value for b.

The substitution of these extreme values in the above equation gives:

$$R = 200 \text{ ohms per kilometer, roughly.}$$

From the fact that C varies inversely and L directly as the altitude of the cloud it follows that, other things remaining equal, the height of the cloud has no effect on the value of R per unit length.

If the altitude is kept constant, and the size of the cloud varied, C will increase directly as the area, and L will increase directly as the natural logarithm of the equivalent radius of the cylinder of return

[1] PETERSEN, W., *A. E. G. Progress*, **6**; 307, 1930; OLENDORF, F., *Archiv. f. Electrotech.* **27**; 169, 1933.

current. Assuming the area of the cloud base to be 1 square kilometer, which certainly is far less than the ordinary size, and computing as above, it is found that

$$R = 850 \text{ ohms per kilometer, roughly.}$$

Again, assuming the base area to be 1000 square kilometers, an area far in excess of that of the base of an ordinary thunderstorm cloud, the result is

$$R = 35 \text{ ohms per kilometer, roughly.}$$

It would seem, therefore, that a resistance along the lightning path of the order of 200 ohms per kilometer, or 0.002 ohm per centimeter, would suffice, in most cases, absolutely, to prevent electrical oscillations between cloud and earth. In reality, the total resistance includes, in addition to that upon which the above calculations are based, the resistance in parallel of the numerous feeders, or branches, within the cloud itself and, finally, from them to the individual charged droplets. In other words, the assumption that the resistance of the condenser plates is negligible is not true in the case of a cloud. Nor is this the only uncertainty, for no one knows what the resistance along the path of even the main discharge actually is; though judging from the resistance of an oscillatory electric spark,[1] it, presumably, is many times greater than the foregoing calculated limiting value; and, if so, then lightning flashes, as we have seen, would have to be unidirectional and not alternating, even if the cloud were a conductor, and all the more certainly so if it were (and it is) a non-conductor with a volume charge.

Direction of Discharge.—When the discharge is between cloud and earth the great majority of the cases consist of relatively long darts of negative electricity from the cloud toward the earth and simultaneous short darts of positive electricity from the earth toward the negative until they meet; and then a rush of positive from the earth up along the ionized path, including the branches, growing feebler, or being neutralized as it goes.

Temperature.—What the effective temperature (not temperature as ordinarily understood) along the path of a lightning discharge is, no one knows, but, obviously, it is high, since lightning frequently sets fire to buildings, trees, and many other objects struck. In an ordinary electrical conductor, the amount of heat generated in a given time, by an electric current, is proportional to the product C^2RT, in which C is the strength of the current, R the ohmic resistance, and T the time in question during which C and R are supposed to remain constant. In a spark discharge of the nature of lightning some of the energy produces

[1] FLEMING, "The Principles of Electric Wave Telegraphy and Telephony," 2d Ed., **80**; 228–237, 1910.

effects, such as decomposition and ionization, other than mere local heating, but as experiment shows, a great deal of heat is generated, according, so far as we know, to the same laws that obtain for ordinary conductors. Hence, extra heavy discharges, like extra large currents, produce excessive heating, and, therefore, are far more liable than are light ones to set on fire any objects that they may hit.

Visibility.—Just how a lightning discharge renders the atmosphere, through which it passes, luminous is not definitely known. It must, and does, make the air path very hot, but probably not enough so to produce the light observed. Hence, it seems likely that the luminosity of lightning flashes is owing, in part at least, to something other than high temperature, probably atomic disturbances induced by the discharge —ionization and recombination.

Spectrum.—Lightning flashes have been reported of every spectrum color,[1] but mainly white, yellow, and pink, or rose. The rose-colored flashes, when examined in the spectro-scope, show several lines due to hydrogen which, of course, is furnished by the decomposition of some of the water along the lightning path. The white flashes, on the other hand, show no hydrogen lines or, at most, but faint ones. Yellow flashes, evidently, are only those that have lost their shorter wave-length components through absorption, owing to distance or intervening clouds. As one might suspect, the spectrum of a light-ning flash and that of an ordinary electric spark in air are practically identical. This is well shown by Fig. 134, copied from an article on the spectrum of light-

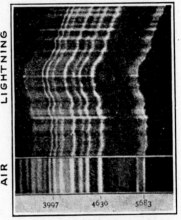

FIG. 134.—Spectrum of lightning. (*Fox.*)

ning, by Fox,[2] in which the upper, or wavy, portion is due to the lightning and the lower, or straight, portion to a laboratory spark in air. Figure 135 is from an exceptionally fine photograph by Steadworthy,[3] of the Dominion Observatory, Ottawa, Canada. The heavy streak across the spectrum is not the parent, but an accidental stray that got in beside the prism.

It is often asserted that the spectrum of streak lightning consists wholly of bright lines, and that sheet lightning gives only nitrogen bands; and, from this, it is argued that the latter is not a mere reflection of the first. This assertion is not supported by Figs. 134–135, the brightest

[1] RUSSELL, S. C., *Quart. J. Roy. Met. Soc.*, **34**; 271, 1908.
[2] *Astrophys. J.*, **18**; 294, 1903.
[3] *J. Roy. Astro. Soc. Canada*, **8**; 345, 1914.

portions of which, the portions that would longest be seen as reflection grew steadily feebler, coincide with strong nitrogen bands.

Thunder.—For a long while no one had even a remotely satisfactory idea in regard to the cause of thunder, and it is not a rare thing, even yet, to hear such a childish explanation as that "it is the noise caused by the bumping or rubbing of one cloud against another."

Nor are all the learned explanations wholly free from error. Thus it has been suggested that thunder is due to the mutual repulsion of electrons along the path of discharge, though there are several objections

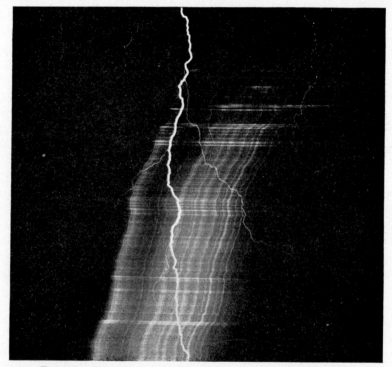

Fig. 135.—Spectrum of lightning; and stray streak. (*Steadworthy.*)

to this pleasing hypothesis. If such repulsion really occurred to the extent indicated, one might, therefore, expect a thread, or rod, of mercury, carrying a current, to spread out. Instead, however, it actually draws together, and, with a strong enough current, even pinches itself in two. Again, if mutual repulsion actually drove the electrons violently asunder, one would expect the discharge instantly to dissipate, producing some kind of a brush effect, instead of concentrating along the familiar streak. Electronic repulsion, therefore, though it must exist to some extent, does not seem adequate, nor, as we shall see presently, is it necessary, for the production of heavy peals of thunder.

Another plausible, but erroneous, hypothesis in regard to the origin of thunder insists that it is caused by the collapse of the partial vacuum produced by the heat generated by the lightning. Obviously, cooling, in this case, must be rapid, especially at the instant the discharge ceases, but, probably, not nearly rapid enough to create sound, nor, therefore, ever to produce any of the crashes and rumblings that always follow heavy lightning.

On the other hand, the heating of the atmosphere along the discharge path is so excessive and the dissociation of molecules into atoms and atoms into electrons and ions, as evidenced by the lightning spectrum, so abundant that the resulting sudden expansion simulates a violent explosion and, therefore, sends out a steep compression wave. Indeed, compression waves generated by electric sparks are so sharply defined that not only they, themselves, but even their reflections may be clearly photographed.[1] A compression wave, therefore, generated in the manner just explained, apparently is an adequate cause of thunder, and, hence, presumably, its only cause.

Rumbling.—Probably the most distinctive characteristic of thunder is its long-continued rumbling and great variation in intensity. Several factors contribute to this peculiarity, among them:

a. Inequalities in the Distances from the Observer to the Various Portions of the Lightning's Path.—Hence, the sound, which ordinarily travels about 330 meters per second in the air, will not all reach one simultaneously, but continuously, over an appreciable interval of time.

b. Crookedness of Path.—Because of this condition, it often happens that sections of the path here and there are, each through its length, at nearly the same distance from the observer or follow, roughly, the circumferences of circles of which he is the center, while other portions are directed more or less radially from him. This would account for, and doubtless in a measure is the correct explanation of, some of the loud booming effects or crashes that accompany thunder.

c. Succession of Discharges.—When, as often happens, several discharges follow each other in rapid succession, there is every opportunity for all sorts of irregular mutual interference and reinforcement of the compression waves, or sound impulses, they send out. Occasionally, they may even give rise to a musical note of short duration.

d. Reflection.—Under favorable conditions, especially when the lightning is at a considerable distance, the echo from hills, and other reflecting objects, certainly is effective in accentuating and prolonging the noise and rumble of thunder. But the importance of this factor, generally, is overestimated, for ordinarily the rumble is substantially the same whether over the ocean, on a prairie, or among the mountains.

---

[1] WOOD, *Phil. Mag.*, **48**; 218, 1899.

Distance Heard.—Thunder seldom is heard over a distance greater than 25 kilometers, and, generally, not more than half so far. Sometimes, when produced at considerable heights, even though directly overhead, or nearly so, it is quite inaudible; partly, no doubt, because all sounds from high levels are relatively faintly perceived, if at all, at the surface, and partly because lightning within, or between, clouds, at such levels, and which does not come below them, often is comparatively feeble.

To most persons familiar with the great distance to which the firing of large cannon is still perceptible, the relatively small distances to which thunder is audible is quite a surprise. It should be remembered, however, that both the origin of the sound and often the air, itself, as a sound conductor are radically different in the two cases. The firing of cannon or any other surface disturbance is heard farthest when the air is still and when, through temperature inversion or otherwise, it is so stratified as, in a measure, to conserve the sound energy between horizontal planes. Conversely, sound is heard to the least distance when the atmosphere is irregular in respect to either its temperature, or moisture distribution, or both, for these conditions favor the production of internal sound reflections and the dissipation of energy. Now the former, or favorable, conditions occasionally obtain during the production of ordinary noises, including the firing of cannon, but never during a thunderstorm. In fact, the thunderstorm is especially likely to establish the second set of the above conditions, or those least favorable to the far carrying of sound.

Then, too, when a cannon, say, is fired, the noise all starts from the same place, the energy is concentrated, while in the case of thunder it is stretched out over the entire length of the lightning path. In the first case, the energy is confined to a single shell; in the second, it is diffused through an extensive volume. It is these differences in the concentration and the conservation of the energy that cause the cannon to be heard much farther than the heaviest thunder, even though the latter, almost certainly, produces much the greater total atmospheric disturbance.

The Ceraunograph.—Various instruments, based upon the principles of "wireless" receivers and known as ceraunographs, have been devised for recording the occurrence of lightning discharges, whether close by, or so far away as to be invisible and their thunder unheard. Of course, the sensitiveness of the instrument, the distance, and the magnitude of the discharge, all are factors that affect the record, but, by keeping the sensitiveness constant, or nearly so, it is possible, with an instrument of this kind, to estimate the approximate distance, progress, and, to a large extent, even the direction and intensity of the storm. Furthermore with direction finders at two or more suitably located stations, the position of the storm at any time can be closely determined. The method and value of such observations are explained in a paper, and the discussions following it, by R. W. Boswell and W. J. Wark.[1]

Apparently, too, all, or nearly all, atmospherics, or statics, are owing to lightning somewhere.[2]

Chemical Effects.—As is well known, oxides of nitrogen are produced along the path of an electric spark and ozone at the point of a brush discharge in the laboratory. Therefore, one might expect an abundant formation, during a thunderstorm, of these same compounds. And this is exactly what does occur, as observation conclusively shows. It seems probable, too, that some ammonia must also be formed in this way, the hydrogen being supplied by the decomposition of raindrops and water vapor.

In the presence of water or water vapor, these several compounds, except the ozone, undergo important changes or combinations. The nitrogen peroxide (most stable of the oxides of nitrogen) combines with water to produce both nitric and nitrous acids, while the ammonia in the main merely dissolves, but, probably, also, to some extent forms caustic ammonia.

Symbolically the reactions seem to be as follows:

$$2NO_2 + H_2O = HNO_3 + HNO_2$$
$$NH_3 + H_2O = NH_4OH.$$

The ammonia and, also, both the acids through the production of soluble salts are valuable fertilizers. Hence, wherever the thunderstorm is frequent and severe, especially, therefore, within the tropics, the chemical actions of the lightning may materially add, as has recently been shown,[3] to the fertility of the soil and the growth of crops.

Explosive Effects.—As already explained, the excessive and abrupt heating, caused by the lightning current, together with the atomic rupturing it effects explosively converts to a hypergas the column of air, or other inadequately conducting substance, through which it passes, and thereby shatters chimneys, rips off shingles, and produces many other similar, and surprising, results. Hence, trees are stripped by it of their bark or utterly slivered and demolished through the sudden volatilization and decomposition of sap and other substances; wire is fused, vaporized, and ionized, and even the vapor blown through a cloth insulation without burning it; holes are melted through steeple bells and other large pieces of metal; and a thousand other seeming freaks and vagaries wrought.

Many of the effects of lightning appear, at first, difficult to explain, but, except the physiological, which, indeed, are but little understood,

[1] *Quart. J. Roy. Meteorol. Soc.*, **62**; 499, 1936.

[2] APPLETON, E. V., WATT, R. A. W., and HERD, J. F., *Proc. Roy. Soc.*, **111**; 615, 1926.

[3] CAPUS, GUILLAUME, *Ann. Géographie*, **23**; 109, 1914.

and, probably, some of the chemical, nearly all depend upon the sudden and intense heating along its path.

Crushing Effects.—One of the more surprising phenomena of the lightning discharge is the crushing of hollow conductors, an effect that gives some idea of the strength of current and quantity of electricity involved, and, therefore, deserves a full discussion.

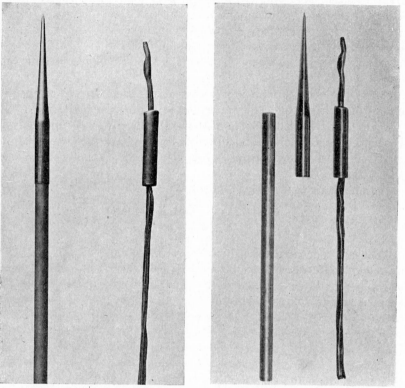

FIG. 136.—Originally duplicate hollow copper lightning rods; one never used, the other crushed by a lightning discharge.

FIG. 137.—Same as Fig. 136, except unused rod is not assembled.

Pollock and Barraclough[1] have described and explained this phenomenon in connection with a hollow copper cylinder; outside diameter 18 mm., inside 16 mm., lap joint 4 mm. wide, 2 mm. thick. In what follows, however, reference will be had to a remarkable, and even more instructive, product of the same phenomenon, kindly lent by West Dodd, of Des Moines, Iowa. Figure 136 shows two originally duplicate (so reported), hollow, copper lightning rods, one uninjured (never in use), the other crushed by a discharge. The uninjured rod consists of

[1] *J. and Proc. Roy. Soc., N. S. Wales,* **39**; 131, 1905.

two parts, shown assembled in Fig. 136, and separate in Fig. 137. The conical cap, nickel plated to avoid corrosion, telescopes snugly over the top of the cylindrical section, and when in place, where it is left loose or unsoldered, becomes the ordinary discharge point.

The dimensions are:

Section	Outside Diameter	Inside Diameter
Cylinder.....................	16.0 mm.	14.65 mm.
Cone shank..................	17.4 mm.	16.0 mm.

Length of conical cap, cylindrical portion, 7 cm., total 19 cm.

Both the cylindrical and the conical portions of the rod are securely brazed along square joints.

The general effects of the discharge, most of which are obvious from the illustrations, were:

1. One or two centimeters of the point were melted off.

2. The conical portion of the top piece and all the cylindrical rod except the upper 2 centimeters, roughly, within the cap, were opened along the brazed joint.

3. The brazing solder appears to have been fused and nearly all volatilized—only patches of it remain, here and there, along the edges.

4. The upper end of the cylindrical rod was fused to the cap just below its conical portion.

5. The rod was fused off where it passed through a staple. Whether a bend in the conductor occurred at the place of fusion is not stated.

6. The collapse of the cylindrical rod extended up about 5 centimeters into the cap.

7. The cylindrical portion of the cap, about 7 centimeters in length, was uninjured; even the brazing was left in place.

What force or forces caused this collapse? Possibly, it might occur to many that it was produced by the reaction pressure from an explosion-like wave in the atmosphere, due to sudden and intense heating. But, however plausible this assumption may seem at first, there, nevertheless, are serious objections to it, some of which are:

a. While explosions, with their consequent pressures, may be obtained by passing a powerful current along a conductor, they seem to occur only with the sudden volatilization of the conductor itself, which, in this case, did not take place.

b. The heating of the enclosed air should have produced a pressure from within, more or less nearly equal to the pressure simultaneously caused from without, and, thereby, have either prevented, or at least greatly reduced, the collapse.

c. The assumption that the crushing of the conductor was due to mass inertia of the sudden heated air offers no solution whatever of the collapse of the rod up into the shank of the cap.

For these reasons it seems that the idea that the collapse of the conductor may have been caused by the reaction pressure of an explosion wave in the atmosphere, due to sudden heating, is untenable.

Probably the correct explanation of the collapse, as already offered by Pollock and Barraclough,[1] an explanation that, at least, must involve an important factor, is as follows:

Each longitudinal fiber, as it were, of the conductor attracted every other such fiber through the interaction of the magnetic fields due to their respective currents, and the resulting magnetic squeeze on the hollow rod, whose walls were weakened by the heating of the current, caused it to collapse in the manner shown.

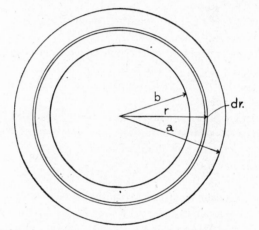

FIG. 138.—Section of a hollow tubular conductor, inner radius a, outer radius b.

As is well known, the force f in dynes per centimeter length, with which a straight wire carrying a current of I amperes is urged at right angles to the direction of the lines of force of a uniform magnetic field of intensity H is given by the equation

$$f = \frac{IH}{10}$$

Also, the value of H, r centimeters from a relatively very long straight conductor carrying I amperes, is given by the relation

$$H = \frac{2I}{10r}.$$

Now, as developed by Northrup[2] in the theory of his heavy-current ammeters, let a (Fig. 138) be the outer, and b the inner radius of a tubular conductor, and let r be the radius of any intermediate tube of infinitesimal

[1] *Loc. cit.*

[2] *Trans. Am. Electrochem. Soc.*, **15**; 303, 1909.

thickness dr. Also, let the conductor as a whole carry a uniformly distributed current of I amperes. Then, the value of the magnetic force, at the end of the radius r, is given by the equation

$$H_r = \frac{2I(r^2 - b^2)}{10r(a^2 - b^2)},$$

which depends upon the fact that only those portions of the current less than r distant from the axis are effective—the forces due to the outer portions neutralizing each other. Also the strength of the current dI carried by the cylinder of radius r and infinitesimal thickness dr is given by the relation

$$dI = \frac{2Irdr}{(a^2 - b^2)}.$$

Hence, under the assumed conditions, the normal pressure dP per unit area on the cylinder of radius r and thickness dr may be determined by the equation

$$dP = \frac{2Irdr}{2\pi r10(a^2 - b^2)} \times \frac{2I(r^2 - b^2)}{10r(a^2 - b^2)}.$$

Hence, the total normal pressure P per square centimeter of the *inner* surface is given by integrating the above expression between the limits b and a. That is,

$$P = \frac{2I^2}{100\pi(a^2 - b^2)^2}\left(\int_b^a rdr - b^2\int_b^a \frac{dr}{r}\right)$$

$$= \frac{2I^2}{100\pi(a^2 - b^2)^2}\left[\frac{1}{2}(a^2 - b^2) + b^2 \log_e \frac{b}{a}\right]$$

$$= \frac{I^2}{100\pi(a^2 - b^2)}\left(1 + \frac{2b^2}{a^2 - b^2} \log_e \frac{b}{a}\right).$$

Substituting for a and b their numerical values, 0.8 and 0.7325 cm., respectively, it is found that

$$P = \frac{I^2}{379.1}.$$

If we assume P, the pressure in dynes per square centimeter of the inner surface, to be 10^6, approximately one atmosphere, then

$$I = 19,470 \text{ amperes, approximately.}$$

If the lightning discharge were alternating, the current density would be greatest in the outer portions of the conductor, and, therefore, the total current would have to be still heavier than the above computed value to produce the assumed pressure. From reasons already given, however, it seems extremely probable that the discharge is unidirectional, and not alternating, and, therefore, that the computed strength of current, though of minimum value, is substantially correct.

Quantity of Electricity in Discharge.—To determine the amount of electricity involved in a lightning discharge, it is necessary to know both its duration and the average strength of current. Both factors, and, therefore, the total charge, vary greatly, though actual measurements have been comparatively few and even these, as a rule, only crudely approximate.

It has often been stated that the duration of a single discharge, or single component of a multiple discharge, is not more than one one-millionth of a second. Some have computed a duration of roughly one-one-hundred-thousandth of a second, while others have estimated that it can not be greater than one-forty-thousandth or, at most, one-thirty-five-thousandth of a second. Doubtless many discharges are as brief as these estimates would indicate, but there is ample reason to believe that others are much longer. Thus, one occasionally sees a streak of lightning that lasts fully ½ second without apparent flicker, while more or less continuous or ribbon discharges are often photographed by moving cameras. Hence, it seems probable that the actual time of a complete discharge, that is, the sum of the times of the several components, of which as many as 50 have been recorded, may occasionally amount to at least 0.01 second.

The second factor mentioned above, the strength of discharge, is even more difficult to determine, and but few estimates of it have been made.

Pockels,[1] adopting the ingenious method of measuring the residual magnetism in basalt, near a place struck by lightning, and comparing these quantities with those similarly obtained in the laboratory, concluded that the maximum strength of current in such discharges amounted occasionally to at least 10,000 amperes. However, the loss of magnetism before the measurements were made, and other unavoidable sources of error, indicate that the actual current strength, probably, was much greater than the estimated value—that the maximum strength of a heavy lightning discharge certainly amounts to many thousands of amperes, occasionally, perhaps, to even 100,000.

Since the above estimates are very rough, it would be well to check them, even though the check itself be equally crude. Hence, it may be worth while further to consider the crushed lightning rod with this particular object in view.

From the dimensions already given of this rod, outside diameter 1.6 centimeters, inside diameter 1.465 centimeters, it follows that its cross-

[1] *Ann. Phys.*, **63**; 195, 1897; **65**; 458, 1898; *Met. Zeit.*, **15**; 41, 1898; *Phys. Zeit.*, **2**; 306, 1901.

sectional area is about 0.325 square centimeter, and its weight, therefore, approximately 2.9 grams per centimeter length. Further, from the fact that the brazed joint was opened and most of the solder removed, apparently volatilized, and the further fact that the rod, itself, in several places, indicates incipient fusion, it would seem that the final temperature may have been roughly 1050° C. If so, the rod must have been heated about 1025° C., since its temperature just before being struck probably was approximately 25° C. But the average specific heat of copper over this temperature range is, roughly, 0.11 and, therefore, the calories generated per centimeter length, about 327.

Now, one ampere against one ohm generates 0.24 calories per second. Hence, since the resistance of the uninjured or check rod, as kindly measured by the Bureau of Standards, is practically that of pure copper, and the average resistance of the crushed conductor over the assumed temperature range probably was about 17 microhms per centimeter length,[1] we have the equation

$$\frac{24}{10^2} I^2 \frac{17}{10^6} t = 327$$

in which I is the average strength of current, and t the actual time of discharge. Assuming that $t = 0.01$ second we get, roughly,

$$I = 90,000 \text{ amperes.}$$

A current of this average value would indicate a maximum value of perhaps 100,000 amperes.

It was computed, above, that a current of 19,470 amperes in the given hollow conductor would produce on it a radial pressure of 10^6 dynes per square centimeter, or about one atmosphere. Hence 100,000 amperes would give a pressure of 2638×10^4 dynes per square centimeter, or, approximately, 400 pounds per square inch; enough, presumably, to produce the crushing that actually occurred.

A current of 90,000 amperes for 0.01 second would mean 900 coulombs or 27×10^{11} electrostatic units of electricity; certainly, an enormous charge, in comparison with laboratory quantities, but, after all, a surprisingly small amount of electricity, since it would electrolyze only 0.084 of a gram of water. It must be distinctly remembered, however, that these estimates are exceedingly rough, and, further, that this particular discharge, presumably, was exceptionally heavy since it produced an exceptional effect.

An interesting method of measuring the resultant electric exchange, between earth and cloud, incident to a lightning discharge, has been used by C. T. R. Wilson.[2] Values up to about 50 coulombs were found, but

[1] NORTHRUP, *J. Franklin Inst.*, **177**; 15, 1914.
[2] *Proc. Roy. Soc.*, **92**; 555, 1916.

it is not stated whether the discharges were single or multiple, nor are their durations given.

From the above various observations and experiments, therefore, it appears that in some cases the strength of current in a lightning discharge probably amounts to many thousands of amperes, and that the total duration of the individual or partial discharges may be several thousandths of a second.

Energy and Power of Discharge.—The energy and power of a lightning discharge obviously vary over a wide range. As an example, presumably near the upper limit, let the discharge be that just computed above, 27×10^{11} electrostatic units; let the potential gradient be 10,000 volts per centimeter, or $33\frac{1}{3}$ electrostatic units; let the length of the path be 1 kilometer; and let the duration of the discharge be 0.01 second. This multiplies up to 9×10^{18} ergs, or 9×10^{20} ergs per second, or 12×10^{10} horsepower. That is, the total energy transformed, or dissipated, by this one discharge would be the equivalent of 14,000 horsepower continuously for 24 hours and the rate of work, that of 60 horsepower for every man, woman, and child on the face of the earth. The values pertaining to the average conspicuous lightning bolt probably are of the order of one-fifth of these.

Danger.—It is impossible to say much of value about danger from lightning. Generally, it is safer to be indoors than out during a thunderstorm, and greatly so if the house has a well-grounded metallic roof or properly installed system of lightning rods. If outdoors, it is best of all to be in a cave, or under an overhanging cliff, and far better to be in a valley than on the ridge of a hill, and it is always dangerous to take shelter under an isolated tree—the taller the tree, other things being equal, the greater the danger. An exceptionally tall tree is dangerous, even in a forest. Some varieties of trees appear to be more frequently struck, in proportion to their numbers and exposure, than others, but no tree is immune. In general, however, the trees most likely to be struck are those that have either an extensive root system, like the locust, or deep tap roots, like the pine, for the very obvious reason that they are the best grounded and, therefore, offer, on the whole, the least electrical resistance.

If one has to be outdoors, and exposed to a violent thunderstorm, it is advisable, so far as danger from the lightning is concerned, to get soaking wet, because wet clothes are much better conductors, and dry ones poorer, than the human body. In extreme cases it might even be advisable to lie flat on the wet ground. In case of severe shock, resuscitation should be attempted through persistent (hour or more, if necessary) artificial respiration and prevention from chill.

As just implied, the contour of the land is an important factor in determining the relative danger from lightning because, obviously, the chance of a discharge between cloud and earth varies somewhat inversely as the distance between them. Hence, thunderstorms are more dangerous in mountainous regions, at least in the higher portions, than over a level country. For this same reason also (inverse relation between distance from cloud to earth and frequency of discharge between them) there exists on high peaks a level or belt of maximum danger, the level approximately, of the base of the average cumulus cloud. The tops of the highest peaks are seldom struck, simply because the storm generally forms, and runs its course, at a lower level.

Clearly, too, for any given region, the lower the cloud the greater the danger. Hence, a high degree of humidity is favorable to a dangerous storm, partly because the clouds will form at a low level, and partly because the precipitation, and probably, therefore, the electricity generated, will be abundant. Hence, too, a winter thunderstorm, because of its generally lower clouds, is likely to be more dangerous than an equally heavy summer one. Finally, as already explained, thunderstorms, incident to cyclonic disturbances, presumably, are more dangerous than those due to local heating; and, therefore, the thunderstorm of middle latitudes is generally more dangerous than one of equal severity in the tropics.

It may also be interesting to note that the front edge of a thunderstorm, probably, is more dangerous than any other portion; more dangerous, because it is immediately beneath the region of most active electrical generation, and because objects here, often, still are dry and, therefore, if struck, more likely to be penetrated and fired than later, when wet, and thus partially shielded by conducting surfaces.

LIGHTNING PROTECTION

If, as seems quite certain, the lightning discharge follows, or tends closely to follow, the instantaneous lines of electric force, then it is obvious that whatever changes the direction of this force must correspondingly alter the path the flash shall take. To the extent, then, that the direction of electric force near the surface of the earth can be changed, but, in general, to only this extent, lightning protection is possible. If, also, the strength of the field could materially be reduced, clearly, the discharges might be rendered less violent and even less frequent, but, as will be explained presently, there is no evidence that the strength of the field can be altered, greatly, by any practicable means. Hence, it appears that protection from lightning must be sought through directional control, which is both possible and practical,[1] rather than through prevention.

[1] PETERS, O. S., "Protection of Life and Property against Lightning." *Technologic Paper*, 56, Bureau of Standards, Washington, D. C., 1915; COVERT, R. N., "Protection of Buildings and Farm Property from Lightning," *Farmers' Bull.* 1512. Department of Agriculture, Washington, D. C., 1926.

Assume, in accordance with observation, that over an extended horizontal surface, a prairie for instance, the lines of electric force are vertical; determine how the field of force will be modified by the presence of a given structure. Obviously, if the structure itself consists of such non-conducting materials as wood and stone, there will be but little directional change of the electric force. If, however, it is made of a conducting substance, the direction of the force will be changed, but to an extent, and over an area, that depend upon the size and shape of the structure in question. In general, this effect is not calculable, but fortunately it may be definitely computed in the special case of a conducting semiellipsoid with vertical axis, and standing, as would a right cone, on the conducting surface—the actual surface, if wet, somewhat below, if dry. The ground and all parts of the conductor, unless actively discharging, will have the same potential. Hence, by varying the values of the three diameters of the semiellipsoid, a fair approximation may be made to many ordinary structures and their effects on the electric field estimated, in some cases roughly, in others with even a high degree of accuracy. Thus, by making each of the horizontal diameters small and the vertical one relatively very large, the modification of the field by a single upright metallic rod may be computed very closely, and its efficiency as a protection against lightning approximately determined. This has been done by Sir J. Larmor and J. S. B. Larmor,[1] who say that:

In fact, if the undisturbed vertical atmospheric field is F, the modified potential

$$V = -F_z + A_z \int_\epsilon^\infty \frac{d\lambda}{(a^2 + \lambda)^{1/2}(b^2 + \lambda)^{1/2}(c^2 + \lambda)^{3/2}}$$

will be null over the ground, and also null over the ellipsoid (a, b, c), provided

$$\frac{F}{A} = \int_0^\infty \frac{d\lambda}{(a^2 + \lambda)^{1/2}(b^2 + \lambda)^{1/2}(c^2 + \lambda)^{3/2}}.$$

For our special case of a thin symmetrical semiellipsoid of height c, this gives

$$V = -F_z + A_z \int_\epsilon^\infty \frac{d\lambda}{\lambda(c^2 + \lambda)^{3/2}}.$$

The value of this integral, however, increases indefinitely toward its lower limit as ϵ falls to zero, when a and b are null. Thus, as the semiellipsoid becomes thinner, the value of A diminishes without limit; that is, the modification of the field of force by a very thin rod is negligible along its sides unless close to it. A thin isolated rod thus draws the discharge hardly at all unless in the region around its summit.

This is not to be taken as a condemnation of lightning rods in general. It only shows that a single vertical rod affords but little protection

[1] *Proc. Roy. Soc.*, **90**; 314, 1914.

to things in its neighborhood, and, thus, explains why kite wires, for instance, are so seldom struck. When, however, the horizontal diameters of the semiellipsoid are of appreciable length, the directions of the otherwise vertical lines of force are greatly changed for some distance on all sides, as illustrated by Fig. 139, adapted from the paper quoted above. Hence, one method, and, so far as known, the only method, of at least partially protecting an object from lightning, consists in surrounding it by a hollow conductor, or by a well-grounded conducting cage. Perfect protection, ordinarily, is not practical, even if possible.

By this method, the lightning that, otherwise, would hit at random, is guided to the conducting system and through it, if all goes well, harmlessly to the ground. It must be clearly remembered, however, that this discharge, though in all probability unidirectional, is extremely

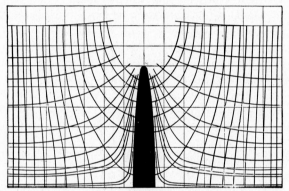

Fig. 139.—Vertical field of electric force disturbed by a conducting, semiellipsoidal column.

abrupt and of great amperage and, therefore, possesses the dangerous voltage and inductive properties of alternating currents of high frequency and large volume. It should also be remembered that although the successive partial discharges that make up the usual lightning flash follow the same ionized path, this path itself, shifted by the winds, probably, often guides one or more of the secondary, or sequent, discharges to an entirely different object from that hit by the first.

From these fundamental principles it is easy to formulate general rules (details may be varied indefinitely) for the construction of an efficient system of lightning protection.

Conductors.—Since lightning discharges occasionally involve very heavy currents, it is necessary that the conductors of the protective system be sufficiently large to prevent fusion. Probably, copper is the best material to use, mainly because non-corrosive, or practically so, in the atmosphere and, therefore, very durable, though aluminum and galvanized iron also are good. If copper, a weight of 370 grams per meter (4 ounces per foot) might suffice, but a greater weight, possibly, would be better. The shape of the cross-section appears to be of comparatively small importance.

Terminals.—Because of the distortion of the electric field due to the object to be protected, house, for instance, and to the system of conductors, each ridge, peak, chimney, and other highest point should be capped, or surmounted, by a conductor that is well grounded.

It would be better if the conductor extended 2 meters or so above each of these salients, though the protection is still fair to good with much shorter projections, or even none at all. Whether or not each projection, in turn, is provided with the customary sharp points, probably, is of small importance—rather a matter of taste or sentiment than a necessity. To be sure, it often is asserted that sharp points discharge so freely that they, thereby, largely *prevent* lightning. But this assumption has little support from observation or experiment. Lodge,[1] for instance, says: "*I find that points do not discharge much till they begin to fizz and audibly spit; and when the tension is high enough for this, blunt and rough terminals are nearly as efficient as the finest needle points.* The latter, indeed, begin to act at comparatively low potentials, but the amount of electricity they can get rid of at such potentials is surprisingly trivial, and of no moment whatever when dealing with a thundercloud." The inefficiency of points to prevent lightning is further obvious from the fact that trees are struck in a forest despite the myriads of pointed leaves all around.

System.—Because a single rod modifies the electric field only in its near neighborhood, and because the wind shifts the ionized, or conducting, path during the interval between successive partial discharges, it is obvious that the smaller the spaces left bare by the conductive covering, the more effective the protection. A steel frame building, with the framing well grounded from its lower portions, and connected at all upper corners, and other places of near approach, to a metallic roof from which, in turn, conductors extend above the chimney tops and other protrusions, would, therefore, appear to be especially well protected from lightning damage.

A stone or wooden building should have electrically continuous rods up each corner to the eave, thence to, and along, the ridge, with such side branches and elevated projections as the size and shape of the building, and other considerations, may require. In general, no place on the roof should be more than 3 meters (10 feet) from some portion of the protective system. Further, the principal and secondary conductors must be so placed that from any point the ground may be reached by a continuous *downward* course.

Protection would also be increased by surmounting each corner with a conducting rod 3 to 4 meters tall, properly connected to the rest of the

[1] "Lightning Conductors and Lightning Guards," p. 370, London, 1892.

system. Architectural considerations, however, might often forbid this additional precaution.

Joints.—To facilitate the discharge, as far as possible, the conductors should be, as nearly as practicable, continuous. Hence, all necessary joints should be electrically good and mechanically secure. Well-made screw joints, turned up tight, appear to be the best.

Bends.—Since electric surges tend to arc across sharp angles, lightning rods must have no short bends. Changes in direction must be avoided, as far as possible, and wherever necessary be made gradually along a curve of 30 centimeters (1 foot) radius, or more; self-induction must be kept at a minimum.

Attachment.—The rods should be attached to the building with holders of the same material as the rod itself. This prevents corrosion, and also secures electrical connection to the roof and sides which usually are wet and conducting during a thunderstorm.

Ground Connections.—Because of the considerable resistance of even very damp earth, ground connections should be as good, and as many, as practicable. Every descending rod, and there would better be one at each corner, and on large buildings even more, should be sunk straight down to perpetually damp earth; if convenient, connected also to underground water pipes, and, of course, protected from injury by a noninductive jacket a couple of meters above ground. Generally, copper is best for this purpose. If iron is used, it should not be packed in coke or charcoal, since either would cause the iron more rapidly to corrode.

Connection to Neighboring Conductors.—The high potential and strong induction of the lightning discharge require that not only gutters, waterspouts, and the like, on the outside, but also all internal conductors of large size, or considerable length, be connected with the outer system at their upper ends and wherever they come within even 2 or 3 meters of it, cross-connected with each other at points of close approach, and, finally, well grounded, from their lower ends, either directly, or by proper attachments, to the main conductors.

It is often stated that leaky gas pipes should be excepted from such connections. Possibly so, but in the first place gas pipes should not be allowed to leak.

Special Dangers.—Overland wires, telephone, telegraph, light and power, necessarily are sources of danger unless provided with proper lightning arresters, and so, also, are radio antennae. However, appropriate devices of this nature, commonly, are installed, and, therefore, danger from electric wires, usually, is negligible. Nevertheless, it must be remembered that this distinctly is a case where the price of protection is proper forethought and adequate precaution.

A much greater source of danger, because seldom, if ever, provided with an efficient lightning arrester, is the harmless-looking wire clothes line running from some part of the house to a convenient tree. The obvious remedy, in this important case, is either to use a cotton, or other fibre, rope, or else to avoid connection with the house altogether.

Still another common source of danger, especially to stock, is the ordinary wire fence. But here, too, approximate safety is easy of attainment. It is only necessary that good ground connections be made at intervals of every 100 meters (20 rods), or less—the shorter the better, so far as safety is concerned.

Finally the question of shade trees is of some importance. None is safe, but, in general, the danger they imply increases both with their own height and with the elevation of the ground above adjacent regions.

PART II
ATMOSPHERIC ELECTRICITY AND AURORAS

CHAPTER I
ATMOSPHERIC ELECTRICITY

Three manifestations of atmospheric electricity, lightning (discussed in connection with the thunderstorm), the aurora polaris, and St. Elmo's fire—a "brush" discharge from elevated objects—have long been known; the first two, of course, from the beginning of human existence, and the last, as an object of the sailor's superstition, certainly, since the days of ancient Greece and Rome.[1] Their identification, however, as electrical phenomena is very modern.

Chief Discoveries.—The following list of contributions to the science of atmospheric electricity, though fragmentary, will, perhaps, give some idea of its slow but accelerated course of development:

a. The suspicion of the electrical nature of lightning, by Hawksbee, who says,[2] "Sometimes I have observed the light to break from the agitated [electrified] glass in as strange a form as lightning," and also,[3] "I likewise observed that . . . it was but approaching my hand near the surface of the outer glass [a rotated open receiver containing an exhausted vessel] to produce flashes of light like lightning in the inner one"; by Wall,[4] . . . "by holding a finger a little distance from the [electrified] amber, a crackling is produced, with a great flash of light succeeding it . . . and it seems, in some degree, to represent thunder and lightning;" by Gray,[5] . . . "this electric fire, which, by several of these experiments, seems to be of the same nature with that of thunder and lightning;" and by many others.

b. The devising, by Franklin,[6] in 1749, of a simple means "to determine the question, whether the clouds that contain lightning are electrified or not."

c. The proof, May 10, 1752, by Dalibard[7] (following Franklin's suggestion), that clouds in which lightning appears are electrified,

[1] BRAND, "Antiquities," Castor and Pollux.
[2] *Phil. Trans.,* 1705.
[3] *Phil. Trans.,* 1707.
[4] *Phil. Trans.,* 1708.
[5] *Phil. Trans.,* 1735.
[6] "Experiments on Electricity," Ed. 1769, p. 66.
[7] FRANKLIN, "Experiments on Electricity," Ed. 1769, p. 107.

and Franklin's confirmation thereof the same summer by drawing electricity from a thundercloud with a kite.

d. The proof, July, 1752, by Lemonnier,[1] that a tall, insulated metallic conductor becomes electrified even when the sky is absolutely clear.

e. The inauguration, in 1757, by Beccaria,[2] of systematic and long continued (15 years) observations of atmospheric electricity.

f. The invention, by Thomson[3] (Lord Kelvin), of the quadrant electrometer, in 1855, and the "water-dropper," about the same time, that greatly increased the delicacy and accuracy of the measurements of atmospheric electricity.

g. The discovery, by Linss,[4] in 1887, that even the most perfectly insulated conductors lose their charges, when exposed to the air, in a manner that shows the atmosphere itself to be a conductor of electricity.

h. The discovery, in 1900, by C. T. R. Wilson,[5] and also by H. Geitel,[6] of spontaneous ionization in the atmosphere.

i. The discovery, in 1902, independently, by Rutherford and Cooke,[7] and McLennan and Burton,[8] of a penetrating radiation in the lower atmosphere, presumably from radioactive substances near the surface of the earth.

j. The invoking, in 1902, by A. E. Kennelly[9] and Oliver Heaviside,[10] of strong ionization in the high atmosphere to account for the bending of radio waves around the earth.

k. The discovery, in 1905, by Langevin,[11] of slow-moving or large ions in the atmosphere.

l. The discovery, by Simpson,[12] in 1908 and 1909, that the electric charge on thunderstorm rain, and precipitation generally, is prevailingly positive.

m. The discovery by Hess,[13] confirmed by Kolhörster,[14] that an extremely hard or penetrating radiation exists in the atmosphere that comes from the outside.

[1] *Acad. Roy. Sci.*, 1752; 233.
[2] "Dell' Elettricità Terrestre Atmospherica a Cielo Sereno," Torino, 1775.
[3] *B. A. Rept.*, **2**; 22, 1855.
[4] *Met. Zeit.*, **4**; 345, 1887.
[5] *Proc. Cambr. Phil. Soc.*, **2**; 52, 1900.
[6] *Phys. Zeit.*, **2**; 116, 1900.
[7] *Phys. Rev.*, **16**; 183, 1903.
[8] *Phys. Rev.*, **16**; 184, 1903.
[9] *Elec. World, Eng.*, **39**; 473.
[10] *Encyclopaedia Britannica*, 10th Ed., **33**, 215.
[11] *C. R.*, **140**; 232, 1905.
[12] *Memoirs Indian Meteorl. Dept.*, Simla, **20**; pt. 8, 1910.
[13] *Phys. Zeit.*, **13**; 1084, 1913.
[14] *Deutsche Phys. Gesel.*, July 30, 1914.

ELECTRICAL FIELD OF THE EARTH

The experiments of Franklin, and others, with kites and insulated vertical rods, revealed a persistent difference of electrical potential between the earth and the atmosphere that soon became, and still is, the object of innumerable measurements.

Instruments.—The instruments essential for accurate measurements of the difference of potential between the earth and any point in the atmosphere, are a "collector" and an electroscope. The "collector" is merely an insulated conductor provided with an adequate means of electric discharge—sharp point, flame, ionizing salt, or "dropper"—that brings it, and all other conductors with which it is electrically connected, to the potential in the air at the point of discharge.

The electrometer, one element of which is connected to the "collector," and thus brought to its potential, while the other is grounded, or connected to a "collector" at a different level, may be any one of several types. Those generally used at present are the Thomson quadrant, Bendorf registering (adaptation of the Thomson quadrant), Wulf bifilar, and Einthoven single-fiber. The quadrant type must be kept stationary, but the others are not so restricted and give good results, even on shipboard and in balloons.

Potential Gradient near the Surface.—The vertical potential gradient near the surface of the earth due to the total charge on the earth plus charges locally induced by clouds or otherwise, varies greatly with location, season, hour, and weather conditions. It even reverses signs, frequently, during thunderstorms and often reaches 10,000 volts per meter, but its general average over the sea and level land areas, during fine weather, appears to be of the order of 100 volts per meter, in response to a negative surface charge.

Location Effect.—Since the earth is a conductor, it is obvious that the distribution on its surface and the resulting vertical potential gradient will be so modified by topography as to be smaller in narrow valleys than on the neighboring ridges. Over level regions of the same elevation, the gradient appears to be largest in the interior of continents of the temperate zones, and least within the tropics, and also, perhaps, in very high latitudes.

Annual Variation.—The annual variation of the vertical potential gradient near the surface of the earth differs greatly from place to place. In general, it is comparatively small in tropical regions, and, also, everywhere on mountain tops, but large, as much in some cases as twice the annual average value, in the temperate zones where the gradient changes are, roughly, as follows: An increase during the fall and early winter to a maximum of perhaps 250 volts per meter, followed by a rapid decrease during spring to a moderately constant summer minimum of, roughly, 100 volts per meter.

Diurnal Variation.—The diurnal variation of the potential gradient, as illustrated by Fig. 140, after Bauer and Swann,[1] changes with place, season and altitude. Its amplitude is greater along middle latitudes, in the interior of continents, than along low latitudes, or anywhere over the ocean; greater during winter, when it is single crested, than summer, when double crested. At moderate elevations, ½ kilometer or less, the

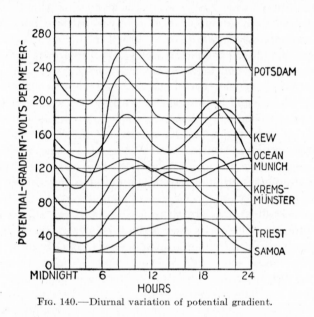

FIG. 140.—Diurnal variation of potential gradient.

gradient has only a single daily maximum and minimum, whatever its surface periods.

From the above facts, it appears that the single daily variation of the potential gradient is fundamental, and that the summer afternoon minimum, that develops a double diurnal variation, is only a shallow disturbance. Furthermore, quoting from Mauchly:[2]

It is found that the preponderance of evidence from observations made aboard the *Carnegie* in each of the major oceans, indicates that *the diurnal variation of the potential gradient over the oceans is primarily due to a 24-hour "wave," which progresses approximately according to universal, rather than local, time.* According to the mean yearly results, from all ocean observations to date, this primary wave has an amplitude of about 15 per cent of the mean-of-day value of the potential gradient and attains its maximum development at about 17.5*h*. g.m.t.

---

[1] *Publication* 175, Vol. III, of the Carnegie Institution of Washington.
[2] *Terr. Mag. and Atmos. Elec.*, **28**; 80, 1923.

Measurements of the potential gradient in the central United States give results very similar to those found on the ocean.[1]

And Whipple[2] has added the significant fact that the diurnal variation of the electric potential gradient over the oceans coincides, roughly, with the like variation of the world's thunderstorms.

It would seem, therefore, that there are two terms in this diurnal variation; one, dominant over continents, that runs with local time and presumably is due to local conditions; and another, dominant over the oceans, that follows universal time, and is owing, perhaps, to the occurrence of thunderstorms as affected jointly by insolation and the distribution of continents and oceans.

Potential Gradient and Meteorological Elements.—Many efforts have been made to find what relations obtain between the potential gradient and the various meteorological elements, but the results, in most cases, are inconclusive, especially in respect to temperature, humidity, and pressure changes. Strength and direction of wind both are important, through their effect on the amount of smoke, dust, factory fumes, etc., in the air at the place of measurement.[3] Fog, rain, and other forms of precipitation are nearly always electrically charged and, therefore, often greatly modify, and, occasionally, even reverse the potential gradient, as do also heavily charged or thunderstorm clouds. Cirrus and other types of high, fair-weather clouds produce little or no effect.

Dust Clouds.—The raising of a dust cloud is accompanied with strong electrification.[4] Acid dust, such as powdered silica, gives the air a negative charge; basic and organic dust give it a positive charge.

Potential Gradient and Elevation.—Measurements of the potential gradient from free balloons have shown that it varies greatly and irregularly through the low dust-laden stratum, and that above this layer it decreases less and less rapidly to a comparatively small value at an altitude of only a few kilometers. If the surface gradient is 100 volts per meter, it may be 25 volts per meter at an elevation of 1.5 kilometers, 10 at an elevation of 4 kilometers, 8 at 6 kilometers elevation, with similar decreases for greater heights. The potential difference between the earth and the highest atmosphere, commonly is estimated to be of the order of 1,000,000 volts.

Surface and Volume Charges, Etc.—From the simple equation

$$\frac{dV}{dn} = \frac{100 \text{ volts}}{\text{meter}} = f = 4\pi\sigma,$$

giving the electric force f or rate of change of potential normal to the

[1] WAIT, G. R., *Terr. Mag. and Atmos. Elec.*, **35**; 137, 1939.

[2] *Meteorol. Mag.*, **59**; 201, 1924.

[3] WHIPPLE, *Quart. J. Roy. Meteorol. Soc.*, **55**, 351, 1929.

[4] RUDGE, W. A. D., *Proc. Roy. Soc.*, **90**; 256, 1914.

surface, in terms of the surface charge σ per unit area, it follows that when the potential gradient at the surface of the earth is 100 volts per meter the charge is 2.65×10^{-4} negative electrostatic units per square centimeter, or 4.5×10^5 coulombs, roughly, for the total surface charge of the earth.

Similarly, from the equation

$$\frac{d^2V}{dn^2} = \frac{df}{dn} = 4\pi\rho$$

between the volume charge ρ and the ratio of change of the electric force to change of elevation, it appears that near the surface of the earth the net charge of the air is roughly 0.1 electrostatic unit of positive electricity per cubic meter.

ELECTRICAL CONDUCTIVITY OF THE ATMOSPHERE

It is well known that an electrified conductor, exposed to the air, gradually loses its charge, however carefully it may be insulated. This phenomenon was first investigated by Coulomb,[1] who found the important law that the rate of loss of charge is proportional to the existing charge, or rate of drop of potential proportional to the existing potential. In symbols,

$$\frac{dQ}{dt} = -aQ \text{ and } \frac{dV}{dt} = -aV,$$

or

$$Q_t = Q_0 e^{-at}$$

and

$$V_t = V_0 e^{-at},$$

where Q_0 and V_0 are the charge and potential, respectively, at any given instant, Q_t and V_t the corresponding values t seconds, or other units of time, later, e the base of the natural logarithms, and a a constant.

The loss of charge was explained by Coulomb, and his explanation was accepted for more than a century, as due to the charging by contact of neutral molecules of air and their subsequent repulsion.

From the work begun by Linss,[2] and extended by others, it is now known, however, that the discharge coefficient a varies more or less from hour to hour and from season to season, and, further, that generally it is not the same for charges of opposite sign. Hence, the loss of charge in addition to that which may be accounted for by imperfect insulation, is due to neutralization by numerous minute charges of the opposite sign normally present in the atmosphere—charges that render it conductive. It is also known that the values of these charges are either that

[1] *Mém. de l'Acad. de Paris*, p. 616, 1785.

[2] *Met. Zeit.*, **4**; 345, 1887.

of the electron or multiples thereof. Swann[1] has shown that whatever the shape of the charged body the rate of its loss of charge is given by the equation

$$\frac{dQ}{dt} = -4\pi Qnev$$

where Q is the charge on the object, n the number of ions per cubic centimeter of sign opposite to that of Q, v the specific velocity of these ions, which decreases with increase of their mass, and e the ionic charge. In other words, the rate of supply of electricity by the ions to the charged

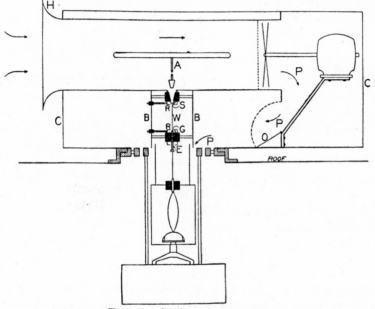

Fig. 141.—Conductivity apparatus.

body is $4\pi\lambda CV$, in which C is the capacitance of the charged object and λ the conductivity of the air for electricity of sign opposite to that of the charge.

The conductivity, therefore, of the atmosphere may be conveniently measured by noting the rate of potential drop of a charged cylinder concentrically surrounded by a relatively large tube through which a good circulation of fresh air is maintained. Figure 141 indicates the equipment used for this purpose on the *Carnegie* during the cruises of 1915–1916.[2] As explained in the publication referred to, if C_1 is the capacitance of the whole apparatus, including the electroscope, and

[1] *Terr. Mag. and Atmos. Elec.*, **19**; 81, 1914.

[2] BAUER and SWANN, *Publication* 175, **3**; 385, of the Carnegie Institution of Washington, D. C.

C_2 the measured capacitance of the concentric cylinders, including that portion of the supporting rod A that is exposed to the air current then

$$-C_1 \frac{dV}{dt} = 4\pi\lambda C_2 V$$

and

$$4\pi\lambda C_2 = \frac{C_1}{T} \log_e \frac{V_1}{V_2}$$

in which T is the time required for the potential to fall from V_1 to V_2. Hence both conductivities, $\lambda +$ and $\lambda -$, corresponding respectively to the positive and negative ions, are easily determinable.

The average value of the conductivities found during the above-mentioned cruise of the *Carnegie* were $\lambda + = 1.44 \times 10^{-4}$ and $\lambda - = 1.19 \times 10^{-4}$. These are also, approximately, the values found over land during clear weather.

Annual Variation.—In general, the conductivity is greater during the summer than during winter—the reverse of the potential gradient.

Diurnal Variation.—The diurnal variation of the conductivity is quite irregular, but is more or less the reverse of the potential gradient, that is, high in the early morning and low in the evening.

Relation to Weather.—The conductivity of the atmosphere is very small when the air is either dusty or foggy; nearly all the ions being then attached to masses so large that the velocity factor v in the current equation, and consequently the current itself, is quite small. On the other hand, when the air is clean and dry, the conductivity is relatively large. Furthermore, the potential gradient generally varies inversely with the conductivity, as it does in the case of other conductors.

Conductivity and Elevation.—Through the first kilometer the conductivity of the atmosphere varies irregularly, owing, presumably, at least in part, to corresponding variations in the dust content, or mass and sluggishness of the ions. Beyond about that level, it generally increases rather rapidly, owing to increase in the number of ions per unit volume and decrease in the ratio of gross to molecular ions, so that at the elevation of 6 kilometers it may have, roughly, twenty times the surface value. At any rate, the resistance of the lowest 4 or 5 kilometers is equal to that of all the rest of the air beyond.

IONIC CONTENT OF THE AIR

Ionic Density.—The number of ions of either sign per unit volume of the atmosphere may be found by passing a known volume of air through a cylindrical condenser, sufficiently charged to catch all the ions of opposite sign, and noting the drop in potential.

Let n_+ and n_- be the number of positive and negative molecular or fast-moving ions, respectively, per cubic centimeter of the air examined, e the ionic charge, V the initial potential, sufficient to clean out the molecular ions, but not great enough materially to affect the large ions mentioned below, and δV the drop in potential on passage of A cubic centimeters of air through the condenser; then, neglecting, or allowing for, the leakage,

$$n_\pm = \frac{C\delta V}{eA}.$$

The value of n varies greatly, being very small during foggy and dusty weather, and relatively large when the air is clear. In general it is larger during summer than winter, larger during the daytime than at night, and larger when the temperature is high than when it is low. It also increases with elevation through at least the first few kilometers, but to what maximum value, and where, is not known.

Through the lower atmosphere the fair-weather values of n_+ and n_-, generally, are of the order of 800 and 680, respectively, per cubic centimeter, or, roughly, one ion to twenty thousand million million molecules of air. In the very high atmosphere, the region called the "ionosphere," or "Kennelly-Heaviside layer," there are everywhere two levels of maximum electron density, and, beneath the sun, a third, the E, F_1 and F_2 layers with, roughly, 18×10^4, 33×10^4, and 10^6 electrons per cubic centimeter, respectively, at around 100, 220, and 300 kilometers above the surface.[1]

Ionic Velocity.—The velocities v_1 and v_2 of the positive and negative ions, respectively, may be computed from the corresponding values of the current n_+ev and ionic density n_+, since the value of e is a known constant. The average value of v_+ in the lower air is of the order of $1 \frac{\text{cm/sec}}{\text{volt/cm}}$, and of v_-, $1.2 \frac{\text{cm/sec}}{\text{volt/cm}}$. Both values increase with decrease of pressure—at half the pressure the velocity is double, approximately—and, therefore, with increase of elevation.

Large, or Langevin, Ions.—After the atmosphere is deprived of all its ions of molecular size, it still is slightly conductive, because, as discovered by Langevin,[2] of the presence of relatively slow moving and, therefore, comparatively massive ions. The number of such ions per cubic centimeter ranges widely. In the open country this number appears to be comparatively small, but it is very great over large cities, usually many times that of the ordinary, or molecular, ions, and more negative than positive. However, the values vary greatly and either sign may prevail.[3]

[1] FLEMING, J. A., Ed., "Terrestrial Magnetism and Electricity," McGraw-Hill Book Company, Inc., 1939.

[2] *C. R.*, **140**; 232, 1905.

[3] ISRAËL, H., *Beiträge Geophys.*, **23**; 144, 1929.

ELECTRIC CURRENTS IN THE ATMOSPHERE

At least four different electric currents exist in the atmosphere—two always, and everywhere, or nearly so, and two sporadically, in time and place. These are:

a. The lightning discharge, roughly, 100 per second for the earth as a whole, with a transfer of 10 to 20 coulombs each.

b. Precipitation currents, or currents due to the falling of charged rain, snow, hail, etc. The average strength of such current may be found from the rate of precipitation and charge, usually positive, per cubic centimeter, say, of the rain, or its equivalent in the case of snow or hail. During non-thunderstorm rains, this current often averages about 10^{-16} ampere per square centimeter of surface. During violent thunderstorms, however, it is far greater, even as much as 10^{-12} ampere per square centimeter for brief intervals has been reported. J. A. Chalmers and E. W. R. Little[1] have recorded, during showers of graupel, currents up to $+3.8 \times 10^{-12}$ amperes per square centimeter, in one case, and -7.3×10^{-12} in another.

c. Convection currents, due to the mechanical transfer of the ions in the atmosphere from one place to another by winds, including vertical convection. The strength of such current per unit area, at right angles to the direction of the wind, is obtained by multiplying the wind velocity by the net density of the charge.

This density may be found either by multiplying the ionic charge by the difference between the numbers of ions of opposite sign per cubic centimeter, or from the equation

$$\rho = -\frac{1}{4\pi} \frac{d^2 V}{dh^2},$$

in which ρ is the density required, and dV/dh the vertical potential gradient.

The value of ρ varies greatly, but through much of the atmosphere the convection current is of the order 10^{-16} ampere per square centimeter cross-section of the wind, per meter/second velocity.

d. Conduction current, due to the downward flow of one set of ions, usually the positive, and the simultaneous upward flow of the other in response to the vertical potential gradient. The density of this current, or strength per square centimeter cross-section, may be computed from the potential gradient and the conductivity, or, with suitable apparatus, may be measured directly. The average value of this conduction current is of the order of 2×10^{-16} ampere per square centimeter of, apparently, the entire surface of the earth. It generally is less during the day than at night, and less in summer than winter. At the Kew Observatory,

[1] *Nature*, **143**; 244, 1939.

however, Scrase[1] finds it to be greater in summer than winter. Always, however, the sum total of the conduction current for the entire earth is roughly 1000 amperes, sufficient to carry off the entire charge of the earth, 45×10^4 coulombs, in 7.5 minutes if it were not continuously replenished. How this constant current, always, on the whole, in the same direction, is maintained—how the earth can so rapidly discharge and, yet, forever be equally charged, like a cataract always falling but never running dry— is the present most urgent problem of atmospheric electricity.

RADIOACTIVE CONTENT OF THE ATMOSPHERE

The first evidence that the atmosphere normally contains one or more radioactive substances was obtained in 1900, when Geitel[2] and C. T. R. Wilson,[3] independently, found that an insulated electrified conductor gradually loses its charge even when inside a closed vessel. Later Elster and Geitel[4] showed that a bare wire exposed to the air and charged negatively to a high voltage, gradually becomes coated with radioactive material. In 1904, Bumstead[5] showed that the radioactive substance of the atmosphere consists essentially of radium and thorium emanations, which, it is now known, occur in widely varying proportions. On the average, however, they appear to produce about the same amount of ionization, that is, near the surface and over land, roughly 2 ions each, of each sign, per cubic centimeter per second.

The emanations, which are heavy, radioactive gases, are several fold more abundant in mines and cellars than in the open, and, obviously, get into the atmosphere by diffusion from the earth where they are generated by the spontaneous decomposition of radium and thorium. They may be absorbed from a known volume of air by cocoanut charcoal, liquified by low temperatures ($-150°$ C. or lower), or caught up by a conductor charged to a high negative potential. In any case the nature of the deposit can be determined from the decay curve, from which, together with the saturation current and the volume of air used, the amount of active material per unit volume may be determined. In this way it has been found[6] that the radioactive emanations in the atmosphere over the Pacific Ocean, Sub-Antarctic Ocean, and land (average), amount to 3.3×10^{-12}, 0.4×10^{-12}, and 88×10^{-12} curie per cubic meter, respectively. Or, since the volume of one curie of emanation at standard temperature and pressure is 0.59 cubic millimeter,[7]

[1] *Geophys. Mem.*, 58, 1933.

[2] *Phys. Zeit.*, **2**; 116, 1900.

[3] *Proc. Camb. Phil. Soc.*, **2**; 52, 1900.

[4] *Phys. Zeit.*, **2**; 590, 1901.

[5] *Am. J. Sci.*, **18**; 1, 1904.

[6] BAUER and SWANN, *Publication* 175, **3**; 422, Carnegie Institution of Washington, D. C.

[7] RUTHERFORD, "Radioactive Substances and Their Radiations," Cambridge University Press, p. 480, 1913.

the emanation gases constitute, in these several regions, 1.95×10^{-19}, 0.24×10^{-19}, and 51.9×10^{-19} of the atmosphere, respectively.

The amount of these emanations appears to be sufficient to account for the measured ionization (ions of molecular size) on the land, but quite insufficient over the oceans to maintain the ionization of these regions. Perhaps, as the slow ions are so very numerous over land areas, it may account for only a small part of the ionization in either case.

PENETRATING RADIATION

It has been found that the air within a closed metallic vessel remains fully conductive, even when deprived of all emanations and when the inner walls of the vessel have been cleaned, as far as possible, of radioactive materials. By surrounding this vessel with thick screens, or sinking it in water, the conductivity of the enclosed air is more or less reduced.[1] It is, therefore, inferred that the conductivity in question is produced by penetrating radiation of the γ type from the outside. Obvious sources of such radiation are the radium and thorium, and their decomposition products, that seem to be more or less prevalent everywhere near the surface of the earth, especially over land.

That a portion, at least, of the ionization giving this conductivity is produced by the γ rays of ordinary radioactive substances in the earth and lower atmosphere, is evident from the fact that it decreases with elevation up to about 1.5 kilometers above the surface.

In addition to this type of radiation there is another, cosmical radiation many times more penetrating,[2] that appears to come from quite outside the atmosphere, and which, possibly, may contribute to the maintenance of the earth's negative charge. A general summary of what is known of cosmic rays has been given by J. C. Stearns and O. K. Froman.[3]

ORIGIN AND MAINTENANCE OF THE EARTH'S CHARGE

Numerous hypotheses have been made to account for the negative charge of the earth, and to explain how that charge is maintained in spite of the current that would exhaust it in a few minutes if it were not, in some way, continually replenished, but no explanation of either has yet been found that meets all the difficulties and is supported by observation and experiment. Ebert[4] attributed them to the positively charged air that comes out of the pores of the earth at the onset of low barometric

---

[1] RUTHERFORD and COOKE, *Phys. Rev.*, **16**; 183, 1903; McLENNAN and BURTON, *Phys. Rev.*, **16**; 184, 1903.

[2] MILLIKAN and CAMERON, *Nature*, **121**; 19–26, 1928; *Science*, **67**; 401, 1928; MILLIKAN, *Phys. Rev.*, **36**; 1595, 1930; KOLHÖRSTER and TUWIM, *Beiträg. Geophys.*, *Ergeb. kos. Phys.*, **1**; 87–179, 1931.

[3] *Amer. Phys. Teacher*, **7**; 79, 1939.

[4] *Phys. Zeit.*, **5**; 135 and 499, 1904.

pressure, and its diffusion by winds and by convection. Lenard[1] ascribed the normal gradient largely to the positive charging of the air by the spray of ocean waves. S. K. Banerji[2] gives strong experimental support to the same idea. Swann,[3] however, has shown that all theories of this kind are inadequate because, among other reasons, convection is too slow to get the positive ions well up in the atmosphere, where they are known to exist abundantly, before being neutralized by the negative earth-air current.

Since the atmosphere is all the time more or less ionized, it seems reasonable to suggest, as many have done, that particles of any appreciable size falling through it would leave it positively charged, owing to the higher velocity and, therefore, likelier capture of the negative ions. This theory is weakened by the fact that, on the whole, more positive electricity appears to be brought down by rain and snow than negative. On the other hand, much negatively charged rain does fall, and some, at least, of that which is positively charged on reaching the earth may be so owing to the mechanical capture of ions of both classes in its course through the air, in which the volume charge normally is positive. Then, too, the large, or Langevin, ions that settle slowly are more numerously negative than positive. The idea, therefore, that the conduction current of negative electricity, away from the earth, may be largely balanced by a gravity return has not yet been conclusively refuted.

Since both the earth and the upper atmosphere, 50 kilometers above the surface, say, and far beyond, are excellent conductors in comparison with the lower air, they constitute a fairly good, even if somewhat leaky, condenser. Presumably, earth and upper air each promptly distributes world wide every charge it receives, except in so far as it may be bound by a localized charge in the intervening dielectric, or lower, air.

This dielectric between the condenser plates contains about 1800 thunderstorms all the time, and is ruptured by, roughly, 100 lightning discharges every second. And since only 1 in 10, perhaps, of these discharges is to the earth, it appears likely that many of them are diffusely to the upper air that is so richly ionized—presumably by insolation. Furthermore, since the charges in a thunderstorm often get separated by winds, or otherwise, with their ions in great measure immobilized by attachment to cloud particles, it seems possible that their separate actions on the conducting upper air render it relatively rich in positive ions, and poor in negative, as the latter, being the more mobile, are the easier pulled down. Evidently, there also is a tendency to produce the same electrical unbalance in the air below the clouds, but this is relatively ineffective owing to poor conductivity. When the cloud droplets

[1] *Ann. Phys.*, **46**; 584, 1892.

[2] *Ind. J. Phys.*, **12**; 409, 1938.

[3] *Terr. Mag.*, **20**; 105, 1915.

evaporate, their charges remain, but, presumably, now attached to the condensation nuclei, which thus become gross ions that, with excess negative charges, slowly settle by gravity to the earth.

In some such manner, perhaps, as here outlined, thunderstorms mainly have established, and maintain, a potential difference of about 1,000,000 volts between the earth and the highly ionized region of the upper air—a difference that is small in comparison with those locally and temporarily produced by these storms within the dielectric between the conducting plates and that cause lightning discharges.

This concept may be very erroneous, but from it practically every important observational fact about atmospheric electricity, such as inverse relation of conductivity and potential gradient, effects of dust, fogs, wind, cloud, time of day, etc., may be deduced. It is, therefore, at least an aid to the memory.

If we insist that gravity actions, such as the falling of rain, bring to the earth more positive electricity than negative, as many observations indicate, and hold with Simpson that lightning usually is positive from cloud to earth, and, finally, that most of the brush discharges from grounded objects are of negative electricity, a comforting explanation, then, is not so easy to find.

But even under these, or practically these, adverse conditions, theories have been evolved, especially the penetrating radiation theory of Swann,[1] in which it is assumed that incoming radiation of high penetrating power not only produces ionization, as it is known to do, but also drives violently forward the electrons it detaches. In this way, it is assumed, the earth is kept negatively charged to such value that the resulting conduction current is, on the average, equal and opposite to the downward driven corpuscular current.

Evidently, then, the maintenance of the earth's electric charge still is the great problem in atmospheric electricity, but it should not, and probably will not, remain so, much longer.

Wormell[2] estimates from measurements made near Cambridge, England, that in the course of a year the surface of the earth in that region obtains, per square kilometer, from:

Fine weather currents............................ + 60 coulombs
Precipitation.................................... + 20 coulombs
Lightning.. − 20 coulombs
Point discharges, mainly under storm clouds........ −100 coulombs

This, he suggests, summed up for the whole world, may account for the earth's prevailingly negative charge. However, his estimates are admittedly very rough, and so the problem of the earths charge is not yet fully solved.

[1] *J. Franklin Inst.*, **188**; 577, 1919.
[2] *Proc. Roy. Soc.*, **127**; 567, 1930.

CHAPTER II

AURORA POLARIS

The aurora polaris is a well-known but imperfectly understood luminous phenomenon of the upper atmosphere, of which Figs. 142 and 143, from Störmer's numerous photographs, are good examples.

Types.—While no two auroras are exactly alike, several types have been recognized, such as arcs, bands, rays, curtains or draperies, coronas, luminous patches, and diffuse glows. All these are well shown in the "Photographic Atlas of Auroral Forms," Oslo, 1930. The arcs normal to the magnetic meridian, often, but not always, reach the horizon. Their under edge is rather sharply defined, so that, by contrast, the adjacent portion of the sky appears exceptionally dark. The rays, sometimes extending upward from an arch, at other times isolated, are parallel to the lines of magnetic force. Many auroras are quiescent, others exceedingly changeable, flitting from side to side like wandering searchlights, and, in some cases, even waving like giant tongues of flame.

Latitude Variation.—The aurora of the northern hemisphere occurs most frequently, about 100 per year, at the latitudes 60° (over the North Atlantic and North America) to 70° (off the coast of Siberia). Its frequency appears to be less within this boundary, while with decrease of latitude it falls off so rapidly that, even in southern Europe, it is a rare phenomenon. At the same latitude it is distinctly more frequent in North America than in either Europe or Asia.

The distribution of auroras in the southern hemisphere is not so well known, but it appears to be similar, in general, to that of the northern.

Periodicity.—It is well established that, on the average, auroras are more numerous during years of sun spot maxima than during years of spot minima. They also appear to be more numerous before midnight than after. Relations of frequency to phase of the moon, season, etc., have also been discussed, but with no conclusive results.

Color.—Many auroras are practically white. Red, yellow, and green, are also common auroral colors. Some streaks and bands are reddish through their lower (northern) portion, then yellowish, and, finally, greenish through the higher portions. Much of the light is owing to nitrogen and oxygen bands, none to the hydrogen lines, while the "auroral line" $\lambda5577.350A$,[1] the brightest of all, is due to atomic

[1] BABCOCK, *Astrophys. J.*, **57**; 217, 1923.

FIG. 142.—Aurora, Feb. 28, 1910.   (*Störmer.*)

FIG. 143.—Aurora, Mar. 3, 1910.   (*Störmer.*)

oxygen,[1] presumably, in a special state, and, probably, is intensified by the presence of helium. The line λ5206, occasionally seen, has been attributed by V. M. Slipher and L. A. Sommer[2] to the neutral nitrogen atom.

There is good evidence that this green light, the light that produces the "auroral line," is always present in the sky, though whether wholly of auroral origin, or due, in part, to bombardment by meteoric dust, or to some other cause, is not known.

Height.—The problem of the height of auroras has been fully solved. By simultaneously photographing the same aurora from two stations against a common background of stars (Fig. 144), and measuring the

Fig. 144.—Parallactic auroral photographs for determining altitude. (*Störmer.*)

parallax obtained Störmer,[3] and Vegard and Krogness[4] have secured many excellent height measurements. The upper limits of strong auroral light vary from, about, 100 kilometers to over 300 kilometers; and the lower limits from, perhaps, 85 kilometers to 170 kilometers, with two well-defined maxima, one at 100 kilometers, the other at 106 kilometers. Recently, Störmer[5] has found diffuse auroras extending to heights of over 1000 kilometers. He also finds[6] that auroras of great height over 400 kilometers, seem to occur only in sunshine.

Cause.—The fact that brilliant shifting auroras are accompanied by magnetic storms renders it practically certain that they, and presumably therefore all auroras, are due to electric discharges; and the further fact, that they vary in frequency with the sunspot period, indicates that this current either comes from, or is induced by, the sun.

[1] McLennan and Shrum, *Proc. Roy. Soc.*, **108**; 501, 1925.

[2] *Am. Astronom. Soc. Pub.*, **6**; 280, 1931.

[3] *Terr. Mag. and Atmos. Elec.*, **21**; 157, 1916.

[4] *Terr. Mag. and Atmos. Elec.*, **21**; 169, 1916.

[5] *Beitr. Geophys.*, **17**; 254, 1927.

[6] *Nature*, **120**; 329, 1927.

All mid-latitude auroras, or, at least, all the strong ones, are accompanied by magnetic storms; those of the auroral belt may or may not be so accompanied. For some time, it was thought probable that auroras are caused by negative particles shot off from the sun, and entrapped by the magnetic field of the earth. On the other hand, Vegard[1] has given strong arguments in favor of the α particle which is positively charged, and Störmer[2] has found at least one case that required the positive charge to account for the observed magnetic disturbance. Still later, Vegard and Krogness,[3] and Vegard,[4] found much evidence that, at least, most auroral forms are caused by negative electrons, or β rays. Ultraviolet radiation

Fig. 145.—Auroral corona. (*Störmer.*)

and photoradiation also have each been championed as the cause of the aurora, but in neither case has the argument been generally accepted. Auroras, then, appear most likely to be due to α and β rays in widely varying proportions in the upper atmosphere, shot off from the sun.

The seeming convergence of the auroral rays on a point far short of the magnetic pole, toward which they actually do converge, is due to perspective. Similarly, their apparent divergence from the magnetic zenith, thus forming a corona (Fig. 145), also is a phenomenon of perspective, for here one is looking out along a bundle, or tube, of rays that, following the lines of magnetic force, surround him in every direc-

[1] *Phil. Mag.*, **23**; 211, 1912; *Ann. Phys.*, **50**; 853, 1916.
[2] *Terr. Mag. and Atmos. Elec.*, **20**; 1, 1915.
[3] The Position in space of the Aurora Polaris," Kristiania, 1920.
[4] *Phil. Mag.*, **42**; 47, 1921.

tion. The rapid, upward pulses of light along these rays, however, are quite real, and due, presumably, to progressive electric discharges.

Most of the auroral literature, and it is voluminous, is just talk, but for reliable and detailed information on this subject the best single source is the *Geofysiske Publikasjoner*, issued by the Norwegian Academy of Sciences at Oslo. However, all literature on this subject has been well summed up by E. W. Hewson.[1]

[1] *Rev. Mod. Phys.*, **9**; 403, 1937.

PART III
METEOROLOGICAL ACOUSTICS

CHAPTER I

METEOROLOGICAL EFFECTS ON SOUND

Introduction.—Meteorological acoustics is concerned with every sound of a distinctly meteorological origin, such as the humming of telegraph wires, the "roaring of the mountain," the rumbling of thunder, and the like; and with every effect meteorological conditions have on the travel, distribution, and audibility of sound. In short, it treats of meteorological sounds and of meteorological effects on sound.

Nature of Sound.—The term "sound," as used in the science of acoustics, means either an external disturbance or a sense impression. In the more restricted field of meteorological acoustics, it has only the former of these meanings; the sensation being referred to, merely, as evidence of the presence and nature of a disturbance in the external medium.

Now, everyone knows: (*a*) by observation, that a tuning fork, bell, violin string, and the like, produce sound only when vibrating; (*b*) by observation, that the hammer is seen to strike, the gun go off, the lightning flash, and innumerable other abrupt causes of sound to occur, before the sound itself is heard, and that this time interval increases with the distance of the observer; (*c*) by experiment, that the sound of a bell, say, mounted on an acoustical insulator within an air pump receiver, grows fainter and fainter to extinction as the exhaustion of the receiver is progressively increased.

From these three facts it is obvious that objective sound, or sound in its physical aspect, consists of traveling disturbances of some kind in a material medium. If this medium is the atmosphere (or any other fluid), it is further obvious that the disturbances in question consist of compressions and rarefactions, for the atmosphere has no tendency to recover from distortion of any kind save that of volume, alone—no tendency to recover from twist or bend, but a resistance to change of volume that increases with the ratio of that change to the initial volume.

Seeing Sound.—Since sound consists of condensations and rarefactions of the atmosphere traveling outward from the source, and since light is unequally refracted by air of different density, it would seem possible to see, and perhaps even to photograph, the front of a sound pulse. And, indeed, this has often been realized. The outermost sound shell, produced by the firing of a cannon, for instance, has repeatedly been seen sweeping across the sky and over clouds, like a narrow fleeting shadow. Similarly, the initial condensation wave, caused by an electric spark, has given numerous beautiful and instructive photographs, of which Fig. 146, from Dr. Foley's remarkable collection,[1] showing both the primary wave and its reflection from a flat surface, is an excellent example.

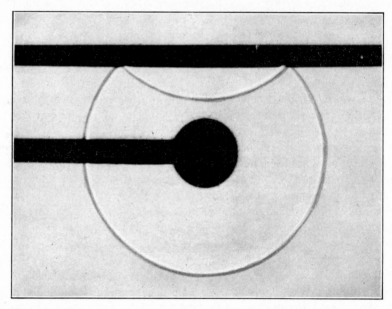

Fig. 146.—Photograph of sound waves—incident and reflected.   (*A. L. Foley.*)

VELOCITY OF SOUND

Velocity of Sound in Still Air.—As stated above, many simple observations show that sound travels through the air with moderate velocity—faster than a mile a minute, and slower than a mile a second. Just what this velocity is, might be determined by careful experiment over a large range of temperatures, pressures, humidities, and other factors, and its relation to each, empirically determined. But, while this has been done to some extent, the collection of an adequate amount of such data would require long and tedious work and the results, in the end, would be only empirical and not rational. Hence, it seems desirable logically to derive equations that show the exact and necessary relation of the velocity of sound to each of the several factors upon which it depends.

[1] *Phys. Rev.*, **35**; 373, 1912.

The following method of computing sound velocity is essentially that of Rankine.[1] It may not be so mathematically elegant as the "velocity potential" method, used by Lord Rayleigh,[2] for instance, but it has the great advantage of revealing, rather than concealing, the physical processes involved.

Consider an ordinary sound wave (great explosions which result in additions to the atmosphere, and, hence, require a modified treatment, are excluded) at some distance from its origin, traveling through the atmosphere. As above explained, this disturbance must consist of longitudinal motions of the air particles in the line of travel of the sound, resulting in alternate compressions and rarefactions. This follows from the fact that the atmosphere is elastic only to changes of volume and not to twists or bends. Furthermore, it is clear that these sound excursions of the air particles are small—not even leaves visibly quiver as any ordinary sound passes—and the pressure changes comparatively slight, too slight indeed to be felt.

Clearly, an atmospheric wave of any form, harmonic or otherwise, can be made to progress unchanged through air at any given speed, by applying to each particle a proper external force, directed along the line of travel, in addition to the internal force already acting on it.

Let the external force be X per square centimeter in the direction of propagation, that is, per square centimeter of a plane wave front over which, of course, all particles are in the same vibration phase, and, hence, subject to exactly equal forces; and let X vary in such manner from phase to phase as to keep the form of the wave unchanged and to give it a uniform velocity v. To further simplify the problem, consider an imaginary tube of unit cross-section, parallel to the line of propagation and extending through the wave front slightly into the undisturbed region on one side, and more or less into the disturbed region on the other. Let this tube be fixed in position, and let the atmosphere flow past it exactly opposite in direction to that of the sound propagation. That is, let the sound waves or that arbitrary portion of a single one, within the tube, though continuously affecting new material, be absolutely fixed in position and condition.

What, under these circumstances, are the relations between the forces involved, internal and external, and the deductions therefrom?

Since the quantity and state of the air within the tube is constant, it is obvious that its momentum is also constant, and also, under the given conditions, wholly along the line of propagation. Hence, the momentum entering the front of the tube during a given interval, one second, say, is equal to the momentum leaving it during the same interval. This momentum *per second* consists of two parts, (*a*) the mass entering,

---

[1] *Phil. Trans.*, **160**; 277, 1870.
[2] "Theory of Sound," **2**; 15.

or leaving, per second, times its velocity, and (b) the pressure upon this mass at the place of entrance or exit, respectively—force is equal to mass times acceleration, which is equal to momentum produced per second in the direction of the force.

Let, now, P be the pressure in the undisturbed atmosphere, and hence at the front end of the tube; $P \pm p$ the pressure at the rear end of the tube (p being either positive or negative, owing to whether this end of the tube is in the compression or rarefaction portion, respectively, of the wave); v the velocity of entry of air of density ρ into the tube; $v \mp u$ and ρ_1 the velocity and density, respectively, of the air as it leaves the tube; and X the assumed sustaining external pressure, constant at each particular phase, and thus constant at the exit end of the tube.

Hence, the momentum entering the tube of unit cross-section per second is, if m is the mass

$$mv + P.$$

Similarly, the momentum leaving the tube per second is, since the mass within the tube cannot change,

$$m \, (v \mp u) + P \pm p + X.$$

But the two momenta are equal therefore

$$mu = \rho v u = p \pm X.$$

If, now, $X = 0$

$$\rho v = \frac{p}{u},$$

and the sound moves on without the aid of any external force with the velocity

$$v = \frac{p}{\rho u}. \tag{1}$$

As above explained,

$$\rho_1 \, (v \mp u) = \rho v,$$

and, if the air remains isothermal, ρ_1 is given by

$$\frac{(P \pm p)}{\rho_1} = \frac{P}{\rho}.$$

Hence, neglecting pu, the product of two relatively small terms,

$$u = \frac{pv}{P}$$

and, substituting in equation (1),

$$v = \sqrt{\frac{P}{\rho}}. \tag{Newton}$$

Or, if the compressional changes take place adiabatically,

$$\frac{(P \pm p)}{P} = \left(\frac{\rho_1}{\rho}\right)^k$$

in which k is the ratio of the specific heat of the air involved at constant pressure to its specific heat at constant volume; and

$$v = \sqrt{\frac{kP}{\rho}}. \qquad \text{(Laplace)}$$

Whether the velocity of sound is in accordance with Newton's equation, or Laplace's, or has, indeed, some distinctly intermediate value (it cannot be outside these theoretical extremes) can, of course, be tested by direct experiment. But here, too, theory is a great help in that it shows[1] the impossibility of a velocity appreciably different from one or the other of the extremes. The non-mathematical form of this reasoning (Stokes gives both) is substantially as follows:

Let an airtight, frictionless, piston oscillate so slowly in a cylinder with thermally conducting walls that the temperature of the enclosed air remains constant. Clearly, then, at each given position of the piston the pressure is the same during expansion as during compression, and the process is without net loss, or gain, of energy. Similarly, if the reciprocal motion of the piston is so rapid that no heat is lost during compression, nor gained during expansion, the pressure, though different from its former value, is again constant for each given position of the piston, and, hence, the total external work zero per cycle.

If, however, the speed of the piston is such that some heat is passed, but not enough to maintain a constant temperature, the pressure at each point will be greater during compression than during expansion, and the process can be maintained only at the expense of external work. Under these conditions, therefore, the sound would be damped out far more rapidly than is the case in nature.

Actually, sound waves are so fleeting (only those of the baser tones require more than one-hundredth of a second to pass) that the slight pressure changes they produce are all but absolutely adiabatic. Hence, to an extremely close approximation,

$$v = \sqrt{\frac{kP}{\rho}} = \sqrt{\frac{1.40P}{\rho}}. \qquad (2)$$

It should be noted, here, that since neither u, p, nor ρ_1, the only factors affected by either the amplitude or frequency of the vibrating air, enter into equation (2), therefore the velocity of sound is independent alike of both loudness and pitch—the same for all sounds of whatever origin.

Relation of Sound Velocity to Condition of Air.—From equation (2) it is likewise clear that all meteorological changes that alter the value of k, or the ratio of P to ρ, or both, affect also the velocity of sound; and that it is independent of every other such change.

[1] STOKES, *Phil. Mag.*, 1; 305, 1851.

Changes in pressure, therefore, do not alter the velocity of sound. They obviously do not affect the value of k, and, by proportionately varying ρ, leave the ratio of P to ρ constant. On the other hand, variations in the temperature do affect the velocity of sound. In fact, this velocity is directly proportional to the square root of the absolute temperature T as is obvious from the fact that when P and k are constant (k constant implies same composition), ρ is inversely proportional to T. Similarly, changes in the absolute humidity also affect the velocity of sound, since they slightly alter the value of k.

The value of k for dry air is 1.40, very closely. Its value for water vapor is not accurately known for ordinary outdoor temperatures, but appears to be 1.30, roughly. Presumably, therefore, in nature

$$k = \frac{1.40 - 0.1e}{P}$$

approximately, in which P is the total atmospheric pressure and e that portion of it due to water vapor.

In terms of the reading of the barometer

$$P = Bg\delta, \; e = wg\delta$$

in which B is the reduced total height of the barometer, w the reduced height due to the water vapor, g and δ the standard gravity acceleration and mercury density, respectively.

Finally, if ρ_0 is the density of dry air at 0° C. and when the reduced height of the barometer is 760 mm., then

$$\rho = \rho_0 \frac{(B - 0.378w)}{760(1 + at)}$$

in which a is the coefficient of gas expansion per degree Centigrade at 0° C., and t the temperature, as read on the Centigrade scale.

On substituting these several values in the equation for the velocity of sound it appears that, in terms of centimeters per second,

$$v = \sqrt{\frac{76gB\delta(1 + at)\left(1.40 - 0.1\dfrac{w}{B}\right)}{\rho_0(B - 0.378w)}}.$$

For dry air at 0° C. this reduces to

$$v = \sqrt{\frac{76g\delta(1.40)}{\rho_0}} = \sqrt{\frac{76 \times 980.665 \times 13.5951 \times 1.40}{0.0012930}},$$

or 331.23 meters per second, which is in close agreement with observations.

The effect of dust, smoke, fog, or any other such foreign substance in the atmosphere, on the velocity of sound is not well known. Presumably, however, the values of both k and ρ, and through them the velocity in question, are altered by all such things. But as the aggregate mass of any such substance is invariably quite small in comparison to that of the atmosphere in which it floats, and since it plays the rôle of a gas to only a limited extent, its effect on this velocity must always be minute, and for most purposes entirely negligible.

Doppler Effect.—Many, if not most of us, have often noticed the change in the pitch of a locomotive whistle, or bell, as the train passed rapidly by us; and also the similar change in pitch of a bell, or other sounding object, as we were carried rapidly past it. This phenomenon, known as the Doppler effect, and dependent on the finite velocity of sound, is easily explained.

Let v be the sound velocity; n the vibration frequency, λ the wavelength, and u the velocity of the sounding body toward, or from, the stationary hearer. If u is zero,

$$\lambda = \frac{v}{n}, \text{ and } n = \frac{v}{\lambda}.$$

If the sounding object is approaching the hearer the resulting wave length λ_1 and frequency n_1 clearly are given by the relations

$$\lambda_1 = \frac{v - u}{n} = \frac{v}{n_1},$$

and

$$n_1 = \frac{nv}{v - u}.$$

Similarly, if the sounding object is receding from the observer,

$$\lambda_2 = \frac{v + u}{n} = \frac{v}{n_2},$$

and

$$n_2 = \frac{nv}{v + u}.$$

Hence,

$$n : n_1 : n_2 = 1 : \frac{v}{v - u} : \frac{v}{v + u}.$$

That is, the pitch is highest when the sounding object is approaching, and lowest when it is receding.

If, then, the sounding body were on a train, say, making 47 miles per hour, the pitch, as perceived by a person at rest near the track, would drop approximately from G (approaching) to F (receding) on the musical scale.

If, however, the hearer is moving with the velocity w and the sounding object is at rest, on approaching the body

$$n_1 = \frac{v + w}{\lambda},$$

and on leaving it,

$$n_2 = \frac{v - w}{\lambda}.$$

Hence, in this case

$$n:n_1:n_2 = v:v + w:v - w.$$

If both object and hearer are in motion the expressions for the pitch ratios are only a little more complex—no new principle is involved.

Sound Perception in the Inverse Order of Sound Production.— Another interesting consequence of the moderate velocity of sound propagation is the occasional perception of sounds in the inverse order of their production. This is especially noticeable in the case of high velocity cannon shells passing close by, or over, one from a considerable distance. Such projectiles often have double the velocity of sound. Hence, the first thing heard is the whine of the shell, then its explosion, perhaps, and, last of all, the firing of the cannon; or, the explosion may be heard last, if far to the rear. All this is obvious when it is recalled that the shell is continuously producing sound far in advance of the initial wave front from the cannon.

It is also interesting to note that when the source moves faster than sound, as do cannon shells, the wave front envelop is a cone whose vertex is at the source, and whose angular opening α is given by the equation

$$\sin \frac{\alpha}{2} = \frac{v}{s},$$

in which v and s are the velocities of sound and of the shell, respectively.

Velocity of Intense Sounds.—Whenever a sound is produced by a violent explosion, such as by the firing of a cannon, the blast itself drives through the air and gives to the sound a velocity which at first, that is, so long as X in the general velocity equation is real and positive, is in excess of that which applies when X is zero.

This excess velocity, however, occurs only relatively near the source of the sound, and rapidly decreases with increase of distance from that source. That is, the external force X is soon reduced to a negligible quantity, after which the velocity becomes constant with the value appropriate to $X = 0$.

SOUND REFLECTION

Reflection by a Rigid Surface.—As above explained, all sounds in the atmosphere are propagated in the form of successive compressions and rarefactions. If, therefore, these air waves should impinge normally on a wall of stone, or other dense material, it is obvious that they could not pass on unaltered. If the wall is absolutely unyielding, a condition solid and liquid boundaries more or less approach with respect to slight variations of atmospheric pressure, evidently the adjacent molecules cannot oscillate in the line of propagation. The pressure actions, then, of the wall on the atmosphere are precisely the same as they would be if it, and not the air, were vibrating with the given period and amplitude.

Hence, sound waves incident on an absolutely rigid wall are wholly reflected, and in such a manner that the surface of this wall is a place of minimum (zero) motion—the incident and the reflected wave having always exactly the same phase at the boundary.

Reflections at a Free Surface.—The effect on sound of a medium of the opposite rigidity extreme, that is, infinitely yielding, such as empty space, is also interesting, though not realizable in the case of the atmosphere. Here the incident compression tends to drive the boundary molecules of the first medium away; if, however, they are restrained from flying off, as is the free end of a vibrating rope, say, or the surface of a liquid, this restraint must be of the nature of a tension. In this way the flux of incident energy is reversed in direction—the waves are reflected. Furthermore, since change of pressure is impossible at a free boundary, the incident waves always have exactly opposite phases at the boundary reflecting surface.

Reflection at an Air Interface.—Let the boundary be between masses of air at the same pressure, but of unequal density, owing to difference

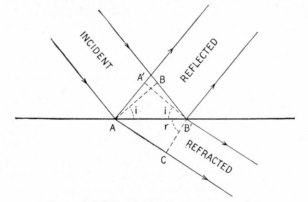

Fig. 147.—Reflection and refraction of sound.

in temperature, or humidity, or both. This case is of especial importance, since it includes the problems of internal atmospheric reflections, and of reflections from fogs and clouds.

Here, too, as in so many other acoustical problems, the most general treatment is given in Lord Rayleigh's "Theory of Sound." But the physical significance of each step in this elegant analysis is, perhaps, not easy to visualise. Hence, a more obvious course of reasoning will be followed, based on Fresnel's theory of the reflection of polarized light.[1]

If none of the energy of the incident sound waves is transformed into heat at the boundary (and there is no evidence of any such transformation) clearly, all of it must be contained jointly in the reflected and the refracted waves.

[1] FRESNEL, "Oeuvres," **1**; 649–653; PRESTON, "Theory of Light."

The laws of the reflection and refraction of sound in still media are the same as those of light. They are given below, but assumed here for convenience.

Let, then, the incident, reflected, and refracted waves be as indicated in Fig. 147; let their amplitudes be a, b, and c, respectively; let the velocity in the first medium be v, and in the second v'; and let the densities of these media be ρ and ρ', respectively. Then, since the energy in the incident wave is divided between the reflected and the refracted waves without loss, and, in each case, is proportional to the volume affected, obviously, and to the square of the respective amplitudes as immediately explained below,

$$v\rho a^2 = v\rho b^2 + v'\rho'c^2 \frac{\cos r}{\cos i}.$$

in which i is the angle of incidence and r the angle of refraction.

To show, as just assumed, that sound energy is proportional to the square of the amplitude, let f be the restorative, or elastic, force; a the amplitude (extreme displacement of a particle from its position of rest) and w the work of displacement. Now, f is proportional to the compression, that is, to the displacement x, say. Hence,

$$dw = f dx$$

but

$$f = kx,$$

k being a constant, and

$$w = k \int_o^a x dx = \frac{k}{2}a^2.$$

Now, $v/v' = \sin i/\sin r$; hence,

$$\rho(a^2 - b^2) \sin 2i = \rho'c^2 \sin 2r.$$

Also, as above explained,

$$\left(\frac{\rho'}{\rho}\right)^{\frac{1}{2}} = \frac{v}{v'} = \frac{\sin i}{\sin r}.$$

Therefore,

$$a^2 - b^2 = c^2 \tan i \cot r.$$

Furthermore, if there is no slipping between the media at their interface, and it seems impossible that there can be, to an appreciable extent, then the algebraic sum of a and b must equal c, or algebraically

$$a + b = c.$$

Hence,

$$a - b = c \tan i \cot r$$

$$b = -a \frac{\sin (i - r)}{\sin (i + r)} = -a \frac{\left\{\left(\frac{\rho'}{\rho}\right)^{\frac{1}{2}} - \frac{\cos i}{\cos r}\right\}}{\left(\frac{\rho'}{\rho}\right)^{\frac{1}{2}} + \frac{\cos i}{\cos r}}$$

and

$$c = \frac{2a \cos i \sin r}{\sin (i + r)} = \frac{2a \cos i}{\left(\dfrac{\rho'}{\rho}\right)^{\frac{1}{2}} \cos r + \cos i}.$$

If, then, sound waves in a clear atmosphere, say, should impinge normally on a fog bank, or a cloud, in which the density of the air at the same pressure is one per cent less—a possible ratio owing to differences in temperature and humidity—the energies in the incident, reflected, and transmitted (refracted), waves will have to each other the following ratios, approximately:

$$v\rho a^2 : v\rho b^2 : v'\rho' c^2 = 160,000 : 1 : 159,999.$$

In making this calculation the small correction due to differences between the specific heats of the two masses was neglected.

If the angle of incidence is not zero, as just assumed, but of considerable size, the reflection obviously is greater, but still small for any angle up to nearly 90°. If, for instance, $i = 80°$ and $\rho'/\rho = 99/100$, as above assumed,

$$v\rho a^2 : v\rho b^2 = 100 : 1,$$

roughly. Clearly, then, reflection from fogs and clouds, or at any sharp boundary of sufficient size (greater than wave-length dimensions) between masses of air at the same pressure but of unequal density, varies from a very small value at normal incidence up to total reflection at

$$i = \sin^{-1} \left(\frac{\rho'}{\rho}\right)^{\frac{1}{2}}.$$

If, as above, $\rho'/\rho = 99/100$,

$$i = 84° \ 15', \text{ nearly.}$$

Hence, a small number of successive total reflections—not likely to occur, though conceivable—might greatly change the direction of the sound.

If the change in density is gradual through a distance of many wave lengths—if the medium has no definite boundary—reflection is practically absent, as the equations show. For instance, there can be no reflection of sound from the gradually attenuating upper layers of the atmosphere, as demonstrated by Lord Rayleigh.[1] The energy is maintained through increase of amplitude with decrease of density, except as reduced, as it all finally is, by viscosity, to heat.

Laws of Sound Reflection.—By careful experiment it has been determined that sound is reflected according to exactly the same laws as those that apply to light, namely:

[1] *Phil. Mag.*, **29**; 173, 1890.

1. The normal, at any point of the reflecting surface, and the directions of incidence, and of reflection at the foot of this normal, all lie in a common plane.

2. If the reflecting surface is flat and its every diameter large in comparison with the wave length, the reflection is regular; that is, the angle of reflection (angle between the direction of reflection and the normal to the surface at the point of reflection) is equal to the angle of incidence.

3. Surfaces with less than wave length diameters do not regularly reflect sound, but merely scatter or diffuse it.

Echo.—It is well known that in the neighborhood of a flat, vertical wall of some size a loudly spoken word, or brief sentence, often is twice, intelligibly, heard; the first time, as coming straight from the speaker, and the second, as if coming from some invisible person in the direction of the wall. This latter sound is the familiar echo (nymph of the poets who pined away until only her voice was left) due to reflection by the wall of the incident condensations and rarefactions in the atmosphere. Parallel walls facing each other, the walls of a canyon, for instance, and separated a few hundred feet, may so reflect and re-reflect the same sound as to cause it to be distinctly heard again and again, through a long fading series. If the reflecting wall is quite irregular, or, especially, if there are walls of various shapes and distances on all sides, the multiplicity of echoes becomes jumbled into a continuous, unintelligible reverberation, a phenomenon most pronounced, perhaps, in certain caves—and auditoriums.

There are, of course, many natural phenomena due to echo, or sound reflection. Some of the more interesting are: (a) the discrete single echo; (b) the discrete multiple echo; (c) the overlapping multiple echo—reverberation; (d) the diffuse echo; due to scattering of the sound by many relatively small objects; (e) the harmonic echo; due to the greater scattering of an overtone than of the fundamental by small objects—the intensity of scattered sound, like that of light, being inversely proportional to the fourth power of the wave length; (f) the musical echo; due to reflection from, or scattering by, a series of objects, such as stair-steps, spaced at uniformly increasing distances from the source.

Obviously, a single sound impulse, such as the crack of a whip, a clap of the hand, and the like, in front of a flight of steps, or just beyond, and a little to one side of, a row of palings, will be scattered by the successive steps, or palings, respectively, in a series of regularly spaced similar pulses. Hence, the "echo" thus produced of any sound pulse is a musical note whose pitch depends not on the parent sound, but on the spacing of the palings or width of stair treads, as the case may be, and position of the observer.

If s is the spacing of the pickets, or distance from center of one to the center of the next, along the path of propagation of the incident sound;

and if the origin of the parent sound impulse is nearly in line with the row of pickets, then the distance between the sound impulses, or wave length l, due to any few successive pickets, is given by the equation

$$l = s(1 + \cos \theta)$$

in which θ is the angle, at the pickets in question, between the origin and observer.

An observer, therefore, at the source, which, as above explained, is beyond the row of pickets and a little to one side, hears a distinctly musical echo of each sharp sound pulse; since at his place the value of cos θ is very nearly the same, unity, for all the pickets, and, hence, the pitch substantially constant. If, however, the observer is off from the middle of a long straight row of palings, and the source of the impulse is located as before, cos θ will vary from nearly -1 to nearly $+1$, and the echo heard sweep down from the inaudible through a considerable range of the shriller notes.

SOUND REFRACTION

Sound Refraction in Still Air of Uniform Temperature.—The direction of propagation of sound is abruptly changed whenever it passes obliquely from one to another mass of air at the same pressure but of different density. This is owing to the fact that the velocity depends on the density, as above explained.

If both masses are quiet and equally humid, the velocity of propagation is inversely proportional to the square root of the density. If then i is the angle of incidence in the air whose density is ρ and r the angle of refraction in the air whose density is ρ', the change in direction, as indicated in Fig. 147, is the difference between i and the corresponding value of r as given by the equation

$$\sin r = \sin i \left(\frac{\rho}{\rho'}\right)^{\frac{1}{2}}.$$

The laws of refraction in this case are identical with those of light, namely:

1. The normal, at any point of the refracting surface and the directions of incidence and of refraction at the foot of this normal all lie in a common plane.

2. The sine of the angle of refraction (angle between the direction of refraction and the normal to the surface at the point of refraction) is to the sine of the angle of incidence as the velocity in the refracting medium is to the velocity in the incident medium; or, inversely, as the square roots of the densities of the respective media, or, directly, as the square roots of their absolute temperatures.

Spread of Sound.—Since the velocity of sound in an atmosphere of homogeneous composition is, as previously explained, directly proportional to the square root of the absolute temperature, and since the atmosphere, when at rest, frequently is horizontally stratified with respect to temperature, it follows that sound cannot always spread in precisely the same manner.

Special cases are interesting:

a. Temperature uniform, air quiet and of constant composition. Under these conditions, which, however, never exist, sound would spread uniformly in every direction.

b. Temperature decreasing uniformly with elevation, air quiet and of constant composition.   These conditions often are approximately fulfilled through a considerable depth of the atmosphere.   They evidently give an oblate ellipsoidal sound shell, with the shorter axis, axis of rotation, vertical.   If the origin is on a horizontal surface, the wave front tends to incline upward, owing to the greater velocity in the lowest and warmest air, and, hence, the sound tends to become faint, or even lost, at points on this surface.

Fig. 148.—Sound confined to an inversion layer.

c. Temperature increasing upwards (temperature inversion), air quiet and of constant composition—conditions that obtain over land on a typical frost night and over water on summer nights especially.

Let the surface be an indefinite plane, such as the surface of a large frozen lake, and let the temperature be 0° C. at the surface and increase rapidly, with elevation, to a maximum of 6° C. at, say, 20 meters elevation, and let a sound be produced near the surface.

The velocity of sound, since it varies as the square root of the absolute temperature, will therefore be about one-one-hundredth greater at the top of this inversion layer (layer through which temperature increases with elevation) than at the surface.   Hence, total reflection will occur for all sound leaving the source between the angles i and $\pi/2$ to the vertical; i being determined by the equation

$$\sin i = \frac{100}{101} \sin 90°,$$

from which $i = 82°$, about.

Hence, the whole volume of sound leaving the source S (Fig. 148), within a horizontal toroidal wedge of angle θ (16° in this case) is confined, by refraction above and reflection below, to the surface layer of 20 meters depth.   At times this inversion layer is much shallower, but whatever its thickness it is, acoustically, a "speaking disk" in which the intensity of sound is inversely proportional, roughly, to the first power only of the distance.   This explains why sounds often carry surprisingly far on still, clear nights.

As a further illustration of this phenomenon let the temperature inversion occur over a river whose banks are free of trees and steep, or canyon-like. Here, not only the vertically spreading sound is constrained to a shallow layer, as above explained, but also, the horizontally spreading portion is roughly confined to the course of the river by reflection from the banks. That is, the river is one wall of a gigantic "speaking tube" through which sounds occasionally are heard at amazing distances.

d. Temperature rapidly decreasing upward for a few meters, air quiet and of constant composition. Under these unstable conditions sounds travel appreciably faster near the surface than at some distance above it. Hence, sounds originating within, or but little above, this relatively high temperature surface layer may pass entirely over one's head, even as close as 100 meters to the source, owing to the greater

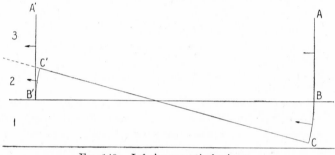

Fig. 149.—Inferior acoustical mirage.

velocities of the lower portions of the sound waves, in proportion to the square roots of the absolute temperatures, and the consequent upward inclination and propagation of these portions of the wave fronts.

Under the given conditions in the lower air and with an approximately constant temperature through the next layer above, a sound front may be shaped substantially as shown at ABC (Fig. 149), and, if so, it must later develop into the front $A'B'C'$. Owing to refraction CC' will not be quite straight, but may be so drawn to represent the general results.

Clearly, then, under the given conditions a person in region 1 will hear only a faint sound, if any at all; at 2 he will hear two identical sounds, probably more or less out of phase, one from the direction of the actual source as given by the undistorted wave front $A'B'$, and the other apparently from some point more or less below the actual source, as indicated by the front $B'C'$. At 3 only one sound is heard, namely, the undisturbed original, and, of course, in its true direction.

The phenomena here described are identical with those of the inferior optical mirage, and are due to the same meteorological conditions. They constitute, therefore, the *inferior acoustical mirage*. Indeed a series of sounding objects arranged vertically might, in position 2, if one were equipped with a suitable sound-pointer, be heard both right side up and upside down.

e. Temperature uniform throughout a shallow layer, then increasing with elevation over several meters to a uniform higher temperature above, air quiet and of constant composition—conditions identical with those that give the superior optical mirage.

The necessary acoustical consequences of this assumed, and sometimes actual, temperature distribution, may be easily inferred by the aid of Fig. 150. After the sound, whose origin is at only a moderate elevation, has traveled for some distance, its wave fronts have some such shape as that indicated by *ABCDE* in the figure, owing to the relation of sound velocity to temperature, as explained above. Farther on, this front obviously transforms into *A'B'C'D'E'* of the figure, from

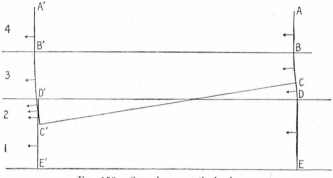

Fig. 150.—Superior acoustical mirage.

which it appears that: In position 1 only a single sound is heard, and in the direction of the source; in position 2, three identical sounds are possible, one in the correct direction, another apparently from a slightly higher point, and inverted if, as explained under (*d*), that be possible, and a third, not inverted, apparently from a still higher point; in position 3, a single sound, apparently from a point distinctly above the true source and, finally, in position 4, also a single sound and again, as in position 1, in the direction of the source.

Since these phenomena are closely analogous to those of the superior optical mirage, and have identical causes, it is suggested that they be called the *superior acoustical mirage*.

Sound Refraction by Straightaway Winds.—Everyone knows, of course, that, in general, winds do not prevent sounds from being heard. Obviously, however, the vibrating portions of the air are carried along with the wind, or, rather, are a portion of it. Clearly, then, the effect of a known wind on the path of a sound ray can be computed with all desired accuracy. Thus, following Barton[1] substantially:

[1] "Textbook of Sound," pp. 99–106, The Macmillan Company, 1908.

Let AB (Fig. 151) be the boundary between two horizontal layers of air; let the wind velocity in the lower layer be u_1, and that of the upper u_2, both in the same direction, and $u_2 > u_1$; let θ_1 and θ_2 be the inclinations of the wave fronts to the horizontal in the lower and upper layers, respectively; let ϕ_1 and ϕ_2 be the corresponding angles between the sound paths in the two layers and the vertical, and let the velocity v of sound in still air be independent of altitude—true, on the average, to about 1 part in 100 between bottom and top of the lowest kilometer, and correspondingly nearer true, in this region, for less depths.

Draw CB' at right angles to the wave front AC, or along a sound path for still air of uniform temperature and composition, and let $B'B$

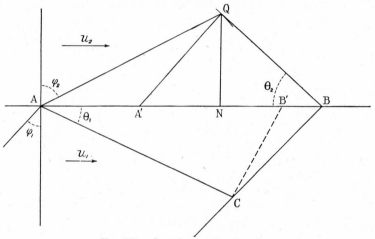

Fig. 151.—Sound refraction by wind.

have such value that $B'B/CB' = u_1/v$. Then CB is the actual sound path in the lower layer.

To find the wave front in the upper layer resulting from the front AC in the lower, draw $AA' = B'B(u_2/u_1)$, describe about A' a circle whose radius $A'Q = CB'$, and draw BQ tangent to this circle. This tangent BQ is the wave front desired. From the figure

$$\operatorname{cosec} QBA' = \frac{BA'}{A'Q} = \frac{B'A - AA' + B'B}{CB'}.$$

Hence,

$$\operatorname{cosec} \theta_2 = \operatorname{cosec} \theta_1 - \frac{u_2 - u_1}{v},$$

and, for any layer whatever,

$$\operatorname{cosec} \theta = \operatorname{cosec} \theta_1 - \frac{u - u_1}{v},$$

or

$$\frac{v}{\sin \theta} + u = \frac{v}{\sin \theta_1} + u_1,$$

in which θ and u apply to the layer in question.

Clearly, then, since the limiting value of the cosecant of an angle is unity, any pair of values of θ_1 and $u - u_1$, which makes cosec θ in the above equation less than unity provides a case of total reflection.

Obviously, the actual path of a sound ray can be traced through the various layers when their speeds and directions of motion, temperatures, and other acoustical factors, are all given. Thus, from the figure, in which QN is perpendicular to AB, it is evident that

$$\frac{AN}{QN} = \frac{A'N}{QN} + \frac{AA'}{QA' \cos \theta_2},$$

and, therefore, that in every layer

$$\tan \varphi = \tan \theta + \frac{u}{v} \sec \theta.$$

If u increases continuously and uniformly with elevation, and if the temperature and composition of the air are the same along the sound path, then it is possible to find an equation for the path, at least in the

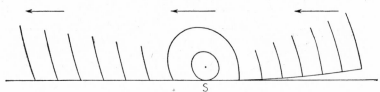

S

FIG. 152.—Distortion by wind of sound fronts.

vertical plane through the origin. But as the conditions specified never strictly obtain, the solution is scarcely more than an abstract mathematical exercise, and therefore will not be given here. (See, however, a valuable paper on this subject, by Milne.)[1]

From the above discussion of the effect of the bodily movement of air on the velocity and direction of travel of sound, it is obvious that its leeward and windward distributions may be radically different.

Let the center of the distorted circle above S (Fig. 152) be the place of origin of a sound, and let the wind be blowing from right to left, as indicated, and increasing with elevation. Obviously, the velocity of the sound, and the consequent distances between the successive compressions and rarefactions will be greatest on the leeward side and least to the windward. The pitch, however, if source and observer are both stationary, will be the same. Furthermore, since the propagation is normal to the wave fronts, the sound is lifted to the windward as indicated in the figure, and thus becomes faint, if not quite inaudible, to one on, or near, the surface in that direction. On the other hand, it is driven down to leeward, in which direction it consequently is heard much farther and louder. All of which are matters of great importance in fog and other

[1] *Phil. Mag.*, **42**; 96, 1921.

sound signaling. Indeed, it is even possible for the lifted sound to windward to strike a shore cliff, or other object, and be reflected back in such manner that the echo alone is heard, and the friendly, warning signal, thereby, transformed into a lure to danger.

From the figure, it is also evident that the sounds are much farther and better heard to the windward from elevated sources than from those near the surface—hence, one of the great advantages in having bells in high steeples rather than near the ground. Likewise, sounds to windward, especially if originating near the surface, often are best heard at elevated points; better in the "crow's nest," for instance, than on the deck.

Another interesting phenomenon in this connection is the carrying of sounds from the windward to the leeward side of a mountain where they sometimes are so distinctly heard as to appear but a little way off. The wind, increasing in speed with distance from the surface, flows parallel,

Fig. 153.—Sound crossing a mountain to leeward.

roughly, to the mountain sides—up one side and down the other. Hence, the forward portion of a wave front tends more and more toward the vertical as it climbs the windward side of the mountain, crosses the ridge upright (if the wind is suitable) and then focuses onto the leeward valley beyond, all as diagrammatically illustrated in Fig. 153, in which S is the source of the sound and F its diffuse leeward focus, determined by the wind currents, as indicated in the figure, by the progressive positions of the wave front.

The acoustical effects of oppositely directed winds in adjacent layers are worth considering, because such opposing winds frequently occur, for instance, when, in middle latitudes, the surface wind is from the east; in places of strong land and sea breezes; and in all trade wind regions.

The general effect in question is quite obvious from Fig. 152. That is, a sound made near the surface, by the firing of a large cannon, say, is first lifted on the windward side as indicated, and later, on getting into the oppositely directed upper current, tipped forward and downward, as readily conceived, though not indicated in the figure. In this way exceptionally loud sounds occasionally are heard 100 miles or more from the source, and over extensive areas beyond a broad silent area.

Zones of Silence.—Occasionally a sound is heard in several widely different directions from the source across an almost, if not quite, continuous zone of silence, an effect that obviously cannot be caused by upper winds. Some, therefore, have attributed the return sound to the change in composition of the upper air with height, and others to a much higher temperature of the stratosphere 40 kilometers or more above the surface. The first of these assumptions appears untenable, owing to the observed nearly constant composition of the air, except in respect to the inconsequential (in this relation) water vapor, up to the height of 20 kilometers, and to the fact that oxygen and nitrogen still are the major constituents of the air, even hundreds of kilometers above the surface. Presumably, therefore, the cause of this phenomenon must be a strong temperature inversion well up in the stratosphere. Careful observations of return sounds have been made by Whipple[1] and others. The major facts that they found are easily explained, though they also may be, and have been, the subjects of elaborate mathematical analyses.

The actual distribution of sound about an explosion center obviously depends, in part, on the strengths and directions of the current winds of the free air, but, since they never are known throughout the path of the sound and, even if they were known, would make the problem of tracing a sound ray tedious, it is here assumed: (1) that the air is calm throughout; (2) that the temperature of the air is constant horizontally but decreases, more or less uniformly, from the surface to the base of the stratosphere; (3) that the temperature of the stratosphere is constant up to a level much above its base; and (4) that beyond this level the temperature rapidly increases to a value greater than that at the surface at the given time and place.

A surface explosion, under these assumed conditions, sends out a hemispherical (becoming oblate) sound, or compression, wave whose rim progressively rises above the earth with expansion and at the same time gives off diffraction waves of sufficient intensity to produce audibility over a considerable area around the source. Beyond a particular distance from this source, determined by the energy of the explosion, the diffraction sound no longer is audible, and the main sound (compression wave) moves on overhead and then, if it encounters a sufficient increase of temperature with height, back to the earth again at a considerably greater distance from its point of origin.

Obviously, the course of a ray of such a sound must be horizontal at its maximum level, lie in a vertical plane, and be symmetrical about the perpendicular through its highest point.

Let e be the angle of elevation of a given sound ray at a particular point and v the velocity of the sound along this ray at that point; then, from the laws of refraction,

$$\frac{v}{\cos e} = \text{constant.}$$

[1] *Quart. J. Roy. Meteorol. Soc.*, **61**; 285, 1935.

But v is proportional to the square root of the absolute temperature of the air. Hence, if the temperature at the surface of the earth is 17° C., say, and $-55°$ at the base of the stratosphere, then the smallest possible angle of elevation a sound ray produced under these conditions can have on entering the stratosphere is given by the equation

$$\cos e_2 = \cos e_1 \sqrt{218/290}$$

and is 29° 53′—pertaining to the ray that starts out horizontally. This is the lowest of all the rays and again is horizontal when it gets back to the earth.

If we knew the angle of elevation at which a return sound ray reaches the earth, we then could deduce certain other interesting facts; and this angle can be determined with two near-by recording stations in line with the sound source, and a few hundred meters apart.

Let, for example, the difference between the times of reception of the descending sound wave, at the two observing stations, be to the time for sound to travel the distance between these stations, in air at the current temperature, as, say, 9 to 10. Then, clearly, if e is the angle of elevation of the descending ray when it reaches the earth,

$$\cos e = 0.9; e = 25° 50′.$$

And since $v/\cos e$ is a constant, it follows that at the highest portion of the curve followed by this ray, when the course is horizontal, the velocity of sound is $\frac{9}{10}$ that at the surface. Furthermore, the absolute temperature of the air at this highest level, when that at the surface is 290°, is $290° \times (10/9)^2 = 358°$ Abs.

Again, e clearly is greatest in the case of the ray that reaches the earth at the innermost edge of the ring of audibility, the ray that obviously has come through warmer air (absolute temperature, T_{max}) than has any other. Let the cosine of this angle be c, and let the absolute temperature at the surface be T; then

$$T_{max} = T/c^2.$$

Finally, the vertical horizontal reflecting surface, from which any particular descending ray seems to come, is at that height where the tangent to this ray at the base of the stratosphere intersects the vertical at the mid-point between the place of origin and place of reception. However, since this height varies from ray to ray, it is clear that the return is not owing to specular reflection, but to gradual refraction. Therefore, the actual maximum height attained by any particular ray is decidedly less than that of its apparent reflector—the ray passing from its ascending portion to the descending along a rather smooth curve.

Why the temperature of the air is so high at levels 40 to 50 kilometers above the earth we do not know. The idea, formerly advanced, that somehow it is owing to the presence of ozone seems to be untenable, since the concentration of ozone is greatest at lower levels than these and at levels at which the air is known to be very cold.

LOCATING BY SOUND

Sound Pointing.—It is well known that a very small difference in the phase of a sound as it enters the two ears, generally, is quite perceptible.[1] If, then, one could actually, or virtually by some artificial aid, stretch his ears far apart, and listen in at widely separated portions of the wave front he, obviously, could determine the direction of the sound arrival with great precision. And this has been done[2] by the aid of long, gently tapering, hollow cones, mounted some distance apart with their axes parallel, quickly adjustable in direction, and supplied, at their smaller ends, with aural tubes.

On correcting for refraction, due essentially to wind and differences in temperature (often impossible to do very accurately), the direction of the source, or, at least, its direction when the received sound was emitted, is determined.

Sound Ranging.—Not only is it possible to determine the direction of the source of a sound, but, by the aid of three listening stations, its exact location as well. In this way the positions of many enemy cannon were located during the World War.[3] The details of sound ranging, as the exact locating of an object by sound is called, are numerous and their variations many. Nevertheless, the underlying principles are very simple.

Let A, B, C (Fig. 154), be three listening stations and O the place of origin, to be determined, of the sound pulse—place of the firing cannon, say. Let v be the velocity of sound in still air appropriate to the current temperature and humidity. Corrections can easily be made for any observed wind, but, for simplicity, it will be assumed that there is no wind, and, hence, no wind corrections. Let the sound pulse, originating at O, be received at A, B, and C, at the times t_1, t_2, and t_3, respectively.

Then, at the time t_1 the pulse is at A, and distant r_1, or $(t_2 - t_1)v$, from B, and r_2, or $(t_3 - t_1)v$, from C. Hence, O is the center of that circle whose circumference passes through A and is tangent to a circle of radius r_1 about B, and also to another circle of radius r_2 about C.

Another method of locating O is to note that it is on the loci of three separate points, the difference of the distances of one of which from A and B is r_1, a constant; of another from A and C is r_2, a constant; and of the third from B and C is $r_2 - r_1$, likewise a constant. That is, it is at the intersection of any two, and, hence, all three, of the hyperbolas whose

---

[1] Stewart, *Phys. Rev.*, **15**; 432, 1920.

[2] Stewart, *Phys. Rev.*, **14**; 166, 1919.

[3] Trowbridge, *J. Franklin Inst.*, **189**; 133, 1920.

foci are A, B; A, C; and B, C, respectively, conditioned by $OB - OA = r_1$; $OC - OA = r_2$; and $OC - OB = r_2 - r_1$, respectively.

Dissipation of Sound.—In an absolutely quiet and homogeneous medium, the intensity of sound must vary inversely as the square of the distance from the source, except in so far as the mechanical energy of the waves is slowly dissipated into heat. In the ordinary atmosphere, however, at least near the surface, the intensity of sound decreases far more rapidly.[1] A portion of the excess in the rate of decrease of the intensity over that required by the inverse square law is due, no doubt, to internal reflections and refractions incident to temperature irregularities. However, the dissipation of sound generally is more pronounced the stronger the wind. Hence, since winds smooth out horizontal tempera-

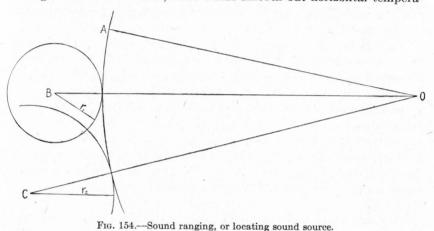

Fig. 154.—Sound ranging, or locating sound source.

ture irregularities and establish an approximately adiabatic cooling with altitude (1° C. per 103 meters) it follows that, at least when there is considerable wind, some other factor than reflection and refraction of the type just mentioned must be effective in dissipating sound. This factor appears to be the ordinary turbulence, or eddy motions, of the lower air.

Since eddy motion is very irregular, both as to speed and direction, and since the velocity of only a moderate wind is several per cent of that of sound (22 miles per hour equals about 3 per cent of the velocity of sound) it follows that a sound front is dimpled and wrinkled on passing through such gusty winds as are common near the surface of the earth. These distortions obviously alter the direction of propagation—normal to the wave front—and, on the whole, increase the dispersion of the sound and rate of its enfeeblement.

To visualize the effect of eddies on sound a little differently, let an instantaneous distribution of atmospheric compressions and rarefactions, constituting a train of sound waves, be fixed in position, except as acted

[1] Stewart, *Phys. Rev.*, **14**; 376, 1919.

on by mass movements of the air. Such inequalities, quickly, would be so intermingled by any moderately strong and turbulent wind as, practically, to obliterate the sound waves, and this same obliterative process is quite as operative, presumably, on traveling, as it would be on stationary waves. The time actually available for such operation is, of course, very brief, but it is sufficiently long, apparently, to permit a great reduction of the sound intensity. Furthermore, the absorption of sound by still air, which absorption is proportional to the square of the frequency of the vibration, increases with temperature and also with decrease of relative humidity until that is reduced to around 15 per cent and then becomes less as the relative humidity is further lowered.[1]

Sounds to and from Elevated Points.—Balloonists, mountain climbers, and others, who have visited quiet places of considerable altitude, have reported two interesting sound observations:

(a) The balloonist, for instance, tells us that the higher-pitched sounds on the surface of the earth are heard to a greater altitude than lower ones of equal initial loudness. A chorus of spring frogs (*hylas*), for example, or the excited cackling of a flock of chickens, is heard after the human voice, of at least equal loudness, has faded away. This is in spite of the fact that the sounds of shorter wave length are more rapidly dissipated by atmospheric irregularities than are those of longer wave length, and due to the greater sensitivity, within certain limits, of the ear to the higher-pitched notes,[2] to our keener perception here, as also in the case of earthquake shocks, of acceleration than of amplitude.

(b) The balloonist may hear and understand persons on the ground while they cannot hear and understand him. This fact is so striking that it has repeatedly evoked wonderment and comments. Its explanation, however, is not, perhaps, immediately obvious. Probably several factors contribute to the final result, among them:

1. Since the density of the atmosphere is less at the level of the balloon than on the ground, it follows that the voice of the balloonist will be correspondingly weaker (carry less energy) than that of a person on the surface. At an altitude of one-half mile, probably about the limit at which vocal communication is possible, the density of the atmosphere is still nine-tenths, roughly, that near the ground. Hence, the density factor, while in the right direction, is not sufficient to account for the commonly observed differences in audibility.

2. The pilot hears both the direct and the reflected portions of the voice below him (whether reflected by the horizontal surface or by objects on it) in substantially the same direction, while the ground observer

---

[1] CHRISLER and MILLER, *J. Research, Nat. Bur. Standards*, **9**; 175, 1932; KNUDSEN, V. O., *J. Acous. Soc. Am.*, **5**; 112, 1933.

[2] SABINE, *Contributions, Phys. Lab. Harvard Univ.*, **No. 8**; 1919. STEWART, *Phys. Rev.*, **14**; 376, 1914.

hears the balloonist's direct voice from overhead, its chief reflection from below, and minor reflections, more or less, from all around, horizontally. Just what the resultant will be in each case is not obvious, but it would seem that, with respect to this factor, also, the ballonist has the better listening position.

3. The balloonist, even when up only ½ kilometer, is in a region, prevailingly, of utter silence, where any occasional sound is most easily perceived. On the other hand, his surface interlocutor is immersed in a flood of sound, where the limit of audibility is soon reached. That this difference in noise environment is an important factor in the cause of the phenomenon under consideration, is evident from the fact that the balloonist often can hear the earth echo of his own voice when he is unable to arrest the attention of persons below him. This echo is loudest over still water and faint over freshly fallen snow, owing to dissipation of the sound energy by microeddies in the myriads of snow interstices—an absorption that largely accounts for the unwanted quiet that accompanies and follows, for a time, any considerable fall of fluffy snow.[1]

[1] KAYE, G. W. C., and EVANS, E. J., *Nature*, **143**; 80, 1939.

CHAPTER II

SOUNDS OF METEOROLOGICAL ORIGIN

CREAKING OF THE SNOW

Probably all, or nearly all, who have experienced a cold winter, are familiar with the cheery cry of the snow as it is pressed against a hard surface by the steel tire of a wagon, for instance, or even onto a pavement by the heels of one's boots.

When the temperature is just a little below the freezing point, the snow, then in fine condition for snowballing, does not creak, and the track of the wheel is marked by a strip of more or less compact ice. On the other hand, when it is so cold that the snow will not ball, its voice is loud, and the track left by the wheel is now marked, not by a strip of compact ice, as before, but by a trail of crushed and powdered crystals.

In the first case, that is, when the temperature is only a little below freezing, the snow crystals obviously melt, to a greater or less extent, as a result of the pressure to which they are subjected, and undergo regelation immediately the pressure is removed. The yielding is gentle and progressive through melting and flowing, and not of that abrupt nature essential to the production of sound.

In the second case, however, or when the snow is too cold to melt under the pressure applied, its yieldings and readjustments are abrupt and jerky, incident to the crushing of the crystals and their slippage in a dry condition over each other. It is these abrupt yieldings, these sudden breaks and slips of its dry crystals, that produce the familiar cold-weather creak and cry of the snow.

THUNDER

Cause.—Thunder, one of the most familiar and, certainly, the most impressive of all meteorological sounds, has been "explained" in many ridiculous ways, but generally, perhaps, just accepted. Any careful observation, however, will soon show that thunder is associated with lightning, and that the lightning flash always precedes the thunder. Clearly, then, thunder is somehow caused by lightning.

Now, it is known that sudden and intense heating and molecular dissociation occur along the path of a lightning discharge. Hence, a corresponding abrupt expansion, simulating a violent explosion, also occurs along this path; and this expansion, in turn, produces a compression wave in the surrounding atmosphere that travels outward exactly as would any other sound wave.

Musical Thunder.—It occasionally happens, when one is near the path of a lightning flash, that the thunder heard begins with a musical note. This is due to the fact that some lightning discharges—the flickering type—consist of a series of rapid flashes that, occasionally, are nearly enough regular, and of such frequency, as to produce a quasi-musical note.

Duration.—The long continuation of thunder is owing, chiefly, to the length, and crookedness, of the lightning path. Sound produced simultaneously, and but momentarily, along a straight course would give, off to the side anywhere, only a single boom; if along a crooked course, the effect would not be so restricted. Hence, when the difference in distance from the nearest and farthest points of a lightning path is 5 miles, say, which it sometimes is, the duration of the thunder, owing to this cause alone, is about 24 seconds. It also is increased, more or less, by reflection.

Rumbling.—The great variations in the intensity of thunder, that constitute its characteristic rumbling, are due:

a. To crookedness of path. The thunder starts from all parts of the discharge path at the same instant, or practically so, and, thus, the observer hears, simultaneously, the thunder from the whole of any portion of the path that happens to be at a constant distance from him. Now, as the path usually is very crooked, it generally happens that many portions of it are at one or another nearly constant distance from any given point. Hence, almost every peal of thunder is of irregular intensity, and as no two lightning paths are alike so, also, each peal of thunder differs from every other.

b. To the sequence of discharges. Obviously, when a number of discharges follow each other in rapid succession—when the lightning is flickering—there is likely to be more or less interference between the several sound pulses resulting, now, in partial neutralization, and, again, in reinforcement, the whole merging into an irregular rumble.

c. To reflection. Reflection by mountains, hills, and other objects, may, occasionally, be effective in prolonging the noise of thunder and accentuating its rumble. Mountains and hills, however, are not nearly so essential to the rumble of thunder as, occasionally, they are said to be, for whether in the valley, over the plain, or on the peak, it is substantially the same.

Distance Heard.—Thunder seldom is heard more than 15 miles. This is much less than the distance to which cannon are sometimes heard. The circumstances in the two cases, however, are radically different. Thus, the sound energy from the cannon is relatively concentrated, since it all starts from a single point and spreads out in a hemispherical shell; whereas, that of thunder starts, not from a single point, but from a crooked line, often miles long. Furthermore, cannon often are fired when the surface air, in which the firing occurs, is very still and, otherwise, in the best state for long transmissions of sound. Thunder, on the other hand seldom occurs except when the winds are turbulent and the general conditions very adverse to sound propagation. Finally, the density of the air is greater at the cannon than along the lightning path, and, hence, its sound energy per unit volume, other things being equal, also correspondingly greater in the former than in the latter case.

BRONTIDES

From time immemorial, low, rumbling, thunder-like noises (brontides, *mistpoeffers*, "Barisal guns," etc.,) of short duration, and that certainly are not thunder, for they often occur when the sky is clear, have been heard in many parts of the world, both singly and in irregular series. They appear to come from a distance, but are of uncertain direction, and are most frequent in actively seismic regions.

Apparently, then, the true brontides (many other sounds have often been mistakenly reported as brontides) are only the rumblings of earthquakes too feeble for registration, or other than aural detection. And this inference is strengthened, if not indeed confirmed, by the fact that earthquake adjustments have been known to occur in a long irregular series of shocks that became feebler and feebler, until only the characteristic low rumbles (then properly called brontides) remained as presumable evidence of their passage.

HOWLING OF THE WIND

One of the compensations for being snowbound on a windy day is the pleasure of listening to the well-known howling of the wind as it sweeps by the chimneys and over the gables, and wondering where it gets its many voices, or, indeed, any voice at all. Nor is the wonderment yet over, for the problem of the howling of the wind has never been completely solved, at least not in the fullness of all the differential equations that tell the whole story. This much, however, is known: the howling, like the other æolian sounds discussed below, is due to eddy motions in the atmosphere immediately beyond the obstructing object. There is no resonance or other organ-pipe action, for the change from one pitch to another is not by jumps, as it is in all pipes, but gradual, through every intermediate value, in response to the varying wind velocity.

Let the direction of the wind make an appreciable angle with the roof and let the latter either project a little beyond the gable wall or, at least, come up flush with it. Under these conditions the wind will have its maximum velocity as it leaves the roof, and there, in only a comparatively thin sheet. This sheet, in turn, immediately it escapes the roof, drags along, through viscosity, some of the air just beneath it, and is, itself, slightly deflected in the direction of the consequent pull. In this way, an abrupt change in the direction of flow is produced at the edge of the roof and, hence, an eddy will immediately start at that place. One effect of such an eddy, since it enters the current from relatively still air, is to slightly decrease the velocity of that current. It is quickly carried on, however, and the eddy-forming conditions, thereby, renewed. In this general manner, presumably, eddy after eddy is formed at the edge of the roof with such frequency, and such approach to regularity, as to produce a more or less musical note whose pitch increases with the wind velocity.

These sounds generally are much better heard indoors than out. This is largely, if not wholly, because one is, there, far less disturbed by the innumerable other outdoor noises, especially the continuous and annoying whisper of the wind right in one's ears—also an eddy effect.

HUMMING OF WIRES

Few things, perhaps, have been more absurdly "explained" than has the well-known humming of telegraph and telephone wires, and that in spite of the fact that the correct explanation has long been at hand.

It was shown, by Strouhal,[1] that wind normal to a cylinder, such as a stretched wire, produces æolian tones, even when the cylinder, itself, takes no part in the vibration; that the pitch of the note thus produced, independent alike of the material, length, and tension of the wire, varies directly as the speed u of the wind and inversely as the diameter d of the obstructing rod; and that the number n of such vibrations per second is given, approximately, by the equation

$$n = \frac{0.185u}{d}$$

the units being the centimeter and second.

Whenever the tone, thus produced, coincides with one of the proper tones (fundamental or a harmonic) of the wire, the wire, itself, if suitably supported, then vigorously vibrates, normal to the direction of the wind, and, thereby, increases the loudness and also holds the pitch fixed over a considerable range of wind velocity. The sound in question, however, that is, the humming of telegraph and telephone wires, is not due to the elasticity of the wires (the pitch changes gradually with wind velocity and not from harmonic to harmonic), but to the instability of the vortex sheets their obstruction introduces into the air, as it rushes by them. This obvious and, indeed, unavoidable deduction from Strouhal's experiments, just referred to, is abundantly confirmed by cinema photographs of water eddies, due to flow past a cylinder, made at the National

[1] *Ann. Phys.*, **5**; 216, 1878. Lord Rayleigh, *Phil. Mag.*, **29**; 433, 1915; Relf, *Phil. Mag.*, **42**; 173, 1921.

Physical Laboratory. Vortex whirls developed at regular intervals, alternately to the right and left of the interfering cylinder, while the

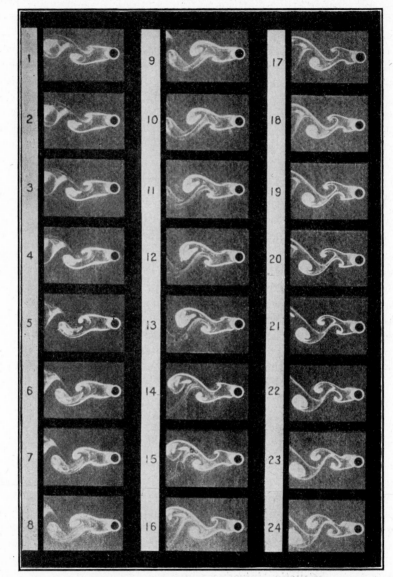

Fig. 155.—Eddies behind cylinder. (*N. P. L.*)

eddy mass vibrated from side to side in the same period, all as shown in Fig. 155, copied from Bairstow's "Applied Aerodynamics."

The complete mathematical analysis of these, and similar, vortices, giving the deduction of Strouhal's rules, and many others, would be both interesting and valuable, but it appears that this important problem has not yet been fully solved.   Much progress, however, towards this solution, has been made by v. Kármán,[1] and by v. Kármán and Rubach,[2] who have shown that evenly spaced vortices, alternately on opposite sides, is a stable arrangement, and the only one.

It is well known that the humming of telegraph and telephone wires is loudest when the wires are tightly stretched, as they generally are during cold weather.   This appears to be because the eddies thus produced in the wind vary the tension on the wire, and, rapidly, the more so the tighter, or straighter, it becomes.   Now, these variations of tension are transmitted to the posts which, in turn, act as sounding boards, analogous to the sounding board of a piano, and, hence, largely increase the volume of the sound, whatever its pitch.

WHISPERING OF TREES

From the experiments of Strouhal, above referred to, it is evident that pine needles, bare twigs, and even the branches of trees, must all

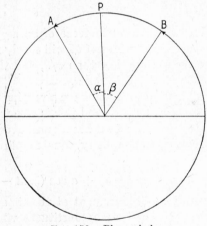

FIG. 156.—Phase circle.

produce æolian notes—that trees must have voices, even voices that are characteristic of the species.   And they do.   The muffled plaint of the oak at the wintry blast, for instance, has but little in common with the sibilant sigh of the pine.   And the reason is obvious; the twigs and branches of the one, because relatively large, and of many sizes, produce a multitude of low tones, while the innumerable fine needles of the other give a smaller range of high-pitched notes.

It may be granted that, as shown by experiment, each twig and other similar obstacle in the wind must produce an æolian note.   But how, one must ask, do a multitude of such notes blend together—how are the

[1] Göttingen Nachrichten, 5; 547, 1912.
[2] Phys. Zeit., 13; 49, 1912.

pitch and loudness of the resultant related to the like properties of the constituents?

To solve this problem, let two sounds have the same amplitude, but differ slightly in period. Let them start together with maximum displacement, or at the top P of the phase circle (Fig. 156). Let the phase position of the quicker, after a few intervals, and at the instant when the resultant displacement towards P is at a maximum, be at A (having described the angle $2n\pi + \alpha$, n being a whole number) and that of the slower at B (having described the angle $2n\pi - \beta$); let s be the velocity along the circumference of the phase circle of the slower, and $s + \delta s$ the corresponding velocity of the quicker. Then, since the combined displacement towards P is at a maximum

$$s \sin \beta = (s + \delta s) \sin \alpha, \text{ and } \beta > \alpha.$$

For the next maximum

$$s \sin (\beta + \delta\beta) = (s + \delta s) \sin (\alpha + \delta\alpha).$$

But

$$\delta\beta < \delta\alpha.$$

Furthermore, since the rate of increase of an angle is greater than that of its sine, the successive values of $\delta\beta$ will slowly increase so long as β and α are greater than 0, and less than $\pi/2$, and then decrease while they are greater than $\pi/2$ and less than π.

In short, the combination tone will have a varying pitch intermediate between those of its constituents. And this is also true of any number of constituent sounds—their resultant has a quasi-average pitch.

Analytically, assuming, for simplicity, equal amplitudes a and initially identical phase,

$$x = a \cos (2\pi mt - \epsilon) + a \cos (2\pi nt - \epsilon)$$

in which x is the resultant displacement at the time t after the initial count, when the phase epoch of each constituent vibration was ϵ, and m and n the respective frequencies.

Since

$$\cos (2\pi nt - \epsilon) = \cos \{2\pi mt - 2\pi(m - n)t - \epsilon\},$$
$$x = a \cos (2\pi mt - \epsilon) + a \cos \{2\pi mt - 2\pi(m - n)t - \epsilon\},$$
$$= r \cos (2\pi mt - \theta),$$

where

$$r^2 = 2a^2[1 + \cos \{2\pi(m - n)t\}]$$

and

$$\tan \theta = \frac{\sin \epsilon + \sin \{2\pi(m + n)t + \epsilon\}}{\cos \epsilon + \cos \{2\pi(m - n)t + \epsilon\}}.$$

That is, the resultant is a quasi-harmonic in r and θ, each of which has the frequency $m - n$, while that of the combination is a varying intermediate between m and n.

A combination of two notes having different amplitudes and different initial phases gives equations substantially the same as the above, though, of course, slightly more complicated. Similarly, a multitude of sounds merge into a quasinote whose pitch is the approximate average of those of the many constituents. Hence, the whisper of a tree, whatever its volume, has substantially the same pitch as that of its individual twigs or needles; just as the hum of a swarm of bees is pitched to that of the average bee, and as the concert of a million mosquitoes is only the megaphoned whine of the type.

The final law of sound, essential to the explanation of the whispering of trees, namely, the intensity of a blend in terms of that of its constituents, has been found, by Lord Rayleigh,[1] in substantially the following manner:

Let the number of individual sounds be n, all of unit amplitude and same pitch, but arbitrary phase—conditions that approach the æolian blend of a tree. Clearly, if all the individual sounds had the same phase, and unit amplitude, at any given point, their combined intensity at that point would be n^2. If, however, half had one phase, and half the exactly opposite phase, the intensity would be zero. Consider, then, the average intensity when all the vibrations are confined to two exactly opposite phases, $+$ and $-$. Now, the chance that all the n vibrations will have the same phase, $+$, say, is $(\frac{1}{2})^n$ and the expectation of intensity corresponding to this condition $(\frac{1}{2})^n n^2$. Similarly, when one of the vibrations has the negative phase and the $n - 1$ others the positive phase, the expectation is $(\frac{1}{2})^n n(n - 2)^2$; and the whole or actual expectation

$$\left(\frac{1}{2}\right)^n \left\{ 1 \cdot n^2 + n(n - 2)^2 + \frac{n(n - 1)}{1 \cdot 2}(n - 4)^2 + \cdots \right\} \qquad (A)$$

The sum of the $n + 1$ terms of this series is n, as may be indicated by a few numerical substitutions; or proved, as Lord Rayleigh (loc. cit.) has shown, by expanding the expression

$$(e^x + e^{-x})^n$$

into the two equivalent series

$$2^n \left(1 + \frac{1}{2} x^2 + \cdots \right)^n \qquad \text{(Maclaurin)}$$

and

$$e^{nx} + n e^{(n-2)x} + \cdots \qquad \text{(Binomial)}$$

developing the exponentials into series of algebraic terms, and, finally, assembling and equating the coefficients of x^2 in the two equivalent series, and solving for n. The value of n thus found is identical with the expression (A).

[1] "Encyclopedia Britannica," 9th Ed., Wave Theory; *Scientific Papers*, **3**; 52.

That is, on the average, the intensity of the resultant of n sounds of unit amplitude, but confined, in random numbers, to two opposite phases, is always n, whatever its numerical value.

If, instead of the numbers of sounds in either of two opposite phases being random, the phases are random, the result, as Rayleigh has shown, is the same.

It should be noted that n is only the mean intensity of a possible range from 0 to n^2, and not the continuous intensity. But when the changes are rapid the fluctuations from the mean are correspondingly inconspicuous.

From the above two laws, namely, (1) that the pitch of a composite note is the approximate average of those of its constituents, and (2) that the mean intensity is the sum of the individual intensities, it appears (*a*) that the pitch of the æolian whisper of a tree is essentially that of its average twig, or needle, if the tree be a pine, and (*b*) that though the note of the twig may be inaudible, even at close range, the tree may often be heard some distance away.

MURMURING OF THE FOREST

Just as the æolian whispers of the myriads of needles on a single pine tree, or of the numerous twigs on an oak, for example, blend into a whisper of the same average pitch but vastly greater volume, so, too, the whisperings of a great many individual trees merge into the well-known murmur of the forest.

ROARING OF THE MOUNTAIN

When a mountain, well wooded along, and near, its top is crossed by a wind approximately at right angles to its axis, as indicated in Fig. 153, it often happens, particularly during winter, when there are no protecting leaves on the trees (or at any time if the forest is pine), that, in the leeward valley, one hears a low sighing or moaning noise which, as the wind over the crest grows to a gale, gradually swells to a cataract roar. This, too, is only another instance, but a most striking one, at times even awe inspiring, of the combined effects of myriads upon myriads of æolian whispers, accentuated, indeed, along the valley through their crude focusing by the descending winds.

ODDS AND ENDS

In addition to the above, there also are numerous other sounds that might, more or less justly, be called meteorological, such as the *rustle of leaves*, due to the rubbing together of the foliage as trees and branches, or stalks, as of corn, are shaken by the wind; the *roar and whir of the tornado*, due to the instability of, and eddies between, different portions of the air involved, as, for instance, between the relatively quiet core and the violently whirling shell, and to the wrecking, when the storm strikes to earth, of all things in its path; to the wind eddies engendered by every obstruction, and to the more or less continuous rumble of thunder; the *patter of rain*, due to the successive falling of innumerable drops onto a roof, pavement, compact soil, and the like, or into a body of water; the *rattle of sleet* (frozen raindrops), due to the driving of the small ice pellets against any hard object—the windowpane, for instance; the *clatter of hail*, due to the fall of relatively large lumps of ice onto a roof, or other hard surface, and even (occasionally reported in connection with severe storms) to the combined swish of many stones falling simultaneously, and possibly also, in some measure, to their striking together in mid-air; the *detonations of meteorites*, due to violent disruptions owing to their sudden and intense heating; the *sizzle of St. Elmo's fire*, the faint crackle of the constant stream of feeble electric discharges from mast tips, or other points thus strangely illuminated; the *swish of the aurora*, really, it seems, the swish of ones own breath as its moisture freezes at very low temperatures;[1] and, of course, many more. But the explanations of all are easy, if not immediately obvious, and, hence, even their further listing is quite unnecessary.

[1] SVERDRUP, *Nature*, **128**; 457, 1931.

PART IV
ATMOSPHERIC OPTICS

CHAPTER I

PERSPECTIVE PHENOMENA

Apparent Stair-step Ascent of Clouds.—The stair-step appearance of the echelon cloud (Fig. 124) is, perhaps, the simplest sky phenomenon due to perspective. The exact manner by which the stair-step, or terrace, illusion is brought about, is shown by Fig. 157, in which O is the position of the observer, H his horizon, 1, 2, 3, etc., evenly spaced flat-bottomed cumuli of the same base elevation—flat bottomed and of constant level because of the approximately uniform horizontal distribution of moisture which gives the same height everywhere for convectional condensation.

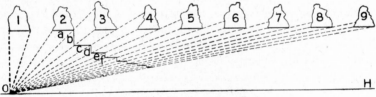

Fig. 157.—Cloud echelon effect.

Since the clouds are at a higher level than the observer, each successive cumulus, as the distance increases, is seen at a lower angle than its predecessor; and the dark bases of any two adjacent clouds appear to be connected with each other by the lighter side of the farther one. Besides, their general resemblance to stair steps often leads one into the error of "seeing" the connection between any two adjacent bases to be at right angles to both. That is, starting with base a, the light side of cloud 3 appears as a vertical surface at b, and its base as a dark horizontal surface at c; the side and base of cloud 4 appear as the next vertical and horizontal surfaces, d and e, respectively, and so on for the other clouds; the whole effect merging into the appearance of a great stairway, consisting of the horizontal treads, a, c, e, etc., connected by the seemingly vertical rises, b, d, f, etc.

Apparent Arching of Cloud Bands.—Occasionally a narrow cloud band is seen to stretch almost, if not entirely, from horizon to horizon, but, although its course is practically horizontal and its direction often nearly straight, it usually appears arched. If even the nearest portion of the cloud, still, is far away, the apparent arching is slight. On the other hand, when the cloud is near, the arching is great. The apparent curve is neither circular nor elliptical, but resembles, rather, a conchoid whose origin is at the observer and whose asymptote is his horizon.

The angle of elevation at which different segments of the cloud are seen obviously varies from a minimum for the more distant portions to a maximum for the nearest. Hence, the phenomenon in question, the apparent arching of the band along its nearest portions, is only an optical illusion, due entirely to the projection of the cloud (above the observer's level) onto the sky.

When several such bands, or streaks, occur in parallel, they appear to start from a common point at, or beyond, the horizon; to terminate, if long enough, in a similar opposite point; and progressively to arch and spread apart as they approach the observer's zenith. They thus form the perspective effect often called "Noah's Ark" or polar bands.

Apparent Divergence and Convergence of Crepuscular Rays (Sunbeams).—Everyone is familiar with the beautiful phenomenon of the "sun drawing water"—sunbeams that, finding their way through rifts in the clouds, are rendered luminous by the dust in their courses. Equally familiar, and equally beautiful, are, also, those streaks and bands of pearly lights (where the lower atmosphere is illuminated) and azure shadows (where only the upper atmosphere is illuminated) that often, at twilight and, occasionally, at dawn, radiate far out from the region of the sun, and, at times, even converge toward the opposite point of the horizon. These, too, are only beams of sunlight and shadow caused by broken clouds or irregular horizon.

All such crepuscular rays, whether their common origin, the sun, be below, or above, the horizon, seem first to diverge, while the few that cross the sky appear, also, to arch on the way and, finally, to converge towards the antisolar point, as anticrepuscular rays.

Here, again, the facts are not as they seem, for the rays, all coming, as they do, from the sun, some 93,000,000 miles away, necessarily are practically parallel. Their apparent divergence, convergence, and arching, are all illusions due to perspective; just as are the apparent divergence, convergence, and arching, of the rails on a long straight track.

Apparent Divergence of Auroral Streamers.—Anyone at all familiar with the appearance of auroral streamers will recall that, at most localities, they seem to radiate from some place far below the horizon. In reality, they do diverge (or converge, if one prefers) slightly, since they follow, approximately, the terrestrial lines of magnetic force. Indeed, their rate of convergence is about the same, on the average, as that of the geographic meridians at the same latitudes, and, therefore, far less than one would infer from their apparent courses. That is, their seeming rapid convergence is only another illusion due to perspective, just as is the apparent divergence of the crepuscular rays, as above explained.

Apparent Shape (Flat Vault) of the Sky.—To everyone, the sky looks like a great, blue dome, low and flattish, whose circular rim rests on the horizon and whose apex is directly overhead. So flat, indeed, does this dome appear to be, that points on it estimated to lie half way between the rim and apex generally have an elevation of but little more than 20° instead of 45°, as they would if it seemed spherical.

That the rim of the sky dome should appear circular is obvious enough. It is, simply, because the horizon, where land and sky come together, itself is circular, except when conspicuously broken by hills or mountains.

To understand the other, and more important, feature, that is, why the dome looks so flat, consider (1) a sky filled from horizon to horizon with high cirrus clouds. These seem nearest overhead for the simple reason that that is just where they are nearest. As the horizon is approached, the clouds merge, through perspective, into a uniform gray cover that appears to rest on the land at the limit of vision, whether this limit be fixed by the curvature of the earth or by haze, and the whole cloud canopy may seem arched just as, and for the same reason that, cloud streaks and crepuscular rays seem arched, as above explained. But (2) even a thin cirro-stratus veil, whose parts are well-nigh indistinguishable, produces a similar effect, the nearest portions appearing nearest largely because they are the most clearly seen. Similarly, when there are no clouds, the sky overhead also appears nearest because it is clearest; and that unconscious inference, based on endless experience, is correct—it is clearest because nearest. As the eye approaches the horizon, the increasing haze produces the impression of greater distance; and this impression is entirely correct, for the blue sky seen in any such direction is farther away than the sky overhead. In short, the spring of a cloudless sky dome is "seen" to rest on the distant horizon and its ceiling to come closer and closer, in proportion to increasing clearness, as the zenith is approached. The shape, then, of this dome should not always appear the same, and it does not—not the same on a clear night, for instance, as on a clear day.

Impressions, therefore, of the "shape" of the sky are, perhaps, not so erroneous as, sometimes, they are said to be. Indeed, they usually conform surprisingly well to the actual facts.

Change with Elevation of Apparent Size of Sun and Moon.—One of the most familiar, as also one of the most puzzling, of optical illusions is the change between the apparent sizes of the full moon, say, or of the sun, at rising or setting, and at, or near, culmination. It is, however, only a phenomenon of perspective.

Since the solid angle subtended at any place on the earth by the moon, as also that subtended by the sun, is sensibly constant throughout its course from rising to setting, it follows that its projection, and, there-fore, its apparent size, must be relatively large, or small, as the place of projection (sky dome) is comparatively far away or nearby. But, as already explained, the sky dome, against which all celestial objects are projected and along which they, therefore, appear to move, seems to be farther away, and is farther away, near the horizon than at places of considerable elevation. Hence, the moon and the sun must look much larger when near the horizon than when far up in the heavens, and the fact that they do so look, is, as stated, merely a phenomenon of perspective.

The familiar fact that the moon appears of one size to one person and a different size to another clearly is also due to perspective. The one who judges it large imagines his comparison object to be at a greater distance than does the one who judges it small. But such estimates usually are very erroneous; the moon may seem 1 foot in diameter, for instance, and 3 miles away, whereas, at that distance, a 144-foot circle would just cover it.

Change, with Elevation, of Apparent Distance between Neighboring Stars.—The generally recognized fact that the distance between neigh-boring stars appears much greater when they are near the horizon than when well up is also a phenomenon of perspective. Its explanation is identical with that of the change, under similar circumstances, of the apparent diameter of the moon, and, therefore, need not be given in further detail.

CHAPTER II

REFRACTION PHENOMENA: ATMOSPHERIC REFRACTION

Astronomical Refraction.—It is well known that, because of astronomical refraction, the zenith distance of a star, or other celestial object, is greater than it seems, except when zero, to an extent that increases with that distance. To understand this important phenomenon, it is necessary to recall two experimental facts: (*a*) that, in any homogeneous medium, light travels in sensibly straight lines, and (*b*) that its velocity (velocity pertaining to any given wave frequency) differs from medium to medium.

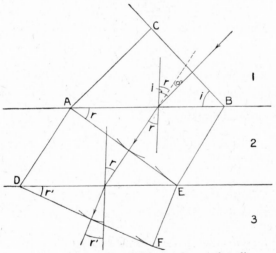

Fig. 158.—Refraction of light on change of media.

Let, then, the parallel lines AB and DE (Fig. 158) be the intersections of the boundaries between three homogeneous media, 1, 2, 3, by a plane normal thereto and to the wave front BC. Let the velocities in these media of a given monochromatic light be v_1, v_2, and v_3, respectively. Hence, when the light disturbance at C has travelled the distance CA in the first medium, that at B will have gone the distance BE in the second, where $CA/BE = v_1/v_2$, and AE will be the new wave front. Similarly, DF will be the wave front in the third medium, and so on, for any additional media that may be traversed.

If i is the angle between the normal to the interface AB and the direction of the light, both in medium 1, and r the corresponding angle in medium 2, then, as is obvious from the figure,

$$\frac{\sin i}{\sin r} = \frac{v_1}{v_2}, \text{ or } \sin i = \frac{v_1}{v_2} \sin r.$$

Similarly, $\sin r = \dfrac{v_2}{v_3} \sin r'$. Hence, $\sin i = \dfrac{v_1}{v_3} \sin r'$. That is, the total change in direction of the light depends solely on its velocities in the first and final media, respectively, and the initial angle of incidence. The optical densities of the intermediate layers may abruptly change by large amounts, as indicated, and, thus, cause the light to follow a per-

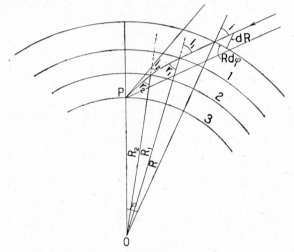

Fig. 159.—Path of light through the atmosphere.

ceptibly broken course, as from air to water, for instance; or they may change so gradually that the path is a smooth curve, even to the closest observation.

Since the ratio of the velocity of light in space to its velocity in any given gas, or definite mixture of gases (the refractive index of that medium), increases directly with density, it follows that all rays of light that cross the atmospheric shell, except those that enter it normally, must follow continuously curved paths, somewhat as shown, to an exaggerated extent, in Fig. 159.

To determine the shape of such a curve through the atmosphere, let ϕ (Fig. 159) be the angle between the radii from the center of the earth at the place of observation and any other point along the course of a refracted ray.

As before,

$$\mu_2 \sin r_1 = \mu_1 \sin i_1$$

in which μ_1 and μ_2 are the refractive indices (with reference to space) of media, or layers, 1 and 2, respectively, i_1 the angle of incidence and r_1 the angle of refraction at the interface between these media or layers. But, corresponding to the radii R_1 and R_2,

$$\frac{\sin i_2}{\sin r_1} = \frac{R_1}{R_2}.$$

Hence,

$$R_1\mu_1 \sin i_1 = R_2\mu_2 \sin i_2,$$

or, in general,

$$R\mu \sin i = C, \text{ a constant.}$$

Further,

$$\frac{dR}{Rd\phi} = \cot i.$$

But

$$\cot i = \frac{\cos i}{\sin i} = \sqrt{\frac{1 - \sin^2 i}{\sin^2 i}} = \sqrt{\frac{\mu^2 R^2}{C^2} - 1}.$$

Hence,

$$\frac{dR}{d\phi} = R\sqrt{\frac{\mu^2 R^2}{C^2} - 1},$$

and

$$\phi = \int_{R_o}^{R} \frac{dR}{R\sqrt{\dfrac{\mu^2 R^2}{C^2} - 1}}.$$

Clearly, then, the value of ϕ corresponding to a definite value of R, or the value of R appropriate to a definite value of ϕ, depends upon the

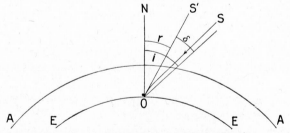

Fig. 160.—Approximate astronomical refraction.

relation of μ to R, or, very nearly, the relation of the density of the atmosphere at any point to the altitude of that point. Hence, refraction curves may be drawn for different angles of incidence, or, if preferred, for different apparent altitudes, according to any assumed distribution of atmospheric density—a distribution fairly well known.

The approximate value of astronomical refraction, that is, its value, generally, to within 1 second of arc, through all zenith distances up to at least 60°, may easily be obtained as follows: Assume the atmosphere to be flat, as it nearly is, over the restricted area through which stars may be seen whose zenith distances are within 60°, or thereabouts. Let O (Fig. 160) be the position of the observer, S the true position of a star and S' its apparent position.

As explained above,

$$\sin i = \mu \sin r$$

in which μ is the refractive index of the air at the point of observation, i the actual and r the apparent zenith distance. But

$$i = r + \delta$$

in which δ is the angle of deviation.

Hence,

$$\sin (r + \delta) = \sin r \cos \delta + \cos r \sin \delta = \mu \sin r.$$

When the angle of incidence is 60°, or less, δ is always very small, and, putting $\cos \delta = 1$,

$$\sin \delta = (\mu - 1) \tan r, \text{ nearly.}$$

Expressed in seconds of arc this gives, writing δ for $\sin \delta$,

$$\delta'' = 206{,}265''(\mu - 1) \tan r$$

in which the numerical coefficient is the approximate number of seconds in a radian.

For dry air at 0° C. and 760 mm. pressure, the average value of μ is about 1.000293.

Hence, also

$$\delta'' = 60''.4 \tan r.$$

But for gases $\mu - 1 = K\rho$, very closely, in which K is a constant and ρ the density.

Hence, finally,

$$\delta'' = \frac{21''.7B}{T} \tan r,$$

in which B is the height of the barometer in millimeters, and T the absolute temperature in degrees C.

As a matter of fact, the atmospheric shell is not plane, even over small areas, but slightly curved, and, therefore, the complete formula for astronomical refraction, such as is needed for the construction of tables to be used in the most accurate measurements of star positions, is rather complicated. Probably the briefest and simplest derivation of a formula adequate for all zenith distances to at least 75° is due to Lord Rayleigh,[1] and is essentially as follows:

Let p_0, p_1, p_2, etc., be the normals from the center of the earth onto the tangents of a ray path through the atmosphere at the points where

[1] *Phil. Mag.*, **36**; 141, 1893.

the refractive indices are μ_0, μ_1, μ_2, etc., respectively. Let i_0, i_1, i_2, etc., be the angles of incidence, and r_1, r_2, etc., the corresponding angles of

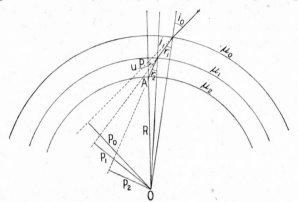

FIG. 161.—Astronomical refraction. (*Lord Rayleigh.*)

refraction. Then (see Fig. 161)

$$\frac{\mu_0}{\mu_1} = \frac{\sin r_1}{\sin i_0} = \frac{p_1}{p_0},$$

$$\frac{\mu_1}{\mu_2} = \frac{\sin r_2}{\sin i_1} = \frac{p_2}{p_1}, \text{ etc.}$$

Hence,

$$\mu p = \text{constant.}$$

Let the tangent to the ray path, where it enters the atmosphere, meet the vertical at the distance C above the point of observation A; let μ_s be the refractive index at A; θ the apparent zenith distance; $\delta\theta$ the total refraction; and R the radius of the earth. Then, since the refractive index of space is 1,

$$\mu_s p_2 = p_0, \text{ or } \mu_s R \sin \theta = (R + C) \sin$$
$$(\theta + \delta\theta) \quad \text{(A)}$$

Obviously, the refraction $\delta\theta$ could be determined from this equation directly if the value of C were known. But

$$C = \frac{u}{\sin \theta}, \quad \text{(B)}$$

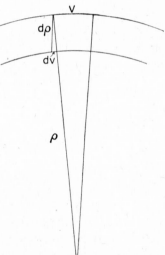

FIG. 162.—Curvature of a light path in the air.

in which u, the total linear deviation of the ray, may be substituted by known terms. Hence, C and, therefore, $\delta\theta$ are determinable.

To determine u, let α be the angle which the ray makes with the direction of most rapid increase of index of refraction (at the surface α

equals θ); z the vertical coordinate; and v the velocity of light. Now, consider a wave front moving through the atmosphere in any direction except vertical. The portion in the higher, or thinner, air will move faster than that in the denser air, and the path will be curved. If ρ is the radius of curvature and $d\rho$ is regarded as positive when measured towards the center, then, as is obvious from Fig. 162,

$$\frac{d\rho}{\rho} = -\frac{dv}{v}$$

by similar triangles.

Also, since the refractive index μ is inversely proportional to the velocity v

$$\frac{d\rho}{\rho} = \frac{d\mu}{\mu}.$$

Hence, calling the path s, and since (Fig. 161)

$$\frac{d\mu}{d\rho} = \frac{d\mu}{dz} \sin \alpha, \text{ and } \cos \alpha = \frac{dz}{ds},$$

$$\therefore \frac{1}{\rho} = \frac{d \log \mu}{d\rho} = \frac{d \log \mu}{dz} \sin \alpha = \frac{d \log \mu}{ds} \tan \alpha,$$

and to a close approximation, since $\dfrac{1}{\rho} = \dfrac{d^2u}{ds^2}$,

$$\frac{du}{ds} = \int \tan \alpha\, d \log \mu = \tan \alpha(\mu - 1) + a,$$

in which a is the constant of integration and $\mu - 1$ is substituted for $\log_e \mu$, μ being but little greater than 1, and

$$u = \tan \alpha \int (\mu - 1)ds + as + b,$$

$$= \frac{\sin \alpha}{\cos^2 \alpha} \int (\mu - 1)dz + as + b \qquad (C)$$

But $\mu - 1$ is directly proportional to the density. Hence, if the height h in "the homogeneous atmosphere" be such that air below it is the same as below z in the actual atmosphere, and if the origin be taken at the surface where $\alpha = \theta$, and $\mu = \mu_s$.

$$u = \frac{\sin \theta}{\cos^2 \theta} \int_o^h (\mu - 1)dz = \frac{\sin \theta}{\cos^2 \theta}(\mu_s - 1)h.$$

For the limit of the atmosphere, and any point beyond, $h = H$, the height of the homogeneous atmosphere, or about 7.990×10^5 cm.

For stars, therefore, viewed from the surface of the earth,

$$u = (\mu_s - 1)H \frac{\sin \theta}{\cos^2 \theta}. \qquad (D)$$

Substituting this value of u in equation (B) we get

$$C = \frac{(\mu_s - 1)H}{\cos^2 \theta}.$$

Hence, substituting in equation (A),

$$\mu_s R \sin \theta = \left\{ R + \frac{(\mu_s - 1)H}{\cos^2 \theta} \right\} \sin \{\theta + \delta\theta\}.$$

With this equation it is only a matter of arithmetic to compute a table of correction,, that is, values of $\delta\theta$ for every value of θ and μ_s; θ being the apparent or observed zenith distance, and μ_s the current refraction at the surface, given by the equation

$$\mu_s = \frac{273\mu_0 B}{760T},$$

in which B is the height of the barometer in millimeters, T the absolute temperature in degrees Centigrade, and μ_0 atmospheric refraction at 0° C. and 760 mm. pressure.

Since $\delta\theta$ is small, we have from equation (A), to a close approximation

$$\delta\theta = \sin \delta\theta = \frac{\mu_s \tan \theta}{1 + \dfrac{C}{R}} - \tan \theta \cos \delta\theta$$

$$= \tan \theta \left(\frac{\mu_s}{1 + \dfrac{C}{R}} - \sqrt{1 - \sin^2 \delta\theta} \right)$$

$$= \tan \theta \left\{ \frac{\mu_s}{1 + \dfrac{C}{R}} - 1 + \frac{1}{2}(\delta\theta)^2 \right\}$$

$$= \tan \theta \left\{ \mu_s - \frac{\mu_s C}{R} - 1 + \frac{1}{2}(\delta\theta)^2 \right\}, \text{ nearly.}$$

But, from the laws of refraction,

$$\mu_s \sin \theta = \sin (\theta + \delta\theta)$$

from which

$$\delta\theta = (\mu_s - 1) \tan \theta, \text{ nearly.}$$

Hence,

$$\delta\theta = (\mu_s - 1) \tan \theta \left\{ 1 - \frac{\mu_s C}{(\mu_s - 1)R} + \frac{1}{2}(\mu_s - 1) \tan^2 \theta \right\}, \text{ approximately.}$$

Substituting for C its value and noting that

$$\frac{1}{\cos^2 \theta} = 1 + \tan^2 \theta$$

this equation reduces to

$$\delta\theta = (\mu_s - 1)\left(1 - \frac{\mu_s H}{R}\right) \tan \theta - (\mu_s - 1)\left(\frac{\mu_s H}{R} - \frac{\mu_s - 1}{2}\right) \tan^3 \theta$$

$$= (\mu_s - 1)\left(1 - \frac{H}{R}\right) \tan \theta - (\mu_s - 1)\left(\frac{H}{R} - \frac{\mu_s - 1}{2}\right) \tan^3 \theta, \text{ nearly.}$$

If $H = 7.990 \times 10^5$ cm.; $R = 6.3709 \times 10^8$ cm.;   and $\mu_s - 1 = 0.0002927$, all closely approximate values, then,

$$\delta\theta = 60''. 29 \tan \theta - 0''.06688 \tan^3 \theta.$$

This is Lord Rayleigh's final equation, and it appears to be exceedingly accurate for all values of θ up to at least 75°, or as far, perhaps, as irregular surface densities generally allow any refraction formula to be used with confidence.

Since the index of refraction varies from color to color, it follows that star images are drawn out into vertical spectra. The amount of this effect, however, is small. Thus, the difference between the refractions of red and blue-green is only about one-one-hundredth of the total refraction of yellow (*D*) light. Hence, the approximate angular distance between the red and blue-green images of a star at the zenith distances, 30°, 45°, 60°, and 75° are $0''.35$, $0''.60$, $1''.04$, and $2''.24$, respectively. Possibly, this may account, in part at least, for the fact that stellar declinations, as determined from the northern and southern hemispheres, respectively, are not quite the same.

Scintillation or Twinkling and Unsteadiness of Stars.—The scintillation or twinkling of stars, that is, their rapid changes in brightness and, occasionally, also in color, especially when near the eastern or western horizon, is a well-known, and, now, well-understood, phenomenon that for many centuries—certainly since the days of Aristotle (384–322 B.C.), who noted the fact that the fixed stars twinkle while the planets shine with comparatively steady lights—has been observed, investigated, and discussed. The most systematic and complete observations, however, of scintillation are those made by Respighi,[1] with a spectroscope, during the years 1868–1869, and which he summed up, substantially, as follows:

1. In the spectra of stars near the horizon, more or less broad and distinct dark and bright bands sweep with greater or less velocity from the red to the violet and from the violet to the red, or oscillate from the one to the other; and this whatever the direction of the spectra from the horizontal to the vertical.

2. When the conditions of the atmosphere are normal, the dark and bright bands of western stars travel regularly from the red to the violet, and of eastern from the violet to the red; while in the neighborhood of the meridian they usually oscillate from the one color to the other, or even are limited to a portion of the spectrum.

3. On examining the horizontal spectrum of a star sensibly parallel dark and bright bands, more or less inclined to the axis (transverse) of the spectrum, are seen passing from the red to the violet or reversely, according as the star is in west or east.

4. The inclination of the bands, or angle between them and the axis (transverse) of the spectrum, depends upon the altitude of the star; increasing rapidly

[1] Assoc. Française pour l'Avancement des Sciences, **1**; 148, 1872.

from 0° at the horizon to 90° at an elevation of 30° to 40°, where they, therefore, are longitudinal.

5. The inclination of the bands, reckoned from above, is towards the violet end of the spectrum.

6. The bands, most distinct at the horizon, become less conspicuous with increase of elevation. Above 40° the longitudinal bands reduce to mere shaded streaks and often can be seen in the spectrum only as slight general changes of brightness.

7. With increase of elevation the movement of the bands becomes more rapid and less regular.

8. On turning the spectrum from the horizontal the inclination of the bands to the transversal continuously diminishes until it becomes zero, when the spectrum is nearly vertical. They also become less distinct, but continue always to move in the same direction.

9. The bright bands are less frequent and more irregular than the dark, and are well defined only in the spectra of stars near the horizon.

10. In the midst of this general and violent movement of light and shade over the spectra of stars, the Fraunhofer lines peculiar to the light of each star remain quiescent, or are subject to only very slight oscillations.

11. When the atmospheric conditions are abnormal, the bands are fainter and more irregular in form and movement.

12. When the wind is strong, the bands usually are quite faint and ill defined; the spectra even of stars near the horizon showing mere changes of brightness.

13. Good definition and regular movement of the bands appear to indicate the continuance of fair weather, while varying definition and irregular motion seem to imply a probable change.

These observations show that the dark bands are due to temporary deflection of light from the object glass, by irregularities in the density of the atmosphere. For stars near the horizon, the linear separation of the rays of different color is so great, as they pass through the atmosphere to the observer, that successive portions of the spectrum may be deflected from, or concentrated onto (light deficiencies in a transparent medium must be balanced by light concentrations, and *vice versa*), the telescope or eye. Hence, the progression of bright and dark bands along the spectra of low altitude stars, and their rapid change of color to the unaided eye.

Further, since the path of the more refrangible light, necessarily, lies above that of the less refrangible (Montigny's principle), it follows that an atmospheric irregularity traveling, or rotating, with the earth, would affect the different-colored rays from the stars in the west in the order of red, green, blue, violet, and rays from stars in the east in the reverse order. If, then, the separation of the extreme rays is large in comparison to the effective dimension of the air irregularity, the resulting band will, at any given instant, cover only a portion of the spectrum.

But the approximate amount of this separation is readily obtained from equation (D), p. 442. Thus, for the limit of the atmosphere,

$$du = H \frac{\sin \theta}{\cos^2 \theta} d\mu_s.$$

Hence, at the zenith distance 80°, the red and violet rays, simultaneously received by the observer from the same star, will be separated at the limit of the atmosphere (assuming the dispersion between these rays to be one-fiftieth the refraction of yellow light) by about 156 centimeters, and proportionately for levels below which definite fractions of the total mass of the atmosphere lie. For the zenith distance 40°, however, the corresponding separation at the limit of the atmosphere is only about 5 centimeters, and for 20° about 2 centimeters. Inequalities in the atmosphere may, therefore, interfere with only a portion at a time of the spectrum of a star near the horizon and, thus, produce the phenomenon of a traveling band, while in the case of a star whose zenith distance is 40°, or less, the interference will include nearly, or quite, the entire spectrum, and thus produce mere changes of brightness.

It is generally stated that the direction of travel of the bands during fine weather, red to violet for stars in the west, violet to red for stars in the east, and irregularly, or simultaneously, over the entire spectrum for stars near the meridian, is directly dependent upon the west to east rotation of the earth. It is correctly stated (on assumption of a stationary atmosphere) that this rotation would cause an atmospheric irregularity to affect the red rays first and the violet last, violet first and red last, and all rays, more or less simultaneously, of stars in the west, east, and near the meridian, respectively. But the order would be the same if the earth were at rest and the air traveling from west to east. As a matter of fact, over most of the earth outside the tropics, the west to east angular velocity of the general winds, as seen by the observer, is several times that of the earth. Hence, the rate at which the disturbance drifts across the line of sight, presumably, depends much more on the direction of the prevailing winds than upon the rotation of the earth. Indeed, in tropical regions, where the prevailing winds are from easterly points, the usual direction of travel of the bands probably (if the above reasoning is correct) is reversed.

The disappearance of distinct bands with high winds is due, of course, to the more complete mixing of the atmosphere at such times.

In the same general way, atmospheric inequalities produce "unsteadiness," or rapid changes in the apparent positions of stars as seen in a telescope. In reality, this is a telescopic form of scintillation which, because never amounting to more than a very few seconds of arc, the unaided eye cannot detect. On the other hand, the great changes in brightness and color, so conspicuous to the naked eye, are scarcely, if at all, noticeable in a large telescope. This is because the object glass is so large that, in general, light deflected from one portion of it is caught in another.

Scintillation of the Planets, Sun, and Moon.—It is commonly stated that the planets do not scintillate—that the light from the several portions of their disks follows such different paths through the atmosphere that not all, nor even any large portion, of it can be affected at any one time. It is true that because of their sensible disks the scintillation of planets is much less than that of fixed stars, but, under favorable circumstances, their scintillation is quite perceptible. Even the rims of the sun and the moon boil, or "scintillate," while, of course, any fine marking on either, or on a planet, is quite as unsteady as the image of a fixed star.

Nature of Irregularities.—It is well known that the atmosphere, generally, is so stratified that with increase of elevation many more or less abrupt changes occur in temperature, composition, density, and, therefore, refrangibility. As such layers glide over each other, billows are formed, and the adjacent layers thereby corrugated. The several layers, frequently, also heat unequally, largely because of disproportionate vapor contents, and, thereby, develop, both day and night, and at various levels, innumerable vertical convections; each moving mass differing, of course, in density from the surrounding air, and by the changing velocity being drawn out into dissolving filaments. Optically, therefore, the atmosphere is so heterogeneous that a sufficiently bright star shining through it would produce on the earth a somewhat streaky pattern of light and shade.

Shadow Bands.—A striking proof of the optical streakiness of the atmosphere is seen in the well-known shadow bands that at the time of a total solar eclipse appear immediately before the second, and after the third, contact, due mainly, perhaps, to quasitotal reflection as the light passes from denser surrounding air into the lighter rising masses.[1]

Terrestrial Scintillation.—A bright terrestrial light of small size, such as an open electric arc, scintillates, when seen at a great distance, quite as distinctly as do the stars and for substantially the same reason, that is, optical inequalities due to constant and innumerable vertical convections and conflicting winds.

Shimmering.—The tremulous appearance of objects, the common phenomenon of shimmering, seen through the atmosphere immediately over any heated surface, is another manifestation of atmospheric refraction, and is due to the innumerable fibrous convections that always occur over such an area.

Optical Haze.—The frequent indistinctness of distant objects on warm days when the atmosphere is comparatively free from dust, and ascribed to optical haze, is due to the same thing, namely, optical hetero-

[1] HUMPHREYS, W. J., *Popular Astronomy*, **34**; 566, 1926.

geneity of the atmosphere, that causes that unsteadiness, or dancing, of star images that so often interferes with the positional and other exact work of the astronomer. Both are but provoking manifestations of atmospheric refraction.

Times of Rising and Setting of Sun, Moon, and Stars.—An interesting, and important, result of astronomical refraction is the fact that the sun, moon, and stars, rise earlier and set later than they, otherwise, would. For places at sea level, the amount of elevation of celestial objects on the horizon averages about 35', and therefore the entire solar and lunar disks may be seen before (on rising) and after (on setting) even their upper limbs would have appeared, in the first case, or disappeared, in the second, if there had been no refraction. This difference in time of rising, or setting, depends on the angle of inclination α of the path to the horizon. In general, it is given by the equation

$$t = 140^s \csc \alpha, \text{ about.}$$

The minimum time, therefore, occurs when the path is normal to the horizon and is about $2^m 20^s$; the maximum obviously occurs at the poles where, for the sun, it is about $1\frac{1}{2}$ days, the time required near equinox for the solar declination to change by 35', and, for the stars, anything from a calculable long time down to the minimum of approximately 100 years for those whose polar distances are changing most rapidly incident to precession, that is, those near the vernal equinox.

Green Flash.—As the upper limb of the sun disappears in a clear sky below a distant horizon, its last star-like point often is seen to change rapidly from pale yellow or orange, to green and, finally, blue, or, at least, a bluish-green. The vividness of the green, when the sky is exceptionally clear, together with its almost instant appearance, has given rise to the name "green flash" for this phenomenon. The same gamut of colors, only in reverse order, occasionally is seen at sunrise.

The entire phenomenon has been described by some as merely a complementary after-image effect, that is, the sensation of its complementary color that frequently follows the sudden removal of a bright light. This explanation, however, cannot account for the reverse order of the colors as seen at sunrise. Neither does it account for the twinkling of the "flash" close observation, now and then, reveals, nor for the fact that when the sun is especially red the "flash" is never seen.

It is not, indeed, a physiological effect, but only the inevitable result of atmospheric refraction, by virtue of which, as a celestial object sinks below the horizon, its light must disappear in the order of refrangibility; the red first, being least refrangible, then the green, and, finally, the blue, or most refrangible. Violet need not be considered, since only a comparatively small portion of it can penetrate so far through the atmosphere.

It may properly be asked, then, why these color changes do not apply to the whole solar disk. The answer is, because the angular dispersion, due to the refraction of the atmosphere, between the several colors is very small—between red and green, for instance, only about 20″, even when the object is on the horizon, so that any color from a given point on the sun is reinforced by its complementary color, thus giving white, from a closely neighboring point. Hence, color phenomena can appear only when there are no such neighboring points, or when only a minute portion of the disk is above the horizon. It must, further, be noted that color effects, due to the general refraction of the atmosphere, occur only when the source (brilliant point) is on the horizon. Stars above the horizon are not permanently drawn out into rainbow bands, and that for the simple reason that the red light by one route is supplemented by the green, blue, etc., by others, and the whole blended into white, yellow, or whatever the real color of the star may be. This multiplicity of routes, and consequent blending of color, is not possible for rays of light from objects just sinking below, or rising above, the horizon, and, therefore, under such circumstances, they pass through a series of color changes.

Terrestrial Refraction.—The curving of rays of light is not confined to those that come from some celestial object, but applies also to those

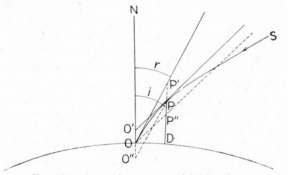

Fig. 163.—Approximate terrestrial refraction.

that pass between any points within the atmosphere, whether at the same or different levels. This latter phenomenon, known as terrestrial refraction, causes all objects on the earth, or in the atmosphere, to appear to be at greater altitudes than they actually are, except when the surface air is so strongly heated as to cause an *increase* of density with elevation and, thus, produce the inferior mirage, described below.

Terrestrial refraction is also a matter of great importance, especially to the geodesist, and its complete analysis, from which practical tables may be constructed, is essentially the same as that of astronomical refraction.[1] It will be instructive, however, to consider a few graphical corrections of apparent elevations.

[1] McLeod, *Phil. Mag.* **38**; 546, 1919.

Let *ON* (Fig. 163) be normal to the surface *OD* of the earth, and let *P* be observed from *O*.   Obviously *P*, whose horizontal distance *OD* may be supposed known, will seem to be at *P'* and, thus, its apparent altitude greater than the actual by the distance *PP'*.   From the angle *r*, the density of the air at the observer's position *O* and the approximate density at *P* (known from the approximate height of *P*) it is easy to draw *OP''* parallel to the tangent at *P* to the refraction curve *SPO*. This gives *P''*, necessarily below *P*.   Hence *P* lies somewhere between *P'* and *P''*.

A more exact determination could be had by drawing the curve of refraction *OPS* corresponding to the angle *r* and noting its intersection with the normal at *D*.

If the observer happens to be at *P*, the point *O* will appear elevated to *O'*.   Clearly, however, from a knowledge of the angle *PO'N*, and the approximate air densities at *P* and *O*, one may draw *PO''* parallel to *P'O*, and thus locate *O* somewhere between the two determined points *O'* and *O''*.   Here, too, it would be more accurate to use the refraction curve *SPO*.

Even initially horizontal rays normally curve down toward the surface of the earth, so that objects at the observer's own level, as well as those above and below it, appear elevated.   To understand this phenomenon, consider a wave front normal to the surface of the earth, and, consequently, moving horizontally.   If, now, the density of the air, at the place in question, decreases with increase of elevation, as it nearly always does, the upper portion of the wave front will travel faster than the lower, and the path will be bent down toward the earth along a curve whose radius depends upon the rate of this density decrease. For example, let the corrected height of the barometer be 760 mm., the temperature 17° C., and the rate of temperature decrease with elevation 5° C. per kilometer; conditions that not infrequently obtain at sea level.   On substituting these values in the density-elevation equation, it appears that the density gradient would be such that, if continuous, the limit of the atmosphere would be reached at an elevation of about 10 kilometers.   Hence, under these circumstances, the velocity of light at an elevation of 10 kilometers would be to its velocity at the surface in the ratio of 1,000,276 to 1,000,000, approximately, since the refractive index of the lower air would be 1.000276, about.   The radius of curvature *r* therefore, is closely given in kilometers by the equation

$$\frac{r}{r + 10} = \frac{1,000,000}{1,000,276}.$$

Hence, *r* = 36,232 kilometers, or approximately 5.7 times the radius of the earth.

It is conceivable, therefore, that the size of a planet and the vertical density gradient of its atmosphere might be such that one's horizon on it would include the entire surface—that he could look all the way round, and, as some one has said, see his own back.

The distance to the horizon, corresponding to a given altitude, obviously depends upon the rate of vertical density decrease in such manner that, when the latter is known, the approximate value of the former can easily be computed. Thus, let the density decrease be such that the radius of curvature of a ray tangent to the surface shall be $5.7R$, $R = 6366$ kilometers, being the radius of the earth; let α be the angle between the radii from the center of the earth to the observer and a point on his unobstructed horizon respectively; let h be the observer's height in meters above the level of his horizon; and let r be the distance, in kilometers, measured over the surface from the horizon to a point on the same level below the observer; then, by trigonometry, to a close approximation;

$$h = 6,366,000 \,(\sec \alpha - 1) - 36,286,200 \left(\sec \frac{\alpha}{5.7} - 1 \right) \sec \alpha$$

and

$$r = 6366 \,\alpha, \, \alpha \text{ in radians.}$$

A few values of the distance to the horizon from different elevations, computed by the above formula, are given in the following table:

DISTANCE TO HORIZON

Distance in kilometers...	1	2	5	10	20	50	100
Elevation in meters.....	0.061	0.263	1.613	6.856	25.901	161.918	647.604

Looming.—Since the extension of the actual, beyond the geometrical, horizon depends, as just explained, upon the density decrease of the atmosphere with increase of elevation, it follows that any change in the latter must produce a corresponding variation of the former. An increase, for instance, in the normal rate of decrease, such as often happens over water in middle to high latitudes, produces the phenomenon of looming, or the coming into sight of objects normally below the horizon, a classical instance of which was described by Latham.[1] Similar changes in the rate of density decrease with increase of elevation also are common in valleys, but here, looming, in the above sense, is rendered impossible by the surrounding hills or mountains.

Towering.—The condition of the atmosphere that produces looming, in the sense here used, or would produce it if the region were level, often gives rise to two other phenomena, namely, unwonted towering, also usually called looming, and the consequent apparent approach of surrounding objects.

[1] *Phil. Trans.*, **88**; 1798; abridged, **18**; 337; EVERETT, *Nature*, **11**; 49, 1874.

The more rapid the downward curvature of the ray paths at the observer the more elevated, clearly, will objects appear to be, and such curvature may, indeed, be very considerable. Thus, a temperature inversion near the surface of the earth of 1° C. per meter change of elevation bends down a ray along an arc whose radius is about 0.16 that of the earth, while an inversion of 10° C. per meter—a possible condition through a shallow stratum—gives a radius of only about 0.016 that of the earth, or, say, 100 kilometers. If, now, as occasionally happens, the inversion layer is so located that rays to the observer from the top of an object are more curved than those from the bottom, it will appear not only elevated but also vertically magnified—it will tower and seem to draw nearer.

Sinking.—Instead of increasing the curvature of rays, the temperature distribution may be such as, on the contrary, to decrease it, and, thereby, cause objects normally on the horizon to sink quite beyond it. Such phenomena, exactly the reverse of looming, are, also, most frequently observed at sea.

Stooping.—Occasionally, rays from the base of an object may be curved down much more rapidly than those from the top, with the obvious result of apparent vertical contraction, and the production of effects quite as odd and grotesque as those due to towering. Indeed, since the refraction of the atmosphere increases, in general, with the zenith distance, it is obvious that the bases of objects nearly always, apparently, are elevated more than their tops, and themselves, therefore, vertically shortened. The normal effect, however, is small and seldom noticed except, perhaps, in connection with the slightly flattened shape of the sun and moon when on the horizon.

Superior Mirage.—It occasionally happens that one or more images of a distant object, a ship for instance, are seen directly above it, as shown in Fig. 164, copied from Vince's[1] well-known description of exceptionally fine displays of this phenomenon.

The image nearest the object always is inverted, and, therefore, appears as though reflected from an overhead plane mirror—hence the name "superior mirage"—and indeed, many seem to assume that this image really is due to a certain kind of reflection, that is, total reflection, such as occurs at the undersurface of water, which, like mirror reflection, causes an abrupt change in the direction of the light. It is obvious, however, that this assumption is entirely erroneous, since the atmosphere can never be sufficiently stratified in nature to produce the discontinuity in density (adjacent layers are always interdiffusible) that this explanation of the origin of the proximate inverted image presupposes. Another apparently simple explanation of mirage phenomena is furnished by drawing imaginary rays from the object along arbitrary

[1] *Phil. Trans.*, **89**; 8 (abridged, 436), 1799.

paths to the observer. But, in reality, this is no explanation at all, unless it is first demonstrated that the rays must follow the paths assumed. It is allowable, of course, to assume any *possible* distribution of atmospheric density and to trace the rays from an object accordingly. If

FIG. 164.—Examples of superior mirage. (*Vince.*)

the assumed distribution follows a simple law, the rays may be traced mathematically, as by Mascart,[1] though such discussions, when at all thorough, necessarily are long.

[1] "Traité d'Optique," **3**; 305–308.

A simple explanation of mirage, that admirably accounts for the phenomena observed, has been given by Hastings,[1] in substance as follows:

Let the air be calm and let there be a strong temperature inversion some distance, 10 meters, say, above the surface—conditions that occasionally obtain, especially over quiet water. Obviously, the ratio of decrease of density to increase of elevation is irregular in such an atmosphere, and, therefore, the velocity of light traveling horizontally through it must increase also irregularly with increase of elevation. Thus, beginning with the undersurface of the inversion layer, the rate of velocity increase with elevation must first grow to a maximum and then diminish to something like its normal small value at, and beyond, the upper surface of this layer. Hence, that portion of an originally

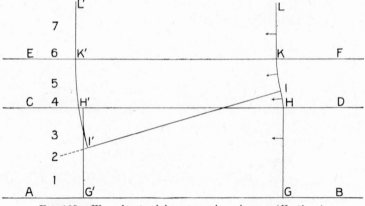

Fig. 165.—Wave fronts giving a superior mirage. (*Hastings.*)

vertical, or approximately vertical, wave front that lies within the inversion layer must soon become doubly deflected, substantially as indicated in Fig. 165.

Let *AB* (Fig. 165) be the surface of water, say, *CD* the under and *EF* the upper surface of a strong inversion layer, and let *GHIKL* be the distorted wave front of light, traveling in the direction indicated, from a distant source. The future approximate positions of the wave front, of which *G′H′I′K′L′* is one, are readily located from the fact that its progress is always normal to itself, and the appearance of the distant object, from which these wave fronts are proceeding, easily determined. At 1, for instance, the object seems upright and at its proper level, no images are seen and the whole appearance is normal; at 2, confused elevated images appear, in addition to the object itself; at 3, the object and two distinct images are seen, the lower produced by the segment *HI* of the wave front inverted, the other erect; at 4, the undersurface

[1] "Light," Chap. VII; Charles Scribner's Sons, 1902.

of the inversion layer, the inverted image blends with the object and disappears; at 5, only the erect image can be seen, and, indeed, may be seen even when the object itself, normally, would be below the horizon; at 6, the upper surface of the inversion layer, the vertical image merges with the object and disappears; while, everywhere beyond the upper surface, only the object itself is visible, as at 1, with no evidence, whatever, of abnormal refraction and mirage.

An additional inversion layer, obviously, might produce other images, while more or less confused layers might produce multiple and distorted images, such as shown in Fig. 166, copied from Scoresby's account[1] of a certain telescopic view of the east coast of Greenland.

FIG. 166.—Telescopic appearance of the coast of Greenland, at the distance of 35 miles, when under the influence of an extraordinary refraction.   July 18, 1820.   Lat. 71° 20′, Long. 17° 30′ W.

Inferior Mirage.—It is a very common thing, in flat desert regions, especially during the warmer hours of the day to see, below distant objects and somewhat separated from them, their apparently mirrored images—the inferior mirage. The phenomenon closely simulates, even to the quivering of the images, the reflection, by a quiet body of water, of objects on the distant shore, the "water" being the image of the distant low sky, and, therefore, frequently leads to the false assumption that a lake or bay is close by. This type of mirage is very common on the west coast of Great Salt Lake. Indeed, on approaching this lake from the west, one can often see the railway over which he has just passed apparently disappearing beneath a shimmering surface. It is also common over smooth-paved streets, provided one's eyes are just above the street level. An undergrade crossing in a level town, for instance, offers an excellent opportunity almost any warm day of seeing well-defined

[1] *Trans. Roy. Soc. Edinburgh*, **9**; 299, 1823.

images that are apt to arouse one's surprise at the careless way his fellow citizens wade through pools of water!

Since the inferior mirage occurs only over approximately level places and, there, only when they are so strongly heated that for a short distance the density of the atmosphere increases with elevation, it follows that its explanation is essentially the same as that of the superior mirage. Of course, the surface air is in unstable equilibrium and rising in innumerable filaments, but its rarefied state is maintained so long as there is an abundant supply of insolation. A wave front, therefore, from an object slightly above the general level, soon becomes distorted through the greater speed of its lower portion, as schematically indicated in Fig. 167.

Let *AB* of this figure be the surface of the earth and *CD* the upper level of the superheated stratum. Let *EFG* be the position of a wave front, traveling, as indicated, the lower portion curved forward as a

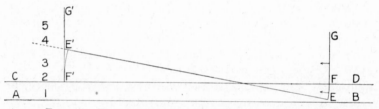

FIG. 167.—Wave fronts giving an inferior mirage. (*Hastings.*)

result of its greater speed in the rarefied layer. One of the consequent later positions of the wave front is shown at *E'F'G'*, from which it follows that, at 1, neither the object in question nor any image of it can be seen; at 2, the object and its inverted image are glimpsed, superimposed; at 3, both the object and its inverted image well below it, are plainly visible; at 4, the image is just disappearing; while at 5, there is no evidence of a mirage, unless of objects more distant than the one under consideration.

Great uncertainty may exist, therefore, in regard to the exact positions of objects seen in (or perhaps hidden by) a mirage. Thus, in his official report of the battle of Apr. 11, 1917, between the English and the Turks in Mesopotamia, Gen. Maude, the British commander, says: "The fighting had to be temporarily suspended owing to a mirage."

Lateral Mirage.—Vertical sheets of abnormally dense, or abnormally rare, atmosphere, obviously, would produce lateral mirages in every way like those due to similar horizontal layers, and, indeed, such mirages are occasionally seen along walls and cliffs whose temperatures differ widely from that of the air a few meters from them.

Fata Morgana.—Morgana (Breton equivalent of sea woman), according to Celtic legend and Arthurian romance, was a fairy, half-sister of King Arthur, who exhibited her powers by the mirage. Italian poets represent her as dwelling in a crystal palace beneath the waves. Hence, presumably, the name Fata Morgana (Italian for Morgan le Fay, or Morgan the fairy) was given, centuries ago, to those complicated mirages that occasionally appear over the strait of Messina though much more frequently in high latitudes, and at Toyama Bay on the northwest coast of Japan, molding the bluffs and houses of the opposite shore into wondrous castles that, alike, tower into the sky and sink beneath the surface; nor is it strange that this poetical name should have become generic, as it has, for all such multiple mirages, wherever they occur.

According to Forel,[1] this phenomenon, to which he has given much attention, results from the coexistence of the temperature disturbances peculiar to both the inferior and superior mirages, such as might be produced by a strong inversion over a relatively warm sea. This, of course, implies a marked increase of density with elevation to a maximum a short distance above the surface, followed by a rapid density decrease— an unstable condition and, therefore, liable to quick and multiform changes. Obviously, too, such a cold intermediate layer, in addition to producing a double mirage, acts, also, as a sort of cylindrical lens that vertically magnifies distant objects seen through it.

No wonder, then, that, under such circumstances, the most commonplace cliffs and cottages are converted, through their multiple, distorted, and magnified images, into magic castles, or the marvellous crystal palaces of Morgan le Fay! Interesting discussions, observational and theoretical, of the mirage are given by Fujiwhara, Oomori, and Taguti[2]; Hidaka[3]; and Futi.[4] Also, an elaborate mathematical treatment of it, supplemented with an extensive bibliography, has been published by Wolf-Egbert Schiele.[5]

[1] *Archives Sciences Phys. Nat.*, **32**; 471, 1911.
[2] *Geophys. Mag.*, **4**; 317, 1931.
[3] *Geophys. Mag.*, **4**; 375, 1931.
[4] *Geophys. Mag.*, **4**; 387, 1931.
[5] *Geophys. Inst.*, Univ. Leipzig, **7**; 101–188, 1935.

CHAPTER III

REFRACTION PHENOMENA: REFRACTION BY WATER DROPS

RAINBOW

Principal Bows.—It may seem entirely superfluous to describe so common a phenomenon as the rainbow, or to offer more than the simple explanation of it that may be found in innumerable textbooks. But rainbows differ, among themselves, as one tree from another, and, besides, some of their most interesting features usually are not even mentioned—and naturally so, for the "explanations" generally given of the rainbow may well be said to explain beautifully that which does not occur, and to leave unexplained that which does.

The ordinary rainbow, seen on a sheet of water drops—rain or spray—is a group of circular, or nearly circular, arcs of colors whose common center is on the line connecting the observer's eye with the exciting light (sun, moon, electric arc, etc.) or rather, except rarely, on that line extended in the direction of the observer's shadow. The lunar bow, though well known, is rarely seen except about great waterfalls and along certain showery coasts.[1] A very great number of rainbows are theoretically possible, as will be explained later, and, doubtless, all that are possible actually occur, though only three (not counting supernumeraries) certainly have been seen on sheets of rain. The most brilliant bow, known as the *primary*, with red outer border of about 42° radius and blue to violet inner border, appears opposite the sun (or other adequate light); the next brightest, or the *secondary* bow, is on the same side of the observer, but the order of its colors is reversed and its radius, about 50° to the red, is larger; the third or *tertiary* bow, having about the same radius as that of the primary, and colors in the same order, lies between the observer and the sun, but is so faint that it is rarely seen in nature. Obviously, the common center of the primary and secondary bows is, angularly, as far below the observer as the source (sun generally) is above, so that, usually, less than a semicircle of these spectral arcs is visible, and never more, except from an eminence.

The records of close observations of rainbows soon show that not even the colors are always the same; neither is the band of any color of constant angular width; nor the total breadth of the several colors at all uniform; similarly, the purity and brightness of the different colors are subject to large variations. The greatest contrast, perhaps, is between the sharply defined brilliant rainbow of the retreating thunderstorm and that ill-defined faintly tinged bow that sometimes appears in a mist, fog, or cloud—the "white bow" or "fog bow."

[1] *Science*, **88**; 496, 1938.

All these differences depend, as will be explained later, essentially upon the size of the drops, and, therefore, inequalities often exist between even the several portions, especially top and bottoms, of the same bow, or develop as the rain progresses. Additional complications occasionally result from the reflection of bows and from bows produced by reflected images of the sun, but, though unusual and, thus, likely to excite wonder and comment, such phenomena are easily explained.

Supernumerary Bows.—Rather narrow bands of color, essentially red, or red and green, often appear parallel to both the primary and the secondary bows, along the inner side of the first and outer of the second. These also differ greatly in purity and color, number visible, width, etc., not only between individual bows but, also, between the several parts of the same bow. No such colored arcs, however, occur between the principal bows; indeed, on the contrary, the general illumination here is perceptibly at a minimum.

Deviation in Direction of Emerging from Entering Ray.—Since a raindrop is spherical, its action on an enveloping wave front may be

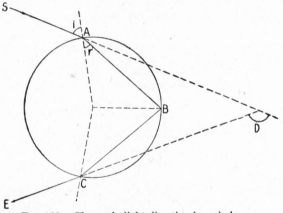

Fɪɢ. 168.—Change in light direction by raindrop.

obtained by determining, first, the effects in the plane of a great circle containing an entering ray, and, then, revolving this plane about that line in it that bisects the angle between the incident and emerged paths of any given ray in the same plane. Let, then, ABC (Fig. 168) be the plane of a great circle of an enlarged raindrop and let $SABCE$ be the path of a ray in this plane, entering the drop at A and emerging at C. The changes in direction at A and C are each $i - r$, in which i is the angle of incidence and r the angle of refraction, and the change at B, as also at every other place of an internal reflection, when there are more than one, is $\pi - 2r$. Hence, the total deviation D is given by the equation

$$D = 2(i - r) + n(\pi - 2r) \tag{1}$$

in which n is the number of internal reflections.

Minimum Deviation.—The above general expression for the deviation shows that it varies with the angle of incidence. There is also a minimum deviation, corresponding to a particular angle of incidence, as may be shown in the usual way. Thus, by equation (1),

$$dD = 2di - 2(n + 1)dr$$

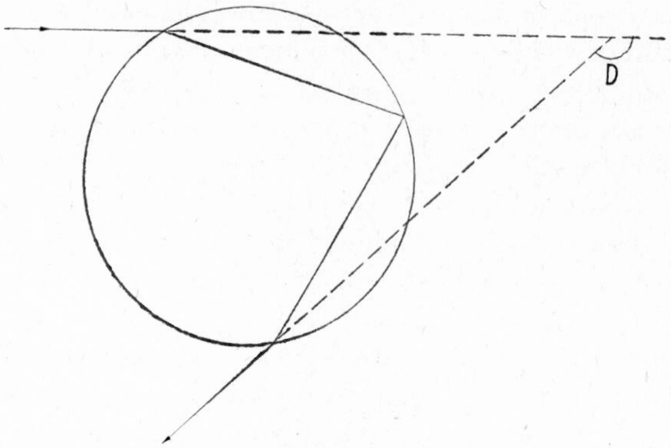

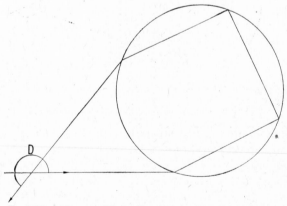

Fig. 169.—Change of light direction in primary rainbow.

which, on putting $dD = 0$, the condition of stationary (maximum or minimum) deviation, gives,

$$di = (n + 1)dr. \tag{2}$$

Fig. 170.—Change of light direction in secondary rainbow.

But

$$\sin i = \mu \sin r, \tag{3}$$

in which μ is the refractive index of water with reference to air, and, therefore,

$$\cos i \, di = \mu \cos r \, dr.$$

Hence, by equation (2)

$$\mu \cos r = (n + 1) \cos i \qquad (4)$$

and, by squaring and adding equations (3) and (4),

$$\cos i = \sqrt{\frac{\mu^2 - 1}{n^2 + 2n}}.$$

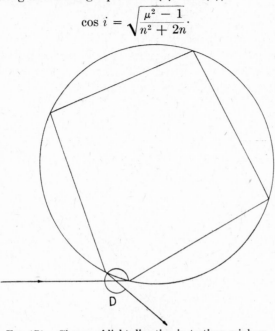

Fig. 171.—Change of light direction in tertiary rainbow.

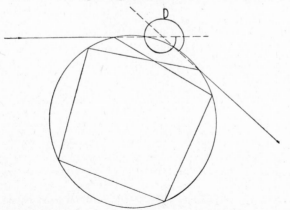

Fig. 172.—Change of light direction in quaternary rainbow.

This value of the angle of incidence corresponds, as stated, to a stationary deviation, but whether of maximum or minimum value may be determined by noting the sign of the second derivative.

$$\frac{d^2D}{di^2} = -2(n + 1)\frac{d^2r}{di^2}.$$

But

$$\frac{dr}{di} = \frac{\cos i}{\mu \cos r},$$

and

$$\frac{d^2r}{di^2} = \frac{(1 - \mu^2) \sin i}{\mu^3 \cos^3 r}.$$

Hence, as μ is greater than unity, this latter value is negative and, therefore, the second derivative of D with respect to i is positive, and the corresponding value of D is a minimum.

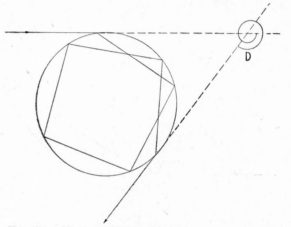

Fig. 173.—Change of light direction in quinary rainbow.

The following table gives these values for the primary, secondary, tertiary, quaternary, and quinary rainbows corresponding to 1, 2, 3, 4, and 5 internal reflections, respectively, as shown in Figs. 169, 170, 171, 172, and 173.

		$n = 1$	$n = 2$	$n = 3$	$n = 4$	$n = 5$
Violet, H......	i	58° 48′	71° 30′	76° 36′	79° 27′	81° 17′
$\lambda = 3968.5$.....	r	39° 33′	44° 54′	46° 23′	47° 2′	47° 22′
$\mu = 1.3435$.....	D	$\pi - 40° 36′$	$2\pi - 126° 24′$	$2\pi - 37° 52′$	$3\pi - 131° 26′$	$3\pi - 45° 50′$
Yellow........	i	59° 23′	71° 50′	76° 50′	79° 38′	81° 26′
$\lambda = 5800.0$,						
about....	r	40° 12′	45° 27′	46° 55′	47° 32′	47° 52′
$\mu = 4/3$.........	D	$\pi - 42° 2′$	$2\pi - 129° 2′$	$2\pi - 41° 40′$	$3\pi - 136° 4′$	$3\pi - 51° 32′$
Red, $H\alpha$......	i	59° 31′	71° 54′	76° 53′	79° 40′	81° 28′
$\lambda = 6562.9$.....	r	40° 21′	45° 34′	47° 2′	47° 39′	47° 59′
$\mu = 1.3311$.....	D	$\pi - 42° 22′$	$2\pi - 129° 36′$	$2\pi - 42° 30′$	$3\pi - 137° 10′$	$3\pi - 52° 5$

Entering and Emerging Rays.—Since a raindrop is spherical, it is obvious that its effect on incident radiation from the sun, or other spherical or point source, is symmetrical about an axis through the center of the drop and the luminous object. Hence, in the study of the rainbow, it is sufficient to use only a single plane containing this axis, tracing the rays incident over one quadrant of the intersection circle and noting the resulting phenomena. It is also obvious that, neglecting sky light, solar rays are parallel to within the angular diameter of the sun, 0.5°, about, and that as a first approximation they may be

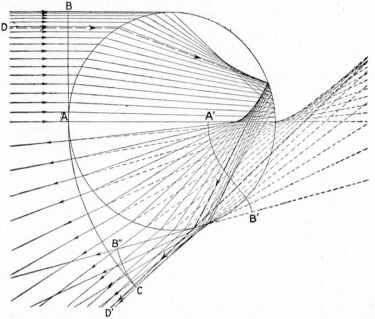

Fig. 174.—Course of light through a raindrop and the corresponding wave fronts.

regarded as strictly parallel. Let, then, the plane of Fig. 174 pass through the centers of a raindrop and the sun, and let *AB* be the wave front of parallel rays incident, as shown, above the normal or axial ray (ray passing through center of drop). An equal amount of light clearly enters below the normal ray, but for simplicity this is omitted. Similarly, that portion reflected from the outer surface is ignored, as is also all that gets through the drop directly, that is, at the place of first internal reflection, and all that is internally reflected more than once. This reduces the problem of the rainbow to its simplest terms, but loses none of its generality, since additional internal reflections merely change angular dimensions and brightness. The heavy line shows the course of the Descartes ray, or ray of minimum deviation for light of air-water refractive index, $\frac{4}{3}$. The courses of other rays are, approximately, as indicated.　Since the deviations of the rays incident between the axial and the Descartes rays are greater than that of the Descartes, it follows that their exits are, as shown, between those of the same two rays.　Similarly, all rays that enter beyond the Descartes ray are likewise more deviated, and, therefore, while they leave the drop beyond this ray, they do so in such direction as, sooner or later, also to come between it and the axial ray, substantially as shown.　Clearly, then, the once reflected light is diffuse and feeble except near the path of minimum deviation, and confined, as indicated, to the region between this path and the axial ray.

Formation of the Bow.—From the course, just given, of light through raindrops, it is clear that maximum brightness will be produced by all illuminated drops along the elements of a right circular cone whose vertex is at the eye, whose axis passes through the sun, and whose angular opening, corresponding to a given number of internal reflections, is determined by the wave length.　Hence, the rainbow exhibits a number of concentric circular arcs of different colors whose centers are angularly as far below the observer as the sun is above him.

Minimum Brightness between Primary and Secondary Bows.—Careful observers often note the fact that the region between the primary

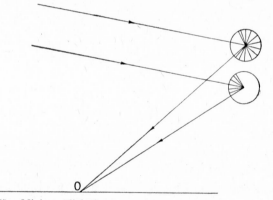

Fig. 175.—Minimum light between primary and secondary rainbows.

and secondary bows is slightly darker than any other in the same general direction.　The explanation of this phenomenon is very simple.　As the deviation of no ray can be less than that of the Descartes, it is clear that all light pertaining to any given number of internal reflections must leave a drop within a cone formed by the rotation of a corresponding Descartes ray about the axial ray, keeping the angle between them constant as shown in Fig. 175 for light of 1 and 2 internal reflections, respectively.　Hence, once reflected light reaches an observer from drops along, and within, his primary bow, but none from those without, while twice reflected light reaches him from along, and without, the secondary bow, but none from within it. The region between the two bows, therefore, and it alone, is devoid of both the once and the twice reflected rays and, in consequence, is comparatively dark.

Origin of Supernumerary Bows.—Since wave fronts are normal to the corresponding rays, it is clear that the incident front AB (Fig. 174) will, at the moment of complete emergence, appear as ACB''—exactly as though it had come from the virtual front $A'B'$ the locus of the terminus of a line of constant length AA' as it travels normally over the emerging wave front ACB''. Further, since the rays here lie on both sides of the one of minimum deviation, it is obvious that this ray divides $A'B'$ into two portions curved in opposite directions. That portion of the front that is convex forward will, of course, remain convex, but with increasing radii of curvature, while the part that is concave forward will

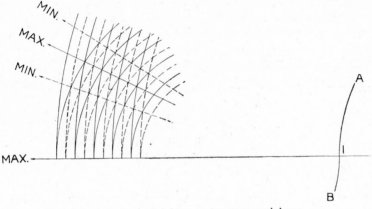

Fig. 176.—Interference giving supernumerary rainbows.

later become convex, and although neither portion is strictly the arc of a circle, the results they produce at a considerable distance, at the position of the observer, for instance, are qualitatively as though they were.

Let AIB, then (Fig. 176), be such a wave front, I being the point of inflection where the front is normal to the ray of minimum deviation. Let the full and dotted curves be opposite phase positions of the resulting cusped wave front. By inspection, it is obvious that, soon after leaving the drop, all the light must lie on one side of the ray of minimum deviation, thus making the observed angular radius of an arc of any given color slightly less than of the Descartes ray. It is also obvious that, with increasing angular distance from the Descartes ray, the two branches of the cusped front are alternately, and with increasing frequency, in opposite and like phases, thus producing alternate arcs of minimum and maximum brightness within and without the circle of the primary and the secondary bow, respectively. These additional maxima, of which several frequently are visible, constitute the familiar supernumerary bows.

Clearly, from Fig. 176, the widths of all the color bands, and the spacing of the maxima, vary inversely with the distance between the centers of the interfering waves, or size of the drop.

Equation of Portion of Outgoing Wave Front near Ray of Minimum Deviation.—In deriving this equation, originally due to Airy,[1] the more direct and elementary method of Wirtinger[2] will be followed with only such modifications as appear to make for clearness.

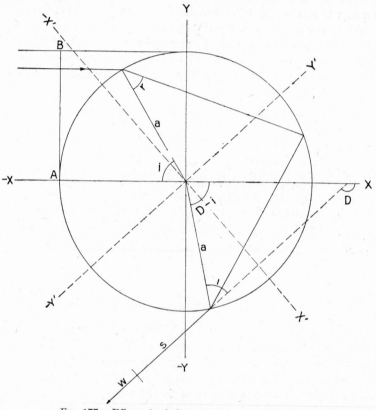

Fig. 177.—Effect of raindrop on shape of wave front.

Let AB (Fig. 177) be an incident wave front tangent to a raindrop of radius a; let w be a small section of the emitted front near the minimum deviation ray—more distant portions of the front need not be considered, as they are formed by rays too divergent to produce anything more than a slight general illumination; let v_1 be the velocity in air of the light under examination and v_1/μ its velocity in water. Clearly, then, from the

[1] *Cambridge Phil. Trans.*, **6**; 380.

[2] Berichte des naturw. medicin. Vereines an der Universität Innsbruck, Vol. xxi, 1896–1897; PERNTER-EXNER, "Meteorologische Optik."

constancy of the time interval between corresponding points on the wave fronts,

$$\frac{a(1 - \cos i)}{v_1} + \frac{4\mu a \cos r}{v_1} + \frac{s}{v_1} = T, \text{ a constant,}$$

in which s is the distance between the drop and the corresponding point on w; i and r the angles of incidence and refraction, respectively.

Let the completely emitted front be also tangent to the drop, as shown in Fig. 174. Then

$$T = \frac{4\mu a}{v_1}$$

and

$$s = a\{4\mu(1 - \cos r) - (1 - \cos i)\}.$$

Let the center of the drop be the intersection of coördinates as indicated. Then, if D is the angle of deflection, a point on w is given by the values,

$$x = a \cos (D - i) + s \cos D,$$

and

$$y = -a \sin (D - i) - s \sin D.$$

By turning the coördinates clockwise through the angle $D_1 - \pi/2$, in which D_1 is the change in direction of the ray of minimum deviation, the projection angles are correspondingly reduced and the new y axis brought parallel to the emerged Descartes ray. Hence, in terms of the new coördinates, writing d for $D - D_1$,

$$x' = -a \sin (d - i) - s \sin d$$
$$-y' = a \cos (d - i) + s \cos d.$$

But, as only rays very near that of minimum deviation need be considered, d is so small that to a sufficiently close approximation,

$$\cos d = 1, \text{ and } \sin d = d.$$

Hence,

$$x' = -ad \cos i + a \sin i - sd,$$

and

$$-y' = a \cos i + ad \sin i + s.$$

From Fig. 174, it is obvious that the small section w (Fig. 177) of the emerged wave front is very nearly parallel to the x' axis, and that the x' coördinate, therefore, is extremely sensitive to changes in y', while the y' coördinate is, relatively, but little affected by the changes in x'. Hence, as d is very small, points on w are sufficiently closely given by the expressions,

$$x' = a \sin i$$

and

$$-y' = a \cos i + ad \sin i + a\{4\mu(1 - \cos r) - (1 - \cos i)\}.$$

Let I and R be the angles of incidence and refraction, respectively, corresponding to the minimum deviation D_1 and let

$$i = I + \alpha, \text{ and } r = R + \beta$$

in which α and β are quite small, since only rays near that of minimum deviation are considered. Further, to make the problem entirely general, let n be the number of internal reflections. Then,

$$x' = a \sin (I + \alpha) = a \sin I + a\alpha \cos I$$

$$-y' = a \cos i + ad \sin i + a\{2\mu(n + 1)(1 - \cos r) - (1 - \cos i)\}$$

$$= 2a\left\{\cos i + \frac{d}{2} \sin i - \mu(n + 1) \cos r + \mu(n + 1) - \frac{1}{2}\right\}.$$

Treating d and β as functions of α and developing by Maclaurin's theorem we get, neglecting powers of α higher than the third,

$$\cos i = \cos (I + \alpha) = \cos I - \alpha \sin I - \frac{\alpha^2}{2} \cos I + \frac{\alpha^3}{6} \sin I + \cdots$$

$$\frac{d}{2} = \frac{1}{2}(D - D_1)$$

$$= (I + \alpha) - (R + \beta) + \frac{n}{2}\left\{\pi - 2(R + \beta)\right\} - \left\{I - R + \frac{n}{2}(\pi - 2R)\right\}$$

$$= \alpha - (n + 1)\beta = \alpha - (n + 1)\left(\frac{d\beta}{d\alpha}\right)_0 \alpha - (n + 1)\left(\frac{d^2\beta}{d\alpha^2}\right)_0 \frac{\alpha^2}{2}$$

$$- (n + 1)\left(\frac{d^3\beta}{d\alpha^3}\right)_0 \frac{\alpha^3}{6}.$$

Since

$$\frac{d}{2} = \alpha - (n + 1)\beta, d\left(\frac{d}{2}\right) = d\alpha - (n + 1)d\beta, \text{ and } \left(\frac{d\beta}{d\alpha}\right)_0 = \frac{1}{n + 1},$$

and, since

$$i = I + \alpha, \text{ or } \sin i = \sin I + \alpha \cos I,$$

therefore,

$$\frac{d}{2} \sin i = -(n + 1)\left(\frac{d^2\beta}{d\alpha^2}\right)_0 \frac{\alpha^2}{2} \sin I - (n + 1)\left(\frac{d^3\beta}{d\alpha^3}\right)_0 \frac{\alpha^3}{6} \sin I \cdots$$

$$- (n + 1)\left(\frac{d^2\beta}{d\alpha^2}\right)_0 \frac{\alpha^3}{2} \cos I \cdots$$

Finally, putting $\cos r = F(\alpha)$ and expanding $F(\alpha)$ by Maclaurin's theorem,

$$\cos r = \cos \{R + f(\alpha)\} = \cos R + \alpha\left(\frac{d \cos r}{d\alpha}\right)_0 + \frac{\alpha^2}{2}\left(\frac{d^2 \cos r}{d\alpha^2}\right)_0 +$$

$$\frac{\alpha^3}{6}\left(\frac{d^3 \cos r}{d\alpha^3}\right) + \cdots$$

But

$$\frac{d \cos r}{d\alpha} = - \sin r \frac{d\beta}{d\alpha} = - \frac{\sin i}{\mu} \frac{d\beta}{d\alpha},$$

$$\frac{d^2 \cos r}{d\alpha^2} = - \frac{\cos i}{\mu} \frac{d\beta}{d\alpha} - \frac{\sin i}{\mu} \frac{d^2\beta}{d\alpha^2}$$

$$\frac{d^3 \cos r}{d\alpha^3} = \frac{\sin i}{\mu} \frac{d\beta}{d\alpha} - \frac{\cos i}{\mu} \frac{d^2\beta}{d\alpha^2} - \frac{\cos i}{\mu} \frac{d^2\beta}{d\alpha^2} - \frac{\sin i}{\mu} \frac{d^3\beta}{d\alpha^3}.$$

Hence,

$$-\mu(n + 1) \cos r = - \mu(n + 1) \cos R - (n + 1)\left(\frac{d\beta}{d\alpha}\right)_0 \left[-\alpha \sin I \right.$$

$$\left. - \frac{\alpha^2}{2} \cos I + \frac{\alpha^3}{6} \sin I \right] - (n + 1)\left(\frac{d^2\beta}{d\alpha^2}\right)_0 \left[-\frac{\alpha^2}{2} \sin I - \frac{\alpha^3}{3} \cos I \right]$$

$$+ (n + 1)\left(\frac{d^3\beta}{d\alpha^3}\right)_0 \left[\frac{\alpha^3}{6} \sin I \right]$$

Hence, by addition of the above terms, remembering that,

$$\mu \cos R = (n + 1) \cos I$$

and that

$$\left(\frac{d\beta}{d\alpha}\right)_0 = \frac{1}{n + 1}.$$

$$-y' = 2a\{1 - (n + 1)^2\} \cos I - a(n + 1)\left(\frac{d^2\beta}{d\alpha^2}\right)_0 \frac{\alpha^3}{3} \cos I +$$

$$a\{2\mu(n + 1) - 1\}.$$

Differentiating the equation

$$\sin i = \mu \sin r$$

we have

$$\cos i = \mu \cos r \frac{d\beta}{d\alpha};$$

and, differentiating again,

$$- \sin i = -\mu \sin r \left(\frac{d\beta}{d\alpha}\right)^2 + \mu \cos r \left(\frac{d^2\beta}{d\alpha^2}\right),$$

or

$$- \sin I = -\mu \sin R \left(\frac{d\beta}{d\alpha}\right)_0^2 + \mu \cos R \left(\frac{d^2\beta}{d\alpha^2}\right)_0$$

$$= - \frac{\mu \sin R}{(n + 1)^2} + \mu \cos R \left(\frac{d^2\beta}{d\alpha^2}\right)_0.$$

But

$$\mu \sin R = \sin I, \text{ and } \mu \cos R = (n + 1) \cos I.$$

Therefore,

$$\left(\frac{d^2\beta}{d\alpha^2}\right)_0 = - \frac{\sin I}{\cos I} \frac{n^2 + 2n}{(n + 1)^3}$$

and

$$-y' = 2a\left[-(n^2 + 2n) \cos I + \mu(n + 1) - \frac{1}{2}\right] + a\alpha^3 \frac{n^2 + 2n}{3(n + 1)^2} \sin I,$$

$$x' = a \sin I + a\alpha \cos I.$$

The first terms in the equations for x' and y' are the coördinates of the point of inflection on the curve w. Taking this point as the origin and calling the coördinates x_1 and y_1 we have for points on w,

$$x_1 = a\alpha \cos I$$

$$y_1 = a\alpha^3 \frac{n^2 + 2n}{3(n+1)^2} \sin I.$$

But

$$\alpha^3 = \frac{x_1^3}{a^3 \cos^3 I},$$

hence,

$$y_1 = \frac{1}{3a^2} \frac{n^2 + 2n}{(n+1)^2 \cos^3 I} x_1^3 \sin I.$$

As previously shown,

$$\cos I = \sqrt{\frac{\mu^2 - 1}{n^2 + 2n}},$$

hence,

$$y_1 = \frac{1}{3a^2} \frac{(n^2 + 2n)^2}{(n+1)^2(\mu^2 - 1)} \sqrt{\frac{(n+1)^2 - \mu^2}{\mu^2 - 1}} x_1^3.$$

Putting

$$\frac{(n^2 + 2n)^2}{(n+1)^2(\mu^2 - 1)} \sqrt{\frac{(n+1)^2 - \mu^2}{\mu^2 - 1}} = h,$$

$$y_1 = \frac{h}{3a^2} x_1^3.$$

This equation, then, represents a curve very nearly coincident with that portion of the wave front to which the rainbow phenomena are due, and, since the effects computed from it substantially agree with those observed when the drops are not too small, as will be seen presently, it is clear that the approximation thus obtained is sufficient for most, if not all, practical uses; indeed, the assumption that raindrops are perfectly spherical involves, perhaps, a greater error.

Intensity and Its Variation with Angular Distance from the Ray of Minimum Deviation.—This, too, was first determined by Airy.[1] The following discussion, however, is essentially that of Mascart[2] and Pernter-Exner.[3]

Let O (Fig. 178) be the point of inflection of an emitted wave front near a drop; let P be a distant point in the direction θ from the ray of minimum deviation. Then, the difference in phase ΔF between the

[1] *Loc. cit.*

[2] *Traité d'Optique,* 1.

[3] "Meteorologische Optik."

light vibrations at P, due respectively to an element ds of the front at O and an equal element M at (x, y) is given by the equation

$$\Delta F = 2\pi \frac{OR - MT}{\lambda} = 2\pi \frac{x \sin \theta - y \cos \theta}{\lambda}$$

in which λ is the wave length.

Hence, substituting for y its value $hx^3/3a^2$, and dx for ds, which is allowable over the effective portion of the wave front, the vibration at P is given by the equation,

$$V = k \int \sin 2\pi \left[\frac{t}{T} - \left(\frac{\frac{hx^3}{3a^2} \cos \theta - x \sin \theta}{\lambda} \right) \right] dx$$

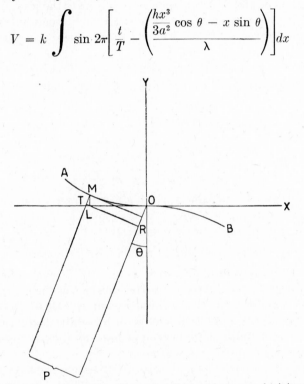

Fig. 178.—Variation of intensity with angular distance from ray of minimum deviation.

in which T is the period and k the amplitude per unit length of front.
Or, putting

$$\frac{2\pi}{\lambda} \left(\frac{hx^3}{3a^2} \cos \theta - x \sin \theta \right) = \delta$$

$$V = k \int \sin \left(2\pi \frac{t}{T} - \delta \right) dx$$

$$= k \int \cos \delta dx \sin 2\pi \frac{t}{T} - k \int \sin \delta dx \cos 2\pi \frac{t}{T}.$$

Since $\cos \delta dx$ and $\sin \delta dx$ appear in this equation as amplitudes it follows, if

$$A = k \int \cos \delta dx$$

and

$$B = k \int \sin \delta dx$$

that the resultant amplitude $C = \sqrt{A^2 + B^2}$.

But to find A and B it is necessary to integrate the given expressions over the effective portion of the wave front, or through limits that produce essentially the same results. Such limits may be determined as follows:

Let x and x_1 be so situated that the difference between their distances from P is $\lambda/2$, and their combined result at that point, therefore, zero. That is, let

$$\frac{h}{3a^2}(x_1{}^3 - x^3) \cos \theta - (x_1 - x) \sin \theta = \frac{\lambda}{2}$$

or

$$x_1 - x = \frac{\lambda}{2 \cos \theta} \cdot \frac{3a^2}{h(x_1{}^2 + xx_1 + x^2) - \tan \theta}.$$

Consider the primary bow in which h has its least value, 4.89, nearly, for $\mu = \tfrac{4}{3}$; assuming the radius a of a drop to be 1 mm., and writing δx for $x_1 - x$, it follows, since θ is small, that

$$x^2 \delta x = 0.0002 \text{ mm.}^3, \text{ roughly, for yellow light.}$$

Hence, δx decreases rapidly with increase of x (even when $x = 0.1$ mm., $\delta x = 0.02$ mm.), and the successive portions of the curve beyond a very short distance from the inversion point O (Fig. 178) completely neutralize each other, and, therefore, no error will be introduced by integrating between infinite limits instead of between the *unknown* limits of the effective portion of the wave front.

Hence,

$$A = k \int_{-\infty}^{+\infty} \cos \delta dx$$

and

$$B = k \int_{-\infty}^{+\infty} \sin \delta dx.$$

But as the sign of B reverses with that of x, while that of A remains unchanged,

$$B = O$$

and

$$A = 2k \int_{0}^{\infty} \cos \frac{2\pi}{\lambda}\left(\frac{hx^3}{3a^2} \cos \theta - x \sin \theta\right) dx.$$

Putting

$$\frac{2h}{3a^2\lambda}x^3\cos\theta = \frac{u^3}{2},$$

from which

$$dx = \left(\frac{3a^2\lambda}{4h\cos\theta}\right)^{\frac{1}{3}}du,$$

and

$$\frac{2x}{\lambda}\sin\theta = \frac{zu}{2}$$

$$A = 2k\int_0^\infty\left(\frac{3a^2\lambda}{4h\cos\theta}\right)^{\frac{1}{3}}\cos\frac{\pi}{2}(u^3 - zu)du,$$

which is Airy's rainbow integral, in which

$$\frac{\pi}{2}(u^3 - zu)du = \delta,$$

the difference in phase.

Putting

$$\int_0^\infty\cos\frac{\pi}{2}(u^3 - zu)du = f(z)$$

$$A = 2k\left(\frac{3a^2\lambda}{4h\cos\theta}\right)^{\frac{1}{3}}f(z) = Mf(z), \text{ say,}$$

and the intensity,

$$A^2 = M^2f^2(z).$$

The evaluation of $f(z)$ is not simple, but it has been accomplished through mechanical quadrature by Airy,[1] and through development in series by both Airy[2] and Stokes.[3] Airy's integral may also be expressed in terms of Bessel functions,[4] and has been tabulated.

The following table and its graph (Fig. 179), both from Pernter-Exner's "Meteorologische Optik," give certain values of z and $f^2(z)$, corresponding to monochromatic light of a particular wave length and drops of a definite size.

It will be noticed that the first maximum does not coincide with $z = 0$, nor, therefore, with $\theta = 0$, the direction of the ray of minimum deviation; that the intensity of the first maximum, corresponding to a principal bow, is much the greatest; and that the succeeding maxima, corresponding to the supernumerary bows, and also the angular intervals between successive maxima, continuously decrease, at a decreasing rate, with the increase of θ.

[1] *Cambridge Phil. Trans.*, **6**; 379.
[2] *Cambridge Phil. Trans.* **8**; 595.
[3] *Cambridge Phil. Trans.*, **9**; Pt. I.
[4] Nicholson, J. A., *Phil. Mag.*, **18**; 6, 1909.

Fig. 179.—Periodic changes of intensity of monochromatic light.

VALUES OF $f^2(z)$ FOR DIFFERENT VALUES OF z

z	$f^2(z)$	z	$f^2(z)$	z	$f^2(z)$
−2.0	0.006	3.4	0.609	8.8	0.189
−1.8	0.011	3.6	0.586	9.0	0.373
−1.6	0.018	3.8	0.436	9.2	0.320
−1.4	0.030	4.0	0.225	9.4	0.100
−1.2	0.048	4.2	0.051	9.6	0.001
−1.0	0.074	4.4	0.003	9.8	0.054
−0.8	0.113	4.6	0.104	10.0	0.240
−0.6	0.168	4.8	0.297	10.2	0.360
−0.4	0.239	5.0	0.465	10.4	0.220
−0.2	0.331	5.2	0.501	10.6	0.022
0.0	0.443	5.4	0.379	10.8	0.013
0.2	0.571	5.6	0.172	11.0	0.170
0.4	0.706	5.8	0.014	11.2	0.338
0.6	0.836	6.0	0.022	11.4	0.270
0.8	0.941	6.2	0.174	11.6	0.050
1.0	1.001	6.4	0.370	11.8	0.004
1.2	0.996	6.6	0.450	12.0	0.140
1.4	0.914	6.8	0.353	12.2	0.320
1.6	0.758	7.0	0.141	12.4	0.256
1.8	0.547	7.2	0.010	12.6	0.045
2.0	0.319	7.4	0.046	12.8	0.006
2.2	0.125	7.6	0.230	13.0	0.136
2.4	0.014	7.8	0.394	13.2	0.314
2.6	0.016	8.0	0.363	13.4	0.202
2.8	0.131	8.2	0.150	13.6	0.013
3.0	0.317	8.4	0.010		
3.2	0.502	8.6	0.038		

MAXIMA AND MINIMA

Maxima	z	$f^2(z)$	Minima	z
1	1.0845	1.005	1	2.4955
2	3.4669	0.615	2	4.3631
3	5.1446	0.510	3	5.8922
4	6.5782	0.450	4	7.2436
5	7.8685	0.412	5	8.4788
6	9.0599	0.384	6	9.6300
7	10.1774	0.362	7	10.7161
8	11.2364	0.345	8	11.7496
9	12.2475	0.330	9	12.7395
10	13.2185	0.318	10	13.6924

Distribution of Colors in the Rainbow.—The above discussion of the distribution of light intensity applies, as stated, to monochromatic light. When the source of light simultaneously emits radiations of various wave lengths, as does the sun, a corresponding number of bows, each consisting of a sequence of maxima and minima, are partially superimposed on each other. In this way different colors are mixed, and thus the familiar polychromatic rainbow produced.

The particular mixing of colors that obtains is the result of several cooperating causes. Thus, the distribution of intensity, as illustrated by Fig. 179, depends on phase difference, as given by the expression,

$$2\pi \frac{\dfrac{hx^3}{3a^2}\cos\theta - x\sin\theta}{\lambda}.$$

The angular intervals between maxima, say, increase, therefore, with λ, and, consequently, coincident distribution of the intensities of any two colors is impossible. Again, since the direction of the ray of minimum deviation varies with the refractive index, as already explained, and that, in turn, with the wave length or color, it follows that the direction of the zero point on the intensity curve, near which the first maximum lies, correspondingly varies. Obviously, then, these two causes, together, produce all sorts of color mixings that in turn arouse widely varied sensations.

To determine, however, just what color mixtures are induced by drops of any given size, it, obviously, is necessary to express the values of the abscissa z of the intensity curve (Fig. 179) in terms of angular deviation from the corresponding principal ray, since the direction of each such ray fixes the position of origin of its particular curve.

Let, then, as before,

$$\frac{zu}{2} = \frac{2x}{\lambda}\sin\theta$$

or

$$z^3 = \left(\frac{4\sin\theta}{\lambda}\frac{x}{u}\right)^3$$

Also, as before, let

$$\left(\frac{x}{u}\right)^3 = \frac{3a^2\lambda}{4h\cos\theta}$$

hence,

$$z^3 = \frac{48a^2}{h\lambda^2}\sin^2\theta\tan\theta.$$

But whatever the value of θ from $0°$ to $30°$

$$\frac{\sin^2\theta\tan\theta}{\theta^3} = 1, \text{ to within } 0.0055.$$

Hence, approximately,

$$z^3 = \frac{48a^2}{h\lambda^2}\,\theta^3,$$

or

$$\theta = \frac{z}{2a^{2/3}}\left(\frac{h\lambda^2}{6}\right)^{1/3}.$$

From this equation it appears that the angular distance between any two successive intensity maxima varies directly as the cube root of the square of the wave length and inversely as the cube root of the square of the diameter, or other linear dimension of the parent drop. That is, this interval is greater for red light than for blue, and greater for small drops than for large ones.

The following table, copied with slight changes, from Pernter-Exner's "Meteorologische Optik," gives the values of θ in minutes of arc per $0.2z$, for lights of different wave length and drops of different size.

ANGLE IN MINUTES PER $0.2z$, PRIMARY BOW

a = in microns	5	10	15	20	25	30	40	50	100	150	250	500	1000
λ, in microns	Angle in minutes												
0.687	85.8	54.0	41.2	34.0	29.3	26.0	21.4	18.5	11.7	8.9	6.32	3.98	2.51
0.656	83.0	52.3	39.9	32.9	28.4	25.1	20.7	18.0	11.0	8.6	6.10	3.84	2.43
0.589	77.0	48.5	37.0	30.5	26.4	23.3	19.3	16.6	10.5	7.9	5.67	3.57	2.26
0.527	71.2	44.9	34.2	28.2	24.4	21.6	17.8	15.4	9.6	7.4	5.25	3.31	2.10
0.494	68.1	42.8	32.6	27.0	23.1	20.6	17.0	14.7	9.3	7.1	5.02	3.15	2.03
0.486	67.2	42.3	32.3	26.7	22.8	20.3	16.8	14.5	9.1	7.0	4.94	3.12	1.99
0.449	63.4	40.0	30.5	25.2	21.7	19.2	15.9	13.7	8.6	6.6	4.67	2.93	1.88
0.431	51.5	38.8	29.6	24.4	21.0	18.6	15.4	13.3	8.3	6.4	4.53	2.87	1.82

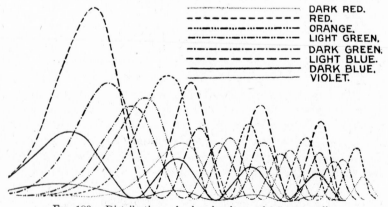

DARK RED.
RED.
ORANGE.
LIGHT GREEN.
DARK GREEN.
LIGHT BLUE.
DARK BLUE.
VIOLET.

FIG. 180.—Distributions of colors by drops of 0.5 mm. radius.

By the aid of this table; a table of intensity distribution $M^2f^2(z)$ along the coördinate z; and the following relative intensities,

λ	0.687	0.656	0.589	0.527	0.494	0.486	0.449	0.431
I	20	86	250	152	121	134	163	74

Pernter has constructed Figs. 180 and 181 that show the intensity distributions of these several colors due to drops of 0.5 and 0.05 mm. radius, respectively.

It still remains to determine the color at any particular point at which the relative intensities of the several colors are known. This can be done by the aid of Maxwell's[1] color triangle, as explained in detail by Pernter-Exner.[2]

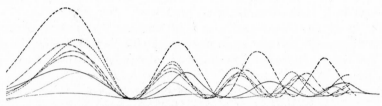

FIG. 181.—Distributions of colors by drops of 0.05 mm. radius.

Relation of Size of Drop and Wave Length to Intensity.—Since the Airy expression for the amplitude of the vibration produced at a distant point by the effective portion of the emitted wave front involves the factor $(\lambda a^2)^{1/3}$ it is evident that the corresponding intensity, which is proportional to the square of the amplitude, will be proportional to $(\lambda a^2)^{2/3}$. This, however, is based on the assumption that the effective light from the drop comes strictly from the *line* of a great circle. As a matter of fact, it actually comes from a narrow belt whose effective angular width, as measured from the center of the drop, is inversely proportional to the curvature, or directly to the radius a, and inversely proportional to the wave length.[3] Hence, the actual intensity is proportional to $\lambda^{-1/3}a^{7/3}$.

A larger fraction of the short wave length light is effective, therefore, than of the long. Further, the rainbow bands produced by very small droplets are not only broad, as previously explained, but also feeble, and as their colors necessarily are faint they frequently are not distinguished—the bow appearing as a mere white band. In fact, the above theory of the rainbow, involving interference from different sections of the brighter or Descartes portion of the wave front, does not apply to droplets of fog size and smaller, since interference either does not occur there or, at best, only at a large angle from the minimum ray. When

[1] *Trans. Roy. Soc.*, p. 57, 1860.

[2] "Meteorologische Optik."

[3] MASCART, *C. R.*, **115**; 453, 1892.

the diameter of the drop is large, in comparison with the wave length of the incident radiation, the resulting distribution of light is practically all due to refraction and reflection, and every one of the conspicuous phenomena is well explained in terms of the wave theory. Similarly, the wave theory fully provides for the scattering of light by particles of molecular, or near molecular, dimensions, as explained, later, in Chap. VI. But when scattering, reflection, and refraction, each is produced, as by fog particles, in appreciable amount, the simple wave theory does not adequately account for the phenomena observed. In such cases, to obtain quantitative results, one must resort to the inclusive, but computationally burdensome, electromagnetic theory, as developed by Lord Rayleigh[1] and heroically used by B. Ray.[2]

Popular Questions about the Rainbow.—A few popular questions about the rainbow need, perhaps, to be answered. "What is the rainbow's distance?" In the sense of its proximate origin, the drops that produce it, it is nearby or far away, according to their respective distances, and, thus, extends from the closest to the farthest illuminated drops along the elements of the rainbow cone. Indeed, the rainbow may be regarded as consisting of coaxial, hollow conical beams of light of different colors seen edgewise from the vertex, and, thus, having great depth, or extent, in the line of sight.

"Why is the rainbow so frequently seen during summer and so seldom during winter?" Its formation requires the coexistence of rain and sunshine, a condition that often occurs during local convectional showers but rarely during a general cyclonic storm, and as the former are characteristic of summer and the latter of winter, it follows that the occurrence of the rainbow correspondingly varies with the seasons.

"Why are rainbows so rarely seen at noon?" As above explained, the center of the rainbow's circle is angularly as far below the level of the observer as the sun is above it, hence, no portion of the bow can be seen (except from an elevation) when its angular radius is less than the elevation of the sun above the horizon. Now, during summer, the rainbow season, the elevation of the sun at noon is, nearly everywhere, greater than 42°, the angular radius of the primary bow, or even 51°, the radius of the secondary bow. A rainbow at noon, therefore, is, except for very high latitudes, an impossible summer phenomenon, and, of course, a rare winter one, for reasons given above, even where possible.

"Do two people ever see the same rainbow?" Theory teaches, and ordinary experience shows, that as the observer remains stationary, or moves, so also, other things being equal, does his rainbow. If, then, two observers, initially close together, should move in opposite directions, each would find his rainbow responding in the same sense as his shadow,

[1] *Proc. Roy. Soc.*, **84**; 25, 1910.
[2] *Proc. Ind. Assn. for the Cultivation of Science*, **8**; 23, 1923.

and, presently, the positions and, therefore, the identity, of the two bows would become unquestionably different, from which it follows, that as the eyes of two observers must always be separated by a greater or less distance, their bows must also be correspondingly separated and different —different in the sense that they have different positions and are produced by different drops. In short, since the rainbow is a special distribution of colors (produced in a particular way) with reference to a definite point—the eye of the observer—and as no single distribution can be the same for two separate points, it follows that two observers do not, and cannot, see the same rainbow.

"Can one see the same rainbow by reflection that he sees directly?" An object seen by reflection in a plane surface is seen by the same rays that, but for the mirror, would have focused to a point on a line normal to it from the eye, and as far back of it as the eye is in front. But, as just explained, the bows appropriate to two different points are produced by different drops; hence, a bow seen by reflection is not the same as the one seen directly.

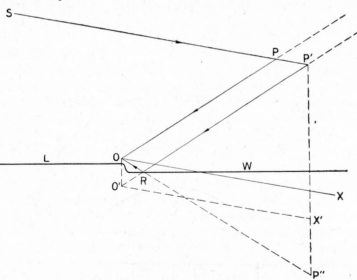

Fig. 182.—Reflected rainbow.

Reflected Rainbows.—Since rainbows occasionally are seen reflected in smooth bodies of water they deserve, perhaps, a somewhat fuller explanation than that just given.

Let an observer be at *O* (Fig. 182). Under proper conditions of rain and sunshine he will see, directly, a primary bow due to drops on the surface of a cone formed by rotating *OP* about *OX*, parallel to *SP*, keeping the angle *POX*, roughly 42°, constant; and by reflection in the surface of the water *W* another primary bow due to drops on the surface of a different cone, one formed by rotating $O'P'$ about $O'X'$, also parallel to SP, keeping the angle $P'O'X'$ constant. The bow seen by reflection necessarily will appear upside down, P' at P'', etc. The arc of the bow seen by reflection, obviously (from the figure), will be less than that of the bow seen directly, and, for that reason, is likely to appear flatter.

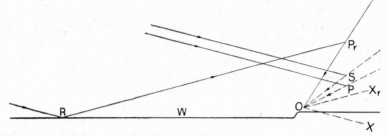

Fig. 183.—Reflection rainbow.

Reflection Rainbows.—A reflection rainbow is here defined as one due to reflection of the light source, the sun, usually, but itself seen directly.

Let the observer be at O (Fig. 183) with the sun and a smooth surface of water W at his back and illuminated rain in front. The direct sunshine will give a primary and a secondary bow along the elements of cones

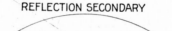

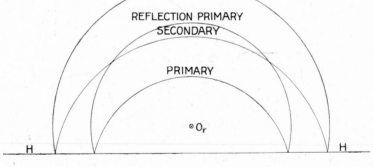

Fig. 184.—Direct and reflection rainbows.

formed by rotating OP and OS, respectively, about the common axis OX parallel to the incident rays, keeping the angles POX and SOX constant and of proper value; while the reflected light will give a primary bow along the elements of a cone formed by the rotation of OP_r about the axis OX_r (OX_r parallel to RP_r), keeping the angle P_rOX_r constant, and equal to POX. Reflection bows, of higher orders than that of the primary, are likely to be too faint to be seen.

The angular elevation of the center (axis really) of the reflection bows, clearly, is equal to the angular depression of the center of the direct bows. Hence, the direct and the reflection bows of the same order intersect on the observer's level, as shown in Fig. 184.

Horizontal Rainbow.—A rainbow, or even a cluster of bows, occasionally is formed by a sheet of drops, fallen from fog perhaps, resting on a smooth water surface, probably oily. The peculiar appearance of such bows is due entirely to the unusual distribution of the parent drops, for there is nothing new in their theory. The position of the direct primary bow, for instance, formed by drops on a horizontal surface below the eye of the observer, obviously, as shown in Fig. 185, is the intersection

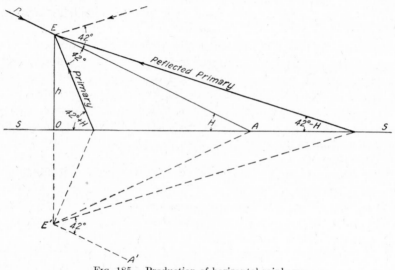

Fig. 185.—Production of horizontal rainbows.

of that surface SS with a right circular cone of 42° angular opening, with vertex at the eye E of the observer and axis EA parallel to the incident radiation R. The reflection primary, produced by light reflected from the horizontal surface before entering the drops, clearly, is located on the intersection of the plane with a cone, exactly like the above, but with vertex at E', directly below the eye, as far beneath the plane as the eye is above it, and with axis $E'A$ parallel to the reflected rays. Hence, the direct primary and the reflection primary almost exactly coincide with each other and are indistinguishably blended. The reflected primary, due to reflection by the horizontal surface of the light after it has left the drops, evidently is on the intersection of the reflecting surface and a cone the same size as the two just mentioned, but with axis $E'A'$ parallel to that of the first, that is, to the initial or incident light, and vertex at E' coincident with that of the second. The locus of each horizontal bow, therefore, is a conic section, ellipse, parabola, or hyperbola, as determined by the angular altitude of the sun. If this altitude is H, and the height of the eye above the surface h, then the distances d and D from O, the foot of the perpendicular from the eye, to the nearest points on the primary and reflected bows, are given by the equations

$$d = h \cot (42° + H),$$

and

$$D = h \cot (42° - H),$$

respectively.

The explanations of all other horizontal rainbows, secondary and supernumeraries, are exactly the same as that of the primary, except as to angular opening of the ray cone—50° for the secondary bow, and whatever is right for each of the others.

A remarkable bunch of horizontal bows, direct primary and, of course, merged reflection primary, reflected primary and direct and merged reflection secondary, was observed on Lake Monroe, Florida, in the spring of 1928, by Dr. E. D. Ball who kindly put his unpublished notes on this interesting phenomenon at my disposal. Similarly, Juday[1] reports the simultaneous occurrence, Oct. 23, 1924, of the primary bow, its first two supernumeraries, and also, the secondary, on the surface of Lake Mendota, Wisconsin.

Why There is No Visible Rainbow without Internal Reflection.— Since more light passes through the raindrop at the place of first internal reflection than anywhere else, it is reasonable to ask why this light, which is refracted as much as any other, instead of giving the brightest of all rainbows, shows none at all.

Clearly, and as is obvious from inspection of Fig. 174, the deviation of this nonreflected light varies from zero, in the case of that which is normal to the drop, to a maximum for the tangential. Its brightness, however, as seen by the observer, gradually decreases, with increase of deviation, to zero at $2(90° - \sin^{-1} 1/\mu)$ from the sun, μ being the air-water refractive index for the wave length under consideration. Hence, owing to superposition of the several colors, all this refracted but nonreflected light is white, except a violet to bluish circular border about 84° from the sun, or other source, and far too faint ever to be seen.

This explains also why, following an ice storm, trees in the general direction of the sun, are purest white, whereas those on the opposite side glow in rainbow colors. The myriads of pendant drops on the tips of the tiny icicles, and the casings of the twigs all have curved surfaces, which, like raindrops, leave the more directly transmitted light diffuse and white and concentrate in spectrum colors from that, and only that, which has been internally reflected.

[1] *Monthly Weather Review,* **44**; 65, 1916.

CHAPTER IV

REFRACTION PHENOMENA: REFRACTION BY ICE CRYSTALS

Introduction.—The cirrus clouds and others formed at temperatures considerably below 0° C. usually consist of small but relatively thick snowflakes with flat bases, or ice spicules with flat or, rarely, pyramidal bases, always hexagonal in pattern and detail, as shown by Fig. 186 from Bentley's remarkable collection of photomicrographs of snow crystals.

Light from the sun, for instance, obviously, takes many paths through such crystals and produces, in each case, a corresponding and peculiar optical phenomenon. Several of these phenomena, the halo of 22° radius, the halo of 46° radius, the circumzenithal arc, parhelia, etc., are quite familiar, and their explanations definitely known. Others, however, have so rarely been seen and measured that the theories of their formation are still somewhat in doubt. Finally, many phenomena, theoretically possible, as results of refraction by ice crystals, appear, so far, to have escaped notice.

Prismatic Refraction.—Since the phenomena caused by the passage of light through ice crystals are numerous, it will be most convenient, in discussing them, first, to obtain general equations for prismatic refraction, and then, to substitute in these equations the numerical constants applicable to each particular case.

Deviation.—Let A (Fig. 187) be the angle between two adjacent faces of a prism; let CE be the path of a ray of light in a plane normal to their intersection (direction of travel immaterial): let i and i' be the angles between the ray and the normals in the surrounding medium and r and r' the corresponding angles in the prism. Then the change in direction D of the ray is given by the equation

$$D = i + i' - (r + r') = i + i' - A. \tag{1}$$

Minimum Deviation.—Minimum deviation occurs when $\dfrac{dD}{di} = 0$ and $\dfrac{d^2D}{di^2} > 0$. But when

$$\frac{dD}{di} = 1 + \frac{di'}{di} = 0, \; di = -di'.$$

and as

$$r + r' = A, \; dr = -dr'.$$

501

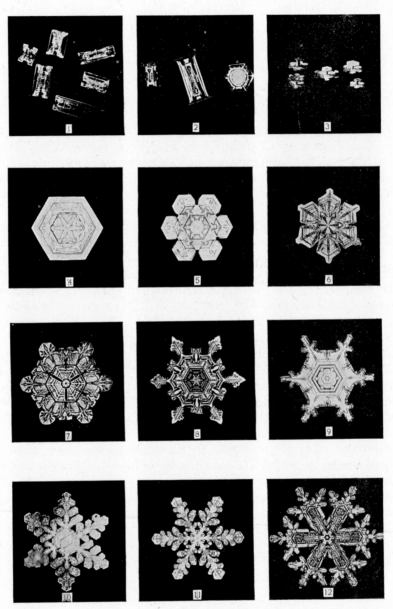

Fig. 186.—Snow crystals.   (*Bentley.*)

Also, from the law of refraction,

$$\sin i = \mu \sin r.$$
$$\sin i' = \mu \sin r'.$$

Hence,

$$\frac{\sin i}{\sin i'} = \frac{\sin r}{\sin r'},$$

or

$$\sin i \sin r' = \sin i' \sin r$$

and, by differentiation and division, if $di = -di'$ and $dr = -dr'$,

$$\frac{\cos i}{\cos i'} = \frac{\cos r}{\cos r'}$$

or

$$\cos i \cos r' = \cos i' \cos r.$$

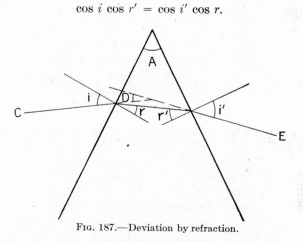

Fig. 187.—Deviation by refraction.

By addition, $\cos (i - r') = \cos (i' - r)$, or $i - r' = i' - r$.

By subtraction, $\cos (i + r') = \cos (i' + r)$, or $i + r' = i' + r$.

Hence, if, as assumed, $\dfrac{dD}{di} = 0$,

$$i = i', \text{ and } r = r' = \frac{A}{2}.$$

From

$$\frac{dD}{di} = 1 + \frac{di'}{di} = 1 + \frac{\dfrac{\mu \cos r' dr'}{\cos i'}}{\dfrac{\mu \cos r dr}{\cos i}} = 1 - \frac{\cos i \cos r'}{\cos i' \cos r},$$

it follows, by a little reduction, that when $\dfrac{dD}{di} = 0$

$$\frac{d^2D}{di^2} = \frac{2\mu \cos^2 r \sin i - 2 \cos^2 i \sin r}{\mu \cos i \cos^2 r}.$$

But

$$\mu > 0, \cos^2 r > \cos^2 i, \sin i > \sin r, \text{ and } \mu \cos i \cos^2 r > 0.$$

Hence, when

$$\frac{dD}{di} = 0, \text{ that is, when } r = r', \frac{d^2D}{di^2} > 0$$

and the deviation has its minimum value.

Writing D_0 for the minimum deviation, it follows that

$$D_0 = 2i - A. \tag{2}$$

Hence, from $\sin i = \mu \sin r$, and $r = \dfrac{A}{2}$, we get

$$\sin \frac{D_0 + A}{2} = \mu \sin \frac{A}{2} \tag{3}$$

Maximum deviation D_m obviously occurs when

$$i \text{ or } i' = 90°,$$

or, for ice for which $\mu = 1.31$, when r or $r' = 49° \ 46'$.
Since

$$D = i + i' - A$$
$$D_m = 90° + i' - A$$

and

$$\sin (D_m + A - 90°) = \mu \sin r' = \mu \sin (A - 49° \ 46'), \text{ for ice,}$$

or

$$\cos [(180° - A) - D_m] = \mu \sin (A - 49° \ 46'). \tag{4}$$

Refraction of Skew Rays.—The above equations apply only to refraction in a plane normal to the intersection of the faces of the prism. When the incident ray is inclined to this plane, the effective angle of refraction is increased, and as such inclination usually occurs in the case of floating ice crystals it is necessary, in the study of halos, to evaluate its effect on the deviation.

Let ABC (Fig. 188) be a principal plane of a prism; let DEF be the plane, perpendicular to the face of incidence, determined by the incident and interior portions of a ray entering the prism at O and leaving it at O'; let GH be the intersection of these two planes; and let ON be normal to the face of incidence at O. Draw OM normal to the principal plane, and connect M with L and K, the points on the intersection GH determined by the interior ray and the incident ray extended, respectively.

Clearly, from the figure, since $\sin i = \mu \sin r$, if, in length,

$$KO = 1,$$

then

$$LO = \mu,$$

and

$$\sin h = \mu \sin k,$$

in which h and k are the angles between the principal plane and the incident and interior rays respectively. That is, these angles are connected by the law of sines.

Similarly,

$$\sin h' = \mu \sin k',$$

in which h' and k' are the angles between the principal plane and the exit and interior rays, respectively. But

$$k' = k, \qquad\qquad \text{hence} \qquad\qquad h' = h.$$

That is, the incident and the exit rays are equally inclined to the principal plane.

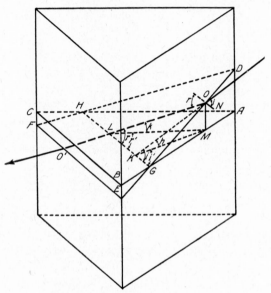

Fig. 188.—Refraction of skew rays.

Furthermore, if i' and r' are the projections of i and r, respectively, onto the principal plane, then

$$\mu \cos k \sin r' = \cos h \sin i',$$

or

$$\frac{\sin i'}{\sin r'} = \mu' = \mu \frac{\cos k}{\cos h}.$$

Hence a ray inclined to the principal plane of a prism of refractive index μ is so bent that the projection of its path on this plane gives the index μ' where

$$\mu' = \mu \frac{\cos k}{\cos h} = (\mu^2 - \sin^2 h)^{\frac{1}{2}}(1 - \sin^2 h)^{-\frac{1}{2}}*$$

* It may be interesting to note that this relation between the inclination of a ray to the principal plane of a prism and its deviation by that prism explains the curvature of spectrum lines as seen in an ordinary straight slit prism spectroscope.

The minimum deviation, therefore, of the projection of such rays D_0' in the principal plane, is given by the equation

$$\sin \frac{D_0' + A}{2} = \mu \frac{\cos k}{\cos h} \sin \frac{A}{2} \qquad (5)$$

and the maximum D_m' by the equation

$$\cos [(180° - A) - D_m'] = \mu \frac{\cos k}{\cos h} \sin (A - \alpha), \qquad (6)$$

in which α is the limiting value of the angle of refraction for the index μ' when

$$\mu' = \mu \frac{\cos k}{\cos h}.$$

The largest or limiting value of h at which light can still pass through the prism obviously is determined by the equation, representing grazing incidence and emergence,

$$\frac{D + A}{2} = 90°,$$

in which D is the (minimum) deviation as projected on the principal plane.

In this case

$$\sin \frac{D + A}{2} = \mu \frac{\cos k}{\cos h} \sin \frac{A}{2} = 1. \qquad (7)$$

Therefore,

$$\frac{1}{\sin^2 \frac{A}{2}} = \mu^2 \frac{(1 - \sin^2 k)}{\cos^2 h} = \frac{\mu^2 - \sin^2 h}{\cos^2 h}$$

and

$$\cos h = \sqrt{\mu^2 - 1} \, \tan \frac{A}{2}.$$

Hence, when $A = 60°$, as between alternate sides of a hexagonal ice prism, or snowflake, the limiting value of h for $\mu = 1.31$, is $60° \, 45'$, and when A is $90°$, as between base and a side, $32° \, 12'$.

Alternative Derivation of Bravais' Laws of Refraction.—Since the laws of refraction outside the principal plane are essential to the discussion of the halo, it is worth while, perhaps, to emphasize them by adding to the above straightforward derivation the following more analytical method of Laville.[1]

Let P (Fig. 189) be the point where a ray passes from one homogeneous medium into another whose index of refraction is μ times that of the first. From the point O, at a unit distance back from P, draw a line parallel to

[1] *J. Phys. Rad.*, **2**; 62, 1921.

the ray in the second medium, intersecting the normal through P at B. Clearly, then, from the figure

$$\sin i = OB \sin r,$$

and

$$OB = \mu.$$

Hence, if from any point two lines be drawn parallel to the paths of a given ray of light in two adjacent homogeneous media, each proportional in length to the corresponding refractive index, and in, or opposite to, the direction of travel, then the straight line joining the ends of these two lines is parallel to the perpendicular to the interface at the point of refraction of the given ray.

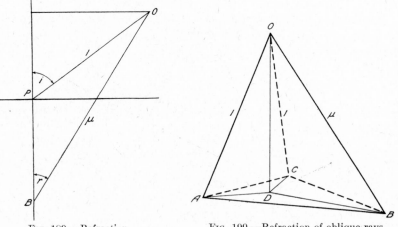

FIG. 189.—Refraction.   FIG. 190.—Refraction of oblique rays.

Draw, then, from O (Fig. 190) the lines OA, OB, and OC parallel to a given ray before entering, within, and after leaving, respectively, a refractive medium—a snow crystal, say, in air. Let the lengths of these lines be 1, μ, and 1, respectively. By this construction AB is parallel to the normal to the interface at the place of entrance of the ray, and BC parallel to the normal at its place of exit. Hence the plane ABC is parallel to the principal plane of the refracting object.

Draw OD perpendicular to the plane ABC. Then clearly

$$\angle OAD = \angle OCD.$$

That is, *the incident and the exit rays are equally inclined to the principal plane.*

Also

$$\sin OAD = \mu \sin OBD.$$

That is, *the inclinations of the incident, or exit, and the interior rays to the principal plane are connected by the law of sines.*

Finally,

$$\frac{BD}{AD} = \frac{\mu \cos OBD}{\cos OAD}.$$

That is, *the ratio of the projection of the interior ray onto the principal plane to that of the incident, or exit, ray is equal to the refractive index of the medium (or ratio of the two indices) times the ratio of the cosines of the angles between the corresponding rays and the principal plane.*

Internal Total Reflection and Its Effect on the Passage of Light through Ice Crystals.—Since the limiting value of the "angle of incidence" is 90°, and the refractive index of ice 1.31, it follows that total reflection of an internal ray occurs at the angle α, given by the equation

$$\sin 90° = 1.31 \sin \alpha = 1.31 \sin 49° \ 46'.$$

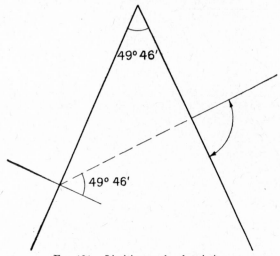

FIG. 191.—Limiting angle of emission.

An internal ray, therefore, cannot leave an ice crystal if the angle it makes with the normal is greater than 49° 46'. Hence, as is clear from Fig. 191, a ray of light in the principal plane, and also most rays out of it, will pass through an ice crystal between faces whose inclination is not greater than 49° 46' at all angles of incidence (measured on the base side of the normal) from 0° to 90°. On the other hand, no light can pass through an ice crystal at any angle of incidence between planes whose inclination is greater than 2 × 49° 46'. In proof of this latter statement, let *AB* (Fig. 192) be a ray grazing the side of a crystal whose angle of refraction is 99° 32' and entering at *B*. It will reach the opposite face at *C*, and either pass out in the direction *CD* or else suffer total reflection. But as *CD* lies along the face of the crystal, it is clear that any decrease of the angle of incidence at *B* from 90°, or increase of the inclination of the crystal faces to each other, each of which increases the angle BCE, causes total reflection at C, and thereby prevents transmission. Refracting angles intermediate between the above extremes obviously transmit light incident through an angular range less than 90° and greater than 0°.

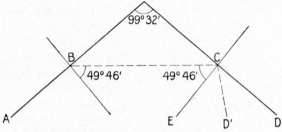

FIG. 192.—Limiting angle of transmission.

The largest angle of incidence clearly is 90°, and the smallest i, as determined by the equation

$$\sin i = \mu \sin r = 1.31 \sin (A - 49° 46')$$

If, then, $A = 60°$, $i = 13°$ 27′, giving a transmission range of 76° 33′; if $A = 90°$, $i = 57° 48'$, range 32° 12′; and similarly for other possible values of A.

General Illumination of the Sky through Ice Crystals.—The deviation of a ray of light through refraction and n internal reflections obviously is given by the equation

$$D = i + i' + n\pi - \Sigma A,$$

in which ΣA is the sum of the several angles passed by the ray in its course through the crystal. If these angles are all equal the equation becomes

$$D = i + i' + n\pi - (n + 1)A.$$

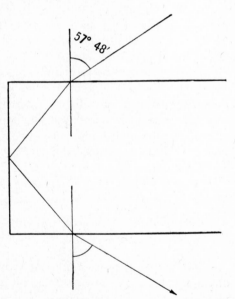

FIG. 193.—Illumination of the sky by flat snow cystals.

If, then, as frequently is the case, the ice crystal is a thick hexagonal disk floating horizontally, the position it oscillates about in falling, both angles passed by a once reflected ray will be 90°, provided the entering and emergent branches lie in the same plane, and the deviation will be

$$D = 2i,$$

as readily seen in Fig. 193.

Hence, such crystals illuminate the sky at all distances from the sun out to 115° 36′. The effect, however, is not sufficiently striking ordinarily to arrest attention.

Parhelia of 22°.—Whenever the air through any depth or at any level contains innumerable hexagonal snow crystals with their sides vertical (the position about which relatively broad crystals oscillate) two colored bright spots, known as parhelia or sun dogs, appear at 22° or more, from the sun, one to the right, the other to the left. Each bright spot is in the direction of maximum light or minimum refraction, and has the same altitude as the sun. When the refraction is in a principal plane, that is, as the sides of the crystal are vertical, when the sun is on the horizon, the angular distance D_0 of each spot, also on the horizon, is given by the equation, derived from equation (3),

$$\sin \frac{D_0 + 60°}{2} = \mu \sin \frac{60°}{2}.$$

For yellow light ($\mu = 1.31$), $D_0 = 21° 50′$; for red light ($\mu = 1.307$), $D_0 = 21° 34′$; and for violet ($\mu = 1.317$), $D_0 = 22° 22′$. The order of the colors, therefore, counting from the sun, is red, yellow, etc., to violet, and the length or dispersion 48′ for a point source. For the sun, diameter 30′, the total length is 1° 18′, and width 30′.

Since the above are minimum angles, it follows that slight changes in either the inclination or orientation of the crystals causes rays of each color to come also from somewhat greater distances from the sun. Hence, the only color thus produced that appears approximately pure is the darker portion of the red. Yellow and green are also moderately distinct, but blue, and especially violet, scarcely perceptible because of so much admixture of colors.

When the angular elevation of the sun is h, the distance D' in azimuth, of each of these parhelia from the sun, is given by the equation, derived from equation (5),

$$\sin \frac{D' + 60°}{2} = \mu \frac{\cos k}{\cos h} \sin \frac{60°}{2}.$$

The angular distance Δ_0 measured on the arc of a great circle, between the sun and each of these parhelia, may be found from the right spherical triangle formed by the three sides: zenith to sun (complement of h); zenith to mid point between sun and a parhelion; "mid point" to sun, $\Delta_0/2$. The angle thus formed at the zenith is $D'/2$, and the angle at the "mid point" 90°. Hence,

$$\sin \frac{\Delta_0}{2} = \cos h \sin \frac{D'}{2}.$$

For $\mu = 1.31$ the following relations[1] exist between h, D', and Δ_0.

[1] PERNTER-EXNER, "Meteorologische Optik," 2d. Ed., p. 362.

h	D'	Δ_0
0°	$D_0 = \Delta_0 = $	21° 50'
5°	22° 2'	21° 56'
10°	22° 30'	22° 10'
15°	23° 20'	22° 32'
20°	24° 34'	23° 4'
25°	26° 22'	23° 50'
30°	28° 44'	24° 49'
35°	31° 56'	26° 3'
40°	36° 20'	27° 38'
45°	42° 30'	29° 42'
50°	51° 30'	32° 26'
55°	66° 2'	36° 26'
60°	98° 48'	44° 38'
60° 45'	120° 0'	50° 4'

All the above values pertain, as explained, to minimum deviation. But as the orientation of the crystals is fortuitous, it follows that all possible deviations from minimum to maximum will occur, and the parhelia, therefore, be drawn out into streaks, the lengths of which depend upon their angular altitude.

The maximum deviation for refraction in a principal plane (for sun on the horizon when the crystal edges are vertical) is given by the equation, derived from equation (4),

$$\cos(180° - 60° - D_m) = \mu \sin(60° - 49° 46').$$

The value of the maximum deviation in azimuth D_m corresponding to the solar altitude h is given by equation (6), and the actual maximum Δ_m by the equation

$$\sin\frac{\Delta_m}{2} = \cos h \sin\frac{D_m'}{2}.$$

The following table[1] gives interesting relations between the quantities indicated:

h	D_m	Δ_m	$\Delta_m - \Delta_0$
0°	43° 28'	43° 28'	21° 38'
5°	43° 38'	43° 26'	
10°	44° 8'	43° 24'	21° 16'
15°	44° 59'	43° 20'	
20°	46° 15'	43° 18'	20° 18'
25°	48° 0'	43° 16'	
30°	50° 17'	43° 10'	18° 22'
35°	53° 15'	43° 4'	
40°	57° 9'	42° 58'	15° 22'
45°	62° 28'	43° 2'	
50°	68° 48'	43° 10'	10° 46'
55°	81° 3'	43° 44'	
60°	104° 54'	46° 44'	2° 6'
60° 45'	120° 0'	50° 4'	0° 0'

[1] PERNTER-EXNER, "Meteorologische Optik," 2d. Ed., p. 364.

From the computed values of $\Delta_m - \Delta_0$, fully supported by observations, it appears that when the angular elevation of a parhelion of 22° is moderate to small, 20° or less, it may extend over an arc, parallel to the horizon, of more than 20°. The end next the sun, produced by minimum deviation, is colored, beginning with red, through a short range. Similarly, the distal end, due to maximum deviation, is also colored, terminating with violet, though always too faint, perhaps, to be distinctly seen. Through the rest of its length the blending of the colors is quite complete, giving white, of course, as the result.

At greater altitudes the possible lengths of the parhelia of 22° become less and less, as shown by the table, though the color distribution remains the same.

Halo of 22°.—When the refracting edges of the ice crystals are vertical, as they tend to be in the case of relatively thin snow-flakes falling through still air, parhelia are produced, as just explained. But in general, these edges lie in all directions, especially at the windy cirrus level and when the crystals are of the short columnar type; and as refracted light reaches an observer in every plane through his eye and the sun (or moon) to which the refracting edges are approximately normal, it follows that the effect produced by fortuitously directed snow crystals must be more or less symmetrically distributed on all sides of the exciting luminary. There may, however, be a maximum brightness both directly above, and directly below, the sun, since ice needles tend to settle with their refracting edges horizontal.

As before, when the refracting angle is 60° and $\mu = 1.31$, corresponding to yellow light, $D_0 = 21°\ 50'$, and is independent of solar elevation. The inner portion of this, the most frequent and best known of all halos, is red, because light of that color is least refracted. Other colors follow, with increase of distance, in the regular spectral sequence, but with decrease of wave length they so rapidly fade that even green is indistinct and blue seldom detected. This is owing to the variation in deviation caused by the tipping of the needles, as previously fully explained.

The brightest portion of the ring, clearly, is at the angle of minimum refraction from the sun. With increase of distance, light produced in this manner gradually fades (not all the crystals are ever simultaneously in position to give minimum refraction) until it ceases to be perceptible at 15° to 20° beyond the inner portion, or, say, 40° from the sun. On the other hand, no such light reaches the observer from places within the ring of maximum brightness, and, therefore, this portion of the sky is comparatively dark, except, and for an entirely different reason, namely, diffraction, near the sun itself.

When the sun is within 10° of the horizon, the halo of 22° and the parhelia of 22° are practically superimposed. At greater altitudes they become distinctly separated, as per the accompanying table[1] for $\mu = 1.31$, in which h = solar elevation, Δ_0 = parhelic angular distance from the sun, and D_0 = angular distance of halo from sun.

h	$\Delta_0 - D_0$
0°	0° 0′
10°	0° 20′
20°	1° 14′
30°	2° 59′
40°	5° 48′
50°	10° 36′
60°	22° 48′
60° 45′	28° 14′

Arcs of Lowitz, or Vertical Arcs of the 22° Parhelia.—On rare occasions oblique extensions of the parhelia of 22°, concave towards the sun and with red inner borders, are seen, in addition to their horizontal tails, above described. These are known as the arcs of Lowitz, after the astronomer who described them[2] as seen in the famous Petersburg halo complex (Fig. 194) of June 29, 1790. Their general explanation is simple, though exact computations of their outlines, and of the relative intensities of their parts for different altitudes of the sun, are rather tedious. As already explained, parhelia and their horizontal extensions are produced by ice crystals whose principal axes are vertical, the former by those set to minimum refraction, and the latter by crystals turned more or less from this unique position.

When, however, the principal axes oscillate about the vertical, as they obviously do in the case of snowflakes, the arcs of Lowitz, or obliquely vertical extensions of the parhelia of 22°, necessarily are produced, though rarely seen, because of the diffusion of their light in the midst of a general glare, as explained on page 501.

Consider, first, for simplicity, the doubly special case in which the sun is on the horizon and the principal axes of the crystals oscillate in a vertical plane passing through the sun. Let C (Fig. 195) be the position of an ice crystal whose principal axis is in the direction CZ. Let an observer be at O and let the incident ray SC lying between Z and P make the angle h with the principal plane CP. On emerging, this ray, in its new direction $S'O$, has the same inclination as formerly to the axis. Hence, SC and $S'C$ may be regarded as elements of a right cone of vertex C and axis CZ and as the plane CZS is vertical, if S is on the horizon, as seen from O, the element CS (lowest element), being parallel to OS, owing to the great distance of S, will lie in a plane tangent to the cone and parallel to the plane of the horizon, while every other element, such as CS', will lie above it. S', therefore, the apparent position of S due to

[1] PERNTER-EXNER, "Meteorologische Optik," 2nd Ed., p. 367.

[2] *Nova. Acta Acad. Petropol.*, **8**; 384, 1794.

refraction of the ray SC by the ice crystal at C is above this plane and, also, as seen from O, at the same angular distance above the horizon. Similarly, when the axis of the crystal is tipped beyond the vertical in the opposite direction, S' drops below the horizon.

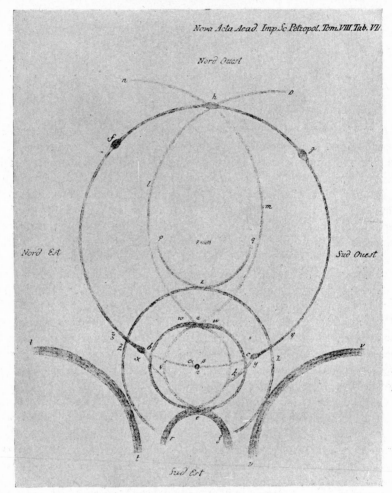

Fig. 194.—Petersburg halo of July 18, 1794.

Further, let ZP and ZP' be arcs of great circles intersecting SC and $S'C$ at B and B', respectively. Then the projection of the deviation SCS', or SOS', on the principal plane is given by the angle D between these arcs, and on bisecting D, thus dividing ZBB' into two equal right spherical triangles, and putting $BB' = \Delta$, it is obvious that

$$\sin \frac{\Delta}{2} = \sin \frac{D}{2} \cos h \tag{1}$$

and

$$\cot B = \tan \frac{D}{2} \sin h. \tag{2}$$

Clearly, then, the locus of S' is given when the arc BB' is known in terms of the angle B.

On eliminating h by squaring equations (1) and (2), and putting $\cos^2 (D/2) = 1\Big/\Big(1 + \tan^2 \dfrac{D}{2}\Big)$, it appears that

$$\cot^2 B = \tan^2 \frac{D}{2} \cos^2 \frac{\Delta}{2} - \sin^2 \frac{\Delta}{2}. \tag{3}$$

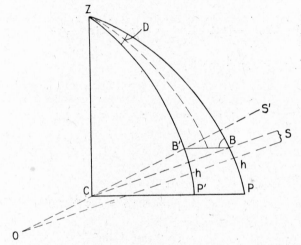

FIG. 195.—Formation of the arc of Lowitz, crystals vibrating in solar vertical.

Hence, that either Δ or B may be found when the other is given, it remains only to express $\tan^2 \dfrac{D}{2}$ in terms of a function or functions of Δ.

But from equation (7) (p. 488), and $\sin h = \mu \sin k$

$$\sin^2 \frac{D + A}{2} = \mu^2 \frac{\cos^2 k}{\cos^2 h} \sin^2 \frac{A}{2}$$

$$= \{1 + (\mu^2 - 1) \sec^2 h\} \sin^2 \frac{A}{2}. \tag{4}$$

Also from equation (3) (p. 486),

$$\mu^2 = \frac{\sin^2 \dfrac{D_0 + A}{2}}{\sin^2 \dfrac{A}{2}}$$

and from equation (1), above,

$$\sec^2 h = \frac{\sin^2 \dfrac{D}{2}}{\sin^2 \dfrac{\Delta}{2}}.$$

Hence, substituting the last two expressions in equation (4),

$$\frac{\sin^2 \dfrac{D+A}{2} - \sin^2 \dfrac{A}{2}}{\sin^2 \dfrac{A}{2}} = \frac{\sin^2 \dfrac{D_0+A}{2} - \sin^2 \dfrac{A}{2}}{\sin^2 \dfrac{A}{2}} \times \frac{\sin^2 \dfrac{D}{2}}{\sin^2 \dfrac{\Delta}{2}}$$

or

$$\sin^2 \frac{\Delta}{2} \sin \left(\frac{D}{2} + A \right) \sin \frac{D}{2} = \sin^2 \frac{D}{2} \sin \left(\frac{D_0}{2} + A \right) \sin \frac{D_0}{2}.$$

Dividing by $\cos \dfrac{D}{2} \cos A$,

$$\sin^2 \frac{\Delta}{2} \tan \frac{D}{2} + \sin^2 \frac{\Delta}{2} \tan A = \frac{\sin \left(\dfrac{D_0}{2} + A \right) \sin \dfrac{D_0}{2} \tan \dfrac{D}{2}}{\cos A}$$

$$= \frac{1}{2} \left\{ \left(1 - \frac{\cos (D_0 + A)}{\cos A} \right) \tan \frac{D}{2} \right\}.$$

Putting

$$\frac{\cos (D_0 + A)}{\cos A} = \cos \beta = \cos 73° 30'$$

$$\tan \frac{D}{2} = \frac{2 \tan A \sin^2 \dfrac{\Delta}{2}}{\cos \Delta - \cos \beta}. \tag{5}$$

On using this value of $\tan \dfrac{D}{2}$, equation (3) reduces to

$$\cot B = \frac{\sin \dfrac{\Delta}{2} \sqrt{4 \sin^2 \dfrac{\Delta}{2} \cos^2 \dfrac{\Delta}{2} \tan^2 A - (\cos \Delta - \cos \beta)^2}}{\cos \Delta - \cos \beta}. \tag{6}$$

From equation (6) B is readily computed for any assumed value of Δ, as is also D from equation (5). Further, h can be found from equation (1) when Δ and D are known, or from equation (2) when B and D are known.

The following table, copied from Pernter-Exner,[1] as are most of the above equations, gives data for drawing the locus of S' when the sun is on the horizon.

[1] *Loc. cit.*, p. 327.

h	Δ	B
0°	21° 50′	90° 0′
5°	21° 55′	89° 5′
10°	22° 10′	88° 1′
15°	22° 38′	86° 54′
20°	23° 04′	85° 45′
25°	23° 51′	84° 19′
30°	24° 49′	82° 38′
35°	26° 3′	80° 38′
40°	27° 38′	78° 5′
45°	29° 42′	74° 36′
50°	32° 26′	69° 43′
55°	36° 26′	61° 58′
60°	44° 38′	44° 41′
60° 45′	50° 4′	33° 29′

Since the value of Δ in this table increases with μ, other things being equal, it follows that these arcs must be colored and that their inner borders must be red, as stated.

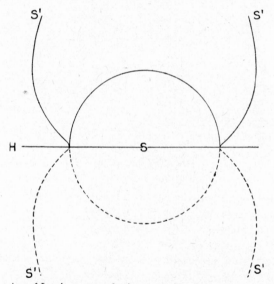

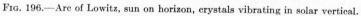

Fig. 196.—Arc of Lowitz, sun on horizon, crystals vibrating in solar vertical.

This table is graphically represented by Fig. 196, in which the circle is the 22° halo, HH the horizon, S the sun, and $S'S'$ the curve in question, dotted below the horizon where, of course, like the under portion of the circle, it is invisible, except from a suitable elevation.

Obviously, the optical effect is independent of the manner by which the inclination of the principal axis of the crystal to the incident ray is produced, and, therefore, crystals tilted in the vertical plane through the sun to an angle $E + h$ to the plane of the horizon give the same result, if E is the solar elevation, as do crystals tilted to only the angle h in this plane when the sun is on the horizon. The points of contact with the halo of 22°, being due to crystals whose principal axes are normal to the incident rays, lie, therefore, at equal altitudes on opposite sides of the halo and in a plane that passes through the sun. Consequently, the angular altitude of these points is less than that of the sun, except when the latter is on the horizon. If, as before, E is the elevation of the sun and E' that of the points of contact in question, then, from the right spherical triangle formed by the radius of the halo and the zenith distances of the sun and point of contact, respectively,

$$\cos (90° - E') = \cos (90° - E) \cos 21° 50'.$$

Figure 197 represents, approximately, the outline of the bright band produced in this manner when the elevation of the sun is 40°; making that of the points of contact 36° 38'. O is the position of the observer, S the

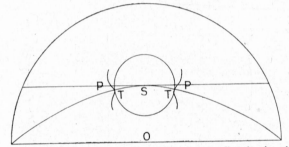

Fig. 197.—Arcs of Lowitz, elevation of sun 40°, crystals vibrating in solar vertical.

center of the halo of 22°, PP parhelia of 22°, TT the points of tangency to this circle of the arcs of Lowitz PT PT. In order that the arc may reach the halo, the tilt of the crystal must at least equal the elevation of the sun, and no portion of the lower branch (part below point of tangency) is given unless the tilt is greater than this elevation. Hence, if the extent of the tilting of snow crystals is less, in the great majority of cases, than 30°, as it probably is, only the upper branch is likely to be produced when the sun is 30° or more above the horizon.

Consider, now, the effect of the vibration of the principal axis in a vertical plane at right angles to the vertical plane through the sun. Let E be the elevation of the sun and i the inclination of the principal axis to the vertical, then the angle h between the incident ray and principal plane is given by the equation

$$\sin h = \sin (90° - i) \sin E.$$

Let $E = 30°$, and $i = 20°$. Then the angular distance from the sun to a parhelion of 22° is 24° 49', or say 3° from the halo of 22°. Also $h = 28° 1'$, and the corresponding distance of image from halo is about

2° 40′, at approximately 20°, measured from center of halo, above or below the parhelion, owing to direction of tip.

Vibrations of the principal axis in intermediate planes give images, of course, in intermediate positions, so that the total effect, when the elevation of the sun is 30°, may be somewhat as represented in Fig. 198, in which tilting is supposed to be restricted to 30° and less from the vertical.

In this figure, *PP* are the parhelia of 22°, *aa*, *bb*, and *cc* the outlines of the images corresponding to minimum refraction when the principal axis is oscillated in a vertical plane through the sun, true tangent arcs; at 45°, roughly interpolated, to this sun plane; and at 90° to it, respectively.

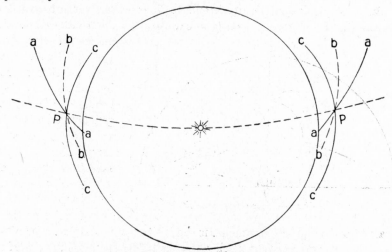

Fig. 198.—Arcs of Lowitz, crystals vibrating at random.

It will be noticed that this light, nearly always too faint to be distinguished from the general glare, would be more concentrated, if the orientation of the ice crystals were fortuitous, which, presumably, often is the case, and consequently brighter below the parhelia than above them. Hence, because of limited tilting, as above explained, and because of the greater concentration of light in its lower branches, this halo, whenever seen at all, appears as short arcs including the parhelia and extending mainly below them. In fact, Pernter's theory, alone, does not seem to afford an adequate explanation of all the observed forms of the Lowitz arcs, and several investigators have attempted to identify them with arcs produced by other modes of tipping of the crystals.[1]

Tangent Arcs of the Halo of 22°.—Obviously, when the sun is on the horizon, ice crystals whose principal axes lie, or oscillate, in hori-

[1] Fujiwhara and Oti, *Bull. Central Meteorol. Obs.*, **3**; No. 1, 1919; Fujiwhara and Nisimura, *Geophys. Mag.*, **1**; 28, 1926.

zontal planes must produce the same optical effects above and below
(theoretically) the halo of 22° that are produced on its sides, as above
explained, by crystals whose principal axes oscillate in the vertical
plane through the sun. Each set of curves might properly be called
tangent arcs of the halo of 22°, but as a matter of fact only those well-
known, and fairly common, arcs that occur above and below the circular
halo are so designated.

Similarly, when the elevation of the sun is E, arcs identical with
those just described and tangent to the halo at its highest and lowest
points, as shown in Fig. 199, are formed by crystals whose principal
axes oscillate in planes normal to the solar vertical and inclined at the
angle E to the plane of the horizon.

But ice spicules, or needles, tend to float with their principal axes
horizontal. Hence, it is necessary carefully to determine the optical
effects of crystals in
this particular posi-
tion, as may be done
by noting the trans-
formations of the tan-
gent arcs as the crystals
are so turned as to
carry their principal
axes from the inclined
to the horizontal plane.
Let, then, the principal
axis of an ice needle lie

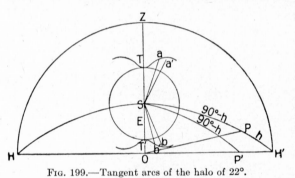

Fig. 199.—Tangent arcs of the halo of 22°.

parallel to OP (Fig. 199) in which O is the position of the observer, HSH' the
inclined plane and S the sun at elevation E. Let h be the inclination of the
principal axis to the incident radiation and let a or b be the position of the
resulting image. Now, let the crystal, as suggested above, be so turned as to
carry its axis from an inclined to a horizontal position, and in such manner
as to keep *constant* the angle between the principal axis and the direction
of the incident ray. That is, change the direction of the axis from parallel
to OP to parallel to OP', with $SP = SP'$. Under these conditions the
refracted ray will turn precisely as does the principal axis. Hence, if a'
and b' are the new positions of a and b, the angle $aSa' = bSb' = PSP'$.

But from the right spherical triangle OSP'

$$\cos OSP' = \sin PSP' = \tan E \cot SP' = \tan E \tan h,$$

and

$$aSa' = bSb' = \sin^{-1} (\tan E \tan h).$$

Since the points of tangency of the "tangent arcs" under consideration are 90° from the corresponding points of the similar "arcs of Lowitz,"
it follows that the angle B, of Fig. 195 and table on page 517 equals
TSa (Fig. 199).

Hence,

$$\left.\begin{array}{c} TSa' \\ T'Sb' \end{array}\right\} \equiv S = B \pm \sin^{-1}(\tan E \tan h).$$

The following table, adapted from Pernter-Exner, "Meteorologische Optik,"[1] gives the necessary data for accurately constructing tangent arcs corresponding to different solar elevations:

VALUES OF ANGLE S

E		5°		10°55'		15°		20°		25°2'	
h	Δ	Top	Bottom	Top	Bottom	Top	Bottom	Top	Bottom	Top	Bottom
0°	21°50'	0° 0'	0° 0'	0° 0'	0° 0'	0° 0'	0° 0'	0° 0'	0° 0'	0° 0'	0° 0'
5	21 55	1 21	0 29	1 50	0 0	2 16	− 0 26	2 45	− 0 55	3 16	− 1 26
10	22 10	2 52	1 06	3 56	0 02	4 42	− 0 44	5 40	− 1 42	6 42	− 2 44
15	22 38	4 27	1 45	6 04	0 08	7 13	− 1 01	8 42	− 2 30	10 17	− 4 05
20	23 04	6 15	2 35	8 27	0 25	10 01	− 1 11	12 02	− 3 12	14 12	− 5 22
25	23 51	8 01	3 21	10 51	0 31	12 52	− 1 30	15 27	− 4 05	18 16	− 6 54
30	24 49	10 16	4 28	13 46	0 58	16 16	− 1 32	19 30	− 4 46	23 01	− 8 17
35	26 03	12 53	5 51	17 08	1 36	20 11	− 1 27	24 08	− 5 24	28 28	− 9 44
40	27 38	16 08	7 42	21 14	2 36	24 55	− 1 05	29 42	− 5 52	34 59	− 11 19
45	29 42	20 25	10 23	26 31	4 17	30 57		36 45	− 5 57	43 16	− 12 28
50	32 26	26 16	14 18	33 34	7 00	38 55	1 39	46 10	− 5 26	54 07	− 13 33
55	36 26	35 13	20 51	44 02	12 02	50 32	5 32	59 21	− 3 17	69 53	− 13 49
60	44 38	54 02	36 36	64 50	25 48	72 58	17 40	84 25	6 13	99 19	− 8 41
60°45'	50 04	65 30	47 32	76 40	36 22	85 06	27 56	97 04	15 28	113 02	0 0

E		29°15'		35°		40°		45°	
h	Δ	Top	Bottom	Top	Bottom	Top	Bottom	Top	Bottom
0°	21°50'	0° 0'	0° 0'	0° 0'	0° 0'	0° 0'	0° 0'	0° 0'	0° 0'
5	21 55	3 44	− 1 54	4 26	− 2 36	5 08	− 3 18	5 56	− 4 06
10	22 10	7 39	− 3 41	9 04	− 5 06	10 30	− 6 32	12 09	− 8 11
15	22 38	11 54	− 5 32	13 51	− 7 43	16 06	− 9 54	18 39	− 12 27
20	23 04	16 11	− 7 21	19 11	− 10 21	22 12	− 13 22	25 46	− 16 56
25	23 51	20 49	− 9 27	24 45	− 13 23	28 43	− 17 21	33 29	− 22 07
30	24 49	26 14	− 11 30	31 12	− 16 28	36 20	− 21 36	42 38	− 27 54
35	26 03	32 27	− 13 43	38 43	− 19 59	45 21	− 26 37	53 48	− 35 04
40	27 38	39 57	− 16 07	47 54	− 24 04	56 40	− 32 50	68 57	− 45 07
45	29 42	49 27	− 18 39	59 50	− 29 02	72 26	− 41 38	105 24	− 74 36
50	32 26	62 09	− 21 35	76 50	− 36 16	110 17	− 69 43		
55	36 26	81 09	− 25 07	118 02	− 61 58				
60	44 38	121 15	− 30 37						
60°45'	50 04	146 31	− 33 29						

E		50°		55°		60°		70°		80°	
h	Δ	Top	Bottom	Top	Bottom	Top	Bottom	Top	Bottom	Top	Bottom
0°	21°50'	0° 0'	0° 0'	0° 0'	0° 0'	0° 0'	0° 0'	0° 0'	0° 0'	0° 0'	0° 0'
5	21 55	6 54	− 5 04	8 06	− 6 16	9 38	− 7 48	14 50	− 13 00	30 40	− 28 50
10	22 10	14 07	− 10 09	16 34	− 12 36	19 46	− 15 48	30 58	− 27 00	91 59	− 88 01
15	22 38	21 44	− 15 32	25 36	− 19 28	30 45	− 24 33	50 31	− 44 19		
20	23 04	29 08	− 21 18	35 45	− 26 57	41 31	− 34 41	94 25	− 85 35		
25	23 51	39 26	− 28 04	47 26	− 36 01	59 34	− 48 12				
30	24 49	50 50	− 36 06	62 54	− 48 07	97 22	− 82 38				
35	26 03	65 55	− 47 11	99 22	− 80 38						
40	27 38	101 55	− 78 05								
45	29 42										
50	32 26										
55	36 26										
60	44 38										
60°45'	50 04										

[1] 2d Ed., pp. 385–386.

The upper and lower tangent arcs change with elevation E of the sun, as indicated by the table and shown in Fig. 200, copied from Pernter-Exner, "Meteorologische Optik." Portions below the natural horizon can only be seen from sufficient heights.

With increase of elevation of the sun from the horizon the branches of the lower tangent arc draw closer together; become pointed; cross,

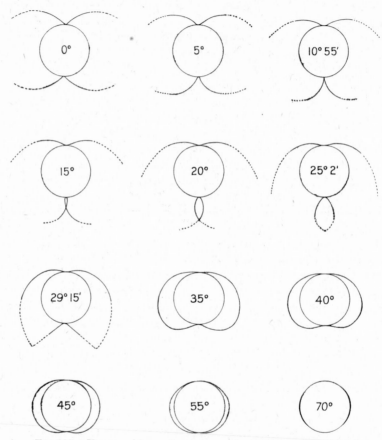

Fig. 200.—Upper and lower tangent arcs at solar elevations indicated.

forming a loop; then open out and turn up where they merge with the drooped branches of the upper tangent arc and thus form an enclosing curve, the circumscribed halo, with red inner border, which, at first, when the elevation is 30° to 35°, is bagged below; then, when the elevation is 50° to 60°, approximately elliptical and occasionally alone, or nearly so[1]; and, finally, at elevations of 75° and more, indistinguishably merged with the circular halo. The brightest portions of these arcs are at, and near, the points of tangency. Hence, when the solar elevation

[1] Hastings, C. S., *M. W. R.*, **43**; 498, 1915; Clarke, G. A., *Meteorol. Mag.*, **73**; 175, 1938.

is 35° to 45° the lower arc, if visible over only its brightest part, appears as an inferior tangent arc, which, indeed, it is, circular, perhaps, and limited to, say, 10° to 20°, which, in reality, it is not.

Frequency of Horizontal and Rarity of Vertical Tangent Arcs.—Since the theory of the formation of the horizontal (upper and lower) tangent arcs of the halo of 22° is identical with that of the vertical (arcs of Lowitz), it will be interesting to consider why, though the former is fairly common, the latter is extremely rare. Obviously, this must somehow be connected with the attitudes, which radically do differ, of the principal axes of the ice crystals that produce them. The horizontal tangent arcs are produced, as already explained, by crystals whose principal axes are horizontal, and, therefore, by columnar crystals, since these, and these alone, tend to assume this as an attitude of maximum frequency and thus produce a corresponding concentration of light.

The vertical tangent arcs (arcs of Lowitz), on the other hand, being produced by crystals whose principal axes oscillate in that particular vertical plane that passes through the sun, nearly always are too faint to be seen, because, in part, this unique attitude can only rarely be assumed by any considerable proportion of the crystals present. Even the combined effect of the crystals in all vertical planes is seldom noticed because, as explained, of its width and consequent faint nebulosity.

Another factor that probably contributes to the contrast between the frequencies of occurrence of the two types of tangent arcs is the fact that columnar crystals whose principal axes tend to lie horizontal probably are far more effective as refractors, or halo producers, than are the tabular crystals whose principal axes tend to stand vertical. This is because the tabular crystals are so filled with air spaces or other heterogeneities, as shown by their photomicrographs, that anything like regular transmission of light through them from edge to edge is hardly possible. The columns, on the other hand, appear to be more nearly homogeneous and, consequently, much more effective as refractors. This is partially confirmed by the fact that halos often are seen close at hand in polar regions when the air is filled with ice needles, and rarely, if ever, seen in ordinary snowstorms consisting essentially of tabular crystals.

The greater efficiency (presumably), then, of the columnar crystal, whose principal axis tends to lie horizontally, as a refractor, over that of the tabular crystal whose principal axis tends to stand vertical, together with the further fact that the orientation of the vertical plane of oscillation must nearly always be fortuitous, seems to explain why the horizontal tangent arc of the halo of 22° is so frequently and the vertical so rarely seen.

It should be remembered, however, that, in apparent contradiction of the above statements concerning the maximum frequency attitudes of the principal axes of ice crystals, there are two special types of columnar crystals whose principal axes tend to stand vertical; namely, those that are shorter than broad (tabular when much shorter than broad), and those that have tabular caps. Perhaps, therefore, all halo phenomena are due essentially to columnar and very little to tabular crystals.

Parry and Parryoid Arcs.—Columnar snow crystals in either of their stable attitudes, that is, with two side faces horizontal (Fig. 201) or vertical (Fig. 201, turned 90°), the stabler of the two,[1] produce, with different altitudes of the sun, a variety of halos,[2] the concentration of light being due not to minimum refraction, the usual cause, but to a most favored, hence most common, attitude of the crystals. All these halos

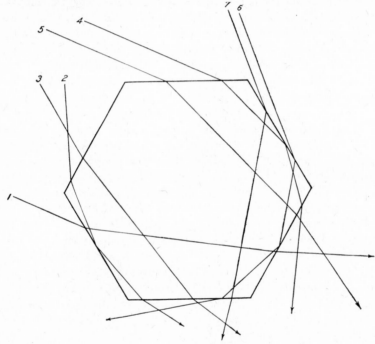

Fig. 201.—Various courses of halo-producing light.

obviously lie outside the familiar one of 22°, or, at most, are just tangent to it in the solar vertical, when the elevation of the sun is exactly such as to cause minimum refraction in the principal plane. Rays 1 and 5 (Fig. 201) produce, as explained by Hastings,[3] the lower Parry arc and the upper Parry arc (Fig. 214f), respectively, so named after the explorer whose descriptions of them[4] are the earliest known. Ray 4 forms the oblique heliac arcs, discussed later. The arcs produced by the remaining

[1] Besson, L., *Annuaire de la Société Météorologique de France*, February, 1907; "Wind Tunnel Experiments," unpublished, Nat. Bur. Standards.

[2] Putniņš, P., *Met. Zeit.*, **51**; 321, 1934.

[3] *M. W. R.*, **48**; 322, 1920.

[4] "First Voyage," p. 164.

rays through crystals in this attitude are very faint and therefore seldom, if ever, seen.

Of the several possible rays through crystals in their other stable attitude, only 3 and 5, as shown in Fig. 201, with the left side turned to top, produce halos of record.

A straightforward method of locating points on either Parry arc, or, indeed, on any arc produced by crystals whose principal planes of refraction are vertical, is as follows:

Let an ice needle (hexagonal rod with flat ends) be at the center C (Fig. 202) of the celestial sphere; let EE be the intersection of this sphere by the top face, say, of the crystal; let S be the position of the sun as

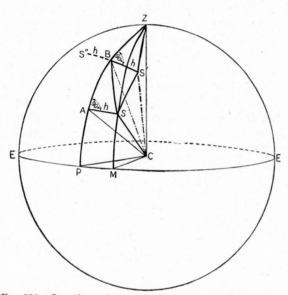

Fig. 202.—Locating points on the Parry and similar halo arcs.

viewed from C, and S' its apparent position as given by the emerging ray; let MZ be the solar vertical; ZP the intersection of the sphere by a principal plane, and SCA any given angle h between the incident ray and this plane; and, finally, ZS the known zenith distance of the sun, or angle of incidence of the ray SC onto the top surface of the crystal. Then, from the right spherical triangle ZAS the corresponding "angle of incidence" ZA of the projection AC of the ray SC onto the principal plane can be computed for any value of h; and with this "angle of incidence" and the "projection index," $\left(\dfrac{\mu^2 - \sin^2 h}{1 - \sin^2 h}\right)^{\frac{1}{2}}$, the "projection deviation" AB can be found, CB being the backward extension of the projection of the emerging ray onto the principal plane. The difference between these two values gives ZB of the right spherical triangle ZBS', whose side BS', according to the first law of oblique refraction, is equal to AS, which is known. Hence, through the triangles indicated, the exact position of S' with reference to S can be found for any assumed value of $h(0 \leqq h \leqq ZS)$, and by taking a sufficient number of such values the arc can be traced with any desired degree of accuracy.

Much of such entering light as may be reflected by a vertical end face of the crystal will pass out through the same side face as that which is not so reflected, and produce an image S'' which, obviously, is symmetrical with S' about the principal plane ZP. The arc thus produced clearly is tangent to the Parry, or other S', arc at the intersection with the solar vertical, but rarely bright enough to be seen.

Parhelia of 46°.—Since the flat ends of columnar snow crystals and the flat faces of tabular ones both are at right angles to the sides, it follows that optical phenomena must occur, produced by refraction at such angles, analogous to those already explained for the 60° angle.

Let, then, the 90° intersection be vertical, as it is, more or less, in the case especially of columnar crystals, and let the orientation be that of minimum refraction. If, now, the sun is on the horizon, the distance from it to either of its refraction images, also on the horizon, corresponding to the angle in question, is given by substitution in the general equation

$$\sin \frac{D_0 + A}{2} = \mu \sin \frac{A}{2}.$$

On putting $\mu = 1.31$, this becomes

$$\sin \left(\frac{D_0}{2} + 45° \right) = 1.31 \sin 45°,$$

from which $D_0 = 45° \ 44'$.

Hence, these images are known as the parhelia of 46°.

With increase of elevation of the sun the inclination h of the incident ray to the vertical face of the crystal is equally increased, as is also the elevation of the images, as we know from previous considerations. Hence, the positions of the parhelia of 46° corresponding to different elevations of the sun may be found in the same manner as those of 22°. On substituting, then, in the equation

$$\sin \frac{D' + A}{2} = \mu \frac{\cos k}{\cos h} \sin \frac{A}{2},$$

in which $\sin h = \mu \sin k$, the proper values of μ and A, namely 1.31 and 90°, respectively, and also computing the corresponding values of Δ_0', one obtains the following table:

h	D_0'	Δ_0'
0°	45° 44'	45° 44'
5°	46° 11'	46° 0'
10°	47° 36'	46° 50'
15°	50° 08'	48° 18'
20°	54° 08'	50° 38'
25°	60° 48'	54° 36'
30°	72° 48'	61° 52'
32° 12'	90° 0'	73° 30'

These parhelia, like those of 22°, also trail off parallel to the horizon, for crystals whose attitudes differ somewhat from that of minimum refraction. Such trails, however, necessarily are very faint, and perhaps never observed. In fact, these parhelia themselves are only rarely seen.

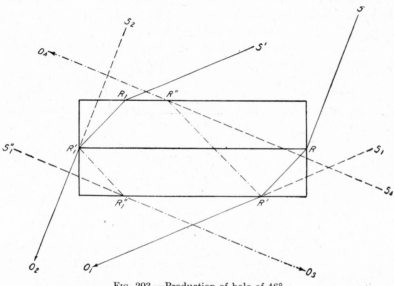

Fig. 203.—Production of halo of 46°.

Halo of 46°.—Since, as just explained, the images S_1, S_2 (Fig. 203) of the sun produced in the principal plane of a 90° refracting angle of an ice crystal, as seen by the observer O_1, O_2 are 45° 44' from the sun S, S' itself ($\mu = 1.31$), it follows that when such crystals are very abundant and set at random in all directions the innumerable images so produced must together assume the shape of a ring about the sun of radius 45° 44'. This is the well-known, though not very common, halo of 46°.

Whenever at all conspicuous, this halo also shows colors (red being nearest the sun) which, because of the greater dispersion produced by the angle of 90° than by the angle of 60°, are more widely separated than in the halo of 22°. Hence, it likewise has the greater width of the two—about 2° 40', corresponding to the diameter of the sun, 30', plus the dispersion, that is, to $30' + D_v$, $(\mu = 1.317) - D_r$, $(\mu = 1.307) = 30' + 47° 16' - 45° 6' = 2° 40'$.

In addition to the colored ring, there is also a broad outer band of diffuse white light corresponding to all refractions other than the minimum, but it is too faint and too uniformly distributed to be conspicuous, or, perhaps, unmistakably seen even when carefully looked for. In so far as the crystals have favored orientations, certain segments, especially the top and bottom, of this halo, as similarly for the 22° halo, are brighter than others, owing to the combined effect of minimum refraction and maximum number of contributing sources. There also are closely adjacent arcs of greater than minimum refraction, due, like the Parry arc, entirely, to a most common attitude of the snow crystal.

Halo of 90°.—Occasionally, a faint white halo, sometimes called the halo of Hevelius, is seen at 90° from the sun.

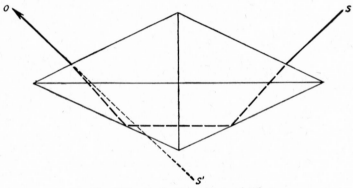

Fig. 204.—Production of halo of 90°.

Several explanations of this halo have been suggested, but none gives it the right distance from the sun or is otherwise satisfactory. The following simple theory of its formation, therefore, is offered, based on the presence of fortuitously directed bipyramidal hexagonal crystals whose pyramidal sides are inclined 24° 51' to the longitudinal axis.

Apparently no exact measurements of pyramidal ice crystals have ever been made.[1] However, by X-ray analysis it has been shown[2] that the oxygen atoms of an ice crystal are arranged in hexagonal patterns and so spaced that the axial ratio (longitudinal to lateral) is almost exactly 1.62.

Clearly, then, from the laws of crystallography, the ratio of the height of the pyramidal end of an ice crystal to the inner radius of its base (a lateral axis) must also be 1.62, or some multiple thereof, expressi-

---

[1] Dobrowolski, *Arkiv för Kemi, Mineralogi och Geologi*, **6**; No. 7, p. 44, 1916.

[2] St. John, A., *Proc. Nat. Acad. Sci.*, **4**; 193, 1918; Dennison, D. M., *Phys. Rev.*, **17**; 20, 1921; Bragg, W. H., *Proc. Phys. Soc.*, **34**; 98, London, 1922.

ble in either a small whole number or a fraction whose numerator and denominator both are small whole numbers.

If, now, we multiply 1.62 by ⅔, a factor entirely allowable, we obtain a pyramid whose sides are inclined 24° 51′ to the longitudinal axis, and since this value satisfies both the 90° halo, and also several "halos of unusual radii," *q. v.*, it will be provisionally accepted as a value that actually occurs in nature.

Light from any source *S* (Fig. 204) entering a face of such a crystal (truncated or pointed, and with, or without, an intervening hexagonal column), in, or near, a plane determined by the longitudinal axis and a

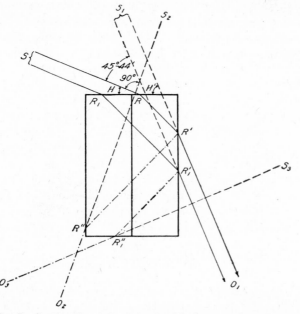

Fig. 205.—Production of antisolar halo of 46° and tangent arcs of halo of 46°.

normal to that face from this axis, will, over a wide range (42° 6′) of the angle of incidence, undergo two internal total reflections and pass out the corresponding face of the abutting pyramid in such direction that an observer at *O* will see the image *S′* very nearly 90° from the source; the total range being, for light of refractive index 1.31, from 89° 28′ where the concentration is greatest, to 88° 2′ where it is least. Light outside this range is relatively too faint to be considered, being enfeebled by at least one reflection that is not total. Minimum refraction, hence, maximum deviation (turning of ray by reflection minus its turning by refraction) and maximum concentration, occurs when that portion of the internal ray that lies between the points of reflection is parallel to the longitudinal axis. This, as above stated, puts the brighter edge of the halo at nearly 90° from the sun or moon. Clearly, too, the red of this halo, contrary to rule, is on the side away from, and not the side nearest to, the parent luminary, and still nearer 90° therefrom, though always, perhaps, too faint to arouse a distinct color sensation.

Antisolar Halo of 44°.—Light that has undergone minimum refraction, one internal reflection, and passed two 90° angles, as indicated in Fig. 205, image S_3 (axis of crystal vertical) is concentrated, too faint to show colors except very rarely, but with red farthest from the sun, along the circle of angular radius $2i - 2r + 90°$. That is, since $r = 45°$ and $i = 67° 52'$, along a circle of 44° 16′ radius about the antisolar point, not the anthelion, or 135° 44′ from the sun.

Antisolar Halo of 38°.—Light that has undergone minimum refraction, one internal reflection, and passed two 60° angles is concentrated, with red, if strong enough to show, farthest from the sun, along a circle of angular radius $2i - 2r + 60°$; that is, since $r = 30°$ and $i = 40° 55'$, along a circle of 38′ 10′ radius about the antisolar point.

Circumzenithal Arc.—Occasionally, an arc of, perhaps, 90°, having its center at the zenith, and, therefore, known as the circumzenithal arc, is seen some 46°, or a little more, above the sun. It generally lasts only a few minutes, about five on the average, but during that time often is so brilliantly colored, especially along that portion nearest the sun—red on the outside, to violet, inclusive—as to be mistaken, by persons unfamiliar with it, for an exceptionally bright rainbow. It occurs most frequently when the altitude of the sun is about 20° and at times when the parhelia of 22° are conspicuous; presumably, therefore, when the principal axes of a large portion of the crystals are practically vertical.

The explanation of this halo, as of many others, was first given by Bravais,[1] and is very simple.

In still, or steadily flowing, air the type of crystals assumed will keep their principal axes substantially vertical. Let, then, H (Fig. 205) be the altitude of the sun above the horizon, and also the angle between the incident ray and the upper horizontal surface of the crystal; let θ be the angle between this surface and the refracted ray, and let H' be the altitude of the solar image, S_1, produced by the 90° prism.

Hence,

$$\cos H = \mu \cos \theta,$$

and

$$\sin H' = \mu \sin \theta = \sqrt{\mu^2 - \cos^2 H}.$$

As previously explained, the angles between a principal plane (plane normal to the refracting edge) and incident and emergent rays are equal. Therefore, since the position of the image is altered by rotation of the crystal about its principal axis while its altitude remains unchanged,

[1] Mémoire sur les halos, *Journal de l'École polytechnique*, 31me cahier, 1845.

it follows that the halo so produced is a limited circular arc whose center is the zenith.

From the equation for minimum refraction,

$$\sin \frac{D_0 + A}{2} = \mu \sin \frac{A}{2},$$

it appears that in the present case, and for $\mu = 1.31$,

$$D_0 = 45° \, 44'.$$

This corresponds to $H = 22° \, 8'$, and to $H' = 67° \, 52'$. In this case

$$H' - H = 45° \, 44',$$

which is the radius of the 46° halo.

With increase or decrease of the altitude of the sun from $22° \, 8'$, the solar distance of the circumzenithal arc increases, but so slowly, at first, that the gain amounts to only about 1° when the sun has sunk to 16°, or risen to 27°. Hence, this arc is also, though erroneously, called the upper tangent arc of the halo of 46°.

When the sun is on the horizon the solar distance of the circumzenithal arc is $57° \, 48'$, and the interval between it and the 46° halo $12° \, 4'$. On the other hand, the arc rapidly converges on the zenith as the altitude of the sun approaches 32°, and is theoretically impossible for solar altitudes greater than $32° \, 12'$.

Kern's Arc.—Kern's arc, so designated from the name of the first observer to report it,[1] occurs exactly opposite the corresponding circumzenithal arc, simultaneously with it. Together they sometimes form a complete colored circle.[2]

Since the rays by which one sees any point on a circumzenithal halo are paralleled over the adjacent region by exactly similar rays (he and his neighbors, each by virtue of a different set of crystals, all seeing at the same time the "same" halo), and, since the faces of the crystals are prevailingly vertical, and the bases horizontal, it follows that by reflection, both internal and external, from these sides each point on the circumzenithal halo is drawn out into a circle about the zenith, precisely as the sun is drawn out into the parhelic circle, *q. v.* This, then, appears to be the explanation of Kern's arc, which, being greatly enfeebled by reflection, seldom is bright enough to be seen.

Circumhorizontal Arc.—A colored arc, red on the upper side, of perhaps 90° in extent, is occasionally seen parallel to the horizon and about 46°, or a little more, below the sun. This arc is produced by light entering snow crystals through vertical sides and passing out through

---

[1] *Koninklijk nederlandsch meteorologisch Instituut. Onweders, optische verschijn., enz., in Nederland*, O. 66, 1895.

[2] LING, *Monthly Weather Review*, **50**; 132, 1922.

horizontal bases, and, therefore, the theory of its formation is identical with that of the circumzenithal arc. On merely substituting "zenith distance" for "elevation" all the numerical values of the one become those of the other. Hence, the circumhorizontal arc cannot appear when the zenith distance of the sun is greater than 32° 12′. Similarly, when this distance is 22° 8′, corresponding to minimum deviation, the solar distance of the circumhorizontal arc is 45° 44′, the radius of the halo of 46°. Further, for all values of the zenith distance of the sun from 16° to 27° the circumhorizontal arc is within 1° of tangency to the halo of 46°. Hence, it is also, though incorrectly, called the lower tangent arc of the halo of 46°.

Lateral Tangent Arcs of the Halo of 46°.—Just as flat-topped crystals with vertical sides produce a circumzenithal arc, when the altitude of

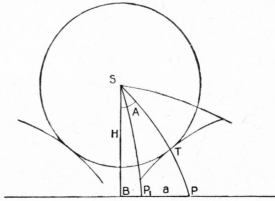

Fig. 206.—Formation of the lateral tangent arcs of the halo of 46°.

the sun is between 0° and 32° 12′, so, too, similar crystals whose axes are horizontal and directed toward any point whose solar distance is between 90° and 57° 48′, or between 0° and 32° 12′, produce a colored arc—red next the sun—about this directive point as a center. And as there are two such points corresponding to each solar distance, one to the right, the other to the left, of the solar vertical, it follows that arcs formed in the above manner are symmetrically situated with respect to this vertical. Further, when the solar distance of the directive point is 67° 52′ or 22° 8′, the resulting arc is tangent to the halo of 46°, and as always some, at least, of the innumerable crystals are turned toward this point, except when the altitude of the sun is greater than these values, respectively, it follows, with the same exceptions, that the blend of the numerous arcs produced by the variously directed crystals is always tangent to the halo of 46°, and, also, that except near the point of tangency, only the red of these blends is reasonably pure.

Obviously, there are two classes of lateral tangent arcs, namely, lower, as seen at S_1 by an observer at O_1 (Fig. 205, but with axis of crystal horizontal), and upper, as seen at S_2 by an observer at O_2. These will next be considered separately as infralateral and supralateral arcs.

Infralateral Tangent Arcs of the Halo of 46°.—Let the circle about S (Fig. 206) be the halo of 46°; let the altitude H of the sun be less than 67° 52', and let the principal axes of the columnar crystals be horizontal and directed towards the point P on the horizon distant 67° 52' from S. As previously explained, the infralateral tangent arcs, convex to the sun, are tangent to this halo at the point T, where it is intersected by the arc SP. The position of T may easily be determined from the value of the angle A, between the vertical SB and the arc SP.

Obviously, from the right spherical triangle SBP

$$\cos A = \tan H \cot 67° 52'.$$

Since refraction by the crystal is limited to solar distances of P between 57° 48' and 90°, it follows that A_1 and A_2, corresponding to the lower and upper ends of the tangent arc, are given by the equations

$$\cos A_1 = \tan H \cot 57° 48'$$

and

$$A_2 = 90°,$$

respectively.

When the altitude of the sun is 57° 48', or a little greater, the two tangent arcs, springing from a common point on the solar vertical, form a wide V.

When the solar altitude equals 67° 52', the two arcs, now merged into a smooth, continuous curve, are tangent to the halo at its lowest point.

Finally, for altitudes of the sun greater than 67° 52', the arcs, still appearing as a single curve, are slightly separated from the circular halo even at its lowest and closest point.

Supralateral Tangent Arcs.—When the altitude of the sun is less than 22° 8', supralateral tangent arcs are produced, concave to the sun and nearly coincident with the halo of 46°.

The point of tangency of the supralateral tangent arc with the halo of 46° is given in terms of the angle A on this halo from its upper point. When the solar altitude H is less than 22° 8',

$$\cos A = \tan H \cot 22° 8'.$$

Similarly, the possible end of the arc is given by the equation

$$\cos A' = \tan H \cot 32° 12'.$$

When the altitude of the sun is 22° 8', both arcs, forming a continuous curve, are tangent to the halo at its highest point.

Finally, for altitudes between 22° 8' and the extreme limit, 32° 12', these arcs are more or less above the halo of 46°.

The following table gives the value of A for different altitudes of the sun.

Infralateral Arcs		Supralateral Arcs	
H	A	H	A
0°	90° 0′	0°	90° 0′
10°	85° 54′	5°	77° 35′
20°	81° 35′	10°	64° 18′
30°	76° 25′	15°	48° 47′
40°	70° 03′	20°	26° 30′
50°	61° 00′	22° 8′	0° 0′
60°	45° 13′	25°	0° 0′
67° 52′	0° 0′	30°	0° 0′
		32° 12′	0° 0′

Halos of Unusual Radii.—Various halos, circular about the sun or moon, and differing in size from those already discussed, have occasion-

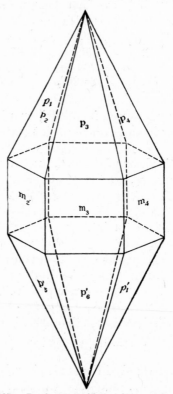

Fig. 207.—Production of halos of unusual radii.

ally been reported.[1] The radii of six of these have been measured, and have been found to be, approximately, 8° (theodolite[2]), 17° (plane-table

[1] Besson, C. R., **170**; 334, 1920.
[2] Piippo, *Monthly Weather Review*, **50**; 534, 1922.

method,[1] and theodolite[2]), 19° (plane-table method[1]), 23° (mercury basin[3]), 24° 37′ (theodolite[4]), and 32°, respectively. Several estimates, not measurements, differing more or less from the above, have also been given, probably erroneous, or, possibly, referring in some instances to coronas. Besides, there often is uncertainty as to what angle was measured, that from the center, or limb, of sun or moon to the inner edge, center, or outer edge of the halo.

Halos of this kind, doubtless, are due to fortuitously oriented pyramidal crystals; whether truncated or pointed, and with or without columns between the pyramidal ends. Such a pointed, bipyramidal crystal, with an intervening hexagonal column (a well-known type), is represented by Fig. 207. Light, obviously, can pass through this crystal in various directions. Those courses that offer refraction, and, hence, produce halos, are listed in the accompanying table, in which the numerical values correspond to an inclination of 24° 51′ of a pyramidal face to the longitudinal axis, a value assumed for the reasons given in the discussion above of the halo of 90°. Such crystals are quite unusual. Scoresby[5] says that he saw pyramidal snow crystals only once, but then in large quantity. Dobrowolski[6] saw both pointed and truncated pyramidal frost crystals in the Antarctic.

In this table, the meanings are: *Incidence face*, that face of the crystal through which the ray in question passes in; *exit face*, that face of the crystal through which the given ray passes out; *refraction angle*, the dihedral angle between the incidence and exit faces, extended; *minimum deviation*, the least difference in direction between the incident and exit branches of any single ray—the deviation corresponding to maximum light, hence, the angular radius of a particular halo.

The pairs of faces listed in this table are merely typical since, obviously, a change in either face of any pair merely requires a corresponding change in the other.

The last three members of this list are the 46°, the 22°, and the 90° halos, previously discussed. The 8°, 17°, 19°, 23° 20′, 24° 37′, and 32° halos are unusual because the pyramidal snow crystal is rare. The 46° halo does not require crystals of pyramid form—only crystals that have faces at right angles to each other. Hence, this halo and several others of the table may be simultaneously seen when there is no trace of the sixth. Finally, the fourth is apt to blend more or less with the 22° halo into a band broader than usual and, thereby, cause the radius of the 32° halo to be underestimated by ordinary observation.

[1] ANDRUS, *Monthly Weather Review*, **43**; 213, 1915.

[2] CAVE, *Nature*, **117**; 791, 1926.

[3] DUTHEIL, *Ann. de l'Obs. de Montsouris*, **12**; 236, 1911.

[4] HUMPHREYS, *M. W. R.*, **61**; 328, 1933.

[5] "Account of the Arctic Regions," Vol. 1, p. 430.

[6] "Results of the Voyage of the Belgica."

CIRCULAR HALOS ABOUT SUN OR MOON, BY PYRAMIDAL CRYSTALS, WHOSE FACES ARE INCLINED 24° 51′ TO LONGITUDINAL AXIS

Incidence face	Exit face	Refraction angle	Minimum deviation (radius of halo— calculated $\mu = 1.31$)	Radius of halo observed
p_1	p_4	49° 42′	17° 06′	17° $\pm$
p_1	p_3	76° 24′	31° 49′	32° 00′
p_1	m_4	24° 51′	7° 54′	8° 12′
p_1	m_3	63° 01′	23° 24′	23° 20*
p_1	$p_6{}'$	53° 58′	18° 58′	19° $\pm$
c	p'	65° 09′	24° 34′	
c	m	90°	45° 44′	
m_1	m_3	60°	21° 50′	
p_1	$p_4{}'$	130° 18′†	89° 28′‡	

* Original value 23° 57′ corrected as per measurement of halo of 22°.

† Not really a refraction angle, but the crystal angle between the incident and exit rays.

‡ Maximum total deviation, corresponding to minimum refraction.

m, face of hexagonal column; p, face of one pyramid; p', face of companion pyramid; c, truncate face, normal to longitudinal axis.

Secondary Halos.—Obviously, each bright spot of the primary halo phenomena, especially the upper and lower points of the 22° circle and its parhelia, must in turn be the source of secondary halos. Doubtless, the 22° halos of the lateral parhelia contribute much to the flaring vertical column through the sun that occasionally has been seen; and, perhaps, the brilliant upper and lower points of the halo of 22° may produce faint secondary parhelic circles. In general, however, very few of the secondary halos are ever bright enough to be seen even when carefully looked for.

Singular Halos.—A few halos not included in any of the above classes have been *once* reported. No satisfactory explanations of them have been offered. Clearly, though, since the ice crystal appears in many modified forms—with flat tabular, and pyramidal ends, for instance—and even in orderly clusters, it is obvious that although only a few halos are well known, a great many are possible.

Horizontal or Surface Halos.—A moderately dense distribution of the right kind of ice crystals over a continuous surface produces, of course, halos on that surface in those directions, point by point, in which they would appear in the sky if that were visible beyond this surface. Thus, the 22° and the 46° halos have been seen[1] on a level snow surface as hyperbolas, each with its vertex toward the observer.

[1] WHITNEY, A. W., *Amer. J. Sci.*, **45**; 389, 1893. RENAUD, ANDRÉ, *C. R.*, **206**; 1750, 1938.

CHAPTER V

REFLECTION PHENOMENA

A few optical phenomena of the atmosphere, usually classed as halos, are produced by simple reflection.

Parhelic Circle.—Occasionally, a white circle, perhaps faint and tending to be diffuse, passes through the sun parallel to the horizon and, therefore, crosses the positions of the parhelia, anthelion, paranthelia, etc. This circle is produced by simple reflection (hence it is white) from vertical faces of ice crystals, as may easily be demonstrated.

To this end, let PP (Fig. 208) be a plane parallel to the horizon and normal to a vertical face of an ice crystal at C. Let SC be an incident

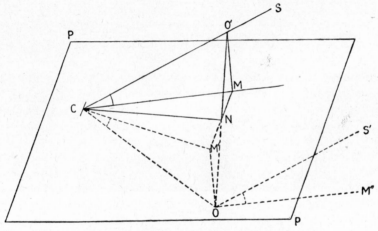

Fig. 208.—Formation of the parhelic circle.

ray reflected to the observer at O. Let CN be normal to the reflecting face, and lie in the plane PP. By the laws of reflection, CS, CN, and CO lie in a common plane, and the angle SCN = the angle OCN. If, now, $CO' = CO$, and $O'M$ and OM' be drawn normal to the plane PP, it is obvious that the triangle NMO' = the triangle $NM'O$, and that MO' = $M'O$. Hence, as the angles CMO' and $CM'O$ are right angles, and CO' = CO, the angle MCO', that is, the elevation of the sun above the plane PP, or above the plane of the horizon to which PP is parallel = the angle $M'CO$, the angle of depression at C of O below the plane PP, or angle of elevation of the crystal C above the observer's horizon.

But C is the position of any *vertical* face that reflects light to the observer at O Hence, the parhelic circle passes through the sun and is parallel to the horizon. Hence, also, it is superimposed upon such parhelia and parhelic tails as may coexist. Occasionally, therefore, one may be unable to distinguish between a portion of a parhelic tail and a segment of the parhelic circle. There can be no doubt, however, in regard to any portion that occurs nearer the sun than the appropriate positions of the parhelia of 22°. Such portion cannot be produced by refraction, and, consequently, must belong to the parhelic circle.

Since the formation of this circle requires a predominance of vertical faces, and since a simple columnar hexagonal prism, longer than broad, tends not only to keep its major axis horizontal but, often, also, one of its faces down, it follows that the required vertical surfaces must be either the flat ends of such crystals, the near end acting by direct reflection

Fig. 209.—Parhelic circle and oblique arcs through the anthelion. (*R. P. Wentworth, photographer.*)

and the far one by internal reflection; or the faces of columnar crystals that are broader than long, and therefore prevailingly vertical, whose farther sides are very bright, owing to total reflection.

Anthelion.—On rare occasions a bright white spot, known as the anthelion, is seen on the parhelic circle opposite the sun. Of course, all crystals in the locus of the anthelion that contribute to the production of the parhelic circle and the anthelic arcs, described later, also add to the brightness of the anthelion, and presumably they alone. That is, the brightness of the anthelion appears to be but the combined brightness of the parhelic circle and the anthelic arcs at their common point of intersection, as shown in Fig. 209, from a photograph taken near the equator at about local noon, Dec. 26, 1938.

Anthelic Borders.—Horizontal, columnar crystals evidently contribute to an anthelion when two of their sides are vertical. If, however, these sides are more or less inclined, the reflected light will come from a point above, or below, and to the right or left, as the case may be, of the anthelion. Only that light which has been totally reflected by the base is at all conspicuous. Nor is this portion uniform, but brighter and brighter as the angle of incidence on the base becomes smaller, and the cross-section of the beam larger, until the limiting angle of total reflection is reached, where the intensity abruptly drops to practically zero. The borders, therefore, of this anthelic light are rather sharply marked and, as stated by Hastings,[1] appear as short arcs crossing at the anthelion.

To locate points along these borders: From

$$\sin h = \mu \sin k$$

in which h and k are the angles between the base of the crystal and the external and internal rays, respectively, we find, at the limit of total reflection, $h = 57° 48'$. Hence, if θ is the angle between the axis of the crystal and the plane of the solar vertical,

$$\cos \theta = \frac{\sin 57° 48'}{\cos H},$$

in which H is the solar altitude. We now tip the horizon equally with the crystal through any definite angle and find the new anthelion (the border point desired) from the new solar vertical and new solar altitude.

The borders cross at an angle of about 30°, due to light passing in and out by the same face, and when the altitude of the sun is 10°; at an angle of roughly 127°, due to light passing in one face and out the second below it, when the altitude of the sun is 30°.

Anthelic Arcs.—When the rays 1, 3, 5, and 7 (Fig. 201) are internally reflected by a base of the crystal, "mirror images" of the corresponding points on the Parry class of arcs are produced. Two of these halos, those due to the internal reflection of the rays 3 and 5, are, as Hastings[2] has explained, the well-known lower and upper anthelic arcs (Fig. 210)—brightest when the altitude of the sun is about 70° and 50°, respectively, when the advantage of minimum refraction is added to that of favored position.

Points on these halos are found, as explained above, under *Parry arcs*.

Oblique Heliac Arcs.—On rare occasions, oblique white arcs are seen to rise from the sun (not cross it), symmetrical about the solar vertical, to which they are inclined nearly 60°. These arcs, which unite in a continuous curve above the sun, and which produce parhelia at their

---

[1] *Monthly Weather Review,* **48**; 322, 1920.
[2] *Loc. cit.*

intersections with other halos, especially with the halo of 22°, are due to reflection by ice needles in a particular position of stability—the major axis and two faces horizontal.

To trace these arcs, let a crystal in this stable attitude be at O (Fig. 211), the center of the celestial sphere; let A be the circle, 30° below the horizon BB, swept out by a normal to the reflecting face as the crystal is turned around a vertical axis; let N be the intersection of this normal with the circle A when the principal axis of the crystal is inclined $90° - \theta$

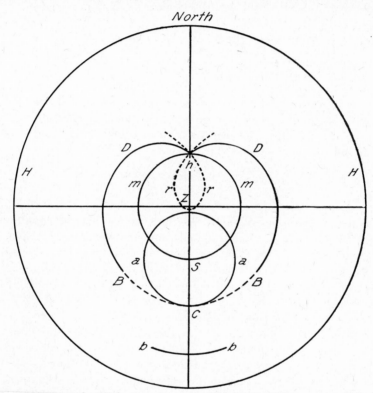

Fig. 210.—Z, zenith; HH, horizon; S, sun; aa, 22° halo; bb, 46° halo; mm, parhelic circle; h, anthelion; DBC, lower oblique arcs passing through the anthelion; rr, upper oblique arcs passing through the anthelion. The dotted arcs were not actually present in this particular observation.

to the plane of the solar vertical; let ZN be the vertical through N, Z being the zenith.

Then, since the incident ray, the reflected ray, and the normal to the reflecting surface lie in a common plane, with the angle of incidence equal to the angle of reflection, the plane of the incident ray SO and the reflected ray OS_1 includes the normal ON, and intersects the sphere in a great circle, and the angle SON is equal to the angle NOS_1. The image S' of S is on S_1O extended.

Clearly, then, to fix S' it is only necessary to know the arc SS' and the angle ZSS'. But

$$SS' = 180° - 2SN,$$

and, from the spherical triangle ZNS, in which $ZN = 120°$ and $ZS = 90° - H$, H being the altitude of the sun,

$$\cos SN = -\sin 30° \sin H + \cos 30° \cos H \cos \theta. \tag{1}$$

Hence, the arc SS' is easily computed for any assumed value of θ and

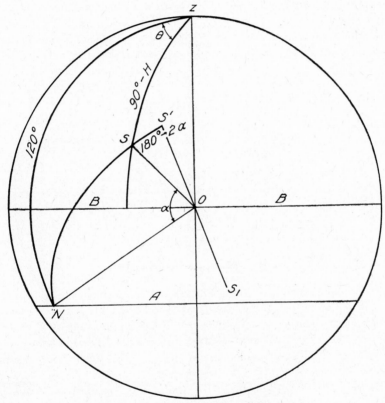

Fig. 211.—Production of oblique heliac arcs.

given value of H. Also,

$$\sin ZSS' = \sin ZSN = \frac{\sin \theta \cos 30°}{\sin SN}, \tag{2}$$

in which θ and SN are the values already assumed and computed, respectively.

By varying θ the entire halo is readily traced for any given altitude of the sun less than 60°, the limiting value for which the halo in question is possible.

The limiting value of θ, its value when $SN = 90°$, or when the reflecting plane passes through the sun, is given by the equation, deduced from equation (1),

$$\cos \theta_0 = \tan 30° \tan H,$$

and the corresponding value of ZSS' by the equation, from equation (2),

$$\sin ZSS' = \sin \theta_0 \cos 30°.$$

Finally, this halo crosses the solar vertical at the distance $120° - 2H$ above the sun.

Parhelia of 120°.—Bright spots that show no trace of color are occasionally seen on the parhelic circle 120° from the sun, in azimuth, or

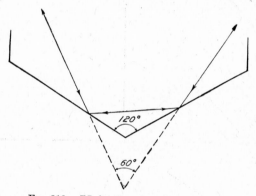

Fig. 212.—Production of parhelia of 120°.

60° from the anthelion. These are known as the parhelia of 120°, and are due, chiefly, to internal total reflection from one, and, thereafter, the other of two adjacent columnar, or hexagonal, faces across an internal angle of 120° (Fig. 212) and, slightly, to external reflection across re-entrant angles of 60°, and similar angles of 120°, both of which are common in snow crystals.

Parhelia of 90°.—The brightish spots that, on rare occasions, are seen on the parhelic circle, midway between the sun and the anthelion, presumably, are owing merely to the intersections of this circle with the halo of 90°.

Parhelia of Variable Position.—Obviously, the intersections of the parhelic circle with the antisolar halos of 38° and 44° produce parhelia whose distances from the anthelion, 38° and 44°, respectively, when the sun is on the horizon, progressively decrease with increase of the solar elevation.

Parhelic Arcs of 120°.—Occasionally, a short colorless arc g (Fig. 214) crosses the anthelic circle obliquely at each anthelion of 120°. These arcs are due, as explained by Hastings,[1] to tipping out of the horizontal of the crystals which, when horizontal, give the parhelia of 120°.

Clearly, the crystals most effective in producing the parhelia of 120° are those which, in addition to being horizontal, have a minor axis parallel, or roughly so, to the plane of the solar vertical. Furthermore, the hexagonal disk crystals, the kind that produce the arcs in question, tip, rock, or rotate, mainly about their minor axes.

Let, then, the crystals under consideration have a minor axis parallel to the plane of the solar vertical, let them be tipped θ degrees about this axis, and, for simplicity of argument, let the plane of the horizon be also, and equally, tipped in the same sense. There will then be a corresponding new parhelic circle, lost in the general illumination of the sky, and new parhelia of 120°, points on the arcs under consideration.

Obviously the arc a on the celestial sphere from the sun to either parhelion of 120° is one side of an isosceles spherical triangle of which the other two sides are each 90° − h, and their included angle 120°, in which h is the altitude of the sun referred to a horizon tipped parallel to the given plane of the crystals.

If H be the true altitude of the sun,

$$\sin h = \sin H \cos \theta,$$

and, by a little reduction,

$$\cos a = \tfrac{1}{2}(3 \sin^2 H \cos^2 \theta - 1).$$

Also, if φ is the angle between the true solar vertical and the arc a, then

$$\varphi = \tan^{-1} \frac{0.5774}{\sin H \cos \theta} \pm \theta,$$

in which the positive sign refers to points on the oblique arcs below the parhelic circle, and the negative sign to points above this circle.

The distance from the sun to either of these arcs is least at the place of its intersection with the parhelic circle, but only a little greater to any other part. Hence, they are sensibly circular about the sun, or antisolar point.

Pillars.—During very cold weather, vertical pillars of white light are often seen extending above and below the sun, when its elevation is small, or merely rising above it, when it is on the horizon. Artificial lights also give this effect, producing at times a forest of glowing, vertical shafts.

The upper and lower portions of these pillars, counting from the light, are owing, as has long been known, merely to reflection by the under and upper surfaces of tabular ice crystals—partial from the nearer surface and largely total from the farther.

[1] *Loc. cit.*

Crosses.—On very rare occasions strips of white light have been seen to intersect over the sun at right angles. This rare phenomenon is owing, presumably, merely to the simultaneous occurrence of a parhelic circle, or segment of it next the sun, and a light pillar. Possibly, it might also be produced by the intersection of the secondary halos of 22°, or even by some combination of "pillar," parhelic circle, and secondary halos. A competent observer, however, could easily distinguish between the several possible causes of a light "cross," and thus determine the actual origin of any particular instance of this phenomenon he might happen to see.

RECENT HALO COMPLEXES

Two unusual halo complexes have recently been reported that, together, show nearly all the well-known phenomena of that kind.

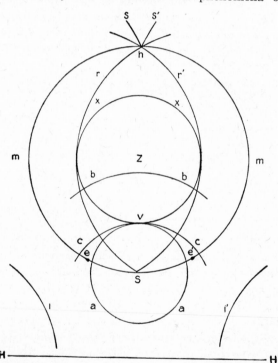

Fig. 213.—Ellendale (North Dakota) halo of Mar. 8, 1920. *H H* horizon; *S* sun; *Z* zenith; *a a* halo of 22°; *e e'* parhelia of 22°; *c c* upper tangent arc of halo of 22°; *b b* portion of halo of 46°; *m m* parhelic circle; *h* anthelion; *r r'* wide-angle oblique arcs of the anthelion; *s s'* narrow-angle oblique arcs of the anthelion; *v* so-called vertical parhelion of 22°; *x x* apparently secondary parhelic circle due to *v*.

They, therefore, are given here, both because of their individual worth and also as a convenient summary of this subject. They are:

1. An exceptional combination, including both the refraction and reflection (primary and secondary) types, observed and independently

measured with theodolites on Mar. 8, 1920, by F. J. Bavendick and W. H. Brunkow,[1] at the Ellendale, North Dakota, aerological station. Its appearance at 1.30 p.m., 90th meridian time, is indicated by Fig. 213, in which the seemingly secondary parhelic circle *xx* is especially interesting. The elevation of the sun, about 38° 15′, made the appearance of the circumzenithal arc impossible; nor was there an opportunity, later, to see it at Ellendale, since in an hour or two the entire halo faded away in a gradually thickening cloud. It was, however, seen in the

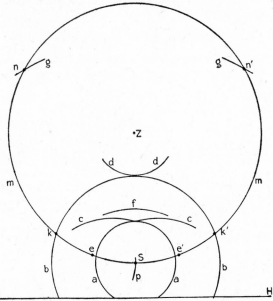

Fig. 214.—Boulder (Colorado) halo of Jan. 10, 1918. *H H* horizon; *S* sun; *Z* zenith; *a a* halo of 22°; *e e′* parhelia of 22°; *p* sun pillar, curved owing to prevailing tip of crystals due, presumably, to light surface winds; *c c* upper tangent arc of halo of 22°; *f* "Parry arc;" *b b* halo of 46°; *k k′* parhelia of 46°; *d d* circumzenithal arc; *m m* parhelic circle; *n n′* paranthelia; *g g* portions of the paranthelic arc.

same cloud sheet over northwestern Iowa, but with a much lower sun and as a portion of a simpler complex.

2. An equally rare combination observed by E. W. Woolard,[2] and others, at Boulder, Colorado, on Jan. 10, 1918; temperature, −20° C. Its appearance at 10 a.m., 105th meridian time, when the altitude of the sun was 19° 50′, is indicated by Fig. 214. The most noteworthy features of this complex are (1) the curvature of the sun-pillar *p*, obviously due to a prevailing tip (eastern edge up) of the reflecting faces, caused, presumably, by gentle surface winds incident to the onset of a cold wave; and (2) the flat arc *f* between the halos of 22° and 46°, and symmetrical about the solar vertical. This latter arc clearly is produced, as explained by

[1] *Monthly Weather Review*, **48**; 330, 1920.
[2] *Monthly Weather Review*, **48**; 331, 1920.

Hastings,[1] and previously by Brand and Wegener,[2] by refraction through ice needles oriented at random in one of their stable positions, that is, with a pair of the side faces horizontal.   Under the given circumstances, the computed Parry arc, with its center 28° 47′ above the sun, is as indicated, and agrees fully with the original sketch.

[1] *Monthly Weather Review*, **48**; 322, 1920.

[2] *Dan. Eksped. til Grönland's Nordöstkyst*, Vol. 2, 1906–1908.

CHAPTER VI

DIFFRACTION PHENOMENA

Coronas.—Coronas consist of one or more sets of rainbow-colored rings usually of only a few degrees radius, concentrically surrounding the sun, moon, or other bright object, when covered by a thin cloud veil. They differ from halos in having smaller (except in rare cases) and variable radii, and in having the reverse order of colors; that is, blue nearest the sun, say, and red farthest away.

Clearly, then, coronas are caused by diffraction, or the distribution of effective (nonneutralizing) quantities of light off the primary path, resulting from the action of cloud particles on radiation incident from a distant source.

Consider, then, the diffractive action of a layer of innumerable water droplets on a parallel beam of monochromatic light.

In this case the wave front, or continuous locus of any given phase, is flat—pits and pimples on it would quickly be smoothed out by dispersion—and everywhere normal to the line of travel. Also the droplets, because of their very short focal lengths and consequent great dispersive power, affect the parallel beam roughly as would so many opaque disks each of the size of a great circle of the corresponding droplet and normal to the line of travel. Furthermore, since the incident light is parallel, the center of the droplets may be regarded as lying in a common plane, each being located where the line of sight to its actual position intersects the plane in question.

The problem, then, as a first approximation, reduces to that of finding the diffraction pattern produced in an isotropic transparent medium by a great many irregularly distributed opaque disks on a plane wave front of monochromatic light.

The key to the solution of this problem is Babinet's principle, which may be explained as follows: When parallel light passes through a large opening in an opaque screen, but little illumination occurs outside the primary beam, and that little owing to rays from the edge of the opening whose angle of deviation from the original direction is very small. If, now, this large opening should be partially covered by a great many opaque disks, as assumed in the problem under consideration, and, if illumination should result, as it does, at places where formerly there was complete shadow, then, if the opaque disks should become transparent

547

and the transparent interspaces opaque, precisely the same illumination in the "shadow region" would obtain as before, but in exactly the opposite phase, as is obvious from the fact that the two illuminations acting together produce darkness.

Babinet's principle, therefore, enables one to use circular openings and opaque disks interchangeably in the solution of diffraction problems. And, as it is easier to discuss the circle mathematically than an irregular area, the above problem will be substituted by its physical equivalent. That is, circular openings in an opaque screen will be substituted for opaque disks on a wave front.

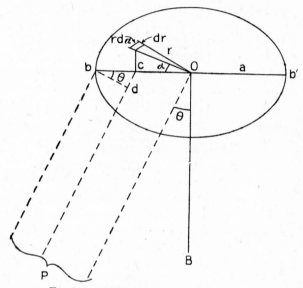

Fig. 215.—Diffraction by a circular opening.

Let O (Fig. 215) be the center of a small circular opening of radius a in an opaque screen, and let parallel light pass through this opening, normal to its plane, in the direction OB. Let the plane fixed by P, the point whose illumination is to be determined, and the line OB intersect the circle in the diameter bb', and let the angle $BOP = \theta$. Finally, let r be the distance of any element of the circle from the center O; c, the foot of the perpendicular from this element onto the diameter bb', and α the angle between r and the radius Ob.

Clearly, then, the difference of phase at P between light from an element of the wave front at b and from any other element is given by the expression.

$$2\pi\frac{cd}{\lambda}, \text{ or } \frac{2\pi}{\lambda}(a - r\cos\alpha)\sin\theta,$$

in which λ is the wave length. Also, since the displacement at P owing to any element $rd\alpha dr$ is

$$\left[\sin\left(\frac{t}{T} - \frac{cd}{\lambda}\right)\right]rd\alpha dr,$$

in which t is the time of travel from b to P and T the period, the total displacement X at P is given by the equation,

$$X = \int_0^{2\pi}\int_0^a \sin 2\pi\left[\left(\frac{t}{T} - \frac{a\sin\theta}{\lambda}\right) + \frac{r\sin\theta}{\lambda}\cos\alpha\right]rd\alpha dr.$$

Hence, developing, and putting

$$\int_0^{2\pi}\int_0^a \cos 2\pi\left(\frac{r}{\lambda}\sin\theta\cos\alpha\right)rd\alpha dr = A$$

and

$$\int_0^{2\pi}\int_0^a \sin 2\pi\left(\frac{r}{\lambda}\sin\theta\cos\alpha\right)rd\alpha dr = B$$

$$X = A\sin 2\pi\left(\frac{t}{T} - \frac{a\sin\theta}{\lambda}\right) + B\cos 2\pi\left(\frac{t}{T} - \frac{a\sin\theta}{\lambda}\right).$$

Therefore, A and B are components at right angles to each other of the resultant amplitude. Hence, the intensity I is given by the equation

$$I = A^2 + B^2.$$

Putting

$$\frac{\pi r\sin\theta}{\lambda} = \beta r$$

$$A = \int_0^{2\pi}\int_0^a \cos(2\beta r\cos\alpha)d\alpha dr$$

$$= \int_0^{2\pi}\int_0^a\left[1 - \frac{(2\beta r\cos\alpha)^2}{1\cdot 2} + \frac{(2\beta r\cos\alpha)^4}{1\cdot 2\cdot 3\cdot 4}\cdots\cdot\right]d\alpha dr$$

But

$$\int_0^{2\pi}\cos^{2n}\alpha d\alpha = \frac{1\cdot 3\cdot 5\cdots(2n-1)}{2\cdot 4\cdot 6\cdots(2n)}2\pi$$

Hence,

$$A = \pi\int_0^a\left[2rdr - \frac{2\beta^2 r^3 dr}{1} + \frac{2\beta^4 r^5 dr}{(1\cdot 2)^2} - \frac{2\beta^6 r^7 dr}{(1\cdot 2\cdot 3)^2} + \cdots\cdot\right]$$

$$= \pi\left[a^2 - \frac{1}{2}\frac{\beta^2 a^4}{1} + \frac{1}{3}\frac{\beta^4 a^6}{(1\cdot 2)^2} - \frac{1}{4}\frac{\beta^6 a^8}{(1\cdot 2\cdot 3)^2} + \cdots\cdot\right]$$

and, putting

$$\beta a = \frac{\pi a\sin\theta}{\lambda} = m.$$

$$A^2 = \pi^2 a^4\left[1 - \frac{1}{2}\frac{m^2}{1} + \frac{1}{3}\frac{m^4}{(1\cdot 2)^2} - \frac{1}{4}\frac{m^6}{(1\cdot 2\cdot 3)^2} + \cdots\cdot\right]^2$$

$$= \pi^2 a^4\left\{\frac{1}{m}J_1(2m)\right\}^2$$

where J_1 is the Bessel function of the first order.

A similar development gives the other component in terms of a series of odd valued sines of α. Hence, as the elements are symmetrically distributed on either side of the diagonal bb', $B = 0$, and

$$I = A^2.$$

On giving m various values, tables and curves of intensity may be constructed from the series or from tables of the Bessel functions. The following table, by Airy, copied from Mascart's "Traité d'optique,"[1] is restricted to that portion of the expression within the brackets.

m	A	I	m	A	I
0.0	1.0000	1.0000	3.0	−0.0922	0.0085
0.1	0.9950	0.9900	3.1	−0.0751	0.0056
0.2	0.9801	0.9606	3.2	−0.0568	0.0032
0.3	0.9557	0.9134	3.3	−0.0379	0.0014
0.4	0.9221	0.8503	3.4	−0.0192	0.0004
0.5	0.8801	0.7746	3.5	−0.0013	0.0000
0.6	0.8305	0.6897	3.6	0.0151	0.0002
0.7	0.7742	0.5994	3.7	0.0296	0.0009
0.8	0.7124	0.5075	3.8	0.0419	0.0017
0.9	0.6461	0.4174	3.9	0.0516	0.0027
1.0	0.5767	0.3326	4.0	0.0587	0.0035
1.1	0.5054	0.2554	4.1	0.0629	0.0040
1.2	0.4335	0.1879	4.2	0.0645	0.0042
1.3	0.3622	0.1312	4.3	0.0634	0.0040
1.4	0.2927	0.0857	4.4	0.0600	0.0036
1.5	0.2261	0.0511	4.5	0.0545	0.0030
1.6	0.1633	0.0267	4.6	0.0473	0.0022
1.7	0.1054	0.0111	4.7	0.0387	0.0015
1.8	0.0530	0.0028	4.8	0.0291	0.0008
1.9	0.0067	0.0000	4.9	0.0190	0.0004
2.0	−0.0330	0.0011	5.0	0.0087	0.0001
2.1	−0.0660	0.0044	5.1	−0.0013	0.0000
2.2	−0.0922	0.0085	5.2	−0.0107	0.0001
2.3	−0.1116	0.0125	5.3	−0.0191	0.0004
2.4	−0.1244	0.0155	5.4	−0.0263	0.0007
2.5	−0.1310	0.0172	5.5	−0.0321	0.0010
2.6	−0.1320	0.0174	5.6	−0.0364	0.0013
2.7	−0.1279	0.0164	5.7	−0.0390	0.0015
2.8	−0.1194	0.0143	5.8	−0.0400	0.0016
2.9	−0.1073	0.0115	5.9	−0.0394	0.0016
3.0	−0.0922	0.0085	6.0	−0.0372	0.0014

The following table of diffraction maxima and minima is also copied from Mascart.[2]

[1] Vol. 1; 310.
[2] *Loc. cit.*, p. 312.

DIFFRACTION MAXIMA AND MINIMA

	$\dfrac{m}{\pi}$	Maxima difference	I	$\dfrac{m}{\pi}$	Minima difference	I
1	0.000		1.00000	0.610		0
		0.819			0.506	
2	0.819		0.01745	1.116		0
		0.527			0.503	
3	1.346		0.00415	1.619		0
		0.512			0.502	
4	1.858		0.00165	2.121		0
		0.504			0.501	
5	2.362		0.00078	2.622		0
		0.500			0.500	
6	2.862		0.00043	2.122		0
		0.500			0.500	
7	3.362		0.00027	3.622		0
		0.500			0.501	
8	3.862		0.00018	4.123		0
		0.500			0.500	
9	4.362		0.00012	5.623		0

It will be noticed that the decrease of intensity from maximum to minimum, though large at first, quickly becomes very small.

From the values of m/π, corresponding to diffraction minima, it is evident that

$$\sin \theta = (n + 0.22)\frac{\lambda}{2a}, \text{ very nearly,}$$

in which n is the order of the minimum, counting from the center.

This important equation gives the angular distance from the light source at which the successive diffraction minima occur for any particular wave length and size of drop or disk. It also gives the diameter of the drop when the wave length, angular distance from the center, and order of the minimum are known. Furthermore, it shows that the longer the wave length, and the smaller the droplet, the larger the diffraction circle, or halo.

The above discussion applies to a single circular disk on the wave front. An exact duplicate disk, obviously, would produce an exact duplicate diffraction pattern. If, then, two such disks occur close together, and if the distance between their centers, or other homologous points is b, and ϕ the angle between the line connecting these points and the line connecting the farthest to the point of observation, then the difference in phase between the two lights at the latter phase is $2\pi\dfrac{b \sin \phi}{\lambda}$, and a secondary diffraction pattern, in addition to the two primary circular ones, is produced, directed at right angles to the line connecting the centers of the disks. Similarly, conspicuous diffraction patterns are produced by any regular geometric distribution of many disks.

Let, however, the disks, or droplets, be numerous, irregularly distributed, and all of the same size (if of various sizes their effects cannot easily be summed up). Let each produce at a given point a disturbance whose amplitude is A, but let the phases be $\epsilon_1, \epsilon_2, \ldots \epsilon_n$, and let R be the resultant amplitude.

Then,

$$R^2 = \Sigma(A \cos \epsilon)^2 + \Sigma(A \sin \epsilon)^2,$$
$$= A^2[\cos \epsilon_1 + \cos \epsilon_2 + \cdots + \cos \epsilon_n)^2 + (\sin \epsilon_1 + \sin \epsilon_2 + \cdots + \sin \epsilon_n)^2]$$
$$R^2 = A^2(\Sigma \cos^2 \epsilon + \Sigma \sin^2 \epsilon + 2\Sigma \cos \epsilon \cos \epsilon' + 2\Sigma \sin \epsilon \sin \epsilon'),$$
$$= A^2 n + 2A^2 \Sigma \cos (\epsilon - \epsilon').$$

But as n is large and the disks irregularly scattered, it is clear that the phase difference, $\epsilon - \epsilon'$, between the innumerable pairs will have all manner of values with, on the whole, the positive and negative well balanced. Hence, as close as can be detected,

$$R^2 = nA^2.$$

That is, the diffraction rings, corona, for instance, produced by a large number n of irregularly distributed neighboring droplets are the same as those produced by any one of them, but n times as bright.

When the incident light is complex, the diffraction patterns produced by the several wave lengths necessarily overlap and produce correspondingly colored rings—red, if present, being the outermost, and blue the innermost.

Aureole.—When the cloud droplets are of various sizes and none is distinctly dominant, the diffraction patterns they produce around the sun or moon so thoroughly misfit each other, so overlap and blend, that the coronal region is everywhere devoid of prismatic colors except close to the luminary. This remaining patch of light is the familiar, fuzzy aureole, brownish red in its outer portion and bluish white over its inner area. It is the first from the center and therefore the least obliterated of the overlapping coronas, and, since it is the first, it evidently is produced by the largest of the droplets that are present in any considerable amount.

Size of Cloud Particles.—Since the diffraction pattern produced by a great many irregularly distributed droplets of uniform size is the same as that due to a single droplet, it is clear that the size of the cloud particles producing coronas may be determined by the equation

$$\sin \theta = (n + 0.22)\frac{\lambda}{2a},$$

in which, as already explained, θ is the angular distance from the center of the corona to the nth minimum corresponding to light of the wave length λ and a the radius to be determined.

Measurements made in this manner have indicated that the radii of corona-producing cloud droplets, though varying over a considerable range, commonly average about 0.007 mm. to 0.010 mm., and the radii of fog droplets about 0.005 mm. The values thus computed, however, are too small, since the Babinet principle does not hold for transparent droplets of this size.[1]

It may be interesting to note, in this connection, that a contracting or decreasing corona implies growing droplets, and, perhaps, the approach of rain; and that an expanding corona implies, on the other hand, decreas-

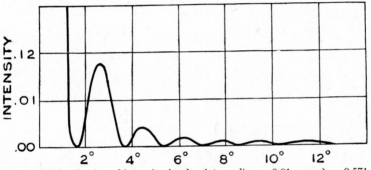

Fig. 216.—Distribution of intensity by droplets, radius = 0.01 mm., $\lambda = 0.571\mu$.

ing or evaporating droplets, and, presumably, the approach of fair weather.

Figure 216, copied from an instructive article by Simpson,[2] gives the angular and intensity distribution of the monochromatic light $\lambda =$ 0.000571 mm. in a corona produced by droplets of 0.01 mm. radius.

Droplets vs. Ice Needles as Producers of Coronas.—When coronas are seen in clouds whose temperature is above 0° C., or in which halos do not form, it is certain that they are due to droplets. It is well known, however, that the most brilliant coronas—those of multiple rings and large diameter—usually are formed by very high clouds whose temperature often must be far below freezing. Naturally, then, it has been inferred that these coronas are produced by the diffractive action of ice needles. Simpson,[3] however, appears to have disproved the probability that they are formed in this manner. "On no occasion," he says, referring to his stay in the Antarctic, "were a corona and halo seen at the same time on the same cloud." Furthermore, he explains, as the axes of the needles are essentially horizontal, this being their stable position, only

[1] WILSON, J. G., *Cambridge Philosoph. Socy.*, **32**; 493, 1936.

[2] *Quart. J. Roy. Met. Soc.*, **38**; 291, 1912.

[3] *Loc. cit.*

those at right angles to radii from the sun, or other luminary, could produce coronas of the kind observed, while the equally numerous crystals of every other orientation would produce such different patterns that the total effect probably could be but little more than white light— certainly nothing approaching the pure brilliant colors often seen in these coronas.

Presumably, therefore, the brilliant coronas of high clouds are due to very small undercooled water droplets of approximately uniform sizes, and not, as has generally been supposed, to ice needles. Köhler[1] reaches about the same conclusion.

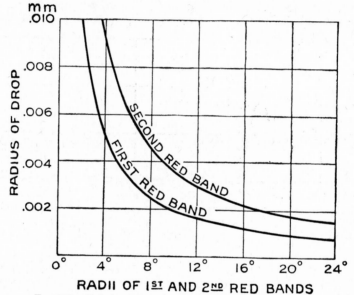

FIG. 217.—Relation between size of drop and size of corona.

Iridescent Clouds.—Thin and, perhaps, slowly evaporating cirro-stratus, cirrocumulus, and other high clouds occasionally develop numerous iridescent borders and patches of irregular shape, especially of red and green, at various distances from the sun up to 30° or more. A brilliantly colored iridescent cloud of considerable area is justly regarded as one of the most beautiful of sky phenomena, but one for which, until recently, there was no satisfactory explanation. Simpson,[2] however, has shown that the colored patches in question, presumably, are only fragments of coronas formed by exceedingly small droplets of approximately uniform size. The relation between the radius of droplet and angular distances from the center to the first and second red bands is shown in Fig. 217, also copied from the paper cited, from

[1] "Untersuchungen über die Elemente des Nebels und der Wolken," Stockholm, 1925.

[2] *Loc. cit.*

which it appears that coronas of the requisite size may occur, and, therefore, that the assumption that iridescent clouds are only fragments of unusually large and exceptionally brilliant coronas, presumably, is correct.

Bishop's Ring.—After the eruption of Krakatoa, in 1883, of Mont Pelé, in 1902, and of Katmai, in 1912, a faint reddish-brown corona was often seen, under favorable circumstances, around the sun. This is known as Bishop's ring, after the Reverend Sereno Bishop, of Honolulu, who first described it.

The width of this ring, as seen after the eruption of Krakatoa, was about 10°, and the distance from the sun to its outer edge, that is, to the first minimum, 22° to 23°. Substituting this value of the angular radius of the first minimum in the equation, explained above,

$$\sin \theta = (n + 0.22)\frac{\lambda}{2a}$$

and letting $\lambda = 0.000571$ mm., it appears that the diameter of the dust particles, assumed either spheres or circular disks of approximately uniform size, that produced this peculiar corona is given by the equation

$$2a = 1.22\frac{0.000571 \text{ mm.}}{\sin 22° 30'}$$
$$= 0.00182 \text{ mm. about.}$$

Glory or Brocken-bow.—When favorably situated, one occasionally may see rings of colored light around the shadow of his own head as cast upon a neighboring fog bank or cloud. This phenomenon, to which several names have been given—glory, Brocken-bow, Brocken-specter, mountain-specter—is produced by the primary "scattering" of the incident light by the directly illuminated droplets of the cloud or fog bank.[1] In the case of a water droplet of fog or cloud size, some light is reflected by the outer surface, but this is feeble, due to both imperfect reflection and wide divergence. Another portion enters the drop, and, after one internal reflection, returns in the form of a cusped wave front cap symmetrical about the line of incidence, as shown in Fig. 174. Furthermore, the forward and rear portions of the cusp, due to such a droplet, are too close together to produce interference, and the effect at any given point of the whole, virtually spherical, cap can be obtained by the Huyghens method, just as the direct corona is computed from circular sections of a flat wave front; or, more exactly, as Ray has done, by laboriously computing the total effect of all the light, no matter how dispersed by the drop, according to the electromagnetic theory. In effect each illuminated droplet is a somewhat smaller hole in an opaque

[1] RAY, B., *Proc. Ind. Assn. for the Cultivation of Science*, **8**; Pt. 1, 1923.

screen normal to a beam of parallel rays. A cluster of such holes produces coronas, as explained above.

Heiligenschein.—It is interesting to observe (and reason why) the luminous, white corona one may see on a bedewed lawn close around and glorifying the shadow of his own head, and none but his own. The explanation is very simple. As a little geometric consideration will show, the light reflected from the outer surface of a dewdrop is brightest directly back along the line of incidence and falls off rapidly as its deviation from that line increases, while that internally reflected is bright only far off in the rainbow direction. Hence, to any given observer, the drops rapidly increase in brightness, due to external reflection, as the shadow of his own head is approached and none other. His head, and his only, is to him, and to him only, crowned with a glory.

CHAPTER VII

PHENOMENA DUE TO SCATTERING: COLOR OF THE SKY

The color of the cloudless sky, though generally blue, may, according to circumstances, be anything within the range of the entire spectrum. At great altitudes the zenithal portions are distinctly violet, but at moderate elevations often a clear blue. With increase of the angular distance from the vertical, however, an admixture of white light soon becomes perceptible, that often merges into a grayish horizon. Just after sunset and also before sunrise, portions of the sky often are distinctly green, yellow, orange, or even dark red, according, especially, to location and to the humidity and dust content of the atmosphere. Hence, these colors and the general appearance of the sky have rightly been used, immemorially, as more or less trustworthy signs of the coming weather.

Early Ideas.—Many attempts have been made to account for the blue of the sky[1]—the other colors being comparatively ignored. Some have held that it is just the nature of the atmosphere, or of particles in it, to reflect the blue of sunlight and to transmit the other colors. But, as they did not explain how the atmosphere, or these particles, happened to have such nature, the mystery actually remained as profound as ever. Another interesting hypothesis, suggested by Leonardo da Vinci, was to the effect that the blue is the resultant of a mixture of more or less white light, reflected by the atmosphere, with the black of space. But the futility of this idea is, immediately, obvious from the fact that gray alone could be produced by any such mixture.

The first logical attempt to explain (as that term is now understood) why the sky is blue, was made by Newton,[2] who supposed it to be due to the same sort of interference between the rays reflected from the front and rear surfaces of transparent objects (in this case minute water drops) that produce the colors of soap bubbles. In fact, he thought that the "blue of the first order," the blue nearest the black central spot of the "Newton's rings," is of the same color as the blue of the sky, and that they were produced in the same way. This explanation, though erroneous, and based only on analogy, was accepted, without modification, for nearly 175 years. At about the end of this period, however, Clausius[3] demonstrated, analytically, that a cloud of droplets, of the

---

[1] DORSEY, summary and bibliography, *Monthly Weather Review*, **28**; 382, 1900.

[2] *Optics*, book II.

[3] *Crell's J.*, **34**; 122, 1847; p. 185, 1848; *Pogg. Ann.*, **72**; 294, 1847.

small size assumed by Newton, would cause the stars, and other celestial objects, to appear enormously magnified. He, therefore, modified Newton's theory by assuming that the droplets are larger, but vesicular, with very thin walls. In this way the magnification trouble is avoided, but the theory is not improved. First, because water droplets are not hollow; and, second, because, as shown by Brücke,[1] the color of the sky differs radically from the blue of the "first order."

Although the above appears to have been the first serious criticism of the Newtonian theory of sky colors, observational and experimental data sufficient to render it untenable had long been known. This consisted of (a) Arago's[2] discovery, in 1811, that sky light is partially polarized and that this polarization is a maximum along a circle about 90° from the sun; and (b) Brewster's[3] discovery, shortly thereafter, that polarization by reflection is a maximum when the tangent of the angle of incidence is equal to the refractive index of the reflector divided by that of the adjacent medium.

If, then, sky light is the result of simple reflection, the angle of polarization (angle of incidence corresponding to maximum polarization) of the reflecting medium must be 45°—since the arc of maximum polarization is 90° from the sun. But the angle of polarization of water in air is about 74°. Hence, the color of the sky cannot be due to reflection from water droplets, as Newton and many others assumed.

Modern Theory.—The real origin of the blue of the sky, scattering of light by particles far too small to reflect specularly, appears to have been first indicated by Brücke's[4] experiments, which showed (a) that a transparent medium, rendered turbid by sufficiently small particles, appears blue when illuminated with white light; and (b) that objects may be seen through such medium clearly and distinctly. A few years later, Tyndall[5] made a large number of experiments on the action of chemically formed "clouds" on incident white light, and found that not only did they scatter blue light when their particles were very small, but also that this light was completely polarized at right angles to the incident beam. Here, then, was the experimental solution of the problem of the blue of the sky and its polarization. About two years later, Lord Rayleigh[6] supplied the necessary theory, and, thus, at last, one of the oldest and most difficult of the many problems of meteorological optics became completely solved. In a later paper, Lord Rayleigh[7] showed that in the

[1] *Pogg. Ann.*, **88**; 363, 1853.
[2] "Oeuvres," Vol. VII; 394 and 430.
[3] *Phil. Trans.*, **33**; 125, 1815.
[4] *Loc. cit.*
[5] *Phil. Mag.*, **37**; 384, 1869; **38**; 156, 1869.
[6] *Phil. Mag.*, **41**; 107, 274, 447, 1871; **12**; 81, 1881.
[7] *Phil. Mag.*, **47**; 375, 1899.

absence of dust of all kinds "the light scattered from the molecules [of air] would suffice to give us a blue sky, not so very greatly darker than that actually enjoyed." And still later, King[1] concluded that:

The analysis of the present paper seems to support the view that at levels above Mount Wilson [1730 meters] molecular scattering is sufficient to account completely both for attenuation of solar radiation and for the intensity and quality of sky radiation.

Whether the scattering be by fine dust, however, or by individual molecules, the theory is the same, and, as developed in Rayleigh's first paper, substantially as follows:

Let a beam of light of wave length λ be incident, say, to be definite, from the zenith. There will be little or no scattering from that portion of the beam in free ether, as is obvious from the facts (a) that extremely distant stars are still visible, and (b) that interstellar spaces are nearly black. From the portion in the atmosphere, however, there is abundant lateral scattering by the innumerable particles of dust and molecules of air, each of which is optically denser than the ether and so small in comparison to λ^3 that the applied force due to the light wave is practically constant throughout its volume. Each such particle merely increases the local inertia of the ether, and, thereby, since the rigidity is not affected, correspondingly reduces the amplitude of a passing light wave. If, then, a force should be applied to each particle, such as to counterbalance the increasing inertia, the light would pass on exactly as in empty space, and, therefore, without scattering. On the other hand, precisely the same force, but reversed in direction, if acting alone on free ether would produce the same effect that the disturbing particle produces. This force obviously must have the same period and direction as the undisturbed luminous vibrations and be proportional to the difference in optical density between the particle and the ether.

The only factors that conceivably can affect the ratio of the amplitude of scattered to incident light are: direction, or, rather, angle between directions of force and point of observation; ratio between the optical densities of the disturbing particle and the ether; volume of particle; distance from particle; wave length; and velocity of light. Hence, in comparing the extents to which lights of different colors are scattered, the first two factors may be neglected, since they apply in equal measure to all. Furthermore, as the ratio in question, like all ratios, is a mere number and, therefore, dimensionless, the last factor must be omitted, since it, and it alone, involves time. There remain, then, only the volume of the particle, distance from it, and the wave length to consider. But, from the dynamics of the problem, it appears that the ratio of the two

[1] *Phil. Trans.*, **212**; 375, 1913.

amplitudes must vary directly as the volume of the particle and inversely as the distance from it. That is,

$$N = \frac{L^3}{L} f(\lambda),$$

in which N is some number, L a unit of length, and $f(\lambda)$ that function of λ that renders the equation dimensionless. Hence,

$$f(\lambda) = \lambda^{-2},$$

and, therefore, the ratio of the two intensities is proportional to λ^{-4}. Obviously, then, light from a serene sky should belong essentially to the blue or short wave-length end of the spectrum.

If, as commonly expressed, the displacement in the incident wave is $A \cos\left(\dfrac{2\pi vt}{\lambda}\right)$, in which A is the amplitude; v the velocity of light, λ the wave length; and t the time since any convenient instant when the displacement was A, then the corresponding acceleration is

$$\frac{d^2}{dt^2} A \cos \frac{2\pi vt}{\lambda} = -A\left(\frac{2\pi}{\lambda} v\right)^2 \cos \frac{2\pi}{\lambda} vt.$$

Hence, the force that would have to be applied to a sufficiently minute particle in order that the wave might pass over it undisturbed is

$$-(D' - D)TA\left(\frac{2\pi v}{\lambda}\right)^2 \cos \frac{2\pi}{\lambda} vt,$$

in which D' and D are the optical densities of the particle and ether, respectively; and T the volume of the particle. And this, as explained, is also the expression for the opposite force which, if operating alone on the ether, would produce the same light effects that actually are induced by the particle in question.

Now it has been shown by Stokes,[1] and also by Lord Rayleigh,[2] that the displacement X produced by the force $F \cos \dfrac{2\pi vt}{\lambda}$ is given by the expression

$$X = \frac{F \sin \alpha}{4\pi v^2 Dr} \cos \frac{2\pi}{\lambda}(vt - r),$$

in which α is the angle between the direction of the force and the radius vector r that connects the center of the force with the point at which the displacement is observed.

On substituting for F its value, one finds that

$$X = A\frac{D' - D}{D}\frac{\pi T}{r\lambda^2} \sin \alpha \cos \frac{2\pi}{\lambda}(vt - r).$$

Hence, the intensity of the light scattered by a single particle is

$$A^2\left(\frac{D' - D}{D}\right)^2 \frac{\pi^2 T^2}{r^2\lambda^4} \sin^2 \alpha,$$

[1] *Camb. Phil. Trans.*, **9**; 1, 1849; *Math. and Phys. Papers, II*, pp. 243–328.
[2] *Phil. Mag.*, **41**; 107, 1871.

and for a cloud—particles at random, hence, phases random and intensities additive,

$$A^2\left(\frac{D'-D}{D}\right)^2 \frac{\pi^2 \sin^2 \alpha}{\lambda^4} \sum \frac{T^2}{r^2},$$

in which $\sum \frac{T^2}{r^2}$ is the sum of the values of $\frac{T^2}{r^2}$ for all the particles in the line of sight, or

$$A^2\left(\frac{D'-D}{D}\right)^2 \frac{\pi^2 \sin^2 \alpha}{\lambda^4} N\left(\frac{T}{r}\right)^2_m$$

in which N is the total number of particles in the line of sight, and $\left(\frac{T}{r}\right)^2_m$ the mean of the several values of $\left(\frac{T}{r}\right)^2$.

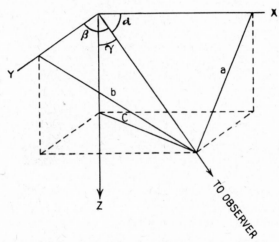

Fig. 218.—Intensity of scattered light in a given direction.

The above equations are based on the assumption that the displacements in the incident wave are all in the same plane—that the incident light is plane polarized. If, however, they lie in all planes, passing through the axis of propagation, that is, if the incident light is unpolarized, we may resolve each displacement, always normal to the line of travel, into two components at right angles to each other and obtain their joint effect in any given direction. Let the line from the center of the force to the point of observation make the angles α, β, and γ with these components and the direction of travel, respectively. Then, since $\sin^2 \alpha + \sin^2 \beta = 1 + \cos^2 \gamma$ (Fig. 218), the intensity of the scattered light at the angle γ from the direction of travel of a nonpolarized beam is

$$\frac{A^2}{2}\left(\frac{D'-D}{D}\right)^2 \frac{\pi^2(1+\cos^2\gamma)}{\lambda^4} N\left(\frac{T}{r}\right)^2_m. \tag{1}$$

According to this equation, the maximum amount of scattered light is along the path—forward and back—of the incident beam, and least (half as great) at right angles to it. However, this equation does not hold for strictly forward scattered light, in which case the intensity is given, not by the arithmetical addition of the individual contributing intensities, but by the square of the geometric sum of the several amplitudes. Also, the intensity is directly proportional to the square of the volume of the disturbing particle, provided it is sufficiently small.

The effect of the size, from small to large with respect to λ^3, on scattering has been theoretically developed for spheres by Bromwich,[1] and others, but the relations found are not simple. The exact modifications necessary to adapt this theory to particles of other shapes, especially the irregular, are not known.

Extinction Coefficient.—The intensity or brightness of solar or other radiation is decreased with increase of air path by (a) scattering, (b) selective absorption, (c) diffraction, (d) reflection, and (e) refraction. When the sky is clear, however, only (a) is particularly effective in the visual region, but here it is quite effective.

Let E be the intensity of the (unpolarized) beam. The amount of radiation scattered by each disturbing particle is, from equation (1),

$$\frac{E}{2}\left(\frac{D'-D}{D}\right)^2 \frac{\pi^2}{\lambda^4} T^2 \int (1+\cos^2\gamma)d\Omega$$

where $d\Omega$ is the elementary solid angle, and the integration is through the whole of angular space; that is,

$$\int (1+\cos^2\gamma)d\Omega = \int_0^{2\pi} d\psi \int^\pi (1+\cos^2\gamma)\sin\gamma d\gamma = \frac{16\pi}{3}.$$

Hence, the amount of light scattered is

$$E\frac{8\pi^3}{3\lambda^4}\left(\frac{D'-D}{D}\right)^2 T^2.$$

Let n be the number of disturbing particles (all alike) per unit volume. Then the depletion per unit cross-section in traveling the distance dx is

$$dE = -Endx\frac{8\pi^3 T^2}{3\lambda^4}\left(\frac{D'-D}{D}\right)^2.$$

If, then, E_0 is the energy in the beam before any scattering takes place, and E the energy remaining after penetrating the distance x into the turbid medium in question,

$$E = E_0 e^{-\epsilon x}$$

in which the extinction coefficient

$$\epsilon = \frac{8\pi^3 n T^2}{3\lambda^4}\left(\frac{D'-D}{D}\right)^2.$$

[1] *Phil. Trans.*, **220**; 175, 1920.

But $D = \mu^2$ (from the equations, $v = \sqrt{\dfrac{\text{elasticity}}{\text{density}}} = \dfrac{1}{\mu}$, density of ether $= 1$, μ for ether $= 1$), $\mu =$ refractive index. Also, in the case of scattering by air molecules, or by any small particles in a medium whose refractive idex is 1,

$$nT\left(\frac{D' - D}{D}\right) = D'' - 1$$

in which $D'' =$ average optical density of the turbulent space. If μ is the refractive index of the medium, air, say,

$$nT\left(\frac{D' - D}{D}\right) = \mu^2 - 1 = (\mu + 1)(\mu - 1) = 2(\mu - 1), \text{ nearly,}$$

since μ differs but little from unity.

Hence, substituting,

$$\epsilon = \frac{32\pi^3}{3n\lambda^4}(\mu - 1)^2, \text{ approximately.}$$

Clearly, then, opacity and glare, the spoilers of good seeing, rapidly decrease with increase of wave length, a fact that justifies the use, on aeroplanes, for instance, of "haze cutters" (filters that transmit only the longer waves) for both visual and photographic work. A fog haze, however, cannot be much cut. This is because the extinction and glare it produces, being due, owing to the relatively large size of the fog droplets, chiefly to diffraction and reflection, are nearly equally effective for all colors.

Sky Brightness.—The scattering of light, by the molecules of the atmosphere and the suspended fine dust particles, decreases the

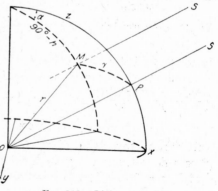

FIG. 219.—Light scattering.

intensity of both the direct insolation and the scattered radiation, but, at the same time, gives to all portions of the sky, except that occupied by the sun, a luminosity that otherwise would not exist, and this in turn increases the brightness of objects on the earth. A first approximation to the amount of skylight incident onto a horizontal unit surface is obtained by summing up all the visible radiation due to primary scattering, assuming that this light is *not* itself scattered, reaching that surface from a hemisphere above it of radius R (20 kilometers, perhaps) filled with dustless air of constant density.

Let O (Fig. 219) be the unit area in question in the xy-plane; z, the zenith distance of the sun S; M the air molecule (elevation h, azimuth

α from the vertical through the sun, and distance r) illuminating O. Clearly, then, the straight lines OPS and MS are parallel to each other, and the angle MOP, or arc MP, the difference in direction between the incident ray at M and the particular scattered ray therefrom that reaches O. Hence, if the surface is dead white (unit albedo) and L its luminosity, we may write, from equation (1),

$$dL = \frac{kn}{r^2}(1 + \cos^2 \gamma) \sin h \, dV \qquad (2)$$

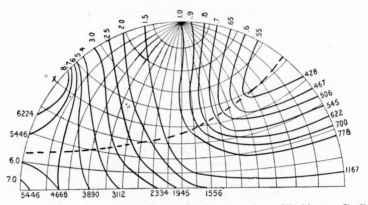

Fig. 220.—Average brightness in millilamberts of a clear sky at Washington, D. C. X, Position of sun.

in which dV is the differential of the volume, n the number of molecules per unit volume, and k the constant, for monochromatic radiation, $\frac{A^2}{2}\left(\frac{D' - D}{D}\right)^2 \frac{\pi^2 T^2}{\lambda^4}$. But, as explained, $\gamma = $ arc MP, hence,

$$\cos \gamma = \sin h \cos z + \cos h \sin z \cos \alpha.$$

Substituting this value of $\cos \gamma$ in equation (2), and for dV its value $r^2\cos h \, d\alpha dr dh$, and integrating throughout the hemisphere, or from $r = 0$ to R, $h = 0$ to $\pi/2$, and $\alpha = 0$ to 2π, we get

$$L = \frac{knR\pi}{4}(5 + \cos^2 z).$$

Under these conditions, the illumination of a horizontal surface, due to sky light alone, is a maximum when the sun is at the zenith, and a minimum—though only one-sixth less—when it is on the horizon.

The illumination of the unit horizontal surface by direct light from the sun is $E \cos z = E_0 \cos z e^{-\epsilon R} \equiv A^2 \cos z f$, in which $f = e^{-\epsilon R}$ and $\epsilon = 16\pi nk/3A^2$.

Hence, the ratio of the sky illumination of a horizontal surface to its direct illumination by the sun on a clear day is

$$\frac{L}{E \cos z} = -\frac{3 \log f(5 + \cos^2 z)}{64f \cos z}.$$

By taking into account secondary scattering, and other corrections, King[1] and Berlage[2] have obtained better expressions for the intensity of sky light. This light, also, has been repeatedly measured with great care; many of the values thus obtained are shown in Figs. 220[3] and 221[4] which are self-explanatory when it is recalled that the "lambert" is the brightness of a perfectly diffusing surface 1 cm. from a point source of light of 1 candlepower. See also a paper by Ray P. Teele.[5]

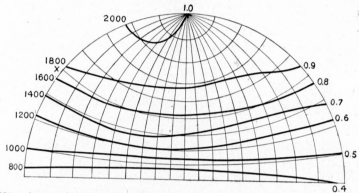

Fig. 221.—Average brightness in millilamberts of a sky covered with dense clouds at Washington, D. C.   X, Position of sun.

Prevailing Color.—If I_0 is the initial intensity and I_1 the remaining intensity after penetrating the uniformly turbid medium, the distance x, then,

$$I_1 = I_0 e^{-\frac{kx}{\lambda^4}}$$

where

$$k = \frac{32\pi^3}{3n}(\mu - 1)^2.$$

This residual light, in turn, is scattered, and if I_2 is the intensity of the light scattered by a single particle at the angle α from the direction of travel, and distance r from the particle,

$$I_2 = I_1 \frac{k'}{\lambda^4}$$

where

$$k' = \frac{\pi^2 T^2}{r^2}\left(\frac{D' - D}{D}\right)^2 (1 + \cos^2 \alpha)$$

and

$$I_2 = I_0 \frac{k'}{\lambda^4} e^{-\frac{kx}{\lambda^4}}.$$

[1] *Phil. Trans.*, **212**; 375, 1913.
[2] *Met. Zeit.*, **45**; 174, 1928.
[3] Kimball and Hand, *Monthly Weather Review*, **49**; 483, 1921.
[4] Kimball and Hand, *Monthly Weather Review*, **50**; 618, 1922.
[5] Stratosphere Flight of 1935, *Nat. Geographic Soc.*

Hence, the ratio of intensity received to initial intensity, or I_2/I_0, is small both for very long and very short wave lengths. Its maximum value occurs at $\lambda^4_m = kx$; and

$$\left(\frac{I_2}{I_0}\right) = \left(\frac{I_2}{I_0}\right)_m \left(\frac{\lambda_m}{\lambda}\right)^4 e^{1-\left(\frac{\lambda_m}{\lambda}\right)^4},$$

or, if I_0 is uniform throughout the spectrum,

$$I_2 = (I_2)_m \left(\frac{\lambda_m}{\lambda}\right)^4 e^{1-\left(\frac{\lambda_m}{\lambda}\right)^4}$$

According to Abbot, Fowle, and Aldrich,[1] the mean energy intensities of I_0, in arbitrary units, are:

λ =	0.39	0.42	0.43	0.45	0.47	0.50	0.55	0.60	0.70
I_0 =	3614	5251	5321	6027	6240	6062	5623	5042	3644

The luminous intensities would show greater contrasts, since the eye is more sensitive to the mid-region of the visible spectrum than to either end.

From these values of I_0, and the equation for the intensity of I_2, it can be shown that the prevailing color of the clear sky, except when the sun is on or below the horizon, is neither violet nor red, but some intermediate color, generally blue, as we know by observation.

Twilight Colors.—As the sun sinks to, and below, the horizon, during clear weather, a number of color changes occur over large portions of the sky, especially the eastern and western. The phenomena that actually occur vary greatly, but the following may be regarded as typical, especially for arid and semiarid regions:

a. A whitish, yellowish, or even bronze glow of 5° or 6° radius that concentrically encircles the sun as it approaches the horizon, and whose upper segment remains visible for perhaps 20 minutes after sundown.

The chief contributing factors to this glow appear to be (1) scattering which is a maximum in the directions forward (nearly) and back, of the initial radiation, and (2) diffraction by the dust particles of the lower atmosphere. In both cases, blue and violet are practically excluded, owing to the very long air paths.

b. A grayish-blue circle that rises above the eastern horizon as the sun sinks below the western. This is merely the shadow of the earth.

c. A purplish arch that rests on the earth shadow and gradually merges into the blue of the sky at a distance of perhaps 10°, and also fades away as the arch rises.

Obviously, any direct sunlight in the lower dusty atmosphere to the east must have penetrated long distances through the denser air and, thus, have become prevailingly red, while that reaching the higher atmos-

[1] *Ann. Astrophys. Obs.*, Smithsonian Institution, **3**; 197, 1913.

phere is still rich in blue and violet. Hence, the observer sees red light scattered from the first of these layers, and blue to violet from the other, and, thereby, gets the effect of the superposition of the opposite ends of the visible spectrum, that is, purple. The effect is most pronounced when the luminous layers are seen more or less "end on." Hence, the light is brightest at the border of the earth shadow. The fact that the red component of the purple is from the lower atmosphere, and the others from the higher, is evident from the bluish crepuscular rays that often radiate, apparently, from the antisolar point—shadow streaks cast through the lower dust-laden air by western clouds or mountain peaks, often below the horizon.

d. A bright segment only a few degrees deep, but many in extent, that rests on the western horizon just after sundown. The lowest portion often is red and the upper yellowish. A product, essentially, of scattered light by the lower and dustier portions of the atmosphere, where the light before being scattered is already reduced, essentially, to the colors seen.

e. A purple glow covering much of the western sky, reaching its maximum intensity when the sun is about 4° below the horizon and disappearing when it is about 6° below. The explanation of this purple glow in the western sky, presumably, is the same as that in the eastern sky, as given above under (c). The crepuscular rays of this region, apparently radiating from the sun, often are greenish-blue.

f. A faint purple glow covering the entire sky when the sun is 6° or more below the horizon, and gradually disappearing in the west when the sun is 16° to 18° below the horizon. This appears to be due to secondary scattering of light from the illuminated atmosphere far to the west.

The foregoing descriptions, applying equally to dawn (not the "false dawn" which appears to be the zodiacal light, transient owing to the greater brightness of the true dawn), are not universally applicable. Indeed, the sky very commonly is greenish instead of purple, probably when the atmosphere is but moderately dust laden. Furthermore, the explanations are only qualitative. A rigid analysis, even if the distribution of the atmosphere and its dust and moisture content were known—which they are not, nor are they constant—would be at least difficult and tedious.

Duration of Twilight.—The duration of twilight, whether civil, that is, the time after sunset or before sunrise during which there is sufficient light for outdoor occupations, or astronomical, the time until or after maximum darkness, varies with the amount of cloudiness and inclination of the ecliptic to the horizon. In the case of clear skies, civil twilight ends, or begins, when the true position of the sun (center) is about 6° below the horizon, and astronomical twilight when it is about 18° below

DURATION OF ASTRONOMICAL TWILIGHT

(Interval between Times When the Upper Edge of the Sun is on and the True Position of Its Center 18° below the Horizon)

Date	North latitude														
	0°	10°	20°	25°	30°	32°	34°	36°	38°	40°	42°	44°	46°	48°	50°
	h.m.	h.m.	h.m.	h.m.	h.m.	h.m.	h.m.	h.m.	h.m.	h.m.	h.m.	h.m.	h.m.	h.m.	h.m.
January 1	1 14	1 15	1 18	1 21	1 26	1 28	1 29	1 31	1 34	1 37	1 41	1 45	1 49	1 53	1 59
11	1 14	1 14	1 18	1 21	1 25	1 27	1 29	1 31	1 33	1 36	1 39	1 43	1 37	1 52	1 57
21	1 13	1 13	1 17	1 20	1 23	1 25	1 28	1 30	1 32	1 34	1 38	1 41	1 45	1 49	1 51
February 1	1 12	1 12	1 15	1 18	1 22	1 24	1 26	1 28	1 30	1 33	1 36	1 39	1 43	1 47	1 52
11	1 11	1 12	1 14	1 17	1 21	1 23	1 25	1 27	1 29	1 32	1 34	1 37	1 41	1 45	1 49
21	1 10	1 11	1 13	1 16	1 20	1 22	1 24	1 26	1 28	1 31	1 33	1 36	1 40	1 44	1 48
March 1	1 10	1 11	1 13	1 16	1 20	1 21	1 23	1 25	1 28	1 30	1 33	1 36	1 39	1 43	1 48
11	1 09	1 10	1 13	1 16	1 19	1 21	1 23	1 25	1 28	1 30	1 33	1 36	1 39	1 43	1 48
21	1 09	1 10	1 13	1 16	1 20	1 22	1 24	1 26	1 29	1 31	1 34	1 37	1 41	1 45	1 50
April 1	1 09	1 11	1 14	1 17	1 21	1 23	1 25	1 27	1 30	1 33	1 36	1 40	1 44	1 49	1 54
11	1 10	1 11	1 15	1 18	1 22	1 24	1 27	1 30	1 33	1 36	1 39	1 43	1 48	1 54	2 00
21	1 11	1 12	1 16	1 20	1 24	1 27	1 29	1 32	1 36	1 39	1 43	1 48	1 54	2 01	2 08
May 1	1 12	1 13	1 18	1 22	1 27	1 30	1 33	1 36	1 39	1 43	1 48	1 54	2 01	2 10	2 20
11	1 13	1 14	1 19	1 24	1 30	1 33	1 36	1 40	1 43	1 48	1 54	2 01	2 10	2 20	2 35
21	1 13	1 15	1 21	1 26	1 32	1 36	1 39	1 43	1 48	1 54	2 01	2 10	2 20	2 35	2 58
June 1	1 14	1 16	1 23	1 28	1 35	1 38	1 41	1 46	1 52	1 59	2 07	2 18	2 31	2 54	
11	1 15	1 17	1 24	1 29	1 36	1 40	1 44	1 49	1 55	2 02	2 12	2 23	2 40	3 11	
21	1 15	1 18	1 24	1 29	1 37	1 41	1 45	1 50	1 56	2 03	2 13	2 25	2 44	3 19	
July 1	1 15	1 17	1 24	1 29	1 36	1 40	1 44	1 49	1 55	2 02	2 12	2 23	2 40	3 10	
11	1 14	1 16	1 23	1 28	1 35	1 38	1 41	1 46	1 52	1 59	2 07	2 18	2 31	2 54	
21	1 13	1 15	1 21	1 26	1 32	1 36	1 39	1 43	1 48	1 54	2 01	2 10	2 21	2 36	3 00
August 1	1 13	1 14	1 19	1 24	1 30	1 33	1 36	1 40	1 44	1 48	1 54	2 02	2 10	2 20	2 35
11	1 12	1 13	1 18	1 22	1 27	1 30	1 33	1 36	1 39	1 43	1 48	1 54	2 01	2 10	2 20
21	1 11	1 12	1 16	1 20	1 24	1 27	1 30	1 33	1 36	1 39	1 43	1 48	1 54	2 01	2 09
September 1	1 10	1 11	1 14	1 18	1 22	1 24	1 27	1 30	1 33	1 36	1 39	1 43	1 48	1 53	2 00
11	1 09	1 11	1 13	1 17	1 21	1 23	1 25	1 27	1 30	1 33	1 36	1 39	1 44	1 49	1 54
21	1 09	1 10	1 13	1 16	1 20	1 22	1 24	1 26	1 29	1 31	1 34	1 37	1 41	1 45	1 50
October 1	1 09	1 10	1 13	1 16	1 19	1 21	1 23	1 25	1 28	1 30	1 33	1 36	1 39	1 43	1 48
11	1 10	1 11	1 13	1 16	1 19	1 21	1 23	1 25	1 28	1 30	1 33	1 36	1 39	1 43	1 48
21	1 10	1 11	1 13	1 16	1 20	1 22	1 24	1 26	1 28	1 31	1 33	1 36	1 40	1 44	1 48
November 1	1 11	1 12	1 14	1 17	1 21	1 23	1 25	1 27	1 29	1 32	1 34	1 38	1 41	1 46	1 49
11	1 12	1 12	1 16	1 18	1 22	1 24	1 26	1 28	1 30	1 33	1 36	1 40	1 43	1 47	1 52
21	1 13	1 13	1 17	1 20	1 24	1 26	1 28	1 30	1 32	1 35	1 38	1 42	1 46	1 49	1 55
December 1	1 14	1 14	1 18	1 21	1 25	1 27	1 29	1 31	1 33	1 36	1 40	1 44	1 47	1 52	1 57
11	1 14	1 15	1 18	1 22	1 26	1 28	1 30	1 32	1 34	1 37	1 41	1 45	1 49	1 53	1 59
21	1 15	1 16	1 19	1 22	1 26	1 28	1 30	1 32	1 35	1 38	1 41	1 45	1 49	1 54	1 59

DURATION OF CIVIL TWILIGHT

(Interval between Times When the Upper Edge of the Sun is on and the True Position of Its Center 6° below the Horizon)

Date	North latitude														
	0°	10°	20°	25°	30°	32°	34°	36°	38°	40°	42°	44°	46°	48°	50°
	m.	m.	m.	m.	m.	m.	m.	m.	m.	m.	m.	m.	m.	m.	m.
January 1	22	22	24	25	27	27	27	28	29	30	32	33	34	36	39
11	22	22	24	25	26	27	28	28	29	30	31	32	33	35	38
21	22	22	23	24	26	26	27	27	28	29	30	32	33	34	37
February 1	22	22	23	24	25	26	27	27	27	28	29	31	32	34	35
11	22	22	22	23	25	26	26	27	27	28	29	31	32	34	35
21	21	22	22	23	24	25	25	26	27	28	28	29	30	32	33
March 1	21	22	22	23	24	24	25	26	27	28	28	29	30	31	33
11	21	21	22	23	24	24	25	26	26	27	27	28	30	31	33
21	21	21	22	23	24	24	25	26	26	27	27	28	30	31	33
April 1	21	21	22	23	24	25	25	26	27	28	28	29	30	32	33
11	21	22	22	23	24	25	26	26	27	28	28	29	31	32	34
21	22	22	22	23	25	25	26	27	28	28	29	30	32	34	35
May 1	22	22	23	24	25	26	27	28	28	29	30	32	33	35	36
11	22	22	23	24	26	27	28	29	29	30	31	33	35	36	39
21	22	22	24	25	27	28	28	29	30	31	33	35	36	38	41
June 1	22	22	24	25	27	28	28	29	31	32	34	36	37	40	43
11	22	23	24	26	28	28	29	30	31	33	34	36	38	41	44
21	22	23	25	26	28	29	29	30	31	33	34	36	38	42	44
July 1	22	23	24	26	28	28	29	30	31	33	34	36	38	41	44
11	22	22	24	25	27	28	28	29	31	32	34	36	37	40	43
21	22	22	24	25	27	28	28	29	30	31	33	35	36	38	41
August 1	22	22	23	24	26	27	28	29	29	30	31	33	35	36	39
11	22	22	23	24	25	26	27	28	28	29	30	32	33	35	36
21	22	22	22	23	25	25	26	27	28	28	29	30	32	34	35
September 1	21	22	22	23	24	25	26	26	27	28	28	29	31	32	34
11	21	21	22	23	24	25	25	26	27	28	28	29	30	31	33
21	21	21	22	23	24	24	25	26	27	27	27	28	30	31	33
October 1	21	21	22	23	24	24	25	26	26	27	27	29	30	31	32
11	21	22	22	23	24	24	25	26	27	28	28	29	30	31	33
21	21	22	22	23	24	25	25	26	27	28	28	29	30	32	33
November 1	22	22	22	23	25	25	26	27	28	28	29	30	31	33	34
11	22	22	23	24	25	26	27	28	28	29	30	31	32	33	35
21	22	22	23	24	26	26	27	28	28	29	30	32	33	34	37
December 1	22	22	24	25	26	27	28	28	29	30	31	33	34	35	38
11	22	22	24	25	27	27	28	28	29	30	32	33	34	36	39
21	22	23	24	25	27	27	28	28	29	31	32	33	34	37	39

RELATIVE ILLUMINATION INTENSITIES

Source of illumination	Intensity	Ratio to zenithal full moon
	Foot-candles	
Zenithal sun..............................	9,600.0	465,000.0
Twilight at sunset or sunrise...................	33.0	1,598.0
Twilight center of sun 1° below horizon...........	30.0	1,453.0
Twilight center of sun 2° below horizon...........	15.0	727.0
Twilight center of sun 3° below horizon...........	7.4	358.0
Twilight center of sun 4° below horizon...........	3.1	150.0
Twilight center of sun 5° below horizon...........	1.1	53.0
Twilight center of sun 6° below horizon...........	0.40	19.0
(End of civil)		
Twilight center of sun 7° below horizon...........	0.10	5.0
Twilight center of sun 8° below horizon...........	0.04	2.0
Twilight center of sun 8° 40' below horizon........	0.02	1.0
Zenithal full moon..............................	0.02	1.0
Twilight center of sun 9° below horizon...........	0.015	0.75
Twilight center of sun 10° below horizon..........	0.008	0.40
Starlight......................................	0.00008	0.004

The tables of twilight duration (pp. 568 and 569) were computed by Kimball[1] from the equation

$$\cos h = \frac{\sin \alpha - \sin \phi \sin \delta}{\cos \phi \cos \delta}$$

in which h is the sun's hour angle from the meridian, α the sun's altitude (negative below the horizon), δ the solar declination, and ϕ the latitude.

Twilight Illumination.—The brightness of twilight changes slowly or rapidly, according as the sun is less or more, respectively, than about 4° below the horizon. The last table above, based on photometric measurements by Kimball and Thiessen,[1] gives the approximate value of a number of clear-sky, twilight, and other natural illumination intensities on a fully exposed horizontal surface. However, as explained in detail by G. Déjardin,[2] no matter how far the sun and the moon may be below the horizon, a clear night never is completely dark, for always the sky is luminous with stars, great and small; with sunlight reflected by zodiacal dust; with a continuous auroral glow; and, perhaps, with some light of still other sources.

[1] *Monthly Weather Review*, **44**; 614, 1916.
[2] *Rev. Mod. Phys.*, **8**; 1, 1936.

CHAPTER VIII

PHENOMENA DUE TO SCATTERING: SKY POLARIZATION

The polarization of sky light, discovered in 1811, by Arago,[1] often is more or less modified by specular reflection from relatively large particles—cloud droplets, coarse dust, etc.—but in general it results from the combination of primarily and secondarily scattered radiation.

Condition of Primarily Scattered Light.—As explained by Lord Rayleigh,[2] the light scattered from an incident beam by an isotropic gas molecule, or other sufficiently small isotropic object, is symmetrically distributed about the line of enforced motion of that particle as an axis, and completely polarized in the plane at right angles to this line. This follows, directly, from the fact that plane polarized light is merely light whose vibrations are all normal to the same plane—the plane of polarization. If, then, the incident beam is nonpolarized, ordinary sunlight, for instance, the scattered light, therefore, will be completely polarized at right angles to the direction of incidence, and partially polarized in other directions. And, since the plane of polarization is fixed by the sun, observer, and point observed, it follows from Fig. 218 that the ratio

$$\frac{\text{polarized light}}{\text{total light}} = \frac{\sin^2 \gamma}{1 + \cos^2 \gamma},$$

where γ = the angular distance of the point observed from the sun. That is, the polarization increases from zero in the direction both of the sun and the antisolar point to a maximum (complete) midway between them, or normal to the incident rays.

Condition of Secondarily Scattered Light.—While primary scattering of ordinary light by gas molecules and fine dust particles accounts for a large part of the observed polarization and other phenomena of sky light, the nonpolarized light that always exists in a greater or less amount at 90° from the sun; the luminosity—partially polarized—of shaded air masses; and the existence of neutral points (small regions whose light is not polarized) are all largely due, as Soret[3] has shown, to secondary scattering, but not wholly. Some of it, as determined by Strutt[4] (present Lord Rayleigh), Cabannes,[5] and others, appears to be owing to the aniso-

---

[1] *Astronomie Populaire*, **2**; 99.

[2] *Phil. Mag.*, **41**; 107, 1871.

[3] *Arch. sci. phys. nat.*, **20**; 429, 1888.

[4] *Proc. Roy. Soc.*, **95**; 155, 1919.

[5] *Ann. Phys.*, **15**; 5, 1921,

tropy of the air molecules. Tertiary and indefinitely higher scattering. obviously, also exist, but their effects are too small to justify consideration,

To determine the nature and magnitude of secondary scattering, let O (Fig. 222) be the position of a particle shielded from direct insolation but otherwise exposed, and consider its effect on the total incoming sky light. Let the sun be on the horizon; let OX be parallel to the solar radiation, OZ vertical, and OY normal to the plane ZX; let m be any particle a unit distance from O; and let Om make the angle ϕ with the vertical, and its projection on the plane XY the angle θ with OX.

As the solar rays are nonpolarized they may be treated as consisting of two parts of equal amplitude l, say, polarized at right angles to each other. For convenience, let the displacements in the light vibration and the consequent movements of m be parallel to OZ and OY, corresponding to polarization in the horizontal and vertical planes, respectively.

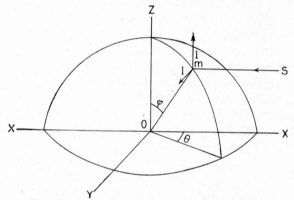

Fig. 222.—Intensity of secondarily scattered light.

These movements of m, in turn, generate a secondary light with displacements in the same direction, hence, of an intensity that varies from a maximum at right angles to that direction to zero along it.

On resolving the vertical amplitude into two components, one normal, the other parallel, to Om and the former (which alone is operative on the particle at O), in turn, into components parallel to the X, Y, and Z axes, respectively, one finds that,

$$l'_X = -l \sin \phi \cos \phi \cos \theta$$
$$l'_Y = -l \sin \phi \cos \phi \sin \theta$$
$$l'_Z = l \sin^2 \phi.$$

Similarly, on resolving the horizontal amplitude into components normal and parallel to the plane OZm, and these in turn parallel to the three axes, one obtains

$$l''_X = l \cos^2 \phi \sin \theta \cos \theta - l \sin \theta \cos \theta = -l \sin^2 \phi \sin \theta \cos \theta$$
$$l''_Y = l \cos^2 \phi \sin^2 \theta + l \cos^2 \theta$$
$$l''_Z = -l \sin \phi \cos \phi \sin \theta.$$

As a crude first approximation, let the distribution of the atmosphere about O be equal in all upward directions and assume all parts to be equally illuminated. Further, let a per unit area be the number of particles that, if distributed over the hemispherical shell, would produce at O the same optical effect that actually obtains. Then, the total intensity components at O (found by squaring the amplitudes and integrating over the hemisphere) are given by the equations

$$I_X = 2al^2 \int_0^{\frac{\pi}{2}} \int_0^{\pi} (\sin^2 \phi \cos^2 \phi \cos^2 \theta + \sin^4 \phi \sin^2 \theta \cos^2 \theta) \sin \phi d\phi d\theta$$

$$I_Y = 2al^2 \int_0^{\frac{\pi}{2}} \int_0^{\pi} (\sin^2 \phi \cos^2 \phi \sin^2 \theta + \cos^4 \phi \sin^4 \theta$$
$$+ 2 \cos^2 \phi \sin^2 \theta \cos^2 \theta + \cos^4 \theta) \sin \phi d\phi d\theta$$

$$I_Z = 2al^2 \int_0^{\frac{\pi}{2}} \int_0^{\pi} (\sin^4 \phi + \sin^2 \phi \cos^2 \phi \sin^2 \theta) \sin \phi d\phi d\theta.$$

Or,

$$I_X = 2\pi al^2 \times \tfrac{2}{15}$$
$$I_Y = 2\pi al^2 \times \tfrac{3}{5}$$
$$I_Z = 2\pi al^2 \times \tfrac{3}{5}.$$

The intensity components of secondary diffusion at the center of a sphere of uniformly distributed particles would be just twice the above, which, as stated, applies to the center of a hemisphere.

Since there is an appreciable amplitude along all three of the rectangular axes, it follows that secondary scattering sends more or less nonpolarized light in all directions, and, therefore, would prevent sky light from being completely polarized at right angles to the direction of insolation, even if the air molecules were strictly isotropic, which, apparently, they are not.

The above assumption that the light-scattering particles are distributed equally along any upward radius from O obviously is not in close agreement with the actual distribution of the atmosphere and its dust content as visible from any given point in it. Let this distribution be $a(n + 1) - an \cos \phi$ particles per unit area of the hemisphere instead of a, as previously assumed, that is, a gradual increase from a in the zenith to $a(n + 1)$ on the horizon. Then,

$$I_X = 2\pi al^2 \left[\frac{2}{15} (n + 1) - \frac{n}{16n} \right]$$

$$I_Y = 2\pi al^2 \left[\frac{3}{5} (n + 1) - \frac{17n}{48} \right]$$

$$I_Z = 2\pi al^2 \left[\frac{3}{5} (n + 1) - \frac{5n}{24} \right].$$

If $n = 12$, that is, if the horizon is thirteen times brighter than the zenith, a common condition,

$$I_X = 2\pi al^2 \times 0.983$$
$$I_Y = 2\pi al^2 \times 3.55$$
$$I_Z = 2\pi al^2 \times 5.3.$$

This distribution of intensities still gives nonpolarized light in all directions. It also gives a preponderant amount of polarization I_z in the horizontal plane, which neutralizes at certain places the polarization in the vertical plane due to primary scattering.

The combination, then, of primarily and secondarily scattered light must produce a variety of polarization and other phenomena which necessarily vary with the altitude of the sun, dust content of the atmosphere, and state of the weather. Many observational studies have been made of sky polarization and the facts found to agree with the above theoretical considerations. The principal facts are:

1. Part of the light from nearly all points in a clear sky is plane polarized, whatever the season, location, altitude of the sun, or other conditions.

2. The polarized portion of sky light, in turn, is divisible into two parts: (a) the positive, due to the first or primary scattering, in which the plane of polarization (plane normal to the vibrations) is given by the source (sun), point of observation, and eye of the observer; and (b) the negative, due to secondary scattering, in which the plane of polarization is normal to that of the primary, and, therefore, because of the ring-like distribution of the atmosphere about any point on the earth's surface, essentially horizontal.

3. Generally speaking, the percentage of polarized light along any great circle connecting the sun and the antisolar point increases from zero near either to a maximum midway between them, which, in turn, increases with the altitude of the point in question.

4. The point of absolute maximum polarization is in the solar vertical and ordinarily about 90°, as stated, from the sun.

5. In general, the percentage of polarization decreases with the amount of light reflected through the sky, whether from the surface or from relatively large particles in suspension. It, therefore, decreases with (a) percentage of snow covering; (b) percentage of cloudiness; (c) dustiness, or anything that itself leads to an increase of dustiness, such as high winds, especially over arid regions, but everywhere during dry weather, strong vertical convection—hence, generally less during summer than winter—volcanic explosions of the Krakatoa type, etc.

6. The percentage of polarization generally increases with the wave length of the light examined.

7. Even shaded masses of air, if exposed to sky radiation, emit perceptible amounts of polarized light.

8. Three small regions of unpolarized light, Babinet's, Brewster's, and Arago's, neutral points, occur on the solar vertical; the first some 15° to 20° above the sun, the second about the same distance below it, and the third 20°, roughly, above the antisolar point.

9. As the sun rises above, or sinks below, the horizon, the antisolar distance of Arago's point increases from about 20° to, roughly, 23°; while the solar distance of Babinet's point decreases from a maximum of, approximately, 20° to, perhaps, 18°, for a solar depression of 5° or 6°, and to 0°, as does also Brewster's point, as the zenith is approached.

10. When the upper atmosphere is greatly turbid, as it has often been after violent volcanic explosions, other neutral points, in addition to those above mentioned, occasionally are observed.

PART V
FACTORS OF CLIMATIC CONTROL

CHAPTER I

GENERAL SUMMARY

Introduction.—The following is a discussion of the principal factors, and the effects of their possible changes, that determine what the climate —the various averages and extremes of weather—of any given place shall be; a discussion of the physics of climate and not of its geographic distribution.

Many people, relying on their memories alone, insist that our climates are now very different from what they used to be. Their fathers made similar statements about the climates of still earlier times, as did also their fathers' fathers, as their several writings show, and so on through the ages; and the bulk of this testimony is to the effect that our climates are getting worse—evidence, perhaps, that flesh has always been heir to ills. The records, however, of the past 100 years show that while there have been several slight and short-period (2 to 3 or 4 years) climatic changes during that time, that will be explained later, there have been no long-period regular cycles, though through roughly the first half of that time there appears to have been a trend to cooler, and through the last half a distinct trend to warmer.[1] There is, however, much evidence that appreciable climatic changes, some to warmer, some to cooler, of many years' duration have occurred within historic times. This evidence, which many do not accept as conclusive, is found in the growth rings of old trees; the known changes in the areas and depths of several inland seas; the records in regard to the breaking up of ice in rivers and the opening of navigation; and in a variety of other more or less significant facts.

But whatever the truth in regard to historic climates may be, nothing is more certain than that during the geologic past there have been many and important climatic changes of great duration. Innumerable fossil remains, both in the Arctic and Antarctic regions, tell of long ages when genial or, at least, temperate climates extended well among the higher latitudes, while deep scorings and ancient moraines, hundreds and even thousands of miles from the nearest existing glacier, tell quite as positively of other ages when vast ice sheets spread far into the zones we now call temperate; and this in spite of the fact (there is no good evidence to the contrary) that from the beginning of geologic records the surface temperatures have been distributed in the same general sense as at

[1] KINCER, J. B., *M. W. R.*, **61**; 251, 1933.

present—highest in equatorial regions and lowest about the poles, though usually with much less contrast than exists at present.

It must be remembered, of course, that the previous existence of comparatively mild climates in limited high-latitude regions does not prove that the average temperature of the world as a whole was then much, if any, higher than it is now, but only that at those places the growing seasons were long enough to permit the, then, indigenous vegetation to mature its seeds (a much more rapid process in high latitudes owing to the greater length of the summer days than in low), and that the temperature of the littoral waters at the same places was such as to foster the local marine life. Both conditions, conceivably, might have been met by a free and, therefore, abundant oceanic circulation; or, perhaps, locally by protection from cold currents and drifting ice. Similarly, local glaciation doubtless often was produced by local causes. But, on the other hand, such extensive glaciation as several times obtained must have required a world-wide lowering of temperature. Indeed, no escape seems possible from the conclusion that the world has experienced many a profound climatic change of both types, local and universal, mild and dry through the long ages when the land was of low level and relatively small extent, and cold and damp during the much briefer periods when mountains were high and numerous and the oceans comparatively restricted in area and circulation.

When this series of climatic changes began, there is no sure means of knowing, for the records, especially those of glacial origin, grow gradually fainter and more scanty with increase of geologic age; so scanty, indeed, as to force the belief that the effects of many of the earlier changes may long since have been completely obliterated. But, however this may be, it is almost certain that, from the time of the earliest known of these changes down to the very present, the series has been irregularly continuous, and the end, one might reasonably assume, is not yet. Change after change of climate in almost endless succession, and even additional ice ages, may still be experienced, though when they shall begin (except in the case of the small and fleeting changes to be noted below), how intense they may be, or how long they shall last, no one can form the slightest idea.

Clearly, then, a matter so fundamental as this, namely, the profound modification of those agencies that not only fashion the face of the earth, but also control its flora and govern its fauna, challenges and deserves every contribution that science can give to its complete or even partial elucidation. Hence it is, that during the past 60 years, or more, numerous attempts, some of them invoking purely terrestrial and others extraterrestrial, or cosmical, conditions, have been made to find a probable and at the same time an adequate physical basis for, or cause of, the known climatic changes of the distant past, and especially for those disastrous changes that brought about the extensive glaciations that prevailed during the so-called ice ages. But nearly all the older suggestions and working hypotheses as to the cause of the ice ages have been definitely and finally abandoned, either because of inconsistency with known physical laws, or abandoned because they were found inadequate to meet the conditions imposed upon them by the results of the very investigations which, in many cases, they themselves had helped to inspire.

FACTS OF CLIMATIC CHANGES

Among the more important facts, with respect to climatic changes, that appear to have been established, and which, presumably, therefore, must be met by any theory that would account for such changes, or explain specifically the origin of ice ages, or, what is equally important, the much longer intervening warm ages, are the following:

a. The number of larger climatic changes were at least several, the smaller many.

b. The greater changes, and, doubtless, many of the smaller also, were simultaneous over the entire earth (there is accumulating evidence in favor of this conclusion), and in the same sense; that is, the world became colder everywhere at the same time (climatically speaking) or warmer everywhere.

c. They were of unequal intensity.

d. They were of irregular occurrence and of unequal duration.

e. They, at least one or more, progressed with secondary variations of intensity, or with advances and retreats of the ice front.

f. There often were centers of maximum intensity—certainly of ice accumulation and, doubtless, of other effects.

g. There were numerous local changes, suggestive of local causes.

h. They have occurred from early, probably from the earliest, geological ages down to the present, and, presumably, will continue irregularly to recur for many ages yet to come.

EXISTING FACTORS OF CLIMATIC CONTROL

Before attempting to find the probable cause, or causes, of climatic changes, it will be convenient first to consider the present factors of climatic control, since the variations of some of these undoubtedly have produced such changes, even, presumably, some, if not all, of those great changes that brought on maxima and minima of glaciation. It is possible, of course, that neither singly nor collectively were the factors in question largely productive of the known changes in geologic climates; but as climate today is subject to a complex control, all terms of which are more or less variable, it is certain that the climates of that portion of the geologic past (the only portion that will here be considered) during which the earth had an atmosphere and a hydrosphere, were also subject to a similar complex control, consisting, certainly, of all the factors that now are effective, and, probably, of no others. Hence, while it is conceivable that some one dominant cause, such as marked and age-long changes in the solar constant, the passage of the solar system through a vast nebula

CHIEF FACTORS OF CLIMATIC CONTROL

Name	Character
1. Latitude	Invariable to within negligible amounts.
2. Brightness of moon and planets.	Widely variable, but of no climatic significance, since they jointly produce a temperature variation of only 0.0001° C., roughly.
3. Solar "constant" at a fixed distance.	Slightly variable. There are small irregular variations that commonly last only a few days, at most, and also a small variation coincident with the 11-year sun spot period. Other changes are not known, but may exist.
4. Solar distance	Slightly variable, with a geologically negligible annual period due to eccentricity of the earth's orbit; and also, for the same reason, both a 100,000-year, roughly (now about 80,000-year), secular period; and a much longer pseudo period. The larger of these eccentricity changes, undoubtedly, are of climatic importance, but, as presently explained in the discussion of Croll's theory, there is strong evidence against the assumption that they were the chief, or even an important, factor in the production of glaciation. There, also, are slight monthly changes in the solar distance due to perturbations by the moon; and other slight changes owing to perturbations by the planets. In any case, however, the climatic effect due to perturbations is negligible—a maximum temperature change (computed) of, roughly, 0.01° C.
5. Obliquity of ecliptic	Slightly variable. According to Sir John Herschel, this variation never exceeds 1° 20' on either side of the mean; and, according to Newcomb, while the limit of variation is still unknown, the amount does not exceed 2° or 3° in 1,000,000 years. In either case, recent geologic climates, including that of the last ice age, could not have been much influenced by this factor.
6. Perihelion phase	Variable through a period of, roughly, 21,000 years. By virtue of this variation the winter of the southern hemisphere, say, may at one time occur, as it now does, at aphelion, and, therefore, be long and cold; and, again, at perihelion, when it must be relatively short and mild. While, however, this is a climatic factor which varies with the eccentricity of the earth's orbit, the period is too short to permit of its being considered as of great influence in the production of either the glacial or interglacial climates.
7. Extent and composition of the atmosphere.	Probably somewhat variable through geological periods, otherwise relatively fixed.
8. Vulcanism	Irregularly variable.
9. Sun spots	Greatly variable, with an 11-year period and probably other periods also, both longer and shorter.
10. Land elevation	Greatly variable through geological periods, otherwise relatively fixed.
11. Land and water distribution.	Greatly variable through geological periods, otherwise relatively fixed.
12. Atmospheric circulation	Largely dependent upon the distribution of land and water, upon land elevation and upon oceanic circulation, and, therefore, in many regions radically variable through geological periods.
13. Ocean circulation	Greatly variable through geological periods, otherwise relatively fixed.
14. Surface covering	Greatly variable, in many places, from season to season; and, also, irregularly so, from age to age.
15. Locations of continents	Generally believed to be practically constant.

and the like, may have produced all the great changes of geologic climates, it seems far safer to assume that climate was then controlled, essentially, as climate is now controlled; and, therefore, that the climatic changes of the past, whatever their nature, intensity, or duration, were due to changes in those factors of climatic control which are now operative and known to be appreciably variable.

The list on p. 580 includes the principal factors of climatic control as they exist today.

Since these are the factors that now control climate, it seems probable, as already stated, that even those profound climatic changes with which the geologist is concerned were also caused by variations in one or more of these same factors. Indeed, certain of these factors—vulcanism, land elevation, and oceanic circulation—are known to have varied greatly during the several geologic periods, while the extent and composition of the atmosphere are suspected also to have changed. It will be well, therefore, to consider what effects such variations probably could have—in some cases surely have had—on our climates. This will constitute the first step in the problem of geologic climates. The next step must be taken by the geologist himself, for he must say whether the climatic changes possible through the supposed causes would be sufficient to account for the observed results, and, especially, whether the known climatic changes, and the known variations in the factors here considered, occurred at such times and places as to permit of the assumption that they were actually related in the sense of cause and effect.

These several factors will be considered in the same order as listed on p. 580.

1. Since the wandering of the pole is limited to only a few meters, it is obvious that the resulting changes in the latitude produce no appreciable climatic effects.

2. The brightness of the moon, and also that of each of the several planets, is known in terms of that of the sun. On the assumption that the heat they supply is in proportion to their light, it appears that, at most, their variations in phase and distance can alter the temperature of the surface of the earth by no more than $0.0001°$ C., an amount that obviously is wholly negligible.

CHAPTER II

PRINCIPAL ICE-AGE THEORIES

FACTORS 3, 4, 5, 6, 7

It would be easy to catalogue perhaps a score of more or less rational hypotheses in regard to the origin of the ice ages, the subject under which the greater climatic changes generally are discussed, and doubtless even a larger number that are quite too absurd ever to have received serious consideration, and to point out, in each case, the known and the suspected elements of weakness. But this would only be a repetition of what, in part at least, has often been done before and, therefore, could serve no good purpose.

As already stated, only a few of these hypotheses still survive, nor do all of even these few really merit the following they have. Indeed, the only ones which still claim a large number of adherents are, respectively:

3. (*a*) **The Solar Variation Theory.**—This is based on the assumption that the solar radiation (the only solar influence that by any known process can affect terrestrial temperatures and terrestrial climates) has waxed and waned, either cyclically or irregularly, through considerable ranges and over long intervals of time.

This theory is seductively attractive—it looks so simple, so sufficient, and so safe from attack. There are, however, two criticisms of it that should be mentioned: (1) A change of the solar constant obviously alters all surface temperatures by a roughly constant percentage. Hence, a decrease of the heat from the sun would, in general, cause a decrease of the interzonal temperature gradients; and this, in turn, a less vigorous atmospheric circulation, and a less copious rain or snowfall—exactly the reverse of the condition, namely, abundant precipitation, most favorable to extensive glaciation. (2) If the solar variation theory is true, it follows as will be shown later, that great solar changes and extensive mountain building must usually, if not always, have been coepochal—a seemingly complete *reductio ad absurdum*.

4, 5, 6. (*b*) **Croll's Eccentricity Theory.**[1]—To make this theory clear, it is necessary to recall two important facts in regard to the earth's movement about the sun: (1) That the orbital position of the earth at any season, that of midsummer, say, progressively changes at such rate as to describe a complete circuit in about 21,000 years. This necessarily

[1] *Phil. Mag.*, **28**; 121, 1864, and elsewhere.

produces a cyclic change of the same period in the length, temperature and contrast of the seasons, and also in the contrast between the climates of the two hemispheres, northern and southern. Thus, when aphelion is attained near midsummer of either hemisphere, as it now is for the northern, that part of the earth enjoys comparatively long, temperate summers, and short, mild winters; while the opposite hemisphere, the southern at present, is exposed to short hot summers, and long, cold winters. Hence, on such occasions, the climatic contrast between the two hemispheres is at a maximum, provided, of course, that their ratios of land to water areas and other factors are the same. After about 10,500 years, another maximum contrast occurs, but with the climates of the two hemispheres interchanged, and so on indefinitely. (2) That the eccentricity of the earth's orbit, never greater than 0.07, and at rare intervals dropping to nearly, or even quite, zero, undergoes irregular but always slow and long cyclic changes. In addition to a change usually, though not always, relatively small, whose average period is roughly 100,000 years (now about 80,000), the eccentricity has, also, a far more irregular, and generally much larger, change whose average period, if a thing so irregular may be said to have a period, is three or four times as great. That is, as a rule, the eccentricity of the earth's orbit is continuously large, within the limit 0.07, or continuously small, for a period of 200,000 years, more or less; but in each case unequally so, because of the shorter period and more regular changes.

The first of these phenomena, the continuous change of the perihelion phase, varies, as explained, the relative lengths and intensities of the summers and winters of the northern and southern hemispheres; while the second, or the change of eccentricity of the earth's orbit, varies the magnitudes of these contrasts.

Now, Croll's theory of the ice ages assumes that when the earth's orbit is very eccentric, or when the earth's maximum solar distance differs largely from its minimum solar distance, ice will accumulate to a great extent over that half of the globe which has its winter during aphelion.

For some time this theory was very generally accepted, and it seems still to have many adherents, despite the destructive criticisms of Newcomb[1] and Culverwell.[2]

The chief objections to Croll's theory are:

1. That the assumption that midwinter and midsummer temperatures are directly proportional to the sun's heat at these times is not at all in accord with observed facts.

2. That each ice age (within a glacial epoch, when eccentricity is large) would be limited to a fraction of the secular perihelion period, 21,000 years, which, according to most geologists, is too short a time.

[1] Am. J. Sci., 2; 263, 1876; Phil. Mag., 17; 142, 1884.
[2] Phil. Mag., 38; 541, 1894.

3. That the successive ice ages would have occurred alternately in the northern and southern hemispheres instead of, as is generally believed to have been the case, in both hemispheres simultaneously.

4. That during the past 3,000,000 years there would have been fully 100 extensive glacial advances and retreats in each hemisphere (eccentricity having been rather large through much the greater portion of this time), a deduction unsupported by confirmatory geological evidence.

5. That the last extensive ice sheet in either hemisphere must have retracted, roughly, to its present limits some 80,000 years ago (eccentricity having become small about that time and remained small ever since), instead of less than 9000 as Gerald de Geer[1] has conclusively demonstrated.

As W. B. Wright[2] puts it:

An almost fatal objection to Croll's famous theory is the date it assigns to the end of the last ice age, which it places at some 80,000 years back. If, as De Geer seems to have clearly established, the ice margin retreated north past Stockholm only about 9000 years ago, this practically excludes any possibility of a connection between glaciation and changes in the eccentricity of the earth's orbit.

That changes in the maximum and minimum distances of the earth from the sun have affected our climates, and that they will continue to affect them, seems too obvious to admit of doubt, but that such changes ever were, or ever will be, of sufficient magnitude to be the sole, or even the chief, cause of an ice age, appears to be flatly contradicted, both by rigid deductions from the laws of physics and meteorology, and by close observations of geological records.

7. (*c*) **The Carbon Dioxide Theory.**—This theory, advocated by Tyndall,[3] Arrhenius,[4] Chamberlin,[5] and others, is based on the selective absorption of carbon dioxide for radiation of different wave lengths, and on its assumed variation in amount.

It is true that carbon dioxide is more absorptive of terrestrial than of solar radiations, and that it, therefore, produces a greenhouse or blanketing effect, and it is also, probably, true that its amount in the atmosphere has varied through appreciable ranges, as a result of volcanic and other additions on the one hand, and of oceanic absorption and chemical combination on the other. But it is not possible to say exactly how great an effect a given change in the amount of carbon dioxide in the atmosphere would have on the temperature of the earth. However,

[1] *Geolog. Congress*, Stockholm, 1910.

[2] *The Quaternary Ice Age*, p. 451, The Macmillan Company, 1914.

[3] *Phil. Mag.*, **22**; 277, 1861.

[4] *Phil. Mag.*, **41**; 237, 1896.

[5] *J. Geol.*, **7**; 545, 1899.

by bringing a number of known facts to bear on the subject it seems feasible to determine its approximate value. Thus the experiments of Schaefer[1] show that, at atmospheric pressure, a column of carbon dioxide 50 cm. long is ample for maximum absorption, since one of this length absorbs quite as completely as does a column 200 cm. long at the same density. Also, the experiments of Angström,[2] and those of E. v. Bahr,[3] show that the absorption of radiation by carbon dioxide, or other gas, increases with increase of pressure, and, what is of great importance, that, both qualitatively and quantitatively, this increase of absorption is exactly the same whether the given higher pressure be obtained by compression of the pure gas to a column of shorter length, or, leaving the column unchanged, by the simple addition of an inert gas.

According to these experiments, if a given column or quantity of carbon dioxide at a pressure of 50 mm. absorbs 20 per cent of the incident selective radiation, then, at 100 mm. it will absorb 25 per cent, at 200 mm. 30 per cent, at 400 mm. 35 per cent, and at 800 mm. about 38.5 per cent.

Now, the amount of carbon dioxide in the atmosphere is equivalent to a column of the pure gas, at ordinary room temperature and atmospheric pressure, of, roughly, 250 cm. in length. Hence, as a little calculation proves, using the coefficients of absorption at different pressures given by the experiments of Angström and E. v. Bahr, just described, the carbon dioxide now in the atmosphere must, under its present vertical distribution, absorb radiation very approximately as would a column 475 cm. long of the pure gas at the barometic pressure of 400 mm. But Schaefer's experiments, above referred to, show that such a column would be just as effective an absorber as a cylinder two or three times this length, and, on the other hand, no more effective than a column one-half or one-fourth as long; in each case, the absorption would be complete in the selective regions of the gas in question.

Hence, finally, doubling or halving the amount of carbon dioxide now in the atmosphere, since this would make but little difference in the pressure, would not appreciably affect the total amount of radiation actually absorbed by it, whether of terrestrial or of solar origin, though it would affect the vertical distribution or location of the absorption.

Again, as explained by Abbot and Fowle,[4] the water vapor always present in the atmosphere, because of its high coefficients of absorption in substantially the same regions where carbon dioxide is effective, leaves but little radiation for the latter to take up. Hence, for this reason, as well as for the one given above, either doubling or halving the present

[1] *Ann. Phys.*, **16**; 93, 1905.
[2] *Arkiv för Matematik, Astron. och Fysik*, Vol. **4**; No. 30, 1908.
[3] *Ann. Phys.*, **29**; 780, 1909.
[4] *Ann. Astroph. Obs.*, Smithsonian Institution, **2**; 172, 1908.

amount of carbon dioxide could alter but little the total amount of radiation actually absorbed by the atmosphere, and, therefore, seemingly,
could not appreciably change the average temperature of the earth, or
be at all effective in the production of marked climatic changes.

Nevertheless, in spite of the above objections, there appears to be at
least one way (variation in absorption at levels above the water vapor)
by which a change, especially if a decrease, in the amount of carbon dioxide
in the atmosphere might affect temperatures at the surface of the earth.
Hence, the above arguments do not, perhaps, fully warrant the idea that
no such change was ever an appreciable factor in the production of an
ice age.

Further consideration of this particular point will be taken up later,
after the discussion of certain other questions essential to a clear understanding of the subject.

These three theories, then, of the origin of the ice ages, namely, the
solar variation theory, the eccentricity theory, and the carbon dioxide
theory, are the only ones that, at present, appear to have many adherents; and even these few seem more likely to lose than to gain in number
and ardency of defenders.   The first is strong only as, and to the extent
that, other theories are disproved or shown to be improbable; the second
has failed utterly under searching criticism; while the third has been
sadly impaired.

CHAPTER III

8. VULCANISM : THEORY

GASEOUS CONTRIBUTION TO THE ATMOSPHERE

Although a variety of gases, vapors, and fumes are given off by active volcanoes, probably only one of them, carbon dioxide, is of sufficient volume and of such nature as to produce any effect on climate. Indeed, besides carbon dioxide, the only atmospheric constituents that are especially effective in modifying the average temperature of the earth are water vapor and, probably, ozone. The former of these, water vapor, except as locally modified by temperature and topography, including location and extent of land and sea, presumably, has varied but little in amount since the formation of the earliest oceans, while a practically continuous series of animal fossils from beyond the earliest paleozoic age to the present is abundant proof of an equally continuous supply of free oxygen. Hence, in an effort roughly to determine what climatic changes might have been caused by variations in the atmosphere, whether produced by vulcanism or otherwise, it would appear that only the amount of carbon dioxide need be considered.

But this has been discussed above, to some extent, and will be taken up again in its proper order. Suffice it to anticipate, here, the general conclusion that while variations in the amounts of carbon dioxide in the atmosphere may have somewhat modified our climates, it, probably, never was the controlling, or even an important, factor in the production of any one of the great climatic changes of the past, nor can be, of any great climatic change the future possibly may bring.

CHANGE IN SURFACE COVERING

The effect of volcanic ejecta, whether in the nature of ash, or lava flow, is to convert the region so covered into a temporary desert, even where rain may be abundant, and, therefore, to subject it to an increased range of temperature extremes, and at the same time, if in a previously vegetated region, slightly to increase its average temperature, owing to decrease of evaporation. It seems highly probable, however, that the areas so deprived of vegetation were never, at any one time, sufficiently large to produce marked effects upon the climate of the world as a whole, nor, indeed, anywhere except over themselves and within their own immediate neighborhoods. Hence, in considering universal climatic changes, it seems safe to neglect this special effect of volcanic activity.

DUST IN THE UPPER ATMOSPHERE

It was suggested, a number of years ago, by the cousins P. and F. Sarasin,[1] that the low temperature essential to the glaciation of ice ages was caused by the absorption of solar radiation by high volcanic dust clouds. But the idea, that dust of this nature, when scattered through the atmosphere, may lower the temperature of the surface of the earth, was already old, having been advanced at a much earlier date, in fact, long before the existence of ice ages had been suspected, much less attempts made to find their cause. Thus, in May, 1784, Benjamin Franklin (and he may not have been the first) wrote as follows:

During several of the summer months of the year 1783, when the effects of the sun's rays to heat the earth in these northern regions should have been the greatest, there existed a constant fog over all Europe, and great part of North America. This fog was of a permanent nature; it was dry, and the rays of the sun seemed to have little effect toward dissipating it, as they easily do a moist fog arising from the water. They were, indeed, rendered so faint in passing through it that, when collected in the focus of a burning glass, they would scarce kindle brown paper. Of course, their summer effect in heating the earth was exceedingly diminished.

Hence, the surface was early frozen.

Hence, the first snows remained on it unmelted, and received continual additions.

Hence, perhaps the winter of 1783–1784 was more severe than any that happened for many years.

The cause of this universal fog is not yet ascertained. Whether it was adventitious to this earth, and merely a smoke proceeding from the consumption, by fire, of some of those great burning balls, or globes, which we happen to meet with in our course round the sun, and which are sometimes seen to kindle and be destroyed in passing our atmosphere, and whose smoke might be attracted and retained by our earth; or whether it was the vast quantity of smoke, long continuing to issue during the summer from Hecla, in Iceland, and that other volcano which arose out of the sea near the island, which smoke might be spread by various winds over the northern part of the world, is yet uncertain.

It seems, however, worthy the inquiry, whether other hard winters, recorded in history, were preceded by similar permanent and widely-extended summer fogs. Because, if found to be so, men might, from such fogs, conjecture the probability of a succeeding hard winter, and of the damage to be expected by the breaking up of frozen rivers in the spring; and take such measures as are possible, and practicable, to secure themselves and effects from the mischiefs that attend the last.[2]

The idea, then, that volcanic dust may be an important factor in the production of climatic changes, is not new, though by what physical process it could produce this result, apparently, has not, formerly, been

---

[1] *Verhandlungen der Naturforschenden Gesellschaft in Basel,* **13**; 603, 1901.

[2] SPARKS, "Life of Benjamin Franklin," **6**; 455–457 (cited in *Proc. Am. Phil. Soc.,* **45**; 127, 1906).

explained, nor has the idea, previously, been specifically supported by a long series of direct observations. This is not to be taken as criticism of the above-mentioned pioneer paper by the Sarasin cousins, for, indeed, the arguments, now easy, necessary to show that it must be a factor, were at that time impossible, because the observations upon which these arguments largely are based, had not then been made. In fact, the absorption of radiation by volcanic dust, by which they supposed the earth's temperature to be lowered, can now be shown to be, of itself alone, not only insufficient, but even productive, in all probability, of the opposite effect—of a warming instead of a cooling of the earth's surface.

To make this point clear: Consider a thin shell of dust above the earth and let I be the average intensity of the normal component of solar radiation on it, and E the average intensity of the normal outgoing radiation just beneath the dust shell, partly reflected solar radiation, but chiefly of terrestrial origin. Further, let a be the average coefficient of absorption of the dust shell for solar radiation, a coefficient independent, presumably, of intensity, and b its coefficient of absorption for the mixed outgoing radiation, reflected solar and direct terrestrial also independent of intensity when the proportions are constant. In the case of equilibrium, all the energy absorbed by the dust is radiated away: half of it, very approximately, to the earth, and half of it to space. Hence, we have,

$$E\left(1 - \frac{b}{2}\right) = I\left(1 - \frac{a}{2}\right); \; E = I\frac{2 - a}{2 - b}. \qquad (A)$$

Hence,

$$E \gtreqless I, \text{ according as } b \gtreqless a.$$

The conclusion, therefore, is: *The total amount of radiation reaching the earth is increased, unchanged, or decreased, owing to absorption by the surrounding dust layer according as the dust's coefficient of absorption of terrestrial radiation is greater than, equal to, or less than, its coefficient of absorption of solar radiation.*

Actually, nearly all, both of the incoming and of the outgoing radiation, is oblique, but as equal portions of each pass through equal thickness of the shell, it follows that the conclusion reached for normal radiation applies also for the oblique radiation.

While this general conclusion is self-evident, and, therefore, might have been stated without the use of symbols, nevertheless equation (A), to be used later on, will be found convenient in attempts to obtain quantitative values.

Now, in the case of many, if not all, rocky materials, such as make up the particles of volcanic dust, the coefficient of absorption is much greater for terrestrial radiation than for solar radiation,[1] or, in terms of the above

[1] COBLENTZ, *Publications of Carnegie Institution of Washington*, Nos. 65 and 97.

symbols, in the case of volcanic dust, b is greater than a. Hence, so far as mere *absorption* of radiation is concerned, the only action mentioned by the cousins Sarasin, a veil of volcanic dust, in all probability, would slightly increase and not, as they supposed, decrease the average temperature of the earth. For example, in western and northern Europe the summer of 1783 was abnormally warm,[1] owing, presumably, to the greater absorption of earth radiation than of solar radiation by the then prevailing pall of volcanic dust, and not exceptionally cold, as Franklin seems to imply in the foregoing quotation. However, the winter of 1783–1784 was cold, as Franklin says it was, wherever observations were made, as were also the three years 1784–1786, owing, it seems, not to the dust from Iceland but to the finer dust from Asama in Japan, as will be explained presently.

As just implied, absorption is not the only effect of a dust veil on radiation; *reflection* and *scattering* both are important, and must be fully considered.

These actions, however, reflection and scattering, depend, fundamentally, upon the ratio of the linear dimensions of the particles concerned to the wave length of the incident radiation, and, therefore, before undertaking to discuss them in this connection, it will be essential to determine the approximate size of the individual grains of floating volcanic dust, and, also, the average wave lengths in the regions of the respective maximum intensities of solar and terrestrial radiation. It will be desirable, also, to consider whether or not, and, if so, how, dust of any kind can remain long suspended in the atmosphere. And this point, involving the structure of the atmosphere, will be examined first, since, obviously, the longer the dust can float, the more important, climatically, it may have been in the past and in the future may, again, become.

Physical Structure of the Atmosphere.—The atmosphere is divisible into the stratosphere, including the ionization layers, and the troposphere; or the isothermal region, from the 11-kilometer level, roughly, up to at least 35 kilometers, and the convective region; or, in other words, that region, in middle latitudes at and beyond about 11 kilometers above sea level, where, because of freedom from vertical convection, ordinary clouds never form, and that other, or turbulent, stormy region below this level, which is frequently swept by clouds and washed by snow and rain. The physical reason for, or cause of the existence of, the isothermal region is well known (see Chap. III, Pt. I), and is such that it is certain that ever since the earth was warmed by solar radiation, as at present, rather than by internal heat, the temperature of its atmosphere beyond a certain level, whatever its composition, must have varied but little, certainly in its lower portion, as it now varies but little, with change of altitude, and, therefore, that this region must

---

[1] BRANDES, H. W., "Beiträge zur Witterungskunde," Leipzig, 1820.

then have been free, as it now is free, from clouds and condensation. Obviously, then, this peculiar physical structure of the atmosphere is of great importance in determining the duration of dust suspension for, clearly, any volcanic or other dust, that—by whatever process—is gotten into, and distributed through, the isothermal region where there are no clouds, or other condensation, to wash it out, must drift about until gravity, overcoming the viscosity of the atmosphere, by slow degrees shall have pulled it down to the region of clouds and storms, where it becomes moisture laden and quickly brought to the earth. How long such process must take depends, of course, upon a number of things, among which the size of the particles is vitally important.

Size of Volcanic Dust Particles.—For two or three years after the eruption of Krakatoa, in 1883, also after the eruption of Mont Pelé, and Santâ Maria, in 1902, and, again, after the eruption of Katmai, in 1912, a sort of reddish-brown corona was often, under favorable conditions, observed around the sun. It was from 10° to 12° wide, and had, to the outer edge, an angular radius of from 22° to 23°. This phenomenon, known as Bishop's ring, clearly was a result of diffraction of sunlight by the particles of volcanic dust in the upper atmosphere, and, therefore, it furnished a satisfactory means for determining the approximate size of the particles themselves. The subject has been rather fully discussed by Pernter,[1] who finds the diameter of the particles, assuming them spherical, to be approximately 185×10^{-6} cm., or 1.85 microns. The equation used has the form (page 549)

$$r = \frac{m}{\pi} \frac{\lambda}{\sin \theta}$$

in which r is the radius of the dust particle, λ the wave length of the diffracted light (here taken as 571×10^{-7} cm., or 0.571 micron), θ the angular radius of the ring, and m a numerical term which for the outer edge of the ring, and successive minima of brightness, has the approximate values (see page 550)

$$\frac{\pi}{2}(n + 0.22)$$

in which $n = 1, 2, 3, \cdots$, respectively.

Now, since the width and angular dimensions of Bishop's ring, as seen at different times and different places, have varied but little, the above value, 1.85 microns, may, provisionally, be assumed to be the average diameter of those particles of volcanic dust that remain long suspended in the atmosphere.

Time of Fall.—The steady or terminal velocity of a minute sphere falling in a fluid, assuming no slip between fluid and sphere, is given by

[1] *Met. Zeit.*, **6**; 401, 1889.

Stokes's[1] equation

$$V = \frac{2}{9}gr^2\left(\frac{\sigma - \rho}{\mu}\right)$$

in which V is the velocity of the fall, g the acceleration of gravity, r the radius of the sphere, σ the density of the sphere, ρ the density of the fluid, and μ its viscosity.

However, there always is slip, so that the actual velocity of fall is, according to Cunningham,[2]

$$V = \frac{2}{9}gr^2\left(\frac{\sigma - \rho}{\mu}\right)\left(1 + A\frac{l}{r}\right)$$

in which l is the free path of the gas molecules, A a constant, and the other symbols as above explained.

Obviously, l, other things being equal, is inversely proportional to the gas density, or pressure, if temperature is constant, and directly proportional to the absolute temperature if the pressure is constant. Hence,

$$V = \frac{2}{9}gr^2\left(\frac{\sigma - \rho}{\mu}\right)\left(1 + \frac{B}{rp}\right) \tag{1}$$

in which B is a constant for any given temperature, p the gas pressure, or, if preferred, barometric height.

For the system air glass, probably a fair approximation to air-volcanic dust, it appears[3] that at 23° C., if p is in terms of millimeters of mercury,

$$B = 0.00629.$$

The value of μ, for dry air, is also closely known from the work of a number of experimenters, all of whom obtained substantially the same results. From a careful review of the whole subject, Millikan[4] finds that at 23° C.,

$$\mu = 1824 \times 10^{-7} \text{ (more recently } 18226 \times 10^{-8}),$$

and that, for the temperature t Centigrade,

$$\mu_t = \frac{150.38T^{3/2}}{T + 124} \times 10^{-7}, \text{ approximately,}$$

where $T = 273.11 + t$.

It is easy, therefore, to compute, by the aid of equation (1), the velocity of fall of volcanic dust, assuming gravity to be the only driving

[1] *Math. and Phys. Papers*, **3**; 59.
[2] *Proc. Roy. Soc.*, **83**; 357, 1910.
[3] MILLIKAN, *Phys. Rev.*, **12**; 217, 1923.
[4] *Ann. Phys.*, **41**; 759, 1913.

force. There is, of course, radiation pressure, both toward and from the earth, as well as slight convective and other disturbances, but presumably gravitation exerts the controlling influence.

The following table of approximate velocities and times of fall for volcanic dust was computed by substituting in equation (1) the given numerical values, namely;

$g = 981 \dfrac{cm.}{sec.^2}$

$r = 0.000092$ cm.

$\sigma = 2.3$, approximate density of Krakatoa dust.

$\rho = 0$, being negligible relative to σ.

$\mu = 1416 \times 10^{-7}$, approximate to $-55°$ C., roughly, the temperature of the isothermal region in middle latitudes.

$B = 0.004632$, approximate to $-55°$ C.

$p = $ millimeters barometric pressure.

According to this table, it appears that spherical grains of sand of the size assumed, 1.85 microns in diameter, would require about 1 year to fall from only that elevation already reached by sounding balloons, 35.08 kilometers,[1] down to the undersurface of the isothermal region, at the height of 11 kilometers.

VELOCITY AND TIME OF FALL

Height in kilometers	Barometric pressure	Centimeters per second	Seconds per centimeter
40	1.84	0.8501	1.176
30	8.63	0.2048	4.883
20	40.99	0.0668	14.970
15	89.66	0.0468	21.368
11*	168.00	0.0390	25.641
0	760.00	0.0249†	40.161

* Isothermal level of middle latitudes.
† Temperature 21° C.

As a matter of fact, volcanic dust, at least much of it, consists of thin-shelled bubbles or fine fragments of bubbles, and, therefore, must settle much slower than solid spheres, the kind above assumed. Indeed, the finest dust from Krakatoa, which reached a great altitude, probably not less than 40 nor more than 80 kilometers, was from $2\frac{1}{2}$ to 3 years in reaching the earth, or, presumably, as above explained, the upper cloud levels.

At any rate, volcanic dust is so fine, and the upper atmosphere above 11 kilometers so free from moisture and vertical convection, that once such dust is thrown into this region, as it obviously was by the explosions

[1] *L'Astronomie,* **27**; 329, 1913.

of Skaptar Jökull, and Asamayama, in 1783; Babuyan, in 1831; Krakatoa, in 1883; Santâ Maria, and Pelé, in 1902; Katmai in 1912; and many others, it must require, as a rule, because of its slow descent, from 1 to 3 years to get back to the earth. And this, clearly, has always been the case since the earth first assumed, substantially, its present condition, or had a cool crust and a gaseous envelope.

Obviously, then, it is only necessary to determine the present action of such dust on incoming solar, and outgoing terrestrial, radiation, in order to reach a logical deduction as to what its effect on climate must have been in the past, if, through extensive volcanic activity, it ever, more or less continuously, filled the upper atmosphere for a long, or even considerable, term of years, as may have happened several times during the geologic ages. And the same conclusion, in regard to the possible effect of dust on the climates of the past, clearly applies, with equal force, to the climates of the future.

Action of Dust on Solar Radiation.—Since solar radiation, at the point of maximum intensity, has a wave length less than 5×10^{-5} cm.,[1] or half a micron, and since fully three-fourths of the total solar energy belongs to spectral regions whose wave lengths are less than 10^{-4} cm., or one micron, it follows that the cubes of solar wave lengths must, on the whole, be regarded as small in comparison with the volume of a volcanic dust particle, the diameter of which, as above explained, is nearly 2 microns. Hence, in discussing the action of volcanic dust on incoming solar radiation, we can, with more or less justification, assume the particles to be opaque through reflection or otherwise, and, therefore, use Rayleigh's[2] arguments as applied to a similar case.

Let r be the radius of the particle, n the number of particles per cubic centimeter, and a the projected joint area of these particles. Then, for random and sparsely scattered particles,

$$a = n\pi r^2.$$

Hence, on dividing a plane parallel to the wave front into Fresnel zones, it is seen that for each centimeter traversed the amplitude of the radiation is reduced in the ratio of 1 to $1 - n\pi r^2$. Therefore, if A is the initial amplitude, and A_x the amplitude after passing through x cm. of the uniformly dusty region, assuming $n\pi r^2$ to be only a small fraction of a square centimeter,

$$A_x = A(1 - n\pi r^2)^x = A e^{-n\pi r^2 x}, \text{ nearly.}$$

Further, if I is the initial and I_x the final intensity, then

$$I_x = I e^{-2n\pi r^2 x}.$$

[1] Abbot and Fowle, *Ann. Astrophys. Obs.*, Smithsonian Inst., **2**; 104, 1908.
[2] *Phil. Mag.*, **47**; 384, 1899.

Hence, in the case of volcanic dust, where, as already explained, $r = 92 \times 10^{-6}$ cm.,

$$A_x = A e^{-n\pi x (92)^2 10^{-12}}$$

and

$$I_x = I e^{-2n\pi x (92)^2 10^{-12}}.$$

Presumably, the particles of dust are not absolutely opaque and, therefore, I_x probably is a little larger than the value here given, though even so this value is at least a first approximation.

Action of Dust on Terrestrial Radiation.—Terrestrial radiation, at the point of maximum intensity, has a wave length of, roughly, 12×10^{-4} cm., and, therefore, the wave lengths of nearly all outgoing radiation are large in comparison with the diameters of those volcanic dust particles that remain long suspended in the atmosphere. Hence, while such particles abundantly *reflect* solar radiation, as is obvious from the whiteness of the sky when filled by them, they can only *scatter* radiation from the earth, according to the laws first formulated by Rayleigh,[1] whose papers must be consulted by those who would fully understand the equations which, here, will be assumed and not derived.

Let E be the intensity of terrestrial radiation as it enters the dusty shell, or as it enters the isothermal region, and E_y its intensity after it has penetrated this region, supposed uniformly dusty, a distance y cm.; then, remembering that the dust particles are supposed to be spherical, according to Rayleigh,

$$E_y = E e^{-hy}$$

where

$$h = 24\pi^3 n \frac{(K' - K)^2}{(K' + 2K)^2} \frac{T^2}{\lambda^4},$$

in which n is the number of particles per cubic centimeter, K the dielectric constant of the medium, K' the dielectric constant of the material of the particles, T the volume of a single particle, and λ the wave length of the radiation concerned.

But $K = 1$, and, since the dust seems generally to be a kind of glass, it may not be far wrong to assume that $K' = 7$. Hence, with these values,

$$h = 11\pi^3 n \frac{T^2}{\lambda^4}, \text{ nearly.}$$

Relative Action of Dust on Solar and Terrestrial Radiation.—To determine whether such a dust layer as the one under discussion will increase or decrease earth temperatures, it is necessary to compare its

[1] *Op. cit.*, p. 375.

action on short wave-length solar radiation with its action on long wave-length radiation from the earth.

In the case of solar radiation, as explained,

$$I_x = Ie^{-2n\pi x(92)^2 10^{-12}}.$$

Clearly, then, the intensity of the solar radiation is reduced in the ratio of 1 to e, or

$$I_x : I = 1 : e$$

when

$$x = \frac{10^{12}}{2n\pi(92)^2} \text{ cm.} = \frac{188}{n} \text{ km., approximately.}$$

On the other hand, in the case of terrestrial radiation, where

$$E_y = Ee^{-11\pi^3 n \frac{T^2}{\lambda^4} y,}$$

the intensity is reduced in the ratio of $1 : e$, or

$$E_y : E = 1 : e,$$

when

$$y = \frac{\lambda^4}{11\pi^3 n T^2} \text{ cm.,}$$

in which

$$T = \frac{4}{3}\pi(92)^3 10^{-18}$$

and

$$\lambda = 12 \times 10^{-4} \text{ cm., the region of maximum intensity.}$$

Hence,

$$y = \frac{5700}{n} \text{ km., approximately.}$$

Therefore, finally,

$$y : x = 30 : 1, \text{ roughly,}$$

or the shell of volcanic dust, the particles all being the size given, is some thirtyfold more effective in shutting solar radiation out than it is in keeping terrestrial radiation in. In other words, the veil of dust produces an inverse greenhouse effect, and, hence, if the dust veil were indefinitely maintained, the ultimate equilibrium temperature of the earth would be lower than it is when no such veil exists.

The ratio 30 to 1 in favor of terrestrial radiation, in its ability to penetrate the dusty atmosphere, may, at first, seem quite too large, but it should be remembered that the dust particles in question are to terrestrial radiation in general as air molecules are to solar radiation, in the sense that, in both cases, little more than mere scattering takes place. Now, it is obvious that the dust particles are manyfold more effective in intercepting solar radiation, which they appear to do chiefly by reflection, than is an equal mass of air molecules which simply scatter it; and, hence, it may well be that the above theoretically determined ratio, 30 to 1, is no larger than the ratio that actually exists, or, at any rate, that it is of the correct order.

It must be distinctly understood that certain of the assumptions upon which the foregoing is based—uniformity of size, complete opacity and sphericity of the dust particles, for instance—are only approximately correct, but they are the best that, at present, can be made, and, doubtless, give at least the order of magnitude of the effects, which, indeed, for the present purpose, is quite sufficient.

It may be well, in this connection, to call attention to the fact that the excessively fine dust particles, or particles whose diameters are one-half, or less, the wave length of solar radiation (region of maximum intensity), and which, therefore, remain longest in suspension, shut out solar radiation manyfold more effectively than they hold back terrestrial radiation. This is because both radiations, solar and terrestrial, are simply scattered by such small particles, and scattered in proportion to the inverse fourth power of the wave length. Indeed, since the ratio of solar wave length to terrestrial wave length (region of maximum intensity in both cases) is, roughly, 1 to 25, and the ratio of their fourth powers as 1 to 39×10^4, about, it follows that the interception of outgoing radiation by the very finest and, therefore, most persistent, dust is wholly negligible in comparison with its interception of incoming solar radiation.

Number of Dust Particles.—The intensity of the solar radiation I_x after it has passed through x cm. of the dust layer of the atmosphere is given, as previously explained, by the equation

$$I_x = I e^{-2n\pi x (92)^2 \times 10^{-12}}.$$

But, according to numerous observations made during the summer and fall of 1912, when the solar radiation had passed entirely through the dust layer at such an angle that it met, roughly, twice as many dust particles as it would have met had it come in normally, or from the zenith, it was reduced by about 20 per cent. That is to say, under these conditions

$$I_x = 0.8I.$$

Hence,

$$10 = 8e^{2n x \pi (92)^2 10^{-12}}.$$

Let $nx = 2N$, the total number of particles passed in a cylinder of 1 square centimeter cross-section. Then

$$10 = 8e^{4N\pi(92)^2 10^{-12}}.$$

Hence the number of particles in a *vertical* cylinder of 1 sq. cm. cross-section is given, roughly, by the equation

$$N = 34 \times 10^4.$$

Temperature Correction Due to Dust Radiation.—With the number and size of the dust particles known it is easy to determine at least an upper limit to the effect of the direct radiation of the particles themselves on the temperature of the earth.

The temperature of the dust particles, obviously, is very nearly that of the upper atmosphere in which they float, that is, approximately $-55°$ C., or 218° Abs. Also, as previously explained, the quantity of radiation from the atmosphere below the isothermal region is substantially that which would be given off by a full radiator at 246° Abs.

Now, assume the dust particles to be concentrated side by side on a common plane, and, further, assume them to be full radiators—conditions that would raise their effect to the theoretical upper limit. Let E be the intensity or quantity per square centimeter of the outgoing planetary radiation, and D the intensity of the incoming dust radiation. Then

$$E:D = (246)^4 : a(218)^4,$$

in which a is the projected area of all the particles in a vertical cylinder of 1 square centimeter cross-section.

But

$$a = 34\pi 10^4 (92)^2 10^{-12} = 9 \times 10^{-3}.$$

Hence,

$$E = 180D.$$

Now, when the radiation D is absorbed by the lower atmosphere, it follows that its temperature will be so increased that, when equilibrium is reached, the intensity of its new radiation will be to that of its old as 199 is to 198. Hence ΔT, the effective temperature increase of the lower atmosphere, is given by the equation

$$\frac{(246 + \Delta T)^4}{(246)^4} = \frac{181}{180},$$

from which

$$\Delta T = 0°.34 \ C.$$

But, as stated above, the dust particles, presumably, are not full radiators, and, therefore, probably 0.2° C. is as great an increase in temperature as may reasonably be expected from this source. But this *increase*, 0.2° C., is small in comparison with the *decrease*, 6° to 7° C., caused by the interception of solar radiation, already explained. *Hence it appears reasonably certain that the sum total of all the temperature effects produced by volcanic dust in the upper atmosphere, equal in amount to that put there by the explosion of Katmai, must be, if long continued, a lowering of the surface temperature by several degrees Centigrade.*

Total Quantity of Dust.—Let $nx = 2N$, the total number of particles passed in a cylinder of 1 square centimeter cross-section. Then, as explained above,

$$10 = 8e^{4N\pi(92)^2 \times 10^{-12}}.$$

Hence,

$$N = 34 \times 10^4$$

roughly = number of particles in a vertical cylinder of 1 square centimeter cross-section.

If A is the entire area of the earth in square centimeters, then the total number of dust particles, assuming the dustiness everywhere as just found, is

$$NA = 1734 \times 10^{21}.$$

But the radius of each particle is 92×10^{-6} cm., and its volume, assuming it spherical, 33×10^{-13} cc. Hence, the total volume of the dust, assuming the particles spherical, is equal, roughly, to a cube 179 meters, or about 587 feet, on the side, an amount that certainly is not prohibitively large.

As just stated, the total quantity of dust sufficient, as explained, to cut down the intensity of the direct solar radiation by 20 per cent, and, therefore, if indefinitely continued, capable, presumably, of producing an ice age, is astonishingly small—only the 174th part of a cubic kilometer, or the 727th part of a cubic mile, even assuming that the particles are spherical. Since, however, in large measure, the particles are more or less flat, it follows that the actual total mass of the dust necessary and sufficient to reduce the intensity of direct solar radiation by 20 per cent probably is not more than the 1500th part of a cubic mile, or the 350th part of a cubic kilometer.

Hence, even this small amount of solid material distributed once a year, or even once in 2 years, through the upper atmosphere, would be more than sufficient to maintain continuously, or nearly so, such low temperatures as soon would cover the earth with a mantle of snow so extensive as to be self-perpetuating, through waste of insolation and otherwise, and thereby initiate at least a cool period or, under the most favorable conditions, even an ice age; nor would it make any great difference where the volcanoes productive of the dust might be situated, provided only that it was driven high into the isothermal region, or stratosphere, since, from whatever point of introduction, the winds of the upper atmosphere would soon spread it more or less evenly over the entire earth.

A little calculation shows, too, that this quantity of dust yearly, during a period of 100,000 years, would produce a layer over the earth only about $\frac{1}{2}$ mm., or $\frac{1}{50}$ inch, thick, and therefore one could hardly expect to find any marked accumulation of it, even if it had filled the atmosphere for much longer periods, and surely none at all if the dust period were only the few consecutive years sufficient, as just explained, to spread self-perpetuating covers of snow over extensive areas.

Whether periods of explosive volcanic activity—and in this case, since the locality of the volcano is a matter of small importance, the whole earth must be considered—occurred at such times as to synchronize with the ice ages and with other epochs of great climatic change is, of course, a problem for the geologist to solve. However, this much appears well nigh certain: Since the beginning of reliable records, say, 160 years ago, the temperature of the earth, as a whole, has distinctly varied, but its average value over that period has been perceptibly lower, possibly as much as 0.5° C., than it would have been if, during all this time, there had been no volcanic explosions violent enough to put dust into the isothermal region of the atmosphere. Similarly, on the other hand, if, during this period, violent volcanic explosions had been three or four times more numerous than they actually were, the average temperatures probably would have been 1° to 2° C. lower, or low enough, if long continued, to depress the snow line roughly 300 meters, and thus to begin a moderate ice age.

Effect of Dust on the Interzonal Gradient.—If I is the initial intensity of radiation of a given wave length and aI its intensity after passing a unit distance through a homogeneous absorbing or scattering medium, then its remaining intensity, after traveling n units distance through this medium, will be Ia^n. But n, in the case of solar radiation passing through the atmosphere, is proportional to the secant of the zenith distance of the sun; and from this in turn it is evident that, in general, variations of dust in the upper atmosphere must change the temperatures of the high latitude regions more than those within the tropics. Hence, an increase of such dust would steepen the interzonal temperature gradients, strengthen the winds, and make heavier the rain and snowfall, a condition favorable to extensive glaciation. Of course, the increased circulation would, in turn, more or less reduce the new temperature difference, but, nevertheless, a portion, at least, of the increase clearly would remain, and with it, the corresponding increases of wind and rain.

CHAPTER IV

VULCANISM: OBSERVATIONAL

It will be interesting and profitable, now, to consider the supplementary portion of the theory of the relation of vulcanism to climate. That is, to consider the observational evidence, pyrheliometric or other kind, bearing on the effect of volcanic dust on solar radiation, and, thus, obtain some idea of those absolute values essential to even a rough determination of the climatic consequence of volcanic dust in the high atmosphere.

Pyrheliometric Records.—Direct measurement of solar radiation by means of the pyrheliometer, an instrument that measures the total

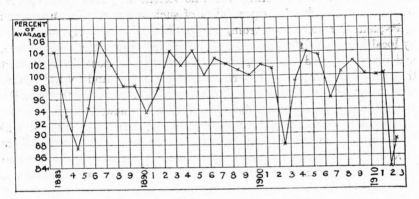

Fig. 223.—Annual average, pyrheliometric values.

heat of sunshine, shows marked fluctuations from year to year in the intensity of this radiation as received at the surface of the earth. This subject has been carefully studied by Dr. H. H. Kimball,[1] of the United States Weather Bureau, who prepared the accompanying table, graphically represented by Fig. 223. Since the yearly values are given in terms of the average value for the entire period, it is obvious that percentages of this average do not represent the full effect of the disturbing causes, of which volcanic dust certainly is the chief.

The intensities given in Table I were computed from observational data obtained at the following stations:

[1] *M. W. R.*, **46**; 355, 1918; **52**; 527, 1924.

A few other stations have been established since 1908.

The marked decrease in the pyrheliometric readings for 1884, 1885, and 1886, doubtless were largely, if not almost wholly, due to the eruption of Krakatoa in the summer of 1883; the decreased values of 1888 to 1892, inclusive, occurred during a period of exceptional volcanic activity, but were probably owing essentially to the violent eruptions of Bandaisan (1888), Bogoslof (1890), and Awoe, on Great Sangir (1892); the low values of 1903 to the eruptions of Santâ Maria (1902), Pelé (1902) and Colima (1903); and the low values of 1912–1913, to the explosion, June 6, 1912, of Katmai. The slight depression in the curve corresponding to the year 1907, during which no violent eruptions were reported (this does not exclude the possibility of such occurrence in remote and unfrequented regions), according to Dr. Kimball, probably was caused by local haze at Washington, D. C., where his observations were made, and elsewhere, and this supposition is partially supported by the fact that his values for the year were not uniformly low, and by the further fact, inferred from a publication by Gorczynski,[1] that during that year the solar radiation was but little below normal at Warsaw, Poland.

By July, 1914, the depression due to the dust from Katmai had fully passed, and from that date to the present (Oct., 1940), there have been no violent volcanic eruptions and the pyrheliometric values have been remarkably constant except for a slight unexplained irregularity in 1920–1921.

There is, then, abundant pyrheliometric evidence that volcanic dust in the upper atmosphere actually does produce that decrease in direct solar radiation that theory indicates it should, and, as the theory is well founded and the observations were carefully taken, this mutual confirmation may be regarded as conclusive both of the existence of volcanic dust in the upper atmosphere (isothermal region) and of its efficiency in intercepting direct radiation from the sun.

It should be remembered, however, in this connection, that the intensity of the solar radiation at the surface of the earth depends not only upon the dustiness of the earth's atmosphere, but also upon the dustiness, and, of course, the temperature, of the solar atmosphere.

Obviously, dust in the sun's envelope must, more or less, shut in solar radiation just as, and in the same manner that, dust in the earth's

[1] *C. R.*, **157**; 84, 1913.

TABLE I.—PYRHELIOMETRIC INTENSITIES

Year	Number of stations	Radiation
1883	1	103
1884	1	92
1885	1	89
1886	1	96
1887	1	105
1888	1	101
1889	1	100
1890	1	96
1891	1	95
1892	2	99
1893	2	104
1894	2	102
1895	2	103
1896	3	103
1897	3	103
1898	3	104
1899	3	103
1900	3	101
1901	3	102
1902	3	99
1903	3	88
1904	3	96
1905	3	100
1906	3	102
1907	5	98
1908	5	99
1909	5	102
1910	5	102
1911	5	103
1912	5	92
1913	5	93

envelope shuts it out. Hence, it follows that when this dust is greatest, other things being equal, the output of solar energy will be least, and when the dust is least, other things being equal, the output of energy will be greatest. Not only may the intensity of the emitted radiation vary because of changes in the transparency of the solar atmosphere, but also because of any variations in the temperature of the effective solar surface, which, it would seem, might well be hottest when most agitated, or at the times of spot maxima, and coolest when most quiescent, or at the times of spot minima.

Now, the dustiness of the solar atmosphere, manifesting itself as a corona, certainly does vary through a considerable range, from a maximum, when the sun-spots are most numerous, to a minimum, when they are fewest; and, therefore, partly because of changes in the transparency of the solar envelope, and partly because of changes in the solar surface temperatures, if, as in all probability they do, such temperature changes take place, we should expect the solar constant also to vary from one value at the time of spot maximum to another at the time of spot minimum, and to vary as determined by the controlling factor, dust or temperature.

If the above reasoning is correct, it follows that pyrheliometric readings are functions of, among other things, both the solar atmosphere and our own terrestrial atmosphere; and as the former is altered chiefly by sun spots or at least varies with their production and existence, and the latter by volcanic explosions, a means is at hand for comparing the relative importance of the two radiation screens.

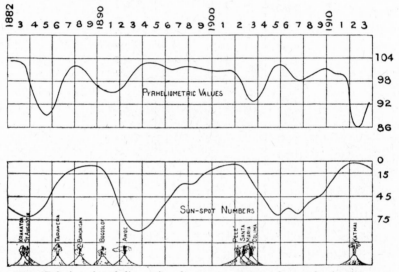

Fig. 224.—Relation of pyrheliometric values to sun-spot numbers and volcanic eruptions.

Figure 224 shows one such comparison. The upper curve gives smoothed annual average pyrheliometric readings (not solar constants, though closely proportional to them) and the lower curve sun-spot numbers. It will be noticed that, in their most pronounced features, the two curves have little in common, and that the great drops in the pyrheliometric values occur simultaneously with violent volcanic explosions, as already explained, and not at the times of sun-spot changes. *Hence, it appears that the dust in our own atmosphere, and not the condition of the sun, is a very important, if not the controlling, factor in determining the magnitudes and times of occurrence of great and abrupt changes of insolation intensity at the surface of the earth.*

Temperatures at the Surface of the Earth.—If a veil of dust actually should intercept as much as one-fifth of the direct solar radiation, as Fig. 223 indicates that, at times, it does, it would seem that in those years the temperature of the atmosphere at the surface of the earth should be somewhat below the normal. Of course, the great supply of heat in the ocean would produce a lag in this effect, particularly over the oceans themselves, and, besides, there must be both an increase of sky light by scattering and some interception of earth radiation by the dust which, since it is at great altitudes, receives the full, or nearly the full, planetary radiation of the earth. This increase of sky radiation, together with the return terrestrial radiation, obviously compensates in some measure for the loss of direct insolation. Measurements, however, made by Abbot,[1] at Bassour, Algeria, during the summer of 1912, show that at this time and place the direct radiation and the sky radiation, which obviously included both the scattered solar radiation and some return terrestrial radiation, were together less by about 10 per cent than their normal combined values; and there is no reason to think that in this respect Bassour was at all different from other places, certainly a large portion of the northern hemisphere, at least, covered by the veil of dust. Clearly, then, if this decrease in the radiation received were universal and should continue indefinitely, the ultimate radiation of the earth would also decrease to the same extent, or 10 per cent. Now, since the earth, or rather the water vapor of the atmosphere, mainly, radiates substantially as a black body, and, therefore, proportionally to the fourth power of its absolute temperature, it follows that a 10 per cent change in its radiation would indicate about a 2.5 per cent change in its temperature. But the effective temperature of the earth as a full radiator, which it closely approaches, is about 246° Abs. Hence a change of 10 per cent in the radiation emitted would imply 6.15° C. change in temperature, an amount which, if long enough continued, would be more than sufficient to produce glaciation equal, probably, to the most extensive of any known ice age.

As above implied, not much lowering of the temperature could be expected to take place immediately; however, some early cooling over land areas might well be anticipated. To test this point, the temperature records of a number of high altitude (together with two or three very dry) inland stations have been examined. High altitudes were chosen because it was thought that the temperature effects of dust in the upper atmosphere probably are most clearly marked above the very and irregularly dusty layers of the lower atmosphere; and the condition that the stations should also be inland was imposed because these are freer, presumably, than many coast stations, from fortuitous season changes. Thus, stations in the eastern portion of the United States were rejected because of the great differences in the winters, for example, of this section depending upon the prevailing direction of the wind,[2] a condition wholly

[1] *Smithsonian Miscellaneous Collections*, Vol. **60**; No. 29, 1913.

[2] HUMPHREYS, *Monthly Weather Review*, **42**; 672, 1914.

independent, so far as known, of variations in the intensity of direct radiation.

The number of stations was still further limited by the available recent data. Hence the records finally selected, and kindly put in shape by the Climatological Division of the United States Weather Bureau, were obtained at the following places:

TABLE II.—STATIONS WHOSE DATA WERE USED

America

Name	Latitude	Longitude	Elevation in feet
Baker, Oregon	44° 46′ N.	117° 50′ W.	3,466
Bismarck, North Dakota	46° 47′ N.	100° 38′ W.	1,674
Cheyenne, Wyoming	41° 08′ N.	104° 48′ W.	6,088
Denver, Colorado	39° 45′ N.	105° 00′ W.	5,291
Dodge City, Iowa	37° 45′ N.	100° 00′ W.	2,509
El Paso, Texas	31° 47′ N.	106° 30′ W.	3,762
Helena, Montana	46° 34′ N.	112° 04′ W.	4,110
Huron, Michigan	44° 21′ N.	98° 14′ W.	1,306
North Platte, Nebraska	41° 08′ N.	100° 45′ W.	2,821
Red Bluff, California	40° 10′ N.	122° 15′ W.	332
Sacramento, California	38° 35′ N.	121° 30′ W.	69
Salt Lake City, Utah	40° 46′ N.	111° 54′ W.	4,360
San Antonio, Texas	29° 27′ N.	98° 28′ W.	701
Santa Fé, New Mexico	35° 41′ N.	105° 57′ W.	7,013
Spokane, Washington	47° 40′ N.	117° 25′ W.	1,929
Winnemucca, Nevada	40° 58′ N.	117° 43′ W.	4,344
Yuma, Arizona	32° 45′ N.	114° 36′ W.	141

Europe

Name	Latitude	Longitude	Elevation in feet
Mont Ventoux	44° 10′ N.	5° 16′ E.	6,234
Obir	46° 30′ N.	14° 29′ E.	6,716
Pic du Midi	42° 56′ N.	0° 8′ E.	9,380
Puy de Dôme	45° 46′ N.	2° 57′ E.	4,813
Säntis	47° 15′ N.	9° 20′ E.	8,202
Schneekoppe	50° 44′ N.	15° 44′ E.	5,359
Sonnblick	47° 3′ N.	12° 57′ E.	10,190

India

Name	Latitude	Longitude	Elevation in feet
Simla	31° 6′ N.	77° 12′ E.	7,232

In Table III, the first column gives the year in question. The second column gives the average departure in degrees Fahrenheit, for the seventeen American stations, of the annual average maximum, as determined from the monthly average maxima, from the normal annual maximum, or average of a great many annual average maxima. The third column gives smoothed values, determined from the actual values in the second column as follows:

$$S = \frac{a + 2b + c}{4},$$

TABLE III.—AVERAGE TEMPERATURE DEPARTURES FROM TEMPERATURE NORMALS
America

Year	Maxima		Minima		Means	
	Actual	Smoothed	Actual	Smoothed	Actual	Smoothed
1880	−1.3	+0.03	−1.8	−0.68	−1.7	−0.50
1881	+0.2	−0.30	+0.6	−0.20	+0.1	−0.48
1882	−0.3	−0.50	−0.2	−0.20	−0.4	−0.50
1883	−1.6	−1.33	−1.0	−0.70	−1.3	−1.15
1884	−1.8	−1.20	−0.6	−0.28	−1.6	−1.05
1885	+0.4	−0.18	+1.1	+0.43	+0.3	−0.30
1886	+0.3	+0.35	+0.1	+0.10	−0.2	−0.03
1887	+0.4	+0.38	−0.9	−0.45	0.0	+0.07
1888	+0.4	+0.53	−0.1	−0.13	+0.5	+0.53
1889	+0.9	+0.63	+0.6	+0.23	+1.1	+0.85
1890	+0.3	+0.15	−0.2	−0.05	+0.7	+0.58
1891	−0.9	−0.58	−0.4	−0.38	−0.2	+0.05
1892	−0.8	−0.85	−0.1	−0.33	−0.1	−0.20
1893	−0.9	−0.73	−0.7	−0.38	−0.4	−0.08
1894	−0.3	−0.55	+0.4	−0.18	+0.6	+0.13
1895	−0.7	−0.35	−0.8	−0.08	−0.3	+0.25
1896	+0.3	−0.18	+0.9	+0.28	+1.0	+0.45
1897	−0.6	−0.30	+0.1	+0.13	+0.1	+0.28
1898	−0.3	−0.65	−0.6	−0.45	−0.1	−0.13
1899	−0.8	−0.13	−0.7	−0.10	−0.4	+0.25
1900	+1.4	+0.78	+1.6	+0.90	+1.9	+1.23
1901	+1.1	+0.83	+1.1	+1.08	+1.5	+1.35
1902	−0.3	−0.13	+0.5	+0.38	+0.5	+0.53
1903	−1.0	−0.43	−0.6	−0.05	−0.4	+0.18
1904	+0.6	−0.15	+0.5	+0.05	+1.0	+0.38
1905	−0.8	−0.30	−0.2	+0.08	−0.1	+0.33
1906	−0.2	−0.30	+0.2	+0.08	+0.5	+0.33
1907	0.0	+0.10	+0.1	+0.10	+0.4	+0.50
1908	+0.6	+0.15	0.0	−0.08	+0.7	+0.43
1909	−0.6	+0.38	−0.4	−0.05	−0.1	+0.55
1910	+2.1	+0.80	+0.6	+0.08	+1.7	+0.75
1911	−0.4	+0.03	−0.5	−0.35	−0.3	+0.05
1912	−1.2	−0.70	−1.0	−0.63	−0.9	−0.53
1913	.....	......	.....	......	−0.1	+0.02
1914	.....	......	.....	......	+1.2	+0.70
1915	.....	......	.....	......	+0.5	+0.40
1916	.....	......	.....	.....	−0.6	−0.23
1917	.....	......	.....	......	−0.2	−0.05
1918	.....	......	.....	......	+0.8	+0.40
1919	.....	......	.....	......	+0.2	+0.33
1920	.....	......	.....	......	+0.1	+0.65
1921	.....	......	.....	......	+2.2	+1.20
1922	.....	......	.....	......	+0.3	+0.83
1923	.....	......	.....	......	+0.5	+0.33
1924	.....	......	.....	......	0.0	+0.58
1925	.....	......	.....	......	+1.8	+1.38
1926	.....	......	....	......	+1.9	+1.60
1927	.....	......	.....	......	+0.8	+0.88

in which S is the smoothed value, b the actual value pertaining to the particular year for which S is being computed, a and c the actual values for the next previous and the next succeeding years, respectively. The fourth and fifth columns give, respectively, the actual and the smoothed average departures of the annual average minima, while the sixth and seventh columns give the corresponding average departures of the annual average means.

Figure 225 shows the graphical equivalents of the smoothed portions of Table III, to, and including, 1912. The values after that date show

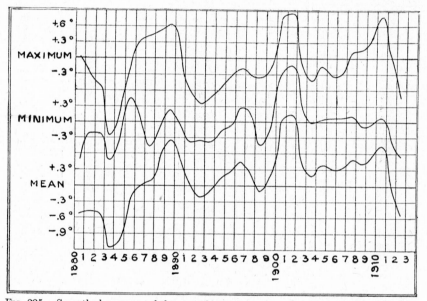

Fig. 225.—Smoothed averages of the annual average temperature departures of 17 American stations.

nothing interesting except, roughly, the usual inverse relation of temperature to sun-spot numbers.

It will be noticed that the three curves of Fig. 225, marked maximum, minimum, and mean, respectively, are, in general, quite similar to each other. Hence, because of this mutual check and general agreement, it seems reasonably certain that any one set of temperature data, the means, for instance, furnishes a fairly safe guide to the actual temperature and climatic fluctuations from year to year, or period to period.

Table IV gives the weighted actual average departures and the smoothed departures in degrees Fahrenheit of the annual mean temperatures of the selected seventeen American, seven European, and one Indian stations listed in Table I.

TABLE IV.—WEIGHTED DEPARTURES OF MEAN TEMPERATURES FROM NORMAL
TEMPERATURES
World

Date	Actual	Smoothed	Date	Actual	Smoothed
1872	−0.78	−0.30	1897	+0.34	+0.45
1873	−0.65	−0.47	1898	+0.61	+0.46
1874	+0.20	−0.34	1899	+0.27	+0.59
1875	−1.12	−0.61	1900	+1.19	+0.76
1876	−0.40	−0.60	1901	+0.40	+0.55
1877	−0.48	−0.32	1902	+0.20	+0.13
1878	+0.07	0.00	1903	−0.30	+0.10
1879	+0.33	+0.04	1904	+0.81	+0.20
1880	−0.50	−0.13	1905	−0.51	+0.01
1881	+0.14	−0.02	1906	+0.23	+0.05
1882	+0.14	−0.16	1907	+0.23	+0.30
1883	−1.04	−0.68	1908	+0.51	+0.21
1884	−0.79	−0.61	1909	−0.43	+0.11
1885	+0.17	−0.09	1910	+0.69	+0.30
1886	+0.11	+0.03	1911	+0.23	+0.09
1887	−0.29	−0.05	1912	−0.80	−0.40
1888	+0.26	+0.24	1913	−0.07	−0.01
1889	+0.74	+0.57	1914	+0.80	+0.45
1890	+0.54	+0.40	1915	+0.25	+0.29
1891	−0.21	+0.06	1916	−0.13	−0.14
1892	+0.10	−0.09	1917	−0.50	−0.12
1893	−0.34	−0.06	1918	+0.74	+0.15
1894	+0.34	+0.03	1919	−0.39	+0.17
1895	−0.21	+0.10	1920	+0.82	+0.52
1896	+0.49	+0.28			

The average departures were calculated in accordance with the
more or less correctly coefficiented equation

$$D = \frac{4A + 2E + I}{7},$$

in which D is the weighted departure, A the smoothed average American,
E the smoothed average European, and I the smoothed Indian, departure
of the mean annual temperature from the normal annual temperature.

Table IV, extended, as well as the scanty early data, mainly from the
given stations, will permit, back to 1872, is graphically represented by
the continuous, light curve at the bottom of Fig. 226. In 1880, and
again in 1901, the curve probably does not very closely represent world-
wide temperature departures, being, presumably, at both places quite
too low, owing, in each case, to an abnormally cold single month in
America.

The dotted curve from 1907 to 1911 gives the average temperature
departures for the American stations only, and, presumably, represents

world temperature departures much more closely than does the continuous light line for the same time. This is because of two or three exceptionally cold summer months in Europe.

The dotted curve from 1872 to 1900 gives the smoothed averages of the annual temperature departures from the normal temperatures of the following stations as computed from the actual departures given by Nordmann;[1] Sierra Leone, Recife (or Pernambuco), Port au Prince, Trinité, Jamaica, Habana, Manila, Hong Kong, Zikawei, Batavia, Bombay, Island of Rodriguez, Island of Mauritius.

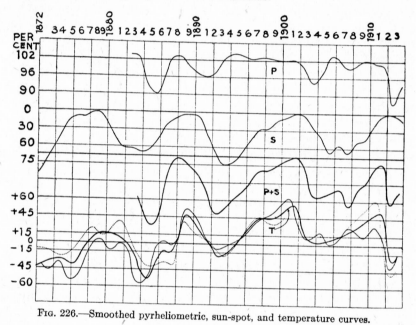

Fig. 226.—Smoothed pyrheliometric, sun-spot, and temperature curves.

All these, or practically all, are low-level stations, and most of them either tropical or semitropical, and, therefore, should show in general, from altitude influence alone, a smaller, and from latitude influence alone, a greater, abnormality than do the stations whose temperature departures are given by the continuous fine-line curve. Hence, all things considered, the average temperature departures as calculated from the two sets of stations agree remarkably well, so that one can say with, presumably, a fair degree of confidence, that the heavy curve T approximately represents the average of the departures of the mean annual temperatures from the normal annual temperatures of equatorial and high altitude regions of the earth, or that T, with the above restrictions, is the curve of world temperatures.

[1] *Revue Générale des Sciences*, pp. 803–808, August, 1903; *Ann. Rept. Smithsonian Institution*, pp. 139–149, 1903.

Much additional statistical evidence bearing on this point and supporting the conclusion just given, has been published by Mielke.[1] This consists of the average annual temperatures from 1870 to 1910 of 487 widely distributed stations, with, however, numerous and extensive breaks—in fact, the records of only a few stations cover the entire period. By grouping these stations according to zones, tropical, subtropical, warm temperate, cold temperate and frigid, and then averaging and smoothing the zonal annual temperature departures, giving all equal weight, values were found which run substantially parallel to those already found but of less (about one-half) amplitude, quite as anticipated from the fact that stations above the dust, fogs, and many clouds of the lower atmosphere, must be more sensitive to variations in the transparency of the outer atmosphere and to solar changes than are those (the great majority) located at, or not more than a few hundred meters above, sea level. Either curve might, therefore, be used in a discussion of the causes and periods of temperature changes, but in what follows the curve of larger amplitudes or the curve of high altitude stations will be used because: (a) data for it, but not for the other, are available through the period of the Katmai veil of dust, (b) it is freer from surface disturbances and, therefore, more representative of solar and high atmospheric conditions, (c) high altitude temperatures are more effective than those of sea level in modifying glacial conditions.

Relation of World Temperatures to Pyrheliometric Values.—Curve P, also of Fig. 226, gives the smoothed course of the annual average pyrheliometric readings, as computed from the actual values given in Fig. 223. The insolation intensity data, covering the whole of the depression that had its minimum in 1885, were obtained at a single place, Montpellier, France, by a single observer, L. J. Eon,[2] who confined himself to noon observations with a Crova actinometer. It may be, therefore, that merely local and temporary disturbances produced a local insolation curve that was not quite parallel to the curve for the entire world. At any rate, the drop in the solar radiation values obviously was due to dust put into the atmosphere by the explosion of Krakatoa in August, 1883, and it would seem that the effects of this dust both on the surface temperatures and on pyrheliometric values must have been greater during the latter part of 1883 and in 1884 than they were in 1885, when much of the dust, certainly, had already settled out of the atmosphere, and this supposition is well supported by the pyrheliometric and temperature drops that immediately followed the volcanic explosions of 1903 and 1912, and their partial recovery within a single year. Nevertheless, the pyrheliometric values must be accepted as obtained. Indeed, this exceptional lag is not quite unprecedented,

---

[1] *Aus dem Archiv der Deutschen Seewarte*, **36**; Nov. 3, 1913.

[2] *Bulletin météorologique du Département de l'Hérault*, 1900.

since the coldest year following the similar, though more violent, explosion of Asamayama, just 100 years earlier, was not the year of the explosion, 1783, nor the following year, but 1785.

It is probable that in the earlier, as certainly in the later, of these unusual cases the dust was thrown to such great altitudes that the finer portions were nearly, or quite, 2 years in reaching the lower level of the isothermal region. Clearly, too, much of this dust, while perfectly dry, probably was so fine as merely to scatter even solar radiation, and yet, on reaching the more humid portions of the atmosphere, the particles may have gathered sufficient moisture to assume reflecting size, and, therefore, seriously to interfere with insolation. This is merely suggested, but in no wise insisted upon, as a possible explanation of the unusual pyrheliometric lag after the explosion of Krakatoa.

It is obvious, from a mere glance, that the pyrheliometric and the temperature curves, or curves P and T, have much in common. This is especially marked by the large and practically simultaneous drops in the two curves in 1912, following the eruption of Katmai. But while a relation between these curves thus appears certain, the agreement is so far from perfect as to force the conclusion that pyrheliometric values constitute only one factor in the determination of average world temperatures.

Sun Spots and Temperature.—It has been known for a long time that the curve of sun-spot numbers, curve S (Fig. 226), and the curve of earth temperatures, curve T, follow or parallel each other in a general way, in the sense that the fewer the spots the higher the temperature, with, however, puzzling discrepancies here and there. Both these facts, the general agreement between the phenomena in question and also their specific discrepancies, are well shown by the curves S and T of Fig. 226, and, while the discrepancies are marked, it is obvious that, on the whole, the agreement is quite too close to leave any doubt of the reality of some sort of connection between sun spots and atmospheric temperatures. Just how, or by what process, this relation, conceivably, may exist will be discussed below.

Combined Effect of Insolation Intensity and Sun-spot Influence on Atmospheric Temperatures.—Since it is obvious that the insolation intensity and the number of sun spots each exerts an influence on the temperature of the earth, it is clear that some sort of a combination of the two curves P and S should more closely parallel the temperature curve T than does either, alone. It is probable that the sun-spot effect is not directly proportional to the actual number of spots, but, however this may be, the direct combination of the curves P and S gives the resultant $P + S$, which, as a glance at the figures shows, actually parallels the curve of temperatures T with remarkable fidelity. Exactly this same combination, from 1880 to 1909, has been made by Abbot and

Fowle,[1] whose lead in this important particular is here being followed, and the resultant curve found to run closely parallel to the curve of "smoothed annual mean departures" of the maximum temperatures of 15 stations in the United States.

Probably the most striking point of agreement, one that must strongly be insisted upon, as shown by Fig. 226, between the combination curve and the temperature, occurs in 1912, when, in spite of the fact that the sun spots were at a minimum, indicating that, according to rule, the temperature should be high, the temperature curve dropped greatly and abruptly; obviously, because of the simultaneous and corresponding decrease in the intensity of solar radiation produced by the extensive veil of Katmai's dust, precisely as happened at spot minima after the explosion of Asama, in 1783. Both cases, since they occurred during spot minima, show distinctly the great influence volcanic dust has on terrestrial temperatures.

Temperature Variations Since 1750 as Influenced by Sun Spots and Volcanic Eruptions.—Sun-spot numbers,[2] month by month, are fairly well known since July, 1749, and so, too, are the annual temperature variations[3] from about the same time, and, therefore, the data at hand for comparing these two phenomena over a continuous period of about 190 years, or from at least the beginning of the year 1750 to the present date. Figure 227 (folded, attached to inside of back cover) makes this comparison easy. The bottom curves give the smoothed annual temperature departures, as computed from Köppen's actual annual departures, using all stations, while the top curve follows Wolfer's annual average sun-spot numbers. Of course, the earlier observations, both of sun spots and of temperatures, were few in number and, more or less, unsatisfactory in comparison with those obtained during the past 50, or even 60 years. Nevertheless, it is clear from Fig. 227 that, at least since 1750, the data of our earliest records, and, presumably, therefore, since an indefinitely distant time in the past, the two phenomena, atmospheric temperature and sun-spot numbers, have in general varied together, with, however, marked discrepancies from time to time. The same relation has continued to hold since 1913 (final year of the figure) to the present, 1939, as previously explained. These discrepancies we shall now consider, and shall show that they occurred, in every important case, immediately after violent volcanic eruptions.

Volcanic Disturbances of Atmospheric Temperature Since 1750.— It must be distinctly remembered that the earlier temperature records, because of their limited number, if for no other reason, give only the general trend of world temperatures. Again, the record, back to 1750,

[1] *Smithsonian Miscellaneous Collections*, Vol. **60**; No. 29, 1913.

[2] WOLFER, *Astronomische Mitteilungen*, **93**; 1902, and later numbers.

[3] KÖPPEN, *Zeit. Oesterreich. Gesell. für Meteorologie*, **8**; 241 and 257, 1873.

of even violent volcanic eruptions is necessarily incomplete; and, besides, *not all great eruptions decrease the surface temperature—only those that drive a lot of dust into the stratosphere*, and, even then, decrease it perceptibly in only those regions, usually extensive and at times world wide, over which the dust spreads. Pronounced and long-continued sky phenomena, therefore, of the type that followed the eruption of Krakatoa, furnish the best evidence of volcanic violence in the sense here used. Finally, there can be no particular test save where the temperature is low in comparison with that which the number of sun spots would indicate. Obviously, then, no matter how close the actual relation between the phenomena may be, the errors and the incompleteness of the recorded data would prevent the discovery of more than a general relation.

Of course, it will naturally occur to one to ask about special cases, such as the cold years of 1783–1784–1785, and, in particular, 1816, the famous "year without a summer," "poverty year," or "eighteen hundred and froze-to-death." The first of these, 1783–1785, followed, as already explained, the great explosion of Asama, in 1783, while the second, the "year without a summer," that was cold the world over, followed the eruption of Tomboro, which killed 56,000 people,[1] and blew up so much dust that "for three days there was darkness at a distance of 300 miles.[2]

There is a detail in the temperature curve, for the years 1886–1887, that needs special attention. The temporary depression where, seemingly, the temperature should be steadily rising, obviously was due to the great eruption of Tarawera (June 10, 1886), in New Zealand. This volcano is a little more than 38° south of the equator, and, therefore, furnishes a good example of an eruption on one side of the equator affecting the temperature far to the other side. Doubtless, however, when the dust gets but a little way into the stratosphere, the effect is greatest on the volcano's side of the equator.

But, if the temperature was decreased by Tarawera, why, one might ask, was not the pyrheliometric curve similarly affected? It was, for several months after the eruption, as the individual monthly values show,[3] but the annual means, plotted in the figure, have the effect of making the pyrheliometric disturbance from Tarawera appear only as a retardation in the recovery from the effects of Krakatoa.

Neglecting the smaller irregularities which may or may not have been of world-wide occurrence, and remembering that, other things being equal, temperature maxima are to be expected at the times of spot minima and temperature minima at the times of spot maxima, the marked discrepancies and their probable explanations may be tabulated as follows:

---

[1] SCHNEIDER, "Die Vulcanischen Erscheinungen der Erde," p. 1, 1911.

[2] *Rept. Krakatoa Committee Royal Society*, p. 393, 1888.

[3] *Bulletin Météorologique du Départment de l'Hérault*, p. 136, 1900.

TEMPERATURE AND SUN-SPOT DISCREPANCIES

Date	Nature of dis-crepancy	Probable cause
1755–1756	Cold	Kötlugia, Iceland, 1755, Oct. 17.
1766–1767	Cold	Hecla, Iceland, 1766. Apr. 15 to Sept. 7. Mayon, Luzon, 1766.
1778–1779	Warm	Maximum number (annual) of sun spots ever recorded and unusually short spot period. Can it be that the solar constant actually was notably greater than usual at this time?
1784–1785–1786	Cold	Asama, Japan, Aug. 2 to 5, 1783, most frightful eruption on record. Skaptar Jökull, Iceland, 1783, June 8 and 18. Vesuvius, Italy, 1785.
1799	Cold	Fuego (?), Guatemala. (Uncertain.)
1809	Cold	St. George (?), Azores, 1808. (Uncertain.) Etna (?), Sicily, 1809. (Uncertain.)
1812–1813–1814–1815–1816	Cold	Soufrière, St. Vincent, 1812, Apr. 30. Mayon, Luzon, 1814. Tomboro, Sumbawa, 1815, Apr. 7 to 12, very great.
1831–1832	Cold	Graham's Island, 1831, July 10 to early in August. Babujan Islands, 1831. Pichincha, Ecuador, 1831.
1836–1837–1838	Cold	Coseguina Nicaragua, 1835, Jan. 20. Awatska, Kamchatka, 1837.
1856–1857	Cold	Cotopaxi (?), and others, 1855–1856. (Uncertain.)
1872–1873	Cold	Vesuvius, Italy, 1872, Apr. 23 to May 3. Merapi, Java, 1872, April.
1875–1876	Cold	Vatna Jökull, Iceland, 1875, Mar. 29 and during April.
1884–1885–1886	Cold	Krakatoa, Straits of Sunda, 1883, Aug. 27, greatest since 1783. Saint Augustin, Alaska, 1883, Oct. 6. Tarawera, New Zealand, 1886, June 10.
1890–1891–1892	Cold	Bogoslof, Aleutian Islands, 1890, February. Awoe, Great Sangir, 1892, June 7.
1902–1903–1904	Cold	Pelé, Martinique, 1902, May 8. Santa Maria, Guatemala, 1902, Oct. 24. Colima, Mexico, 1903, February and March.
1912–1913	Cold	Katmai, Alaska, 1912, June 6.

For the sake of completeness, as well as for such little value and interest it may have, the following list is added, of still earlier great volcanic eruptions and the kinds of seasons that history[1] reports to have

[1] HENNIG, *Abhand. kgl. preuss. Met. Inst.*, Bd. II, No. 4, 1904.

followed. Taken by themselves these ancient or preinstrumental records help but little to connect effect with cause. Nevertheless, it is at least pleasing to know that they report precisely those general weather or seasonal conditions which from later and reliable instrumental observations we infer must have happened, provided only that the explosions were sufficiently great.

Date of eruption	Volcano	Type of season, etc.
79, Aug. 24..........	Vesuvius. (Destruction of Pompeii.)	About 80, severe drought for several years in middle Asia. (Accords with low temperature but signifies very little.) Very cold in England.
1631, Dec. 16........	Vesuvius. (Most violent since 79. Height of ash cloud, measured by Braccini, 48 kilometers.)	1632, Apr. 27, destructive snow in Transylvania (Siebenbürgen); May 17, frost in Saxony; hot dry summer in Italy; Oct. 4, very cold in France, 37 soldiers frozen between Montpellier and Baziers. 1633, severe winter; May 22, snow and severe cold in Transylvania.
1636, May 18 to winter	Hecla.............	1637, long, severe winter.
1680................	Celebes...........	1681, severe drought and cold spring (Evelyn's Diary).
1693, Feb. 13 till August	Hecla.............	1694, hard, snowy winter in both Italy and Spain; May 17, all vineyards of Troyes destroyed by frost.
1694................	Celebes.........	
1694................	Amboyna.......	1695, long, severe and dry winter; cool summer.
1694, Nov. 20 till 1695, April........	Gunong Api.....	
1707, May 20 to August	Vesuvius..........	1708, very mild winter; cold summer; Dec. 10 to 20, very heavy snow in France.
1707................	Japanese volcano	1709, from Jan. 6, for a month and a half extraordinary severe cold in nearly all Europe; Adriatic Sea and Thames frozen; snow 10 feet deep in Spain and Portugal; 50 days frost in England from Dec. 25, 1708 till March 12, 1709; mild winter in Constantinople, but very severe in eastern North America; May 17, snow in Oedenburg; May 17 and 18, frost in Alsace; cool, rainy summer.
1707, May 25 and July 25	Santorin.......	
1721, May 11 till autumn	Kotlugia..........	1722, cool, wet year.

Confining attention to the first of the above lists, since the value of the second in this connection is doubtful, it will be seen that excepting some ill-defined cases, all of the seeming irregularities in the temperature curve, and all of the known volcanic eruptions, are satisfactorily accounted for.

It may be concluded, therefore, that the variations in the average temperature of the atmosphere of the kind and magnitude shown by actual records depend jointly upon volcanic eruptions, through the action of dust on radiation, as already explained, and upon sun-spot numbers, through, presumably, some intermediate action they have upon the atmosphere—possibly of the nature explained in the next chapter.

Magnitude and Importance of Actual Temperature Changes.—The actual temperature range from sun-spot maximum to sun-spot minimum varies, roughly, from 0.5° to 1° C., or possibly more, while the effect of volcanic dust appears to be fully as great—on rare occasions, even much greater. In some ways, and in respect to many things, a range of average temperatures of even 1° C. is well nigh negligible, and, therefore, however important the results may seem to the scientist, the ultra-utilitarian would be justified in asking, "What of it?"

Much of it, in a distinctly practical, as well as in a purely scientific, sense, as is true of every fact of nature. For instance, during the summer, or growing season, a change of 0.5° C. produces a latitude shift of the isotherms by fully 80 miles. Hence, if there is little or no volcanic dust to interfere, during sun-spot minima, cereals, and other crops, may be successfully grown 50 to 150 miles farther north (or south in the southern hemisphere) than at the times of sun-spot maxima. This, alone, is of great practical importance, especially to those who live near the thermal limits of crop production.

In addition to changing the area over which crop production is possible, a change of average temperature also affects, in some cases greatly, the time of plant development. Thus, Walter[1] has shown that a change of only 0.7° C. may alter, and in Mauritius has been observed actually to alter, by as much as an entire year, the time required for the maturing of sugar cane. Hence, the temperature changes that normally accompany sun-spot variations, though small in absolute magnitude, are of great importance, and, by availing ourselves of the reasonable fore-knowledge we have of these changes, may easily be made of still greater importance.

In forecasting these small, but important, climatic changes, it must be distinctly remembered that to the fairly periodic, and, therefore, predictable, sun-spot influence must be added the irregular, and unpre-

[1] "On the Influence of Forests on Rainfall and the Probable Effect of 'Déboise-ment' on Agriculture in Mauritius," 1908.

dictable, volcanic effects. But even here, the case is not bad for the forecaster, because the fine volcanic dust always produces, qualitatively, the same effect—a cooling—and because both the amount of this cooling and its duration (generally only 1 or 2 years, as already explained) approximately may be estimated from the nature of the volcanic explosion itself.

CHAPTER V

OTHER FACTORS OF CLIMATIC CONTROL

(9, 10, 11, 12, 13, 14)

9. Sun Spots.—As already stated, the average temperature of the earth as a whole varies inversely with the frequency of sun spots.

How Sun Spots May Change Earth Temperatures.—If the solar constant should remain the same from spot maximum to spot minimum it clearly would not be easy to see at a glance why the surface temperature of the earth should vary as it does with spot numbers; and the situation is still more difficult if, as observations appear to indicate, the lowest temperatures occur when the solar constant is greatest and the highest temperatures occur when this constant is least. There is, however, a possible explanation of the paradox, and, while it may not contain the whole truth, it nevertheless is sufficient to show *a priori* that in all probability our temperatures do change from spot maxima to spot minima without a corresponding change in the solar constant, and also to show that a decrease in our surface temperatures may accompany even a slight increase in the solar constant.

The explanation in question has already been given elsewhere,[1] and the original paper must be consulted by those who wish to weigh all the details of the argument. Briefly, however, the argument is as follows:

1. At the times of spot maxima the solar corona is denser and more nearly spherical than at the times of spot minima—a well-known observation.

2. This corona consists, in part at least, of reflecting particles, as many eclipse observations have shown, and so may be regarded as dust in the solar atmosphere.

3. The brightness of the sun, as every solar observer knows, drops off from center to limb.

4. This drop, as reported by various observers, is greater the shorter the wave length, and due, almost certainly, to diffuse scattering.

From the observational facts it follows that during spot minima, other things being equal, the solar spectrum must necessarily be richer in violet and ultraviolet radiation than it is during spot maxima.

But, as experiment has shown,[2] ultraviolet radiation of shorter wave length than λ1850 is strongly absorbed by oxygen, with the result that

---

[1] HUMPHREYS, *Astrophys. J.*, **32**; 97, 1910.

[2] LYMAN, *Astrophys. J.*, **27**; 87, 1908.

some of the oxygen is converted into ozone. Hence, since the atmosphere of the stratosphere is cold and dry (conditions favorable to the stability of ozone), and since of the gases of the upper atmosphere only oxygen is appreciably absorptive of radiations between λ1250 and λ1900,[1] the stratosphere was believed to contain more or less ozone, a belief now fully confirmed by several observers,[2] and long ago virtually confirmed by Ångström.[3] In so far, then, as this ozone is produced by the action of ultraviolet solar radiation, it is also logical to expect it to be greater in quantity when the short wave-length radiation, to which it is due, is most intense, or, presumably, therefore, at the times of spot minima. Now, according to the experiments of Ladenburg and Lehmann,[4] while ozone is somewhat absorptive of solar radiation it is severalfold more absorptive of terrestrial radiation. Hence, in this case, as in the case of the absorption of radiation by dust, already considered, equation (A) (page 589) is applicable.

In this equation let a be the coefficient of absorption of the ozone in the stratosphere for solar radiation, and b its coefficient of absorption for earth radiation. To be definite, let $a = 0.02$ and $b = 0.10$ at the time of spot maximum, and for a spot minimum let $a = 0.03$ and $b = 0.15$, quantities that would require really very little ozone. Then, since the earth radiates practically as a full radiator, or black body, at the absolute temperature 246°, if $T_{max.}$ and $T_{min.}$ are the equilibrium temperatures at the time of spot maximum and spot minimum, respectively,

$$\left(\frac{T_{max.}}{246}\right)^4 = \frac{198}{190}; \ T_{max.} = 248°.55,$$

and

$$\left(\frac{T_{min.}}{246}\right)^4 = \frac{197}{185}; \ T_{min.} = 249°.90.$$

That is, under these conditions, and if the solar constant should remain exactly the same, the virtual temperature at the time of spot minimum would be 1°.35 C. higher than at the time of spot maximum. Hence, even a slight increase in the solar constant at the time of spot maximum might still leave the temperature a trifle lower than at the time of spot minimum.

But observations[5] indicate that, on the contrary, there is surprisingly more ultraviolet radiation at the times of spot maxima than at spot

[1] LYMAN, *loc. cit.*

[2] FABRY and BUISSON, *C. R.*, **156**; 782, 1913: *J. Phys.*, **3**; 196, 1913; FOWLER and STRUTT, *Proc. Roy. Soc.*, **93**; 577, 1917; FOWLE, *Smithsonian Miscellaneous Collections*, Vol. **68**; No. 8, 1917.

[3] *Arkiv för Matematik, Astronomi och Fysik*, **1**; 395, 1904.

[4] *Ann. Phys.*, **21**; 305, 1906.

[5] ABBOT, *Beiträge zur Geophysik*, **16**; 373, 1927.

minima. If so, and if the ozone varies, as one would suppose, in the same sense there must be some additional factor affecting the temperature of the earth. Such a factor might be a corresponding change, as has been reported, in the amount of cirrus haze which, like volcanic dust, interferes more with incoming than with outgoing radiation.

Evidently the paradox: "The hotter the sun the cooler the earth," has an explanation; but what it is, exactly, cannot be determined without further observations.

INFLUENCE OF CARBON DIOXIDE ON TEMPERATURES

It was stated in the early part of this discussion, under the carbon dioxide theory of ice ages, that the question of the possible effect a change in the amount of carbon dioxide in the atmosphere might have on temperatures would be taken up later. The way to this is now open through the above discussion of ozone. Like ozone, carbon dioxide also is more absorptive of terrestrial radiation than of solar energy. Hence, increasing the carbon dioxide in the atmosphere, and, thereby, increasing its amount in the stratosphere where it can be treated as a shell external to the radiating earth, obviously, must have the same general effect on the temperature of the earth as increasing the ozone of this region would have. That is, other things being equal, a greater or less temperature increase would follow the introduction into the atmosphere of a larger amount of carbon dioxide.

Because of the constant mixing caused by vertical convection, it is probable that the percentage of carbon dioxide is very nearly as great at the under surface of the stratosphere as it is at the surface of the earth. If so, then the carbon dioxide of the upper atmosphere is equivalent, roughly, to a layer 40 cm. thick at normal atmospheric pressure. In high latitudes, where the stratosphere is low, the equivalent layer probably is thicker than this, and in equatorial regions probably thinner. Now, according to the experiments of Schaefer,[1] a layer of carbon dioxide 40 cm. thick is sufficient to produce very nearly full absorption, and, therefore, no increase in the amount of carbon dioxide in the atmosphere could very much increase its temperature.

An approximate idea of the possible temperature change of the lower atmosphere as a result of the presence of carbon dioxide in the stratosphere can be obtained from known data. Thus, Abbot and Fowle[2] have computed that carbon dioxide may absorb 14 per cent of the radiation from a black body at the temperature of $282.2°$ Abs. But as this is not many degrees, 25 or so, above the effective temperature of the earth as a radiator, it follows that 14 per cent is, roughly, the upper

---

[1] *Ann. Phys.*, **16**; 93, 1905.

[2] *Ann. Astrophys. Obs., Smithsonian Inst.*, **2**; 172, 1908.

limit to which terrestrial radiation can be absorbed by carbon dioxide in the stratosphere while its absorption of solar radiation is very nearly negligible.

Assuming that the present amount of carbon dioxide in the stratosphere absorbs 1 per cent of the solar radiation and 10 per cent of the outgoing earth radiation (values that seem to be, roughly, of the correct order), and using equation (A (page 589)), it will be seen, if the experiments here referred to and the assumptions are substantially correct, that doubling or even multiplying by severalfold the present amount of carbon dioxide, which would leave the absorption of solar radiation practically unchanged, and increase the absorption of terrestrial radiation at most to only 14 per cent, could increase the intensity of the radiation received at the surface of the earth about one-half of 1 per cent, and, therefore, the average temperature by no more than about 1.3° C. Similarly, reducing the carbon dioxide by one-half could decrease the temperature by no more than approximately the same amount, 1.3° C.

It is not certain to what extent the percentage of carbon dioxide in the atmosphere has actually varied during the geologic past, but, if the above reasoning is correct, it seems that surface temperatures could never have been much increased above their present values through the action of this particular agent alone. Furthermore, the fact, so far as known, that within the tropics, at least, plant growth was quite as vigorous during the ice ages as it is now, shows that for a very long time, even in the geological sense, carbon dioxide has been abundant in the atmosphere—probably never much less abundant than at present. Hence, it seems likely that a decrease in temperature of a fraction of 1° is all that can reasonably be accounted for in this way.

Finally, if the above reasoning is correct, it seems that changes in the amount of carbon dioxide in the atmosphere might have been a factor in the production of certain climatic changes of the past, but that it could not, of itself, have produced the great changes of temperature that actually occurred.

10. Land Elevation.—Since many changes in land elevation are known to have taken place during the different geologic ages it is necessary, in considering the climates of the past, to inquire what climatic effects such variations in level would of themselves produce. Changes in area will be considered later.

The substantial answer to this question obviously is found in the present effects of elevation on climate. That is to say, the effects of elevation must then have been distant, local, and universal, just as they now are. The distant effects obviously often extended, as they now extend, many hundreds of miles to the leeward of favorably situated high mountain ranges and consisted, as they now consist, essentially in a decrease of precipitation, owing to the extraction of moisture from the atmosphere by forced convection and the consequent tendency towards or even culmination in, desert conditions beyond. The second, or local, effects, clearly, were both an increase in the local precipitation, especially on the windward side, and an average decrease in the temperature, approximately the same as at present, of about 1° C. for each 180, 200, and 250 meters difference in elevation on mountains, hills, and plateaus, respectively.[1]

In one important case, namely, when the surface is extensive and snow covered (probably to some extent also when bare), this relation of temperature decrease between mountain, hill, and plateau, does not hold, as is obvious from the following consideration. During long, clear winter nights, such as obtain in high latitudes, the surface becomes greatly chilled through comparatively free radiation to the still colder air far above and even to empty space beyond. Hence, the surface air also is chilled and its density made correspondingly greater. It, therefore, flows away to lower levels and at the same time its temperature is increased through increase of pressure, or at least prevented from falling so low as it otherwise would. When the slope is steep, as it usually is on the sides of hills and mountains, this flow clearly must be more or less rapid, especially along narrow valleys or ravines, and, therefore, an approach established, within this portion of the air current, to the adiabatic temperature gradient of about 1° C. per each 100 meters' change in elevation. On the other hand, when the slope is very gentle, as it is over the interior of Greenland and over much of the explored portion of the Antarctic continent, air drainage necessarily is sluggish and the dynamic heating, therefore, less than the surface cooling. Hence, in such cases the change of temperature with change in elevation (counting from sea level) can be, and usually is, far greater than adiabatic, or 1° C., about, per 100 meters. Hence, such regions, when there are no higher surrounding mountains, can and often do establish: (1) a circulation of the upper air from the ocean to the higher portions of the plateau; (2) a well-defined surface temperature inversion, or, for the first few hundred meters, an increase of temperature with increase of elevation; (3) a slow settling of this air onto the cold surface below; (4) the precipitation, without cloud, of fine snow crystals—"frost snow;" (5) drainage of this chilled and relatively dense air to lower levels; (6) drifting of the snow with the winds and the consequent extension, so far as temperature and other conditions will permit, of the ice-covered, or glaciated, area.

All these conditions obtain today over the two great glaciers that still remain, that of Greenland and that of Antarctica, and, presumably, therefore, must also have obtained to a greater or less extent over all great glacial fields wherever, and whenever, they occurred. Mere changes

[1] HANN AND SÜRING, "Lehrbuch der Meteorologie," 4th Ed., p. 125.

in level, therefore, might cause, and doubtless often have caused, somewhat corresponding fluctuations in the climates of both local and leeward regions, and especially in the extent and depth of local glaciations; but this obvious fact does not in the least justify the assumption that either the universal low temperatures and extensive glaciations of ice ages or the world-wide genial temperatures of the intervening periods had, on the whole, any such origin.

It may be worth while, in this connection, to call attention to the fact that the thickness or depth of a glacial sheet cannot continue indefinitely to increase with increase of elevation, but, on the contrary, for each given locality must have a level of maximum development, above which it somewhat rapidly decreases.

An important if not the chief contributing factor to this result is the relation of saturation to temperature, illustrated by Fig. 74, which shows by its shaded areas the relative amounts of precipitation for each 5-degree decrease in the temperature of saturated air, assuming the volume to remain constant. Now as the wind blows up and over a mountain range its temperature decreases somewhat regularly with increase of elevation, and, therefore, at whatever temperature precipitation begins it must, as Fig. 74 shows, continue to decrease in amount as the cloud reaches higher and higher elevations—the effect of the accompanying volume increase on vapor capacity being much less than the effect of the temperature decrease.

If the precipitation always began at the same level, it is obvious that this would be the level not only of initial but also of maximum precipitation. But as the level of initial precipitation actually varies through a considerable range, it follows that the level of maximum catch lies somewhere within this range, probably, too, well within its lower half. Obviously, then, the level of maximum snowfall is not at, nor even close to, the tops of very high mountains, but far down near the lower snow limit.

In addition to this, the generally increasing steepness of the higher reaches causes more frequent avalanches and a greater speed of flow. In short, the higher mountain levels not only catch less snow than do the somewhat lower, but also more rapidly shed what they do catch.

A full discussion of this subject would, of course, require an account of the rate of melting, evaporation, drift, glacial flow, and probably other phenomena; but the above, presumably, is sufficient to make it clear why maximum glaciation is not at the greatest elevations, but, on the contrary, at distinctly lower levels.

The universal climatic effect of land elevation, mentioned above, a greater or less lowering of the average temperature over, perhaps, the entire earth, is a logical consequence of the other two. As is well known, water vapor is by far the world's greatest conservator of heat. Hence, anything that diminishes the average amount of this substance in the atmosphere obviously must somewhat lower surface temperatures.

Now precipitation through which the average humidity is lowered is induced chiefly by vertical convection, a condition which mountain ranges vigorously and extensively produce, (*a*) by mechanical deflection of the winds, (*b*) by updrafts induced on their sides during summer insolation, and (*c*) by the air drainage down their valleys of clear nights. The first two types of convection are very efficient in removing moisture from the atmosphere, while the third spreads the cold of the exposed higher levels—exposed in the sense that they are above much of the protecting vapor blanket, and, therefore, subjected to more rapid cooling.

Clearly, then, assuming the same total extent of land area, the average temperature of the world is lower when there are a number of high mountain ranges than when there are but few or none—lower because the exposed heights themselves are cold, because they drain their cold air over adjacent regions, and because they dry the atmosphere and thus prevent other portions of the earth from having as efficient protection from heat loss as they, otherwise, would.

This lowering of the average temperature necessarily decreases the rate of evaporation and the saturation quantity, and, thereby, presumably, further accentuates the cooling. Hence, high mountain ranges, especially when along the coasts of extensive continents, lead to low temperatures, local and windward glaciation, and reduced leeward precipitation. On the other hand, the absence of mountain ranges insures a relatively humid atmosphere, extensive cloudiness, equable temperature, and moderate general precipitation.

Conceivably, therefore, the great world-wide climatic changes of the past originated in corresponding changes of level, gradual or cataclysmic. Nevertheless, it seems most improbable (apparently it has not yet been definitely proved one way or the other) that all the several glaciated continents rose and sank together—that there is not, nor ever was, a simultaneous swing, up and down, of all, or nearly all, continental areas on the one hand and ocean beds on the other; at least not to any such extent as this hypothesis would demand. To be sure, there is much and increasing evidence[1] that in, geologically, very recent times there has been an increase of sea level relative to that of the land of, roughly, 50 meters in many tropical and subtropical regions where, so far as known, glaciers have never existed. But the simplest interpretation of this appears to be, not that so extensive and such different ocean beds have everywhere sunk to substantially the same extent and at about the same time, but rather that the phenomenon is only the inevitable result of the melting of the extensive glacial sheets of the quaternary ice age.

[1] VAUGHAN, *Bull. Am. Geographic Soc.*, **46;** 426, 1914; DALY, *Am. J. Sci.*, **41;** 153, 1916.

It will be assumed, therefore, that all effects, of whatever kind, that changes in land elevation may have had on climate, local and leeward, were essentially as above explained, and, hence, that such changes, however important as contributory factors, constituted neither the sufficient initiating nor the whole sustaining cause either of the glacial or of the interglacial climates if, as is generally believed, these were simultaneously world wide.

11. Changes in Land Area.—In addition to changes in land elevation, and largely because of such changes, there have also been many variations in land extent and, consequently, in the ratio, both local and world wide, of water surface to land surface. The importance of this phenomenon may be inferred from the fact that, according to Schuchert,[1] North America alone has been submerged at least 17 times over areas that range from 154,000 to 4,000,000 square miles, or fully half its present extent. Hence, in a discussion of how the climates of the past have varied, and why, it is necessary to take this additional factor into consideration. An exact, or quantitative, evaluation of this factor is impossible, but its qualitative effect, and even a rough approximation to its numerical value, may be inferred from the present climates, along the same latitudes, of continents and of islands, and also from the climatic contrast between the northern and the southern hemispheres, as shown in Fig. 65, by the mean annual isotherms. That is, any appreciable increase in the ratio of land to ocean surface, presumably, accentuated the seasonal contrasts, or made the summers warmer and the winters colder than they otherwise would have been. It must also have accentuated the latitude contrast or made warm regions warmer and cold ones still colder, as is also illustrated by Fig. 65. In short, any increase of land area must, in general, have rendered the local climate more continental and less marine, and all this for the obvious reason that while the solid portions of the earth, rock, sand, and soil, have no power of avoiding great temperature ranges through either evaporation, convection, or flow to other latitudes, all three methods belong abundantly to the ocean.

From this, in turn, since the range of animal species is partly restricted and delimited by the extremes of temperature, and that of vegetable species both by these extremes and by the length of the growing season, it follows that an age of great land extent must, through its fossils, give evidence of an excessive zonal climatic contrast, or appear in middle and higher latitudes to have been one of harsh climates, while one of small land extent, even though the world as a whole had the same average temperature as before, must similarly record a much less zonal contrast and a spread of genial climates to far higher latitudes.

In the above, attention has been confined strictly to land surfaces, their elevation and their areas, but continental mountain ranges and

[1] *Bull. Geol. Sec. Am.*, **20**; 601, 1910.

plateaus are not the only portions of the earth subject to changes in elevation and extent. Ocean beds and submarine ridges must also vary in both particulars, and, in turn, profoundly modify both local temperatures and zonal contrasts. Some of these ridges, doubtless, have alternately risen quite to the surface, perhaps, at times, much higher, and again sunk to considerable depths, and in each case, inevitably, have produced greater or less climatic changes through the resulting alterations in the oceanic and atmospheric circulations, and, perhaps, in other ways.

12. 13. Atmospheric and Oceanic Circulation.—As everyone knows, practically the entire amount of heat that maintains the surface temperature of the earth is the result of the absorption of solar energy, chiefly by the lower atmosphere and by the various superficial coverings of the surface —vegetation, soil, rock, and water. On the average, the daily supply of this heat per unit area is much greater within the tropics than it is at high latitudes, a condition that maintains two distinct, though largely interdependent, systems of perpetual circulation, the atmospheric and the oceanic, that in, roughly, even measure, the one with the other, tend to equalize the temperatures of the earth—that keep the tropical regions from becoming unbearably hot and the frigid zones from being unendurably cold.

Clearly, then, any modification of either of these circulations would produce a corresponding change of climates, and the cause of this modification might properly be regarded as the cause of the given climatic changes themselves. But, preliminary to a consideration of the probable climatic effects of any such modification it will be necessary, first, briefly to examine both circulations as they now exist.

Present Atmospheric and Oceanic Circulations.—Despite innumerable disturbances, great and small, the fundamental circulation of the atmosphere is from equatorial toward polar regions and return, over a surface that moves from west to east with a linear velocity that gradually decreases with increase of latitude. As a result of these conditions the prevailing winds of latitudes higher than 32°, roughly, N. and S., blow from the west toward the east, or, to be exact, have a west to east component, while the winds between these latitudes, in the neighborhood, therefore, of the equator and the tropics, commonly blow, in the same general sense as above, from the east toward the west.

Now, the rotation of the earth has forced it to take the shape of an oblate spheroid—has bulged it at the equator and flattened it at the poles—and this distortion from the perfect sphere is such that an object on the surface is in equilibrium, so far as moving north or south is concerned, only when it has the same angular velocity about the axis of the earth that the earth itself has, or, in short, when it has no motion over the surface east or west. Obviously, then, an object moving from west to east, or with an angular velocity exceeding that of the earth, would be in equilibrium on a bulge greater than that which actually exists, and hence all winds with an eastward component, and, therefore, as stated, the prevailing winds outside latitudes 32° N. and S., must tend to climb up towards the equator. On the other hand, an object moving from east to west, or with an angular velocity less than that of the earth, as do the prevailing winds between latitudes 32° N. and S., must tend to slide down towards the adjacent or nearest pole. These opposite drifts of the winds, therefore, the drift of the winds of high latitudes toward the equator and the drift of the tropical winds toward the adjacent pole, obviously, produce the two belts of relatively high barometric pressure that roughly parallel the equator, the one at about latitude 32° N.; the other at approximately latitude 32° S.

Each belt of high pressure is greatly disturbed where it crosses a continental area, owing chiefly to temperature inequalities, but it also happens that, even on the oceans, the belts are of unequal intensity, and, what is of especial importance, have relatively fixed absolute pressure maxima or anticyclonic centers.

These permanent or nearly permanent centers of high pressure, or centers of action as they have been called, are five in number, as a reference to Fig. 62 will show; two in the northern hemisphere, one off the coast of southern California, the other near the Azores; and three in the southern hemisphere, one off the coast of Chile, another just west of South Africa, and a third between South Africa and Australia. Further, as is shown by Fig. 65, there is, in the region of each of these permanent anticyclonic centers, a marked equatorial deflection of the annual average isotherms, showing clearly that while each high pressure belt as a whole is caused by the mechanical squeeze of the opposite air drifts, above explained, the additional pressure that produces each maximum is a result of the local relatively low temperature, which causes a corresponding contraction and, therefore, increased density of the local atmosphere. And, finally, these particular low air temperatures, in turn, are caused by cold ocean currents, as is obvious from Fig. 66, and again from Fig. 67 which shows the interrelations here considered between barometric pressure, air isotherms, and ocean currents.

That both the mere existence of these anticyclonic centers and their several geographic locations are of great importance to the climates of neighboring regions, through their directing influence on the prevailing winds, is obvious from Figs. 63 and 64, that give the directions and indicate the average force and steadiness of ocean winds at different seasons. But all this influence on the winds, however vital to many a local climate, can properly be said to be only one of the important climatic effects of the existing ocean currents.

In addition to the several permanent anticyclonic centers there are, also (see Figs. 63 and 64), one permanent cyclonic center, the Icelandic "low," and one semipermanent or winter cyclonic center, the Aleutian "low," both of which are strongly influenced by ocean currents, the first by the Gulf Stream and the second by the Japan Current. The Icelandic "low" results from the temperature contrast between the air over the relatively warm water and that over the glacial fields of Greenland and Iceland, in consequence of which there is established a circulation in the sense of an overflow from the warm region and counter underflows from both the adjacent cold regions. This thermally induced circulation, in conjunction with the rotation of the earth, produces cyclonic conditions, and as the temperature contrasts are permanent (the Icelandic and the Greenland glaciers remain throughout the year and indefinitely), the cyclonic conditions themselves of this region are also permanent.

The Aleutian "low," on the contrary, that is flanked by the Alaskan peninsula and the peninsulas of northeastern Siberia, has a circulation similar to that of the Icelandic "low," and for similar reasons, only while the adjacent land areas are covered with ice and snow and, therefore, are relatively cold. In the spring, when the snow melts away, the cyclonic conditions also disappear, there then being nothing to sustain them.

But the formation and geographic location of the above cyclonic and anticyclonic conditions— direction and force of winds, nature and frequency of storms, and the like—do not exhaust the more important climatic effects of existing ocean currents, as a glance at the annual average isotherms and ocean currents of the North Atlantic (Fig. 67) will show. In fact, the January isotherm of Chicago, Buffalo, and Boston (very approximately on the latitude of Rome), though not particularly cold, passes, under the influence of the Gulf Stream, through Iceland and on well beyond the Arctic Circle to the north of Norway and Sweden; while, under the same influence, frost is practically unknown and semitropical vegetation flourishes on the Scilly Isles in the latitude of northern Newfoundland. Similarly, it is said that because of the Japan Current frost rarely, if ever, occurs on one or two of the Aleutian islands.

Obviously, then, as the above several examples show, the ocean currents, driven by the winds, deflected by the rotation of the earth and by continental and island barriers, and otherwise modified by various minor causes, are both directly and indirectly of the greatest importance to the climates of many parts of the world; directly through the immense thermal interchange they establish between the torrid and the frigid zones, and, indirectly, through the centers of action, the permanent and semipermanent "highs" and "lows," they create and maintain.

Possible Changes in Oceanic Circulation and the Obvious Climatic Results.—Clearly, if the immense system of hot water heating by which the temperature of the whole surface of the earth tends to become equalized should be greatly modified, say, by the opening of a valve here or the closing of another there, correspondingly great climatic modifications surely would have to follow. And there are several, perhaps many, such valves that have been opened or closed, irregularly, and from time to time, since the beginning of geological records. One such valve now partially open, perhaps at one time closed and at another still wider open than at present, lies between South America and the Antarctic continent. Another, now but a little way open, is Bering Strait, which doubtless has greatly changed from one to another geologic age. Still another, now wholly closed, but at one time probably wide open, is the Central American region between the Caribbean Sea and the Pacific Ocean. This particular valve, if now widely opened, would, on the one hand, obliterate the Gulf Stream proper, and probably diminish the Antilles current, and, on the other, greatly increase the Japan Current; and, of course, in each case induce widespread and marked climatic changes. Yet another valve, now rather wide open, that merits special mention, a valve that may have suffered many changes and have undergone its latest opening only in recent times, geologically speaking, is found in that ridge which, by way of Iceland and the Faroe Islands, connects Greenland with north Scotland.

With this Greenland-Scotland valve closed and even with all the other valves, channels of flow, and deflecting obstructions, substantially as they now are, it is well nigh certain that the Icelandic "low" would shift to some point between Greenland and Newfoundland; that Labrador and the Hudson Bay region would receive a greatly increased precipitation; that the Norwegian Sea would become largely, if not wholly, ice covered; and, finally, that Norway and Sweden, since they have the same latitude as Greenland, would be swept by winds of practically Arctic temperature and, therefore, eventually would become, like Greenland itself, almost wholly ice capped. Indeed, any decided change in either the average intensity or average position of the Icelandic "low," if continued for even a few weeks, seems to produce a marked influence on the weather of west and north Europe. In general, whenever the average position of this "low" during a winter month is considerably to the west of its normal place, as occasionally happens, the average temperature of north Europe is likely to be several degrees below normal.[1] That is, the above conclusion that a permanent or age-long shift of the Icelandic "low" far to the west of its present position would lead to, or, at least, permit, the reglaciation of portions of north Europe appears to be abundantly supported by direct observation. Nor would these be all the profound climatic changes that probably, indeed well nigh certainly, would follow the closing of the Greenland-Scotland valve, but they are sufficient, if granted, to indicate how vitally important the

[1] Hann and Süring, "Handbuch der Meteorologie," 4th Ed., pp. 637, 644.

direction and magnitude of the ocean currents are to our climates and to local glaciation.

Doubtless many other valves and courses, such as the broad seaways from the Persian Gulf and the Gulf of Mexico to the Arctic Ocean, have contributed their part in the control of the earth's great water circulation and the regulation of its climatic details, but it would be tedious to take all of them up individually, and, for the present purpose, unnecessary, since it is desired, here, only to make clear the fact that oceanic circulation is a vital factor in the production and control of many a local climate.

14. Surface Covering.—The contrast between land and water in respect to their climatic effects obviously is largely owing to the inequality of their surfaces both as radiators and as absorbers. The values of these properties are approximately known for the ocean, but not for the continents. In fact, there are no fixed values for land areas; nor can there be, since their surfaces undergo many and great changes. Bare soil, luxuriant vegetation, and snow, for instance, are among the surface coverings that have very unequal powers of radiation and absorption; and, therefore, the changes from one to the other over any extensive area, necessarily, are a matter of climatic importance.

To illustrate an extreme, but seemingly possible, climatic effect due to change of surface, assume: (1) That continental areas are unusually extensive; (2) that mountains are abundant and high; (3) that during a period of a few years volcanic explosions are frequent (one a year, say), and of such nature as to put large quantities of dust in the upper atmosphere, as did the Krakatoa and other explosions of historic times.

The low temperatures incident to the volcanic dust would lead to an abnormal extent of continental snow covering, and this, in turn, by its power of reflection—70 per cent, roughly, whereas that of water and of snow-free land is, for vertical radiation, only about 7 per cent—would render the insolation correspondingly less effective—would virtually decrease the solar constant, for all the reflected radiation that passes directly to space might as well never have reached the earth at all, so far as producing any heating is concerned. In this way, an ice covering of the land areas, far more extensive than previously existed, might be initiated by only a few rightly timed violent volcanic explosions, and then *perpetuated* over long periods, if not even added to, by the highly reflecting snow cover. This initial gain of snow and ice, and the further lowering of temperature owing to increase of reflection and decrease of absorption of insolation, would be most pronounced in the high latitudes, and polar ice caps might form on water that previously had been open. The surface winter temperatures over the polar seas, then, would be far below the freezing point instead of, as formerly, rather above that value, while the summer temperatures would be lowered much less, the top of the ice and snow coming to about 0° C.   Over the adjacent land areas, on the other hand, the summer temperatures would be more depressed than those of winter, rising but little above that of melting ice so long as the snow cover was extensive, instead of approaching tropical values, as they often do, when the snow is all gone.   The winter cooling would be owing, mainly, to frigid winds from the ice covered seas, instead of, as formerly, milder breezes from open water, and the greater extent of the snow field.   Thus, during both winter and summer, the horizontal temperature gradient, and with it the pressure gradient, would be increased, and, therefore, also the storminess and precipitation.   A cooler period would thus be begun, possibly even an ice age, if the land area was unusually high and extensive and the warmer ocean currents restricted to middle and lower latitudes; to last, perhaps, until, by erosion of the continents and the opening of the ocean lanes, the world was, again, well on the way toward its normal state of equable temperatures and mild climates.

Unfortunately it is not possible to make quantitative calculations in accordance with the above assumptions.   It would not be extravagant, however, to assume enough dust in the stratosphere for several consecutive years to lower the average temperature of the earth at least 5° C. And this, if the other conditions—height and extent of land areas, and condition of oceanic circulation—were already favorable might be sufficient to abruptly start a long, and marked, climatic change.   It is not claimed that the cold periods were thus caused, but it is insisted that at least some of them might have been.   Those, if any, so caused must have begun abruptly and eventually disappeared gradually.   Perhaps the geologist can tell us something of the speed of the onset, and rate of the decline, of one or more of the past cold periods.

15. Locations of Continents.—The theory that throughout geologic time the continents have drifted, and still are drifting, hither and yon over the surface of the earth, becoming glaciated when near the poles and hot and humid when across the equator, was first clearly stated by F. B. Taylor and later elaborately discussed by Alfred Wegener, whose name it now commonly bears.   At first thought this may seem to be an acceptable explanation of all great climatic changes, but, since the known climates of the past can be plausibly explained without invoking this radical assumption and since no force adequate to effect an interdrift of the continental platforms has been found, it now generally is believed, and therefore here assumed, that no appreciable climatic change ever was so caused.

CHRONOLOGICAL RELATION OF GEOLOGICAL EVENTS

It is rarely possible to state in terms of years, even approximately, when any prehistoric geological event occurred or, similarly, to measure its duration, but it is possible, in large measure, accurately to decipher the order of their occurrence and to learn their chronological relations to each other.

Our present knowledge of geological chronology has been summarized by several geologists—Schuchert in his "Climates of Geologic Time,"[1] for instance—all of whom, though differing in details, have much in common. In the course of his summary Schuchert[2] says:

The data at hand show that the earth since the beginning of geologic history has periodically undergone more or less widespread glaciation, and that the cold climates have been of short geologic duration. So far as known, there were seven periods of decided temperature changes, and of these at least four were glacial climates. The greatest intensity of these reduced temperatures varied between the hemispheres, for in earliest Proterozoic and Pleistocene time it lay in the northern, while in late Proterozoic and Permic time it was more equatorial than boreal. The three other probable periods of cooled climates are as yet too little known to make out their centers of greatest intensity.

Of the four more or less well-determined glacial periods, at least three (the earliest Proterozoic, Permic, and Pleistocene) occurred during or directly after times of intensive mountain making, while the fourth (late Proterozoic) apparently also followed a period of elevation. The Table Mountain tillites of South Africa, if correctly correlated, fall in with the time of the making of the great Caledonian Mountains in the northern hemisphere. On the other hand, the very marked and world wide mountain-making period, with decided volcanic activity, during late Mesozoic and earliest Eocene times, was not accompanied by a glacial climate, but only a cooled one. The cooled period of the Liassic also followed a mountain-making period, that of late Triassic time. We may, therefore, state that cooled and cold climates, as a rule, occur during or immediately follow periods of marked mountain-making—a conclusion also arrived at, independently, by Ramsay.[3]

From the above, with which most geologists are in accord, it appears that neither cold nor even cool climates ever occurred except when mountains were either building or at least geologically young, and, also, so far as may be judged from the Strand line of North America, when the ratio of land area to ocean was relatively large. This coincidence appears to have occurred too frequently to admit of the idea that it was mere chance or due to anything less than some sort of causal relation— surely not that the cold climates produced the mountains, nor necessarily that mountain building was wholly responsible for glaciation, but rather that crustal uplift and the other geological phenomena, whatever they were, that went with it, so combined as to produce, at one time a small, and at another a great, climatic change. If, also, as supported by geological evidence, vulcanism (only violently explosive volcanoes are of especial

---

[1] Carnegie Institution of Washington, *Publication* 192, p. 285, 1914.

[2] *Loc. cit.*, p. 286.

[3] "Oversigt af Finska Vet.-Soc. Forhandl.," **52**; 1–48, 1910.

climatological importance), was, in general, most active during the epochs of mountain building, but unequally so for different mountain systems, then it follows that at each of these particular times there obtained to a greater or less degree precisely those formations and conditions—high mountains, extensive land area, restricted oceanic circulation and much volcanic dust—which are known to be effective to-day in reducing temperature, and which, presumably, are entirely sufficient, when properly cooperating, to produce not only a cool climate, such as, relatively speaking, now prevails, but even climates that are severely glacial. Which of these several causes was most effective in producing the low temperatures of any given age in the past (they must have been unequally active at different epochs) it may be impossible to determine.

But, whatever else geologic chronology, as it is now understood, may teach in regard to the climatic changes of the past, the practical coincidence of cold ages with mountain-building epochs appears at once, and irretrievably, to negative the entire group of cosmical ice-age theories— those that assume all great climatic changes to depend upon the sun, a condition in space, or anything else wholly outside the earth. Such theories, any solar theory, for instance, must also assume that those external changes, solar changes, say, which caused a marked lowering of terrestrial temperatures, occurred only at or about the times of mountain building. That is, they must assume that either (a) the solar changes caused the mountain building, or (b) that mountain building caused the solar changes, or, finally (c) that both had some unknown but simultaneously acting common cause. But each of these assumptions is wholly untenable—it has no support whatever in the logic of cause and effect—and, therefore, it seems that any theory that implicitly, or otherwise, is definitely hung on the horns of this dilemma, as is every cosmical ice-age theory, nebular, or what not, must itself be abandoned.

This is not intended in the least to deny, or even to question, the existence of small solar changes of comparatively short duration, but only to emphasize the fact that forces within the earth itself suffice to modify its own climate, and that there is much, and accumulating, evidence that these, and these alone, have actually caused great changes, time and again, in the geologic past; done so by building mountains, and by tearing them down; by emerging continents, and by submerging them; by restricting ocean currents, and by making wide their paths; by filling the atmosphere with volcanic dust, and by clearing it up; and by every possible combination of these, and other such phenomena.

CONCLUSION

It appears from various considerations that, with a constant or nearly constant output of solar energy, the earth itself possesses the inherent ability to modify profoundly its own climates, whether only local or world wide. Thus, a mere change in land elevation, whether of plateau or of mountain range, a thing that appears often to have happened, must alter both the local and the leeward climates, and, by reducing the general humidity, somewhat lower the average temperature. Besides, a change in land elevation of any considerable extent is pretty certain to be accompanied by a somewhat corresponding variation in continental area, and such modification of shore lines and ocean beds that greater or less changes must follow in the directions, temperatures, and magnitudes of ocean currents, in the location and intensity of permanent "highs" and permanent "lows," in the direction, force and temperature of local winds, in the amount and kind of local precipitation, and in a host of other meteorological phenomena.

Again, as the laws of radiation truly indicate, and as observations, at least back to 1750, the date of the earliest reliable records, show, the temperature of the lower atmosphere depends, in part, upon the amount of dust in the upper air, in the sense that when this amount is great the average temperature at the surface of the earth is below normal, and when the dust is absent this temperature is comparatively high. Hence, as there appear to have been several periods of great volcanic activity in the past with intervening periods of volcanic quiescence, it is inferred that volcanic dust in the upper atmosphere was at least one important factor in some, if not all, of the great and universal climatic changes that have left their records in abandoned beaches and forsaken moraines.

How these various causes of climatic changes were related to each other, during the geologic past, is not yet entirely clear. This the geologist, most interested and most competent to judge, must determine. May it be that extensive upheavals and great volcanic activity often were synchronous? If so, the climatic effects of each, obviously, were added to those of the other, and, hence, it may be that the greatest of our past climatic changes were caused by the roughly synchronous variations in continental level and volcanic activity; universal cold periods coming with increase in vulcanism, increase in elevation and the obstruction of interzonal oceanic circulation; universal mild periods when volcanic dust seldom veiled the skies, when the continents had sunk or been eroded to low levels and when there was great freedom of oceanic circulation from equatorial to polar regions; mild universal climatic oscillations with temporary changes in vulcanism; and mere local climatic changes with variations in such local climatic controls as nearby elevations and neighboring ocean currents. Finally, as the past is the pledge of the future, it is but reasonable to suppose that the world is yet to know many another climatic change, in an irregular but well nigh endless series, often local and usually slight, though always important, but occasionally, it may be, as in the ages gone—whether towards the auspiciously genial or into the fatefully disastrous—universal, profound, and momentous.

APPENDIX I

GRADIENT WIND VELOCITY TABLES

To be used only in the absence of local disturbances—thunderstorms, line squalls, and the like—or strong horizontal temperature gradients, and when the isobars, as drawn, are free from any considerable reduction or other errors. Also to be used with discretion in the case of east winds in the middle latitudes, since at an altitude of 1 kilometer or more their actual velocities are likely to be less than the computed, as explained on page 115.

To find from the following tables the probable wind velocity at $\frac{1}{2}$ kilometer, elevation over any given place, one notes (a) the current system of winds, cyclonic or anticyclonic, at that place (this determines which table to use); (b) the latitude of the place in question (this determines the latitude division of the table in which the desired value is to be found); (c) the pressure gradient shown on the concurrent weather map in terms of the difference of the barometer reading in millimeters per 100 kilometers at right angles to the nearest isobar (this, through the closest tabulated gradient, locates the gradient division of the value sought); and, finally, (d) the radius of curvature, in kilometers, of this isobar (a sufficiently close practical value of r) at the place in question, on line with which the desired velocity is given in meters per second, kilometers per hour, and miles per hour. The wind at the given level is roughly parallel to the corresponding surface isobar, and so directed that on following it one will have the lower pressure to his left.

In using these tables in conjunction with weather maps whose barometric interval is 0.1 inch the interval used in the United States, it is only necessary in taking step c to note the number of miles between the 0.1 inch isobars and then select from the second expressions in the first columns the nearest to an equal gradient.

The actual gradient, radius of curvature, density, and latitude usually will all differ somewhat from the tabulated values, but as the latter, except the density, which may be computed approximately, are given for small intervals it would be easy to add, with their proper signs, interpolated corrections. In practice, however, this will hardly be necessary, partly because of the great number of intervals directly supplied by the tables themselves, and partly because actual velocities and computed gradient velocities are likely to differ too much to justify minute corrections. They differ because the atmosphere never attains to a fixed or steady state of motion; because the actual density is likely to differ from that assumed; and because the gradient at the level for which computation is made is not, as a rule, exactly the same as that given on the maps.

In regions of great elevation, 1 kilometer or more, the isobaric lines, if drawn, as they commonly are, in accordance with values obtained by reduction of the barometer to sea level, may be seriously in error during both unusually warm and exceptionally cold weather. Obviously, therefore, it is not safe, at such times and places, to use the reduced distribution of isobars for the calculation of gradient winds—nor, indeed, for any other purpose.

The first line in each section of the anticyclonic table gives the maximum velocity for the given density and pressure gradient and the corresponding radius of curvature of the path. It will be noticed that this limiting radius grows smaller as the gradient is decreased, in accordance with the fact that steep gradients and strong winds can not occur near the center of an anticyclonic region.

TABLE I.—GRADIENT WIND VELOCITY FOR CYCLONIC MOVEMENT

(Computed for $\rho = 0.0011$, a density that obtains at an elevation of about 1 kilometer above sea level)

$\dfrac{\varDelta B(mm.)}{100\ km.}$ = barometric gradient, or difference of barometric reading in millimeters per

$$100\ \text{kilometers at right angles to isobars} = \frac{\varDelta B(\text{tenths } in.)}{158\ mi.}.$$

r = radius of curvature of isobars in kilometers.

$V\dfrac{m}{s}$ = velocity in meters per second.

$V\dfrac{km}{hr}$ = velocity in kilometers per hour.

$V\dfrac{mi}{hr}$ = velocity in miles per hour.

Latitude 25°

$\dfrac{\varDelta B(mm.)}{100\ km.}$	r	$V\dfrac{m}{s}$	$V\dfrac{km}{hr}$	$V\dfrac{mi}{hr}$	$\dfrac{\varDelta B(mm.)}{100\ km.}$	r	$V\dfrac{m}{s}$	$V\dfrac{km}{hr}$	$V\dfrac{mi}{hr}$
$\dfrac{0.2\ mm.}{100\ km.} = \dfrac{0.1\ in.}{789\ mi.}$	100	2.73	9.83	6.11	$\dfrac{0.6\ mm.}{100\ km.} = \dfrac{0.1\ in.}{263\ mi.}$	100	5.99	21.56	13.40
	200	3.13	11.27	7.00		200	7.38	26.57	16.51
	300	3.33	11.99	7.45		300	8.18	29.45	18.30
	400	3.45	12.42	7.72		400	8.71	31.36	19.49
	500	3.53	12.71	7.90		500	9.10	32.76	20.36
	600	3.58	12.89	8.01		600	9.40	33.84	21.03
	700	3.63	13.07	8.12		700	9.64	34.70	21.56
	800	3.66	13.18	8.19		800	9.83	35.39	21.99
	900	3.69	13.28	8.25		900	9.99	35.96	22.34
	1000	3.71	13.36	8.30		1000	10.13	36.47	22.66
	1200	3.74	13.46	8.36		1200	10.35	37.26	23.15
	1500	3.78	13.61	8.46		1500	10.58	38.09	23.67
	2000	3.81	13.72	8.53		2000	10.84	39.02	24.25
	3000	3.85	13.86	8.61		3000	11.12	40.03	24.87
	∞	3.93	14.15	8.79		∞	11.79	42.44	26.37
$\dfrac{0.4mm.}{100\ km.} = \dfrac{0.1\ in.}{395\ mi.}$	100	4.53	16.31	10.13	$\dfrac{0.8mm.}{100\ km.} = \dfrac{0.1\ in.}{197\ mi.}$	100	7.24	26.06	16.19
	200	5.45	19.62	12.19		200	9.06	32.62	20.27
	300	5.95	21.42	13.31		300	10.15	36.54	22.70
	400	6.27	22.57	14.02		400	10.90	39.24	24.38
	500	6.49	23.36	14.52		500	11.46	41.26	25.64
	600	6.66	23.98	14.90		600	11.90	42.84	26.62
	700	6.79	24.44	15.19		700	12.25	44.10	27.40
	800	6.90	24.84	15.43		800	12.54	45.14	28.05
	900	6.98	25.13	15.62		900	12.78	46.01	28.59
	1000	7.05	25.38	15.77		1000	12.99	46.76	29.05
	1200	7.17	25.81	16.04		1200	13.32	47.95	29.79
	1500	7.29	26.24	16.30		1500	13.69	49.28	30.62
	2000	7.42	26.71	16.60		2000	14.11	50.80	31.57
	3000	7.55	27.18	16.89		3000	14.58	52.49	32.62
	∞	7.86	28.30	17.58		∞	15.72	56.59	35.16

Latitude 25° (*Continued*)

$\dfrac{\Delta B(mm.)}{100\ km.}$	r	$V\dfrac{m}{s}$	$V\dfrac{km}{hr}$	$V\dfrac{mi}{hr}$	$\dfrac{\Delta B(mm.)}{100\ km.}$	r	$V\dfrac{m}{s}$	$V\dfrac{km}{hr}$	$V\dfrac{mi}{hr}$
$\dfrac{1.0\ mm.}{100\ km.}=$	100	8.35	30.06	18.68	$\dfrac{2.5\ mm.}{100\ km.}=$	100	14.59	52.52	32.63
	200	10.58	38.09	23.67		200	19.21	69.16	42.97
$\dfrac{0.1\ in.}{158\ mi.}$	300	11.94	42.98	26.71	$\dfrac{0.1\ in.}{63\ mi.}$	300	22.28	80.21	49.84
	400	12.90	46.44	28.86		400	24.60	88.56	55.03
	500	13.63	49.07	30.49		500	26.44	95.18	59.14
	600	14.20	51.12	31.76		600	27.97	100.69	62.57
	700	14.67	52.81	32.81		700	29.27	105.37	65.47
	800	15.06	54.22	33.69		800	30.40	109.44	68.00
	900	15.39	55.40	34.42		900	31.38	112.97	70.20
	1000	15.67	56.41	35.05		1000	32.26	116.14	72.17
	1200	16.13	58.07	36.08		1200	33.74	121.46	75.47
	1500	16.65	59.94	37.25		1500	35.50	127.80	79.41
	2000	17.24	62.06	38.56		2000	37.64	135.50	84.20
	3000	17.92	64.51	40.08		3000	40.34	145.22	90.24
	∞	19.65	70.74	43.96		∞	49.13	176.87	109.90
$\dfrac{1.5\ mm.}{100\ km.}=$	100	10.75	38.70	24.05	$\dfrac{3.0\ mm.}{100\ km.}=$	100	16.23	58.43	36.31
	200	13.87	49.93	31.03		200	21.49	77.36	48.07
$\dfrac{0.1\ in.}{105\ mi.}$	300	15.87	57.13	35.50	$\dfrac{0.1\ in.}{53\ mi.}$	300	25.04	90.14	56.01
	400	17.32	62.35	38.74		400	27.74	99.86	62.19
	500	18.44	66.38	41.23		500	29.92	107.71	66.93
	600	19.35	69.66	43.28		600	31.73	114.23	70.98
	700	20.11	72.40	44.90		700	33.28	119.81	74.45
	800	20.75	74.70	46.42		800	34.64	124.70	77.49
	900	21.30	76.68	47.65		900	35.83	128.99	80.15
	1000	21.78	78.41	48.72		1000	36.89	132.80	82.52
	1200	22.59	81.32	50.53		1200	38.71	139.36	86.59
	1500	23.50	84.60	52.57		1500	40.88	147.17	91.45
	2000	24.58	88.49	54.99		2000	43.56	156.82	97.44
	3000	25.87	93.13	57.87		3000	47.01	169.24	105.16
	∞	29.48	106.13	65.95		∞	58.96	212.26	131.90
$\dfrac{2.0\ mm.}{100\ km.}=$	100	12.79	46.04	28.61	$\dfrac{4.0\ mm.}{100\ km.}=$	100	19.15	68.94	42.84
	200	16.70	60.12	37.36		200	25.57	92.05	57.20
$\dfrac{0.1\ in.}{79\ mi.}$	300	19.26	69.34	43.09	$\dfrac{0.1\ in.}{39\ mi.}$	300	29.99	107.96	67.08
	400	21.16	76.18	47.34		400	33.39	120.20	74.69
	500	22.65	81.54	50.67		500	36.17	130.21	80.91
	600	23.88	85.97	53.42		600	38.51	138.64	86.15
	700	24.92	89.71	55.74		700	40.53	145.91	90.67
	800	25.80	92.88	57.71		800	42.31	152.32	94.65
	900	26.58	95.69	59.46		900	43.89	158.00	98.18
	1000	27.26	98.14	60.98		1000	45.31	163.12	101.36
	1200	28.40	102.24	63.53		1200	47.77	171.97	106.86
	1500	29.74	107.06	66.52		1500	50.75	182.70	113.52
	2000	31.34	112.82	70.10		2000	54.51	196.24	121.94
	3000	33.31	119.92	74.52		3000	59.48	214.13	133.05
	∞	39.31	141.52	87.94		∞	78.61	283.00	175.85

Latitude 30°

$\dfrac{\Delta B(mm.)}{100\ km.}$	r	$V\dfrac{m}{s}$	$V\dfrac{km}{hr}$	$V\dfrac{mi}{hr}$	$\dfrac{\Delta B(mm.)}{100\ km.}$	r	$V\dfrac{m}{s}$	$V\dfrac{km}{hr}$	$V\dfrac{mi}{hr}$
$\dfrac{0.2\ mm.}{100\ km.}=$ $\dfrac{0.1\ in.}{789\ mi.}$	100	2.48	8.93	5.55	$\dfrac{0.8\ mm.}{100\ km.}=$ $\dfrac{0.1\ in.}{197\ mi.}$	100	6.86	24.70	15.35
	200	2.79	10.04	6.24		200	8.43	30.35	18.86
	300	2.93	10.55	6.56		300	9.32	33.55	20.85
	400	3.01	10.84	6.74		400	9.92	35.71	22.19
	500	3.07	11.05	6.87		500	10.35	37.26	23.15
	600	3.10	11.16	6.93		600	10.68	38.45	23.89
	700	3.13	11.27	7.00		700	10.94	39.38	24.47
	800	3.15	11.34	7.05		800	11.16	40.18	24.97
	900	3.17	11.41	7.09		900	11.33	40.79	25.35
	1000	3.19	11.48	7.13		1000	11.48	41.33	25.68
	1200	3.21	11.56	7.18		1200	11.72	42.19	26.22
	1500	3.23	11.63	7.23		1500	11.98	43.13	26.80
	2000	3.25	11.70	7.27		2000	12.26	44.14	27.43
	3000	3.28	11.81	7.34		3000	12.57	45.25	28.11
	∞	3.32	11.95	7.43		∞	13.29	47.84	29.73
$\dfrac{0.4\ mm.}{100\ km.}=$ $\dfrac{0.1\ in.}{395\ mi.}$	100	4.22	15.19	9.44	$\dfrac{1.0\ mm.}{100\ km.}=$ $\dfrac{0.1\ in.}{158\ mi.}$	100	7.95	28.62	17.78
	200	4.96	17.86	11.10		200	9.90	35.64	22.15
	300	5.34	19.22	11.94		300	11.04	39.74	24.69
	400	5.58	20.09	12.48		400	11.82	42.55	26.44
	500	5.74	20.66	12.84		500	12.40	44.64	27.74
	600	5.86	21.10	13.11		600	12.84	46.22	28.72
	700	5.95	21.42	13.31		700	13.20	47.52	29.53
	800	6.02	21.67	13.47		800	13.49	48.56	30.17
	900	6.08	21.89	13.60		900	13.74	49.46	30.73
	1000	6.13	22.07	13.71		1000	13.95	50.22	31.21
	1200	6.21	22.36	13.89		1200	14.28	51.41	31.95
	1500	6.28	22.61	14.05		1500	14.65	52.74	32.77
	2000	6.37	22.93	14.25		2000	15.06	54.22	33.69
	3000	6.56	23.62	14.68		3000	15.51	55.84	34.70
	∞	6.64	23.90	14.85		∞	16.61	59.80	37.16
$\dfrac{0.6\ mm.}{100\ km.}=$ $\dfrac{0.1\ in.}{263\ mi.}$	100	5.63	20.27	12.60	$\dfrac{1.5\ mm.}{100\ km.}=$ $\dfrac{0.1\ in.}{105\ mi.}$	100	10.32	37.15	23.08
	200	6.80	24.48	15.21		200	13.12	47.23	29.35
	300	7.44	26.78	16.64		300	14.85	53.46	33.22
	400	7.85	28.26	17.56		400	16.07	57.85	35.95
	500	8.15	29.34	18.23		500	17.00	61.20	38.03
	600	8.37	30.13	18.72		600	17.73	63.83	39.66
	700	8.54	30.74	19.10		700	18.33	65.99	41.00
	800	8.68	31.25	19.42		800	18.84	67.82	42.14
	900	8.79	31.64	19.66		900	19.27	69.37	43.10
	1000	8.89	32.00	19.88		1000	19.63	70.67	43.91
	1200	9.04	32.54	20.22		1200	20.24	72.86	45.27
	1500	9.20	33.12	20.58		1500	20.92	75.31	46.80
	2000	9.37	33.73	20.96		2000	21.69	78.08	48.52
	3000	9.55	34.38	21.36		3000	22.58	81.29	50.51
	∞	9.97	35.89	22.30		∞	24.92	89.71	55.74

Latitude 30° (Continued)

$\dfrac{\Delta B(mm.)}{100\ km.}$	r	$V\dfrac{m}{s}$	$V\dfrac{km}{hr}$	$V\dfrac{mi}{hr}$	$\dfrac{\Delta B(mm.)}{100\ km.}$	r	$V\dfrac{m}{s}$	$V\dfrac{km}{hr}$	$V\dfrac{mi}{hr}$
$\dfrac{2.0\ mm.}{100\ km.}=$ $\dfrac{0.1\ in.}{79\ mi.}$	100	12.34	44.42	27.60	$\dfrac{3.0\ mm.}{100\ km.}=$ $\dfrac{0.1\ in.}{53\ mi.}$	100	15.77	56.77	35.27
	200	15.90	57.24	35.57		200	20.64	74.30	46.17
	300	18.16	65.38	40.62		300	23.85	85.86	53.35
	400	19.79	71.24	44.27		400	26.24	94.46	58.70
	500	21.06	75.82	47.11		500	28.13	101.27	62.93
	600	22.08	79.49	49.39		600	29.85	107.46	66.77
	700	22.93	82.55	51.29		700	31.00	111.60	69.34
	800	23.64	85.10	52.88		800	32.14	115.70	71.89
	900	24.26	87.34	54.27		900	33.12	119.23	74.09
	1000	24.79	89.24	55.45		1000	33.99	122.36	76.03
	1200	25.68	92.45	57.45		1200	35.46	127.66	79.32
	1500	26.71	96.16	59.75		1500	37.19	133.88	83.19
	2000	27.89	100.40	62.39		2000	39.27	141.37	87.84
	3000	29.30	105.48	65.54		3000	41.84	150.62	93.59
	∞	33.22	119.59	74.31		∞	49.84	179.42	111.49
$\dfrac{2.5\ mm.}{100\ km.}=$ $\dfrac{0.1\ in.}{63\ mi.}$	100	14.14	50.90	31.63	$\dfrac{4.0\ mm.}{100\ km.}=$ $\dfrac{0.1\ in.}{39\ mi.}$	100	18.67	67.21	41.76
	200	18.38	66.17	41.12		200	24.68	88.85	55.21
	300	21.13	76.97	47.27		300	28.73	103.43	64.27
	400	23.15	83.34	51.78		400	31.88	114.77	71.32
	500	24.74	89.06	55.34		500	34.26	123.34	76.64
	600	26.05	93.78	58.27		600	36.31	130.72	81.23
	700	27.12	97.63	60.66		700	38.06	137.02	85.14
	800	28.05	100.98	62.75		800	39.59	142.52	88.56
	900	28.85	103.86	64.54		900	40.93	147.35	91.56
	1000	29.55	106.38	66.10		1000	42.12	151.63	94.22
	1200	30.74	110.44	68.63		1200	44.16	158.98	98.79
	1500	32.11	115.60	71.83		1500	46.48	167.33	103.98
	2000	33.73	121.43	75.45		2000	49.59	178.52	110.93
	3000	35.70	128.52	79.86		3000	53.41	192.28	119.48
	∞	41.53	149.51	92.90		∞	66.45	239.22	148.64

Latitude 35°

$\dfrac{\Delta B(mm.)}{100\ km.}$	r	$V\dfrac{m}{s}$	$V\dfrac{km}{hr}$	$V\dfrac{mi}{hr}$	$\dfrac{\Delta B(mm.)}{100\ km.}$	r	$V\dfrac{m}{s}$	$V\dfrac{km}{hr}$	$V\dfrac{mi}{hr}$
$\dfrac{0.2\ mm.}{100\ km.}=$ $\dfrac{0.1\ in.}{789\ mi.}$	100	2.28	8.21	5.10	$\dfrac{0.4\ mm.}{100\ km.}=$ $\dfrac{0.1\ in.}{395\ mi.}$	100	3.94	14.18	8.81
	200	2.52	9.07	5.64		200	4.55	16.38	10.18
	300	2.62	9.43	5.86		300	4.85	17.46	10.85
	400	2.68	9.65	6.00		400	5.04	18.14	11.27
	500	2.72	9.79	6.08		500	5.16	18.58	11.55
	600	2.75	9.90	6.15		600	5.24	18.86	11.72
	700	2.77	9.97	6.20		700	5.31	19.12	11.88
	800	2.78	10.01	6.22		800	5.36	19.30	11.99
	900	2.79	10.04	6.24		900	5.41	19.48	12.10
	1000	2.80	10.08	6.26		1000	5.44	19.58	12.17
	1200	2.82	10.15	6.31		1200	5.49	19.76	12.28
	1500	2.83	10.19	6.33		1500	5.55	19.98	12.42
	2000	2.85	10.26	6.38		2000	5.61	20.20	12.55
	3000	2.86	10.30	6.40		3000	5.67	20.41	12.68
	∞	2.90	10.44	6.49		∞	5.79	20.84	12.95

Latitude 35° (*Continued*)

$\frac{\Delta B(mm.)}{100\ km.}$	r	$V\frac{m}{s}$	$V\frac{km}{hr}$	$V\frac{mi}{hr}$	$\frac{\Delta B(mm.)}{100\ km.}$	r	$V\frac{m}{s}$	$V\frac{km}{hr}$	$V\frac{mi}{hr}$
$\frac{0.6\ mm.}{100\ km.}=$ $\frac{0.1\ in.}{263\ mi.}$	100	5.32	19.15	11.90	$\frac{1.5\ mm.}{100\ km.}=$ $\frac{0.1\ in.}{105\ mi.}$	100	9.93	35.75	22.21
	200	6.31	22.72	14.12		200	12.45	44.82	27.85
	300	6.83	24.59	15.28		300	13.95	50.22	31.21
	400	7.16	25.78	16.02		400	15.00	54.00	33.55
	500	7.39	26.60	16.53		500	15.77	56.77	35.28
	600	7.55	27.18	16.89		600	16.38	58.97	36.64
	700	7.68	27.65	17.18		700	16.87	60.73	37.74
	800	7.78	28.01	17.40		800	17.28	62.21	38.66
	900	7.87	28.33	17.60		900	17.61	63.40	39.39
	1000	7.94	28.58	17.76		1000	17.90	64.44	40.04
	1200	8.04	28.94	17.98		1200	18.36	66.10	41.07
	1500	8.16	29.38	18.26		1500	18.88	67.97	42.24
	2000	8.28	29.81	18.52		2000	19.46	70.06	43.53
	3000	8.41	30.28	18.82		3000	20.11	72.40	44.99
	∞	8.69	31.28	19.48		∞	21.72	78.19	48.58
$\frac{0.8\ mm.}{100\ km.}=$ $\frac{0.1\ in.}{197\ mi.}$	100	6.51	23.44	14.57	$\frac{2.0\ mm.}{100\ km.}=$ $\frac{0.1\ in.}{79\ mi.}$	100	11.93	42.95	26.69
	200	7.88	28.37	17.63		200	15.18	54.65	33.96
	300	8.62	31.03	19.28		300	17.19	61.88	38.45
	400	9.11	32.80	20.38		400	18.61	67.00	41.63
	500	9.45	34.02	21.14		500	19.69	70.88	44.04
	600	9.71	34.96	21.72		600	20.55	73.98	45.97
	700	9.91	35.68	22.17		700	21.25	76.50	47.53
	800	10.07	36.25	22.52		800	21.84	78.62	48.85
	900	10.20	36.72	22.82		900	22.34	80.42	49.97
	1000	10.31	37.12	23.07		1000	22.77	81.97	50.93
	1200	10.49	37.76	23.46		1200	23.48	84.53	52.52
	1500	10.68	38.45	23.89		1500	24.27	87.37	54.29
	2000	10.88	39.17	24.34		2000	25.18	90.65	56.33
	3000	11.10	39.96	24.83		3000	26.22	94.33	58.61
	∞	11.58	41.69	25.90		∞	28.96	104.26	64.78
$\frac{1.0\ mm.}{100\ km.}=$ $\frac{0.1\ in.}{158\ mi.}$	100	7.59	27.32	16.98	$\frac{2.5\ mm.}{100\ km.}=$ $\frac{0.1\ in.}{63\ mi.}$	100	13.72	49.39	30.69
	200	9.31	33.52	20.83		200	17.63	63.47	39.44
	300	10.27	36.97	22.97		300	20.10	72.36	44.96
	400	10.92	39.31	24.43		400	21.89	78.80	48.96
	500	11.38	40.97	25.46		500	23.26	83.74	52.03
	600	11.74	42.26	26.26		600	24.37	87.73	54.51
	700	12.02	43.27	26.89		700	25.29	91.04	56.57
	800	12.24	44.06	27.38		800	26.06	93.82	58.30
	900	12.43	44.75	27.81		900	26.72	96.19	59.77
	1000	12.59	45.32	28.16		1000	27.30	98.28	61.07
	1200	12.84	46.22	28.72		1200	28.25	101.70	63.19
	1500	13.11	47.20	29.33		1500	29.34	105.62	65.63
	2000	13.41	48.28	30.00		2000	30.41	109.48	68.03
	3000	13.73	49.43	30.71		3000	32.10	115.56	71.81
	∞	14.48	52.13	32.39		∞	36.20	130.32	80.98

Latitude 35° (Continued)

$\dfrac{\Delta B(mm.)}{100\ km.}$	r	$V\dfrac{m}{s}$	$V\dfrac{km}{hr}$	$V\dfrac{mi}{hr}$	$\dfrac{\Delta B(mm.)}{100\ km.}$	r	$V\dfrac{m}{s}$	$V\dfrac{km}{hr}$	$V\dfrac{mi}{hr}$
$\dfrac{3.0\ mm.}{100\ km.}=$ $\dfrac{0.1\ in.}{53\ mi.}$	100	15.34	55.22	34.31	$\dfrac{4.0\ mm.}{100\ km.}=$ $\dfrac{0.1\ in.}{39\ mi.}$	100	18.22	65.59	40.76
	200	19.86	71.50	44.43		200	23.87	85.93	53.39
	300	22.77	81.97	50.93		300	27.59	99.32	61.71
	400	24.91	89.68	55.73		400	30.37	109.33	67.93
	500	26.57	95.65	59.43		500	32.57	117.25	72.86
	600	27.91	100.48	62.44		600	34.38	123.77	76.91
	700	29.04	104.54	64.96		700	35.91	129.28	80.33
	800	30.00	108.00	67.11		800	37.22	133.99	83.26
	900	30.82	110.95	68.94		900	38.37	138.13	85.83
	1000	31.55	113.58	70.58		1000	39.38	141.77	88.09
	1200	32.76	117.94	73.28		1200	41.10	147.96	91.94
	1500	34.15	122.94	76.39		1500	43.11	155.20	96.44
	2000	35.79	128.84	80.06		2000	45.54	163.94	101.87
	3000	37.76	135.94	84.47		3000	48.54	174.74	108.58
	∞	43.44	156.38	97.17		∞	57.92	208.51	129.56

Latitude 40°

$\dfrac{\Delta B(mm.)}{100\ km.}$	r	$V\dfrac{m}{s}$	$V\dfrac{km}{hr}$	$V\dfrac{mi}{hr}$	$\dfrac{\Delta B(mm.)}{100\ km.}$	r	$V\dfrac{m}{s}$	$V\dfrac{km}{hr}$	$V\dfrac{mi}{hr}$
$\dfrac{0.2\ mm.}{100\ km.}=$ $\dfrac{0.1\ in.}{789\ mi.}$	100	2.11	7.60	4.72	$\dfrac{0.6\ mm.}{100\ km.}=$ $\dfrac{0.1\ in.}{263\ mi.}$	100	5.04	18.14	11.26
	200	2.30	8.28	5.14		200	5.90	21.24	13.27
	300	2.38	8.57	5.33		300	6.33	22.79	14.10
	400	2.43	8.75	5.44		400	6.60	23.76	14.76
	500	2.46	8.86	5.51		500	6.78	24.41	15.17
	600	2.48	8.93	5.55		600	6.91	24.88	15.46
	700	2.49	8.96	5.57		700	7.01	25.24	15.68
	800	2.50	9.00	5.59		800	7.08	25.49	15.84
	900	2.51	9.04	5.62		900	7.15	25.74	15.99
	1000	2.52	9.07	5.63		1000	7.20	25.92	16.11
	1200	2.53	9.11	5.66		1200	7.28	26.21	16.29
	1500	2.54	9.14	5.68		1500	7.37	26.53	16.49
	2000	2.55	9.18	5.70		2000	7.46	26.86	16.69
	3000	2.56	9.22	5.73		3000	7.55	27.18	16.89
	∞	2.58	9.29	5.77		∞	7.75	27.90	17.34
$\dfrac{0.4\ mm.}{100\ km.}=$ $\dfrac{0.1\ in.}{395\ mi.}$	100	3.71	13.36	8.30	$\dfrac{0.8\ mm.}{100\ km.}=$ $\dfrac{0.1\ in.}{197\ mi.}$	100	6.23	22.43	13.94
	200	4.22	15.19	9.44		200	7.41	26.68	16.58
	300	4.46	16.06	9.98		300	8.04	28.94	17.98
	400	4.61	16.60	10.31		400	8.44	30.38	18.88
	500	4.70	16.92	10.51		500	8.72	31.39	19.50
	600	4.77	17.17	10.67		600	8.92	32.11	19.95
	700	4.82	17.35	10.75		700	9.08	32.69	20.31
	800	4.85	17.46	10.85		800	9.21	33.16	20.60
	900	4.89	17.60	10.94		900	9.31	33.52	20.83
	1000	4.91	17.68	10.99		1000	9.40	33.84	21.03
	1200	4.95	17.82	11.07		1200	9.53	34.31	21.32
	1500	4.99	17.96	11.16		1500	9.67	34.81	21.63
	2000	5.03	18.11	11.25		2000	9.82	35.35	21.97
	3000	5.08	18.29	11.36		3000	10.09	36.32	22.57
	∞	5.17	18.61	11.56		∞	10.34	37.22	23.13

Latitude 40° (*Continued*)

$\dfrac{\Delta B(mm.)}{100\ km.}$	r	$V\dfrac{m}{s}$	$V\dfrac{km}{hr}$	$V\dfrac{mi}{hr}$	$\dfrac{\Delta B(mm.)}{100\ km.}$	r	$V\dfrac{m}{s}$	$V\dfrac{km}{hr}$	$V\dfrac{mi}{hr}$
$\dfrac{1.0\ mm.}{100\ km.}=$ $\dfrac{0.1\ in.}{158\ mi.}$	100	7.28	26.21	16.29	$\dfrac{2.5\ mm.}{100\ km.}=$ $\dfrac{0.1\ in.}{63\ mi.}$	100	13.34	48.02	29.84
	200	8.80	31.68	19.69		200	16.96	61.06	37.94
	300	9.63	34.67	21.54		300	19.20	69.12	42.95
	400	10.17	36.61	22.75		400	20.79	74.84	46.50
	500	10.55	37.98	23.60		500	21.99	79.16	49.19
	600	10.83	38.99	24.23		600	22.95	82.62	51.34
	700	11.06	39.82	24.74		700	23.73	85.43	53.08
	800	11.24	40.46	25.14		800	24.38	87.77	54.54
	900	11.39	41.00	25.48		900	24.94	89.78	55.79
	1000	11.51	41.44	25.75		1000	25.42	91.51	56.86
	1200	11.71	42.16	26.20		1200	26.20	94.32	58.66
	1500	11.91	42.88	26.64		1500	27.09	97.52	60.60
	2000	12.14	43.70	27.15		2000	28.09	101.12	62.83
	3000	12.38	45.57	28.32		3000	29.26	105.34	65.45
	∞	12.92	46.51	28.90		∞	32.30	116.28	72.25
$\dfrac{1.5\ mm.}{100\ km.}=$ $\dfrac{0.1\ in.}{105\ mi.}$	100	9.60	34.56	21.47	$\dfrac{3.0\ mm.}{100\ km.}=$ $\dfrac{0.1\ in.}{53\ mi.}$	100	14.95	53.82	33.44
	200	11.87	42.73	26.55		200	19.17	69.01	42.88
	300	13.19	47.48	29.50		300	21.83	78.59	48.83
	400	14.09	50.72	31.52		400	23.74	85.46	53.10
	500	14.74	53.06	32.97		500	25.21	90.76	56.40
	600	15.25	54.90	34.11		600	26.39	95.00	59.03
	700	15.65	56.34	35.01		700	27.36	98.50	61.21
	800	15.98	57.53	35.75		800	28.18	101.45	63.04
	900	16.25	58.50	36.35		900	28.88	103.97	64.60
	1000	16.48	59.33	36.87		1000	29.49	106.16	65.96
	1200	16.86	60.70	37.72		1200	30.50	109.80	68.23
	1500	17.26	62.14	38.61		1500	31.65	113.94	70.80
	2000	17.71	63.76	39.62		2000	32.97	118.69	73.75
	3000	18.21	65.56	40.74		3000	34.50	124.20	77.17
	∞	19.38	69.77	43.35		∞	38.77	139.57	86.72
$\dfrac{2.0\ mm.}{100\ km.}=$ $\dfrac{0.1\ in.}{79\ mi.}$	100	11.57	41.65	25.88	$\dfrac{4.0\ mm.}{100\ km.}=$ $\dfrac{0.1\ in.}{39\ mi.}$	100	17.82	64.15	39.86
	200	14.55	52.38	32.55		200	23.14	83.30	51.76
	300	16.35	58.86	36.57		300	26.58	95.69	59.46
	400	17.60	63.36	39.37		400	29.11	104.80	65.12
	500	18.52	66.67	41.43		500	31.08	111.89	69.53
	600	19.26	69.34	43.09		600	32.69	117.68	73.12
	700	19.84	71.42	44.38		700	34.04	122.54	76.14
	800	20.33	73.19	45.48		800	35.18	126.65	78.70
	900	20.74	74.66	46.39		900	36.18	130.25	80.93
	1000	21.10	75.96	47.20		1000	37.05	133.38	82.88
	1200	21.67	78.01	48.47		1200	38.50	138.60	86.12
	1500	22.31	80.32	49.91		1500	40.20	144.72	89.93
	2000	23.02	82.87	51.49		2000	42.19	151.88	94.37
	3000	23.83	85.79	53.31		3000	44.60	160.56	99.86
	∞	25.84	93.02	57.80		∞	51.69	186.08	115.62

Latitude 45°

$\dfrac{\Delta B(mm.)}{100\ km.}$	r	$V\dfrac{m}{s}$	$V\dfrac{km}{hr}$	$V\dfrac{mi}{hr}$	$\dfrac{\Delta B(mm.)}{100\ km.}$	r	$V\dfrac{m}{s}$	$V\dfrac{km}{hr}$	$V\dfrac{mi}{hr}$
$\dfrac{0.2\ mm.}{100\ km.} =$ 0.1 $in.$ 789 $mi.$	100	1.97	7.09	4.41	$\dfrac{0.8\ mm.}{100\ km.} =$ 0.1 $in.$ 197 $mi.$	100	5.96	21.46	12.87
	200	2.13	7.67	4.77		200	7.01	25.24	15.68
	300	2.19	7.88	4.90		300	7.55	27.18	16.89
	400	2.23	8.03	4.99		400	7.89	28.40	17.42
	500	2.25	8.10	5.03		500	8.12	29.23	18.16
	600	2.27	8.17	5.08		600	8.29	29.84	18.54
	700	2.28	8.21	5.10		700	8.42	30.31	18.83
	800	2.29	8.24	5.12		800	8.52	30.67	19.06
	900	2.29	8.24	5.12		900	8.60	30.96	19.24
	1000	2.30	8.28	5.14		1000	8.67	31.21	19.39
	1200	2.31	8.32	5.17		1200	8.78	31.61	19.64
	1500	2.32	8.35	5.19		1500	8.89	32.00	19.84
	2000	2.33	8.39	5.21		2000	9.01	32.44	20.16
	3000	2.33	8.39	5.21		3000	9.14	32.90	20.44
	∞	2.35	8.46	5.26		∞	9.40	33.84	21.03
$\dfrac{0.4\ mm.}{100\ km.} =$ 0.1 $in.$ 395 $mi.$	100	3.52	12.67	7.87	$\dfrac{1.0\ mm.}{100\ km.} =$ 0.1 $in.$ 158 $mi.$	100	7.40	26.64	16.55
	200	3.94	14.18	8.81		200	8.36	30.10	18.70
	300	4.14	14.90	9.26		300	9.08	32.69	20.31
	400	4.26	15.34	9.53		400	9.54	34.34	21.34
	500	4.33	15.59	9.69		500	9.86	35.50	22.06
	600	4.39	15.80	9.82		600	10.10	36.36	22 59
	700	4.43	15.95	9.91		700	10.28	37.01	23.00
	800	4.46	16.06	9.98		800	10.43	37.55	23.33
	900	4.49	16.16	10.04		900	10.55	37.98	23.60
	1000	4.50	16.20	10.07		1000	10.65	38.34	23.82
	1200	4.53	16.31	10.13		1200	10.80	38.88	24.16
	1500	4.56	16.42	10.20		1500	10.97	39.49	24.54
	2000	4.60	16.56	10.29		2000	11.15	40.14	24.94
	3000	4.63	16.57	10.36		3000	11.33	40.79	25.35
	∞	4.70	16.92	10.51		∞	11.75	42.30	26.28
$\dfrac{0.6\ mm.}{100\ km.} =$ 0.1 $in.$ 263 $mi.$	100	4.81	17.32	10.76	$\dfrac{1.5\ mm.}{100\ km.} =$ 0.1 $in.$ 105 $mi.$	100	9.28	33.41	20.72
	200	5.55	19.98	12.42		200	11.36	40.90	25.41
	300	5.92	21.31	13.24		300	12.54	45.14	28.05
	400	6.13	22.07	13.71		400	13.32	47.95	29.79
	500	6.28	22.61	14.05		500	13.88	49.97	31.05
	600	6.39	23.00	14.29		600	14.31	51.52	32.01
	700	6.47	23.29	14.47		700	14.65	52.74	32.77
	800	6.53	23.51	14.61		800	14.92	53.71	33.37
	900	6.58	23.69	14.72		900	15.15	54.54	33.89
	1000	6.62	23.83	14.81		1000	15.34	55.22	34.31
	1200	6.69	24.08	14.96		1200	15.64	56.30	34.98
	1500	6.75	24.30	15.10		1500	15.97	57.49	35.72
	2000	6.82	24.55	15.25		2000	16.33	58.79	36.53
	3000	6.90	24.84	15.43		3000	16.72	60.19	37.40
	∞	7.05	25.38	15.77		∞	17.62	63.43	39.41

Latitude 45° (*Continued*)

$\dfrac{\Delta B(mm.)}{100\ km.}$	r	$V\dfrac{m}{s}$	$V\dfrac{km}{hr}$	$V\dfrac{mi}{hr}$	$\dfrac{\Delta B(mm.)}{100\ km.}$	r	$V\dfrac{m}{s}$	$V\dfrac{km}{hr}$	$V\dfrac{mi}{hr}$
2.0 *mm.* $\dfrac{}{}$ = 100 *km.* 0.1 *in.* 79 *mi.*	100	11.24	40.46	25.14	3.0 *mm.* $\dfrac{}{}$ = 100 *km.* 0.1 *in.* 53 *mi.*	100	14.59	52.52	32.63
	200	14.00	50.40	31.32		200	18.55	66.78	41.50
	300	15.61	56.20	34.92		300	21.00	75.60	46.98
	400	16.72	60.19	37.40		400	22.72	81.79	50.82
	500	17.53	63.11	39.21		500	24.04	86.54	53.77
	600	18.16	65.38	40.62		600	25.08	90.29	56.10
	700	18.67	67.21	41.76		700	25.93	93.35	58.00
	800	19.08	68.69	42.68		800	26.64	95.90	59.59
	900	19.43	69.95	43.47		900	27.24	98.06	60.93
	1000	19.72	70.99	44.11		1000	27.77	99.97	62.12
	1200	20.20	72.72	45.23		1200	28.62	103.03	64.02
	1500	20.72	74.59	46.35		1500	29.58	106.49	66.17
	2000	21.30	76.68	46.78		2000	30.68	110.45	68.63
	3000	21.94	78.98	49.08		3000	31.94	114.98	71.45
	∞	23.49	84.56	52.54		∞	35.24	126.86	78.83
2.5 *mm.* $\dfrac{}{}$ = 100 *km.* 0.1 *in.* 63 *mi.*	100	12.99	46.76	29.05	4.0 *mm.* $\dfrac{}{}$ = 100 *km.* 0.1 *in.* 39 *mi.*	100	17.45	62.82	39.03
	200	16.37	58.93	36.62		200	22.48	80.93	50.29
	300	18.41	66.28	41.18		300	25.68	92.45	57.45
	400	19.83	71.37	44.35		400	27.99	100.76	62.61
	500	20.90	75.24	46.75		500	29.78	107.21	66.62
	600	21.74	78.26	48.63		600	31.23	112.43	69.86
	700	22.41	80.68	50.13		700	32.42	116.71	72.52
	800	22.97	82.69	51.38		800	33.44	120.38	74.80
	900	23.44	84.38	52.43		900	34.31	123.52	76.75
	1000	23.85	85.86	53.35		1000	35.06	126.22	78.43
	1200	24.51	88.24	54.83		1200	36.32	130.75	81.25
	1500	25.25	90.90	56.48		1500	37.77	135.97	84.49
	2000	26.07	93.85	58.32		2000	39.45	142.02	88.25
	3000	27.01	97.24	60.42		3000	41.43	149.15	92.68
	∞	29.37	105.73	65.70		∞	46.99	169.16	105.11

Latitude 50°

$\dfrac{\Delta B(mm.)}{100\ km.}$	r	$V\dfrac{m}{s}$	$V\dfrac{km}{hr}$	$V\dfrac{mi}{hr}$	$\dfrac{\Delta B(mm.)}{100\ km.}$	r	$V\dfrac{m}{s}$	$V\dfrac{km}{hr}$	$V\dfrac{mi}{hr}$
0.2 *mm.* $\dfrac{}{}$ = 100 *km.* 0.1 *in.* 789 *mi.*	100	1.86	6.70	4.16	0.4 *mm.* $\dfrac{}{}$ = 100 *km.* 0.1 *in.* 395 *mi.*	100	3.34	12.02	7.47
	200	1.99	7.16	4.45		200	3.72	13.39	8.32
	300	2.04	7.34	4.56		300	3.89	14.00	8.70
	400	2.07	7.45	4.63		400	3.98	14.33	8.90
	500	2.09	7.52	4.67		500	4.04	14.54	9.04
	600	2.10	7.56	4.70		600	4.09	14.72	9.15
	700	2.11	7.60	4.72		700	4.12	14.83	9.22
	800	2.12	7.63	4.74		800	4.15	14.94	9.28
	900	2.13	7.67	4.77		900	4.17	15.01	9.33
	1000	2.13	7.67	4.77		1000	4.18	15.05	9.35
	1200	2.14	7.70	4.79		1200	4.21	15.16	9.42
	1500	2.14	7.70	4.79		1500	4.23	15.23	9.46
	2000	2.15	7.74	4.81		2000	4.26	15.34	9.53
	3000	2.15	7.74	4.81		3000	4.28	15.41	9.59
	∞	2.17	7.81	4.85		∞	4.34	15.62	9.71

Latitude 50° (Continued)

$\dfrac{\Delta B(mm.)}{100\ km.}$	r	$V\dfrac{m}{s}$	$V\dfrac{km}{hr}$	$V\dfrac{mi}{hr}$	$\dfrac{\Delta B(mm.)}{100\ km.}$	r	$V\dfrac{m}{s}$	$V\dfrac{km}{hr}$	$V\dfrac{mi}{hr}$
$\dfrac{0.6\ mm.}{100\ km.}=$ $\dfrac{0.1\ in.}{263\ mi.}$	100	4.61	16.60	10.31	$\dfrac{1.5\ mm.}{100\ km.}=$ $\dfrac{0.1\ in.}{105\ mi.}$	100	9.01	32.44	20.16
	200	5.27	18.97	11.79		200	10.92	39.31	24.43
	300	5.58	20.09	12.48		300	11.98	43.13	26.80
	400	5.76	20.74	12.89		400	12.67	45.61	28.34
	500	5.89	21.20	13.17		500	13.16	47.38	29.44
	600	5.97	21.49	13.35		600	13.53	48.71	30.27
	700	6.04	21.74	13.51		700	13.82	49.75	30.91
	800	6.09	21.92	13.62		800	14.06	50.62	31.45
	900	6.13	22.07	13.71		900	14.25	51.30	31.88
	1000	6.17	22.21	13.80		1000	14.41	51.88	32.24
	1200	6.22	22.39	13.91		1200	14.66	52.78	32.80
	1500	6.27	22.57	14.02		1500	14.93	53.75	33.40
	2000	6.33	22.79	14.16		2000	15.23	54.83	34.07
	3000	6.38	22.97	14.27		3000	15.54	55.94	34.76
	∞	6.51	23.44	14.57		∞	16.26	58.54	36.38
$\dfrac{0.8\ mm.}{100\ km.}=$ $\dfrac{0.1\ in.}{197\ mi.}$	100	5.73	20.63	12.82	$\dfrac{2.0\ mm.}{100\ km.}=$ $\dfrac{0.1\ in.}{79\ mi.}$	100	10.95	39.42	24.49
	200	6.68	24.05	14.94		200	13.51	48.64	30.22
	300	7.15	25.74	15.99		300	14.99	53.96	33.53
	400	7.44	26.78	16.64		400	15.98	57.53	35.75
	500	7.63	27.47	17.07		500	16.70	60.12	37.36
	600	7.77	27.97	17.38		600	17.25	62.10	38.59
	700	7.88	28.37	17.63		700	17.69	63.68	39.57
	800	7.97	28.69	17.83		800	18.04	64.94	40.35
	900	8.03	28.91	17.96		900	18.34	66.02	41.02
	1000	8.09	29.12	18.09		1000	18.59	66.92	41.58
	1200	8.18	29.45	18.30		1200	18.99	68.36	42.48
	1500	8.27	29.77	18.50		1500	19.43	69.95	43.47
	2000	8.36	30.10	18.70		2000	19.91	71.68	44.54
	3000	8.46	30.46	18.93		3000	20.44	73.58	45.72
	∞	8.67	31.21	19.39		∞	21.69	78.08	48.52
$\dfrac{1.0\ mm.}{100\ km.}=$ $\dfrac{0.1\ in.}{158\ mi.}$	100	6.76	24.34	15.12	$\dfrac{2.5\ mm.}{100\ km.}=$ $\dfrac{0.1\ in.}{63\ mi.}$	100	12.69	45.68	28.38
	200	7.99	28.76	17.87		200	15.86	57.10	35.48
	300	8.63	31.07	19.31		300	17.73	63.83	39.66
	400	9.02	32.47	20.18		400	19.02	68.47	42.55
	500	9.29	33.44	20.78		500	19.97	71.89	44.67
	600	9.50	34.20	21.25		600	20.71	74.56	46.33
	700	9.65	34.74	21.59		700	21.30	76.68	47.65
	800	9.77	35.17	21.85		800	21.79	78.44	48.74
	900	9.87	35.53	22.08		900	22.21	79.96	49.68
	1000	9.96	35.86	22.28		1000	22.55	81.18	50.44
	1200	10.09	36.32	22.57		1200	23.12	83.23	51.72
	1500	10.22	36.79	22.86		1500	23.74	85.46	53.10
	2000	10.36	37.30	23.18		2000	24.47	88.09	54.74
	3000	10.52	37.87	23.53		3000	25.21	90.76	56.40
	∞	10.84	39.02	24.25		∞	27.11	97.60	60.65

Latitude 50° (*Continued*)

$\dfrac{\Delta B(mm.)}{100\ km.}$	r	$V\dfrac{m}{s}$	$V\dfrac{km}{hr}$	$V\dfrac{mi}{hr}$	$\dfrac{\Delta B(mm.)}{100\ km.}$	r	$V\dfrac{m}{s}$	$V\dfrac{km}{hr}$	$V\dfrac{mi}{hr}$
$\dfrac{3.0\ mm.}{100\ km.}=$	100	14.28	51.41	31.95	$\dfrac{4.0\ mm.}{100\ km.}=$	100	17.12	61.63	38.29
	200	18.01	64.84	40.29		200	21.90	78.84	48.99
$0.1\ in.$	300	20.27	72.97	45.34	$0.1\ in.$	300	24.89	89.60	55.67
$\overline{53\ mi.}$	400	21.85	78.66	48.88	$\overline{39\ mi.}$	400	27.03	97.31	60.47
	500	23.03	82.91	51.52		500	28.66	103.18	64.11
	600	23.96	86.26	53.60		600	29.97	107.89	67.04
	700	24.72	88.99	55.30		700	31.04	111.74	69.43
	800	25.34	91.22	56.68		800	31.95	115.02	71.47
	900	25.87	93.13	57.87		900	32.72	117.79	73.19
	1000	26.33	94.79	58.90		1000	33.39	120.20	74.69
	1200	27.07	97.45	60.55		1200	34.50	124.20	77.17
	1500	27.89	100.40	62.39		1500	35.75	128.70	79.97
	2000	28.81	103.72	64.45		2000	37.19	133.88	83.19
	3000	29.86	107.50	66.80		3000	38.87	139.93	86.95
	∞	32.53	117.11	72.77		∞	43.37	156.13	97.01

Latitude 55°

$\dfrac{\Delta B(mm.)}{100\ km.}$	r	$V\dfrac{m}{s}$	$V\dfrac{km}{hr}$	$V\dfrac{mi}{hr}$	$\dfrac{\Delta B(mm.)}{100\ km.}$	r	$V\dfrac{m}{s}$	$V\dfrac{km}{hr}$	$V\dfrac{mi}{hr}$
$\dfrac{0.2\ mm.}{100\ km.}=$	100	1.77	6.37	3.96	$\dfrac{0.6\ mm.}{100\ km.}=$	100	4.44	15.98	9.93
	200	1.88	6.77	4.21		200	5.03	18.11	11.25
$0.1\ in.$	300	1.93	6.95	4.32	$0.1\ in.$	300	5.30	19.08	11.86
$\overline{789\ mi.}$	400	1.95	7.02	4.36	$\overline{263\ mi.}$	400	5.46	19.66	12.22
	500	1.96	7.06	4.39		500	5.57	20.05	12.46
	600	1.97	7.09	4.41		600	5.64	20.30	12.61
	700	1.98	7.13	4.43		700	5.70	20.52	12.75
	800	1.99	7.16	4.45		800	5.74	20.66	12.84
	900	1.99	7.16	4.45		900	5.77	20.77	12.91
	1000	1.99	7.16	4.45		1000	5.80	20.88	12.97
	1200	2.00	7.20	4.47		1200	5.85	21.06	13.09
	1500	2.00	7.20	4.47		1500	5.89	21.20	13.17
	2000	2.01	7.24	4.50		2000	5.94	21.38	13.29
	3000	2.02	7.27	4.52		3000	5.99	21.56	13.40
	∞	2.03	7.31	4.54		∞	6.08	21.89	13.60
$\dfrac{0.4\ mm.}{100\ km.}=$	100	3.20	11.52	7.16	$\dfrac{0.8\ mm.}{100\ km.}=$	100	5.54	19.94	12.39
	200	3.53	12.71	7.90		200	6.40	23.04	14.32
$0.1\ in.$	300	3.68	13.25	8.23	$0.1\ in.$	300	6.82	24.55	15.25
$\overline{395\ mi}$	400	3.76	13.54	8.41	$\overline{197\ mi.}$	400	7.07	25.45	15.81
	500	3.81	13.72	8.53		500	7.24	26.06	16.19
	600	3.85	13.86	8.61		600	7.36	26.50	16.47
	700	3.88	13.97	8.68		700	7.45	26.82	16.67
	800	3.90	14.04	8.72		800	7.52	27.07	16.82
	900	3.91	14.08	8.75		900	7.58	27.29	16.96
	1000	3.93	14.15	8.79		1000	7.63	27.47	17.07
	1200	3.95	14.22	8.84		1200	7.70	27.72	17.22
	1500	3.97	14.29	8.88		1500	7.77	27.97	17.38
	2000	3.99	14.36	8.92		2000	7.85	28.26	17.56
	3000	4.01	14.44	8.97		3000	7.94	28.58	17.76
	∞	4.06	14.62	9.08		∞	8.11	29.20	18.14

Latitude 55° (Continued)

$\dfrac{\Delta B(mm.)}{100\ km.}$	r	$V\dfrac{m}{s}$	$V\dfrac{km}{hr}$	$V\dfrac{mi}{hr}$	$\dfrac{\Delta B(mm.)}{100\ km.}$	r	$V\dfrac{m}{s}$	$V\dfrac{km}{hr}$	$V\dfrac{mi}{hr}$
$\dfrac{1.0\ mm.}{100\ km.} =$ 0.1 in. 158 mi.	100	6.55	23.58	14.65	$\dfrac{2.5\ mm.}{100\ km.} =$ 0.1 in. 63 mi.	100	12.43	44.75	27.81
	200	7.68	27.65	17.18		200	15.41	55.48	34.47
	300	8.24	29.66	18.43		300	17.15	61.74	38.36
	400	8.59	30.92	19.21		400	18.22	65.59	40.76
	500	8.83	31.79	19.75		500	19.19	69.08	42.92
	600	9.01	32.44	20.16		600	19.85	71.46	44.40
	700	9.14	32.90	20.44		700	20.38	73.37	45.59
	800	9.25	33.30	20.69		800	20.82	74.95	46.57
	900	9.33	33.59	20.87		900	21.18	76.25	47.38
	1000	9.40	33.84	21.03		1000	21.49	77.36	48.07
	1200	9.51	34.24	21.28		1200	21.98	79.13	49.17
	1500	9.63	34.67	21.54		1500	22.52	81.07	50.37
	2000	9.74	35.06	21.79		2000	23.12	83.23	51.72
	3000	9.87	35.53	22.08		3000	23.77	85.57	53.17
	∞	10.14	36.50	22.68		∞	25.35	91.26	56.71
$\dfrac{1.5\ mm.}{100\ km.} =$ 0.1 in. 105 mi.	100	8.77	31.57	19.62	$\dfrac{3.0\ mm.}{100\ km.} =$ 0.1 in. 53 mi.	100	14.00	50.40	31.32
	200	10.55	37.98	23.60		200	17.54	63.14	39.23
	300	11.51	41.44	25.75		300	19.65	70.74	43.96
	400	12.13	43.67	27.14		400	21.00	75.60	46.98
	500	12.56	45.22	28.10		500	22.18	79.85	49.62
	600	12.89	46.40	28.83		600	23.03	82.91	51.52
	700	13.14	47.30	29.39		700	23.70	85.32	53.02
	800	13.35	48.06	29.86		800	24.26	87.34	54.27
	900	13.51	48.64	30.22		900	24.73	89.03	55.32
	1000	13.65	49.14	30.53		1000	25.13	90.47	56.22
	1200	13.87	49.93	31.03		1200	25.79	92.84	57.69
	1500	14.10	50.76	31.56		1500	26.50	95.40	59.28
	2000	14.35	51.66	32.10		2000	27.30	98.28	61.07
	3000	14.62	52.63	32.70		3000	28.20	101.52	63.08
	∞	15.21	54.76	34.03		∞	30.42	109.51	68.05
$\dfrac{2.0\ mm.}{100\ km.} =$ 0.1 in. 79 mi.	100	10.70	38.52	23.94	$\dfrac{4.0\ mm.}{100\ km.} =$ 0.1 in. 39 mi.	100	16.84	60.62	37.67
	200	13.10	47.16	29.30		200	21.40	77.04	47.87
	300	14.45	52.02	32.32		300	24.21	87.16	54.16
	400	15.35	55.26	34.34		400	26.10	93.96	58.38
	500	16.00	57.60	35.79		500	27.70	99.72	61.96
	600	16.48	59.33	36.87		600	28.91	104.08	64.67
	700	16.88	60.77	37.76		700	29.88	107.57	66.84
	800	17.19	61.88	38.45		800	30.70	110.52	68.67
	900	17.45	62.82	39.03		900	31.39	113.00	70.22
	1000	17.67	63.61	39.53		1000	31.99	115.16	71.56
	1200	18.02	64.87	40.31		1200	32.95	118.62	73.70
	1500	18.39	66.20	41.14		1500	34.08	122.69	76.24
	2000	18.80	67.68	42.05		2000	35.34	127.22	79.55
	3000	19.25	69.30	43.06		3000	36.79	132.44	82.29
	∞	20.28	73.01	45.37		∞	40.56	146.02	90.73

Latitude 60°

$\dfrac{\Delta B(mm.)}{100\ km.}$	r	$V\dfrac{m}{s}$	$V\dfrac{km}{hr}$	$V\dfrac{mi}{hr}$	$\dfrac{\Delta B(mm.)}{100\ km.}$	r	$V\dfrac{m}{s}$	$V\dfrac{km}{hr}$	$V\dfrac{mi}{hr}$
$\dfrac{0.2\ mm.}{100\ km.}=$ $\dfrac{0.1\ in.}{789\ mi.}$	100	1.69	6.08	3.78	$\dfrac{0.8\ mm.}{100\ km.}=$ $\dfrac{0.1\ in.}{197\ mi.}$	100	5.38	19.37	12.04
	200	1.79	6.44	4.00		200	6.17	22.21	13.80
	300	1.83	6.59	4.10		300	6.54	23.54	14.63
	400	1.85	6.66	4.14		400	6.77	24.37	15.14
	500	1.86	6.70	4.16		500	6.92	24.91	15.48
	600	1.87	6.73	4.18		600	7.02	25.27	15.70
	700	1.88	6.77	4.21		700	7.10	25.56	15.88
	800	1.88	6.77	4.21		800	7.17	25.81	16.04
	900	1.89	6.80	4.23		900	7.22	25.99	16.15
	1000	1.89	6.80	4.23		1000	7.26	26.14	16.24
	1200	1.90	6.84	4.25		1200	7.32	26.35	16.37
	1500	1.90	6.84	4.25		1500	7.38	26.57	16.5¹
	2000	1.90	6.84	4.25		2000	7.45	26.82	16.67
	3000	1.91	6.88	4.28		3000	7.53	27.11	16.85
	∞	1.91	6.88	4.28		∞	7.60	27.36	17.00
$\dfrac{0.4\ mm.}{100\ km.}=$ $\dfrac{0.1\ in.}{395\ mi.}$	100	3.08	11.09	6.89	$\dfrac{1.0\ mm.}{100\ km.}=$ $\dfrac{0.1\ in.}{158\ mi.}$	100	6.37	22.93	14.25
	200	3.38	12.17	7.56		200	7.42	26.71	16.60
	300	3.51	12.64	7.85		300	7.93	28.55	17.74
	400	3.58	12.89	8.01		400	8.25	29.70	18.45
	500	3.63	13.07	8.12		500	8.46	30.46	18.92
	600	3.66	13.18	8.19		600	8.61	31.00	19.26
	700	3.68	13.25	8.23		700	8.73	31.43	19.53
	800	3.70	13.32	8.28		800	8.82	31.75	19.73
	900	3.72	13.39	8.32		900	8.90	32.04	19.91
	1000	3.73	13.43	8.34		1000	8.96	32.26	20.05
	1200	3.74	13.46	8.36		1200	9.05	32.58	20.24
	1500	3.76	13.54	8.41		1500	9.15	32.94	20.47
	2000	3.78	13.61	8.46		2000	9.25	33.30	20.69
	3000	3.80	13.68	8.50		3000	9.37	33.73	20.96
	∞	3.80	13.68	8.50		∞	9.50	34.20	21.25
$\dfrac{0.6\ mm.}{100\ km.}=$ $\dfrac{0.1\ in.}{263\ mi.}$	100	4.29	15.44	9.59	$\dfrac{1.5\ mm.}{100\ km.}=$ $\dfrac{0.1\ in.}{105\ mi.}$	100	8.57	30.85	19.17
	200	4.83	17.39	10.81		200	10.24	36.86	22.90
	300	5.07	18.25	11.34		300	11.12	40.03	24.87
	400	5.22	18.79	11.68		400	11.68	42.05	26.13
	500	5.31	19.12	11.88		500	12.08	43.49	27.02
	600	5.37	19.33	12.04		600	12.37	44.53	27.67
	700	5.42	19.51	12.12		700	12.59	45.32	28.16
	800	5.46	19.66	12.22		800	12.77	45.97	28.56
	900	5.49	19.76	12.28		900	12.92	46.51	28.90
	1000	5.51	19.84	12.33		1000	13.05	46.98	29.19
	1200	5.55	19.98	12.42		1200	13.23	47.63	29.60
	1500	5.59	20.12	12.50		1500	13.44	48.38	30.06
	2000	5.63	20.27	12.59		2000	13.65	49.14	30.53
	3000	5.67	20.41	12.68		3000	13.88	49.97	31.05
	∞	5.70	20.52	12.85		∞	14.25	51.30	31.88

Latitude 60° (*Continued*)

$\dfrac{\Delta B(mm.)}{100\ km.}$	r	$V\dfrac{m}{s}$	$V\dfrac{km}{hr}$	$V\dfrac{mi}{hr}$	$\dfrac{\Delta B(mm.)}{100\ km.}$	r	$V\dfrac{m}{s}$	$V\dfrac{km}{hr}$	$V\dfrac{mi}{hr}$
$\dfrac{2.0\ mm.}{100\ km.} =$	100	10.48	37.73	23.44	$\dfrac{3.0\ mm.}{100\ km.} =$	100	14.77	53.17	33.04
	200	12.75	45.90	28.52		200	17.14	61.70	38.34
0.1 *in.*	300	14.01	50.44	31.34	0.1 *in.*	300	19.12	68.83	42.77
79 *mi.*	400	14.83	53.39	33.17	53 *mi.*	400	20.48	73.73	45.81
	500	15.42	55.51	34.49		500	21.47	77.29	48.03
	600	15.86	57.10	35.48		600	22.24	80.06	49.75
	700	16.21	58.36	36.26		700	22.86	82.30	51.14
	800	16.49	59.36	36.88		800	23.36	84.10	52.26
	900	16.72	60.19	37.40		900	23.79	85.64	53.22
	1000	16.92	60.91	37.85		1000	24.15	86.94	54.02
	1200	17.22	61.99	38.52		1200	24.73	89.03	55.32
	1500	17.56	63.22	39.28		1500	25.38	91.37	56.77
	2000	17.92	64.51	40.08		2000	26.08	93.89	58.34
	3000	18.30	65.88	40.94		3000	26.87	96.73	60.10
	∞	18.99	68.36	42.48		∞	28.49	102.56	63.73
$\dfrac{2.5\ mm.}{100\ km.} =$	100	12.20	43.92	27.29	$\dfrac{4.0\ mm.}{100\ km.} =$	100	16.59	59.72	37.11
	200	15.03	54.11	33.62		200	20.96	75.46	46.89
0.1 *in.*	300	16.66	59.98	37.27	0.1 *in.*	300	23.63	85.07	52.86
63 *mi.*	400	17.75	63.90	39.71	39 *mi.*	400	25.00	91.80	57.04
	500	18.54	66.74	41.47		500	26.90	96.84	60.17
	600	19.14	68.90	42.81		600	28.01	100.84	62.66
	700	19.62	70.63	43.89		700	28.91	104.08	64.67
	800	20.01	72.04	44.76		800	29.66	106.78	66.35
	900	20.34	73.22	45.50		900	30.29	109.04	67.76
	1000	20.61	74.20	46.10		1000	30.84	111.02	68.98
	1200	21.05	75.78	47.09		1200	31.73	114.23	70.98
	1500	21.53	77.51	48.16		1500	32.72	117.79	73.19
	2000	22.05	79.38	49.32		2000	33.83	121.79	75.68
	3000	22.63	81.47	50.62		3000	35.11	126.40	78.54
	∞	23.74	85.46	53.10		∞	37.98	136.73	84.96

TABLE II.—GRADIENT WIND VELOCITY FOR ANTICYCLONIC MOVEMENT
Latitude 25°

$\dfrac{\Delta B(mm.)}{100\ km.}$	r	$V\dfrac{m}{s}$	$V\dfrac{km}{hr}$	$V\dfrac{mi}{hr}$	$\dfrac{\Delta B(mm.)}{100\ km.}$	r	$V\dfrac{m}{s}$	$V\dfrac{km}{hr}$	$V\dfrac{mi}{hr}$
$\dfrac{0.2\ mm.}{100\ km.}=$ 0.1 *in.* 789 *mi*	255.1	7.86	28.30	17.59	$\dfrac{0.8\ mm.}{100\ km.}=$ 0.1 *in.* 197 *mi*	1020.4	31.44	113.18	70.33
	300	5.67	20.41	12.68		1200	22.67	81.61	50.71
	400	4.91	17.68	10.99		1500	20.09	72.32	44.94
	500	4.63	16.67	10.36		2000	18.50	66.60	41.38
	600	4.47	16.09	10.00		3000	17.35	62.46	38.81
	700	4.38	15.77	9.80		∞	15.72	56.59	35.16
	800	4.31	15.52	9.64					
	900	4.26	15.34	9.53	$\dfrac{1.0\ mm.}{100\ km.}=$ 0.1 *in.* 158 *mi*	1275.5	39.30	141.48	87.91
	1000	4.22	15.19	9.44		1500	28.34	102.02	63.39
	1200	4.17	15.01	9.33		2000	24.54	88.34	54.89
	1500	4.11	14.78	9.18		3000	22.36	80.50	50.02
	2000	4.07	14.65	9.10		∞	19.65	70.74	43.96
	3000	4.02	14.47	8.99					
	∞	3.93	14.15	8.79	$\dfrac{1.5\ mm.}{100\ km.}=$ 0.1 *in.* 105 *mi*	1913.3	58.96	212.26	131.89
						2000	48.80	175.68	109.16
$\dfrac{0.4\ mm.}{100\ km.}=$ 0.1 *in.* 395 *mi*	510.2	15.72	56.59	35.16		3000	36.81	132.52	82.34
	600	11.34	40.82	25.36		∞	29.48	106.13	65.95
	700	10.34	37.22	23.13					
	800	9.82	35.35	21.97	$\dfrac{2.0\ mm.}{100\ km.}=$ 0.1 *in.* 79 *mi*	2551	78.62	283.03	175.87
	900	9.48	34.13	21.21		3000	56.68	204.05	126.79
	1000	9.25	33.30	20.69		∞	39.31	141.52	87.94
	1200	8.94	32.18	20.00					
	1500	8.68	31.25	19.42					
	2000	8.44	30.38	18.88					
	3000	8.23	29.63	18.41					
	∞	7.86	28.30	17.58					
$\dfrac{0.6\ mm.}{100\ km.}=$ 0.1 *in.* 263 *mi*	765.3	23.58	84.89	52.75					
	800	19.52	70.27	43.66					
	900	17.01	61.24	38.05					
	1000	15.89	57.20	35.54					
	1200	14.72	52.99	32.93					
	1500	13.87	49.93	31.03					
	2000	13.21	47.56	29.55					
	3000	12.66	45.58	28.32					
	∞	11.79	42.44	26.37					

Latitude 30°

$\frac{\Delta B(mm.)}{100\ km.}$	r	$V\frac{m}{s}$	$V\frac{km}{hr}$	$V\frac{mi}{hr}$	$\frac{\Delta B(mm.)}{100\ km.}$	r	$V\frac{m}{s}$	$V\frac{km}{hr}$	$V\frac{mi}{hr}$
0.2 mm. = 100 km. 0.1 in. 789 mi.	182.25	6.64	23.90	14.85	0.8 mm. = 100 km. 0.1 in. 197 mi.	729	26.58	95.69	59.46
	200	5.12	18.43	11.45		800	20.48	73.73	45.81
	300	4.08	14.69	9.13		900	18.51	66.64	41.41
	400	3.82	13.75	8.54		1000	17.48	62.93	39.10
	500	3.70	13.32	8.28		1200	16.34	58.82	36.55
	600	3.62	13.03	8.10		1500	15.48	55.73	34.63
	700	3.57	12.85	7.98		2000	14.79	53.24	33.08
	800	3.54	12.74	7.92		3000	14.21	51.16	31.79
	900	3.51	12.64	7.85	∞	13.29	47.84	29.73	
	1000	3.49	12.56	7.80					
	1200	3.46	12.46	7.74	1.0 mm. = 100 km. 0.1 in. 158 mi.	911.25	33.22	119.59	74.31
	1500	3.43	12.35	7.67		1000	25.60	92.16	57.26
	2000	3.40	12.24	7.61		1200	22.29	80.24	49.86
	3000	3.38	12.17	7.56		1500	20.43	73.55	45.70
	∞	3.32	11.95	7.43		2000	19.12	68.83	42.77
						3000	18.11	65.20	40.51
0.4 mm. = 100 km. 0.1 in. 395 mi.	364.5	13.28	47.81	29.71		∞	16.61	59.80	37.16
	400	10.24	36.86	22.90					
	500	8.74	31.46	19.55	1.5 mm. = 100 km. 0.1 in. 105 mi.	1367.9	48.84	179.42	111.49
	600	8.17	29.41	18.27		1500	38.40	138.24	85.90
	700	7.85	28.26	17.56		2000	31.89	114.80	71.33
	800	7.65	27.54	17.11		3000	28.68	103.25	64.16
	900	7.50	27.00	16.78		∞	24.92	89.71	55.74
	1000	7.40	26.64	16.55					
	1200	7.24	26.06	16.19	2.0 mm. = 100 km. 0.1 in. 79 mi.	1822.5	66.44	239.18	148.62
	1500	7.11	25.60	15.91		2000	51.20	184.32	114.53
	2000	6.98	25.13	15.62		3000	40.85	147.06	95.76
	3000	6.86	24.70	15.35		∞	33.22	119.59	74.31
	∞	6.64	23.90	14.85					
0.6 mm. = 100 km. 0.1 in. 263 mi.	546.75	19.94	71.78	44.60	2.5 mm. = 100 km. 0.1 in. 63 mi.	2278.1	83.06	299.02	185.80
	600	15.36	55.30	34.36		3000	55.72	200.59	124.64
	700	13.58	48.89	30.38		∞	41.53	149.51	92.90
	800	12.76	45.94	28.55					
	900	12.26	44.14	27.43					
	1000	11.91	42.88	26.64	3.0 mm. = 100 km. 0.1 in. 53 mi.	2733.8	99.68	358.85	222.98
	1200	11.49	41.36	25.70		3000	76.79	276.44	171.77
	1500	11.09	39.92	24.81		∞	49.84	179.42	111.49
	2000	10.76	38.74	24.07					
	3000	10.47	37.69	23.42					
	∞	9.97	35.89	22.30					

Latitude 35°

$\dfrac{\Delta B(mm.)}{100\ km.}$	r	$V\dfrac{m}{s}$	$V\dfrac{km}{hr}$	$V\dfrac{mi}{hr}$
0.2 mm. / 100 km. = 0.1 in. / 789 mi.	138.5	5.80	20.88	12.88
	200	3.73	13.43	8.35
	300	3.34	12.02	7.47
	400	3.20	11.52	7.16
	500	3.13	11.27	7.00
	600	3.09	11.12	6.91
	700	3.06	11.02	6.85
	800	3.03	10.91	6.78
	900	3.02	10.87	6.75
	1000	3.00	10.80	6.71
	1200	2.98	10.73	6.67
	1500	2.97	10.69	6.64
	2000	2.95	10.62	6.60
	3000	2.93	10.55	6.56
	∞	2.90	10.44	6.49
0.4 mm. / 100 km. = 0.1 in. / 395 mi.	277.0	11.58	41.69	25.90
	300	9.07	32.65	20.30
	400	7.46	26.86	16.61
	500	6.95	25.02	15.55
	600	6.68	24.05	14.94
	700	6.52	23.47	14.58
	800	6.41	23.08	14.34
	900	6.32	22.75	14.14
	1000	6.26	22.54	14.01
	1200	6.17	22.21	13.80
	1500	6.09	21.92	13.62
	2000	6.01	21.64	13.45
	3000	5.93	21.35	13.27
	∞	5.79	20.84	12.95
0.6 mm. / 100 km. = 0.1 in. / 263 mi.	415.5	17.38	62.57	38.88
	500	12.31	44.32	27.54
	600	11.18	40.25	25.01
	700	10.61	38.20	23.74
	800	10.26	36.94	22.95
	900	10.02	36.07	22.41
	1000	9.85	35.46	22.03
	1200	9.61	34.60	21.50
	1500	9.39	33.80	21.00
	2000	9.19	33.08	20.56
	3000	9.01	32.44	20.16
	∞	8.69	31.28	19.48
0.8 mm. / 100 km. = 0.1 in. / 197 mi.	554.0	23.16	83.38	51.81
	600	18.14	65.30	40.58
	700	15.91	57.28	35.59
	800	14.90	53.64	33.33
	900	14.30	51.48	31.99
	1000	13.89	50.00	31.07
	1200	13.36	48.10	29.89

$\dfrac{\Delta B(mm.)}{100\ km.}$	r	$V\dfrac{m}{s}$	$V\dfrac{km}{hr}$	$V\dfrac{mi}{hr}$
0.8 mm. / 100 km. = 0.1 in. / 197 mi.	1500	12.92	46.51	28.90
	2000	12.52	45.07	28.01
	3000	12.17	43.81	27.22
	∞	11.58	41.69	25.90
1.0 mm. / 100 km. = 0.1 in. / 158 mi.	692.5	28.96	104.26	64.78
	700	26.24	94.46	58.70
	800	21.19	76.28	47.40
	900	19.57	70.45	43.78
	1000	18.63	67.07	41.68
	1200	17.55	63.18	39.26
	1500	16.71	60.16	37.38
	2000	16.01	57.64	35.82
	3000	15.43	55.55	34.52
	∞	14.48	52.13	32.39
1.5 mm. / 100 km. = 0.1 in. / 105 mi.	1038.7	43.44	156.38	97.15
	1200	31.79	114.44	71.11
	1500	27.95	100.62	62.52
	2000	25.66	92.38	57.40
	3000	24.02	86.47	53.73
	∞	21.72	78.19	48.58
2.0 mm. / 100 km. = 0.1 in. / 79 mi.	1385.0	57.92	208.51	129.56
	1500	45.36	163.30	101.47
	2000	37.26	134.14	83.33
	3000	33.41	120.28	74.70
	∞	28.96	104.26	64.78
2.5 mm. / 100 km. = 0.1 in. / 63 mi.	1731.2	72.40	260.64	161.95
	2000	52.98	190.73	118.51
	3000	43.87	157.93	98.13
	∞	36.20	130.32	80.98
3.0 mm. / 100 km. = 0.1 in. / 53 mi.	2077.5	86.88	312.77	194.35
	3000	55.89	201.20	125.02
	∞	43.44	156.38	97.17
4.0 mm. / 100 km. = 0.1 in. / 39 mi.	2770.0	115.84	417.02	259.12
	3000	90.72	326.59	202.93
	∞	57.92	208.51	129.56

Latitude 40°

$\frac{\Delta B(mm.)}{100\ km.}$	r	$V\frac{m}{s}$	$V\frac{km}{hr}$	$V\frac{mi}{hr}$
0.2 *mm.* = 100 *km.* 0.1 *in.* 789 *mi.*	110.25	5.16	18.58	11.55
	200	3.10	11.16	6.93
	300	2.88	10.37	6.44
	400	2.79	10.04	6.24
	500	2.74	9.86	6.13
	600	2.72	9.79	6.08
	700	2.70	9.72	6.04
	800	2.68	9.65	6.00
	900	2.67	9.61	5.97
	1000	2.66	9.58	5.95
	1200	2.65	9.54	5.93
	1500	2.63	9.47	5.88
	2000	2.62	9.43	5.86
	3000	2.61	9.40	5.84
	∞	2.58	9.29	5.77
0.4 *mm.* = 100 *km.* 0.1 *in.* 395 *mi.*	220.5	10.34	37.22	23.13
	300	6.83	24.59	15.28
	400	6.19	22.28	13.84
	500	5.92	21.31	13.24
	600	5.76	20.74	12.89
	700	5.66	20.38	12.66
	800	5.59	20.12	12.50
	900	5.53	19.91	12.37
	1000	5.49	19.76	12.28
	1200	5.43	19.55	12.15
	1500	5.37	19.33	12.01
	2000	5.32	19.15	11.90
	3000	5.27	18.97	11.79
	∞	5.17	18.61	11.56
0.6 *mm.* = 100 *km.* 0.1 *in.* 263 *mi.*	330.75	15.50	55.80	34.67
	400	10.95	39.42	24.50
	500	9.80	35.28	21.92
	600	9.29	33.44	20.78
	700	8.98	32.33	20.09
	800	8.78	31.61	19.64
	900	8.64	31.10	19.32
	1000	8.53	30.71	19.08
	1200	8.38	30.17	18.79
	1500	8.23	29.63	18.41
	2000	8.10	29.16	18.12
	3000	7.98	28.73	17.85
	∞	7.75	27.90	17.34
0.8 *mm.* = 100 *km.* 0.1 *in.* 197 *mi.*	441.0	20.68	74.45	46.26
	500	15.39	55.40	34.42
	600	13.65	49.14	30.53
	700	12.86	46.30	28.77
	800	12.38	44.57	27.69
	900	12.06	43.42	26.98
	1000	11.83	42.95	26.46

$\frac{\Delta B(mm.)}{100\ km.}$	r	$V\frac{m}{s}$	$V\frac{km}{hr}$	$V\frac{mi}{hr}$
0.8 *mm.* = 100 *km.* 0.1 *in.* 197 *mi.*	1200	11.52	41.47	25.77
	1500	11.24	40.46	25.14
	2000	10.98	39.53	24.56
	3000	10.75	58.70	24.05
	∞	10.34	37.22	23.13
1.0 *mm.* = 100 *km.* 1.0 *in.* 158 *mi.*	551.25	25.84	93.02	57.80
	600	20.12	72.43	45.01
	700	17.69	63.68	39.57
	800	16.59	59.72	37.11
	900	15.93	57.35	35.64
	1000	15.48	55.73	34.63
	1200	14.89	53.60	33.31
	1500	14.39	51.80	32.19
	2000	13.96	50.26	31.23
	3000	13.58	48.89	30.38
	∞	12.92	46.51	28.90
1.5 *mm.* = 100 *km.* 0.1 *in.* 105 *mi.*	826.9	38.76	139.54	86.71
	900	30.18	108.65	67.51
	1000	27.38	98.57	61.25
	1200	24.89	89.60	55.68
	1500	23.22	83.59	51.94
	2000	21.95	79.02	49.10
	3000	20.94	75.38	46.84
	∞	19.38	69.77	43.35
2.0 *mm.* = 100 *km.* 0.1 *in.* 79 *mi.*	1102.5	51.68	186.05	115.61
	1200	40.23	144.83	89.99
	1500	34.13	122.87	76.35
	2000	30.96	111.46	69.26
	3000	29.77	107.17	66.59
	∞	25.84	93.02	57.80
2.5 *mm.* = 100 *km.* 0.1 *in.* 63 *mi.*	1378.1	64.60	232.56	144.50
	1500	50.29	181.04	112.50
	2000	41.48	149.33	92.79
	3000	37.23	134.03	83.28
	∞	32.30	116.28	72.25
3.0 *mm.* = 100 *km.* 0.1 *in.* 53 *mi.*	1653.75	77.54	279.14	173.45
	2000	54.76	197.14	122.50
	3000	46.43	167.15	103.86
	∞	38.77	139.57	86.72
4.0 *mm.* = 100 *km.* 0.1 *in.* 39 *mi.*	2205.0	103.38	372.17	231.25
	3000	68.25	245.70	152.67
	∞	51.69	186.08	115.62

Latitude 45°

$\dfrac{\Delta B(mm.)}{100\ km.}$	r	$V\dfrac{m}{s}$	$V\dfrac{km}{hr}$	$V\dfrac{mi}{hr}$
0.2 mm. $=$ 100 km. 0.1 in. 789 mi.	91.33	4.70	16.92	10.51
	100	3.62	13.03	8.10
	200	2.70	9.72	6.04
	300	2.56	9.22	5.73
	400	2.50	9.00	5.59
	500	2.47	8.89	5.52
	600	2.45	8.82	5.48
	700	2.43	8.75	5.44
	800	2.42	8.71	5.41
	900	2.41	8.68	5.39
	1000	2.41	8.68	5.39
	1200	2.40	8.64	5.37
	1500	2.39	8.60	5.34
	2000	2.38	8.57	5.33
	3000	2.36	8.50	5.28
	∞	2.35	8.46	5.26
0.4 mm. $=$ 100 km. 0.1 in. 395 mi.	182.66	9.40	33.84	21.03
	200	7.24	26.06	16.19
	300	5.78	20.81	12.93
	400	5.41	19.48	12.10
	500	5.23	18.83	11.70
	600	5.12	18.43	11.45
	700	5.05	18.18	11.30
	800	5.00	18.00	11.18
	900	4.97	17.89	11.12
	1000	4.94	17.78	11.05
	1200	4.89	17.60	10.94
	1500	4.85	17.46	10.85
	2000	4.81	17.32	10.76
	3000	4.77	17.17	10.67
	∞	4.70	16.92	10.51
0.6 mm. $=$ 100 km. 0.1 in. 263 mi.	274.0	14.10	50.76	31.54
	300	10.86	39.10	24.30
	400	9.02	32.47	20.18
	500	8.43	30.35	18.86
	600	8.11	29.20	18.14
	700	7.92	28.51	17.72
	800	7.78	28.01	17.40
	900	7.69	27.68	17.20
	1000	7.61	27.40	17.03
	1200	7.50	27.00	16.78
	1500	7.40	26.64	16.55
	2000	7.31	26.32	16.35
	3000	7.21	25.96	16.13
	∞	7.05	25.38	15.77

$\dfrac{\Delta B(mm.)}{100\ km.}$	r	$V\dfrac{m}{s}$	$V\dfrac{km}{hr}$	$V\dfrac{mi}{hr}$
0.8 mm. $=$ 100 km. 0.1 in. 197 mi.	365.33	18.80	67.68	42.05
	400	14.48	52.13	32.39
	500	12.36	44.50	27.65
	600	11.55	41.58	25.84
	700	11.11	40.00	24.85
	800	10.82	38.95	24.20
	900	10.61	38.20	23.74
	1000	10.46	37.66	23.40
	1200	10.25	36.90	22.93
	1500	10.05	36.18	22.48
	2000	9.87	35.53	22.03
	3000	9.70	34.92	21.70
	∞	9.40	33.84	21.03
1.0 mm. $=$ 100 km. 0.1 in. 158 mi.	456.66	23.50	84.60	52.57
	500	18.10	65.16	40.49
	600	15.76	56.74	35.26
	700	14.77	53.17	33.04
	800	14.19	51.08	31.74
	900	13.80	49.68	30.87
	1000	13.52	48.67	30.24
	1200	13.14	47.30	29.39
	1500	12.81	46.12	28.66
	2000	12.50	45.00	27.96
	3000	12.23	44.03	27.36
	∞	11.75	42.30	26.28
1.5 mm. $=$ 100 km. 0.1 in. 105 mi.	685.0	35.24	126.86	78.83
	700	30.54	109.94	68.31
	800	25.50	91.80	57.04
	900	23.64	85.10	52.88
	1000	22.55	81.18	50.44
	1200	21.28	76.61	47.60
	1500	20.23	73.01	45.37
	2000	19.45	70.02	43.51
	3000	18.76	67.54	41.97
	∞	17.62	63.43	39.41
2.0 mm. $=$ 100 km. 0.1 in. 79 mi.	913.33	46.98	169.13	105.09
	1000	36.20	130.32	80.98
	1200	31.52	113.47	70.51
	1500	28.89	104.00	64.62
	2000	27.04	97.34	60.48
	3000	25.61	92.20	57.29
	∞	23.49	84.56	52.54
2.5 mm. $=$ 100 km. 0.1 in. 63 mi.	1141.66	58.74	211.46	131.39
	1200	47.93	172.55	107.22
	1500	39.40	141.84	88.14
	2000	35.46	127.66	79.32
	3000	32.86	118.30	73.51
	∞	29.37	105.73	65.70

Latitude 45° (*Continued*)

$\frac{\Delta B(mm.)}{100\ km.}$	r	$V\frac{m}{s}$	$V\frac{km}{hr}$	$V\frac{mi}{hr}$	$\frac{\Delta B(mm.)}{100\ km.}$	r	$V\frac{m^{\bullet}}{s}$	$V\frac{km}{hr}$	$V\frac{mi}{hr}$
3.0 *mm.*	1370.0	70.48	253.73	157.66	4.0 *mm.*	1826.66	93.98	338.33	210.23
$\overline{100\ km.}$ =	1500	54.30	195.48	121.46	$\overline{100\ km.}$ =	2000	72.40	260.64	165.53
0.1 *in.*	2000	45.10	162.36	100.89	0.1 *in.*	3000	57.77	207.97	129.23
$\overline{53\ mi.}$	3000	40.56	146.02	90.73	$\overline{39\ mi.}$	∞	46.99	169.16	105.11
	∞	35.24	126.86	78.83					

Latitude 50°

0.2 *mm.*	77.66	4.34	15.62	9.71	0.6 *mm.*	1500	6.78	24.41	15.17
$\overline{100\ km.}$ =	100	2.94	10.58	6.57	$\overline{100\ km.}$ =	2000	6.71	24.16	15.01
0.1 *in.*	200	2.43	8.75	5.44	0.1 *in.*	3000	6.64	23.90	14.85
$\overline{789\ mi.}$	300	2.33	8.39	5.21	$\overline{263\ mi.}$	∞	6.51	23.44	14.57
	400	2.29	8.24	5.12					
	500	2.26	8.14	5.06	0.8 *mm.*	310.66	17.34	62.42	38.79
	600	2.24	8.06	5.01	$\overline{100\ km.}$ =	400	11.78	42.41	26.35
	700	2.23	8.03	4.99	0.1 *in.*	500	10.74	38.66	24.04
	800	2.23	8.03	4.99	$\overline{197\ mi.}$	600	10.24	36.86	22.90
	900	2.22	7.99	4.96		700	9.94	35.78	22.23
	1000	2.21	7.96	4.95		800	9.74	35.06	21.79
	1200	2.21	7.96	4.95		900	9.59	34.52	21.45
	1500	2.20	7.92	4.92		1000	9.48	34.13	21.21
	2000	2.19	7.88	4.90		1200	9.31	33.52	20.83
	3000	2.19	7.88	4.90		1500	9.18	33.05	20.54
	∞	2.17	7.81	4.85		2000	9.04	32.54	20.22
0.4 *mm.*	155.33	8.68	31.25	19.42		3000	8.91	32.08	19.93
$\overline{100\ km.}$ =	200	5.89	21.20	13.17		∞	8.67	31.21	19.39
0.1 *in.*	300	5.12	18.43	11.45	1.0 *mm.*	388.33	21.68	78.05	48.50
$\overline{395\ mi.}$	400	4.87	17.53	10.89	$\overline{100\ km.}$ =	400	18.51	66.64	41.41
	500	4.74	17.06	10.60	0.1 *in.*	500	14.72	52.99	32.93
	600	4.66	16.78	10.43	$\overline{158\ mi.}$	600	13.60	48.96	30.42
	700	4.61	16.60	10.31		700	13.01	46.84	29.11
	800	4.57	16.45	10.22		800	12.63	45.47	28.25
	900	4.54	16.34	10.15		900	12.36	44.50	27.65
	1000	4.52	16.27	10.11		1000	12.17	43.81	27.22
	1200	4.49	16.16	10.04		1200	11.90	42.84	26.62
	1500	4.46	16.06	9.98		1500	11.65	41.94	26.06
	2000	4.42	15.91	9.89		2000	11.43	41.15	25.57
	3000	4.40	15.84	9.84		3000	11.24	40.46	25.14
	∞	4.34	15.62	9.71		∞	10.84	39.02	24.25
0.6 *mm.*	233.0	13.02	46.87	29.12	1.5 *mm.*	582.5	32.52	117.07	72.75
$\overline{100\ km.}$ =	300	8.83	31.79	19.75	$\overline{100\ km.}$ =	600	27.76	99.94	62.10
0.1 *in.*	400	7.90	28.44	17.67	0.1 *in.*	700	23.07	83.05	51.60
$\overline{263\ mi.}$	500	7.52	27.07	16.82	$\overline{105\ mi.}$	800	21.38	76.97	47.83
	600	7.30	26.28	16.33		900	20.41	73.48	45.66
	700	7.16	25.78	16.02		1000	19.76	71.14	44.20
	800	7.06	25.42	15.80		1200	18.94	68.18	42.36
	900	6.99	25.16	15.63		1500	18.25	65.70	40.82
	1000	6.94	24.98	15.52		2000	17.66	63.58	39.51
	1200	6.86	24.70	15.35		3000	17.14	61.70	38.34
						∞	16.26	58.54	36.38

Latitude 50° (Continued)

$\frac{\Delta B(mm.)}{100\ km.}$	r	$V\frac{m}{s}$	$V\frac{km}{hr}$	$V\frac{mi}{hr}$	$\frac{\Delta B(mm.)}{100\ km.}$	r	$V\frac{m}{s}$	$V\frac{km}{hr}$	$V\frac{mi}{hr}$
$\frac{2.0\ mm.}{100\ km.}=$	776.66	43.38	156.17	97.04	$\frac{3.0\ mm.}{100\ km.}=$	1165.0	65.06	234.22	145.54
0.1 in.	800	37.02	133.27	82.81	0.1 in.	1200	55.53	199.91	124.22
79 mi.	900	31.65	113.94	70.80	53 mi.	1500	44.17	159.01	98.80
	1000	29.45	106.02	65.88		2000	39.52	142.27	88.40
	1200	27.21	97.96	60.87		3000	36.51	131.44	81.67
	1500	25.60	92.16	57.27		∞	32.53	117.11	72.77
	2000	24.34	87.62	54.44					
	3000	23.31	83.92	52.15	$\frac{4.0\ mm.}{100\ km.}=$	1553.33	86.74	312.26	194.03
	∞	21.69	78.08	48.52	0.1 in.	2000	58.90	212.04	131.75
$\frac{2.5\ mm.}{100\ km.}=$	970.8	54.22	195.19	121.29	39 mi.	3000	51.19	184.28	114.51
0.1 in.	1000	46.27	166.57	103.50		∞	43.37	156.13	97.01
63 mi.	1200	37.72	135.79	84.38					
	1500	34.05	122.58	76.17					
	2000	31.57	113.65	70.62					
	3000	29.75	107.10	66.55					
	∞	27.11	97.60	60.65					

Latitude 55°

$\frac{\Delta B(mm.)}{100\ km.}$	r	$V\frac{m}{s}$	$V\frac{km}{hr}$	$V\frac{mi}{hr}$	$\frac{\Delta B(mm.)}{100\ km.}$	r	$V\frac{m}{s}$	$V\frac{km}{hr}$	$V\frac{mi}{hr}$
$\frac{0.2\ mm.}{100\ km.}=$	67.9	4.06	14.62	9.08	$\frac{0.6\ mm.}{100\ km.}=$	203.7	12.16	43.78	27.20
0.1 in.	100	2.59	9.32	5.79	0.1 in.	300	7.77	27.97	17.38
789 mi.	200	2.24	8.06	5.01	263 mi.	400	7.16	25.78	16.02
	300	2.16	7.78	4.83		500	6.88	24.77	15.39
	400	2.12	7.63	4.74		600	6.71	24.16	15.01
	500	2.10	7.56	4.70		700	6.61	23.80	14.79
	600	2.09	7.52	4.67		800	6.53	23.51	14.61
	700	2.08	7.49	4.65		900	6.48	23.33	14.50
	800	2.07	7.45	4.63		1000	6.43	23.15	14.38
	900	2.07	7.45	4.63		1200	6.37	22.93	14.25
	1000	2.06	7.42	4.61		1500	6.31	22.72	14.12
	1200	2.06	7.42	4.61		2000	6.25	22.50	13.98
	1500	2.05	7.38	4.59		3000	6.19	22.28	13.84
	2000	2.05	7.38	4.59		∞	6.08	21.89	13.60
	3000	2.04	7.34	4.56	$\frac{0.8\ mm.}{100\ km.}=$	271.6	16.22	58.39	36.28
	∞	2.03	7.31	4.54		300	12.41	44.68	27.76
$\frac{0.4\ mm.}{100\ km.}=$	135.8	8.12	29.23	18.16	0.1 in.	400	10.36	37.30	23.18
0.1 in.	200	5.18	18.65	11.59	197 mi.	500	9.68	34.85	21.65
395 mi.	300	4.66	16.78	10.43		600	9.33	33.59	20.87
	400	4.48	16.13	10.02		700	9.10	32.76	20.36
	500	4.40	15.84	9.84		800	8.95	32.22	20.02
	600	4.32	15.55	9.66		900	8.84	31.82	19.77
	700	4.27	15.37	9.55		1000	8.75	31.50	19.57
	800	4.25	15.30	9.51		1200	8.63	31.07	19.31
	900	4.22	15.19	9.44		1500	8.52	30.67	19.06
	1000	4.20	15.12	9.40		2000	8.41	30.28	18.82
	1200	4.18	15.05	9.35		3000	8.30	29.88	18.57
	1500	4.15	14.94	9.28		∞	8.11	29.20	18.14
	2000	4.13	14.87	9.24					
	3000	4.10	14.76	9.17					
	∞	4.06	14.62	9.08					

Latitude 55° (*Continued*)

$\dfrac{\Delta B(mm.)}{100\ km.}$	r	$V\dfrac{m}{s}$	$V\dfrac{km}{hr}$	$V\dfrac{mi}{hr}$	$\dfrac{\Delta B(mm.)}{100\ km.}$	r	$V\dfrac{m}{s}$	$V\dfrac{km}{hr}$	$V\dfrac{mi}{hr}$
1.0 mm. = 100 km. 0.1 in. 158 mi.	339.5	20.28	73.01	45.37	2.0 mm. = 100 km. 0.1 in. 79 mi.	1200	24.45	88.02	54.69
	400	14.60	52.56	32.66		1500	23.31	83.92	52.15
	500	12.95	46.62	28.97		2000	22.37	80.53	50.04
	600	12.23	44.00	27.34		3000	21.58	77.69	48.27
	700	11.81	42.52	26.42		∞	20.28	73.01	45.37
	800	11.53	41.51	25.79					
	900	11.34	40.82	25.36	2.5 mm. = 100 km. 0.1 in. 63 mi.	848.7	50.70	182.52	113.41
	1000	11.19	40.28	25.03		900	40.94	147.38	91.58
	1200	10.98	39.53	24.56		1000	36.50	131.40	81.65
	1500	10.79	38.84	24.13		1200	32.90	118.44	73.60
	2000	10.61	38.20	23.74		1500	30.56	110.02	68.36
	3000	10.44	37.58	23.35		2000	28.83	103.79	64.49
	∞	10.14	36.50	22.68		3000	27.45	98.82	61.40
						∞	25.35	91.26	56.71
1.5 mm. = 100 km. 0.1 in. 105 mi.	509.2	30.42	109.51	68.05					
	600	21.90	78.84	48.99	3.0 mm. = 100 km. 0.1 in. 53 mi.	1018.5	60.84	219.02	136.09
	700	19.99	71.96	44.71		1200	43.80	157.68	97.98
	800	18.98	68.33	42.46		1500	38.84	139.82	86.88
	900	18.34	66.02	41.02		2000	35.78	128.81	80.04
	1000	17.89	64.40	40.02		3000	33.56	120.82	75.07
	1200	17.30	62.28	38.70		∞	30.42	109.51	68.05
	1500	16.78	60.41	37.54					
	2000	16.33	58.79	36.53	4.0 mm. = 100 km. 0.1 in. 39 mi.	1358.0	81.12	292.03	181.45
	3000	15.92	57.31	35.61		1500	62.04	223.34	138.78
	∞	15.21	54.76	34.03		2000	51.78	186.41	115.83
2.0 mm. = 100 km. 0.1 in. 79 mi.	679.0	40.56	146.02	90.73		3000	46.62	167.83	104.28
	700	34.57	124.45	77.33		∞	40.56	146.02	90.73
	800	29.20	105.12	65.32					
	900	27.12	97.63	60.66					
	1000	25.89	93.20	57.91					

Latitude 60°

$\dfrac{\Delta B(mm.)}{100\ km.}$	r	$V\dfrac{m}{s}$	$V\dfrac{km}{hr}$	$V\dfrac{mi}{hr}$	$\dfrac{\Delta B(mm.)}{100\ km.}$	r	$V\dfrac{m}{s}$	$V\dfrac{km}{hr}$	$V\dfrac{mi}{hr}$
0.2 mm. = 100 km. 0.1 in. 789 mi.	60.75	3.82	13.75	8.55	0.4 mm. = 100 km. 0.1 in. 395 mi.	121.5	7.60	27.36	17.00
	100	2.36	8.50	5.28		200	4.72	16.99	10.56
	200	2.09	7.52	4.67		300	4.33	15.59	9.69
	300	2.03	7.31	4.54		400	4.18	15.05	9.35
	400	2.00	7.20	4.47		500	4.10	14.76	9.17
	500	1.98	7.13	4.43		600	4.05	14.58	9.06
	600	1.97	7.09	4.41		700	4.02	14.47	8.99
	700	1.96	7.06	4.39		800	3.99	14.36	8.92
	800	1.96	7.06	4.39		900	3.98	14 33	8.90
	900	1 95	7.02	4.36		1000	3.96	14 26	8.86
	1000	1 95	7.02	4.36		1200	3.94	14.18	8.81
	1200	1.94	6.98	4.34		1500	3.92	14.11	8.77
	1500	1.94	6.98	4.34		2000	3.90	14.04	8.72
	2000	1.93	6.95	4.32		3000	3.87	13.93	8.66
	3000	1.93	6.95	4.32		∞	3.80	13.68	8.50
	∞	1.91	6.88	4.28					

Latitude 60° (Continued)

$\dfrac{\Delta B(mm.)}{100\ km.}$	r	$V\dfrac{m}{s}$	$V\dfrac{km}{hr}$	$V\dfrac{mi}{hr}$	$\dfrac{\Delta B(mm.)}{100\ km.}$	r	$V\dfrac{m}{s}$	$V\dfrac{km}{hr}$	$V\dfrac{mi}{hr}$
$\dfrac{0.6\ mm.}{100\ km.} =$ 0.1 in. 263 mi.	182.25	11.40	41.04	25.50	$\dfrac{1.5\ mm.}{100\ km.} =$ 0.1 in. 105 mi.	455.6	28.50	102.60	63.75
	200	8.87	31.93	19.84		500	22.17	79.81	49.59
	300	7.08	25.49	15.84		600	19.30	69.48	43.17
	400	6.62	23.83	14.81		700	18.09	65.12	40.46
	500	6.40	23.04	14.32		800	17.37	62.53	38.85
	600	6.27	22.57	14.02		900	16.90	60.84	37.80
	700	6.19	22.28	13.84		1000	16.56	59.62	37.05
	800	6.13	22.07	13.71		1200	16.10	57.96	36.02
	900	6.08	21.89	13.60		1500	15.69	56.48	35.09
	1000	6.05	21.78	13.53		2000	15.31	55.12	34.25
	1200	5.99	21.56	13.40		3000	14.98	53.93	33.51
	1500	5.94	21.38	13.29		∞	14.25	51.30	31.88
	2000	5.89	21.20	13.17					
	3000	5.84	21.02	13.06	$\dfrac{2.0\ mm.}{100\ km.} =$ 0.1 in. 79 mi.	607.5	37.98	136.73	84.96
	∞	5.70	20.52	12.85		700	28.14	101.30	62.94
						800	25.74	92.66	57.58
$\dfrac{0.8\ mm.}{100\ km.} =$ 0.1 in. 197 mi.	243.0	15.20	54.72	34.00		900	24.44	87.98	54.67
	300	10.69	38.48	23.91		1000	23.59	84.92	52.77
	400	9.43	33.95	21.10		1200	22.53	81.11	50.40
	500	8.94	32.18	20.00		1500	21.66	77.98	48.45
	600	8.66	31.18	19.37		2000	20.92	75.31	46.80
	700	8.49	30.56	18.99		3000	20.26	72.94	45.32
	800	8.37	30.13	18.72		∞	18.99	68.36	42.48
	900	8.28	29.81	18.52					
	1000	8.21	29.56	18.37	$\dfrac{2.5\ mm.}{100\ km.} =$ 0.1 in. 63 mi.	759.4	47.48	170.93	106.21
	1200	8.11	29.20	18.14		800	39.14	140.90	87.55
	1500	8.01	28.84	17.92		900	34.37	123.73	76.88
	2000	7.92	28.51	17.72		1000	32.18	115.85	71.99
	3000	7.84	28.22	17.54		1200	29.86	107.50	66.80
	∞	7.60	27.36	17.00		1500	23.17	101.41	63.01
						2000	26.83	96.59	60.02
$\dfrac{1.0\ mm.}{100\ km.} =$ 1.0 in. 158 mi.	303.75	19.00	68.40	42.50		3000	25.72	92.59	57.53
	400	12.87	46.33	28.79		∞	23.74	85.46	53.10
	500	11.79	42.44	26.37					
	600	11.27	40.57	25.21	$\dfrac{3.0\ mm.}{100\ km.} =$ 0.1 in. 53 mi.	911.25	56.98	205.13	127.46
	700	10.95	39.42	24.49		1000	44.34	159.62	99.18
	800	10.73	38.63	24.00		1200	38.61	139.00	86.37
	900	10.58	38.09	23.67		1500	35.38	127.37	79.14
	1000	10.46	37.66	23.40		2000	33.12	119.23	74.09
	1200	10.29	37.04	23.02		3000	31.37	112.93	70.17
	1500	10.13	36.47	22.66		∞	28.49	102.56	63.73
	2000	9.99	35.96	22.34					
	3000	9.85	35.46	22.03	$\dfrac{4.0\ mm.}{100\ km.} =$ 0.1 in. 39 mi.	1215.0	75.96	273.46	169.92
	∞	9.50	34.20	21.25		1500	53.44	192.38	119.54
						2000	47.18	169.85	105.54
						3000	43.32	155.95	96.90
						∞	37.98	136.73	84.96

APPENDIX II

CONSTANTS AND EQUIVALENTS

The following numerical values are taken, chiefly, from the Smithsonian Meteorological Tables, 4th Ed., 1918:

STANDARD VALUES

Gravity acceleration.................. 980.665 centimeters per second per second.

Gram weight........................ 980.665 dynes.

Atmospheric pressure................ 1,013,250.144+ dynes per square centimeter; that is, the pressure of a mercury column at standard gravity and 0° C. 760 millimeters high.

Bar (meteorological)................. 1,000,000 dynes per square centimeter.

TEMPERATURE SCALES

The temperatures of melting ice, and of boiling water (steam just over boiling water), each at standard atmospheric pressure, are indicated as follows:

Freezing: 32° F.; 0° R.;   0° C.; 273°.13 A_c. ±
Boiling: 212° F.; 80° R.; 100° C.; 373°.13 A_c. ±

Hence,

$$\frac{C°}{5} = \frac{F° - 32°}{9} = \frac{R°}{4},$$

and, on the perfect gas scale, or after correction,

$$A_c° = C° + 273.13 \pm.$$

LINEAR EQUIVALENTS

1 meter	= 39.3700 inches[1]	= 3.280833+ feet.
1 foot	= 0.3048006 meter.	
1 kilometer	= 0.621370 mile.	
1 mile	= 1.609347 kilometer.	

VELOCITY EQUIVALENTS

1 meter per second = 2.236932 miles per hour = 196.85 feet per minute.
1 mile per hour   = 0.4470409 meters per second.

WEIGHT EQUIVALENTS

1 avoirdupois pound	= 453.5924277	grams.
1 kilogram	= 2.204622	avoirdupois pounds.
1 gram	= 15.432356	grains.
1 grain	= 0.06479892	gram.

[1] U. S. statutory equivalent.

Densities (Grams per Cubic Centimeter)

Mercury, at 0° C.. 13.5951.

Air, dry, free from carbon dioxide, at standard atmospheric
pressure and 0° C....................................... 0.0012928.

Air, dry, containing 3 volumes carbon dioxide per 10,000 (normal
amount) at standard atmospheric pressure and 0° C........... 0.0012930.

Weight of standard dry air................................. 1.2930 kilograms
per cubic meter;
1.29152 ounces
per cubic foot.

Pressure Equivalents

1 mm. mercury, 0° C. and standard gravity .... = 1.333224 millibars.
1 inch mercury, 0° C. and standard gravity .... = 33.863953 millibars.

Black-body Radiation

$I = \sigma T^4$: T = absolute temperature.   For total or "hemispherical" radiation.

$\sigma = 8.22 \times 10^{-11}$ gram calories per square centimeter per minute.
1 gram calorie = 4.185×10^7 ergs = 4.185 joules, at 15° C.
1 joule   = 10^7 ergs.
1 watt   = 1 joule per second = 10^7 ergs per second.
1 horsepower = 746 watts = 746×10^7 ergs per second.

Wind Pressure

(Based on Dryden and Hill, *Scientific Paper* 523, U. S. Bureau of Standards, Washington, D. C., 1926.)

If the wind is normal to a face of a rectangular column of appreciable size the pressure on the front side *plus* the suction on the rear side (roughly equal to each other, and both always present) is about 1.5 times the "velocity pressure" or "impact pressure," that is, 1.5 times $\frac{1}{2}\rho V^2$, where ρ is the density of the air and V the true wind speed.   For standard dry air, $\rho = 0.001293$,

$$P = 0.004V^2, \text{ roughly,}$$

in which P = pressure *plus* suction in pounds per square foot of flat surface normal to the wind, and V = actual (not average) wind speed in miles per hour.

In the case of cylindrical objects, such as smokestacks, the toppling force due to the wind is very much less—of the order, perhaps, of one-half the value the above formula would give, on the assumption that the virtual area normal to the wind is the maximum vertical cross-section.   There is no universally applicable coefficient of wind pressure; it varies widely with the shape and size of the obstacle.

INDEX